THE EMPEROR FREDERICK II
OF HOHENSTAUFEN

1. The Empress Constance leaves the infant Frederick II in Foligno in the care of the Duchess of Spoleto, as she sets out for Palermo to rejoin the Emperor

THE EMPEROR
FREDERICK II
OF HOHENSTAUFEN

Immutator Mundi

BY

THOMAS CURTIS VAN CLEVE

OXFORD
AT THE CLARENDON PRESS
1972

Oxford University Press, Ely House, London W. 1

GLASGOW NEW YORK TORONTO MELBOURNE WELLINGTON
CAPE TOWN IBADAN NAIROBI DAR ES SALAAM LUSAKA ADDIS ABABA
DELHI BOMBAY CALCUTTA MADRAS KARACHI LAHORE DACCA
KUALA LUMPUR SINGAPORE HONG KONG TOKYO

Printed in Great Britain
at the University Press, Oxford
by Vivian Ridler
Printer to the University

DEDICATED
TO THE MEMORY OF
HERBERT C. F. BELL
ESTEEMED COLLEAGUE
AND FRIEND
IN WAR AS IN PEACE

PREFACE

THIS book was designed to explore as fully as possible the appropriateness of the phrase *immutator mundi*, or 'transformer of the world', as applied by contemporaries to Frederick II of Hohenstaufen; to establish the relationship of his many-sided achievements to those of his Norman and Hohenstaufen antecedents; to describe the circle of associates who participated in his manifold activities; and, finally, to seek the origin and to trace the course of the unremitting hostility of contemporary popes to him and to his concept of empire.

Although conceived as a scholarly project many years ago and intended as the culmination of studies first materializing in my *Markward of Anweiler and the Sicilian Regency* (Princeton, N.J., 1937), the work has been repeatedly interrupted by my overseas service in Africa and Europe during World War II, and further delayed, after the war, by special work for the War Department and while writing my 'The Fifth Crusade' and 'The Crusade of Frederick II', which appeared in vol. ii of the *History of the Crusades*, edited by Setton, Wolff, and Hazard (Philadelphia, Pa., 1962).

Because of the numerous and varied activities of Frederick II, I have felt that in the interest of clarity a topical organization of some parts of the book would be desirable. This is especially true where his literary, artistic, scientific, and fiscal interests are concerned. It has often occurred to me while reading various studies of Frederick II that a common fault has been the want of topical analyses of such interests and activities, a fault which has often resulted in vagueness and confusion.

Absolute consistency in the spelling of proper names has not always been desirable. Generally, the name Petrus has been rendered as Peter, as for example, Peter Capoccio. To avoid complications both French and Italian proper names such as Jean de Brienne are rendered as John of Brienne, John of Ibelin, Ezzelino of Romano, Roffrido of Benevento, etc. The names of some literary personages are retained in the form in which they are universally used: Piero della Vigna, Pietro da Eboli, Aimeric de Péguilhan, Rambaut de Vaqueiras, etc.

Although constantly tempted to shift the emphasis from the more immediate consideration of Frederick II to the papal–imperial conflict in its broadest sense, I have limited myself to the conflict as it manifested itself in Frederick's relations with the various popes as individuals. Whatever may have been Frederick's innermost convictions concerning the doctrines of the Popes and the extreme canonists respecting the supreme authority of the Pope, he affected to ignore them, directing his attacks, instead, at the Popes as individuals.

Notwithstanding the earlier treatment of the regency of Innocent III in my *Markward of Anweiler and the Sicilian Regency*, I have felt that a rapid sketch of that unhappy era is essential to the understanding of the problems which later claimed the attention of Frederick II upon his succession to the kingship and after his elevation as Emperor. It is not enough merely to dismiss the conflicts, intrigues, hostilities, and alliances as hopelessly confused or as of little relevance to the future of Frederick II. It is in the effort to interpret them that one finds the explanation of Frederick's Sicilian policies as King and Emperor.

Another digression from the main theme has seemed to be desirable because of the close interrelationship between the Norman-Sicilian era and that of Frederick II. It becomes increasingly apparent as one analyses the political, the administrative, the economic, and the cultural features of Frederick's reign, that they were deeply rooted in and nourished by the precedents of his Norman predecessors. Although devoting a separate chapter to the 'Norman Cultural Heritage of the Sicilian Court of Frederick II', I have dealt with the political, judicial, economic, and administrative systems, not in separate chapters, but in their appropriate places in relation to the systems of Frederick II.

It has been my constant effort to examine critically and to employ judiciously all available contemporary chronicles, letters, official documents, polemical writings, and all other pertinent materials which either directly or indirectly bear upon the subject. If to some readers there may appear to be a plethora of citations, this must be attributed to my confirmed conviction that by no other means can a biographer prevent the introduction of extraneous materials and misleading interpretations. In short, I have tried to keep constantly before me the rule of Frederick II himself in the writing of his *De Arte Venandi cum Avibus*: 'to present things that are as they are'. This rule, so essential to the scientist, has all too often been ignored by the biographer, either wittingly or unwittingly, because of religious or other dogmatic convictions or preoccupations. In the recognition of this, I have dealt with all personalities, whether lay or sacerdotal, with the same objectivity when their activities were solely temporal. The book is in no wise concerned with the spiritual motivation of the priesthood. This approach presents special difficulties to the medievalist, who is confronted always by the far-reaching influences and traditions of the Church, by its half-temporal, half-spiritual attributes, and by the greatly accentuated temporal claims of the Popes and the extreme canonists between the pontificate of Innocent III and that of Boniface VIII.

While the sources employed in the preparation of the original draft of the book were obtained during several extended visits to Germany, France, Switzerland, Northern Italy, and Sicily, during the final stages of the preparation of the manuscript and throughout the process of verification and revision the facilities of Widener Library of Harvard University have been made available to me repeatedly. After my retirement from Bowdoin College and while I was living in Washington the Library of Congress afforded a limited, though useful, opportunity for further verification and for keeping abreast of recent publications. Also, while I was living in the South during the winter months many courtesies were extended to me by the libraries of the University of North Carolina and of Duke University.

As to the employment of secondary sources, due attention has been given to all full-scale biographies, monographs, essays, and all other pertinent materials. Anyone undertaking a study of Frederick II must immediately recognize the invaluable contributions of the late Professors Ernst Kantorowicz, Karl Hampe, and Charles Homer Haskins, to say nothing of the pioneer works of Raumer, Höfler, Winkelmann, Schirrmacher, Huillard-Bréholles, and others. To Haskins, above all, one is especially indebted for his exhaustive researches into the scientific and cultural development of the eras of the Norman Sicilians and Frederick II. More recently also, the works of F. Baethgen, especially with reference to the minority of Frederick II, and C. A. Willemsen, on the architecture, sculpture, and lyric poetry of the Frederican era, have provided new and fresh orientations. Especially in his *Triumphtor zu Capua*, Professor Willemsen has most nearly sensed the intended significance of the sculptural ornaments of that splendid structure.

I wish also to express my obligation to my former colleague, the late Professor Charles H. Livingston, Longfellow Professor of Romance Languages of Bowdoin College, whose excellent private collection of works of Old French and Provençal was made available to me and proved to be of the greatest usefulness. I am indebted also to my Bowdoin colleagues, Professor Fritz Carl Augustus Koelln, George Taylor Files Professor of Modern Languages, who very graciously read several of the early chapters of the manuscript and edited my translations of two of the *Sprüche* of Walther von der Vogelweide, and to Professor Ernst Christian Helmreich of the department of history for useful suggestions.

For the several plates from the manuscript of Pietro da Eboli, *Liber ad Honorem Augusti* (MSS. del Cod. di Berna 120), I am indebted to the Chief Librarian and other officials of the Burgerbibliothek, Berne. I am especially grateful to the Curator of the Medieval Section of the Statens Historika Museum, Stockholm, for arranging for the photographing of the reliquary constructed at the order of Frederick II for the skull of St. Elizabeth of Thuringia, and to Professor C. A. Willemsen of the University of Bonn who very kindly permitted me to make use of several photographs previously appearing in his books describing the Capuan portal and towers.

Finally, I am indebted to the generous policy of the Presidents and Trustees of Bowdoin College, which, over a long period of years, has afforded me the opportunity to do essential research in the libraries of Europe and to visit the places intimately associated with the life and activities of Frederick II. More recently also, the interest of President James Stacy Coles and of his successor, President Roger Howell, Jr., has made possible the publication of this book.

Other Acknowledgements

To the Cambridge University Press (London and New York) for permission to quote a passage from F. W. Maitland's translation of Otto Gierke, *Political Theories of the Middle Ages* (Cambridge, 1900), and from S. C. Aston, *Pierol, Troubadour of Auvergne* (Cambridge, 1953).

To J. M. Dent & Sons Ltd., Publishers, for permission to quote several passages from Dante's *De Monarchia*, the *Divine Comedy*, and *De Vulgari Eloquentia* (all of the Temple Classics edition).

To Basil Blackwell, Publisher, Oxford, for permission to quote from G. Barraclough, *Medieval Germany* (2 vols., Oxford, 1938).

THOMAS C. VAN CLEVE

Bowdoin College

CONTENTS

List of Maps   xv

List of Illustrations   xvii

Abbreviations   xix

The Background: Italy and the Kingdom of Sicily in the
Purview of the Hohenstaufen   1

PART I

MINORITY OF FREDERICK II: THE REGENCY OF INNOCENT III

I. The Parentage of Frederick II: The Story of his Birth in
Legend and in History   13

II. The Neglected 'Boy of Apulia'   28

III. Struggle for the control of Sicily: The German Pretenders,
a Sicilian Chancellor, and the Heirs of Tancred   38

PART II

FREDERICK II, KING OF SICILY AND KING OF THE ROMANS

I. Frederick II comes of Age: First years as King of Sicily   61

II. Repudiation of Otto IV: Frederick II as German King   72

III. Submission of Northern Germany: Coronation at Aachen   89

IV. Death of Otto IV: Submission of the Welfs to Frederick II   107

PART III

FREDERICK II CROWNED AS EMPEROR: KING OF SICILY AND KING OF JERUSALEM

I. The Italian Expedition: The Imperial Coronation   123

II. Sicily, the 'Mirror of Empire': Reorganization of the Kingdom   139

III. Frederick II, King of Jerusalem   158

PART IV

FREDERICK II AS CRUSADER

i. Preliminary to the Crusade: The Recalcitrant Lombards 179

ii. Frederick II turns back: His Excommunication 194

iii. Frederick II, Diplomat or Crusader? 208
  A. The Kingdom of Sicily during Frederick's absence 208
  B. Frederick regains the Kingdom of Jerusalem 213

iv. The End of the Crusade: The Conquest of Sicily, Reconciliation with the Pope 222

PART V

FREDERICK II, TYRANT OF SICILY

i. Frederick II's *Liber Augustalis: Justitia* 237

ii. The Kingdom of Sicily: Despotic Bureaucracy 251

iii. The Fiscal Administration of the Kingdom of Sicily: Sources of Revenue 255

PART VI

FREDERICK II, PATRON OF THE ARTS AND SCIENCES

i. The Norman Cultural Heritage of the Sicilian Court of Frederick II 283

ii. The Pursuit of Learning at the Court of Frederick II 299

iii. Antecedents of the Sicilian Literary Style and the Advent of the 'Sicilian School' of Poetry 319

iv. Frederick II, Patron of Art 333

PART VII

FREDERICK RETURNS TO GERMANY

i. The German Regency and the Succession of Henry (VII) 349

ii. Henry (VII) in Rebellion against the Emperor 365

iii. Deposition of Henry (VII): The Advent of a New Empress 377

PART VIII

FREDERICK'S SECOND EXPEDITION AGAINST THE LOMBARDS

I. From Vicenza to Cortenuova 391

II. Continued Conquest of the Lombard Communes 410

PART IX

THE RIVALRY FOR EMPIRE: FREDERICK II *v.* GREGORY IX

I. The Second Excommunication of Frederick II 427

II. Frederick II at the Gates of Rome 442

III. Frederick II and the Choice of a Successor to Pope Gregory IX 451

PART X

THE CLOSING YEARS: DEATH OF THE EMPEROR

I. Pope Innocent IV flees to Lyons 473

II. The Council of Lyons: Deposition of Frederick II 480

III. Frederick's Final Effort against the Lombards: His Defeat at Parma 498

IV. From Adversity to the Threshold of Victory: Death of the Emperor 513

Epilogue 531

SOURCES AND BIBLIOGRAPHY

Commentary on the Primary Sources 543
    I. The German Sources 543
    II. The Italian Sources 547
    III. Other Sources 552

Bibliography—Part I: Primary Sources 556

Bibliography—Part II: A Classified List of Secondary Works 569

INDEX 599

LIST OF MAPS

1. Italian cities and castles mentioned in the text   *page* 141
2. The Po Valley   169
3. The Kingdom of Jerusalem after 1229   221
4. Site of the battle of Cortenuova   406
5. Italy in the era of the Hohenstaufen   *facing page* 540

TEXT FIGURE

Genealogical Table showing the relation of Walter of Brienne to the heirs of Tancred   43

LIST OF ILLUSTRATIONS

1. The Empress Constance leaves the infant Frederick II in Foligno in the care of the Duchess of Spoleto, as she sets out for Palermo to rejoin the Emperor

Frontispiece

Between pp. 332 *and* 333

2. Henry VI, at Salerno, receives the ambassadors from Palermo. Queen Sibylla weeping near the castle window as she loses her crown. Below: Triumphal entry of Henry VI into Palermo

3. Henry VI, attended by Fortune, Virtue, and Justice, occupies the throne in Palermo (Illustrations 1, 2, 3, 7, and 8 are from MS. Pietro da Eboli, *Liber ad Honorem Augusti* [late 12th and early 13th centuries] (MSS. del Cod. di Berna 120, fos. 45, 41, 53), in the Burgerbibliothek in Berne and are used by permission of the Library)

4. Head of Frederick II in profile. (Photographed from his gold coin, the *Augustalis*, from the coin collection in the Walker Art Museum, Bowdoin College, Brunswick, Maine)

5. Crown, found in the sarcophagus of the Empress Constance of Aragon, consort of Frederick II, in Palermo, now plausibly identified as that of the Emperor rather than that of the Empress, as formerly assumed

6. The eagle of Frederick II's gold coin, the *Augustalis*, showing the characteristic elongated head and beak of exaggerated proportions, the heavily chiselled scale-like feathers, and other features reflecting the medieval heraldic influence. (From the coin collection of the Walker Art Museum, Bowdoin College)

7. In the second archway from the left, a Saracen notary at the Norman-Sicilian court. (From Pietro da Eboli, fo. 8. See no. 3 above)

8. An Arab astrologer at the Norman-Sicilian court. (From Pietro da Eboli, fo. 4. See no. 3 above)

9. Bird's-eye view of a conjectural reconstruction of the portal and the bridge-towers of Capua. (From C. A. Willemsen *Kaiser Friedrichs II. Triumphtor zu Capua* (Wiesbaden, 1953), Plate 105. By permission of the author)

10. A wax impression of a cameo from a relief of the head of Frederick II, said to have been modelled from a plaster cast of the head before it was severed from the statue above the portal of the bridge-tower of Capua. (By permission of the Museo Provinciale Campano, Capua)

11. Attempted reconstruction of the façade of the bridge-towers and portal of Capua, showing the arrangement of the busts and statues according to C. A. Willemsen's interpretation. (Figure 106, *Triumphtor*. By permission of the author)

12. Probable arrangement of the head and busts in the circular niches beneath the seated statue of Frederick II. The female head is believed to symbolize *Justitia*, while the two busts below are believed to represent the imperial justices, Piero della Vigna below and to the right of Justitia, and Thaddeus of Suessa to the left

13. Sketch of a part of Castel del Monte, showing the portal, the Gothic windows, and the octagonal towers at the corners of the main structure. (From H. W. Schulz, *Denkmäler*, Atlas, Fig. XXX)

14. At top: Distant view of Castel del Monte. Below: Details of the portal. The steps on either side have been covered by debris. (From D. Salazaro, *Studi sui Monumenti dell'Italia meridionale*, Atlas, I, Plate XXIII. Private photograph)

15. The mutilated remnants of what appears to have been an equestrian statue in the Castel del Monte suggesting a marked resemblance to the equestrian statue at the entrance of the Georgian choir of Bamberg Cathedral

16. The Bamberg Cathedral equestrian statue, *Der Reiter*, mentioned above. (From W. R. Valentiner, *The Bamberg Rider*, Plate LXVII.) (By permission of Zeitlin and Ver Brugge, Booksellers, Los Angeles, California)

17. Reliquary, constructed from a chalice and a crown by order of Frederick II for the skull of St. Elizabeth of Thuringia. (By courtesy of the Medieval Section of the Statens Historika Museum, Stockholm)

ABBREVIATIONS

BFW, *Reg. V*	*Regesta imperii V. Die Regesten des Kaiserreichs unter Philipp, Otto IV., Friedrich II., Heinrich (VII), Konrad VI., Heinrich Raspe, Wilhelm und Richard, 1198–1272* (Neu hrsg. und ergänzt von J. Ficker und E. Winkelmann. 5. Abt. Innsbruck, 1881–1901).
Böhmer, *Acta*	J. F. Böhmer, *Acta imperii selecta* (Innsbruck, 1870).
Böhmer, *Fontes*	J. F. Böhmer, *Fontes rerum Germanicarum* (4 vols., Stuttgart, 1843–68).
Deutsches Archiv	*Deutsches Archiv für Geschichte* [later *Erforschung*] *des Mittelalters* (hrsg. von dem Reichsinstitut für ältere Geschichtskunde [later: hrsg. namens der Monumenta Germaniae Historica], Munich, 1937 ff.). A continuation of *Neues Archiv.*
DZfG	*Deutsche Zeitschrift für Geschichtswissenschaft* (hrsg. von L. Quidde, Freiburg i/B, 12 vols., 1889–96. NF. hrsg. von G. Seeliger, 2 vols., 1897–8). (Cont. as *Hist. Vierteljahrschr.* Leipzig after 1898.)
EHR	*English Historical Review.*
Epist.	*Epistolae Innocentii III papae* (Migne, *PL* 214–17). Cited by book, number, and column, as: *Epist.* I, i. 1. (Books I–VI in Migne, *PL* 214, books VII–XI in ibid. 215, and books XII– in ibid. 216.)
Eracles	*L'Estoire de Eracles Empereur* (*RHC, Hist. occ.* ii).
Ernoul	*Chronique d'Ernoul et de Bernard le Trésorier* (ed. M. L. de Mas-Latrie, Paris, 1871).
Fonti	*Fonti per la storia d'Italia* (Rome, 1887 ff.).
FzDG	*Forschungen zur deutschen Geschichte* (Munich, Göttingen, 1862 ff.).
GGA	*Göttingische Gelehrten Anzeigen* (1783 ff.).
Hist. Vierteljahrschr.	*Historische Vierteljahrschrift* (Leipzig, 1898 ff.).
Hist. Zeitschr.	*Historische Zeitschrift* (Munich, 1859 ff.).
Horoy	C. A. Horoy, *Honorius III Romani Pontificis Opera Omnia* (5 vols., Paris, 1879–82).
Huillard-Bréholles	J. L. Huillard-Bréholles, *Historia Diplomatica Friderici Secundi* (6 vols. in 12, Paris, 1852–61).
MGH	*Monumenta Germaniae historica* (ed. G. H. Pertz, T. Mommsen, *et al.*, Hanover, 1826 ff.). [*SS.* = *Scriptores*; *Const.* = *Constitutiones et Acta*; *Deutsch. Chron.* = *Deutsche Chroniken*; *Epist. Pont.* = *Epistolae saec. XIII, e Regestis Pontificum Romanorum Legum*, 1835.]
Migne, *PL*	*Patrologiae latinae cursus completus* (ed. J. P. Migne, 221 vols., Paris, 1844 ff.).
MIöG	*Mitteilungen des Instituts für österreichische Geschichtsforschung* (Innsbruck, 1880–1920, 1944 ff.).

MöIG	*Mitteilungen des österreichischen Instituts für Geschichts-forschung*, 1921–43.
Muratori, *Antiq.*	*Antiquitates Italicae Medii Aevi* (ed. L. A. Muratori, 6 vols., Milan, 1738–42).
Muratori, *RIS*	*Rerum Italicarum Scriptores* (ed. L. A. Muratori, 25 vols. in 28, Milan, 1723–51).
Muratori, *RIS*, new edn.	*Rerum Italicarum Scriptores* (new edn. of above, in progress, Città di Castello, 1900 ff.).
Neues Archiv	*Neues Archiv der Gesellschaft für ältere deutsche Geschichtskunde*, 1876–1936, then see *Deutsches Archiv*.
Pressutti	P. Pressutti, *Regesta Honorii Papae III* (2 vols., Rome, 1888–95).
QF	*Quellen und Forschungen aus italienischen Archiven und Bibliotheken* (hrsg. vom Preussischen Hist. Inst. in Rom, Rome, 1898 ff.).
RHC	*Recueil des historiens des croisades: Académie des Inscriptions et Belles-Lettres* (16 vols., Paris, 1841–1906).
RHC, Hist. occ.	*Historiens occidentaux.*
RHC, Hist. or.	*Historiens orientaux.*
RHGF	*Recueil des historiens des Gaules et de la France* (ed. M. Bouquet *et al.*, Paris, 1738–1904).
ROL	*Revue de l'Orient latin* (12 vols., Paris, 1893 ff.).
RNI	*Registrum Domini Innocentii III super Negotio Romani Imperii* (Migne, *PL* 216, Paris, 1855).
Sb. Bayer. Ak.	*Sitzungsberichte der Kgl. Akademie der Wissenschaften zu München: Phil.-hist. Klasse* (Munich, 1871 ff.).
Sb. Ber. Ak.	*Sitzungsberichte der Kaiserlichen Akademie der Wissenschaften* (Berlin, 1882 ff.).
Sb. H. Ak.	*Sitzungsberichte der Heidelberger Akademie der Wissenschaften: Phil.-hist. Klasse* (Heidelberg, 1910 ff.).
Sb. W. Ak.	*Sitzungsberichte der Kaiserlichen Akademie der Wissenschaften zu Wien: Phil.-hist. Klasse* (Vienna, 1848 ff.).
SRG in usum scholarum	*Scriptores Rerum Germanicarum in usum scholarum ex MGH separatim editi* (Hanover, 1839 ff.).
Stumpf K. F. Stumpf-Brentano	*Die Reichskanzler vornehmlich des X., XI. und XII. Jahrhunderts nebst einem Beitrag zu den Regesten und zur Kritik der Kaiserurkunden dieser Zeit* (3 vols., Innsbruck, 1865–83).
Winkelmann, *Acta*	E. Winkelmann, *Acta Imperii Inedita Saeculi XIII* (2 vols., Innsbruck, 1880, 1885).
ZfbK	*Zeitschrift für bildende Kunst* (hrsg. von C. von Lützow, Leipzig, 1866 ff.).
ZfKirch. Gesch.	*Zeitschrift für Kirchengeschichte* (1877 ff.).
ZfRG	*Zeitschrift für Rechtsgeschichte* (13 vols., Weimar, 1861–1880 — Fortgesetzt u. d. T.: *Zeitschrift der Savigny-Stiftung für Rechtsgeschichte. Germanische Abteilung*, Weimar, 1880 ff.).

THE BACKGROUND

ITALY AND THE KINGDOM OF SICILY IN THE PURVIEW OF THE HOHENSTAUFEN

Rex ut Aquisgrani Carlorum sede resedit.
Ordine legitimo Jermania prorsus hobedit,
Finibus Italie rex sua signa dedit.
Godfrey of Viterbo, *Pantheon* (*MGH, SS.* xxii), 265.[1]

SINCE the Carolingian era Italy had occupied a place of varying importance in the medieval concepts of empire. But, like the idea of the *imperium* itself, the importance of Italy had been but vaguely and uncertainly recognized for nearly a century following the death of Charlemagne. It was with the era of the Ottos, notably with Otto III and his tutor Gerbert, that a concept of empire, free of past uncertainties, revived. In defiance of traditions originating with the so-called Donation of Constantine, Otto III made the city of Rome the seat of the imperial residence. Influenced both by the ancient Roman and the Carolingian Empires, and guided by Gerbert who, in the year 1000, became Pope Sylvester II, the Empire of Otto III was oriented towards an *imperium christianum* with the Emperor in the role of protector of Christianity, the *servus Jesu Christi*, responsible, above all, for the expansion of Christendom. Reflecting the characteristics of both these former Empires, the Ottonian Empire was universal in its aims. There is a suggestion here of the Byzantine prototype with the Emperor as sovereign hierarch, the responsible leader of the *societas christiana*, to whom the Pope, like the Patriarch, was subordinate but indispensable. The principle of universality, the activating force of Otto III's concept of sovereignty, was to be achieved through identifying his aims with those of the catholic or universal Church.[2]

It is remarkable that Otto III's concept of universality and his insistence upon Rome as the centre of the universal Christian Empire did not persist under his immediate successors. Instead, the Empire's essentially Teutonic or Frankish character was revived and, for the time being, the emphasis was primarily upon the development of the Frankish Kingdom. Only with the early Salian kings, Conrad II and his son Henry III,

[1] When the King sat again on the throne of Charles, Germany did obedience precisely as directed by law. The King sent his tokens to the lands of Italy.
[2] See especially R. Folz, *L'Idée d'empire en occident du Vᵉ au XIVᵉ siècle*, 76 ff.

is there some evidence of the revival of a vague concept of universality; it was more akin, however, to a hegemony than to imperial sovereignty.

With the Hohenstaufen the concept of universality assumed its definitive form, incorporating some, if not all, of the aims originally projected by Otto III, and tacitly ignoring the traditions originating in the Carolingian era as to the rights of the Pope in the city of Rome and in Italy. While there is general agreement among historians that the Hohenstaufen Emperors aimed at the restoration of the Empire to its ancient strength and dignity, there have been widely differing opinions as to their ambitions to establish 'World Empire'. A conservatively stated opinion would probably suggest that their concept of sovereignty, originating with Frederick Barbarossa, contemplated a universal Empire of Christendom subject always to continuous expansion. It is apparent also that they considered Italy, and the city of Rome itself, essential to the achievement of their aims. If this was not fully apparent at the time of Barbarossa's first expedition to Italy (1153–5), it was unmistakable a few years later when, in 1157, he asserted that, 'through the grace of Divine Providence we hold the governance of the city and the world' (*urbis et orbis*).[1] Even more emphatic was his enunciation of his sovereign authority when later, while refuting what he interpreted as a papal claim to the right to confer the imperial crown as a *beneficium*, he wrote: 'We hold the Kingdom and Empire, through election by the princes, from God alone. . . . Therefore, whoever says that we hold the imperial crown as a fief (*beneficium*) from the Pope contradicts the teachings of Peter and is guilty of falsehood.'[2]

Throughout the era of the Hohenstaufen the Emperors were concerned with four problems the solutions of which were essential to the achievement of their common goal, the restoration of the imperial authority. These problems were: the settlement of the conflict of interests of the Emperors and the Popes; the checking of the spirit of independence of the communes; the reclaiming of the regalian rights; the crushing of the resistance of the kings of Sicily to imperial authority. Each of these problems had become increasingly serious during the long absence from Italy of a firm imperial control. In Northern Italy the Lombard cities, taking advantage of the absence of imperial authority, had appropriated the regalian rights and otherwise strengthened their position of independence at the expense of both episcopal and imperial authority. Since the middle of the eleventh century also lower Italy and Sicily had become consolidated into the powerful Norman-Sicilian Kingdom, dominating the sea and threatening the territorial claims of both the Pope and the Emperor. In the mid twelfth century a revolutionary movement among the citizens of Rome menaced the Pope, forcing him

---

[1] *MGH, Const.* i. 224.   [2] Ibid. i. 231.

to leave the city. This threat became all the more serious when Arnold of Brescia assumed the leadership of the revolution. It was not a mere formality, therefore, when Pope Eugenius III, in reply to Frederick Barbarossa's announcement of his election as King of the Romans, not only expressed his satisfaction but reminded the newly elected Emperor of his obligation to defend the Church and the persons of the clergy.[1] Perhaps at no time had the Pope and Curia felt greater need for the protection of a powerful Emperor.

Barbarossa was quick to seize this opportunity offered by the conditions in Italy and to initiate his own plans for the reassertion of the imperial authority. It is apparent in many of his statements and in his acts throughout his reign that Frederick Barbarossa regarded the Empire as eternal and continuous, accepting the laws of his predecessors as divinely inspired. In language born of this conviction he proclaimed his veneration for the laws of his 'divine predecessors', Constantine, Justinian, and Valentinian, as well as Charlemagne and Louis the Pious, as divine oracles.[2]

In the mind of Frederick Barbarossa no distinction as to ultimate purpose existed between the Roman Empire of antiquity, the Frankish Empire, or the successor of these, the German Empire of his own era. The *Imperium Romanorum* had merely shifted across the Alps to become first the *Imperium Francorum*, and thereafter it continued as the *Imperium Teutonicorum*. To him the imperial laws promulgated in each of these eras were equally valid and, in this belief, he did not hesitate to order his own laws to be inserted in the *Corpus Juris* alongside those of his predecessors.[3]

Thus Frederick Barbarossa set his seal of approval upon a concept of *imperium* that was to be even more insistently emphasized by Henry VI, and which was to come near to its realization under Frederick II. It would be erroneous, however, to treat the Hohenstaufen Empire as merely a continuity. Certainly the concepts of universality, of absolute sovereignty, and of sacredness were continuous, but there existed also under Frederick Barbarossa and, indeed, throughout the Staufen era as a whole, certain revolutionary features, well characterized as a 'secularization of the whole of human life'. While this is apparent in all aspects of life in the late twelfth and thirteenth centuries, it became of paramount importance in the political sphere.[4] How threatening the aims of the Emperor had become from the point of view of the Pope and Curia is seen in his assertion: 'Since by Divine ordinance I am

---

[1] Ibid. i. 193 f.   [2] Ibid. i. 322.

[3] He ordered his *Privilegium Scholasticum* to be inserted 'inter imperiales constituciones'. (*MGH, Const.* i. 249.)

[4] Albert Brackmann, in his 'Der mittelalterliche Ursprung der Nationalstaaten', trans. G. Barraclough, *Medieval Germany*, ii. 298–9, has described the revolutionary features of this era.

designated, and am, Roman Emperor, I would be merely the shadow of a sovereign and bear but an empty title without substance, if authority over the city of Rome were taken from my hands.'[1] If, indeed, this claim of Barbarossa had been successfully substantiated (and it was to appear as a real threat on more than one occasion during the Hohenstaufen era), it would have reduced the Pope to the status of an imperial bishop.[2] The plans of the Hohenstaufen, as exemplified by Barbarossa, contemplated extending the imperial dominance over the whole of Italy and Sicily, over regions which the Pope and Curia regarded as belonging to the Church of Rome.[3] It was in opposition to what they conceived to be the aggressiveness of the Hohenstaufen that they unleashed new forces of resistance that were to destroy all hopes of peaceful coexistence and co-operation between the popes and emperors. The study of canon law, so flourishing in the era of the Hohenstaufen, was destined to accentuate past differences and to introduce new causes of antagonism.

No less threatening were the policies of Barbarossa to the rapidly developing communes with their demands for independence, including the continued enjoyment of the regalian rights. It is not the place here to review the details of his futile conflict with the Lombard communes between his first expedition to Italy in 1154 and the Peace of Constance in 1183. After repeated efforts, when it became apparent that he could no longer expect the Germans to respond to his call for the renewal of the conflict with the Pope and communes, he wisely yielded to a peaceful settlement, first in a tentative cessation of hostilities by the Peace of Venice and subsequently in a more definite settlement at Constance in 1183, in which Frederick Barbarossa at last recognized the local autonomy of the communes and contented himself with a nominal recognition of his sovereignty, while conceding to the communes most of the regalian rights.[4] It is no great exaggeration to conclude that the Peace of Constance was, in fact, Frederick's admission of the failure of the Italian policies he had pursued prior to 1183.[5] These causes of failure would subsequently reappear to nullify the efforts of Frederick's successor to continue his policies, except where lower Italy and Sicily were concerned.

If there was much that was disappointing in his failure to achieve his original goals, however, it was no little compensation when, shortly after the Peace of Constance, Frederick was able to assert his claim to the lands of the Countess Matilda which provided the foundation for an

---

[1] *MGH, Const.* i. 250–1.

[2] J. Haller, *Das Papsttum*, ii, part ii, pp. 133 ff.

[3] See especially K. Wenck, 'Die römischen Päpste zwischen Alexander III und Innocenz III' (*Papsttum und Kaisertum*, ed. A. Brackmann), pp. 415 ff.

[4] *MGH, Const.* i. 400 ff.

[5] G. von Below, *Die italienische Kaiserpolitik des deutschen Mittelalters*, 119.

imperial territory in Central Italy. Despite the opposition of Pope Lucius III, who had succeeded Alexander III in August 1181, Barbarossa was firmly resolved to retain possession of these lands. He found further compensation through a peace settlement with the King of Sicily, providing for a future foothold in lower Italy and Sicily which, before the end of the Hohenstaufen era, was to make of the Sicilian Kingdom the nucleus of the expanding Empire.

As early as 1174 Barbarossa had contemplated the securing of this important Mediterranean region, to which he believed the Germans had a just claim since the era of Otto the Great. He endeavoured to achieve this through a marriage alliance of his son with the sister of William I. His earlier negotiations are said to have failed chiefly because they were displeasing to Pope Alexander III.[1] Subsequently the plan was revived when William II, despairing of a direct heir, recognized his aunt, Constance, as his legitimate successor and agreed to her betrothal to Frederick's son Henry, Duke of Swabia. The formal betrothal took place in Augsburg on 29 October 1184, and the marriage was celebrated in a brilliant ceremony in Milan on 27 January 1186.[2]

Meanwhile, serious reversals in Syria and Jerusalem were a constant reminder of the urgent need of a new crusade, all the more so when in 1187 reports arrived of the fall of Jerusalem. Moreover, with the seemingly favourable outcome of his negotiations with the Pope, the communes, and the King of Sicily, Frederick Barbarossa felt himself in a position to take the cross and to assume the leadership of a new crusade.[3]

The sudden death of Barbarossa on 10 June 1190, while *en route* to Syria, and the staggering losses which his army had sustained since the day it had set out from Regensburg, made the army progressively weaker. The future crusading plans, like the exploitation of the Italian policies, must be left henceforth in the hands of Henry VI, who had been entrusted with the governance of the Empire upon the departure of his father to the Orient. But before entering upon a crusading expedition, Henry VI must first concern himself with the conquest of the heritage of his consort, Constance, in Sicily. Since the beginning of the negotiations between William II and Barbarossa for the marriage alliance, there had been an irreconcilable Sicilian party opposed to German interference in Sicily. This party had elected as king Count Tancred of Lecce, an illegitimate son of Duke Roger of Apulia, brother of the first

---

[1] *Romualdi Salernitani Chronicon* (Muratori, *RIS*, new edn., vii, part 1), 265–6.

[2] T. Toeche, *Kaiser Heinrich VI*, 38.

[3] For the deteriorating conditions in Jerusalem between 1174 and 1189 see especially M. Baldwin, 'The Decline and Fall of Jerusalem, 1174–1189', *History of the Crusades*, vol. i: *The First Hundred Years* (ed. M. Baldwin), 590 ff. For Frederick's role see E. N. Johnson, 'The Crusades of Frederick Barbarossa and Henry', *History of the Crusades*, vol. ii: *The Later Crusades* (ed. R. L. Wolff *et al.*), 89 ff.

William, known as William the Bad.[1] Peaceful succession to the heritage
of Constance was thus made impossible and Henry was compelled,
between 1189 and 1194, to make good his claim by force of arms. Upon
his succession, following the death of Frederick Barbarossa, the conquest
of the Sicilian Kingdom thus became an essential step in the continuation of the Hohenstaufen policy that looked to the restoration and
expansion of the Empire.[2]

Henry's first expedition, undertaken in 1191, ended in failure. The
Genoese fleet and the land troops of the King had failed to co-ordinate
their efforts during the siege of Naples, and a pestilential fever had im-
mobilized the army and attacked the Emperor so violently as to give
rise to rumours of his death. As a final blow, the Empress Constance was
taken captive by Salernitans hostile to the imperial claims and was
delivered into the hands of Tancred in Messina.[3] Although temporarily
checked by these reverses in Sicily and, even more, by the disquieting
news of a Welf revolt in Germany, Henry's departure from Italy represented a postponement rather than the abandonment of the conquest.
At the close of the year 1191 he was again in Germany. More than two
years were to pass before he was able to resume his conquest.

During these years in Germany he was successful in crushing the
revolt of the Welfs, which was all the more threatening because of its
support by England and the Netherlands. Moreover, a series of unfortunate quarrels with the German clergy, culminating in the murder
of Albert of Brabant, one of the candidates for the vacant bishopric of
Liège, had further jeopardized his position at home. By a timely seizure
of Richard I of England, returning from a crusade, Henry VI extricated
himself from the threatening situation, not only saving his crown but,
through imposing a heavy ransom, finding the means to resume his
conquest of Sicily.[4]

It was during these years in Germany that the grandiose plans for
universal Empire, never wholly absent from the thoughts of Henry VI,
received their most vigorous stimulus. The imprisonment of Richard
Cœur de Lion provided an irresistible temptation to make England a
feudal dependency of the Empire. The claims of England to large areas
of France made plausible also the ultimate extension of the imperial
dominance there. Indeed, Pope Innocent III appears to have regarded
the complete subjugation of the Kingdom of France by the Emperor as
an imminent possibility.[5] Where Frederick Barbarossa was primarily

---

[1] *Breve chronicon de rebus Siculis* (Huillard-Bréholles, i, part ii), 888.

[2] See especially the observations of K. Hampe, *Kaisergeschichte*, 222. (All citations are
from the 10th edn.)   [3] *Annales Casinenses* (*MGH, SS.* xix), 314 f.

[4] Hampe, *Kaisergeschichte*, 224. For the Liège murder and its political significance see
C. Trautmann, *Heinrich VI. und der Lütticher Bischofsmord*, 40 ff.

[5] *RNI*, no. lxiv, col. 1071: 'et regnum Francorum sibi disponeret subjugare, sicut olim,

concerned with the restoration of the Empire, Henry VI, almost from the outset, seemed to contemplate a more ambitious plan suggesting World Empire.[1] When, therefore, conditions in Germany were such as to give assurance of future stability there, Henry VI could return hopefully to his reconquest of Sicily—an enterprise the success of which would determine, in large measure, his future plans. It was also with bitter recollections of his earlier and disastrous experience that he set out once more (in 1194) to claim the heritage of his Norman queen.

For the Empress Constance, returning to Sicily with the Emperor nearly two years after papal intervention had compelled her release by Tancred, this expedition must have evoked mixed feelings of pleasure and anxiety. It is unfortunate that we have little or no information about her residence in Germany after her release, or about the mood in which she had departed from her imprisonment in Sicily. Had either or both of these experiences altered her feelings towards the Germans, or had they caused her to look with suspicion upon plans of the Emperor which could result only in the sacrifice of Sicily to the interests of the Empire? Her captivity in Palermo had not been an entirely unhappy experience. Hers had been an honourable detention, attended by every courtesy and by every comfort commensurate with her exalted station as Empress. The aim of Tancred appears to have been to employ her as an intermediary between himself and the Emperor and, in so far as this was possible, to identify her with the nationalist and patriotic interests of Sicily. The lines of the contemporary poet, Pietro da Eboli, a rabid Hohenstaufen partisan, depicting Sibylla, the spouse of Tancred, as advising the murder of Constance as a means of destroying the validity of Henry's claims, may be dismissed as fanciful.[2] Neither Tancred nor Sibylla could have doubted the intention of Henry to return with the strongest army possible and with the determination that this second expedition must succeed at any cost. Nor could they have doubted that the murder, or even the suspicion of murder, of the Empress would have brought upon the nationalist party in Sicily the full vengeance of the Emperor. Whatever his object may have been, Tancred's detention of Constance had served only to demonstrate the loyalty of the citizens of Palermo to the legitimate line of Roger II. For, much to the discomfiture of Tancred, the Empress was honoured in that city as the rightful heiress of the kingdom.[3]

obtento regno praedicto, disposuerat frater ejus imperator Henricus, affirmans quod te de caetero ad fidelitatem sibi compelleret exhibendam.'

[1] G. von Below, *Italienische Kaiserpolitik*, 119 f.

[2] For Sibylla's alleged 'Letter to Tancred' see Pietro da Eboli (*Fonti*), 66 f. As to the honourable detention of the Empress, see *Sicardi Episcopi Cremonensis Cronica* (*MGH, SS.* xxxi), 174.

[3] *Gisleberti Chronicon Hanoniense* (*MGH, SS.* xxi), 575; Pietro da Eboli (*Fonti*), p. 65, lines 885 ff.

Now in 1194, as she was again returning to her native land, the recollection of that demonstration of affection and loyalty to her Norman ancestors in Palermo must have reminded her that she, as the legitimate heiress of the Hautevilles, was not without obligations towards the nationalist and patriotic party. Already she was aware that a few months hence she would give birth to a child, possibly a son, of the Hohenstaufen, a name hateful to the ears of her Sicilian compatriots. During the nine years of her married life with Henry VI, ten years her junior, she had been denied offspring, and now, in her fortieth year, she must have had serious forebodings as to the future, both of her unborn child and of the Sicilian Kingdom. Loyalty to the memory of her Norman ancestors could not make her Sicilian subjects oblivious of the danger that the Sicily of the future might well become but a province of the Hohenstaufen Empire. Were such thoughts as these provoking already the bitterness and hatred towards the Germans which later, shortly after the birth of her son, would lead her to sacrifice his claims to Germany and to the Hohenstaufen heritage?[1]

On 29 May the imperial party was received with great ceremony by the citizens of Milan, where the Empress was a guest in the monastery of Meda. It is from a brief notice in the *Memoriae* of Milan that we have the first report of her pregnancy: 'And the same year [1194] the abovementioned Constance came to Milan and was a guest in the monastery of Meda, and at that time she was pregnant with Frederick.'[2] Leaving the Empress in Milan to follow more leisurely, Henry proceeded first to Pavia and Piacenza and then to the field of Roncaglia where the army awaited his arrival.[3] He hastened next to Genoa and Pisa where, by the renewal of promises of generous privileges, he sought to ensure support for his conquest of Sicily.[4] His preparations now moved rapidly. By the middle of August a Genoese fleet was in readiness and sailed from the harbour, soon to be joined by thirteen Pisan galleys. In early September the joint fleets anchored in the harbour of Messina to await the arrival of the Emperor with the army.[5]

The delay in Henry's arrival was caused in part by his siege and plundering of Salerno in retaliation for the mistreatment of the Empress Constance during the first expedition in 1191. After a brief siege the citizens capitulated and yielded to the pitiless vengeance of the Emperor.

---

[1] See below, pp. 36 ff.

[2] *Memoriae Mediolanenses* (*MGH, SS.* xviii), 400.

[3] *Notae sancti Georgii Mediolanenses* (*MGH, SS.* xviii), 387; *Annales Placentini Guelfi* (ibid.), 419; see also John Codagnellus (*SRG in usum scholarum*), 22. When not otherwise indicated, future references will be made to the latter rather than to *MGH, SS.* xviii.

[4] *Annales Janvenses* (*Fonti*), ii. 45–6; P. Tronci, *Memorie istoriche della città di Pisa*, 158.

[5] *Annales Janvenses*, loc. cit. See also the enlightening article of D. R. Clementi, 'Some Unnoticed Aspects of the Emperor Henry VI's Conquest of the Norman Kingdom of Sicily' (*Bulletin of the John Rylands Library*, xxxvi, 1953–4), 328–59.

Those who had not made good their escape were condemned to death, to outlawry, or to imprisonment. The wealth of the citizens and the treasures of the church, estimated at 100,000 ounces of gold, were distributed as booty among the soldiers. The walls of the city were razed, its buildings plundered and burned.[1] The fate of Salerno was enough to convince other cities of the futility of further resistance, and they opened their gates to the Abbot of Monte Cassino who had preceded the Emperor as plenipotentiary in Apulia. Despite his delay, the Emperor was received in Messina with honours such as had never before been witnessed there.[2] On 20 November he made his triumphal entry into Palermo where, on Christmas Day 1194, in the cathedral he received the crown of Sicily.[3] Meanwhile the Empress, *en route* to join the Emperor in Palermo, was compelled to delay her journey at Jesi in the March of Ancona in the expectation of the imminent birth of her child.[4]

Henry's successes in the conquest of Apulia and Sicily, together with his ceremonial coronation, gave added impetus to his imperialistic plans. Already it was apparent that he looked upon the Kingdom of Sicily as a pivotal point in the expansion of the Hohenstaufen *imperium* over the whole of the Mediterranean basin. While one seeks in vain at this time for positive evidence as to his intentions toward the Byzantine Empire,[5] his future conduct leaves little room for doubt as to his aggressive intentions there.[6] The obvious feebleness of the once splendid Greek Empire was an open invitation to conquest and a warning to regions formerly its subjects. The Kingdoms of Cyprus and Armenia, seeking a greater security as vassals to the triumphant Western Emperor, willingly received their crowns as fiefs from Henry VI. In the eyes of contemporary Greeks the future intentions of the Hohenstaufen Emperor were all too apparent. They saw him already as 'the Lord of all Lords and the Emperor of all Emperors'.[7]

For the moment, however, Henry was too deeply engrossed in preparations for a crusade to divulge his ultimate plans respecting the Eastern Empire. With this more immediate object in view, he awaited the arrival of reinforcements from Germany for his crusading army while at the same time endeavouring to strengthen his hold upon his newly won Kingdom of Sicily.

[1] *Annales Cavenses* (*MGH, SS.* iii), 193; Richard of San Germano (Muratori, *RIS.*, new edn., vii, part. ii), 12.   [2] Roger of Hoveden (Rolls Series), iii. 269–70.
[3] Ralph of Diceto (Rolls Series), iii. 270.   [4] See below, p. 13.
[5] E. Traub, *Der Kreuzzugsplan Kaiser Heinrichs VI. in Zusammenhang mit der Politik der Jahre 1195–1197*, 51–2.
[6] For a judicious treatment of this long highly controversial question see K. Hampe, *Kaisergeschichte*, 232. I have previously dealt with this in detail in my *Markward of Anweiler and the Sicilian Regency*, 13 ff.
[7] Nicetas Choniates, *Historia* (ex recensione Imanuelis Bekkeri: *Corpus scriptorum historiae byzantinae*, Bonn, 1835), 627.

PART I

MINORITY OF FREDERICK II
THE REGENCY OF INNOCENT III

I

THE PARENTAGE OF FREDERICK II
THE STORY OF HIS BIRTH IN
LEGEND AND IN HISTORY

> Nascitur Augusto, qui regat arma, puer.
> Felix namque pater, set erit felicior infans;
> Hic puer ex omni parte beatus erit.
>
> Pietro da Eboli, *Liber ad Honorem Augusti (Fonti)*, lines 1370–2.[1]

THE small city of Jesi, the *Aesis* of the ancient Romans, stands on an elevation overlooking the river Esino on the highway traversing Central Italy from Falconaro, through Fabriano and Foligno, towards Rome. It was there that the Empress Constance, on her way to join the Emperor in Palermo, was compelled to pause for the birth of her child. On 26 December 1194, the day after the coronation of Henry VI in Palermo, she gave birth to the future Frederick II of Hohenstaufen. Shortly afterwards the Emperor announced the arrival of his heir in a letter to his intimate friend Walter, Archbishop of Rouen, in which he wrote: 'By the grace of God we now hold peacefully the whole of the Kingdom of Apulia and Sicily', and at the same time rejoiced 'that our dear Consort, Constance, illustrious and august Empress, bore us a son on the Day of the Blessed Protomartyr, Stephen' (i.e. 26 December 1194).[2]

If Henry rejoiced at the news of the birth of an heir, many of his contemporaries heard of the event with astonishment and incredulity. A chronicler, writing during the lifetime of Frederick II, took note of the popular scepticism regarding Frederick's birth, characterizing it, because of the advanced age of the Empress, as 'contra opinionem'.[3] Andrea Dandolo (1307–54) reports the contemporary gossip that Constance was fifty years old at the time of Frederick's birth and that Henry, when informed of the pregnancy of his aged spouse, was himself

---

[1] To Augustus is born a son who will excel at arms.
Though fortunate the father, the son will be more so;
In every way he will be blessed.

[2] Ralph of Diceto (Rolls Series), ii. 125. For Jesi in the era of Frederick II see W. Hagemann, 'Jesi im Zeitalter Friedrichs II.' (*QF*. xxxvi. 1956), 138 ff.

[3] *Continuatio Chronici ex Pantheo excerpti* (*MGH, SS.* xxii), 368.

incredulous and was reassured only when the Calabrian prophet, Joachim, interpreting a prophecy of Merlin and the Erythraean Sibyl, declared that Frederick was Henry's son and that Constance was the mother.[1] Although the Empress was born some time after February 1154 and was, therefore, in her fortieth year, the birth of a son at that age was sufficient in the twelfth century to evoke general astonishment and to give rise to a multitude of legends. A typically improbable tale is that of the *Annales Stadenses*, which relate that Constance had already reached the age of sixty at the time of her marriage and that the Emperor, fearing the Kingdom would be without an heir, appealed to physicians to make use of remedies which would overcome sterility. Thereupon, the physicians employed medicines in such manner that the Empress developed a marked corpulence, thus deceiving the Emperor into the belief that his spouse was pregnant. At the moment of simulated *accouchement* a new-born infant of spurious origin was said to have been introduced into the palace and made to appear as the child of the Empress. Gossip described the infant variously as the son of a physician, a miller, a falconer, or a butcher.[2]

The legend of the supposititious origin of Frederick II was most widely publicized by the contemporary chronicler, Salimbene (*c.* 1221–89), who often included irresponsible gossip in his chronicles. It was he who gave currency to the story that Frederick was the son of a butcher of Jesi, deceitfully represented by Constance as her own after a period of simulated pregnancy. As if he were suspicious of the tale, Salimbene gave three reasons to justify its inclusion in his chronicle: first, because he was aware that women were wont to do such things, secondly, because Merlin had prophesied that the second Frederick would come into being 'miraculously and unexpectedly', and, finally, because King John of Jerusalem, Frederick's father-in-law, had once, in a fit of anger, called him 'son of a butcher', exclaiming in French, 'Fi di becer diable!'[3]

Closely associated with these legends were other stories, alleged prophecies, divulging that Constance was destined to bring ruin upon the Kingdom of Sicily. It was this prophecy that caused her brother William I to summon his friends and wise men to a council to determine what was to be done with his sister in order that disaster might be averted. According to this legend, it was agreed that Constance must be put to death, and only the intervention of Tancred, Duke of Lecce and Taranto, a natural son of Roger, Duke of Apulia, and one of the counsellors, dissuaded William from this unnatural act of cruelty. As a measure of security, however, the legend recounts further that Constance was

---

[1] *Andreae Danduli Chronicon* (Muratori, *RIS*, new edn., xii, part 1), 274.
[2] *Annales Stadenses* (*MGH, SS.* xvi), 357.
[3] *Cronica Fratris Salimbene* (*MGH, SS.* xxxii), 42 f.

compelled to become a nun.[1] The Cistercian Annals, compiled much later by Angello Manrique, identify the convent as that of San Salvatore in Palermo.[2] While it is highly probable that Constance was accustomed to retreat from time to time to San Salvatore or other convents, there exists no adequate evidence to confirm the legend that she had taken the veil. Certainly the marriage of a nun, necessitating the dissolution of the most sacred vows, could not have passed unnoticed by contemporary chroniclers or, indeed, by the Pope himself. Even Dante, to whom Constance, like Piccarda Donati, was 'as spotless, pure and eternal as the upper regions of the moon', appears to have drawn solely on the common gossip of his time when he depicted her as having been torn violently, as was the unhappy sister of Corso Donati, from her beloved cell, and compelled by force to marry. It was this legend also that inspired the poet to say: 'Thou hast heard from Piccarda that Constance retained affection for her veil.'[3]

Other legends relate that young Frederick was of demoniacal origin—that his mother, like Atia, the mother of Octavianus, who was said to have been seduced by a serpent, had unwittingly been made pregnant by a demon. Evil dreams of both Constance and her mother Beatrice presaged the birth of an evil spirit, the fire-brand of Italy.[4] Constance's age as well as the nun legend contributed inevitably to the growth of still more colourful legends in the course of time. It was undoubtedly her knowledge of this widespread disbelief in her ability to bear a child that caused the Empress to take extraordinary measures to give proof of her fecundity. While several of the stories regarding her efforts to convince her Sicilian subjects of the authenticity of her parenthood are hardly credible, it is apparent that she took action of such a nature as to give rise to exaggerated accounts of it by hostile contemporaries or near contemporaries. It can hardly be doubted that she took an oath in the presence of a legate of the Pope with her hand upon the Gospels that Frederick was born of the legitimate marriage of Henry and herself.[5] In view of the widespread scepticism and the obvious dangers to which such doubts would expose her son, it is probable also that she invited witnesses to observe the actual birth of the child, thereby giving rise to several of the exaggerated and highly coloured accounts of some of the later chronicles, especially. One such account is that of Pandolf

[1] *Thomae Tusci Gesta Imperatorum et Pontificum* (*MGH, SS.* xxii), 498.

[2] *Annales Cisterciensium*, iii. 169–70. It is to be noted, however, that this and *De rebus Siculis decades duae* (Palermo, 1558), Lib. VII, cap. 6, which also reports the nun legend, are of much later date and appear to employ no source other than the common gossip.

[3] *Paradiso*, Canto IV, lines 97 f. Corso Donati, leader of a powerful Guelf faction in Florence, forced his sister, for selfish reasons, to leave the convent and to marry.

[4] Suetonius, *Augustus*, c. 94. *Anonymi Vaticani* (Muratori, *RIS* viii), col. 778; *Cronica Pontificum et Imperatorum S. Bartholomaei in Insula Romani* (*MGH, SS.* xxxi), 224.

[5] Roger of Hoveden, *Chronica* (Rolls Series), iv. 31.

Collenuccio (1444–1504) in his *Compendium* which relates that the Empress ordered a tent to be erected in the public square of Jesi and invited all barons, nobles, and all the women of that region who wished to do so to witness the birth.[1] These accounts are often questionable because of inaccuracies and contradictions. Some of them attribute to the Empress the more generous gesture of inviting all who would to be present, while others, apparently restrained by a sense of modesty, describe her as extending the invitation only to the women of the vicinity of Jesi. Others, as though repeating inaccurately an oft-told bit of gossip, describe the birth as taking place not in Jesi, but in the Piazza Palermo.[2] The story of the public birth is rendered suspect also by the frequency with which the Joachimites associated Frederick II with the Antichrist whose birth was usually depicted in the mystery plays as taking place publicly.[3] Indicative of the origin of the legend in the common gossip of the time are the conflicting ages attributed to the Empress.[4] Equally questionable, although illustrative of the persistence of such gossip, is the legend that Constance, desiring that the people of the realm as well as the Roman Church be assured of her authentic motherhood, went into various cities revealing to the incredulous her naked breasts distended with milk.[5]

In evaluating these legends concerning the Empress it should not be overlooked that many of them, perhaps most of them, had their origin in the partisan conflicts that arose in Sicily when it became apparent that William II, recognizing that he would have no direct heir, agreed to the proposal of Frederick Barbarossa for a marriage alliance between Constance (who was at that time regarded as the legitimate successor to the Sicilian crown) and his son Henry, Duke of Swabia. The party favouring this alliance was led by Walter Ophamil, Archbishop of Palermo, who, as an outsider of English origin, elevated to the highest ecclesiastical office in Sicily, and therefore relatively uninfluenced by local patriotism or dynastic traditions, could advise a realistic approach.

The rival of the Archbishop and his bitter personal enemy, Matthew of Salerno (traditionally known as Matthew 'd'Ajello'), had become a

---

[1] *Compendio dell'istoria del regno di Napoli, di Pandolfo Collenuccio ... di Mambrino Roseo ... et di Tommaso Costo*, ii. 201–2. Cited hereafter as Collenuccio.

[2] See also the following: *La Cronaca di Giovanni Villani: Illustri storici Italiani dal secolo XIII al XIX*, vol. i, ch. xvi, 63; D. Agostino Inveges, *Annali di Palermo*, Pars Terza, 494. The latter says: 'in medio cuiusdam plateae Panormi'. See also the similar account in Antonius archiepiscopus Florentinus, *Chronicon sive Opus historiarum sive summa historialis ab O.C.–1547*, iii. 126.

[3] H. Preuss, *Die Vorstellungen vom Antichrist im späteren Mittelalter bis Luther*, p. 37, note 3.

[4] Thus Collenuccio, loc. cit., states that other authors hold that Constance was past the child-bearing age: 'per essere secondoche egli dice, di cinquantacinque o, come altri hanno detto di sessanta anni quando genero Federico.'

[5] *Anonymi Vaticani* (Muratori, *RIS* viii), col. 779.

member of the Council of Regency during the minority of William II. Apart from his personal animosity towards Walter Ophamil, he was devoted to the monarchy of the Norman rulers. Mutual jealousies of these two counsellors reached the breaking-point during the marriage negotiations with Frederick Barbarossa, when Walter effectively supported the marriage of Constance to Henry of Swabia and championed her right to succeed her nephew as the legitimate heiress of Sicily, which Matthew so actively and eloquently opposed. In the bitterness of his opposition Matthew made full use of the anti-German sentiment which was widespread through Sicily and Apulia. Typical of this feeling of hatred of the Germans is a contemporary letter, *Epistola ad Petrum*, addressed to the treasurer of the Church of Palermo and probably intended by its author to fall into the hands of the Archbishop. In vivid language it depicts the horror and the sufferings which would descend upon Apulia and the neighbouring provinces if the Kingdom of Sicily should be permitted, through the marriage of Constance, to fall into the hands of the Germans. The author tells how the peace and quiet of the blessed island would be shattered by the clash of arms; how cities would be sacked and devastated and the citizens driven into exile. He depicts the suffering and abuse of the populace, the hardships of venerable men, the degradation of matrons robbed of their silken raiment and reduced to the beggarly attire of sackcloth; of boys and girls terrified by the crude and raucous sound of a barbarous language. In short, his letter is a forceful representation of the calamities of a captive people deprived of their cherished way of life, of their accustomed ease and plenty, and plunged into poverty; reduced from joyousness to sorrow, from honour to ignominy, from the pinnacle of happiness to the extreme of wretchedness.[1]

Another contemporary, the poet Pietro da Eboli, describes with tolerable accuracy, although not without exaggeration, the intrigues of the partisan leaders at the court of Palermo. He relates in detail the activities of Matthew 'd'Ajello'. In language often similar to that of the *Epistola*, he depicts Matthew haranguing the populace on the dangers of the German succession to the Sicilian throne. The zealous Matthew emphasized not only the royal lineage of Tancred, but insisted upon the importance of maintaining the integrity of Norman Sicily.[2] Fear of the union of the Kingdom with the Empire could be relied upon also to enlist the support of the Pope and Curia for Tancred's candidacy. When at length the anti-German faction succeeded in bringing about Tancred's

---

[1] Hugo Falcandus, *La Historia o Liber de Regno Sicilie e la Epistola ad Petrum Panormitane Ecclesie Thesaurarium* (ed. G. B. Siragusa: *Fonti*, xxii). See also *Cronica Pontificum et Imperatorum S. Bartholomaei in Insula Romani* (*MGH, SS*. xxxi), 224.

[2] See especially Pietro da Eboli, *Liber ad Honorem Augusti* (*Fonti*), 13.

election, he was crowned and anointed at Palermo, 'with the favour and consent of the Church'.[1]

This atmosphere of bitterness and hatred was all too favourable for the spread of propaganda that was far less concerned with truth than with discrediting the Hohenstaufen succession to the Sicilian throne. The facts that can be derived from dependable contemporary sources tend to destroy most of these improbable tales. Constance of Sicily was the daughter of King Roger II and his third and surviving Queen, Beatrice, daughter of Count Gunther of Rethel and Countess Beatrice of Namur. Beatrice of Rethel was married to Roger II of Sicily on 19 September 1151.[2] Their daughter Constance was born during the year 1154, and some time after 26 February, the date of her father's death.[3] Despite the persistent efforts of later chroniclers to associate her intimately with the Church and to stress her religious life, the best available evidence indicates that from her earliest years Constance was reared amidst the luxuries and affluence of the royal court. She was educated as befitted a Sicilian princess of that era, although given little instruction in affairs of state.[4] Her character also, as depicted by the chronicler Salimbene, is not that of one who would seek the cloistered life or depart reluctantly from her convent cell. He describes her as a perverse woman who troubled her brothers' wives and their entire families. Indeed, he compares her with the woman of whom Solomon said: 'It is better to dwell in a corner of the house top, than with a brawling woman in a wide house.'[5] In so far, therefore, as reliable contemporary evidence permits of a conjecture, it is that Constance, whatever her preferences may have been, accepted the marriage arrangement as the measure of expediency best serving the interests of the Kingdom of Sicily.

The birth of Frederick in the fortieth year of his mother, and after nine years of marriage without offspring, although somewhat unusual, was in no sense improbable or miraculous.[6] The pregnancy of Constance was apparent during her short visit to Milan in May 1194, and the birth took place in due course at Jesi in the March of Ancona on the day after Christmas.[7]

---

[1] *Annales Casinenses* (*MGH, SS.* xix), 314.

[2] *Gisleberti Chronicon Hanoniense* (*MGH, SS.* xxi), 508; *Sigeberti Gemblacensis Continuatio Aquicinctina* (*MGH, SS.* vi), 423; *Romualdi Annales* (Muratori, *RIS*, new ed., vii), 231. Constance's family history has been traced, not without minor errors, by S. K. von Stradowitz in the *Familiengeschichtliche Blätter*, 22 (1924), 45–50. For essential corrections, however, see A. Hofmeister in *Hist. Zeitschr.* 130 (1924), 350–1. *Chronica Albrici Monachi Trium Fontium* (*MGH, SS.* xxiii), 851 f., contains the genealogy of Constance.

[3] As Godfrey of Viterbo, *Gesta Heinrici VI* (*MGH, SS.* xxii), says: 'Postuma post patrem materno ventre relicta . . .'

[4] Falcandus, *Historia*, 174.

[5] Salimbene, *Cronica*, 358. Proverbs 21: 9.

[6] See G. M. Gould and W. L. Pyle, *Anomalies and Curiosities of Medicine*, pp. 38–40.

[7] The facts appear to be adequately covered by the simple statement of *Annales Casinenses*

The legends pertaining to Frederick, although originating with the partisans of Matthew 'd'Ajello', were later revived, augmented, and widely circulated by his Welf opponents in Germany and, frequently also, by the later Joachimite prophets and votaries of the legend of the Antichrist. The chronicler Salimbene was greatly influenced by Joachim of Floris, whose prophecies he frequently included in his writings. It was from the Calabrian seer that Salimbene derived his conception of Frederick as the Antichrist. With equal conviction of the predestined wickedness of the last of the Hohenstaufens, Salimbene relates that when Henry VI asked Joachim about the future of his infant son, the prophet is said to have replied: 'Thy son is perverse, thy son and heir is evil, O Prince! By God! he will plunge the world into confusion and treat with contempt the saints of the Most High!' It was Salimbene also, obsessed as he was with the idea that Frederick was the Antichrist, who said of him long after his death: 'This Frederick was a wicked and profligate man, a heretic, and a sensualist, corrupting the whole world by sowing the seeds of discord and disunity in Italy which endure even to the present day.'[1]

But more friendly prophets of the reign of Frederick were not wanting. In a poem attributed to a continuator of Godfrey of Viterbo and addressed to Henry VI, the new-born infant is depicted as the future Caesar who would have the Empire, the Kingdom, and the monarchy.[2] This prophecy is also reflected in the lines written by the Emperor's court astrologer, Michael Scott, who says of Frederick:

> The Fates decree, the stars and the flight of birds reveal
> That Frederick will be the hammer of the world.
>
> . . . .
>
> And the boy of Apulia will hold the lands in peace.[3]

The *Fourth Eclogue* of Virgil, long interpreted during the Middle Ages as foretelling the coming of Christ,[4] now became the inspiration for the prophecies of Pietro da Eboli, who saw in the birth of Frederick the

---

(*MGH, SS.* xix), 318: 'Constancia imperatrix filium parit in Marchia Anconitana'; or by Richard of San Germano (Muratori, *RIS* vii), 17: 'Tunc [imperatrix in Hesii civitate] Marchie filium peperit nomine Fredericum, mense decembris in festo sancti Stephani.'

[1] Salimbene, *Cronica*, 31 and 174.

[2] Godfrey of Viterbo, *Gesta Heinrici VI* (*MGH, SS.* xxii), 336, lines 95–6:
> Est futurus cesar, sic est vaticinatum,
> Habebit imperium, regnum, monarchatum.

[3] O. Holder-Egger, 'Italienische Prophetieen des 13. Jahrhunderts', part ii (*Neues Archiv*, xxx, 1904–5), 364–5:
> Fata monent, stelleque docent aviumque volatus,
> Quod Fredericus malleus orbis erit.
>
> . . . .
>
> Et puer Apulie terras in pace tenebit.

See also Salimbene, *Cronica*, 362.

[4] D. Comparetti (tr. E. F. M. Benecke), *Vergil in the Middle Ages*, p. 99 and note 10.

'promised boy', precursor of a new era, whose deeds would surpass those of his grandsires Frederick and Roger. He would be a sun without a cloud, never to suffer eclipse.[1]

The early life of the 'puer Apulie' is further obscured by the action of his mother who, doubtless in order to emphasize his Norman heritage through herself, named him Constantine.[2] It was under this name that he was at first elected by the princes of Germany as King of the Romans.[3] Two years later, at the time of his baptism, he was given the names of his paternal and maternal grandfathers, Frederick and Roger. The occasion of his baptism was a brilliant one, at which fifteen cardinals and bishops are said to have been present.[4] The delay of several years before the baptism was probably the result of the persistent efforts of Henry VI to have his son baptized and crowned simultaneously by the Pope, and to the uncompromising opposition of the Pope and Curia to any such plan, which might result, even in the remote future, in the union of the Kingdom of Sicily with the Empire. Henry had spared no pains in his attempts to induce the princes of Germany to accept the principle of hereditary monarchy, as established in France and other European kingdoms.[5] While the princes stubbornly opposed the principle of hereditary monarchy, they voluntarily chose the infant Constantine, i.e. young Frederick, to be successor to Henry VI.[5] Accordingly when Henry sent an embassy to negotiate an agreement with the Pope, desiring that he baptize his son and that he anoint him king it can hardly be doubted that he was, in fact, asking for the coronation of his son as King of the Romans.[6] The yielding to his request by the Pope would have served to overcome much of the opposition of the German princes and could have resulted, ultimately, in the realization of the plan, which Frederick Barbarossa had so nearly achieved long before through negotiations with Pope Lucius III and which appears to have been successfully resisted by the cardinals.[7]

Shortly after her son's birth, the Empress continued her journey southward to join the Emperor in the newly conquered Palermo. She left the

---

[1] *Liber ad Honorem Augusti (Fonti)*, pp. 95 f., lines 1377 ff. It is interesting to compare these early friendly prophecies with the later encomiums of Nicholas of Bari. See R. M. Kloos, in *Deutsches Archiv*, xi. 166 ff.

[2] *Annales Stadenses (MGH, SS.* xvi), 353.

[3] *Cronica Reinhardsbrunnensis (MGH, SS.* xxx), 558.

[4] Roger of Hoveden (Rolls Series), iv. 24; and *Annales Stadenses (MGH, SS.* xvi), 352. *Annales Casinenses (MGH, SS.* xix), 318.

[5] *Annales Marbacenses (SRG in usum scholarum)*, 68: 'sicut in Francie vel ceteris regnis, iure hereditario reges sibi succederent . . .' (Unless otherwise indicated, future references will be made to this edition.)

[6] *Annales Marbacenses*, loc. cit.: 'quod filium suum baptizaret . . . et quod in regem ungeret'. For the generally accepted opinion that coronation as King of the Romans is meant, see K. Hampe, *Kaisergeschichte*, 229, note 1.

[7] *Annales Stadenses (MGH, SS.* xvi), 350.

infant in Foligno in the care of the Duchess of Spoleto, wife of Conrad of Urslingen who had recently become Duke of Spoleto, where he remained until the death of Henry VI.[1] Throughout his life Frederick recalled with gratitude his early years in Foligno, saying of the city: 'In Foligno our refulgent childhood began and we, therefore, cherish that city as the place that nurtured us.'[2] Only to Jesi the place of his birth did he pay a more affectionate, if somewhat presumptuous, tribute, calling it 'our Bethlehem, not the least of the cities of the March ... where our Divine Mother brought us into the world'.[3]

While Constance was still in Jesi, and only a few days after the coronation of the Emperor in Palermo, an event took place which was to have serious repercussions upon the future relations of the Empress with the Sicilian subjects and, probably, with her imperial spouse as well. A monk was said to have revealed a conspiracy against the Emperor's life. It was alleged that letters were intercepted by imperial agents giving details of the conspiracy and implicating many Sicilian nobles as well as the family of King Tancred.[4]

Although Sicilian sources describe these letters as forgeries or as fictitious,[5] the established facts of the conspiracy agree substantially with Henry's account of it in a letter to his friend, the Bishop of Rouen:

> When some of the magnates of the Kingdom obtained from us our pardon they afterwards organized an abominable conspiracy against our person. Because, however, that which is secret cannot remain hidden, that conspiracy was revealed through Divine Grace and made known to us by the duplicity of one of the conspirators and, accordingly, all without discrimination were captured and ordered to be incarcerated.[6]

Sibylla, widow of King Tancred, together with her son and daughters, were exiled and imprisoned in Germany—the son in the castle of Hohenems, near the Lake of Constance, where he died shortly afterwards, and the mother and daughters in Alsace, where they were detained in the cloister of Hohenburg. The Archbishop of Salerno and several Sicilian barons, the alleged leaders of the conspiracy, were imprisoned in the royal castle of Trifels.[7]

During the early months of 1195 Henry was actively engaged in strengthening his hold upon the Kingdom. He is traceable in various

[1] *Breve chronicon de rebus Siculis* 892; *Gesta Innocentii* (Migne, *PL* 214), xxi, col. xxxi.
[2] Piero della Vigna, *Epist.*, Lib. II, no. 21 (*c*. Jan. 1240); Huillard-Bréholles, v. 662.
[3] Huillard-Bréholles, v, part i, 378.
[4] Pietro da Eboli, *Liber ad Honorem Augusti* (*Fonti*), 93.
[5] *Annales Casinenses* (*MGH, SS.* xix), 317; *Annales Ceccanenses* (ibid.), 292.
[6] Ralph of Deceto, ii. 125.
[7] *Annales Argentinenses* (*MGH, SS.* xvii), 89. See also Otto of St. Blaise, *Chronica* (ibid. xx), 326 (also in an improved edition in *SRG in usum scholarum*, 66). Henceforth, unless otherwise indicated, the latter edition of Otto will be cited.

documents emanating from the vicinity of Palermo and Messina until the month of February, when he crossed the strait into Calabria on his way to Lombardy and Germany, leaving the governance of the Kingdom to the Empress and to his Chancellor Conrad of Hildesheim, the latter charged especially with obtaining necessary supplies and ships for a crusading expedition.[1] With the island of Sicily now apparently firmly in his grasp and with the imperial possessions of the mainland made secure by dependable German lieutenants, the Emperor was in a position to pursue his plans for the conquest of the Orient. Among his most faithful supporters were his German associates, now rewarded with possessions in Sicily and Apulia: Conrad of Urslingen, Duke of Spoleto, Philip of Swabia, Duke of Tuscany, Markward of Anweiler, Duke of Ravenna and the Romagna and Margrave of Ancona, and Dipold of Schweinspeunt, Count of Acerra.[2]

Frederick Roger, heir to the Sicilian throne and elected by the German princes as successor to the German kingship, offered what appeared an exceptional opportunity for the adoption of the hereditary principle in Germany. Such an arrangement, obviously long contemplated by Henry VI, would dispose of the conflicting policies of the German princes and prevent future interference by the Pope and Curia with the succession to the German crown.[3]

The achievement of this objective, this fundamental change in the German constitution or customary procedure, would have been possible only if Henry could obtain the support of either the German princes or the Pope. With the support of one of these he might hope, in time, to bring about the acquiescence of the other. Henry's activities in Germany during 1195, and until the summer of 1196, were devoted to the achievement of this objective. Already, however, the privileges of both temporal and ecclesiastical princes were so extensive that there was little that the Emperor could offer as a *quid pro quo*. He offered to the temporal princes what was tantamount to the right of direct hereditary succession within their respective feudal principalities, not only in the male line, but in the female members and in collateral branches of the family.[4] Many princes already possessed these rights through special grants of privileges and had little or nothing to gain by the extension of similar privileges to all imperial fiefs. To the spiritual princes Henry promised the abolition

---

[1] *Arnoldi Chronica Slavorum* (*MGH, SS.* xxi), 192, 202. Also revised in *SRG in usum scholarum*, 195.

[2] *Burchardi et Cuonradi Urspergensium Chronicon* (*MGH, SS.* xxiii), 364. The same is also in *Burchardi Praepositi Urspergensis Chronicon* (*SRG in usum scholarum*), 72–3. The latter, an improved edition, is cited hereafter unless otherwise stated.

[3] K. Hampe, *Kaisergeschichte*, 227–8. See also G. Fasoli, *Aspetti della politica italiana di Federico II*, 31 ff.

[4] *Cronica Reinhardsbrunnensis* (*MGH, SS.* xxx), 556; *Annales Marbacenses*, 66 f.; *Sächsische Weltchronik* (*MGH, Deutsch. Chron.* ii), 235.

of the 'right of spoil', the royal custom of seizing the property of deceased bishops, which had long been regarded by them as a burdensome exaction that should be abolished without concessions on their part. Opposition to the principle of hereditary succession was especially strong in the lower Rhineland and, under the leadership of the Archbishop of Cologne, a bloc was formed which succeeded ultimately in preventing favourable action by the princes. Before a decision could be reached, Henry returned to Italy to complete preparations for the crusade, hoping that on the way he could persuade the Pope to crown Frederick as King of the Romans and, probably, to sanction the hereditary principle. Meanwhile, as the opposition to the plan stiffened in Germany, Henry wisely accepted a compromise by which his son was elected King of the Romans without recognition of the hereditary principle, an action which would ensure the *de facto* union of Kingdom and Empire for a generation.[1]

Henry saw that the achievement of this radical change in customary procedure must await a more propitious time. He continued his negotiations with the Pope and Curia, however, while in the latter half of 1196 he made his return journey to Sicily. It was not until after the Feast of Epiphany, probably about 10 February 1197, that the Emperor began his final negotiations with the Pope. His embassy was given the fullest authority possible to consider a peace with the Curia that would be compatible with the honour of the Emperor and Empire and the Kingdom of Sicily.[2] These negotiations also proved futile, and by early April at least a part of the embassy had rejoined the Emperor in Palermo.[3]

The events of the following summer were to bring to an end the hope of conciliation between the Pope and the Hohenstaufen. In May 1197 the leaders of the anti-German faction in Sicily once more made a desperate effort to throw off the imperial yoke. A conspiracy to which both the Pope and the Empress appear to have been parties had as its aim the murdering of Henry VI while engaged in his favourite pastime of hunting in the vicinity of Messina. An army of some 30,000 soldiers was said to have been in readiness to attack the Germans.[4] Through the treachery of one of the participants the conspiracy was made known to the Emperor and he was able to take refuge in Messina, where he rejoined Markward of Anweiler and Marshal Henry of Kalden, two of his ablest military leaders. Although the number of the imperial troops

---

[1] K. Hampe, *Kaisergeschichte*, 227 ff. See also H. von Kap-Herr, 'Die unio regni ad imperium' (*DZfG*[1], 1889), 107 ff. I have treated this subject in my *Markward of Anweiler and the Sicilian Regency*, 55 ff. and 59–60. [2] *MGH, Const.* i. 525–6.

[3] Stumpf, nos. 5058, 5060. V. Pfaff, *Kaiser Heinrichs VI. höchstes Angebot an die römische Kurie, 1196*, 65.

[4] *Arnoldi Chronica Slavorum* (*SRG in usum scholarum*), 197, says of the origin of the conspiracy: 'Nam de traditione imperatricis et aliorum nobilium illius terre ei constabat.'

was small, for as yet only a part of the crusading army had arrived, mercenaries, hastily enlisted, enabled the Marshal and the Seneschal to attack speedily and effectively. The rebel forces were routed before the walls of Catania and the city was captured and burned. As the street fighting progressed, the unfortunate citizens sought refuge in the Church of St. Agatha. But the Emperor, alarmed by the seriousness of this second revolt, was in no mood for restraint. The church, with its refugees, was reduced to ashes. The conspiring barons were pursued to their strongholds and taken captive to await the vengeance of the victorious Emperor. Contemporaries are in agreement that this vengeance was without mercy. Constance herself was compelled to witness the gruesome punishments inflicted upon her guilty compatriots. The lord of the castle of S. Giovanni, probably Jordanus de Sicilia, the last of the conspirators to yield, described as a pretender to the throne, had a red-hot crown placed upon his head and affixed with iron nails driven into the skull. Some of the conspirators were burned at the stake, flayed alive, or smeared with tar and set ablaze. Others were hanged or put to the sword, impaled, or cast into the sea.[1]

Whether or not the breach between the Empress and her spouse had developed earlier, as appears likely, either during the first conspiracy of 1194 or during the Emperor's absence in Germany, these acts of unrestrained vengeance must have made impossible all hopes of a reconciliation. It would be difficult to doubt the statement of one of the best-informed contemporary sources that by these acts Henry VI 'incurred the bitterest hatred toward himself, not only of the inhabitants but of others who came to know of these things'.[2] It was the unfortunate feature of this unstatesmanlike act of vengeance that it was not Henry VI but his German associates who had to suffer the unyielding hatred of the Sicilians. Henry himself, long weakened in health, became seriously ill only a short time after the rebellion of 1197. While awaiting the arrival of his brother, Philip of Swabia, to accompany the young Frederick to Germany to receive the crown,[3] Henry died suddenly in Messina on 27 September 1197, thus fulfilling the alleged prophecy of Merlin and the Erythraean Sibyl, that Henry would die 'in partibus Malacii'.[4] The death of Henry VI resulted in widespread turbulence and unrest, the beginning of an era of 'wickedness and war' that long endured.[2] In a letter to Pope Innocent III, Philip of Swabia told of these chaotic conditions: how the Kingdom was torn asunder and convulsed in all of its members so that 'prudent men could doubt that, in our time,

[1] Van Cleve, *Markward of Anweiler*, 65–6.
[2] *Annales Marbacenses*, 70.
[3] Otto of St. Blaise, *Chronica*, 71; *Annales Marbacenses*, loc. cit.
[4] *Andreae Danduli Chronicon* (Muratori, *RIS*, new edn., xii, part i), 274.

it would be possible to restore former conditions'. He compared Germany with a sea whipped and torn by winds from all directions.[1]

Henry was aware that he had alienated the Pope, many of the princes of Germany, his spouse Constance, and the great body of the Sicilian barons. As his faithful supporters he could reckon only upon his German followers in Sicily, including Markward of Anweiler, Conrad of Spoleto, Dipold of Acerra, and, above all, his young brother, Philip of Swabia, now temporarily absent in Germany. It had long been apparent that the aims of the Emperor and Empress had little in common. The speed with which Constance acted to achieve her own ends when she was free to do so strongly suggests that she acted in conformity with plans long contemplated, if not matured. It was undoubtedly the suspicion, if not the actual knowledge, of the differences between herself and the Emperor that gave rise to the gossip that she was responsible for Henry's death by means of poisoning. A contemporary chronicler of Goslar was positive in his statement that 'Emperor Henry was poisoned by his own wife'.[2] Other contemporary German chroniclers, obviously doubting the allegation of poisoning, qualify their statements with the familiar 'some say', or 'it is said'.[3] Sicilian chroniclers, while noting briefly Henry's death, give no reason to assume that it resulted from other than natural causes.[4] It is obvious that Constance had become more and more sympathetic to the traditional Norman interests and, by the time of Henry's death, she was quite ready to sever all ties with the Empire. Henry VI, on the other hand, regarded Sicily as an acquisition essential to the control of the Mediterranean and as a stepping-stone to the expansion of his power politics in the East.[5]

Before his death Henry recognized that the education of his son, if he was to carry on the Hohenstaufen tradition, must be entrusted to Germans and, if possible, to his kinsmen. Philip, the youngest of his brothers, was the most eligible for the guidance of the boy. Already two of Henry's brothers, Frederick of Swabia and Conrad of Rotenberg, had died, the former of sickness at Acre while on the Third Crusade, and the latter, who had meanwhile succeeded as Duke of Swabia, murdered while on a military expedition against Duke Berthold of Zähringen.[6] A third brother, the Count Palatine of Burgundy, was not

---

[1] *MGH, Const.* ii, no. 10, p. 11.

[2] *Chronik des Stiftes, S. Simon und Judas in Goslar* (*MGH, Deutsch. Chron.* ii), 596: 'Dussem sulven Hinrike kesisere wart vorgeven van siner egen husfruwen, darvan he starf.'

[3] See, for example, *Cronica Reinhardsbrunnensis* (*MGH, SS.* xxx), 558; Hermann Altahensis, *Annales* (*MGH, SS.* xvii), 385; *Burchard Chronicon*, 75.

[4] Richard of San Germano (Muratori, *RIS* new edn., vii, part ii), 18; *Annales Casinenses* (*MGH, SS.* xix), 318. Typical is the entry of the *Annales Ceccanenses* (ibid.), 294: 'Hoc anno Henricus imperator obiit in Sicilia.'

[5] See the interpretation of Henry's policies in K. Hampe, *Kaisergeschichte*, 211, 222, 233.

[6] Ch. Staelen, *Wirtembergische Geschichte*, ii. 120, 129–30.

only fully occupied in his own territory but was wanting in the personal qualities that could have recommended him as a fitting guardian for his nephew.[1]

Philip, who had been made Duke of Swabia after the murder of Conrad in 1196, was originally designated by his father for the Church. A poet at the court of Barbarossa, addressing prophetic verses to this youngest of Barbarossa's sons, wrote:

> What future title of honour can I promise you?
> Shall I call you count, king, duke, or indeed, perhaps bishop?
> For rumour says 'tis this your awesome father has ordained
> And what beforehand he has thus decreed
> Is not accustomed to fail, or to be unnoticed by the order of things.[2]

But Philip's clerical career was destined to be brief. Henry was urgently in need of his brother's services in Italy, and entrusted him with the important Duchy of Tuscany and with the administration of the lands of Matilda, the most controversial region in the conflict between the papacy and the Empire.[3] The negotiation of a marriage alliance between Philip and Irene, daughter of the Byzantine Emperor and widow of Roger III of Sicily, was intended to facilitate the prosecution of Henry's plans for the future in the Orient. While active in Italy, Philip incurred the displeasure of the Pope and Curia; he sought to extend his dominion, if we may believe the statement of Innocent III, 'even to the Tiber'.[4] Meanwhile, the Emperor continued his negotiations with the German princes in an effort to bring about the constitutional change that would introduce the principle of hereditary succession into Germany. As the newly created Duke of Swabia, Philip was sent to Germany to conclude the negotiations with the German princes. His arrival in Germany was brilliantly celebrated at the Gunzenle, a sepulchral mound for Swabian heroes near Augsburg, where on 28 May, in the presence of his own countrymen, he received his *adoubrement* and was formally married to Princess Irene to whom he had been affianced in Palermo.[5] The appropriateness of the choice of Philip as special emissary of the Emperor was amply attested at the Gunzenle, not only by the brilliance of the ceremony but also by the unstinted admiration of those in attendance for Irene, the 'rose without a thorn, a dove devoid

---

[1] Édouard Clerc, *Essai sur l'histoire de la Franche-Comté*, i. 386–8.

[2] Gunther of Paris (?), *Ligurinus sive de Rebus Gestis Imper. Caes. Friderici* (Migne, *PL* 212), cols. 334–5. As to Philip's clerical education, see also *Contin. Weingartensis* (*MGH, SS.* xxi), 478. The attribution of the poem to Gunther of Paris is questionable. See M. Manitius, *Geschichte der lateinischen Literatur*, IX, ii. 3, p. 699, and E. Assmann, 'Bleibt der Ligurinus anonym?' (*Deutsches Archiv*, xii, 1956), 453–72.

[3] *Burchardi Chronicon*, 73, and Ficker, *Forschungen zur Reichs- und Rechtsgeschichte Italiens*, ii. 203.

[4] *RNI*, no. xxix, col. 1030.   [5] Otto of St. Blaise, *Chronica*, 70.

of gall'.[1] Already something of that admiration for the young Hohenstaufen couple was apparent which, shortly afterwards, was to influence
the princes to forget 'the boy of Apulia' and, instead, to bestow upon
Philip of Swabia 'des rîches zepter und die krône'.[2] His activity on
behalf of his brother's plan for hereditary succession revealed him as a
man of exceptional skill and gave proof to the Emperor of his ability and
his loyalty. Already, in September 1197, after entrusting the Duchy of
Swabia to the care of Diethelm von Krenkingen, Bishop of Constance,
Philip, accompanied by 300 knights, set out for Apulia where young
Frederick was still in the care of the Duchess of Spoleto (at Foligno), to
escort him to Germany.[3] Philip had proceeded only as far as Montefiascone in the *patrimonium*, some fifty miles north of Rome, when news
reached him of the Emperor's sudden death. The pent-up hostility of
the Italian towards the Germans found full expression when it became
generally known that Henry VI was dead. Only with difficulty was
Philip able to make his way across the Alps against the opposing forces
of the Italians bent upon vengeance on the hated Staufen. Many of his
followers, including the faithful *ministerialis*, Frederick of Tanne, were
slain, while the remainder succeeded in returning to Germany, not without danger and effort.[1]

[1] *Walther von der Vogelweide* (10th edn. by Lachmann–Kraus), 24, line 13.
[2] Ibid. 19, line 10.
[3] *Hugonis Chronici Continuatio Weingartensis* (*MGH, SS.* xxi), 479; Otto of St. Blaise, *Chronica*, 70–1.
[4] *Burchardi Chronicon*, 76.

II

THE NEGLECTED 'BOY OF APULIA'

dô liez der chaiser Hainrich
ain sünlîn, hiez Friderich—
grôz êre hernâch an im gelit,
daz sait daz buoch, sô des wirt zît,—
daz chint von Pülle man in hiez.

*Kaiserchronik—Erste Bairische Fortsetzung (MGH,
Deutsch. Chron.* i), 401, lines 279 ff.[1]

THE absence of Philip of Swabia from the bedside of his dying brother and his failure to conduct the boy to Germany before the Emperor's death proved fateful for the future of young Frederick II. Henceforth, the heir of Henry VI was to be reared, not as the scion of the Hohenstaufen, but as the 'boy of Apulia', successor to the Norman kings of Sicily. In these last hours of his life Henry VI must have been painfully aware of the difficulties that awaited the future of his son when, in the absence of Philip, he was compelled to rely, not upon his most trusted kinsman, but upon his German captains in Sicily, in particular Markward of Anweiler, as executor of his 'testament'. He could have had no doubt of the hostility of the Empress Constance towards these Germans, or of her want of interest in the ultimate realization of the Hohenstaufen plans, nor could he have doubted that the Pope would seize this opportunity to establish his hold upon Sicily as a papal fief, and upon regions of Central Italy that he claimed as the Papal State.

When at length Philip of Swabia succeeded in crossing the Alps he was immediately confronted with the task of persuading the German princes to respect their oaths to support his nephew. Undoubtedly some of them had originally taken the oaths of fealty to the Hohenstaufen heir as a matter of expediency or because it would have been hazardous to their own interests to oppose the will of the late Emperor. Many were only too ready to accept the somewhat devious argument of Innocent III that 'the oaths were illegal and the election unwise. For they elected

[1] At that time the Emperor Henry left
a little son, called Frederick—
great honour would come to him—
so says the Book, and it came to pass.
He was called the boy of Apulia.

a person unsuited not only as Emperor, but for any other office, that is to say, a boy scarcely two years old and not yet reborn through the holy water of baptism.'[1] From the outset Philip was made aware that he could not ignore the sentiments of these princes, nor could he achieve, without their loyal support, that which Henry VI had desired: the coronation of his heir in Germany as King of the Romans. From the moment of his brother's death Philip was prepared to assume the guardianship in accordance with German law, which recognized this as a right and duty of the nearest agnate.[2] In the south and in the upper valley of the Rhine the princes, both lay and ecclesiastic, were disposed to recognize him as the legal guardian of his nephew. Although Frederick was less than three years old, the German princes had already committed themselves by oath to support him. Philip had every reason to expect the full loyalty of the princes, since many of them, now on a crusade, had renewed their oaths of fealty while still in Beirut.[3]

As Philip endeavoured to carry out his mission in Germany he was confronted with several difficulties which, in the light of all the known facts, must have appeared almost insuperable. First there was the unfavourable reaction of many German princes to the long dominant and all too powerful family of Hohenstaufen. The determined efforts of Henry VI to bring about a constitutional change that would perpetuate the kingship in the house of Hohenstaufen had served to accentuate the opposition to the family. Ever present also was the threat of the Welf faction among the princes, all the more dangerous if, in the course of time, its candidate should become acceptable to the not too scrupulous Adolf, Archbishop of Cologne. By no means the least of these difficulties was the anxiety of some princes arising from the infancy of Frederick II, a sentiment recognized by Innocent III when, in his *Deliberatio*, he quoted the words of Ecclesiastes (10: 16): 'Woe to thee, O land, whose King is a child.'

It was one of the greatest misfortunes that the brother of Philip, the Count Palatine, Otto of Burgundy, through his inability to live in peace with his princely neighbours, had succeeded in heightening the latent hostility to the Hohenstaufen. The annalist of Marbach relates in detail the misdeeds of this third son of Barbarossa, and tells of his greed and faithlessness which led the princes at length to ignore their obligations to the Hohenstaufen. At the instigation of the influential Bishop of Strassburg a war of vengeance in which Duke Berthold of Zähringen, the Bishop of Basel, and numerous counts and lords of that region

---

[1] *Deliberatio domini papae Innocentii super facto imperii de tribus electis. RNI*, no. xxix, col. 1025.
[2] G. Waitz, *Deutsche Verfassungsgeschichte*, vi. 277.
[3] *Gesta Episcoporum Halberstadensium* (*MGH, SS.* xxiii), 112; *Annales Stadenses* (*MGH, SS.* xvi), 353.

participated, was waged against Otto of Burgundy.[1] Upon his arrival in Germany, Philip hastened to this war-torn region and entered into negotiations with Bishop Conrad of Strassburg, the instigator of the revolt and leader of the foes of Otto of Burgundy. It was at this time also that Philip gave assurance that he would take over the government, not for himself, but as vicegerent of his nephew. Presumably also the Bishop was induced to attend a meeting at Hagenau to which Philip had summoned his supporters for late December.[2]

For the moment it appeared that Philip's arrival would succeed in restoring peace and remove the threat to Hohenstaufen interests there. But the prospect of peace was shattered by the activities of the Archbishop of Cologne, now leader of the anti-Hohenstaufen party in Germany. It was this same Adolf of Cologne, for five years archbishop of that archdiocese, who had led the opposition to Henry VI's plan to introduce the principle of hereditary monarchy into the constitution.[3] Among German princes his influence was second only to that of the Duke of Swabia and was all the more dangerous because of the traditional alliance between Cologne and England. This close relationship with England had been strengthened by the Archbishop's friendliness towards Richard Cœur de Lion, on whose behalf he had intervened after Richard's capture by Henry VI.[4] As a counter-move to the supporters of Philip at Hagenau, Adolf and the Archbishop of Trier invited Bishop Conrad of Strassburg and other princes and magnates hostile to the Hohenstaufen to Andernach for the purpose of arranging for a general council of princes to meet in Cologne in early March for a new election. Although an embassy from Philip endeavoured to dissuade them, the adherents of Adolf of Cologne proceeded with their plans.[5] Bernhard of Saxony was at first preferred as their candidate.[6] But when he declined, the more influential of the princes agreed, in return for a substantial money payment, to name Berthold of Zähringen as their candidate. Regarded by his contemporaries as a marauder, murderer, and plunderer, for whom Satan had especially reserved the glowing crater of Mount Etna, Berthold owed his selection solely to the cupidity of the conspirators.[7] He was to make his appearance before the princes in March for the formal election. Even before the negotiations with Berthold of Zähringen, Adolf of Cologne must have given some con-

---

[1] *Annales Marbacenses*, 70–1.   [2] Ibid. 71; *Burchardi Chronicon*, 76.
[3] See above, pp. 20, 23.   [4] Th. Toeche, *Heinrich VI*, 294.
[5] *Burchardi Chronicon*, 79.
[6] Concerning him see the extraordinary explanation of the miracle of the five parts of the sun in Caesar of Heisterbach, *Dialogus Miraculorum* (ed. J. Strange), vol. ii, ch. xxiii, 235 f. See also *Chronica regia Coloniensis* (*SRG in usum scholarum*), 162. (This improved edition is regularly referred to when not otherwise indicated.)
[7] Caesar of Heisterbach, *Dialogus*, Bk. XII, no. 13. He is similarly characterized by the *Chronica Albrici Monachi Trium Fontium* (*MGH, SS.* xxiii), 907.

sideration to a proposal from King Richard of England that the Welf, Henry of Saxony, eldest son of Henry the Lion, be accepted.[1]

These persistent efforts on the part of the Archbishop of Cologne and his adherents caused the Hohenstaufen partisans, who as yet had made no decision at Hagenau, to hasten their plans to check this growing threat to their interests. During the early months of 1198 further meetings were held at Arnstadt and Ichtershausen in the vicinity of Erfurt. At first the princes had been content to support Philip merely as 'Defender of the Empire' (*defensor imperii*), with the intention that he would act in that capacity 'until his nephew should arrive in Germany'.[2] Conscious, however, of the dangers of a regency in the face of continued threats from the adherents of Adolf of Cologne, they appealed urgently to Philip to accept election as King and future Emperor. At last, persuaded by Bishop Diethelm of Constance, always the faithful adherent of the Hohenstaufen, Philip reluctantly consented, first at Ichtershausen, and subsequently at Mühlhausen, where the formal election took place on 8 March 1198.[3]

Even as the choice of Philip was being made in early March, the adherents of Archbishop Adolf assembled for the meeting at Cologne. Not only the princes of the Lower Rhine were present, but also representatives of the English King, Richard Cœur de Lion, who was considered an imperial vassal because he had sworn the oath of homage to the Emperor Henry VI.[4] At the insistence of Adolf of Cologne, negotiations with Berthold of Zähringen were resumed only to find that, despite his earlier commitment, he had been dissuaded from accepting the election and had transferred his support to Philip.[5]

Dismayed by the defection of Berthold of Zähringen, the adherents of Adolf of Cologne now heard with greater favour the proposals of the ambassadors of the English King. The rich gifts accompanying Richard's embassy were doubtless a decisive factor, although it must have been apparent to all that the election of the Swabian Philip made it desirable, if not imperative, to choose a Welf to oppose him. Henry of Saxony, the candidate of King Richard, was still absent in the Orient and considered unavailable, but his brother, Otto of Brunswick, formerly Count of Poitou, youngest son of the late Henry the Lion, was chosen instead, and on 9 June 1198 he was formally elected.[6] Henceforth for many years

[1] Roger of Hoveden, *Chronica*, iv. 38.

[2] Otto of St. Blaise, *Chronica*, 73.

[3] Conrad of Fabaria, *Casus S. Galli* (*MGH, SS.* ii), 168. The circumstances of Philip's election are set forth with exceptional clarity in *Gesta Treverorum Continuatio Quarta* (*MGH, SS.* xxiv), 390.

[4] J. Ficker, *Vom Reichsfürstenstande* (2nd edn., Innsbruck, 1932), 224. Roger of Hoveden, iv. 37.

[5] *RNI*, no. cxxxvi, col. 1133.

[6] Roger of Hoveden, iv. 38. *Chronica regia Coloniensis*, 164.

Germany was to be torn by civil strife during which the 'boy of Apulia' was forgotten and the traditional foes, the Welfs and the Weiblingen, led respectively by Otto of Brunswick and the Swabian Philip, contended for the German crown.

The German people, who now faced the inevitable consequences of protracted civil war, had scarcely emerged from more than two years of devastation and famine brought on by disastrous floods, recurrent since the summer of 1195. The sufferings of the 'Hungerjahren' were again in prospect as civil war was envisaged in the fateful year of 1198.[1] It was in these days of death and devastation in Germany, when men and beasts suffered the bitter consequences of famine and war, that the Minnesinger, Walther von der Vogelweide, sensitive alike to the world of nature and to the follies of mankind, wrote the pessimistic lines:

> I heard the water murmuring
> And saw the fishes swimming.
> I saw all things within the world:
> Forest and field, leaf, reed, and grass,
> All things that crawl and fly
> Or tread the earth with feet.
> These things I saw, and thought:
> Not one of these lives free of hate.
> Wild beasts and creeping things
> Engage in violent quarrellings.
> Among themselves even the birds contend.
> Yet in one thing they are agreed:
> That their destruction is decreed
> Unless they build firm governments.
> They create kings and laws;
> Establish lords and servants.
> Yet what of you, you German folk?
> What of your arrangements?
> Tho' every insect has its king
> Your very honour's perishing.
> Take heed! Take heed!
> These petty princes grow too proud,
> Beggarly kinglets threaten you.
> Place the imperial crown on Philip's head,
> And bid these kinglets step aside.[2]

Save for motives of greed and selfishness or, perhaps, because of his

---

[1] The sufferings of the German people are vividly described by numerous contemporary sources. See especially *Sigeberti Gemblacensis Continuatio Aquicinctina* (*MGH, SS.* vi), 433 f.; *Annales Marbacenses*, 71; *Reineri Annales* (*MGH, SS.* xvi), 652; *Chronica regia Coloniensis*, 158; Caesar of Heisterbach, *Dialogus* iv, 65 f., x, no. 47.

[2] For the original see Lachmann-Kraus, *Die Gedichte Walthers von der Vogelweide* (10th edn.), 10: 'Ich hôrte ein wazzer diezen', etc.

implacable hatred of the Hohenstaufen, the Archbishop of Cologne could have had no plausible reason either for his repudiation of his oath to support the son of Henry VI or for his obstinate refusal to accept the decision of the majority of the princes to choose Philip of Swabia. With but few exceptions, contemporary sources are in agreement that Philip's actions throughout these negotiations were honourable, and that he made every effort possible, consistent with the interests of the Kingdom, to protect the rights of his nephew. Philip's own statement of his motives, set forth simply and sincerely some years later (1206) in a letter to Pope Innocent III, explains adequately the wisdom of his decision. At that time he wrote in substance as follows:

In the beginning we worked so wholeheartedly in the interests of the boy that we were reproached by many of the princes and our friends with want of courage in not being willing to accept the imperial dignity. These same princes said also that no one else among them could take on the burden of the Empire or was sufficiently wealthy to measure up to its dignity. We saw also that if we had not accepted the *imperium* a choice would have had to be made from among those who had long been hostile to our family and with whom we could have no peace and tranquillity . . . Conscious of our faith in Jesus Christ, through whom we hope for salvation, we say, therefore, that we have been impelled to this action neither by ambition for honour nor by pride in power and glory, nor yet by greed for riches. We would never have sought or accepted the burden and toils of imperial rule for all these things. Certainly, however, you may believe, or rather be certain, that none among all the princes is wealthier, more powerful, or more noble than ourselves. For we have vast and widely scattered estates and strong and impregnable fortresses. We have also so many *ministeriales* that we are scarcely able to reckon their numbers exactly. We have castles, cities, villages, and rich towns. We have incalculable treasures in gold, silver, and many precious stones. We have also in our possession the Holy Cross, the lance, the crown, the imperial robes, and all the insignia of the Empire. . . . No one could have been chosen King who would not have greater need of our support than we of their goodwill.[1]

No less fateful for the future of the heir of Henry VI than the bitter conflict between Philip of Swabia and Otto of Brunswick was the death of the aged Pope Celestine III and the immediate succession on 8 January 1198 of the youthful and ambitious Lothar, of the family of the Conti of Segni, as Innocent III. From the outset, the new Pope regarded his office as one which 'God himself had recognized as the prince of all the lands of the earth'.[2] Innocent himself could say of his election:[3] 'The agreement of our colleagues was so complete in their desire to fill the vacancy of the papal office . . . that all, animated by but a single will,

---

[1] *MGH, Const.* ii, no. 10, 11–12.
[2] *Epist.* I, i, col. 1; *Epist.* II, ccix, col. 759.   [3] *Epist.* I, xi, col. 9.

elected us unanimously as Pope, on the day of the burial of our pre-decessor.'

From the beginning of his pontificate it became apparent that Innocent III's concept of the papal office extended far beyond that of universal spiritual dominance; it embraced also the continuous influ-ence upon the temporal Empire of the spiritual, a concept to be carried to its logical conclusion by Innocent IV and the canonists of his era.[1] Just as Innocent conceived of the Apostle Peter as having been entrusted with temporal governance, so he looked upon himself as the heritor of the Petrine power.[2] Also it was with Innocent III that the concept of the vicariate of Peter as synonymous with the vicariate of Christ was fully developed.[3] While this concept of the papal office was in no sense original with Innocent III (it is implicit in the writings of Nicholas I in the ninth century and of Bernard of Clairvaux in the twelfth), it was he who first applied it practically, establishing it as fundamental in the political thought of the twelfth- and thirteenth-century canonists. Versed as he was both in theology and in the canon law as interpreted in the *Summa* of Huguccio and others of the Bolognese canonists, he made the most of the dictum of Pope Nicholas I that the world is an *ecclesia*, emphasizing this with no less certainty than he did his pronounce-ment that the Roman Church is the fundamental law of the whole of Christendom.[4] As the Vicar of Christ, Innocent III insisted further that temporal things are of necessity subservient to the spiritual.[5] It was only a final step in a subtle evolutionary process that extended from Pope Leo 'the Great' and Gelasius I, through Nicholas I, Bernard of Clairvaux, and Gregory VII, when at length Innocent III clearly enunciated the obligation of the sacred authority of the Pope to examine the person chosen as King of the Romans and Emperor Elect.[6] Innocent's ideal was a form of theocratic imperialism, through which he, as Vicar of Christ, undertook to regulate the relations of peoples with their sovereigns.[7] While reserv-ing to himself the right to intervene in temporal matters, he denied the lay ruler such rights in spiritual things, comparing the Pope in this

---

[1] See especially J. A. Watt, *The Theory of Papal Monarchy in the Thirteenth Century: The Con-tribution of the Canonists*, pp. 34 ff., 58 ff., for a plausible treatment of Innocent III's role in transforming the canonists' understanding of the relation of the powers, and for the relation of the views of Innocent IV to those of Innocent III. See also H. von Eicken, *Geschichte und System der mittelalterlichen Weltanschauung*: 'Das System des Gottesstaates', 392 ff., and E. W. Meyer, 'Staatstheorien Papst Innocenz III' (*Jenäer Historische Arbeiten*, Heft ix, 1919), 51 f., and especially P. Brezzi, *Il Papato* (2nd edn., Rome, 1947), 122.

[2] *Epist.* II, ccix, col. 759; *Epist.* XI, ccviii, col. 1525.

[3] W. Ullmann, *The Growth of Papal Government in the Middle Ages*, especially pp. 84–5, note 2, and 284, has fully exploited this subject. See also P. Brezzi, *Il Papato*, loc. cit.

[4] *Epist.* II, ccxvii, col. 776.

[5] *RNI*, no. xviii, col. 1013. See also M. Maccarrone, *Chiesa e Stato nella Dottrina di Papa Innocenzi III.*

[6] *Sermo III* (Migne, *PL* 217), col. 658.   [7] L. Hahn, *Das Kaisertum*, 107.

respect to Melchisedek, who 'with the Lord at his right hand doth crush kings in the day of his wrath'. It would be erroneous to assume, however, that Innocent III had as yet become the advocate of the extreme hiero-cratic system that was to dominate the canonistic thinking during the last half of the thirteenth century. When Innocent III declared, as he did on more than one occasion, that Peter had conferred power not only over the Church but over the whole world, he employed this phraseo-logy not in the sense of World Empire, but merely in the liturgical sense.[1] And yet it is obvious that already the claims of Innocent III were diametrically opposed to the concept of Empire of the Hohen-staufen—a concept that originated in a revival of the traditions of Roman antiquity that had influenced the Emperor as a result of his close relations with the interpreters of the Roman law in Bologna.[2] It was inevitable that these conflicting views of imperial sovereignty would manifest themselves strongly in the efforts of Pope and Emperor to dominate Italy, for Innocent III insisted that Italy, by divine dis-position, was pre-eminent over all other regions. The authority of the central government of Rome extended over all the *societas christiana*, whose subordinate rulers, in their conflicts with one another, must sub-mit to the judgements of the Pope.[3] Conditions were favourable in Italy for the ambitious Pope to demonstrate by decisive action the efficacy of his lofty concept of power, for an infant only three years old was heir to the Kingdom of Sicily and Apulia. The imperial throne itself was vacant and might well remain so for several years. Sweeping aside the traditional rights of German princes and ignoring the German consti-tution or customary procedure, Innocent III in his *Deliberatio* greatly advanced the concept of an *ecclesia universalis* as comprehending the *plenitudo potestatis*, as it came to be understood by the canonists of the late thirteenth century. While theoretical expression or implications of such power may be detected in treatises antedating Pope Innocent III, certainly in Bernard of Clairvaux and in the *Dictatus Papae*, it was he who gave practical significance to the words of the Scriptures: 'By me Kings reign and princes decree justice.'[4] Such were

---

[1] Psalms 110: 4. See first P. Brezzi, *Il Papato*, 122 f. and *Epist.* VI, cciii, col. 516; also *Sermo VII* (Migne, *PL* 117), col. 481, and then, R. Folz, *L'Idée d'empire en occident du Vᵉ au XIVᵉ siècle*, 94–5; and especially, A. M. Stickler, 'Sacerdozio e Regno nelle nuove richerche attorno ai secoli XII e XIII nei Decretisti e Decretalisti fino alle decretali Gregorio IX' (*Misc. hist. pont.* 18, Rome, 1954), 1–27.

[2] A. Brackmann, 'Der mittelalterliche Ursprung der Nationalstaaten', tr. G. Barraclough, *Medieval Germany*, ii. 291.

[3] *Epist.* I, cccci, col. 377. See also K. Wenck, 'Die römischen Päpste zwischen Alexander III und Innocenz III' (*Papsttum und Kaisertum*), 415.

[4] See G. B. Ladner, 'The Concepts of "ecclesia" and "christianitas" and their Relation to the Idea of papal "plenitudo potestatis" from Gregory VII to Boniface VIII' (*Misc. hist. pont.*, 18, 1954), 49–77.

the concepts of authority of Innocent III, destined to dictate his relations not only with Philip of Swabia in Germany but also with the Empress Constance and her son in the Kingdom of Sicily and Apulia. But the activities of Philip of Swabia and the determined efforts of Pope Innocent III to prevent the union of Sicily and Germany under a single sovereign were of little interest to Constance. She was concerned solely with safeguarding the future of her son in his hereditary Kingdom of Sicily. In view of her immitigable anti-German sentiment, it is doubtful that she could have done otherwise than play into the hands of the Pope.

Soon after Henry's death, Constance sent Berard, the Archbishop of Messina, to Rome to begin negotiations with the Pope. Among other things, the Archbishop was especially authorized to petition the Pope 'that Frederick, son of the aforesaid Emperor, might be crowned King of Sicily'.[1] It was during these negotiations also that Constance is said to have 'made oath, touching the Gospels, that Frederick was born of the lawful marriage of the aforesaid Emperor Henry and herself'. In addition to attesting the legitimacy of her son on oath Constance is said to have agreed to pay 1,000 marks of silver to the Pope and 1,000 marks to the cardinals, after which the Pope would consent to the coronation, 'if it pleased his colleagues, the cardinals'.[2] Nothing so clearly reveals the helplessness of the Empress as her recognition of the right of the Pope to sanction the election of her son as King of Sicily. Long before, it had been agreed with the Norman kings of Sicily that succession to the Sicilian throne did not require papal sanction.[3]

The coronation of young Frederick took place on Whit Sunday (17 May 1198), and was proclaimed in accordance with the traditional formula, 'Christus vincit, Christus regnat, Christus imperat': 'Grant, O Christ, to our Lord, King Frederick, august, triumphant, invincible, life everlasting! Grant thou this, O Christ, Saviour of the world! Sustain him, thou world Redeemer!' Then were invoked the blessings of the Holy Trinity, the Virgin, St. Michael, St. Gabriel, St. John the Baptist, and a host of other saints.[4] How complete was the triumph of Constance of Sicily, perhaps indeed of the Pope also, is mutely revealed in the change in the title of the young King which appears in official documents before and after his coronation. At the end of April 1198 he is referred to by his mother as 'Illustrious King of the Romans and of Sicily', while shortly after the coronation his habitual titles are 'Frederick, King of Sicily', or else 'King of Sicily, of the Duchy of Apulia, and of the Principality of Capua'. The omission of 'illustris

---

[1] Roger of Hoveden, iv. 31.

[2] Ibid., 'quod Fredericus natus fuit de legitimo matrimonio praedicti Henrici imperatoris et ipsius' (iv. 31).   [3] J. Ficker, *Über das Testament Heinrichs VI.*, 7.

[4] See the transcript of this coronation ritual taken from Amato, *De principe templo Panormitano*, 425, and reprinted in Huillard-Bréholles, i, part i, 9.

Romanorum regis' leaves little doubt that Constance had repudiated the Hohenstaufen heritage of her son and that Innocent III had at last found what he believed to be a permanent safeguard against the 'unio regni ad imperium'.[1]

In her implacable hatred of the Germans and in her quest for protection for her son, Constance had sacrificed not only his German heritage but had acknowledged also the suzerain rights of the Pope and Curia over Sicily and Apulia. Henceforth, the King must acknowledge himself as vassal to the Pope in 'the Kingdom of Sicily, the Duchy of Apulia, and the Principality of Capua with all its appurtenances, Marcia and the other lands beyond Marcia, to which the royal pair have a right'.[2] She had attempted, through her ambassadors to the Pope, to retain the ecclesiastical rights granted to William I and William II, including the right of control over appeals to Rome, the calling of synods, the sending of legates, and the election of prelates. The Pope, however, now demanded the unconditional surrender of such privileges as a *sine qua non* of his granting these lands to herself and her son as fiefs of the Church.[3]

At the time of her death, which was to take place in the midst of her final negotiations with the Curia, on 27 November 1198, Constance abrogated the rights of the heir to Sicily through a testament which not only made of the Kingdom a feudal dependency but also made her son a ward of the Pope. In the exercise of his guardian rights Innocent III was to receive 30,000 *tarens* annually from the royal treasury and compensation for all expenditures made in defence of the Kingdom.[4] These concessions, in sharp contrast to the policies of Frederick Barbarossa and Henry VI who held firmly to the position that the dignity of the Empire did not permit of their swearing homage and fealty to the Church, were now possible in that Constance had renounced all imperial claims of her son.[5]

As Constance surrendered the future of Sicily into the hands of the Pope, so also she determined to rid the Kingdom of all remnants of the government of Henry VI. The Chancellor of the Kingdom, Walter of Palear, was dismissed and probably imprisoned. Markward of Anweiler and all Germans previously established by Henry VI were ordered to leave the Kingdom. Intervention of Pope Innocent III compelled the restoration of the powerful Walter of Palear to the chancellorship,[6] but the Empress, fully supported by the Pope and Curia, pursued her relentless policy towards the hated Germans.

[1] For the changes of title see: Huillard-Bréholles, i, part i, 8 (30 Apr.); and pp. 10–11 (June).
[2] Ibid. i, part i, 17. [3] *Epist.* XI, ccviii, col. 1524.
[4] The complete testament is not extant, and we are dependent upon such fragments as are included in the *Gesta Innocentii III* (Migne, *PL* 214), cols. xxxviii–xxxix.
[5] *RNI*, no. xxix, col. 1026. [6] *Gesta*, XXIII, col. xxxviii.

III

STRUGGLE FOR THE CONTROL OF
SICILY: THE GERMAN PRETENDERS
A SICILIAN CHANCELLOR, AND
THE HEIRS OF TANCRED

Erit inter capram laniandus et non absorbendus.
Breve chronicon de rebus Siculis (Huillard-Bréholles, i,
part ii), 892.[1]

Ho w greatly Constance had erred in her hopes for the future
security of her son was soon to be only too apparent. For neither
the Hohenstaufen party in Germany nor the Germans in Italy
and Sicily were disposed to accept the arrangements of the Empress or
to recognize the far-reaching territorial claims or the regency of the
Pope. Henry VI himself, in his so-called testament, which in reality
appears to have been merely a body of instructions for the guidance of
his executor in his negotiations with the Pope,[2] had certainly not intended to surrender legitimate claims of the Hohenstaufen on the mainland of Italy or in the island of Sicily. His object seems to have been,
above all else, to obtain by means of liberal concessions the recognition
of his son's right to succeed to both the imperial crown and the Kingdom
of Sicily. He could not have anticipated that, before the negotiations
were concluded, the conciliatory Celestine III would be dead or that
his successor would be the forceful and uncompromising Innocent III.
Meanwhile, the princes of Germany had repudiated their allegiance to
the infant Frederick and had chosen in his stead Henry's brother, Philip,
Duke of Swabia.

There can be little doubt that it was the intention of Philip, as it was
of his supporters in Germany, to hold fast to the imperial possessions in
Italy and to continue to look to Markward of Anweiler and his German
associates as representatives of the Hohenstaufen interests in Italy and
Sicily. As early as 28 August 1198, Markward had recognized Philip as
his lord[3] and in May of the following year the princes of Germany

---

[1] In the midst of sheep [literally, goats] he will be lacerated, though not devoured.

[2] Van Cleve, *Markward of Anweiler*, 67.

[3] BFW, *Reg.* v, Abt. iv, no. 12167. See also P. Compagnoni, *La Reggia Picena, overo de' Presidi
della Marca Historia Universale*, 78; and J. Ficker, *Forschungen*, iii, par. 318, pp. 442–3.

appealed to the Pope to bestow his goodwill and favour upon Markward, 'our devoted friend and faithful supporter of our lord King
Philip'.[1] Devoted as Markward had been to the interests of Henry VI,
nothing could have been more futile than an attempt to support the
claims of the infant Frederick after the German princes had felt compelled, in the face of the opposition of the Welfs, to recognize Philip of
Swabia as the legally elected king. In common with other Germans in
Sicily, Markward must have shared the belief that no one could rule the
Sicilian Kingdom who did not receive the crown and Kingdom from
the Roman Emperor.[2] There is ample reason to assume that Markward
was fully aware of the circumstances under which Philip of Swabia had
yielded to the pressure of the German princes and had permitted himself to be chosen King. Obviously, Philip had no intention of recognizing the claims of Innocent III as guardian over his nephew. Indeed, it
appears most doubtful that Philip recognized the suzerain rights of
Innocent over Sicily. For, since the time of Henry III, Sicily had been
widely, if not generally, regarded as part of the Empire.[3] It will become
increasingly apparent, therefore, that the long conflict which Innocent
III and the Curia carried on with Markward and his German associates
in Italy was inseparable from their opposition to Philip of Swabia and
the Hohenstaufen party in Germany.

Constance herself was certainly aware before her death of how little
personal direction the Pope could give either to the education of his
ward or to the regency of Sicily. It was this that caused her to place in
the hands of the Council of *familiares*, the old Central Governing Council,
so active in the days of William II, the veritable administration of the
Kingdom.[4] It was with this council of *familiares* that Innocent III
established relations early in December, after receiving intelligence of
the Emperor's death. He informed the members that he expected soon
to visit the Kingdom with the object of restoring order and securing
obedience to the young King.[5] But these papal plans were altered in
view of the announced intention of Markward of Anweiler to return to
the Kingdom, certainly as the representative of Philip of Swabia, despite
his earlier obedience to the order of Constance expelling him.[6]

Markward made his appearance first in Molise, his Sicilian fief, where
he found faithful supporters, especially Dipold of Vohberg, Count of
Acerra, and other German adherents of the late Emperor, Henry VI,

---

[1] *RNI*, no. xiv, col. 1009.   [2] *Chronica regia Coloniensis*, 186.
[3] H. von Kap-Herr, 'Die unio regni ad imperium', 104–5. See also the excellent treatment of this in F. Baethgen, *Die Regentschaft Papst Innozenz III. im Königreich Sizilien*, 3–4.
[4] Baethgen, *Die Regentschaft Papst Innozenz III*, 6.
[5] *Epist.* I, dlxiii, cols. 518 ff. Van Cleve, *Markward of Anweiler*, 125 f.
[6] *Gesta*, XXIII, col. xxxviii. The following account of Markward's activities is based upon
my *Markward of Anweiler and the Sicilian Regency*, 97 ff. and 108 ff.

who had refused to obey the orders of the Empress to leave the Kingdom. It was in Molise also that he announced himself as regent of Sicily, although he did not at this time reveal the document, the so-called testament allegedly entrusted to him by Henry VI, upon which he based his claim. Here in Central Italy he lost valuable time seeking to overcome the resistance of Abbot Roffrido of Monte Cassino, who had previously taken an oath to support the papal claims.

During these operations in the vicinity of San Germano, Markward continued his efforts to negotiate with the Pope, at the same time maintaining his relations with Philip of Swabia and the Hohenstaufen party in Germany. It was during these negotiations that Markward is alleged to have declared, in his desire to obtain the crown of Sicily for himself, that Frederick was not the legitimate son of Henry VI and Constance. Suspicion is immediately cast upon this charge in that such an allegation would have alienated Philip from Markward; whereas, on the contrary, the relations between the two men became even closer during the succeeding years. On every occasion that the Pope mentioned Markward in his letters, he associated him with Philip and the Hohenstaufen party. Between 28 May 1199, when the German princes made their appeal to the Pope on behalf of Markward, and 11 December 1203, months after the latter's death, Innocent continued to declare that Philip, through the agency of Markward, had sought to deprive Frederick of his kingdom.[1] In his *Deliberatio*, referring to the disputed election in Germany, Innocent III said: 'Moreover, since we have frequently excommunicated Markward and all other German and Italian supporters of Philip, he himself, the author of their sins, is surely subject to the same sentence.' The Pope sent forth manifesto after manifesto, striking examples of the epistolary style of the early thirteenth-century papal chancery. In flowing rhetoric these letters recalled the gruesome scenes that had characterized Henry VI's conquest of Sicily, associating Markward and his supporters with the atrocities of the late Emperor. The excommunication pronounced against Markward was to be read and re-read every Sunday and every feast-day.

We excommunicate, anathematize, curse and damn him, as oathbreaker, blasphemer, incendiary, as faithless, as a criminal and usurper, in the name of God the almighty Father, and of the Son, and of the Holy Ghost, by the authority of the blessed apostles Peter and Paul, and by our own. We order that anyone who henceforth gives him help or favour, or supplies him or his troops with food, clothing, ships, arms, or anything else which he can benefit from, shall be bound by the same sentence; any cleric moreover, of whatever order or dignity, who shall presume to say the divine service for

---

[1] *RNI*, nos. xiv, xxix, cols. 1009, 1030; *Epist.* II, ccxxi, col. 781.

him, may know that he has incurred the penalty due to one of his rank and order.[1]

The trials and tribulations of the year 1199, so frustrating to the hopes and plans of the Pope, had their origin not merely in Markward of Anweiler, but also in the activities of the Governing Council in Palermo, guided by the Chancellor of Henry VI, Walter of Palear, who was sympathetic to the claims of neither Philip of Swabia nor the Pope. The papal legate, Gregory of Santa Maria in Porticu, had been delayed in his arrival in Sicily and when at length he did appear, his reception was not favourable to the successful carrying out of his mission. Walter of Palear, the Chancellor, long accustomed to the free exercise of authority, was but little disposed to yield to the legate. Wisely the latter judged it expedient to leave the island and return to Rome, where he again appeared early in July.[2] Evidently Innocent determined shortly afterwards, probably as a result of Gregory's experience, to leave the Sicilian Council a free hand in the carrying on of the administration.[3] In the same letter, however, in which he revealed this intention to the Council he voiced his dissatisfaction, saying: 'We understand that for some time you have been giving much of the royal domain as fiefs to various persons.'[4]

Relations of the Pope with the Council deteriorated even further as a result of the changes in its constituency, changes always more favourable to the interests of Walter of Palear. It is impossible to determine how some of the appointments were made, whether by the Pope or through the influence of the Chancellor. The appointment of Gentile of Palear, the Count of Manupello, the Chancellor's brother, somewhat later, leads to the suspicion that even at this time Walter chose as councillors whomsoever he wished.[1] Indeed, whatever pretences Walter of Palear may have made at this time of co-operation with the Pope as guardian of the young King, there were, in fact, three contenders for the dominance of Sicily: Philip of Swabia, acting through his agent Markward of Anweiler, the Pope, and Walter of Palear himself. Throughout the continuous conflict between the Pope and Council the intentions of the Chancellor are obscure—whether or not they were wholly selfish, or were merely evidence of his opposition to both the Pope and Philip of Swabia, or of his recognition of his obligation to safeguard the interests of the rightful heir. Subsequent relations between Frederick and the

[1] *Epist.* II, clxxix, col. 730.

[2] Potthast, *Regesta*, i. 466.

[3] *Epist.* II, clxxxvii, col. 736: 'Vos tamen administrationem ejus fere totam libere permiserimus exercere.'

[4] Ibid., 'Jamdudum autem audivimus quod vos multa de dominio regis diversis personis in beneficium assignastis.'

[5] *Gesta*, XXXI, col. lv: 'quin etiam familiares instituebat regios quos volebat . . .'

Chancellor after Frederick's release from the papal guardianship suggest that he considered his own interests would be best served by loyalty to the young King.[1]

Some time during the month of October 1199 Markward of Anweiler, aided by the ships of Admiral Grasso, a Genoese seaman formerly employed by the Emperor Henry VI, crossed over to the island of Sicily, landing at Trapani on the west coast of the island.[2] Immediately after his arrival he informed Philip of Swabia of his successful crossing.[3] He quickly won the support of the Saracens in the western part of the island, the former allies of Emperor Henry VI. His German associates on the mainland could also report at least minor successes there, causing a contemporary to write of them: 'One could hardly live there without fear and trembling.'[4] The Pope himself, conscious of the growing seriousness of the threat from the Germans, not only to the Kingdom but to the Papal State also, proclaimed a crusade against them, offering the same privileges and immunities to those who fought against Markward and his allies that they would enjoy if they crossed the sea to fight the infidel.[5] Despite repeated appeals and threats from the Pope, it was not until March (1200) that the promised papal army made its appearance in Calabria *en route* to Messina.[6] Large numbers of Sicilian barons through preference, fear, or in the hope of greater personal benefits supported Markward.

In the face of these developments it is understandable that Innocent III should begin, somewhat frantically, to search for aid outside the Kingdom. It was especially distressing to the Pope that there was but little enthusiasm among the Sicilians or the inhabitants of the Papal State to join the forces being assembled for the army under the leadership of Marshal James. It could have been only in desperation that Innocent determined to invite the support of the heirs of the illegitimate Tancred, obviously the greatest possible threat to the interests of his ward. The marriage of Alberia, the eldest daughter of the late King Tancred and his Queen Sibylla, to the French nobleman Walter of Brienne appeared to the Pope to provide the means by which much-needed aid could be obtained for the reconquest of Sicily.[7] According to the papal version of this unfortunate incident, so little to the credit

[1] See below, pp. 126 ff.
[2] *Breve chronicon de rebus Siculis*, 899. Richard of San Germano, 21, erroneously gives the landing-place as Palermo.
[3] *Epist.* II, ccxxi, col. 781.
[4] *Annales Casinenses*, 318.
[5] *Epist.* II, ccxxi (24 Nov.), col. 782. See also J. R. Strayer, 'The Political Crusades of the Thirteenth Century', *History of the Crusades*, ii (ed. R. L. Wolff), 346.
[6] For the fixing of this date see E. Winkelmann, *O. von B.*, p. 23, note 3.
[7] The somewhat conflicting sources for this action of the Pope are, first, the *Gesta Innocentii III*, XXXV, cols. xlvii ff., Ernoul, 329, and *Eracles*, 234.

of the judgement of Innocent III, Alberia and her new-found spouse, after their marriage in France, arrived in Rome, where they appealed to the Pope as guardian of the young King to restore to them as royal fiefs the Principality of Taranto and the County of Lecce. These fiefs had

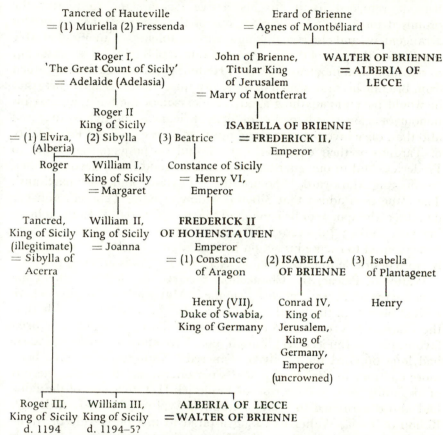

Genealogical tables showing the relation of Walter of Brienne to the heirs of Tancred

formerly been granted by Henry VI to Sibylla, the mother of Alberia, and her heirs shortly after his conquest of Sicily. Later, however, because of the alleged participation of Sibylla and her son in the rebellion of 1194, these lands were confiscated by the Emperor, and the family of Tancred was exiled and imprisoned in Germany,[1] where they remained until released by the Pope after the death of Henry VI.

The visit of Alberia and Walter of Brienne to Rome took place in the spring of 1200, when Innocent was desperately trying to mobilize troops for the papal army under the command of Marshal James. Seeing an

---

[1] See above, p. 21.

opportunity to obtain much-needed assistance for his Sicilian interests, not only from Walter and his immediate following, but from the crusaders from Flanders and Champagne *en route* to the Orient, Innocent yielded to their entreaties. Thus assured of papal support, Walter of Brienne returned hastily to his native Champagne to recruit the promised forces. Obviously conscious of the dangers inherent in this arrangement, and also recognizing the inevitableness of an unfavourable reaction on the part of the Governing Council of Sicily, Innocent sought to reassure them in a lengthy letter. He told them how he had obtained from Brienne his most sacred oath, sworn upon the cross and relics, that he would never do anything against the person of the King, against his honour, or against the Kingdom of Sicily. Brienne is said to have declared also that, once invested with the County of Lecce and the Principality of Taranto or their equivalents, he would do homage and fealty to Frederick, 'aid in our guardianship and, in good faith, devote himself to opposing Markward, Dipold, Otto of Laviano, and their partisans'. The Pope then added that Sibylla, widow of King Tancred, and her daughter, the spouse of Brienne, had taken similar oaths. In the following year also (3 July 1201), in a letter to his royal ward, the Pope endeavoured to excuse his action by explaining that he had considered it more desirable to have Brienne as a friend than as an enemy.[1]

Walter of Palear, the Chancellor, received the letter of the Pope announcing his agreement with Brienne in May while in Messina, where he had been with the papal legate since March.[2] It is unthinkable that the Chancellor's reaction to this decision of the Pope could have been favourable. As Innocent III himself must have known, Walter of Palear had long opposed the family of Tancred.[3] Nothing could have been more contrary to Walter of Palear's personal interests, to the interests of his family, or to the interests of Frederick II. Other acts of the Pope had also contributed to the alienation of Walter of Palear. Although Bishop of Troja, Walter had long aspired to the loftier title of Archbishop of Palermo. The Pope refused to sanction his translation, although he permitted him, while occupying the see of Troja, to assume the additional title of Administrator of the Church of Palermo.[4] Shortly afterwards, certainly in June 1200, and for reasons which we do not know, Walter abandoned all ecclesiastical titles, styling himself merely: Walter, *Chancellor of the Kingdom of Sicily*. The breach between the Chancellor and the Pope now appeared to be irreparable. The same source relates that 'Walter was greatly shaken and, assembling the

---

[1] Huillard-Bréholles, i, part i, 80 ff.   [2] *Gesta*, XXV, col. xlix.

[3] P. Lejeune, *Walther von Palearia Kanzler des normannisch-staufischen Reiches*, 16.

[4] P. Scheffer-Boichorst, 'Urkunden und Forschungen zu Regesten der staufischen Periode' (*Neues Archiv*, xxvii, 1902), p. 120. In a letter, *Gesta*, XXIX, col. liii, Innocent III authorizes Walter to add this title 'si vellet'.

people, he attacked the motives of the Pope in the sharpest possible manner, seeking to slander him'.[1] Despite his disappointment, it was only reluctantly that the Chancellor determined to break with the Pope and Curia and to begin negotiations with Markward of Anweiler and his German associates.[2]

Taking advantage of the Chancellor's indecision and the inactivity of the papal army, Markward continued his operations on the island virtually unopposed and seized many cities and castles.[3] On 27 June 1200 he began the siege of Palermo. It was doubtless the knowledge of these activities of Markward in the vicinity of the capital city that compelled the papal forces to move from Messina to Palermo. But day after day the battle for the possession of this city was delayed. At length, however, when the battle began near Monreale, Markward was defeated and routed. He himself fled, as the Pope was informed, 'none knows whither', leaving in the hands of the papal forces his personal baggage in which, in addition to considerable treasure, was found the so-called testament of Henry VI.[4]

The defeat of Markward of Anweiler might well have been decisive, eliminating the German threat and leaving to the Pope and Curia control of the Kingdom, but for the attitude of Walter of Palear and several of the councillors who had opposed the papal alliance with Brienne. By his agreement with the heirs of Tancred, Innocent III had alienated many of his Sicilian adherents. His appeals to the nobles, the barons, and the citizenry as a whole, in which were invariably included the most extravagant charges against Markward as oppressor of the Church and the Sicilian people, now failed to evoke a sympathetic response. The papal troops under the leadership of Marshal James remained unpaid, and, tormented by the excessive summer heat and by the accompanying sickness, they withdrew from the island.[5] Despite his defeat at Monreale, Markward now found that his position in Sicily had improved, although a contemporary Sicilian chronicler certainly exaggerates when he says 'that he [Markward] obtained possession of all places in Sicily, save the city of Palermo'.[6]

The negotiations between the Chancellor and Markward were resumed immediately after the battle of Monreale. An agreement was reached by the end of October or early November 1200,[7] and the in-

---

[1] *Gesta*, XXIX, col. xlix.

[2] K. Hampe, 'Aus der Kindheit' (*MIöG*, xxii, 4 Heft, 1901), 578–9.

[3] *Epist.* III, xxiii, col. 902.

[4] This episode is treated in detail in my *Markward of Anweiler*, 153 f.

[5] *Gesta*, XXVIII, col. lii f. *Epist.* III, xxiii, col. 902.

[6] *Breve chronicon de rebus Siculis*, 893.

[7] This is apparent from Innocent's letter, *Epist.* III, xxiii, col. 902. See K. Hampe, 'Kindheit', 578 ff.

habitants of Sicily were called upon to accept it in the name of the King. The administration of the Kingdom was divided: Markward assumed authority on the island while Walter of Palear was permitted a free hand on the mainland. As a seal to this agreement, a marriage alliance was arranged between relatives of the contracting parties.[1] Although conceding to Markward virtually unlimited authority on the island of Sicily, the Chancellor, as a precautionary measure, entrusted the person of the young Frederick to his brother, Gentile of Palear, Count of Manupello. Also the city of Palermo, at least for a time, remained in the hands of the Central Governing Council.[2]

The outlook for the papal cause brightened during the following May (1201) when Walter of Brienne, after a year's absence in France, returned to Rome. He had succeeded in obtaining some funds from King Philip Augustus of France[3] and promises of assistance from a few of the French crusaders who agreed to accompany him to Italy. While the troops actually accompanying him into Apulia were not numerous, their prowess was such that he was able to obtain an unexpected victory over Dipold of Acerra, the most powerful of the German allies of Markward on the mainland.[4] The news of this victory of Brienne was to have an immediate effect upon the plans of both Markward of Anweiler and his new ally, the Chancellor, Walter of Palear. Disappointed by the failure of German allies on the mainland, Markward now took steps to strengthen his hold upon the island of Sicily and to secure possession of the person of Frederick. Whatever considerations had led Markward to respect his agreement with Palear not to seize the city and to permit Frederick to remain in the custody of Gentile of Manupello, they could no longer prevent him from doing what he believed essential to ensure his future dominance of the island. In October (1201) he began the siege of Palermo and on the 18th the garrison yielded, opening the gates of the city to the besiegers. Gentile of Manupello, evidently judging his forces too weak to resist the triumphant Markward, made no effort to prevent the capture of the young King. Whatever the motives of Gentile, he was not present at the surrender of the castle. It was the castellan, one 'B. of Accarino', who, at 10 o'clock on All Saints' Day 1201, opened the castle gate and permitted the capture of Frederick and his tutor William Franciscus.[5]

[1] *Gesta*, XXXII, col. lvi.

[2] Ibid., loc. cit.: 'Cancellarius . . . dimisso rege in custodia fratris sui, transfretavit in Calabriam et Apuliam.' According to the *Gesta* XXXV, col. lxii, it was only later that Markward 'Panormum obtinuit, et tam palatium quam regem in suam potestatem accepit.'

[3] *Eracles*, 235.

[4] *Gesta*, XXX, col. liii, says of Brienne's following that they were 'non multis quidem, sed strenuis'.

[5] K. Hampe, 'Kindheit', 593 f. The *Gesta*, XXXIV, col. lxii, accuses Gentile of accepting a bribe: 'recepta pecunia, sicut publice dicebatur.'

Reginald, Archbishop of Capua, who probably heard the details of the incident from Frederick's tutor, reports them with dramatic vividness in a letter to the Pope. When the castle gates were opened, Frederick and his tutor concealed themselves in the innermost part of the castle. But the castellan revealed their hiding-place and the boy suddenly found himself confronted by the man whom he had been taught to think of as his would-be murderer and the plunderer of his heritage. Papal propaganda had done its work all too well. Frederick's conduct was that of a high-spirited boy confronted by something that he had been taught to fear. As Markward was on the point of seizing him, Frederick leaped upon him with all his fighting energies aroused. His helplessness was soon apparent, and, with disgust and a sense of outraged dignity, he angrily cast aside his robes, rent his clothing, and tore his own flesh with his nails. Reginald of Capua saw in this outburst of the royal child the prophecy of the future man—the revelation of a 'noble royal sentiment', the proud disdain of Mount Sinai when touched by a beast of prey.[1] The taking of Palermo and the seizure of the person of the King placed Markward of Anweiler in the forefront of those who were to shape the future of the heir of Sicily. No longer in control of the boy, Walter of Palear was not in a position to play a significant role in the government of the Kingdom. During the remaining ten months of his life Markward, on the other hand, could view the future with satisfaction. Unfortunately, however, we have little information about the life of Frederick during this period of supremacy of his German captors. We know that the predictions of the Pope as to the bloodthirsty intentions of Markward failed to materialize and, in so far as we can ascertain, the life of the boy, perhaps even his education, proceeded as before. It would be most erroneous to treat as peculiar to this period of Markward's ascendancy the statement of one contemporary that so great was the need of the boy that 'he had scarcely enough for subsistence'.[2] Certainly he continued to live as the ward of Markward of Anweiler, although the author of the *Gesta Innocentii III* could explain this only by Markward's fear of Brienne, the nearest heir to the throne in the event of Frederick's death.[3] Despite the propagandist accusation of Markward as potential usurper of the kingship and as would-be murderer of the King, the true cause of the hostility of the Pope and Curia appears to have been that Markward, in the tradition of Frederick Barbarossa and Henry VI, and now as the representative of Philip of Swabia in Italy, was the chief

[1] Exodus 19: 12; Hebrews 12: 20: 'If even a beast touches the mountain, it shall be stoned.' See Hampe, 'Kindheit', 593 f.

[2] *Breve chronicon de rebus Siculis*, 892: 'Et ad tantam devenerunt inopiam quod vix haberet quid comederet.' This statement, probably a rhetorical exaggeration, could apply equally to any of the years following the death of the Empress.

[3] *Gesta*, XXXV, col. lxii.

barrier to the temporal ambitions of the Pope, both in the Kingdom of Sicily and in the Papal State.

For Walter of Palear, the Chancellor, also the unexpected success of Brienne was a stimulus to action. Under the circumstances he could find no solution save joint action with Dipold, the ally of Markward, and his German associates, against the papal forces. On 22 October 1201, on the ancient battlefield of Hannibal, at Cannae, the combined forces of Walter of Palear and his German allies met the followers of Brienne in decisive conflict. The forces of Dipold and the Chancellor were superior in number and the outcome appeared most doubtful to the papal partisans. But again Brienne was victorious and the opposing forces were routed.[1] This defeat proved a shattering blow to the alliance of Walter of Palear and Markward. The alliance, at best a temporary expedient, entered into in the hope of crushing the papal forces, had failed to achieve its objective. Thanks to the efforts of Brienne, the authority of the Pope was now re-established over parts of the mainland, and he could devote his attention to restoring a regular administrative system there. Walter of Brienne was made Grand Justiciar, exercising authority, under the papal regency, over the mainland with the exception of Calabria.[2] For the moment, the Chancellor was eliminated, both as a useful ally of Markward of Anweiler and as a formidable opponent of the plans of Innocent III and the heirs of Tancred.

On his side, Markward now felt free to extend his efforts to the mainland, seeking, in the name of the King, to obtain recognition of his authority there. He was not without some success, at least in the Duchy of Amalfi, and perhaps also in Gaeta.[3] But he had delayed too long in his decision to extend his efforts beyond the island and, at best, his gains were meagre.

Even less successful were the efforts of Innocent III on the island of Sicily itself. It was in vain that he urged his protégé, Walter of Brienne, to make the necessary conquest of the island. The Frenchman was reluctant to leave his hard-won fiefs of Lecce and Taranto exposed to attacks by the Germans. The papal sources, in the bitterness of their disappointment at the inactivity of their champion, did not hesitate to assert that Markward of Anweiler, at this critical moment, endeavoured through bribery to induce Walter of Brienne to abandon his conquests and leave the Kingdom.[4]

Confronted with this reluctance of Brienne to continue his conquests,

---

[1] The date of the battle is established by K. Hampe, *Mitteilungen aus der Capuaner Briefsammlung* (*Sb. H. Ak.*, 1911, 5 *Abhandl.*), i. 6 ff.

[2] *Epist.* V, lxxxiv, col. 1070.

[3] See especially the letter of Innocent III to the Archbishop of Amalfi, *Epist.* V, lxxvi, col. 1061. As to Gaeta, see P. Kehr, 'Das Briefbuch des Thomas von Gaeta Justitiars Friedrich II.' (*QF* viii, 1905), 20.   [4] *Gesta*, XXXV, col. lxii.

Innocent looked for assistance in another quarter. He now took up an old plan of the Empress Constance having as its object the marriage of Frederick with a Spanish princess, a sister of the King of Aragon.[1] The proposed marriage agreement called for substantial military assistance for the liberation of the Kingdom to be provided at the expense of the Spanish King, Pedro II, whose sister was the intended bride.[2] Although the plan failed for the time being, Innocent continued to recognize its advantages and, some years later, actually brought about the realization of a similar plan. Meanwhile, he continued his efforts to induce the reluctant Brienne to enter the island, even offering to ensure the adequate protection of Lecce and Taranto during the Count's absence.[3]

Innocent was still trying to overcome Brienne's reluctance when, in the autumn of 1202, Markward of Anweiler, on the eve of receiving the surrender of Messina, the one stronghold still resisting his rule in the island, died suddenly at Patti some thirty miles west of Messina.[4] The news of the death of Markward, symbol of German wickedness and injustice, came to the Pope as a profound relief.[5] At first regarded by Innocent III as removing the chief barrier to his two cherished goals—the restoration of peace in Sicily and the firm establishment of the Papal State—it actually afforded him but little relief from his trials and tribulations. For Dipold of Acerra, staunchest of the German allies of Markward, although no longer a major threat, now returned to the mainland to harass the Terra di Lavoro.[6] On the island of Sicily there appeared, immediately after the death of Markward, another German, one William Capparone, who gained possession of both the royal palace and the person of young Frederick. Little is known of his origin or of his earlier life, although he seems to have been one of several Germans, formerly with Henry VI, who had defied the order of the Empress Constance in 1198 to leave the Kingdom.[7] He now assumed the title Defender of the King and Grand Captain of Sicily. Actually his position was that of a usurper, having no authority either from the Pope, as guardian of the King, or from Philip of Swabia and the imperial party in Germany. Already Philip had designated Conrad of Uerslingen, Duke of Spoleto, as successor to Markward in Sicily.[8] It is indicative of the extent of the collapse of orderly government in the Kingdom that, under these circumstances, Capparone could have maintained a position of some authority for several years. It was only towards the close of the year 1206 that young Frederick was taken from his custody and restored to the care of the papal legate.

---

[1] *Epist.* XI, iv, col. 1342.
[2] Ibid. V, li, col. 1018.
[3] Ibid. V, lxxxiv, col. 1071.
[4] *Breve chronicon de rebus Siculis*, 893.
[5] *Epist.* V, lxxxix, col. 1075.
[6] *Annales Casinenses*, 318 f.
[7] *Gesta*, XX, XXXVI, cols. xxxi and lxii f.
[8] *RNI*, no. lxxx, col. 1087.

Walter of Palear, disappointed in his alliance with the Germans, together with his brothers Gentile and Manerio, and his brother-in-law Peter of Celano, appealed to the Pope for absolution and reconciliation. Innocent III, evidently feeling the need of a strong leader to check the growing chaos on the island, yielded to their pleas and restored Walter to his office as Chancellor of the Kingdom.[1] Walter's recent experience had served as a sobering influence. In contrast with his former resentment at the interference of Pope and Curia in the affairs of Sicily, he now humbly requested that the Pope send a legate to assist in the rehabilitation of the Kingdom. In compliance with this request, the Pope, in April 1204, named as legate Cardinal Deacon Gerhard Allocingola, whom he described as 'a prudent and honest man', authorized to act 'in our behalf in spiritual as in temporal affairs'.[2]

Negotiations were also being carried on between the Curia and William Capparone, although no evidence is available as to which side took the initiative.[3] It was only after the arrival of the legate that an agreement was finally reached, absolving Capparone from the ban and accepting his oath of submission to the Pope. He is said to have promised obedience in all things (*in omnibus obediret*), and, accordingly, it may be assumed that he permitted free access of a tutor to the boy, Frederick.[4]

On the mainland Dipold and his associates continued a form of guerrilla warfare, all the more successful because of the growing hostility of the inhabitants to the papal ally, Walter of Brienne. It was a major triumph for the Germans, therefore, when in June 1205, while Brienne was besieging one of their strongholds at Sarno, he was so incautious as to be trapped and slain. During the night, having failed to take precautionary measures to safeguard his person, he was surprised in his tent and suffered serious wounds from which he died on 14 June. The *Chronique d'Ernoul*, a continuation of that of William of Tyre and especially well informed with regard to the family of Brienne, gives the following somewhat different account of Walter's death:

> Dipold followed Count Walter to the place where he was camped near the city. During the night, while Brienne slept, Dipold, together with some knights, entered the camp secretly. Going directly to the tent of Count Walter, they cut the tent ropes and allowing the tent to collapse upon him, they slew him.[5]

The death of Brienne removed one of the chief causes of unrest from the Kingdom. The passing of the Frenchman left the way open for the reconciliation of many Sicilian and Apulian barons with the Pope.

[1] *Epist.* VI, lxxi, col. 67.   [2] *Epist.* VII, xxxvi, col. 319.
[3] Baethgen, *Regentschaft*, 85–6.   [4] *Gesta*, XXXVI, cols. lxiv–lxv.
[5] *Ernoul*, 329–30. See also *Annales Ceccanenses*, 292, lines 160 ff.

Above all it made it possible for the Chancellor, although already nominally reconciled, to co-operate whole-heartedly with the Pope and Curia.

While these changes were taking place in Italy changes of equal importance were occurring in Germany. About this time many of Otto's staunchest supporters were falling away and joining the forces of the Staufen. Among them were Adolf of Cologne, hitherto the most powerful of Philip's opponents, Duke Henry of Brabant, and, most significant of all, Otto's brother, Henry Count Palatine of the Rhine. The latter, alienated by his brother's unwillingness to reward him adequately for his services, deserted on the eve of battle near the village of Bergdorf in the early spring of 1204.[1] The Duke of Brabant and the Archbishop of Cologne made their formal submission to Philip at Coblenz on 11 November of the same year. A few weeks later, on 6 January 1205, the Archbishop presided at the ceremonial coronation of Philip at Aachen.[2]

This second coronation of Philip was, in a sense, a formal repudiation by the German princes of papal efforts to dominate the election of the German King. It had been the contention also of the supporters of Otto that Philip's first coronation at Magdeburg on Christmas Day 1199 was invalid because it had not taken place in the church of Aachen where such ceremonies had been conducted since the time of Charles the Great, and that the consecration had not been performed, as was customary, by the Archbishop of Cologne. Accordingly, this second coronation gave to Philip of Swabia a more secure position as duly elected King. The lines of Walther von der Vogelweide, probably written six years before in celebration of the Magdeburg coronation, would have been even more appropriate on this Day of Epiphany, 1205:

> There walked an emperor's brother and an emperor's son
> Clad in one robe, and yet three titles joined in one:
> He bore the royal sceptre, wore the crown.
> Gently he trod, untroubled was his mien:
> Behind him lightly moved his high-born queen,
> A rose without a thorn, a dove devoid of gall.
> Such loyalty never before was anywhere;
> Thuringians and Saxons too did homage there.
> And this could only pleasing be to wise men all.[3]

It was doubtless Philip's confidence in his now unassailable position in Germany that influenced his decision to send Bishop Lupold of Worms as his special agent to regain control of the provinces of Central Italy

---

[1] *Arnoldi Chronica Slavorum* (*SRG in usum scholarum*), Lib. VI, par. 6, 226 f.
[2] *Chronica regia Coloniensis*, 174; BFW, *Reg.* v, Abt. i, no. 86 b.
[3] Translated from the original in Lachmann-Kraus, *Die Gedichte Walthers von der Vogelweide*, p. 24: 'dâ gienc eins keisers bruoder / und eins keisers kint', etc.

and to re-establish his roles as guardian of the interests of Frederick and as regent of the Kingdom of Sicily.[1] Lupold's arrival in Italy, suggesting the possibility of a union of his forces with those of the German captains in Sicily and Apulia, may well have been construed by the Pope and Curia as a threat, not only to the regency of the Pope, but even more as a challenge to the authority of the Holy See in the provinces constituting the Papal State. While the traditional claim of the Pope rested somewhat nebulously on the Donations of Pepin and Charlemagne, it is significant that Innocent III based his claim, notably to the March of Ancona, upon the so-called testament of Henry VI.[2] He seized the opportunity following the death of Henry VI to establish and organize the Papal State as a tangible reality, possessing both definite boundaries and an organized administration—a more or less integrated state extending across Central Italy, separating Northern Italy from the Kingdom of Sicily and Apulia.

How seriously Innocent III regarded Lupold's mission is apparent in the measures taken by him to oppose it. To oppose the invading forces he chose not only his Chamberlain, Cardinal Cinthius of San Lorenzo in Lucina, but also a competent military force of *familiares* and *amici*. The troops of Lupold were quickly crushed and he, together with his shattered army, fled. Lupold himself was recalled to Germany.[3]

Meanwhile, active negotiations between the Pope and Philip of Swabia had long been in progress, but always with the papal insistence upon the recall of Lupold from Italy. It would be erroneous, however, to construe the defeat of Lupold as the main cause of Philip's more amenable attitude towards a *rapprochement* with the Pope. Undoubtedly Philip recognized that the Pope himself, seeing that his plans for Otto of Brunswick had failed in Germany, would welcome a reconciliation.

Still another factor may have served as a warning to the Pope against further delay in the recognition of Philip. This was a plan, first divulged in 1204, to bring about the marriage of Frederick and Maria, daughter of the Duke of Brabant. Such defiance of the interests of the Pope, like the expedition of the 'stone-hearted' Lupold, was construed as having no object other than to ensure the future union of Kingdom and Empire. How bitterly Innocent III resented this interference with his own cherished plan is revealed in his letter to the Duke of Brabant setting forth the long-standing arrangement for the marriage of

---

[1] For Lupold's expedition see H. Tillmann, *Papst Innocenz III.*, 120 ff. Pertinent also is her article 'Das Schicksal der päpstlichen Rekuperationen nach dem Friedensabkommen zwischen Philipp von Schwaben und der römischen Kirche' (*Hist. Jahrbuch*, li, 1931), 341 ff. For an excellent brief summary see D. Waley, *The Papal State in the Thirteenth Century*, 47 ff.

[2] *Epist.* VII, ccxxviii, col. 549: 'ex testamento . . . Henrici.'

[3] *Chronica regia Coloniensis*, 173; Huillard-Bréholles, ii, part i, 593. See also the old but excellent work of S. Sugenheim, *Entstehung und Ausbildung des Kirchenstaates*, 137 ff.

Frederick to a sister of King Pedro II of Aragon.[1] The proposed Brabantine marriage alliance assumes special significance as an effort of Philip
to identify his nephew more closely with Germany and as a demonstration of his intention to maintain his guardianship over the young King.
Certainly also, there is a suggestion that, as guardian, he anticipated
the probable future succession of Frederick as King of the Romans.

The sudden recall of Lupold from Italy and the abandonment of the
Brabantine marriage plan came about largely because both Philip and
Innocent III were disposed to abandon hostilities that had proved of
little advantage to either side and to resort to negotiations. Philip could
be reasonably sure of his future absolution, of the repudiation of Otto
by the Pope, and of his own recognition as King of the Romans and as
Emperor. Innocent III, after the defeat of Lupold, could look forward
to the security of the Papal State. Unfortunately, we do not have the
precise terms of the agreements that were finally reached, but it is a fair
conjecture that they were similar to the agreements made between the
Pope and Otto of Brunswick in 1201.[2] Moreover, such concessions were
less difficult for Philip, since Frederick was now securely established in
his Sicilian heritage, and the corridor through the Duchy of Spoleto
and the March of Ancona was no longer of primary interest to Philip.[2]

There can be little doubt that knowledge of these negotiations influenced the sudden decision of Dipold and his German associates in Italy
to accept reconciliation with the Pope. Unfortunately, contemporary
sources are singularly silent as to the motives that prompted this action
of the Germans in Sicily. It is highly probable that the negotiations of
Philip with the Pope, incomprehensible to Dipold and his associates,
led them to assume that they had been abandoned by the Staufen party.
Whether or not this was the cause, they now determined to make their
peace independently with the Pope. Although it may be questioned
whether the initiative came solely from Dipold rather than from the
Curia, it must have been apparent that the greater advantage was on
the side of the Pope. Dipold and his companions were absolved from the
ban and ostensibly reconciled with the Pope. They were said also to
have promised not to lend aid and support to Philip of Swabia.[3]

Following his release from the ban, Dipold went to Rome towards the
close of the year 1206; here plans were made for the future roles of himself and his associates. Whatever else these plans included, chief among
them was the restoration of Frederick to the care of the papal legate. It is
perhaps the greatest of tributes to the cunning of Dipold that shortly
after his absolution he obtained from Capparone a promise to surrender

[1] *RNI*, no. iii, cols. 1114 ff.
[2] See the observation of D. Waley, *The Papal State*, 50.
[3] *Gesta*, XXXVIII, col. lxviii.

the royal palace and, at the same time, succeeded in releasing young Frederick from William's control, delivering him safely into the hands of the legate, Cardinal Gerhard, and the Chancellor. Contemporary gossip attributed little sincerity to these actions of the German, seeing in them but another of Dipold's schemes to usurp authority in Sicily, after first putting to death his rivals, Walter of Palear and William of Capparone. But the Chancellor, no less cunning than the scheming Dipold and aware of the current gossip, acted swiftly to forestall his rival. Ostensibly as a friendly gesture designed to celebrate the general pacification of the warring factions, he invited Dipold and some of the latter's intimate associates to a banquet. In the midst of the festivities, Walter ordered the arrest of the German leader and his son. On the following night, however, the prisoners eluded their guards and escaped to Salerno, where, once more united with his German followers, Dipold resumed his operations against the papal forces.[1]

Henceforth, Walter of Palear could feel secure in his office of Chancellor and could devote himself, despite serious obstacles, to rescuing the Kingdom from its chaotic condition. His French opponent had been removed by death; Dipold, although still capable of minor operations in various parts of the mainland, need no longer be treated as a serious threat; and the heir to the Kingdom, the source of the Chancellor's authority, was now safely in his hands. Moreover, Walter was restored to his former ecclesiastical dignity, authorized by the Pope to assume the office of Bishop of Catania.[2] But, despite his seemingly secure position, the Chancellor was compelled to meet the obstinate resistance of Capparone, who, in violation of his promise, held tenaciously to the royal palace. Fortunately, the resistance of Capparone and his allies proved less formidable than had been anticipated and they were decisively routed.[3]

On the mainland a German associate of Dipold, Conrad of Marlenheim, once described by a contemporary as the 'most incorrigible and the most perfidious' who, since 1191, had been castellan of the stronghold Rocca Sorella, continued his devastating forays into the Terra di Lavoro, the Campagna, and neighbouring regions. It was not until January 1208 that Abbot Roffrido of Monte Cassino, with the secret aid of some of the citizens, succeeded in gaining entrance to the city of Sora with a considerable body of troops and compelling its surrender. Soon afterwards the castle of Sorella and other neighbouring castles yielded. Conrad of Marlenheim himself, recognizing the hopelessness

---

[1] Richard of San Germano, 24; *Gesta*, XXXVIII, cols. lxviii–lxix.

[2] *Epist.* XI, clxiii, col. 1472.

[3] This conflict is described in a letter of unknown origin, but obviously by an eyewitness, to be found in K. Hampe, 'Kindheit', 596–7. See also 590; and A. Schaube, *Handelsgeschichte*, 484.

of his position, surrendered voluntarily to the leader of the papal forces, Richard Conti, a brother of Innocent III.[1]

Even more threatening to the Kingdom were the numerous private feuds among the barons and the conflicts of the cities with one another. In the absence of a strong central government, individual barons endeavoured to extend their dominions and to usurp the sovereign power. It was this lawlessness that evoked from Innocent III the sharp letter of protest in the autumn of 1207:

> We had thought . . . that the sting of enduring tribulations would have taught the noblemen of Sicily to travel the path of justice. But sorrowfully we are compelled to say that some of them appear to be so hardened under the hammer blows of misfortune that they abstain even less from evil, rather that the harshness of their persecution increases.[2]

But neither papal protests nor efforts of the Governing Council of the Kingdom could check the encroachments upon the royal domains by the lawless magnates. It was to be one of the chief tasks of Frederick II at the end of the regency to dislodge these usurpers from their ill-gotten possessions.

Notwithstanding encroachments of individual barons, after the collapse of the resistance of Conrad of Marlenheim, the Pope was able for the first time to fulfil his long-delayed promise to enter the Kingdom in person for the purpose of implementing the plans that he had announced to the Governing Council at the beginning of the regency. In June 1208, Innocent III, accompanied by several cardinals, arrived in San Germano. There, on the 23rd, he assembled the counts and other magnates of the Kingdom, urging them to support the young King and to aid in the restoration of peace within the realm. In order to further these efforts towards the pacification of the Kingdom before releasing it to his ward, now nearing the legal age for succession to the throne, Innocent appointed Count Peter of Celano as Grand Justiciar of Apulia and the Terra di Lavoro and Richard of Aquilia as Governor of Naples. He then appealed to all present to obey the newly appointed officials and faithfully to observe the peace, abstaining from conflicts with one another. He directed that future differences were to be placed before these officials for adjudication and that anyone refusing to accept their mediation should be treated as a public enemy and punished by all. He announced also that in the following September 200 armed knights would be sent to Sicily to aid and support the interests of the Kingdom. The expenses of these troops were to be paid by the citizens in accordance with estimates to be made by arbiters designated by the Pope for that

---

[1] *Annales Casinenses*, 319; *Gesta*, XXXIX, cols. lxx–lxxii.
[2] *Epist.* X, cxii, col. 1207.

purpose. Pleading as an excuse the excessive summer heat for not going in person into Apulia, he called upon the residents there to obey the mandates of his representatives.[1] In a separate communication addressed to counts, barons, citizens, and others in the Kingdom, he called upon them to participate in the maintenance of the public peace and, especially, to forbid all attempts on the part of individuals to punish encroachments or other acts of injustice. In case of injury a just settlement was to be sought from the officials designated for the various regions for that purpose as grand captains.[2]

Although the efforts of the Pope to restore order in the distracted Kingdom were made ostentatiously, including the ceremonial visit of Innocent III to San Germano, they accomplished but little. The Kingdom had been left too long without adequate central administration. At best the arrangements made at San Germano were but long-delayed first steps towards an orderly government. More positive accomplishments must await the taking over of the Kingdom by Frederick himself. Indeed, it would be no exaggeration to say that the actual rehabilitation of the Kingdom was to be delayed even further, until Frederick, after his coronation as Emperor in 1220, at last found the resources to repair the heavy damages which had been inflicted upon Sicily during the years of his minority. The grand captains appointed by the Pope, intended as the chief agents for the desired restoration of peace, were soon engaged in conflicts with one another, thus permitting the Germans, under the indefatigable leadership of Dipold, to continue their depredations.[3]

Once more the Pope found himself compelled to look to the outside for effective support for the interests of his ward. For some years Innocent III had sought a marriage alliance for the young Frederick with a sister of King Pedro II of Aragon, first with Princess Sancha and, subsequently, with her elder sister Constance of Aragon, widow of the late King Emmerich of Hungary. Yet, in 1208, the marriage agreement had not been concluded. Innocent now appealed most urgently to King Pedro for the completion of the alliance. Why the King of Aragon had hesitated so long we do not know. Perhaps the expense and the hazards involved would provide a sufficient explanation, although there is evidence that King Pedro was not fully satisfied as to the nobility of Frederick's origin. For, in his letter to the King of Aragon early in 1208, Innocent urged him not to hesitate because of such doubts. Insistently he pleaded on behalf of his ward, emphasizing the nobility of one whose father and grandfather had been emperors, and whose mother had been

---

[1] *Annales Ceccanenses*, 319; *Gesta*, XL, cols. lxxiv f.
[2] *Epist.* XI, cxxxiii, col. 1449.
[3] See especially Baethgen, *Regentschaft*, 106.

both queen and empress. At the same time he informed King Pedro of his intention to send the Bishop of Mazzara to conduct the bride. In another letter also he urged the Queen Mother of Aragon to accompany her daughter to Sicily in order that the King and Kingdom might have the benefit of her wisdom. At length the Bishop succeeded in obtaining from King Pedro his agreement to the marriage, which Innocent ratified on 8 August 1208.[1]

About four months after the concluding of the marriage agreement, on 26 December 1208, when Frederick had reached his fourteenth year, recognized both by canon and Sicilian feudal law as the legal age for succession to his heritage, Pope Innocent III gave up the regency.[2]

[1] *Epist.* XI, iv and cxxxiv, cols. 1342 f. and 1449.
[2] As to the ending of the regency, see especially BFW, *Reg.* v, Abt. i, 598a; and J. B. Sägmüller, *Lehrbuch des katholischen Kirchenrechts*, ii. 148.

PART II

FREDERICK II, KING OF SICILY
AND
KING OF THE ROMANS

I

FREDERICK II COMES OF AGE
FIRST YEARS AS KING OF SICILY

non expediat ipsum imperium obtinere, patet ex eo quod per hoc
regnum Sicilie uniretur imperio et ex ipsa unione confunderetur
Ecclesia.

Deliberatio (Huillard-Bréholles, i, part i), 70.[1]

WHEN, in the last weeks of December 1208, Frederick as a
fourteen-year-old boy assumed the responsibilities of the Sicilian
kingship the prospects for his future success were far from bright.
Since the death of his mother in November 1198, the once prosperous
Kingdom had been weakened, if not permanently damaged, by the
prodigality of its governing officials, including the Chancellor himself,
and by raids upon the royal domain by a host of petty counts and
barons.[2] The Pope, as regent, had been more zealous for the interests of
the Church than for the prosperity of the Kingdom. While stoutly
denying the charge that he had encroached upon the domain of the
King,[3] Innocent III did not hesitate to claim as his own certain rights
and privileges which, under the Norman kings of the twelfth century,
had been a source of strength and unity to the Sicilian Kingdom.[4] The
royal treasury also had been impoverished and the revenues impaired by
grants of privileges and immunities, depriving the central government
of a lucrative source of income.[5]

The outlook must have appeared bleak to this high-spirited youth as
he contemplated the future and as he considered the golden days of his
Norman ancestors and the brilliant achievements and ambitious plans
of his Hohenstaufen forebears. Because of these adversities and the near-
poverty of his early years there has been a persistent tendency to
exaggerate the neglect and deprivations from which he suffered. It is
perhaps only natural that contemporary chroniclers writing of conditions in the Kingdom of Sicily at that time, the turbulent governments,

[1] It is not expedient that he [Frederick] obtain the *imperium*, because thereby the Kingdom
of Sicily would be united with the Empire and from such a union the Church would be co-
founded.

[2] *MGH, Epist. Pont.* i, no. 296, p. 219.

[3] *Epist.* VII, cxxiv, col. 409.   [4] See above, pp. 37 ff.

[5] P. Scheffer-Boichorst, *Zur Geschichte des XII. und XIII. Jahrhunderts,* 244 ff.

the impoverishment of the treasury, the ceaseless conflicts, should associate these things intimately with the person of the young King, observing that so great was his need that he scarcely had the necessities of life. Some of the contemporary accounts also are responsible for what, in course of time, became a colourful legend, depicting young Frederick as depending for his livelihood upon the citizens of Palermo, wandering from home to home or else living as a waif in the narrow streets and market-places of the city. In an effort to account for the superior learning that distinguished him from his contemporaries, he is depicted as the self-educated waif, who, by virtue of his superior endowments and extraordinary precociousness, and without extraneous aid, blossomed suddenly before his fourteenth year into a man of mature judgement and imperturbable self-reliance.[1] On the contrary, there are reasons to assume that the education of the boy, despite the unquestionable poverty of the Kingdom, proceeded more or less systematically, not only during the lifetime of his mother, but afterwards, whether under the care of the Chancellor, Walter of Palear, under Markward of Anweiler, or William Capparone. It was of the utmost importance, however illegally their official positions were acquired, that these temporary rulers maintain possession of the heir to the Sicilian throne. To permit him to wander in the streets and market-places of Palermo would be to expose him to probable capture by the rival contenders for control of the government. Only through him and in his name could they exercise their authority. Moreover, at the end of October 1202, when taken into the custody of Markward of Anweiler, Frederick, then less than eight years of age, was accompanied by his tutor William Franciscus, and there is evidence that William may have continued with him, at least intermittently, for the next several years.[2] Further evidence of the continuity of his education is found in a letter of October 1204 in which Innocent III expressed his gratification at the progress of his ward in wisdom and virtue.[3] This could have been a tribute either to the superior guidance of William Franciscus or to other tutors who had been permitted access to the young King after Markward's death and during the regime of William Capparone.[4] About two years later the Pope

---

[1] This improbable picture of the young Frederick derives largely from over-emphasis on the remarks of two contemporary sources, the *Breve chronicon de rebus Siculis*, 892, and Nicholas of Jamsilla, *Historia* (Muratori, *RIS* viii), col. 494. See also E. Kantorowicz, *Kaiser Friedrich der Zweite*, 31 ff., who has accepted this account of Frederick's early life uncritically.

[2] A plausible assumption based upon H. Niese, 'Materialien zur Geschichte Kaiser Friedrichs II.' (*Nachrichten von der königlichen Gesellschaft der Wissenschaften zu Göttingen: Phil.-hist. Klasse*, 1912), 388 and 398–9.

[3] Huillard-Bréholles, i, part i, 106.

[4] Winkelmann's assumption that the tutor who accompanied Allocingola to Palermo was Gregory of San Galgano (see above, pp. 50 f.) is erroneous, as shown by Baethgen, *Regentschaft*, 141–3.

observed, with obvious pride, the progress of Frederick's education 'in the lap of the Apostolic See'.[1] Again, in a letter to King Pedro of Aragon during the marriage negotiations involving the King's sister, Innocent related how Frederick, after reaching the age of puberty, passed swiftly to his years of discretion, for, as he says, 'with the Caesars, maturity is attained before its time'.[2]

From his sixth to his fifteenth year, therefore, the evidence, meagre though it is, justifies the assumption that his formal education proceeded more or less systematically, if not continuously. There were brief intervals when it was probably suspended or neglected, but such periods could not have been of long duration. The sole detailed description by a contemporary[3] of Frederick's youth, written towards the end of his fourteenth year, gives every reason to assume that he had cultivated self-reliance to an exceptional degree. On the other hand, many of the characteristics and attainments that impressed this observer were not of a nature attainable even to the most precocious, save through systematic training of both brain and brawn. Physically, the youth is described as neither tall nor short of stature, with firmly knit and robust body, the result of his passionate devotion to physical exercise. He is depicted as imperious in appearance and of majestic bearing, giving the impression of one born to rule. And yet, in some measure offsetting these characteristics were his sensitive and mobile features, his amiable countenance, and his lively spirit. He was skilled in the knowledge and in the use of arms, especially the sword and the bow. He is said to have wielded the sword with dexterity, displaying at times an almost savage exultation in his swordsmanship. As horseman, he admired noble and swift steeds, priding himself both on his skill and endurance in the saddle and, in later years, upon his knowledge of the treatment and healing of the sicknesses and wounds of horses.[4] The author of the letter relates also that the boy was an avid student, of history especially, which he often read far into the night. It is apparent that there were signs of boorishness in the youth, attributable to the rough and undisciplined life which, at times, he had been compelled to lead. The author hastens to add, however, that Frederick was conscious of these defects and that he was disposed to correct them. Above all he was jealous of his freedom, rebellious towards restraints, demanding to be treated not as a child, but as a king. Other sources that touch upon the early period of his life as well as his adult years are agreed as to his medium stature and as to the ruddiness of his complexion. Some of these sources over-emphasize

---

[1] *Epist.* IX, clviii, col. 985.
[2] *Epist.* XI, iv, col. 1343.
[3] See the letter in the collection by K. Hampe, 'Kindheit', 597.
[4] See below, p. 312, and note 3.

the smallness of his stature and, in general, his undistinguished appearance.[1]

It is all the more striking, therefore, that Salimbene, one of the most hostile critics of Frederick throughout his lifetime, offers the following objective portrait of Frederick in his adult years:

> As to faith in God, he had none. He was an adroit man, cunning, greedy, wanton, malicious, bad-tempered. But at times he was a worthy man, when he wished to reveal his good and courtly qualities, consoling, witty, delightful, hard-working. He could read, write, and sing and he could compose music and songs. He was a handsome man, well built but of medium stature. I have seen him, and at one time I esteemed him highly. For on my behalf he wrote a letter to Brother Elias, minister general to the Brothers Minor, requesting that he return me to my father. Also he could speak many different languages. In short, if he had been a good catholic, and loved God and His Church, and his own soul, he would have had few equals among the emperors of the world.[2]

Perhaps only his extreme youth and the self-confidence born of rare physical stamina and skill in the use of arms made it possible for Frederick to face with equanimity the difficulties that confronted him immediately upon coming of age. However conscientious Innocent III may have been in his last-minute efforts to secure the integrity of the Kingdom and to preserve the peace, most of these efforts failed. The grand captains established in their offices by the Pope at San Germano failed in their responsibilities; they concerned themselves, instead, with the promotion of their private interests. German leaders in the Kingdom, once the faithful supporters of the Emperor Henry VI, were the relentless enemies of his heir, only too ready to ally themselves with any contender for power who might offer them greater opportunities for self-preservation and prosperity. Native counts and barons, also wavering in their loyalty to the young King, saw in his helplessness a fortuitous opportunity for self-aggrandizement.[3]

Scarcely had Frederick taken over the reins of government when it became apparent that the Pope was ever alert to check the first signs of any effort on the part of the King to regain the prerogatives surrendered to the papacy by the Empress Constance. The first clash with the Pope came as the result of a vacancy in the archbishopric of Palermo. The cathedral chapter had obtained permission from the King to choose

---

[1] *Disputatio Carmine Conscripta inter Romam et Papam de Ottonis IV. Destitutione* (G. W. Leibnitz *Scriptorum Brunsvicensia Illustrantium*), ii. 529. *Ricobaldi Ferrariensis Historia Imperatorum* (Muratori, *RIS* ix), col. 132. At the time of Frederick's Crusade in 1229 he was described by an Arab source as ruddy of complexion, beardless, and of weak vision. See Badr-ad-Dīn al-ʿAinī *ʿIqd al-jamān* (*RHC, Hist. or.* ii), 193, and below, 224 f.

[2] *Cronica*, 348–9.

[3] *Annales Casinenses*, 319; *Breve chronicon de rebus Siculis*, 892 f.

a new archbishop, evidently intending to follow the precedent established when Pope Hadrian IV had granted to William I the right to
confirm all such elections. Some of the chapter members, however,
recalling the revocation of the ecclesiastical privileges by the Pope,
refused to agree to the election and appealed to Rome. In a letter to the
young King, Innocent expressed his astonishment and blamed the
King's evil advisers for this 'tyrannical' act, this 'usurpation' of papal
authority. He advised the King in no uncertain terms to content himself with the temporal sovereignty that the Pope had placed in his hands,
and admonished him not to covet the spiritual authority. He reminded
the King of the agreement of the Apostolic See with the Empress, 'your
mother', and warned him not to lend ear to advice of false counsellors
which could lead only to injury to 'you and to your Kingdom'.[1] However
greatly Frederick may have resented the action of the Pope in taking
advantage of the helplessness of his mother in order to revoke the
traditional rights of the kingship, he was obviously in the wrong in his
interference with the election. He was compelled, at least temporarily,
to yield to the Pope, to permit the banished chapter members to return
to the Kingdom, and to defer in such matters, in the future, to the
advice of the papal legate. This set-back to the sovereign aspirations of
the King of Sicily was but the prelude to the perennial conflicts that
were to follow between King and Curia.

Although failing to obtain the support of many of the counts and
barons of the Kingdom, Frederick had some success in his efforts to
regain his lost domain. His first conquest was the result of an expedition
directed against the north-eastern quarter of the island, a triangular
region, the base of which was a line extending from Palermo to Catania,
and the apex in Messina. The expedition was undertaken certainly in
the spring and early summer of 1209, and before the arrival of Constance
of Aragon and the military assistance from her brother, King Pedro.[2]
Frederick himself, in a letter to his vassals reflecting his gratification at
the success of his expedition, says of it: 'the whole country, now pacified,
is saved from destruction and exults in the abundance of secure peace.'
In the same letter he was also able to inform his subjects that in the
midst of his 'triumph and glory in Messina' he had received the news of
the landing of his future consort in Palermo on 15 August.[3] Upon the
receipt of this news he returned hastily to Palermo.

With Constance was her brother, Count Alfonso of Provence, and
some 500 knights given to her by King Pedro to assist in the restoration

---

[1] *Epist.* XI, ccviii, cols. 1523–5.
[2] K. Hampe, 'Beiträge zur Geschichte Kaiser Friedrichs II.', (*Hist.Vierteljahrschr.* iv, 1901),
161 ff.
[3] Ibid. 172.

of royal authority in Sicily. Unfortunately, the Queen Mother, who had been expected to accompany her daughter to Sicily, had died some time in the previous November.[1] Frederick met his fiancée and her escort in Palermo and the marriage took place immediately thereafter. We are given but few details of the wedding by Italian and Sicilian sources, most of which dismiss the event with a bare factual statement that 'Frederick took as wife the sister of the King of Aragon'.[2] A French source, a continuation of the *Chronicle* of William of Tyre, gives an account of the event which in most respects corroborates that of Frederick's letter. Of Constance and her retinue he says: 'When they had set out from Aragon they came to a city which had the name of Palermo, where the King of Sicily was. When they arrived and disembarked, the King went there to meet them and received them well; and immediately after their arrival he married the lady.'[3] The absence of any mention of festivities and the drabness of all contemporary accounts are perhaps indicative of the poverty and of the general unrest in the Kingdom.

To the contemporary chroniclers it was not the marriage itself that was of primary interest, but rather the military aid which was now thought to be at the disposal of Frederick for pushing his conquest beyond the island and into Apulia. No sooner had the marriage been celebrated than Frederick and his queen, accompanied by Alfonso and the 500 mounted troops, resumed the conquest of the Kingdom, moving across the north-east of Sicily from Palermo to Messina, the region recently subdued by Frederick. Their goal was obviously the mainland where the German followers of Dipold and many of the local counts and barons continued to defy the sovereign authority of the young King.[4] While in Messina, or else while *en route* there from Palermo, the Spanish troops were decimated by a plague, which caused the death of most of them, including Alfonso the Queen's brother, and the departure of the remainder for Aragon.[5] The Spanish alliance thus failed in its chief object, the providing of military support for the King in his reconquest of the Kingdom. The marriage had been arranged from the outset solely as a matter of political expediency. Constance was the widowed Queen

---

[1] A. Schott *et al.*, *Hispaniae Illustratae*, iii. 64.

[2] *Annales Casinenses*, 319, says merely that: 'Fredericus rex Siciliae duxit in uxorem sororem regis Ragonensis.' Richard of San Germano, 28, is equally brief: 'Fredericus rex Sicilie uxorem duxit Constantiam sororem regis Arragonum.'

[3] *Eracles*, 298. See also *Ernoul*, 399.

[4] The account of *Ernoul*, 399, is substantially correct, save for the statement that on the journey from Palermo to Messina they conquered everything (*tot conquerant*). The conquest of that region had obviously been completed by Frederick himself and the destination of this expedition must have been the mainland. See also *Eracles*, loc. cit.

[5] *Breve chronicon de rebus Siculis*, 893. See also *Ernoul*, 399, and *Eracles*, 299. Similar also is the Aragonese account, *Hispaniae Illustratae*, iii. 64.

of the late King Emmerich of Hungary and was at least ten years older than the youthful Frederick. Moreover, it was only with difficulty that Innocent III had persuaded his ward to agree to the marriage.[1] It is all the more remarkable that there developed between Frederick II and Constance mutual appreciation and respect, if not genuine affection. There is abundant evidence that throughout their marriage and until her death in 1222, Constance of Aragon enjoyed the complete confidence of the King. Mute witness of his devotion to her appeared in 1781, when the sarcophagus of Constance was opened and a richly jewelled helmeted or *camelaucum* crown was found within—not, as was long believed, the crown of the Empress herself, but of her spouse, Frederick II. The splendour of its ornamentation, its size, and shape preclude the possibility that it was merely the customary 'burial crown', or that it could have been the crown of the Empress. Most plausible is a conjecture by the author of a recent study of this splendid relic that Frederick placed his crown in the tomb of his consort as a part of himself, symbolizing thereby the indissoluble union of their destinies.[2]

In the final conquest of the Kingdom and in its governance Constance enjoyed, henceforth, full partnership. While the extant documents do not permit of the assumption that she was consulted in all matters pertaining to the future of the Kingdom, the few bits of evidence indicate that from the early weeks of their marriage she participated actively in the administration.[3] But a much more substantial assistance than the sympathy and wise counsel of his able consort was needed. At the moment when his hopes of aid from the Aragonese troops faded, and when the recalcitrant Sicilian nobles were in renewed revolts against him, a still greater threat came from the recently chosen Welf Emperor, Otto IV. The circumstances that led to the involvement of Frederick II once more in the affairs of Germany and the Empire are of such importance in his future history that they must be sketched in some detail before entering upon the next phase of his life.

To the mind of Innocent III the death of Philip of Swabia had not opened the way to a new election. It was merely an opportunity to complete the elevation of his favourite, Otto IV, to the German kingship and, ultimately, to the imperial throne. It was this attitude that made it possible for him to write to Otto in the summer of 1208: 'Since now, however, your opponent is out of the way, we are sparing no pains

---

[1] *Epist.* XI, iv, col. 1342.

[2] See the report on J. Deér's contribution, 'Der Kaiserornat Friedrichs II.', in P. E. Schramm, *Kaiser Friedrichs II. Herrschaftszeichen*, 14.

[3] An early illustration of this, as Winkelmann, *O. von B.*, p. 94, note 5, has previously observed, is to be seen in an unpublished document for the Bishop of Patti, an extract of which is included in R. Pirri, *Sicilia sacra*, ii. 776.

to ensure that another shall not be elevated in opposition to you, although Philip's nephew is set up already as your opponent. . . .'[1] Years later, Frederick, as Emperor, was to remind the Curia in terms of unmistakable bitterness that they had failed in this opportune moment to support his claim and that, instead, they had insisted upon the election of the traditional enemy of his family.[2]

Few of the princes of Germany were disposed to rekindle the fires of civil war in the interest of the 'boy of Apulia'. Meanwhile, Archbishop Siegfried of Mainz, supported by a number of temporal princes, called for an assembly of all the princes, ecclesiastical as well as lay, to convene at Frankfurt on 11 November.[3] Notwithstanding Innocent's conception of Otto as a counter-king, chosen by the Pope and Curia and now to be accepted as rightful King, his status was more accurately described by a contemporary who says that 'Otto was elected King by all the princes without dispute'.[4] Now, as legally recognized King, Otto received from the hands of Conrad of Scharfenberg, Bishop of Speyer and Metz, the royal insignia.[5]

At Frankfurt also Beatrice, the eldest daughter of Philip of Swabia, in a dramatic appearance before the assembled princes, made her formal charges against the Count Palatine, Otto of Wittelsbach, and his alleged accomplice, Henry of Istria, as the murderers of her father. Moved by her pathetic appeal, and conscious also of the unwarranted nature of the deed, those present were quick in their condemnation of its perpetrators. The culprits were outlawed and their properties declared confiscated. Henry of Kalden, long the faithful servant of the Hohenstaufen, pursued Otto of Wittelsbach to his place of hiding in a barn near Regensburg, and there put him to the sword, severing his head from his body and casting it into the Danube.[6] Meanwhile the unfortunate queen, widow of Philip of Swabia, who had known little but tragedy as the daughter of the Byzantine Emperor, Isaac, had died on 27 August 1208. Only in her marriage with Philip following the imprisonment and death of her former spouse, young Roger III, had she found a few years of affection and relief from sorrow. Now, as an expectant mother, she received the news of Philip's murder. Conscious of her helplessness in a strange land, and broken in spirit by this final tragedy, she sought retreat in the family castle of Staufen, where,

---

[1] *RNI*, no. cliii, col. 1147. See also ibid., nos. cliv, clvii, in which he warns various prelates against the anointment or coronation of anyone else.

[2] Huillard-Bréholles, ii, part i, 590 and iii. 38.

[3] *Chronica S. Petri Erfordensis moderna* (*MGH, SS.* xxx), 381.

[4] *Annales S. Trudperti* (*MGH, SS.* xvii), 292.

[5] *Annales Marbacenses*, 80, 171; *Chronica regia Coloniensis*, 227: 'diadema cum lancea imperiali ei assignatur.'

[6] *Chronica regia Coloniensis*, 228; *Arnoldi Chronica Slavorum* (*MGH, SS.* xxi), 245; *Annales Marbacenses*, 78; *Burchardi Chronicon* (*MHG, SS.* xxiii), 370.

during the premature birth of her fifth child, she joined the stillborn infant in death.[1]

To the German princes, weary of ceaseless civil war, a marriage alliance between Otto IV and Beatrice, eldest daughter of Philip of Swabia, appeared to open the way to a permanent peace. Difficulties arising from the kinship of Otto with his future bride were removed by a special dispensation of the Pope who was acutely aware of the expediency of such a marriage.[2] Whatever doubts Otto may have entertained on account of consanguinity were dissipated less by the papal consent than by the prospect of the rich Staufen patrimony, which he immediately took over as a result of the marriage agreement.[3] As these arrangements were completed, the German heritage of young Frederick of Sicily appeared to be lost for ever—now the possession of the Saxon house of Welf, the traditional enemies of the Swabian Hohenstaufen.

The success of Otto after years of declining fortune made it imperative that John Lackland, the English king, who had wavered from time to time in his willingness to support his nephew, should now give him his whole-hearted support. John's interest in the fortunes of Otto of Brunswick had its origin, not in the obligation of kinship, but in his need for an ally against Philip Augustus of France. Even when Otto's prospects were at their lowest in 1207, and he hastened to England to plead for assistance, King John is said to have given his nephew 6,000 marks of silver.[4] Following Otto's election in 1208 and his subsequent coronation as Emperor it became the established policy of King John to maintain and strengthen the alliance with his nephew in a joint effort to resist Philip Augustus of France, the relentless enemy of each of them.[5] Knowing how close this alliance was, and well aware of its object where Philip Augustus was concerned, Innocent revealed an astonishing *naïveté* when he wrote to the King of France:

Furthermore, you have added that Otto cannot be elected to the Empire without damaging your Kingdom and Church. Now indeed your Kingdom is united to the Church by such love and devotion that neither can suffer harm unless the other do also. Which we are certainly aware of; and we have sought in these matters to preserve the safety of you and your Kingdom, not immediately because of your request, but for the love we bear you, so that we have gained a definite assurance from the same Otto, sealed with

---

[1] *Annales Marbacenses*, 79.

[2] *RNI*, nos. clv, clxix, 169.

[3] *Chronica regia Coloniensis*, 227.

[4] Roger of Wendover (ed. Coxe), iii. 210 and note 1. Matthew Paris, *Historia Minor* (Rolls Series), ii. 109. For the 6,000 marks instead of 5,000 see Winkelmann, *P. von S.*, p. 406, note 1.

[5] King John found even greater comfort in his alliance with Otto during the quarrel between the Pope and the Emperor. See especially Walter of Coventry, *Memoriale* (Rolls Series), ii. 202.

a golden bull and strengthened by an oath, that making and keeping peace with you he will follow in all things our wishes and judgement.[1]

Of vital significance as a precedent in the future relations of Pope and Emperor were the concessions that Otto made to the Pope on 22 March 1209 as a condition of his coronation as Emperor. These concessions would be required of Frederick II when, subsequently, he was called by the Pope to oppose Otto IV. Substantially, his oath was as follows:

Therefore, most reverent father and lord, Pope Innocent, . . . we will show to you and to your catholic successors and the Church of Rome, (always with a humble heart and a devout spirit,) all the obedience, honour, and reverence which our predecessors, catholic kings and emperors, are known to have shown to your predecessors. We wish in no wise to diminish, but rather to enlarge these, to the end that our devotion may be clearly manifest. We renounce as wilful abuse that which some of our predecessors have formerly claimed with regard to the election of prelates, and we concede and sanction that elections of prelates shall be free and canonical so that whoever is entrusted with the headship of the vacant Church shall be chosen by the whole chapter or by the majority thereof. Moreover, appeals in ecclesiastical causes shall be freely made to the Apostolic See and the prosecution and disposition of such causes shall in no wise be impeded. We renounce and will refrain from the abuse of appropriating the properties of deceased prelates, or the revenues of vacant churches . . . We relinquish to the Sovereign Pontiff and to other prelates of the Church the free disposition of all spiritualities, in order that, duly apportioned, the things which are Caesar's may be rendered to Caesar and the things that are God's to God.[2]

Equally momentous in the succeeding relations of Pope and Emperor, and in the future of Frederick II, was the promise of Otto to restore freely and peacefully the properties of the Church which had been retained by his predecessors. In the restoration of such properties he promised to exert himself diligently. The regions in question, previously mentioned in the oath of Otto of 8 June 1201,[3] and here repeated, included the entire area from Radicofani to Ceperano, the March of Ancona, the Duchy of Spoleto, the lands of the Countess Matilda, the County of Bertinoro, the Exarchate of Ravenna, the Pentapolis, with other adjacent regions that had been bestowed upon the Roman Church through many privileges from the time of Louis the Pious. In short, Innocent III was here demanding the regions of Italy which, throughout his pontificate, he endeavoured to have recognized as the Papal State. Finally, Otto pledged himself to aid and defend the Kingdom of Sicily as a papal possession, and, in order to guarantee this and other privileges in perpetuity, he continued: 'We have ordered the finished privilege to be affixed with the golden seal of our majesty.'[4]

[1] *RNI*, no. clxv, col. 1155.   [2] *RNI*, no. clxxxix, col. 1169.
[3] Ibid., no. lxxvii, col. 1082.   [4] Ibid., no. clxxxix, cols. 1169–70.

After Otto had actually received the imperial crown—on Sunday, 4 October 1209[1]—these expressions of obedience and the attitude of exaggerated deference which he had cultivated so assiduously just before his elevation gave way to the arrogant manner characteristic of his future relations with the Pope and with the prelates and princes of Germany. By his predatory acts and evil habits, by his arrogance and injustice towards the counts and barons, he alienated many of his former adherents. Moreover, a contemporary chronicler relates that during one of Otto's visitations to the region of the Rhine he terrified the inhabitants of Swabia in particular by his rapacious and criminal deeds. Also he treated with disrespect the count, barons, and princes of that region who came into his presence. In several instances valuable fiefs that had previously been granted by Philip of Swabia to ecclesiastical princes were confiscated. He offended them still more by conferring upon his foreign favourites, Saxon and English, both lay and cleric, various fiefs and benefices.[2]

Even during these last months in Germany before setting out for Rome and his coronation as Emperor, there were forebodings of the rising tension between Otto and the princes of Germany and of the conflict of interests between himself and the Pope.

[1] For the details of the coronation see E. Winkelmann, *O. von B.*, 198 f.

[2] This change in the attitude of Otto IV is particularly well depicted by *Burchardi Chronicon*, 97; *Cronica Reinhardsbrunnensis*, 576–7.

II

REPUDIATION OF OTTO IV
FREDERICK II AS GERMAN KING

Poenitet me quod constituerim Saul regem: quia dereliquit me, et
verba mea opere non implevit.

Liber Primus Samuelis, xv. 11.[1]

IN the course of time the arrogance and injustice of Otto were to
benefit Frederick II, who, as the last male heir of the Hohenstaufen,
was to become the instrument for the ending of the Welf tyranny.
The Pope himself was repeatedly offended by Otto IV. Soon it became
apparent that Otto had determined to repudiate the solemn oath
through which he had restored to the Holy See the ecclesiastical rights and
privileges formerly enjoyed by the Emperors and by the Kings of Sicily.
Within a few months following his coronation and as he moved through
Italy in 1209, with the object of restoring the imperial properties, each
step revealed that his policies where Italy and Sicily were concerned
were essentially those of Henry VI in 1197.[2] Although such policies may
have been but vaguely conceived at the moment of Otto's coronation,
they assumed a positive form during the early months of 1210, if not
during his visit to Pisa on 20 November 1209. It was there that he came
under the influence of the German captains who, since the time of
Henry VI, had continued their support of the imperial interests in Italy
and Sicily.[3] Chief among them was Dipold of Acerra whose support of
Otto had been generously rewarded with the office of Grand Captain
of Apulia and the Terra di Lavoro, as well as the title Duke of Spoleto.[4]
Innocent III must have seen from this obviously offensive act how
readily Otto would repudiate the terms of the oath that he had taken in
return for his imperial coronation. Moreover, shortly after his coronation, Otto, in open defiance of his promises at Neuss and Speyer, granted
privileges to various individuals and communes in the provinces of the
Papal State. The most offensive of these and the most damaging to the

---

[1] It repenteth me that I have set up Saul to be king: for he is turned back from following
me, and hath not performed my commandments.

[2] K. Hampe, *Kaisergeschichte*, 250–1.

[3] K. Hampe, 'Beiträge' (*Hist. Vierteljahrschr.* iv, 1901), 176.

[4] J. Ficker, *Forschungen*, iv. 277; *Annales Casinenses*, 319.

papal interests were privileges granted by Otto in the March of Ancona, the Duchy of Spoleto, and in the lands of Matilda, regions which Innocent III believed to have been firmly secured as provinces of the Papal State.[1] Equally offensive to the Pope and certainly in defiance of his promises was Otto's raising of troops with the intention of proceeding against Frederick II. In contemplation of an attack on Sicily by sea as well as by land, he obtained the support of Pisa through grants of commercial advantages and freedom from custom duties in 'Sicily, Calabria, Apulia, and in the Principatum'.[2]

No longer could the Pope and Curia doubt the intentions of Otto. Innocent complained that Otto, not content with his seizure of the family property of the Hohenstaufen, 'now extends his hand to seize the Sicilian Kingdom'. In early February, probably as early as 1 February, he said in a remarkable letter to Philip Augustus of France: 'If only, dearest son, I had known the character of Otto who now calls himself Emperor, as well as you knew it!' Then, after describing to Philip the wrongs that Otto had committed, his ingratitude, his duplicity, his unfailing arrogance, and, above all, his intention to take from young Frederick the Kingdom of Sicily, the Pope continued: 'It is with shame that I write this to you who so well prophesied what has come to pass.'[3]

When at length Otto actually crossed the border into the Kingdom of Sicily, Innocent proclaimed his excommunication on 18 November 1210.[4] As the Pope now moved against Otto with this extreme measure it was to his advantage that he was well informed about the unsympathetic, if not hostile, attitude of some of the German princes towards Otto's German and Italian policies. Before October 1210 he was in intimate correspondence with a group of German princes, several of whom were to assume active leadership in the German opposition to the Emperor. Among these the Pope mentions the Archbishops of Mainz and Magdeburg, the Bishop of Bamberg and, among lay princes, the King of Bohemia, the Landgrave of Thuringia, and Duke Otto of Meran.[5] From the moment that he had proclaimed the ban Innocent determined to make full use of this unrest among the German princes as

---

[1] For some of the more important of these grants see C. Acquacotte, *Memorie de Matelica*, ii. 231; M. Fantuzzi, *Monumenti Ravennati*, v. 304; Ficker, *Forschungen*, iv, no. 222, p. 274) and no. 254, pp. 301 f. An excellent recent treatment of these acts of Otto is D. Waley, *The Papal State*, 59 ff.

[2] *Chronicon Tolosani* (*Documenti di Storia Italiana . . . Cronache dei Secoli XIII e XIV*, i), 691. BFW, *Reg.* v, Abt. i, no. 411.

[3] M. de la Porte du Theil, Art. IX (*Notices et Extraits des Manuscrits de la Bibliothèque du Roi*, ii, Paris, 1789), 282 f. See also Huillard-Bréholles, i. 164–5.

[4] *Annales Casinenses* (*MGH, SS.* xix), 320. See also *MGH, Epist. pont.* i. 233.

[5] B. Bretholz, 'Ein päpstliches Schreiben gegen Kaiser Otto IV von 1210, October 30, Lateran' (*Neues Archiv*, xxii, 1896–7), 293 ff., in which Innocent speaks (p. 294) of 'Nuncciis [*sic*] et literis vestris'.

a means of exerting pressure upon Otto. In a second letter in mid November, intended for the German princes as a whole, a copy of which was sent to Philip Augustus, Innocent III set forth at length the reasons for the excommunication, employing the familiar charges that Otto had opposed the Roman Church, that he had attacked the Kingdom of Sicily. He told also of the Emperor's ingratitude, his infidelity, and his impiety. He called upon them, 'to seek an immediate remedy before it is too late, and while yet the time is opportune'.[1]

Obviously, the 'remedy' thus suggested was a new election, although Innocent refrained from mentioning an appropriate candidate. At this time, as in his relations with Philip Augustus of France, the Pope revealed his readiness to reconcile himself swiftly with the views of those with whom he had previously disagreed. He now turned to his former enemy Adolf of Cologne as one of his allies in Germany in opposing the Emperor. Although still withholding from Adolf his dignity as bishop, Innocent III restored to him much that he had taken away.[2] But long before this reconciliation with Adolf, Innocent had found it expedient to rely upon Philip Augustus, the persistent enemy of the Welfs and friend of the Hohenstaufen, as his chief agent for influencing the German princes. Above all, Innocent desired that Philip incite the princes of Germany to revolt against the Emperor, and in a manner so threatening as to compel Otto to abandon the conquest of Sicily.[3]

The common interests of Philip Augustus and Innocent III now drew them into an intimate alliance of such strength and durability that, in the end, Otto IV would be routed and both King and Pope would emerge triumphant with the elevation of Frederick II as King of the Romans and as Emperor. The activities of the King of France were directed towards a secret alliance among the princes, finding support especially in Siegfried, Archbishop of Mainz, subsequently to be named as papal legate (March 1212), who, together with the Landgrave of Thuringia, the King of Bohemia, the Dukes of Austria and Meran, and several other princes, lay as well as ecclesiastic, met secretly, apparently in September 1210, to formulate the details of this plan.[4] Meanwhile, Innocent had appealed urgently to Philip Augustus for military aid. While insisting that military aid was impossible, Philip revealed that he was fully aware of the activities of the German princes and that he was confident that progress had been made in Germany. He suggested also that the German princes wished to be reassured that the Pope and cardinals would undertake no further negotiations with Otto. He insisted

---

[1] Böhmer, *Acta* no. 921. For the date see BFW, *Reg.* v, Abt. iii, 6099.
[2] *Epist.* XIII, clxxvii, col. 346 f.
[3] A. Cartellieri, *Philipp II*, iv. 289 f.
[4] B. Bretholz, in *Neues Archiv*, xxii, 1896–7, 296.

that everyone must be released from his oath of fealty to Otto and that a new election must be held.[1] It is apparent both in the letter of Philip Augustus and in that of the German princes that they feared the Pope might suddenly reverse his policies towards the Emperor and thus leave them exposed to his vengeance. That such fears were well grounded is apparent in the reluctance of Innocent, after he had actually proclaimed the ban, to discontinue the negotiations, presumably in the vain hope that the Emperor would seek reconciliation through complete submission to the papal demands. Because of this vain hope, or else because of serious pressure from several of the dissenting cardinals, Innocent continued the negotiations until February 1211.[2]

When Otto rejected all peaceful proposals, Innocent at last abandoned further efforts towards a reconciliation and devoted himself to bringing about the downfall of Otto in Germany. On 31 March 1211 the excommunication of the Emperor and his followers was widely publicized, his subjects were absolved from their oath of fealty, and all places where he stayed were declared under the interdict.[3]

Throughout the early months of 1211 the Pope, Philip Augustus, and the conspiring princes in Germany worked actively towards the achievement of their common end: a revolt in Germany as well as in Italy against Otto, and the choice of his successor. It is highly probable that Philip Augustus and the German princes from the moment of their earliest intrigues in 1210 accepted as a matter of course the succession of the Hohenstaufen heir.[4] As was to be expected, the Swabian princes were especially gratified at the progress of the revolt, while in Saxony there was general indignation. There was, however, by no means unanimity of opinion among the spiritual princes, who might have been expected to fall in with the papal desires, and many of them strongly opposed the excommunication.[5]

While the Pope was engaged in his deliberations and in his self-justification, two Swabian barons, Henry of Neifen and Anselm of Justingen, were employed by the German princes at a cost of some 1,500 marks, to be paid from the royal treasury, to undertake the journey to Italy and Sicily in order to inform Frederick of his election and to persuade him to accept the crown.[6]

---

[1] L. Delisle, *Catalogue des actes de Philippe-Auguste*, no. 1251; K. Hampe, 'Beiträge' (*Hist. Vierteljahrschr.* iv, 1901), 190.   [2] E. Winkelmann, *O. von B.*, 258.

[3] *Continuatio Admuntensis* (*MGH, SS.* ix), 591–2; Richard of San Germano (Muratori, *RIS*, VII), 33. See also the letter of Innocent to the Archbishop of Naples (Huillard-Bréholles, i, part i), 188; *Cronaca Altinate* (Muratori, *RIS* vii), 910.

[4] *Canonicorum Pragensium Contin. Cosmae.* (*MGH, SS.* ix), 170; *Annales Breves Wormatienses* (*MGH, SS.* xvii), 75.

[5] Conrad of Fabaria (*MGH, SS.* ii), 170; *Annales Sancti Rudberti Salisburgenses* (*MGH, SS.* ix), 780.

[6] *Burchardi Chronicon* (*MGH, SS.* xxiii), 373; *Breve chronicon de rebus Siculis*, 894.

Meanwhile the enemies of Otto in northern Italy—princes, cities, and the lesser nobles—rallied to the support of Frederick. Chief among them was the city of Cremona and its allies, the Margrave of Este, and Counts Louis and Richard of S. Bonifazio in Verona.[1] As was to be expected, the city of Milan and its allies continued to support Otto. So serious, however, was the revolt in Germany that the brother of the Emperor and his friends urged him to return.[2] Just as Otto was set to invade Sicily, the seriousness of the news from Germany induced him to abandon his plans for the immediate conquest and to return to his homeland. This was a timely relief for the young King of Sicily; for it was generally believed that Frederick's cause was lost. A galley stood ready for his escape in the harbour of Palermo near the Castellamare against the time when the forces of Otto succeeded in crossing to Sicily.[3] Frederick himself never forgot the near miracle of his escape. On more than one occasion he was to express his gratitude to the Divine Creator that it had been granted him to live and reign.[4]

Otto's departure from the south of Italy in early November 1211 was not so hasty, as he moved northwards, as to prevent his pausing to ensure the continued support of the Italian magnates who had previously declared for him. Before leaving Italy the Emperor also endeavoured to strengthen the position of Dipold, recently made Duke of Spoleto, who once again was to remain in Italy as the chief support to the imperial interests.[5] In Lombardy he found his strongest support when, in his court at Lodi on 15 January 1212, he met the magnates of that region, together with the rectors of the Lombard cities and other representative citizens. Here also he outlawed Azzo of Este, who had deserted to the side of the Pope, and here he supported the city of Crema against the unfriendly Cremona. In early February Otto was received with special honours by the citizens of Milan; during a fifteen-day visit to the city, he sought to strengthen his hold on that region by bestowing generous privileges upon his supporters.[6]

Continuing his journey via Como and thence across the Alps into Germany, he proceeded to Frankfurt where, in mid March, he held court, attended by a number of princes and nobles. It was here that he made his formal complaint of the injustice of his excommunication.[7] Although the number of spiritual princes witnessing the imperial docu-

---

[1] *Riccardi comitis Sancti Bonifacii vita* (Muratori, *RIS* viii), col. 124.
[2] John Codagnellus (*SRG in usum scholarum*), 38–9.
[3] *Albert von Beham und Regesten Papst Innocenz IV* (*Bibliothek des Litterarischen Vereins in Stuttgart*, xvi. 2), 74.
[4] Huillard-Bréholles, ii, part i, 122 f., and iii. 39.
[5] J. Ficker, *Forschungen*, iv. 301, no. 254; BFW, *Reg.* v, Abt. i, nos. 451, 454.
[6] John Codagnellus (*SRG in usum scholarum*), 38–9.
[7] *Chronica regia Coloniensis*, 188, 232.

ments in Frankfurt at this time was small, it is apparent, from the considerable numbers of temporal princes and nobles, that Otto's position was not yet so weakened as to be beyond hope of recovery. Moreover some princes who had previously wavered in their loyalty had now returned to the side of the Emperor.[1] This active support for Otto, and the wavering of some princes who formerly had acquiesced in the invitation to Frederick, may have been due to fear and suspicion of the continued interference of Pope and Curia in the election of the King. To many the question must have occurred, as it did to the ever-observant Walther von der Vogelweide: Who in truth creates kings—is it God or is it the Pope?

> God gives as King whom he pleases;
> In this I am not much surprised,
> But we laymen wonder about the clergy's teaching.
> They taught us something a short while ago
> And now they ask us to believe the opposite.
> Now let them, for God's honour and their own,
> Tell us truly and unequivocally
> In which one of these statements we are deceived.
> Let them make one of them decisive:
> The old one or the new one.
> To us it seem that one is a lie.
> Two tongues fit badly in one mouth.[2]

At Midsummer 1212 it seemed possible that Otto IV, like his predecessor, could successfully resist the papal opposition and regain in Germany his lost prestige, achieving, perhaps, a firmer hold upon the Empire. Walther von der Vogelweide, observing these changing tides of German sentiment, could write at this time:

> Welcome, Lord Emperor!
> The title of king is taken from you.
> And yet your crown outshines all others,
> Your hand is strong and rich in lands,
> And whether for good or for evil
> It avenges or rewards each of them.
> Also I have more to tell you:
> The princes are submissive to you,
> They have patiently awaited your return
> And even Meissen's lord, submits to you—
> One of God's angels would sooner be seduced.[3]

---

[1] *Origines Guelficae*, iii. 807 f.
[2] Translated from the verse of Walther from the original in Lachmann-Kraus, *Gedichte Walthers von der Vogelweide*, 15. [3] Ibid. 14.

But in this moment of ascending fortune, while in camp at Weissensee near Erfurt, Otto received news in a letter from the Patriarch, Wolfgar of Aquilea, that Frederick was in Genoa *en route* to Germany. Although feigning little interest in this ominous report, and ridiculing his boyish rival, Otto must have recognized that the presence of Frederick might well be the occasion for widespread desertions. To those assembled around him, however, he merely remarked with scorn: 'Listen to the latest: the Pope-Emperor is on his way and intends to expel us.'[1]

The report reminded him that although Beatrice, the daughter of the late Philip of Swabia, had been formally betrothed to him the marriage had not yet been consummated. In this moment when German nobles and *ministeriales* were ready to shift their allegiance from Staufen to Welf or from Welf to Staufen, as circumstances favoured one or the other, what better assurance of Swabian support could be found than the faithful fulfilment of his marriage pledge? As one contemporary chronicler astutely remarks: 'In order to provide security for himself, he [Otto] solemnly took as wife the daughter of his former adversary, the late King Philip.' The same chronicler concludes also that Otto hoped, through the issue of this marriage, to secure the Duchy of Swabia by hereditary succession.[2] At Nordhausen on 22 July 1212 the marriage took place, but the hopes of Otto for an heir were shattered soon afterwards when his young queen died and was buried in Brunswick.[3] The death of Beatrice marked the end of the prospective conciliation of Welf and Staufen partisans. The Swabian *ministeriales*, upon hearing of Beatrice's death and of the coming of Frederick of Sicily, abandoned their baggage and secretly left the imperial camp during the night. Shortly afterwards they were joined by Bavarians and others. Thus suddenly and seriously weakened Otto was compelled to abandon his assault upon Weissensee and hasten southwards to forestall, if possible, the successful entry of his rival into Germany.[4]

The wheel of fortune, so meaningful in the symbolism of thirteenth-century Europe, was henceforth to move Otto inexorably to his fall. In the early months of the year 1212, as he struggled vainly to maintain his position of strength in Italy and Germany, Frederick II in Palermo was considering the invitation of the German princes. On reaching Italy, the ambassadors of the princes, Henry of Neifen and Anselm of

---

[1] *Magdeburger Schöppenchronik* (*Die Chroniken der deutschen Städte*, vii), 136–7.

[2] Walter of Coventry, *Memoriale*, ii. 204–5.

[3] *Sächsische Weltchronik* (*MGH, Deutsch. Chron.* ii), 239: 'In deme selven orloge nam de keiser Otto sin wif to Northusen, des koning Philippus dochter; du starf unlange darna.'

[4] The chief source for this defection of his troops is *Cronica S. Petri Erfordensis* (*MGH, SS.* xxx, part i), 383. Cf. *Magdeburger Schöppenchronik* (*Die Chroniken der deutschen Städte*, vii), 137: 'des nachtes scheiden de ammechtlude van keiser Otten unde togen to koning Frederike'; *Sächsische Weltchronik* (*MHG, Deutsch. Chron.* ii), 239: 'Do karden van deme keisere almeistich des rikes dienestman, darna de vorsten al êntelen.'

Justingen, had undertaken two preliminary tasks before proceeding to the Kingdom of Sicily. Henry had paused in Verona, evidently seeking support in Lombardy for Frederick, while Anselm had gone to Rome, where, not without difficulty and delay, he gained approval from Innocent III and the Curia for the German princes' action.[1] The delay of Anselm in Rome was undoubtedly occasioned by the Pope's refusal to agree to some details of the terms proposed by the emissary of the princes, notably their right to choose the King of the Romans independently, without papal approval. The negotiations were so oriented by Innocent III as to obtain assurance from the princes that neither his suzerain rights in Sicily nor his claim to the regions constituting the Papal State would be jeopardized. Certainly it was with a feeling of hopefulness and relief that he could tell the citizens of Rome to proclaim Frederick as Emperor.[2]

Early in 1212, having completed his negotiations with the Pope, Anselm proceeded to the court of Frederick II in Palermo. There his mission was no less difficult than that which he had carried out in Rome. However greatly Frederick may have been tempted by the promises of the German and the imperial crowns, there were obvious difficulties to be overcome. Queen Constance, with the wisdom of superior years and experience, and as the mother of a recently born son whose future might also be at stake, sought to dissuade her youthful spouse from accepting the invitation. No less opposed to his acceptance were the Sicilian magnates whose past experience with the German leaders Henry VI, Markward of Anweiler, and the cunning Dipold, Duke of Spoleto, had made them suspect fraudulent intentions.[3] Though we do not know the details of the opposition of the queen and of the magnates of the Kingdom, they certainly emphasized that, while the crown of Sicily was still insecure, the hazards of seeking the crowns of Germany and the Empire were far too great. Moreover, the Kingdom of Sicily, disunited by the long period of civil strife, was still torn by feuds among the local nobility, weakened by the encroachments of the great commercial cities of Italy, and threatened by the revolting Saracens. And who could foretell the dangers awaiting the young King in Germany? The princes who now sought him as their future King and Emperor had already demonstrated how fragile were their sacred oaths, how readily they could repudiate their promises of aid. Only recently, several, if not many, who had joined in the invitation to Frederick had returned to the side of Otto. Indeed, would the Pope himself, now that he had obtained full recognition of the suzerain rights of the Roman Church over Sicily and what

---

[1] *Burchardi Chronicon* (*MGH, SS.* xxiii), 373.

[2] See especially H. Bloch, *Die staufischen Kaiserwahlen und die Entstehung des Kurfürstentums* 89 ff. and 92–5.   [3] *Burchardi Chronicon*, 99 f.

he believed to be security for the Papal State, exert himself whole-heartedly to obtain the elevation of his former ward to the imperial throne?

But the restless and indomitable spirit of the Hohenstaufen now asserted itself. Frederick was no longer the 'boy of Apulia', he was the scion of an imperial house, destined to restore its greatness. The prestige of the imperial crown, the desire of the young King for vengeance against an opponent who had sought to deprive him of his maternal heritage, the call to adventure on a bigger stage than the narrow limits of Sicily—all these compelled him to plunge ahead. Years later, in 1227, he said of the reasons that led him to accept: 'Because no one else appeared who wished to accept the proffered imperial dignity in opposition to ourselves and our just claim . . . and because the princes at that time summoned us, and because the crown is ours by virtue of their choice. . . .'[1]

Nothing now remained save his formal reassurances with regard to certain ecclesiastical privileges: the suzerain rights of the Church of Rome in the Kingdom, and positive safeguards against the future union of Kingdom and Empire. In three documents issued in February 1212 from Messina,[2] Frederick sanctioned the rights which the Pope and Curia claimed in the Kingdom of Sicily and in the State of the Church. He pledged himself to take no part in aggressions against Innocent III or his successors, to protect the Patrimony of St. Peter, and, in the event of Innocent's predeceasing him, Frederick pledged himself to recognize the legally elected successor. In the second Messinese document, he stated that, in the presence of the legate of the Apostolic See, Cardinal Gregory of S. Theodore, he had taken the feudal oath of his ancestors, with the traditional obligation of vassalage, for the Kingdom of Sicily and for Apulia, promising also to complete the oath of homage in person in the presence of the Pope. Finally, he sanctioned the agreement, essentially the same as that entered into with the Curia by his mother, guaranteeing free and canonical elections.

Following his decision to accept the invitation of the German princes, the first acts of Frederick were to have his infant son, Henry, crowned as King of Sicily, in obedience to the papal mandate, and to name his Queen, Constance, vicegerent of the realm.[3] In the second week of March 1212 as 'Emperor Elect' he set out with a few ships from Messina on his journey to Germany, accompanied by Anselm of Justingen, the emissary of the German princes, the constable of Sicily, Walter Gentile,

---

[1] Huillard-Bréholles, iii. 39.

[2] Ibid. i, part i, 200–3.

[3] *MGH, Const.* ii. 72, no. 58, and 82, no. 70. On the naming of Constance as vicegerent see BFW, *Reg.* v, Abt. i, no. 659a. See also Huillard-Bréholles, i, part i, 241 f., 253 f., 265 f., 282 f., for the activity of Constance as vicegerent.

Andreas the Justiciar, Archbishop Berard of Bari, the Archbishop-elect Parisius of Palermo, and several of the Chancery personnel.[1] On 17 March the ships entered the harbour of Gaeta, where the King was honourably received. Outside the harbour lurked hostile Pisan vessels sent there to prevent Frederick's progress northwards, causing a delay of nearly a month.[2] Finally, in mid April, the seventeen-year-old boy, gay of spirit although a 'beggar and pauper', arrived in Rome to be warmly received by the Pope and by the citizens. There to greet him also were several of the magnates of Italy, including the Marquis Azzo of Este, Peter Traversara of Ravenna, formerly supporters of Otto, and many others.[3] In accordance with traditional Norman custom, the King took the oaths of homage and fealty to the Pope in the presence of the cardinals and many other people, after which the Pope confirmed the election.[4] As a gesture of goodwill towards his young visitor, the Pope assumed all expenses incurred during Frederick's stay in Rome, bestowed upon him a sum of money to aid him in the remainder of his journey, and gave him every encouragement for the successful completion of his mission.[5]

The presence of Otto's garrisons north of Rome made the overland route too hazardous; accordingly, transports were provided for the journey to Genoa by sea. It was not until 1 May that the transports arrived in the Genoese harbour. Here, as in Rome, Frederick was received with great ceremony and with every honour by the clergy and by the people. A Genoese annalist relates that the royal party was delayed for three months in that city and that during the King's stay the commune provided some 2,400 *libras* to cover his expenses.[6] This financial aid was, however, not entirely a disinterested act of generosity; in return the citizens received Frederick's promise to ratify the privileges granted by his predecessors. He promised also to pay to the commune 9,200 ounces of pure gold in five annual instalments.[7] It was not until 15 July that the 'boy from Sicily', accompanied by the papal legate

---

[1] E. Winkelmann, *O. von B.*, p. 317, notes 3–6, and Erläuterungen, ii, pp. 473 f., has identified these as Frederick's travelling companions. Contemporary sources give the number of ships variously as four or six. *Breve chronicon de rebus Siculis*, 894: 'cum sex galeis iter marinum arripuit.' *Eracles*, 299: 'si fist apareiller .IIII. galies et entra enz et ala a une soe cité, qui est au chief de sa terre a .IIII. jornees de Rome, qui a non Gaete.'

[2] *Annales Ceccanenses*, 300.

[3] *Thomae Tusci Gesta*, 510; *Sicardi Episcopi Cremonensis Cronica* (*MGH, SS.* xxxi), 180. For the magnates who met him in Rome, John Codagnellus, *Annales*, 39.

[4] Years later, in 1245, Pope Innocent IV, recounting this incident, said 'et venit ad urbem, coram eodem Innocentio suisque fratribus cardinalibus et aliis multis presentibus ligum hominium in ejus faciens manibus innovavit' (Huillard-Bréholles, vi, 322).

[5] *Annales Ceccanenses*, 300. *Breve chronicon de rebus Siculis*, 894: 'Et ipse animavit et confortavit eum ad eundum.'

[6] *Ernoul*, 400; *Annales Janvenses* (*Fonti*), ii. 122.

[7] Huillard-Bréholles, i, part i, 212 f.

Berard of Bari, the Marquis of Montferrat, the Count of St. Bonifazio, the representatives of Cremona and Pavia, and others, resumed the hazardous journey from Genoa to Pavia.[1]

The delay in Genoa may well have resulted from intelligence concerning the activities of the Milanese and Piacentines whose concerted efforts were to render Frederick's crossing into Germany so difficult. As a precautionary measure a circuitous route was chosen, leading westwards some forty-five miles to Asti and the friendly land of the Marquis of Montferrat and, thereafter, in a north-easterly direction to Pavia, across the Lambro river south of Lodi, to Cremona. North of the line of march the Milanese troops were on the alert, and to the south the Piacentines were keeping a sharp look-out even to the extent of searching the small river boats which plied the Po and its tributaries. The first stage of the journey was made under the protection of the Marquis of Montferrat who successfully conducted the royal party to Asti. From here they proceeded on 20 July towards Pavia. Sworn to protect the King against all supporters of Otto, the Pavians set out with their royal guest at vespers on 28 July, riding all night towards the rendezvous with the Cremonese on the banks of the Lambro. Meanwhile, the Milanese, learning of these plans, pursued the Pavians and their guest; they overtook them near the point of rendezvous and killed or took captive large numbers of the royal escort. Frederick, eluding his pursuers, escaped by mounting a horse and riding bareback across the Lambro to the protection of the waiting Cremonese who guided him safely to the city.[2] Behind him on the river bank stood the jeering Milanese, thwarted in their mission by the prompt action of their quarry and compelled to seek what satisfaction they could from the recollection that, 'Roger Frederick had washed his breeches in the Lambro'.[3]

On 30 July Frederick arrived safely in Cremona, where he was received with great rejoicing by the citizens. Here he remained, in the security of the city walls, until 20 August, when he proceeded via Mantua, a city allied with Cremona, to Verona.

From Verona Frederick proceeded northwards along the Adige, the customary route to the Brenner pass, until he reached Trent. There he was compelled once more to leave the main thoroughfare in order to avoid the hostile territory in possession of the Dukes of Meran and Bavaria, supporters of Otto. His course now swerved westwards through

---

[1] John Codagnellus, *Annales*, 40. *Breve chronicon de rebus Siculis*, 894. I follow the *Annales Janvenses*, loc. cit., as to the date: 'Die .xv julii' rather than the *Annales Placentini Guelfi*, which give the date as 'Die veneris XIIII, mensis Julii'.

[2] The details of this journey are taken from John Codagnellus, *Annales*, 40 f., *Thomae Tusci Gesta*, 510–11.

[3] *Annales Mediolanenses minores* (*MGH, SS.* xviii), 398: 'Rugerius Federicus balneavit sarabulum in Lambro.'

barren and precipitous Alpine country to the friendly territory of the Archbishop of Chur.[1] He was received by Archbishop Arnold, formerly Count of Matsch, Abbot Ulrich of St. Gall, and Henry of Sax, all of whom, in obedience to the papal command, guided the King safely across Mount Ruppen (Ruggebain) to the monastery of St. Gall and thence to the city of Constance.

This final stage of the journey to St. Gall and Constance was obviously made in great haste and in the knowledge that Otto, since abandoning the siege of Weissensee, was moving southwards to prevent Frederick's entrance into Germany. Triumph or disaster would now be determined by the young King's success or failure in entering Constance before the arrival of Emperor Otto, known to be at Überlingen on the opposite shore of Lake Constance. The Archbishop of Constance, perhaps less sure of his obligation to obey the papal mandate than the Archbishop of Chur and the Abbot of St. Gall, hesitated to open the gate to the royal party. Frederick's future was now held in the balance by the wavering Archbishop. Thus, suddenly, Constance became Frederick's gateway to Germany. In front of him, and only a few miles away, his implacable foe was advancing. To the rear stood the Alps, the main thoroughfare blocked by the Italian allies of Otto. Was this the point of no return, the insuperable obstacle that had appeared as a vague premonition to Frederick's apprehensive Queen? Once again luck favoured the King. In the company of Frederick throughout the journey was Archbishop Berard of Bari, authorized as papal legate. In forceful language he reminded the Archbishop of Constance that Otto was an excommunicate and that a loyal churchman had no recourse other than to obey the papal mandate. Thus prevailed upon, and impressed also by the accompanying armed troops, the Archbishop yielded; the gate was opened and the King and his escort were received within the city walls. The bridge across the Rhine was fortified and all entrances to the city blocked to the imperial troops.[2] Meanwhile Otto had planned to enter the city on that same day. Already he had sent in advance his servants and cooks, who were in the act of preparing food for the imperial table when Frederick, accompanied by a small body of armed troops, occupied the city. One contemporary chronicler, the biographer of Philip Augustus, reports of the King's entrance into Constance that it was said 'if Frederick had delayed three hours he could never have entered Germany'.[3] Eager to engage the King in battle, Otto arrived shortly afterwards, but he found the bridge across the Rhine closed and fortified and his own forces already weakened by desertions from his

---

[1] John Codagnellus, *Annales*, 40; BFW, *Reg.* v, Abt. i, no. 670a; *Burchardi Chronicon*, 108 f.

[2] Conrad of Fabaria, 171.

[3] Guillelmus Armoricus, *De Gestis* (*RHGF*. xvii), 85.

small following and was compelled to turn back.[1] In a few hours, or perhaps even less, the city shifted its allegiance to the Hohenstaufen, while the forces of Otto retreated, pursued by the vituperation of the populace.

Relying now on aid from the Duke of Zähringen, the Emperor hastened to Breisach where he hoped to establish an effective barrier against the advance of Frederick down the Rhine. But the licentiousness and insolence of his diminishing following soon provoked an uprising among the citizens and necessitated the precipitous flight of Otto and his troops.[2] To one contemporary this ignominious flight of Otto 'was the beginning of his sorrow, for henceforth not a single day passed without disappointment and grief, without jeopardy of body and of soul'.[3] As Otto's following fell away and as disappointment dogged his retreating steps, Frederick's entry into southern Germany was a triumphal progress. As he moved from Constance to Basle he was joined by the Count of Kyburg and other nobles and magnates tempted by his generous promises of money or lands from his patrimony. The Bishop of Strassburg also provided some 500 armed men to augment the young King's following.[4] Already in these early days in Germany, Frederick revealed the quality of generosity so greatly praised by the troubadours and minnesingers. For to them no characteristic so well became a good sovereign as open-handedness. The troubadour Aimeric de Péguilhan rejoiced that:

> Worth which was wasted and spoiled is saved
> And largess is cured of the illness which had seized it.[5]

Like many a prince and magnate of Germany, Walther von der Vogelweide, whose loyalty waxed and waned according as his lord or sovereign was generous or parsimonious, could sing in praise of Frederick:

> I have my fief! O all the world, I have my fief!
> No longer do I fear the hoar frost on my toes,
> No longer run to grudging princes for relief.
> The noble King, the generous King, has cared for me:
> In summer I'll have cooling breeze, in winter, heat.
> My neighbours think me now so well provided for,
> Look not upon me as a ghost, as once they did.
> Methinks that I have been poor too long, without my reward:
> I was so filled with hatred that my breath was foul,
> The King has made it pure, and so also my song.[6]

---

[1] *Andreae Danduli Chronica*, 338. *Burchardi Chronicon*, 109.
[2] Guillelmus Armoricus, *De Gestis*, 85.
[3] *Richeri Gesta Senoniensis Ecclesiae* (*MGH, SS.* xxv), 293.   [4] *Burchardi Chronicon*, 109.
[5] From the translation in W. Shepard and F. M. Chambers, *The Poems of Aimeric de Péguilhan*, 146, 148.
[6] Lachmann-Kraus, *Gedichte*, p. 37, lines 31 ff.: 'Ich hân mîn lehen . . .'

It was this generosity so lavishly displayed that explains, in part, the speed with which Frederick's following was recruited. Each day the growing assurance of Frederick's triumphant future gave added security to his promises of lands, of money, and of privileges. Word of his generosity had spread abroad, and his promises of substantial monetary rewards—'as soon as we, with God's help, have the money'—served as a magnet to attract the former supporters of Otto to his side. Thus all barriers were removed and the Apulian lad moved northwards through Alsace without serious hindrance. The castle of Hagenau remained briefly in the hands of an imperial garrison, but yielded to Frederick with little resistance.[1] As Frederick moved triumphantly from city to city, Otto, abandoning the upper Rhine to his opponent, continued northwards to the friendly city of Cologne, where he remained during the greater part of October and November.[2] It was during his stay in Cologne, in mid October, that Otto summoned his supporters to the city of Aachen some forty miles from Cologne.

If the object of the meeting at Aachen was to prevent the election of Frederick or to check his further progress, it proved a disappointment. It is probable that during the Aachen meeting, or even before, Otto had been forced to the conclusion that his triumph over Frederick, if it was to be achieved at all, was dependent upon the outcome of the conflict between Philip Augustus of France, the powerful ally of the Hohenstaufen, and King John of England, Otto's uncle and chief financial support. Just as Otto was dependent upon England for financial aid, so Frederick must look to the King of France for the funds necessary to ensure the loyalty of his German following. A meeting of Frederick and his French patron was arranged through the mediation of Bishop Conrad of Speyer and Metz, to be held in the vicinity of Vaucouleurs, probably at Maxey-sur-Vaise. Philip Augustus, however, delayed at Châlons-sur-Marne, sent instead the Dauphin, Louis, attended by a group of magnates.[3] The journey to Vaucouleurs was beset with dangers for the young King. One contemporary chronicler relates that a murderer, said to have been employed by Otto, was sent to kill Frederick as he moved towards the French border. A clever, if somewhat melodramatic ruse, said to have been suggested by an attendant knight, saved him. Following the informer's advice, a servant occupied the bed prepared for the King, and the murderer, thinking his intended victim to be sleeping there, slew the unfortunate servant.[4] The meeting near Vaucouleurs resulted first of all in a renewal of the agreements formerly made by

[1] *Annales Marbacenses*, 84; *Reineri Annales* (*MGH, SS.* xvi), 665: 'Haghenon ingreditur Octobri mense.' See also BFW, *Reg.* v, Abt. i, no. 673*b*.
[2] *Chronica regia Coloniensis*, 234.
[3] Guillelmus Armoricus, *De Gestis*, 85. See also L. Clouët, *Histoire de Verdun*, ii. 362.
[4] *Ernoul*, 401 f.

Barbarossa and Louis VII. Frederick pledged himself also not to make peace with John of England, Otto, or with their supporters, except with the agreement of Philip, and, in so far as it was possible, not to allow the enemies of the King of France to enter his realm. Of special importance to the impoverished Frederick was a grant to be made in the near future of 20,000 silver marks.[1] This gift seems to have been employed immediately for the fulfilment of the numerous promises and pledges made by the King since his arrival in Germany. It is said that when he was asked by his Chancellor where this money was to be kept, Frederick replied that neither this nor any other money was to be sequestered but was to be distributed among the princes of the realm.[2] It was character-istic of Frederick's insight that he perceived at once upon his arrival in Germany that a policy of generosity towards the princes, however greatly it might tax the resources of the Kingdom, was essential to his ultimate triumph. For nothing had been more offensive in the policies of Otto, especially to the spiritual princes, than his parsimoniousness and avarice. A contemporary could say of Frederick: 'After the munifi-cence of the King was noised abroad, there arose a voice of universal approval in his favour.'[2] Accordingly, on 5 December 1212 at Frankfurt, in an assembly of the princes and in the presence of French ambassadors and papal legates, Frederick was officially elected as King of the Romans. A few days later, on Sunday 9 December, he was crowned and anointed in Mainz by the Archbishop of Mainz, the papal legate. The traditional emblems of sovereignty were still in the possession of Otto, where they were to remain until after his death. Although imitation insignia were employed, the official ceremony left no doubt that Otto had been definitively repudiated; as the Archbishop of Speyer and Metz wrote to Philip Augustus, 'if our forementioned sovereign Frederick, King of the Romans and always august, should be removed from this life, which may God prevent! we will never accept Otto as lord, king, emperor, or regent'.[3]

When, in these festive days of December 1212, the 'boy of Apulia' was elected and ceremoniously crowned King of the Romans, he was a few days removed from his eighteenth birthday. And yet, young as he was, the events of the months that had passed since his departure from Sicily had revealed already the character of the man. It would be difficult to exaggerate the significance of that moment in his life when, after months of hardship and anxiety, he stood at last upon the friendly soil of Alsace, or made his triumphal progress northwards to Hagenau. Here at every step were memorials of the deeds of his ancestors. At strategic points

[1] Huillard-Bréholles, i, part i, 227; Mencken, *Scriptores rerum Germanicarum*, iii. 241.
[2] *Cronica S. Petri Erfordensis moderna*, 383.
[3] Huillard-Bréholles, i, part i, 230.

along the route from Basle to Mainz his great-grandfather, Duke Frederick of Swabia, had erected castle after castle, so that it was still said of him: 'Duke Frederick always carried a castle at his horse's tail.'[1] Thereafter this picturesque country had assumed the outward aspect of a Staufen land. Here, near the river Moder, with its fortified towers along the river banks, stood the castle of Hagenau, renovated by Frederick Barbarossa for his favourite residential palace. Here too were the 'sacred forest', esteemed as a hunting preserve, the red marble chapel, long the repository of the imperial emblems of sovereignty, the palace library, the haunt of Godfrey of Viterbo, panegyrist of the Hohenstaufen and tutor of Henry VI.[2] As he saw for the first time this land so intimately associated with his German forebears Frederick must have been conscious of his own identity with the deeds and aspirations of his paternal ancestry. How deeply he was impressed is apparent in a remark made in one of his letters a quarter of a century later, when he wrote of Alsace as the land 'which, among all others of our rightful patrimony, we hold most dear'.[3]

It would have been singular indeed if, in these surroundings, he had failed to visualize something of his destined future, no longer limited by the bounds of his Sicilian Kingdom, but ever broadening in scope, centring in the valley of the Rhine and extending far beyond—a future no less expansive than that contemplated by his grandfather, Barbarossa. However vaguely he had glimpsed this future as he made his way through Italy and across the Alps, he could now feel, as he stood triumphant in the palace of Hagenau, a growing certainty of his destiny. Here in this friendly land the princes flocked to his standard. In the early months of 1213 some of the bishops who had been less eager at first to support the King were with him in his courts at Regensburg and Nürnberg, including Conrad of Regensburg, Otto of Freising, Mangold of Passau, and Hartwich of Eichstädt.[4]

Not only could he find satisfaction in the increasing support from spiritual and temporal princes, often purchased at so high a price, but also in the sympathy and admiration of the populace. To the inhabitants of the cities and towns of southern Germany he had come as the heroic prince, a David come forth to meet Goliath. They saw in him the embodiment of the freshness of youth, one destined to garner the fruits of praise, the rewards of wisdom and discernment.[5] To chroniclers and

---

[1] Otto of Freising, *Gesta Friderici Imperatoris* (*MGH, SS.* xx), Book I, ch. 12, p. 359.

[2] See especially F. Schneider, 'Kaiser Friedrich II. und seine Bedeutung für das Elsass' (*Elsass-Lothringisches Jahrbuch*, ix, 1930), 137 f. and R. Wackernagel, *Geschichte des Elsass*, 90 ff., especially, pp. 95–8.

[3] Huillard-Bréholles, v, part i, 60 f.: 'quem inter alia iura nostra patrimonialia cariorem habemus.'   [4] BFW, *Reg.* v, Abt. i, nos. 687*a*, 688*f*.

[5] This attitude of the masses is reflected in the language of the troubadours. See especially

poets alike he was the 'boy of Apulia', the 'boy of Sicily', the 'child of Apulia', or 'the boy'. Years after he became Emperor he was referred to as 'the Emperor Frederick who was once called the boy'. A contemporary observing his triumphal reception in southern Germany could truthfully say that 'he was esteemed by all'; and the *Kaiserchronik* could tell of the general satisfaction at his coming.[1] It is perhaps the greatest tribute to his popularity that attempts to discredit him by reviving the Sicilian gossip about his alleged spurious origin were effectively belied by his heroic achievements and his noble bearing.[2] This attitude of general approval is again reflected, perhaps somewhat extravagantly, in the praise which the troubadour Aimeric de Péguilhan heaped upon him when he sang of his prowess, his open-handedness, his comeliness and charm. To this unhappy and disillusioned poet the coming of the young King was as the dawning of a new day. To him Frederick was the skilled physician, come from the renowned school of Salerno, and sent by a gracious God to heal the sickness of the world. For he had come not merely to regain his lost Empire but to restore its health and vigour. 'Well becomes him the name Frederick, for his words are good and his deeds are noble. O Medicine, hail the noble doctor, Master Frederick, say to him not to postpone too long the practice of the healer's art!'[3] Little wonder that in the friendly land of his forebears this gay-spirited youth was transformed swiftly into a man, clear-headed, forceful, conscious of a great destiny. No longer the provincial Sicilian, hampered by restraints imposed upon him by his mother, he was now stirred to new endeavour.

F. Wittenberg, *Die Hohenstaufen im Munde der Troubadours*, 54, and the lines quoted by him from Guillem de Figueira, 95:

> Reis Frederics, vos etz frugz de joven
> E frugz de pretz et frugz de conoisseusa
> E si manjatz del frug de penedensa
> Feniretz be lo bon comensamen.

[1] *Reineri Annales*, 665; *Kaiserchronik*, Anhang v (*MGH, Deutsch. Chron.* i), 404, lines 494 ff.

[2] *Cronica S. Petri Erfordensis moderna* (*MGH, SS.* xxx, part i), 384.

[3] See especially Fr. Diez, *Leben und Werke des Troubadours*, 353; see also Shepard and Chambers, *Poems of Aimeric de Péguilhan*, 146 ff.

III

SUBMISSION OF NORTHERN GERMANY
CORONATION AT AACHEN

chaiser Otte hete das rîch fürwâr niht volle vier jâr. dâ wart er von
vertriben Frideriche dez rîche was beliben.

Kaiserchronik (MGH, Deutsch. Chron. i), 403.[1]

THESE successes of Frederick during his first months in Germany,
gaining for him such wealth of praise for his graciousness and
generosity, proved to be crucial in the future history of the Empire.
When at last his position was secure and his rival no longer living, could
he regain the heavy losses and sacrifices which this open-handedness
had entailed? Could he have regained the Staufen hold upon Germany
or, indeed, the imperial title itself without these sacrifices of lands, of
money, and of privileges? Intimately associated with these questions is
another: were his policies directed towards the pacification of Germany
merely to obtain a greater freedom of action for his Italian plans? Or,
on the contrary, were these sacrifices the necessary preliminaries to a
vast project of World Empire the centre of which would be Franconia
and Swabia, but which in time would embrace not only all Germany,
but the whole of the Mediterranean basin?

It is highly probable that during his first months in Germany, or
perhaps during the first several years, Frederick was over-optimistic
about the possibilities of Germany as the centre of such an empire. His
experience, however, during his eight years there must have convinced
him that at best he could hope only for the establishment of order and
peace while looking to the Kingdom of Sicily as the more promising
nucleusof his future empire. His primary aim, like that of his father
and grandfather was the continued expansion of the Hohenstaufen
Hausmacht and 'crown principality' in Germany as a check upon the
powerful rival principalities and as the nucleus through which they
could be absorbed into the Empire. For the moment he must concentrate
on the subjugation of the regions of northern Germany that remained
loyal to his Welf rival.

After celebrating Christmas in the palace at Hagenau Frederick began

[1] In truth, Emperor Otto had ruled the Empire less than four years when he was deposed.
Frederick was beloved of the Empire.

a series of visitations in various parts of the Kingdom, obviously intended to restore order and to punish the disturbers of the peace who
had become increasingly bold during the absence of Otto in Italy and
as a result of the ensuing conflict over the throne. Contemporary
observers were impressed by the speed and the thoroughness with which
the young King accomplished this. One of them, commending Frederick
for his decision to make a royal progress through the realm, tells how he
was able to bring to the judgement-seat robbers, arsonists, and other
vicious men, and how such criminals were decapitated, broken on the
wheel, hanged, or mutilated, thus making the highways of the Kingdom
safe for the merchants who travelled them.[1]

During the weeks of his royal progress, while holding court at
Hagenau, Regensburg, Nürnberg, Augsburg, Constance, and Eger,
Frederick was engaged also in paying the price of victory through
territorial grants, sanctioning of privileges, or the conferring of jurisdictional rights. Chief among the beneficiaries were the spiritual princes
and the cities of Northern Italy whose aid and protection had made
possible the hazardous passage of Frederick into Germany. Even more
strikingly does he appear in midsummer of 1213 at Eger as the bounden
debtor come to liquidate a heavy obligation to an exacting creditor, his
'protector and benefactor', Innocent III, to whom he acknowledged
his indebtedness for 'great and innumerable benefits'. In the presence of
the papal legate and with the German princes as witnesses Frederick
now renewed the promise made before his departure from Messina. His
oath at Eger was, in large part, a repetition of that which Otto had
sworn in 1209. He promised all honour, reverence, and obedience to
Innocent III and to his successors, and to the Holy Church of Rome,
'our true mother', just as 'our predecessors, Kings and Catholic
Emperors, have shown towards your predecessors'. He swore to maintain the concessions made by his predecessors concerning ecclesiastical
property; to recognize the freedom of election and of appeals. Again he
renounced the right of spoils, the right to seize the properties of deceased
prelates. He promised further, as 'true son and Catholic Prince', to aid
the Apostolic See in the maintenance of its domains and in the restoration of lands fallen into the hands of others, naming specifically the lands
previously mentioned in Otto's oaths, i.e. Ceperano northwards to
Radicofani, Spoleto, and Ancona, the lands of Matilda, the County of
Bertinoro, the Exarchate of Ravenna, and the Pentapolis. He promised
also, in a second document, to support the Pope and his successors in
these possessions and in their suzerain rights over Sicily, and agreed to
a renewal of these promises, under oath, at the time of his coronation

---

[1] *Richeri Gesta Senoniensis Ecclesiae* (*MGH, SS.* xxv), 301; *Annales Sancti Georgii in Nigra Silva*
(*MGH, SS.* xvii), 297.

as Emperor. The Pope required not only Frederick's personal oath but the supporting oaths of the German princes as well.[1]

While Frederick was thus engaged in paying his debts to the Pope and princes, Otto, despite his loss of southern Germany, did not remain inactive. The King of England, John Lackland, hard pressed by threats from Philip Augustus and the Pope, was desperately in need of help from his nephew. Otto could therefore count on substantial financial support from him in return for promised military assistance. On 28 January 1213 Otto received from England a generous grant of 9,000 marks.[2] Moreover, he could still feel assured of the military support of many northern German princes. Had Otto been willing to concentrate his efforts and to employ his resources systematically rather than sporadically he could have offered a serious, if not definitive, check to Frederick's progress. His activities appear instead to have been directed towards the punishment of his local enemies, especially those of Saxony and Thuringia, who had deserted to the side of Frederick. The Archbishop of Magdeburg and the Landgrave of Thuringia were the special objects of his vengeance. For nearly a month Otto lingered in the territory of the Archbishop, laying waste the land and burning and pillaging. At length the prelate was taken captive by one of his own vassals and treacherously confined as the Emperor's prisoner in the near-by castle of Groneberg. Shortly afterwards, however, following the return of the Burgrave, Gebhard of Querfurt, from Eger (where he had been with Frederick), the citizens of Magdeburg, under the Burgrave's leadership, freed the Archbishop. As an act of vengeance for the loss of his valuable prisoner, Otto attacked the suburbs of the city and burnt its outer fortifications.[3]

These punitive measures of Otto, taking place while Frederick was on his progress through southern Germany, may well have been among the subjects he considered with the princes at Eger and were doubtless a determining factor in the development of his plans for the Saxon invasion.

The forces of Frederick, estimated at 60,000 men, far outnumbered the troops of Otto, who, unable to cope with such odds, withdrew to his well-fortified capital, Brunswick. Frederick had evidently determined to make his decisive assault from near Quedlinburg, some thirty-three miles south-west of Magdeburg, and in October he had established his camp outside the city.[4] But a short time before, while raiding in the

---

[1] *MGH, Const.* ii, nos. 46, 47, pp. 57 ff., no. 72, pp. 84 ff.

[2] *Origines Guelficae*, iii, no. cccxvi, 816.

[3] *Magdeburger Schöppenchronik*, 138–9. See also *Chronicon Montis Sereni* (*MGH, SS.* xxiii), 184; and *Braunschweigische Reimchronik* (*MGH, Deutsch. Chron.* ii), 547, line 7091:

> dhe wart ghegen Magdheburch gekart
> uf dhen biscoph mit grozer macht.

[4] *Cronica S. Petri Erfordensis moderna*, 384.

vicinity of Zeitz and Naumburg, Otto had gone as far south as Quedlinburg, where he seized and fortified a convent as an act of vengeance
against kinsmen of the nuns who had deserted to the side of Frederick.[1]
The convent, heavily garrisoned under the leadership of one Caesarius
an imperial captain, was able to resist Frederick's assault successfully,
chiefly because the countryside, devastated by Otto, afforded no food
supplies for the maintenance of his large army through the winter
months. Accordingly, Frederick abandoned his operations in the Saxon–
Thuringian region and moved south.[2] As his huge army, laden with
booty but half-starved, moved southwards, Frederick must have recognized the seriousness of this failure in its effect upon the German princes
and magnates whose loyalty in times past had so often depended upon
the prospects of victory by their sovereign. It was during this withdrawal
up the Rhine valley and while he was at Speyer for the Christmas
festivities of 1213 that, influenced by his Chancellor, Frederick had the
body of his uncle, Philip of Swabia, fetched from Bamberg and buried
among his kinsmen in the royal tomb of the cathedral of Speyer.[3] Whatever the motive for this gesture may have been, it could not have failed
to influence the former adherents of Philip and to strengthen the feeling
of unity and continuity among the supporters of the Hohenstaufen.

It became increasingly apparent in the early months of 1214 that the
outcome of the conflict between Frederick and Otto would be determined, not in Germany but rather by the success or failure of the
Emperor, in alliance with his uncle, John Lackland, in opposing Philip
Augustus. Both Otto and John Lackland, under the ban of the Holy
See, could hope to emerge triumphant in their conflicts with Innocent
III by crushing Philip Augustus, the chief instrument of the Pope in
his punitive measures against them. The opening of the year 1214, therefore, witnessed an alignment of the forces in a conflict which could be
no less decisive for the papacy and Germany than for the future of
France and England. Already Philip Augustus had obtained an advantage when, at the bidding of the Pope, he had assembled a large fleet
with the intention of carrying out an invasion of England.[4] Threatened
by this danger, King John, capable of acting wisely under compulsion,
suddenly made peace with the Pope, yielding completely to the demands
of Innocent III by subjecting both England and Ireland to the Holy See,
and receiving them back as a fief from the Pope.[5] The Pope, having thus

[1] *Annales Marbacenses*, 84. See also *Chronica regia Coloniensis*, 190.

[2] The chief source for these operations in the vicinity of Quedlinburg continues to be the
Schöppenchronik, 140. See also *Sächsische Weltchronik* (*MGH, Deutsch. Chron.* ii), 240.

[3] Huillard-Bréholles, i, part i, 283–5; *Reineri Annales*, 670.

[4] Walter of Coventry, *Memoriale*, ii. 209.

[5] Roger of Wendover, iii. 275 ff. See also the letter of Innocent III, *Epist.* XVI, lxxvii, cols.
878 f.

gained what he had thought to obtain only with the naval and military support of Philip Augustus, now forbade his French ally to carry out the invasion of England, ignoring the fact that Philip had already expended some £60,000 in preparation for the expedition.[1] In the hierocratic system of Innocent III, Philip Augustus, like other temporal princes, was useful only as the wielder of the temporal sword, to be employed or withheld in the service of the spiritual authority at the behest of the Vicar of Christ. Years before, in a letter to the French King, urging him to employ the material sword to punish heretics, Innocent had described the two offices which God had ordained as bulwarks of the Church, one to cherish its children, the other to destroy its adversaries, one to administer spiritual punishments, the other to employ the temporal sword in behalf of the interests of the Church.[2] Innocent III never ceased to insist that the secular power is a *beneficium* conferred upon the prince by the Pope, and that only the Pope, as the director of the *universitas fidelium*, can say when it is to be used or withheld.[3]

Although greatly angered (*valde iratus*) by the action of the Pope, Philip felt compelled to abandon his naval expedition against England until first he had overcome the threat from Count Ferdinand of Flanders, whose interests were so closely allied with those of the English King that he had refused to participate in the projected expedition. This diversion, although successful, proved fatal to Philip's fleet which awaited him in the harbour of Damme. On 30 May the fleet, guarded only by a skeleton crew, was annihilated by the English and the plans for a naval invasion were shattered. Philip now recognized that a decision must be sought on the soil of France.[4]

The impending conflict, unlike earlier ones between France and England, was not primarily feudal in character as in the days of Louis VI, when the counts of Flanders loyally supported the King of France against the English. The new conflict involved, above all, the economic interests of the whole of the region of the lower Rhine, not merely of Cologne, the traditional ally of England, but Flemish cities such as Ghent, Bruges, Brussels, and Ypres. The predilection of this region for England was apparent in the changing policies of Count Ferdinand of Flanders, the Duke of Brabant, the Counts of Holland and Boulogne, as well as lesser magnates subject to the influence of the more powerful princes.[5]

---

[1] Roger of Wendover, iii. 256.   [2] *Epist.* VII, lxxix, cols. 361 f.
[3] See also W. Ullmann, *Growth of Papal Government*, 418–19.
[4] Roger of Wendover, iii. 258. See also Guillelmus Armoricus, *De Gestis*, 89; A. Cartellieri, *Philipp II*, iv, part ii, 374.
[5] For this English–Flemish alliance see A. Cartellieri, *Philipp II*, iv, part ii, 378 f. For the support of the Flemish princes in the time of Louis VI see especially Suger, *Vie de Louis VI le Gros* (ed. and tr. H. Waquet), 105 and 111.

It was this alliance that now, in the early months of 1214, gave an apparent advantage to King John and, indirectly, to the cause of his ally, Otto IV. It was in recognition of this advantage and in the midst of rejoicing over the disaster of the French fleet that King John resolved to employ his army, originally assembled for the defence of the island, for an attack on France itself. The contemplated plan was threefold, involving simultaneous operations in Flanders, in Poitou, and an invasion by Otto IV of the eastern part of France. While strengthening the striking power of Count Ferdinand in Flanders, King John would land at La Rochelle in Poitou; Otto meanwhile would proceed via Aachen, where in mid May he had solidified his alliance with the northern princes through his marriage with the daughter of the Duke of Brabant.[1] With his Flemish allies he would then continue southwards to a rendezvous with the forces of King John. This conjunction of forces was prevented, however, when the Dauphin, sent to check the northern progress of the English, forced John to seek safety in a hasty retreat. An additional reason for King John's flight was the untrustworthiness of many of his own troops. Philip Augustus, spurred on by the success of his son in Poitou, hastened northwards and in the decisive encounter at Bouvines, on 27 July, he crushed the combined forces of the Emperor and his Flemish and Brabantine allies, capturing several of the leaders, including the Counts of Flanders and Boulogne, and putting the others to flight.[2]

During these activities in northern France, Frederick II was to undertake a second military expedition into the lower valley of the Rhine designed to weaken the effectiveness of Otto in France and to cut off his line of communication with Germany.[3] But Frederick was still engaged in the assembling of troops for this expedition when on 27 July Philip Augustus shattered the forces of his enemies at Bouvines and thus, once again, changed the future outlook for Frederick no less than for himself. It was not until mid August that Frederick, with a huge army of Swabians, Bohemians, and Franconians, moved northwards across the Moselle.[4]

The prestige of Otto among the princes of Lower Lorraine had been irreparably shattered by the disaster of Bouvines, and one after another the princes submitted to Frederick, 'so that no one opposed him and he crossed their land peacefully'.[5] He continued north-westwards across the

---

[1] BFW, *Reg.* v, Abt. i, no. 498f. *Reineri Annales,* 671.

[2] Roger of Wendover, iii. 287–92; Guillelmus Armoricus, *De Gestis,* 93, 99; *Reineri Annales,* 672.

[3] On the contemplated role of Frederick see *Cronica S. Petri Erfordensis moderna,* 384; *Chronica regia Coloniensis,* 191. See also Cartellieri, *Philipp Augustus,* iv. 409.

[4] *Chronica regia Coloniensis,* 192; *Reineri Annales,* 672.

[5] *Chronica regia Coloniensis,* loc. cit.

Meuse where the Duke of Brabant, the most powerful of the lower Rhine princes, yet notorious for his wavering loyalties, submitted to the King. Although he found it expedient to forgive his old foe, Frederick required that the Duke's son should accompany him as security for the future allegiance of his father.[1]

As the battle of Bouvines was decisive in favouring the fortunes of Frederick, so it crushed the hopes of Otto IV. One contemporary said of its outcome: 'Henceforth the fortune of Otto, toppling from the loftiest pinnacle, declined incredibly and without prospect of recovery.' Similarly the chronicler of Lauterberg lamented: 'From this time the reputation of the Germans sank ever lower in the eyes of the French.'[2] Symbolic of this humiliation of the Welfs, and prophetic of the ascending fortune of the 'boy of Apulia', was the gift of the captured imperial golden eagle presented by King Philip Augustus to his young ally, after the battle of Bouvines.[3]

Cologne still remained loyal to Otto, and there, following the battle of Bouvines, he with his recent bride had taken refuge. He had come as one shorn of everything, a heavy burden for the merchants to carry, all the more irksome because of the passionate addiction of his Brabantine spouse to gambling.[4] But Otto's uncle, King John of England, would grant trading privileges to the Colognese only so long as they agreed to support his nephew; the merchants were thus compelled to pay the unfortunate Emperor 700 marks. Otto lived as a guest of the city, 'but he was never known to leave his domicile'.[5]

Apart from the Saxon homeland, which remained loyal to the Emperor, only Kaiserswerth, Aachen, and Cologne continued to resist Frederick. He had failed to take Aachen during his expedition into Lower Lorraine. But Frederick had learned from this experience that, before venturing again into Saxony, he must build up his alliances with the neighbouring princes. Accordingly, late in December 1214 while holding court at Metz, with the concurrence of the princes he concluded a treaty with Waldemar II of Denmark, recognizing the claims of the Danish king to the region north of the Elde and the Elbe which had been conquered by the Danes in 1201. Few of Frederick's actions have evoked more adverse criticism than this sacrifice of strategically and economically valuable territory of the Empire.[6]

---

[1] *Reineri Annales*, 672. See also Huillard-Bréholles, i, part i, 311, for Frederick's grant to the Duke of Brabant and his son Henry.

[2] *Cronica S. Petri Erfordensis moderna*, 384. *Chronicon Montis Sereni*, 186: 'Ex quo tempore nomen Teutonicorum satis constat apud Gallicos viluisse.'

[3] Guillelmus Armoricus, *Philippidos* (*RHGF* xvii), 271.

[4] *Cronica S. Petri Erfordensis moderna*, 384.   [5] *Reineri Annales*, 672.

[6] Huillard-Bréholles, i, part ii, 497. For the judgements of German historians as to the significance of this territorial sacrifice see D. Schäfer, *Deutsche Geschichte*. i. 330 f. See also E. Winkelmann, *O. von B.* 388 f. K. Hampe, *Kaisergeschichte*, 254: 'durch abermalige Preisgabe.'

During a visit to Thuringia, obviously in quest of a general pacification, 'the Saxon magnates, with a few exceptions, made peace with King Frederick'. He remained in Thuringia until the end of February, returning then to Franconia and Swabia and, after celebrating Easter at Hagenau, he proceeded to Andernach where he had summoned the princes for 1 May 1215, to consider ways and means of obtaining the subjugation of Aachen and Cologne. An armed expedition against Aachen proved to be unnecessary. To many of the inhabitants the powerlessness of Otto, and consequently the hopelessness of successful resistance to Frederick, was obvious and, despite the opposition of some, they determined to spare the city the sufferings of a long siege. Hohenstaufen partisans imprisoned the resisting imperial officials and invited Frederick to enter the city.[1] On the same day that Aachen opened its gates, Kaiserswerth, long under siege and stoutly defended by the Welf garrison, fell into Frederick's hands.[2]

On 24 July 1215 Frederick made his ceremonial entrance into the city of Aachen, escorted by large numbers of princes and nobles, by representatives of the King of France, and by the papal legates. On the following day he was crowned in the cathedral of Aachen by the Archbishop of Mainz, the papal legate.[3]

After the service a priest preached a crusade against the Muslims in the name of the Sovereign Pontiff, appealing to the noble lords to take the cross in order that the Holy Land might be recovered. To the astonishment of all present, Frederick was first to sign himself with the holy emblem. A contemporary wrote of the action of the King:

Immediately after the celebration of Mass, and unexpectedly, the King accepted the sign of the living cross and, both in his own person, and with the support of the crusading preachers, he admonished all princes and nobles of the Kingdom to do likewise; and thus he influenced many to join with him. On the following day which was Sunday, while the King sat in the church from early morning until mid afternoon (*hora nona*), the preachers busied themselves with preaching the word of the cross with the result that many, not only princes but also people of the lower classes, took the sign of the cross by the grace of God.[4]

If the action of Frederick in taking the cross astonished those present at the coronation ceremonies, it was no less surprising, if not displeasing, to Innocent III. Not only did the Pope ignore the action of the young King, but years later Pope Gregory IX revealed something of the dis-

---

[1] *Reineri Annales*, 672–3; Huillard-Bréholles, i, part ii, 394 f.

[2] *Chronica regia Coloniensis*, 193.

[3] For the traditional coronation service see *Coronatio Aquisgranensis: Ordo Coronationis* (*MGH, Legum*, ii), 384 f.

[4] *Reineri Annales*, 673; see also *Chronica regia Coloniensis*, 236.

pleasure of the Curia when he reminded Frederick 'that he had acted spontaneously, not with the advice, but without the knowledge of the Apostolic See'.[1] Innocent III conceived of the Fifth Crusade as a papal enterprise, the details of which were arranged by the Lateran Council, the leader to be the Pope himself. Frederick's action, certainly a brilliant diplomatic stroke, placing him automatically at the head of a great European movement, was equally the expression of a deep sense of gratitude for the many blessings bestowed upon him by divine favour. Years later, in 1227, he said of his action:

> Moreover, considering devoutly how we might repay God for the many gifts conferred upon us, as soon as we had received the crown at Aachen, we took the cross, though this was not an equal payment to him, offering ourselves and our power not just in sacrifice but in the holocaust to God, with pure and sincere spirit, that we might work for the recovery of the Holy Land with the efforts we had vowed and owed.[2]

On the following Monday he gave further symbolic meaning to his coronation when he had the body of Charles the Great, which his grandfather had once before taken from its tomb, placed in a magnificent sarcophagus, made of gold and silver by the citizens of Aachen. In humble tribute to his great predecessor, he cast aside his royal robes, mounted the scaffold with the workmen and, in the sight of all, seized the hammer and drove in the nails sealing the sarcophagus.[3]

Two days after the conclusion of the ceremonies at Aachen Frederick held court there, and the inhabitants of that city 'next in honour and dignity after Rome', were generously rewarded with all rights and privileges originally bestowed upon them by 'our glorious predecessor, Charles the Great', as well as those given by 'our father and grandfather and by other predecessors'.

As these ceremonies were being concluded in the sacred city of Aachen, Cologne, long intimately identified with the interests of Otto of Brunswick, prepared for its peaceful submission to this Hohenstaufen. Otto of Brunswick had secretly left his refuge there after the citizens, agreeing to assume all his debts, gave him some 600 marks to meet the expenses of himself and the Empress on their journey to Brunswick.[4] The surrender of Aachen opened the way for the submission of most of the cities of the lower Rhine. As the ceremonies were being concluded in Aachen, the Archbishop of Trier and the Duke of Brabant, serving as mediators, persuaded the citizens of Cologne, who realized they could no longer continue their resistance, to submit to the young King. The

[1] Huillard-Bréholles, iii. 25: 'Nam sponte, non monitus, sede apostolica ignorante, crucem suis humeris affixit.'
[2] Ibid. iii. 39.
[3] *Reineri Annales*, 673.　　　　　　　　[4] Guillelmus Amoricus, *De Gestis*, 107.

ban was lifted and on 4 August, Frederick made his peaceful entry into the city.[1]

Just as the events following the battle of Bouvines had signalized the firm establishment of Frederick's hold upon Germany, so also had the affairs of Innocent III prospered. The extent of the papal triumph was brilliantly revealed in the great oecumenical council of the Lateran which assembled on 11 November 1215. There Innocent could gather the fruits of his patient efforts since his elevation in 1198. He could now feel that he had secured his suzerain rights in Sicily as well as his claim to the Papal State; that he had demonstrated his power, and exemplified his right to create kings and emperors; that he had seen the destruction of the threatening alliance of John Lackland and Otto of Brunswick. Above all, he had witnessed the successful unfolding of his plans for a general crusade against the Muslims, and finally, the sentence depriving Otto of his imperial throne was confirmed, as was the choice of Frederick II as Otto's successor.[2]

The eight years between 1212, when Frederick first appeared in Germany, and 1220, the occasion of his coronation as Emperor, were to constitute his longest continuous residence in the land of his paternal ancestors. They were crucial as the formative years of his policies as King of the Romans while, at the same time, they revealed the existence of new tendencies in Germany that were to distinguish his reign from those of his predecessors. One of these tendencies had checked the normal evolution of the temporal sovereignty which, under Barbarossa, had made substantial gains; it thus afforded a unique opportunity for the strengthening of clerical influence both in the central administration and in the principalities of the territorial princes. This tendency was further stimulated and effectively guided by Pope Innocent III, who had made the most of the chaotic conditions in Germany following the death of Henry VI in 1198; he extended the papal influence so that it not only affected the choice of the national sovereign but also encouraged the development of the independent sovereignty of the territorial princes.

The second of these tendencies confronting Frederick was the vigorous corporate movement accelerated by the shifting of the trade routes from east to west to include Germany, especially the routes along the upper Danube, via the Alpine passes, and the valley of the Rhine from the Lake of Constance to the North Sea.[3] The shifting of the routes of trade was inevitably accompanied by a growth of urban communities and

---

[1] *Chronica regia Coloniensis*, 193, 236.

[2] Richard of San Germano, 62. See especially Mansi, *Sacrorum Conciliorum Collectio*, xxii, 1058–67.

[3] See especially *The Cambridge Economic History of Europe*, ii. 184 ff.; H. Pirenne, *Histoire de l'Europe*, 168 ff.; Engl. tr., 228 ff.

the extension of economic development which 'overflowed widely in Germany and reached as far as the Vistula'.[1] This corporate tendency with its accompanying expansion expressed itself in something akin to patriotism, an ethnic self-consciousness which at times defied the interference even of the See of Rome in the affairs of Germany. The high point of this tendency had been attained in the era of Frederick Barbarossa during which the energies of the German people were directed towards the improvement of their material well-being and the promotion of intellectual and artistic interests—in short, towards elevating the prestige of Germany throughout the Western world. The brilliant Diet of Mainz in 1184 had afforded an opportunity for the tangible expression of German ethnical self-consciousness in the courtly poetry of Heinrich of Veldeke and others.[2] To the historian this twelfth- and early thirteenth-century literary development is of especial interest as a reflection of the lay attitude towards the events and movements of the day. In the long and bitter years of the throne conflict following the death of Emperor Henry VI it bore witness to the nostalgic yearning for a return to the unity and solidarity of the Barbarossa era. Above all, it gave expression to an ethnic pride, if not patriotism, which became a favourite theme of the lyricist Walther von der Vogelweide, whose *Sprüche* so often warned of the threatening disunity of Germany and of the growing weakness and corruption of the medieval Church. His verses were no less hostile to the particularistic tendencies of the territorial princes, the 'poor kings' (*die armen künege*) who stood in the way of the unity of the Kingdom during the conflict over the throne.[3] In the spirit of the true patriot, Walther lamented the sad state of Germany where 'disloyalty reigns supreme and might prevails on the highways', where 'peace and justice are much impaired'.[4] To this much-travelled and patriotic poet there was nothing to compare with the German court: 'May evil befall me, if ever my heart should tempt me to prefer alien customs! German culture takes precedence over all other. . . . From the Elbe to the Rhine and then back again to Hungary is by far the best that I have known in the world.'[5]

[1] H. Pirenne, *Medieval Cities*, 107.

[2] F. Koch, *Geschichte deutscher Dichtung*, 50 f.; and H. Schneider, *Heldendichtung, Geistlichendichtung, Ritterdichtung*, 195 ff. and 250 ff.

[3] Lachmann-Kraus, *Walther von der Vogelweide*, 10: 'die armen künege dringent dich.'

[4] Ibid.: 'Untriuwe ist in der sâze, gewalt vert ûf der strâze: fride unde reht sint sêre wunt.'

[5] As pointed out by C. von Kraus, *Walther von der Vogelweide: Untersuchungen*, 225–6, the above verses have been over-emphasized at times in the sense of a *Nationalhymne* or poem in praise of Reich and Kaiser. It is probable, however, that Kraus may place too restricted an interpretation on the lines when he says: 'dass innerhalb der von Walther genannten Grenzen *wol die besten* sein mögen, die er in der Gesellschaft kennengelernt habe, dass die Frauen hier *bezzer* sind als anderwärts, dass man *in unserer lant* kommen solle, um *tugent* und *reine minne* zu finden.' Even if one accepts this narrower interpretation, the sentiment of patriotism is implicit in the lines.

With the poet's intuitive insight Walther sensed the dangers inherent in the conflict for the throne. To him the superior culture of the court circle, its ladies who *bezzer sint danne ander frouwen* and its men who *sint wol gezogen*, represented the ideal Germany. For it was in this court circle during the late twelfth and early thirteenth centuries that German heroic and lyric poetry of the Middle Ages attained their full development in the works of Wolfram von Eschenbach and Hartmann von der Aue, as well as in a host of lyric poets. Germany's location at the heart of Central Europe also favoured the development of an indigenous art which, while retaining its individuality, was receptive to influences from the West, from Lombardy, and from the Byzantine-Antique.[1] And yet in these same decades counteracting forces were at work which ultimately were to place a check upon German unity and solidarity and to decree, instead, a conglomerate mass of independent principalities powerful enough to obtain from the last of the Hohenstaufen official sanction of their independence. At no time could Frederick II lose sight of the fact that he had come to Germany at the invitation of these princes, of the ecclesiastical princes in particular, and that his success there depended upon their goodwill. The attainment of imperial sovereignty could be achieved only with their support, always purchasable through the granting of generous privileges. The era of the throne conflict that preceded Frederick's arrival had witnessed the acceleration of a constitutional revolution which Frederick was powerless to check. This revolution was characterized by a retarding of the growth of the unity of the Kingdom, so active under Barbarossa. It is most apparent in the altered status of the ecclesiastical princes who, under the powerful influence of Frederick Barbarossa and his Chancellor, Reginald of Dassel, had once been recognized as 'pillars of the realm', devoted above all else to the interests of the German state and to the sovereign authority of the King and Emperor.[2] But the ensuing conflict for the throne had made it possible for Innocent III to destroy this solidarity, rebuilding the ecclesiastical structure of Germany so that the bishops ceased to be one of the chief supports of the central authority and looked instead to the advancement of their principalities. No longer were these ecclesiastical princes content to be the 'core of a feudal aristocracy'; they aspired to be independent sovereigns in their respective princely domains, willing servants of the see of Rome and lending their support to the King only in return for a substantial *quid pro quo*.[3] It was the altered status of this estate under the powerful influence of Innocent III,

---

[1] K. Hampe, *Das Hochmittelalter*, 321 ff. See also A. Koberstein, *Geschichte der deutschen Nationalliteratur*, 88 f.

[2] W. von Giesebrecht, *Geschichte der deutschen Kaiserzeit*, v. 557–8. See also K. Hampe, *Kaisergeschichte*, 158 ff.

[3] J. Haller, *Die Epochen der deutschen Geschichte*, 93–4.

particularly during the conflict between Philip of Swabia and Otto of Brunswick, that deprived the Crown of much of its authority in Germany and necessitated further sacrifices in order to make Frederick's position secure as King and Emperor.

There has been a persistent tendency among historians to criticize Frederick II for failing to utilize the instruments at hand in strengthening the royal or centralized sovereignty in Germany. Such criticism invariably minimizes the essential fact that (as will be seen below) Frederick's chief preoccupation was not with the advancement of German sovereignty but with an imperial sovereignty transcending any concept of local or national kingship. Frederick himself repeatedly emphasized his lofty aims, as when he wrote: 'From our earliest days . . . our heart has never ceased to burn with the desire to re-establish in the position of their ancient dignity the founder of the Roman Empire and its foundress, Rome herself.'[1] Above all Frederick conceived his aim to be the restoration of the rights of the Empire, and to this end his policies were consistently directed. A close analysis of these policies can leave no doubt that he sought to attain this goal through a series of steps by which absolute sovereignty, comparable to that of ancient Rome, would be established first in Sicily, secondly in Central and Northern Italy, and finally, after its realization in these regions, in Germany. While his aim in Central and Northern Italy is but vaguely discernible at the time of his coronation, it was unmistakable after his return from the crusade and throughout his long conflict with Gregory IX, Innocent IV, and the Lombard League. The prior re-establishment of sovereignty in Germany was not necessarily a prerequisite of this higher goal, which might conceivably be more easily achieved through the gradual absorption of the territorial principalities. Certainly Sicily afforded the most favourable conditions for complete absolutism, while Italy, never wholly separated from the classical tradition, might conceivably be visualized as yielding, in course of time, to imperial authority. With the *imperium* thus restored to the heart-land of the old Roman Empire, Germany itself might ultimately be brought into the framework of the restored Empire.[2]

Frederick II perceived upon his arrival in Germany that conflict with the individual ecclesiastical princes would, under the altered conditions, be futile. Already their subserviency to the Pope and Curia was such that the successful restoration of sovereign authority would be possible only by making the Pope 'the chief metropolitan within the state'. Indeed, there is much to be said in favour of the observation that:

The precise way in which this problem was to be solved seems to have been

[1] Huillard-Bréholles, v, part ii, 761.
[2] For an interesting treatment of this see Klingelhöfer, op. cit. 225.

a matter of indifference, provided that Frederick could succeed in making the whole ecclesiastical organization, which threatened to become an *imperium in imperio*, an integral part of the imperial machine. . . . Frederick II therefore directed his attack against Rome, boldly attempted to lay hold of the hierarchical organization of the Church at its very centre, and sought to bring it as a whole within the constitutional structure of the state.[1]

Great as were the sacrifices that Frederick II was compelled to make in these early years in Germany, there is not sufficient evidence to warrant the persistent assumption that he looked upon Germany merely as a tributary land, an 'appurtenance of the Empire'.[2]

Temporarily, and pending the re-establishment of the Empire, the movement towards German consolidation must emanate from a Hohenstaufen *territorium* or principality comparable to that of the Capetian Île de France. It must be powerful enough to limit the neighbouring princes strictly to their respective territories and capable of consolidating the far-flung imperial possessions in southern and eastern Germany. Throughout these regions the policy of Frederick, even when he was compelled to make sacrifices, was to surrender the rights of the feudal lord in return for sovereign rights.[3] With the acquisition of increased sovereign authority within the princely *territorium* it became possible to institute royal officials who exercised authority, not as feudal vassals, but as direct agents of the King, variously designated as *advocatus*, *Schultheiss*, *Burggraf*. Already this administrative system had demonstrated its capacity to absorb other provincial regions and, 'the policy of "concentration concentrique" . . . was justifying itself as fully in the hands of the Hohenstaufen as it had already justified itself in the hands of the Capetians'.[4] Conditions were such upon Frederick's arrival in Germany that he was primarily a territorial prince among numerous other territorial princes; their opposition to him, as it manifested itself from time to time, was not because of his royal authority *per se* but because of his advantageous position as a territorial prince.[5] Their resentment, as revealed in the *Privilegium* of 1200 and the *Statutum* of 1232, was not directed so much towards the royal power as towards Frederick's ever-

---

[1] Otto Freiherr von Dungern, 'Die Staatsreform der Hohenstaufen', tr. G. Barraclough, *Medieval Germany 911–1250*, ii. 224–5.

[2] Such is the view of B. Schmeidler, 'Die Stellung Frankens im Gefüge des alten deutschen Reiches bis ins 13. Jahrhundert', tr. G. Barraclough, op. cit., p. 92 and note 19. To be accepted only with critical caution is the dogmatic statement of H. Pirenne, *A History of Europe*, 315, that Frederick's policy 'was exclusively Italian; it was hardly in any sense Imperial'. See also the conclusions of H. Mitteis, 'Zum Mainzer Reichslandfrieden von 1235' (*ZfRG* lxii, 1942), 56, for an opposing view, and E. Kantorowicz, *Kaiser Friedrich II.*, 352 ff. (and the Lorimer English tr., 384 f.). See also ibid. 79 f.

[3] H. Niese, *Die Verwaltung des Reichsgutes im 13. Jahrhundert*, 56.

[4] Barraclough, *Medieval Germany*, i. 117.

[5] Ibid. i. 131.

increasing principality, which, they believed, was capable of absorbing much of their territories within his consolidated demesne. It was to offset this opposition that Frederick pursued a policy resulting in concessions of privileges which contributed to the often exaggerated portrayal of Germany as an agglomeration of ecclesiastical and secular principalities. The aims of the territorial princes were in many instances identical with those of Frederick within their respective principalities. Only the future could reveal whether or not the wielder of an imperial sovereignty over extensive regions of the world who was, at the same time, the most powerful of the territorial princes could force the lesser principalities of Germany into the framework of a World Empire.

In the pursuit of his imperial goal, Frederick was immediately confronted, upon his arrival in Germany, by preliminary tasks necessary to the re-establishment of order. First of all, he must obtain the fullest possible support from the German princes, especially the ecclesiastical princes who, as the agents of Innocent III, were responsible for the election of Frederick as King of the Romans. Secondly, he must continue the policies of his father and grandfather, looking to the union of Kingdom and Empire, by bringing his son Henry from Sicily and conferring upon him the princely dignity of Duke of Swabia as a first step towards his choice as German King. Thirdly, he must crush all further efforts of the Welfs to regain the throne. Fourthly, he must make provision for the effective carrying out of the crusade as an imperial, rather than as a papal, enterprise. And, finally, he must obtain the imperial crown on terms which he himself would dictate and which the Pope and Curia must be induced to accept. These then are the aims and purposes that gave motivation to Frederick's policies throughout his eight years' residence in Germany.

Apart from the growth of the great territorial principalities during the preceding decades, the most radical change was the social and economic evolution attendant upon the inclusion of Germany within the enlarging commercial sphere. Of special importance were the prosperous urban communities demanding greater freedom from both the King and the territorial princes upon whose domains they had emerged.

It might have been expected that, coming from Sicily and Apulia, where such cities as Naples, Messina, and Palermo were showing signs of developing in conformity with the pattern previously shaped by the Lombard cities, or else were being dominated by the latter, Frederick would be no stranger to the commercial motivation. In Germany, however, the emergence of these communal commercial centres had just begun and as yet neither precedent nor laws existed to retard or to advance their freedom.[1] Even more than the Capetians, Frederick II

---

[1] A. Heusler, *Der Ursprung der deutschen Stadtverfassung*, 218. Many aspects of this subject

must have recognized in these cities potential allies, and yet circumstances were such in early thirteenth-century Germany that he was compelled to favour the interests of the princes, especially the ecclesiastical princes, who had determined already to check the pretensions to freedom of the aggressive burgher class. It was the misfortune of the rising German cities that the King, who was disposed to favour them, was wholly dependent upon the goodwill of their chief opponents, the ecclesiastical princes. *Realpolitiker* that he was, Frederick was compelled to accept the latter as his allies just as he was compelled to recognize the Pope and Curia as his benefactors. Many of them, including the Archbishops of Mainz and Worms, among the earliest of his supporters, lost no time in appealing to the royal authority to secure their dominance over their burghers.[1] In obedience to this policy Frederick felt obliged to deny or else to revoke the privileges of the burghers to hold their own municipal courts without prior sanction of the archbishops of their respective dioceses.[2] Although he would have liked to grant the continuance of rights, liberties, 'good customs', and privileges, previously allowed some of the cities by his father and grandfather, he was compelled by ecclesiastical pressure to revoke or to deny them.[3]

Frederick's true policy towards the cities must be sought in his dealings with the imperial cities. Towards them he displayed a consistent liberality, leaving to them their local customs and extensive autonomy in the administration of justice. In such cities also the *Schultheiss* was chosen by the Crown from among local families. An early example of this liberality was offered at Aachen at the time of his coronation, when he granted its citizens freedom from personal services and taxes, with full trading privileges throughout the realm. He stipulated that judges instituted by the King should be bound by previous judgements of the local magistrate. He conferred similar liberal privileges upon other imperial cities in 1219. Typical of such cities were Frankfurt, Goslar, Anweiler, Nürnberg, Freiburg, Dortmund, Donauwörth, Gelnhausen, and Molsheim[4]. With the extinction of the Zähringen family the number of imperial cities was increased when Frederick, at the Diet of Ulm, as his share of the heritage, obtained possession of Bern, Zürich, Laupen, Murten, Solothurn, and Schaffhausen.[5] It was characteristic of his policies also that villages in well-favoured regions such as Alsace were

---

are covered by F. Knöpp, *Die Stellung Friedrichs II. und seiner beiden Söhne zu den deutschen Städten.*

[1] BFW, *Reg.* v, Abt. i, nos. 675, 676. See also G. L. von Maurer, *Geschichte der Stadtverfassung*, iii. 294.

[2] For examples see Huillard-Bréholles, i, part i, 226, 293; part ii, 558, 560.

[3] Ibid., part i, 310; part ii, 401, 402 f., 407.

[4] For the grants of privileges to such cities as these see Huillard–Bréholles, i, part ii, 643 ff., 659 f., 673 f., 680 f., 700 f., 736 f., 777 f., 812 ff., 814, 816 f.   [5] See below, p. 111.

often protected by walls and raised to the status of cities. Among them were Kolmar, Kaisersberg, Schlettstadt, and Neuburg which, in their turn, received the special protection of the Emperor so that the highways employed by them in their trade relations were made safe for merchants.[1] It was clearly the policy of Frederick II during these early years in Germany to further, in so far as possible, the growth of the imperial cities. Towards the territorial cities his inclination was also to encourage the utmost freedom, except where such encouragement would alienate the princely overlords, especially the ecclesiastical princes.

How fully Innocent III had determined to influence the course of events in Germany is best illustrated in the activities of his legates. During the first years of the conflict between Frederick II and Otto of Brunswick the papal interests had been cared for by the Archbishops of Magdeburg and Mainz. Shortly after the meeting of the Fourth Lateran Council in 1215, Innocent sent as his special legate Peter of Sasso, Cardinal Deacon of the Church of Santa Pudentiana, who was present at the Diet of Würzburg in early May 1216 (when he appears to have participated in ending the schism at Cologne), which resulted in the elevation of Engelbert of Berg in place of the aspirants, Dietrich of Hengebeck and Adolf of Altena.[2] The extraordinary clerical influence of this Diet is further emphasized by the guarantees of the regalian rights and the renunciation of the 'right of spoils' to the Archbishops of Cologne and Magdeburg.[3]

The readiness with which Frederick made these concessions is indicative of his preoccupation with future imperial plans which would require the full support of both the Pope and the German princes. The imperial Chancellor, Conrad of Metz, in preparing the document in which these concessions were made, has Frederick say that he granted them 'in reverence for the cross whose emblem we wear upon our body' and that 'they had their origin in the plenitude of our goodwill'.[4] The seemingly generous policy pursued at Würzburg was much more in the nature of a series of gestures calculated to remove the last vestige of clerical opposition to Frederick's imperial plans. It may not be overlooked that already at this time, as a few years later at Frankfurt, Frederick was endeavouring through negotiations to obtain the consent of the Pope to the coronation of his son as King of the Romans. This was a most delicate subject for papal-imperial diplomacy, for Henry had already received the Sicilian crown and was thus in a position to circumvent the carefully laid plans of the Pope to prevent the union of the

[1] *Richeri Gesta Senoniensis*, 301; *De Rebus Alsaticis Ineuntis Saeculi XIII* (*MGH, SS.* xvii), 236. See also R. Wackernagel, *Geschichte des Elsass*, 106 ff.

[2] Huillard-Bréholles, i, part ii, 452; *Chronica regia Coloniensis*, 237.

[3] Huillard-Bréholles, i, part ii, 456 ff., 462; Böhmer, *Acta*, 239.

[4] Huillard-Bréholles, i, part ii, 457.

Kingdom of Sicily with the Empire. Unfortunately, we can only conjecture as to the subject of these negotiations, but the secrecy surrounding them and the long delay before the emissary's return with a
favourable report 'to the King and princes' suggest that they had to do
with the coming of Frederick's son to Germany and his coronation as
king.[1]

[1] Here again we have only the vague statement of Conrad of Fabaria, 171: 'Finito negocio
pro quo venerat, multis apostolico xeniis transmissis, auctus benedictione ipsius, ad propria
remeavit, regi ac principibus bonum, pro quo ierat, nuncium reportans.'

IV

DEATH OF OTTO IV: SUBMISSION OF THE WELFS TO FREDERICK II

Obiit Otto dictus imperator, qui cum fuisset potentissimus, et ab
Innocentio papa sublimatus et consecratus, factis suis exigentibus ab
ipso est humiliatus et destitutus, et per sententiam in generali concilio
depositus; et Fredericus in regem Romanorum confirmatus.

Reineri Annales (MGH, SS. xvi), 676.[1]

IT was only after the Fourth Lateran Council had sanctioned the
excommunication of Otto and approved the election of Frederick
II that the latter sent Archbishop Berard of Palermo and Albert of
Everstein, a kinsman of Constance of Aragon, to fetch his consort and
son. It was many months later, towards the end of July 1216, that
Constance and her son began their journey to Germany.[2] The cause
of this long delay was probably the difficulty that Frederick's ambassador to Rome, Ulrich of St. Gall, found in satisfying the papal objections
to the possible coronation of young Henry as King of the Romans.
Certainly the promises which Frederick felt compelled to make were
not in accord with his plans for the ultimate union of the Kingdom and
Empire in the hands of his son. Indeed, the language employed in the
official document setting forth these promises would appear to preclude
the possibility of such a union:

Desiring to provide for the interests of the Roman Church as well as for
the Kingdom of Sicily, we promise and concede that after we have received
the imperial crown we will release from our paternal authority our son
Henry whom, in obedience to your command, we had crowned King of
Sicily. Also we will relinquish the entire Kingdom of Sicily on both sides of
the strait to be held by him from the Church of Rome just as we hold it, to
the end that we shall neither be nor yet speak of ourselves as King of Sicily

---

[1] Otto, the so-called Emperor, died. Although he had been most powerful and elevated
and consecrated by Pope Innocent, as the result of his own actions he had been humiliated
and abandoned by the same Pope and deposed by decree of a General Council, and Frederick
was confirmed as King of the Romans.

[2] The chief source for the journey, *Breve chronicon de rebus Siculis*, 894 f., obviously errs in
giving June (*mense junii*) as the month. That it was July, not June, is indicated by the fact
that Constance was still in Messina in July when she issued a document in favour of Archbishop Nicholas of Salerno. See E. Winkelmann, *O. von B.*, p. 439, note 3.

but, pending his coming of age, we shall permit it to be governed by a competent person agreeable to you. Such person shall be responsible for all rights and privileges to the Roman Church inasmuch as the lordship over that Kingdom is known to appertain only to her. This will be done lest because we are by divine ordinance called to the office of Empire, it should be thought at any time that the Kingdom was united to the empire, if we held both at the same time.[1]

As if suspecting that these promises might not be sufficient to convince the Pope of his sincerity, Frederick concluded by saying that such an inference 'could bring about injury to the Apostolic See as well as to our heirs'. While the sincerity of this statement need not be questioned, in view of the traditional opposition of the princes to the principle of hereditary succession, it is doubtful that it would continue to express Frederick's sentiment if, in time, the princess could be induced to approve the imperial succession in the Hohenstaufen family. In that case it would be inconceivable that Frederick would be satisfied merely with a personal union through the coronation of his son, already King of Sicily, as King of the Romans.[2] Indeed it is no less inconceivable that the Curia at any time—whether under Innocent III, Honorius III, or any other Pope—could have assumed that Frederick would have excluded his son from the imperial succession because he wore already the Sicilian crown. Every aspect of this question must have been discussed fully by Frederick's ambassador, Ulrich of St. Gall, and Innocent III. Meanwhile, the official draft of Frederick's promises drawn up on 1 July 1216 never reached Innocent III, who died on 16 July.

Ten days after the death of Innocent III, Constance and her five-year-old son were *en route* to Germany.[3] Travelling by separate routes, they arrived in Germany early in December 1216.[4] Frederick lost little time in investing his son with the Duchy of Swabia and giving him the status of an imperial prince.[5] Although not openly opposing this action of Frederick, which brought the King of Sicily into intimate association with Germany, the Pope and Curia could not have been oblivious of the shrewdness of the move as a first step towards the elevation of Henry as King of the Romans.

The passing of the inflexible Innocent III marked the disappearance of a serious obstacle to Frederick's plans. Frederick had been deeply

---

[1] Huillard-Bréholles, i, part ii, 469–70.

[2] In his subsequent correspondence with the Pope, notably in a letter of 13 July 1220 (ibid. i, part ii, 802), he assured Honorius III that he had striven from the beginning to have his son crowned as King of the Romans.

[3] See above, p. 107, note 2.

[4] BFW, *Reg.* v, Abt. i, 884*a*; *Reineri Annales*, 675.

[5] So mentioned in Feb. 1217. Huillard-Bréholles, i, part ii, 499 f.

indebted to Innocent III, but he was under no such obligations to the mild and conciliatory Cencius Sevelli who had succeeded to the papal throne as Honorius III. Although as Cardinal the new Pope had demonstrated exceptional ability as an administrator and as author of the *Liber Censuum Romanae ecclesiae*, he was wanting in both the youth-fulness and the astounding physical vigour of his predecessor. The one enterprise of Innocent III to which Honorius devoted himself sedu-lously was the Fifth Crusade. In other respects his naturally easy-going disposition seems to have guided his actions, thus affording Frederick II a much-needed opportunity for carrying out his plans.

Despite these satisfactory developments during 1216–17, the opposi-tion of the Welfs in the north was such as to require the constant vigi-lance of the King. His ally in Saxony, the Archbishop of Magdeburg, who had long been a faithful supporter of Frederick, was taken prisoner by Otto. Thanks to the efforts of Count Burchard of Mansfield, for-merly a supporter of Otto, and a hastily assembled group of followers, the Archbishop was released from his prison and returned to Magdeburg.[1] It was only in such attacks that Otto was now effective. His supporters, even in Saxony, were falling away or were being removed by death.[2] It was at this time also that King Waldemar of Denmark, with whom Frederick had made peace, demonstrated his effectiveness as an ally. Through a swift manœuvre, facilitated by the long duration of the ice in the late winter of 1216, he succeeded in dominating both banks of the Elbe, thereby not only depriving Otto of the use of the river mouth but threatening also his control of the lower valley of the Weser.[3]

Faced by these serious reverses, Otto made a final effort to regain his control of northern Germany by means of a liberal use of money. It is said that Hermann, Landgrave of Thuringia, an early supporter of Frederick II, was sorely tempted, despite his serious illness, by an offer of a substantial bribe by Otto IV. Before the negotiations were completed, however, death overtook him. His successor Louis IV, a youth of only seventeen, did homage to Frederick by whom he was confirmed in his possession of the Landgravate.[4] With the failure of this and similar attempts at bribery, Otto, now 'remaining in Saxony, was deprived of all support save that of the Marquis of Branden-burg'.[5]

Why did Frederick not take advantage of these conditions to deliver a decisive blow against the Welfs? The explanation must be sought in his preoccupation with other projects, especially the crusade of 1217,

[1] *Magdeburger Schöppenchronik*, 139 f.
[2] Pressutti, i, no. 119, p. 22, and no. 184, pp. 34–5.
[3] *Annales Ryenses* (*MGH, SS.* xvi), 406; *Annales Bremenses* (ibid. xvii), 858.
[4] *Cronica Reinhardsbrunnensis*, 589.
[5] *Reineri Annales*, 675.

which deprived him of a considerable part of his military support. How heavily the crusading burden now rested upon Germany is apparent in the urgency with which the Pope exhorted the German crusaders to be in the ports of embarkation earlier than the date designated by the Fourth Lateran Council.[1] Meanwhile, the efforts of crusading preachers such as the *scholasticus* Oliver had inspired huge numbers of Germans to take the cross.[2] In many regions of Germany there was unrest; often the result of local disputes, it was capable of developing into widespread confusion and offered a constant temptation for the enemies of the Hohenstaufen to strengthen their opposition. These local conflicts were so numerous as to provide a major resistance to the maintenance of central authority. Many of them arose among ecclesiastical princes or among the burghers in opposition to their territorial lords. Typical was the opposition to Frederick's faithful Ulrich of St. Gall, who had recently been elevated to the important bishopric of Passau.[3] About the same time serious ecclesiastical quarrels in Regensburg, originating in the opposition to certain monastic reforms instituted by Archbishop Eberhardt of Salzburg, threatened the peace of the archdiocese.[4] More serious and certainly a greater threat to relations between Frederick II and the Pope was a conflict between the King of Bohemia, a staunch ally of Frederick, and the Bishop of Prague, who was supported by the Pope.[5]

Of especial concern to Frederick were conflicts over the possession of various border lands between Germany and France, notably on the left bank of the Saône and in trans-Jural Burgundy where rivalry between Otto of Meran and Stephen II of Auxonne created a continuous state of unrest.[6] In Lorraine and in Champagne rival claimants compelled both Philip Augustus and Frederick II to intervene. Following the death of Theobald I (the Duke of Lorraine) his widow, contrary to the wishes of Frederick II, was affianced to Theobald IV, claimant to the succession in Champagne, thus jeopardizing the future of some of the imperial possessions in Lorraine. That these, together with other border disputes, were of serious concern to Frederick is revealed in a letter to the Pope explaining his delay in departing for Rome.[7]

In the north a long-standing feud between Counts William of Holland and Louis of Loos involved both the Pope and Frederick II and threatened the peace of the Kingdom until Louis of Loos died

[1] Pressutti, i, no. 284, p. 51.
[2] T. C. Van Cleve, 'The Fifth Crusade', *A History of the Crusades*, vol. ii (ed. R. Wolff), 381.
[3] *Continuatio Cremifanensis* (*MGH*, *SS*. ix), 549. See also *Annales Mellicenses* (*MGH*, *SS*. ix), 507.
[4] *Annales Sancti Rudberti Salisburgenses*, 780.
[5] *Annales Pragenses* (*MGH*, *SS*. iii), 121.
[6] E. Clerc, *Histoire de la Franche-Comté* i. 401, 403.
[7] Huillard-Bréholles, i, part ii, 805.

suddenly on the eve of his departure for the crusade of 1217.[1] Further
unrest in the Low Countries grew out of the efforts of the recently
elevated Archbishop Engelbert of Cologne to recover possession of
various properties of the archdiocese that had been illegally appropriated during the turbulent years preceding his election.[2]

The death of Berthold V of Zähringen, Duke of Burgundy, without
a direct heir caused problems for Frederick in Germany. Chief of the
various contenders for the Zähringen properties were Berthold's two
sons-in-law, Egeno of Urach and Ulrich of Kyburg, and the Duke of
Tek, member of a collateral branch of the family. Frederick II also
advanced a dubious claim based upon a distant relationship of his
mother, Constance, to the Zähringen family.[3] Frederick purchased
outright the claim of the Duke of Tek.[4] Although other conflicts over
this estate arose, the King successfully pacified the most formidable of
the claimants at the Diet of Ulm, while retaining for himself the cities
of Bern, Zurich, Murten (Morat), and Freiburg. Subsequently he
also bestowed upon his son, Henry, the rectorship of Burgundy.[5]
Petty as some of these conflicts were, each was a threat to the royal and
imperial interests as long as Otto IV remained alive. Moreover,
Frederick's serious preoccupation with these conflicts serves to contra-
dict the charge that he was careless and indifferent towards his German
heritage.

During 1217 and 1218 Frederick made no determined effort to strike
the final blow against Otto IV. He doubtless recognized that it was
only a matter of time until the last of Otto's supporters fell away,
leaving him isolated in his Saxon stronghold. How desperate Otto's
situation had become is apparent in the defection of the long-faithful
citizens of Bremen and their coming to terms with the Pope. In retaliation, Otto made an expedition into the province, devastating the
countryside; he failed however, in his main objective, the capturing of
the coastal region. In that effort he was successfully opposed by the
King of Denmark, the ally of Frederick II and the friend of the recently
elevated Bishop Gerhard of Bremen.[6]

Thwarted in that region, Otto turned once more to the domains of
his old enemies, the Archbishop of Magdeburg and the Margrave
Dietrich of Meissen. He besieged Kalbe and devastated the Magdeburg

---

[1] *Reineri Annales*, 677. For the Pope's involvement see Pressutti, i, no. 457, p. 81.

[2] J. Ficker, *Engelbert der Heilige, Erzbischof von Köln und Reichsverweser*, 66 ff.

[3] This claim through Constance is described in *Reineri Annales*, 676.

[4] Huillard-Bréholles, i, part ii, 682. See also C. Frey, *Schicksale des königlichen Gutes in Deutschland unter den letzten Staufern seit König Philipp*, 153 and 177 f.

[5] Huillard-Bréholles, i, part ii, 717.

[6] *Annales Stadenses*, 356; *Annales Bremenses*, 858. See also *Mecklenburgisches Urkundenbuch*, i, no. 238.

possessions on the left bank of the Elbe. With reinforcements from his brother, Henry of Saxony, and the Margrave of Brandenburg he crossed the Elbe, attacking in the region of Burg some twelve miles north-east of Magdeburg. Driven back from there, his forces suffered heavily while recrossing the river.

Meanwhile Frederick, moved by reports of these renewed activities of the Emperor, hastened to the aid of his Saxon friends. Crossing the Harz Mountains, he was joined by the Archbishop of Magdeburg with many troops. But before Otto could be engaged, he again took refuge behind the fortifications of Brunswick.[1]

Fortunately, Saxony was soon to be relieved of the misery and suffering inflicted upon it by the futile efforts at vengeance of the vanquished Emperor. He suffered a serious illness—apparently a severe attack of dysentery, aggravated by an overdose of a medicinal purge—and died on 13 May 1218, in the Harzburg.[2] It would be idle to recount here the gruesome spectacle of his deathbed repentance when he insisted upon the rigorous scourging of his emaciated body.[3] Despite this penance, however, he clung tenaciously to his imperial title, defending to the last his right to wear the crown and demanding that he be buried in the accoutrements of an emperor. In his testament he required that his brother Henry retain the emblems of sovereignty, the cross, the lance, the crown, and the 'tooth of St. John the Baptist', for twenty weeks following his death. Thereafter the insignia and relics were to be bestowed upon one who was duly elected by the princes or upon Frederick II, provided the princes were united in support of him.[4] Some eight months later, when writing to Pope Honorius III about his crusading plans, Frederick asked the Pope to compel Henry of Brunswick to surrender the imperial emblems by threatening him with excommunication and by imposing the interdict upon the city of Brunswick in the event of Henry's refusal.[5] In compliance with this request, the Pope notified Frederick that he was sending as his representative the Prior of Santa Maria Nova de Urbe to require of Henry the surrender of the imperial emblems, authorizing the excommunication of Henry and an interdict on Brunswick if he failed to comply.[6] Henry recognized the futility of further resistance and yielded, and at Goslar the following July he surrendered the imperial emblems and was reconciled with Frederick.

The way was now open for Frederick to prepare for the expedition to

---

[1] *Sächsische Weltchronik* (*MGH, Deutsch. Chron.*), ii. 241.

[2] Ibid.: 'darna ward he siek to Hartesborch unde starf'; *Chronica regia Coloniensis*, 195.

[3] *Origines Guelficae*, iii. 840 f. E. Winkelmann, *O. von B.* 464 f., has dealt with this scene in all its revolting details.

[4] *MGH, Const.* ii. 51 f.   [5] Huillard-Bréholles, i, part ii, 584 f.

[6] Pressutti, i, no. 1862, p. 308.

Rome and for the undertaking of the crusade under conditions which would exalt his prestige as King of the Romans and as Emperor. It was only after the death of Otto that the young King had been permitted to appear in the foreground of the crusading enterprise. Honorius III, like his predecessor, at first ignored the crusading pledge of Frederick. Not until the latter part of 1218 did he reverse this seemingly studied policy, now urgently insisting upon the immediate fulfilment of the pledge. The reasons for this sudden change are at best conjectural. Certainly the death of Otto had removed one of the chief difficulties in the way of Frederick's departure from Germany. A more probable cause was the worsening situation of the crusading army in Damietta, where reinforcements as well as a strong leadership were urgently needed. There could be no doubt that the Fifth Crusade as a papal enterprise had been a disastrous failure. The Pope's appeal to Frederick is not extant, but the latter's reply of 12 January 1219 suggests that Honorius III had endeavoured to impress upon the young King the urgency of the need for assistance. Frederick's letter reveals that he was fully aware of the extent of the stalemate at Damietta; already in December 1218, in a diet at Fulda, he had summoned the princes to a meeting to be held at Magdeburg in the succeeding March for the express purpose of arranging the details of a crusading expedition and for the choice of a vicegerent during his absence.

The change in the attitude of the Pope gave Frederick a renewed sense of his power as a leader of the crusading movement. It was he who suggested, in his reply to the Pope's letter, the policy to be pursued with respect to the German crusaders. He advised that all who had taken the cross should be made liable to excommunication if they failed to fulfil their crusading vows by 24 June following. Only those individuals who were considered by the King and princes to be essential to the security of the realm were to be released from their vows.[1]

That Honorius now felt himself dependent upon Frederick is apparent in the readiness with which he put these suggestions into effect. Meanwhile, the meeting at Magdeburg mentioned in Frederick's letter failed to take place, probably because the legate sent by the Pope to deal with Henry of Saxony had not yet completed his mission. It was during this interval of waiting that Frederick requested a further postponement of the expedition, to 29 September. In a letter of 18 May 1219 Honorius agreed to the postponement. Only a few days before the sending of the Pope's letter, Frederick had made known his desire to have his son crowned King of the Romans before he himself departed for the Holy Land.[2] Without Honorius' letter of 14 June

[1] Huillard-Bréholles, i, part ii, 585–6; Winkelmann, *Acta*, i, no. 151, pp. 127 ff.
[2] Huillard-Bréholles, i, part ii, 629 (10 May 1219); ibid. 630 ff.

1219 it is impossible to be sure what was his reaction to this request, but Frederick's reply thanking the Pope for the postponement suggests that Honorius either offered no objection to the request or else simply ignored it. In early September Frederick probably again took up the subject of his son's coronation in a letter in which he requested a further postponement of his expedition, to 21 March 1220.[1] Again the Pope yielded to the request for postponement in his reply of 1 October, although he warned the King that another delay would incur excommunication.[2]

During the summer and autumn of 1219 Frederick learned that the Pope and Curia had grown suspicious of his motives with regard to several of his policies. They were especially concerned over what they believed to be his intention to violate his promise that he would not seek to unite the German and Sicilian Kingdoms. Honorius suspected also that Frederick was encroaching upon the possessions of the Church when he permitted the son of Conrad of Uerslingen to employ the title of Duke of Spoleto in his signature to a royal document. Suspicion also was ever uppermost in the minds of Pope and Curia that Frederick, in the manner of his predecessors, was disposed to interfere with the freedom of ecclesiastical elections.

Frederick defended himself in two letters against these charges, giving detailed rebuttals of each. If, perchance, his son should be chosen as German King through due deliberation of the princes, this would be done, he argued, not with the idea of uniting the two Kingdoms, but to the end that the Kingdom might be better governed 'during my absence' and in order that 'my son, in case of my death, might inherit his patrimony more easily'. As to the title *Duke of Spoleto*, employed by the son of Conrad of Uerslingen, this was merely in accordance with the German custom which permitted the son of a duke to employ the title even though he possessed no duchy. In addition, Frederick attempted to placate the Pope and Curia by explaining that royal letters and mandates sometimes found their way into the State of the Church because of the ignorance of the German chancery of the location of these places or because of their unawareness of the rights which appertained to them.[3]

This exchange of letters between Frederick and the Pope, together with the reassuring report of the papal legate, Alatrin, concerning Frederick's intention, served—at least for the moment—to lessen the tension between Pope and Emperor. But the Pope and Curia could have little doubt, however distasteful it might be, that Frederick in-

---

[1] See R. Röhricht, *Beiträge zur Geschichte der Kreuzzüge*, i. 7 and 58, note 37.
[2] Huillard-Bréholles, i, part ii, 691 f.
[3] Ibid. 628 f. and 674; see also BFW, *Reg.* v, Abt. i, nos. 1014 and 1049.

tended to persevere in his efforts to have his son chosen as German King. The perennial question of the future of Sicily was thus again brought into focus. But Honorius would concede no more than a conditional agreement: if Frederick's son Henry, who already, in accordance with the wishes of the former Pope Innocent III, had been crowned King of Sicily, died without leaving an heir or brother, Frederick could rule both kingdoms during his lifetime. As King of Sicily, however, he would rule as the vassal of the Roman Church and would bind himself to do this by the usual feudal oath.[1] So unyielding was the Curia on this question that Frederick no longer endeavoured to achieve his real object—the unconditional sovereignty in Sicily during his lifetime— through the exchange of letters; he determined to rely instead upon oral negotiations, employing what he believed a convincing assurance, for, he asked: 'Who would be more obedient to the Church than one who had been suckled at her breast? . . . Who would be more loyal, more mindful of received benefits . . . than one who, conscious of his indebtedness, tries to pay his debt according to the will and order of his benefactor?'[2]

At this time the King revealed that two diets, one in Nürnberg and another in Augsburg, had been held for the purpose of arranging the details of the crusade and for obtaining from the princes their oaths that they would accompany him on this expedition. He was compelled to report, however, that the princess showed little enthusiasm for the enterprise. Accordingly he urged the Pope to supplement his general appeal with individual letters threatening the recipients with the ban in the event of a delay beyond the prescribed date. He assured the Pope of his intention to work whole-heartedly for the undertaking. He suggested also that, while he himself might conceivably find it necessary to delay his departure, he would send the princes in advance. Once more, apparently in recognition of the apathy of the German princes, Honorius authorized a delay of Frederick's departure to 1 May 1220. He did not fail to warn the King, however, that three times already his requests for delays had been granted. Although obviously displeased that a fourth request for a delay had been made, he insisted that he yielded in the spirit of friendship and not as an antagonist.[3]

It was during this exchange between Honorius and Frederick that the latter sent the Abbot of Fulda to Rome to negotiate with regard to the imperial coronation. In a letter of 10 April 1220 the Pope expressed some dissatisfaction that only an abbot had been sent to deal with a matter of such importance, saying that in similar cases Frederick's

---

[1] See BFW, *Reg.* v, Abt. i, nos. 1091, 1092, and, for the reservations, Huillard-Bréholles, *Rouleaux de Cluny*, 296.

[2] Winkelmann, *Acta* i, no. 173, p. 151.   [3] Huillard-Bréholles, i, part ii, 746.

predecessors would have sent an archbishop or a bishop. He would, however, make no difficulty about this for he considered Frederick's elevation as Emperor essential to success in the Holy Land and to the freeing of the Church, as well as to the uprooting of heresy and the establishment of peace.[1]

As these negotiations proceeded through the last months of 1219 and into 1220, it must have become apparent to both the Curia and Frederick that an almost insuperable barrier to a *rapprochement* was the King's insistence upon the coronation of his son before his own departure on a crusade. It was Frederick who succeeded in solving this difficulty by winning over both the temporal and the spiritual princes to the acceptance of his son as King. It was the spiritual princes, now the dominant element in the princely class, that offered the greater resistance. To the temporal princes the chief objection was the fear of the establishment of the principle of hereditary succession. The same fear had caused them to oppose similar proposals from both Frederick Barbarossa and Henry VI. That they finally yielded is attributable, not so much to concessions made to them as a class or to grants of privileges to individual princes, as to the prospect that, in the absence of Frederick on a crusade and during the long years of minority of his youthful heir, their own condition might be substantially improved. On the other hand, the spiritual princes, already the recipients of so many benefits as the sponsors of Frederick's own election, could be brought to abandon their opposition only through extensive concessions, giving to them a degree of independence as a class hitherto unknown. Although the price was high, Frederick did not long hesitate to pay. For only if it is seen as a necessary concession can the generous grant of privileges contained in the *Confoederatio* or *Privilegium in Favorem Principum Ecclesiasticorum* of 26 April 1220[2] be satisfactorily explained.

The constitutional significance of these eleven articles, although unquestionably entailing sacrifices, has been over-emphasized as 'a Magna Carta for the territorial administration'. It is true that, like Magna Carta, the *Privilegium* must be interpreted, not as a revolutionary innovation, but as a summation of previously existing customs and a universal application of privileges formerly granted to individual princes. Perhaps its greatest importance is its recognition of the ecclesiastical princes as the predominant princely class and its sanctioning of the first of a series of imperial laws that would ultimately recognize the independent sovereignty of the principalities.

A privilege long sought by the ecclesiastical princes was the abandonment of the 'right of spoil', now achieved, not merely as an individual

---

[1] Pressutti, i. 397, no. 2392; Huillard-Bréholles, i, part ii, 750 f.
[2] *MGH, Const.* ii. 86 ff.

right granted to single princes, but as a law applicable to all ecclesiastical princes. Henceforth, neither the King nor any other layman could legally lay claim to the property of a deceased ecclesiastical prince. Moreover, such property was to go to the incumbent's successor or, if he had made a will, to his designated heir. Violators of this procedure were to be punished by outlawry.

No less important to the ecclesiastical princes was the guarantee of protection against damage to the properties of churches and monasteries by *advocati* or stewards whose original function had been to safeguard such properties and to administer justice in cases involving rape, homicide, arson, or other crimes where violence or bloodshed was present.[1] Gradually departing from their original functions, however, the *advocati* had extended their authority, claiming the right to build castles or other fortifications, seizing church lands, holding courts illegally, and imposing fines arbitrarily. These abuses had become all the more destructive in that the office of *advocatus* was hereditary.[2] Like the territorial lords, the King also acquired such jurisdictions, finding in the royal *advocati* as his deputies convenient agents for the extension of his estates.[3] Henceforth, the erection of buildings, castles, or cities on ecclesiastical lands in the interest of the *advocati* (*vel occasione advocati*), or upon any other pretext, save with the consent of those to whom the land belonged, was forbidden, and such structures were to be destroyed by authority of the King.

Of comparable advantage to the ecclesiastical princes was the guarantee of their 'right' to seize the fiefs of their vassals who had violated feudal law and the assurance that the King would not lay claim to the fiefs of these princes which had been vacated by death. Of paramount importance also was the safeguarding of the mint and the toll rights through the King's renunciation of the practice of granting new mints and new tolls within the territories or jurisdictions of ecclesiastical princes. Moreover, by virtue of this article of the *Privilegium*, the King pledged his protection of long-established mints and tolls, and forbade anyone to cheapen or imitate the authorized coins of a principality. This privilege was made even more comprehensive by forbidding royal officials to claim jurisdiction over tolls, mints, or other 'rights' of

---

[1] See *De Advocatis Altahensibus* (*MGH, SS.* xvii), 373 ff.

[2] This aspect of the subject has been fully exploited by K. Weller, 'Die staufische Städtegründung in Schwaben' (*Württembergische Vierteljahrshefte für Landesgeschichte*, Neue Folge, 1922), 145 ff. E. Klingelhöfer, *Reichsgesetze*, 31 ff., has synthesized much of the material of Weller, together with that of H. Geffcken, *Die Krone und das niedere Deutsche Kirchengut unter Kaiser Friedrich II. 1210–1250*, 21; H. Mitteis, *Der Staat des hohen Mittelalters*, 118 ff.; H. Niese, *Die Verwaltung des Reichsgutes im 13. Jahrhundert*, ch. iii, 67 ff.; G. Waitz, *Deutsche Verfassungsgeschichte*, iii. 320 ff.; and others. A valuable supplement to the above-mentioned work of H. Niese in particular is W. Metz, *Staufische Güterverzeichnisse* (Berlin, 1964).

[3] J. Berchtold, *Landeshoheit*, 135.

ecclesiastical princes, 'save during the session of the public courts and eight days preceding or following the convening of the court'. This and other articles of the *Privilegium* were intended to ensure the protection of the regalian rights which had passed from the royal authority to the ecclesiastical princes.

A marked social change was gradually taking place in Germany, as elsewhere in Europe, as a result of the accelerated rise of the towns and the consequent opportunity for the serf to improve his condition by migrating to one of the new municipalities. One article of the *Privilegium* was designed to prevent such migrations and thus to protect the ecclesiastical princes against the loss of their serfs.

Perhaps no articles of the *Privilegium* were more important than those which denied to an excommunicate the right to give testimony, to render judgement, or to bring suit against others, while giving assurance also that the imperial ban should follow automatically within six weeks if the excommunicate was not absolved. Double assurance as guarantee of this procedure was contained in the King's promise to support and defend the prince 'by our authority in all cases'.

Superficially, the *Privilegium* appears to be a serious sacrifice of sovereignty by the King, and, in consequence, a substantial gain of sovereign independence by the ecclesiastical princes. But it must be evaluated first in the light of the precedents upon which it is based and, secondly, within the framework of Frederick II's policies as a whole as opposed to his strictly German policies. Few, if any, of the articles of the *Privilegium* or *Confoederatio* can be described as innovations. Thus, in early grants of privileges to individual princes, the 'right of spoil', or royal custom of seizing the goods of deceased bishops, was recognized by German kings as an *abusus*.[1] So also the articles concerning the *advocati* and the fugitive serfs were significant, not as innovations, but as efforts to limit the *advocati* to their original functions as guardians of church property, and to prevent their encroachments upon such properties by the building of castles.[2] Protection of coinage and toll rights had been granted to individual princes repeatedly since the time of Frederick Barbarossa.[3]

Such innovations, or apparent innovations, as appear in the *Privilegium* are in the more rigorous penalties levied in the event of violation. A striking example of this is the placing of excommunicated persons under imperial outlawry, 'until the excommunication is withdrawn'.

---

[1] *MGH, Const.* ii. 9: 'Omnes abusus, quos antecessores nostri in ecclesiis habuerunt, utputa mortuis prelatis bona ipsorum vel ecclesiarum eorum accipiebant, perpetuo relinquam.' See also BFW, *Reg.* v, Abt, i. nos. 120, 239, for similar precedents under Philip of Swabia and Otto IV.   [2] See especially J. Berchtold, *Landeshoheit*, 133.

[3] *MGH, Const.* i, no. 194, pp. 272 ff.; Stumpf, no. 4650; BFW, *Reg.* v, Abt. i, nos. 200 and 144.

This close association of excommunication and outlawry bears witness to the pressure that the canon law was able to exert, excluding the excommunicate not only from all spiritual but also from all civil benefits.[1]

The final article of the *Privilegium* or *Confoederatio* reveals how fully the princes were aware of their advantage. Only in Frederick's recognition of his dependence upon their support can one find an adequate explanation for his willingness to decree that these privileges were granted in perpetuity and to call upon his successor to 'preserve and enforce them on behalf of the Church'.

Nothing in the history of the medieval Empire has offered greater opportunities for confused judgements and conflicting opinions than Frederick's policies respecting the ecclesiastical princes. The basic cause of these conflicting opinions is the persistent tendency to characterize him as the 'first foreigner on the German throne',[2] to associate him too narrowly with the German kingship which he is alleged to have neglected while devoting his attention to his Sicilian heritage. This interpretation regards the *Privilegium* and its sequel laws not only as crucial in the development of territorial sovereignty but as a catastrophe of such proportions as to destroy the foundation of the German Kingdom.[3] This narrowly nationalistic or particularistic interpretation has been all the more firmly incorporated in German historiography by virtue of the argument that at the time of Frederick's first sojourn in Germany a re-establishment of the German state was still possible and only his 'irresponsible' acts permitted the passing of the last opportunity to bring about a restoration.[4] Implicit in such criticisms is the moral condemnation of Frederick for his failure to honour his promise and his oath.[5] Over-emphasis upon his 'foreign origin' and upon the fact that he resided longer in Sicily than in Germany has led to the assumption that he carelessly sacrificed his sovereign rights, thus indicating his intention to treat the latter as of secondary or subsidiary importance. A more plausible interpretation of his attitude is that he was, in fact, the authentic promoter of the policies inaugurated by his grandfather, Frederick Barbarossa.[6] The difference between the policies

---

[1] J. B. Sägmüller, *Kirchenrechte*, ii. 356. The most satisfactory treatment of this subject, the outlawry of an excommunicate, is that of E. Eichmann, *Acht und Bann im Reichsrecht des Mittelalters*, especially 122 ff.

[2] J. Haller, *Die Epochen der deutschen Geschichte*, 81.

[3] G. Schröder von Künssberg, *Lehrbuch der deutschen Rechtsgesch.* 643; and Haller, *Epochen*, 93: 'Wohl aber hat er die alten Grundlagen des Königtums vollends zerstört.'

[4] J. Ficker, in BFW, *Reg.* v, Abt. i, xvi.

[5] J. Berchtold, *Landeshoheit*, p. 74, note 77.

[6] H. Mitteis, 'Zum Mainzer Reichslandfrieden von 1235' (*ZfRG* lxii, 1942), 56. This opinion is opposed, although I believe unsubstantially, by G. Kallen, 'Friedrich Barbarossas Verfassungsreform und das Landrecht des Sachsenspiegels' (ibid. lviii, 1938), 561, 567.

of the two great Staufen is that Barbarossa was the more favoured in that he found the German princes willing instruments in the promotion, not merely of his sovereign power in Germany, but in the Empire, while Frederick II, thanks to the altered status of the princely estate during the throne conflict, was compelled to purchase their support through extensive grants of privilege. It is precisely here that one finds the true meaning of the *Privilegium* of 1220, the *Statutum* of 1232, and, in some measure, of the *Mainzer Landfriede* of 1235.[1]

Recent historians recognize Frederick's unique position as 'Roman Caesar and Emperor and Divus Augustus'.[2] In his relations with the German princes, with the Popes, with the Lombard communes, with Central Italy, and with the Kingdom of Sicily between 1212 and 1250, the consistent aim of Frederick II was the re-establishment of the Empire, the reassertion of universal sovereignty. He considered himself neither a Sicilian nor a German sovereign, but the temporal head of Christendom, as Emperor.

While the *Privilegium* was a concession to the princes, it was such only in so far as it made applicable to all ecclesiastical princes privileges which previously had been granted to individuals or which, during the long period of weakness of the central government, had become established customs. It was, as Schirrmacher long ago observed, a 'clothing of these individual privileges in the inviolable vestment of the law'.[3] In so far as a duly sanctioned and promulgated law has greater efficacy than a body of widely scattered privileges, the *Privilegium* or *Confoederatio* of 1220 was a positive gain by the princes. It should not be overlooked, however, that Frederick II had obtained not only the election of his son but, what was even more essential to his ultimate plans, the support of the ecclesiastical princes. Whether or not his sacrifice was greater than his gain could be determined only in the future if and when his dream of a restored Empire was realized.

---

[1] See also F. Knöpp, *Die Stellung Friedrichs II. und seiner beiden Söhne zu den deutschen Städten*, 81.
[2] E. Kantorowicz, *Kaiser Friedrich der Zweite*, 353.　　　　[3] *Kaiser Friedrich II.* i. 121.

PART III

FREDERICK II CROWNED AS EMPEROR
KING OF SICILY
AND KING OF JERUSALEM

I

THE ITALIAN EXPEDITION
THE IMPERIAL CORONATION

Post plurimos laboriosos agones in quibus imperii virtus et gloria
imperatorie majestatis enituit, decet nos omnium creatorem per quem
vivimus, movemur et sumus, per quem imperialis culminis optatis
felicitatibus gubernamur, toto corde, tota mente et omni virtute diligere
et ei devotissime omnibus viribus totaliter adherere . . .

> Frederick's letter of 10 February 1221, addressed to *universis
> ejus fidelibus* (Huillard-Bréholles, ii, part i, 123).[1]

OSTENSIBLY the Diet of Frankfurt had been called for the purpose
of making final arrangements for the expedition to Rome and
for the crusade that was to follow the imperial coronation. It
was also a function of this Diet to provide ways and means of maintaining peace and order in Germany during Frederick's absence.[2] The
major accomplishment, however, was to make possible the diplomatic triumph that Frederick achieved in the election of his son as
German King. It may well be true, as Frederick wrote to the Pope, that
the election of his son took place in his absence and without his knowledge.[3] But the nature of the *Confoederatio* or *Privilegium*, granted to the
princes just before the election of his son, permits of no doubt that he
had complete assurance beforehand of the favourable action of the
princes, and that the document was designed primarily to meet the
demands of the ecclesiastical princes as compensation for their support.

The explanatory letter of Frederick to Honorius III, dated 13 July
1220, was intended to placate the Pope and to defend Frederick against
criticisms that had been made in the Curia. In substance, he wrote at
that time:

> Through reports of several persons we hear that the Church, our mother,
> is not a little disturbed over the election of our dear son, and that she blames

---

[1] After so many laborious struggles in which the power of Empire and the renown of
imperial majesty shone forth, it behoves us to worship the CREATOR OF ALL THINGS, through
whom we live, move, and have our being, through whom we are guided with desired good
fortune to the summit of Empire, and to cling to him unreservedly and with complete
devotion, with our whole heart, our whole mind, and all our strength.

[2] *Chronica regia Coloniensis*, 196; *Reineri Annales*, 677 f.

[3] Huillard-Bréholles, i, part ii, 803: 'nobis insciis et absentibus, elegerunt eumdem.'

us for failing to announce his election after it took place, because long ago we had confided him to your care and had promised, after releasing him entirely from our paternal authority, to concern ourselves no further with him: also because we are guilty of delaying our arrival, so often announced to your sanctity, until now. We will explain these things to you directly and truthfully. For we must admit without equivocation that we have worked zealously for the election of our only son, whom we cannot refrain from loving with the tenderness of a father. Until now, however, we have not been in a position to obtain it. At this time, while holding court with the princes of the realm at Frankfurt in preparation for our imminent departure for Rome, thence to begin the journey [to Palestine], an old conflict was resumed between the Archbishop of Mainz and the Landgrave of Thuringia and, because of mutual distrust, the opposing forces grew to such proportions as to threaten the entire realm. Because of this, the princes vowed they would not leave the place until they had settled the feud and we sanctioned this decision in writing. When, however, the efforts of the mediators remained without success and it was apparent that, following our departure, the conflict would continue greatly to the damage of the whole Empire, then, unexpectedly, the princes, even those who had previously opposed the election of our son, elected him as King during our absence and without our knowledge.

Frederick then explained that he had withheld his approval of these proceedings because they had not been previously made known to the Pope. Moreover, he had required that each elector set forth his decision in a sealed letter to the end that the election might be more acceptable to 'Your Holiness'. He asserted further that the Bishop of Metz, who had been chosen by the princes as their representative to journey to Rome and there to explain and verify everything, had, unfortunately, been delayed by illness. As to the chief reason for which the Holy Father could take umbrage, i.e. that the election might lead to the union of the German and Sicilian Kingdoms, it should neither be feared nor suspected, since 'our object is to separate these realms in every respect'. Far from seeking to unite the two kingdoms, he assured the Pope that in the event of his own death without heir he would greatly prefer to bequeath the Kingdom of Sicily to the Pope rather than to the Empire. As to the continued delay of the expedition to Rome and the departure on the crusade, he gave as his chief excuse the various internal conflicts which urgently required his continued presence in Germany, emphasizing especially the threatening conditions in Lorraine arising from the marriage of the widow of the late Duke to the Count of Champagne, a foreigner, who had established himself in possession of the imperial fief.[1]

The effectiveness of Frederick's self-defence was strengthened by the joint letter of the princes which had been sent on 23 April giving

[1] Huillard-Bréholles, i, part ii, 802 ff.

their assurance that the Empire would never be united with or have jurisdiction over the Kingdom of Sicily.[1] Notwithstanding these efforts to reassure the Pope and Curia, Frederick's victory was complete. Although probably contrary to the spirit of previous treaties and promises, it did not constitute a legal violation. And yet the prospect of a personal union of Empire and Kingdom was clearly established. There was no legal difficulty in the way of Frederick's son becoming the personal sovereign of both Germany and Sicily. Meanwhile, the son, now only eight years of age, could not assume the reins of government for several years. It was apparent also that Frederick himself would be *de facto* ruler during this minority. The Curia had been trapped by the skilful manœuvring of Frederick. The sole element of victory remaining to the Curia was Frederick's acknowledgement of Sicily's feudal dependency on the Holy See.

The King had paid liberally for his victory, perhaps too liberally. But there is always the possibility of a grave error in measuring his sacrifices in terms of German sovereignty. In fact there is no moment in Frederick's relations with Germany in which he permitted his sovereign position in Germany to take precedence over his imperial sovereignty. In no sense, however, does this minimize his recognition of Germany as a vital part of his lofty concept of empire. Whatever sacrifice of sovereignty he may have made at this time did not preclude the possibility that, when the restoration of the Empire became a *fait accompli*, he could re-establish whatever degree of sovereign authority was necessary for the attainment of the Caesarism which never ceased to be his goal.

Even as he was seeking to achieve this settlement with the territorial princes, Frederick was making every effort to prepare for his expedition to Rome. Following the Diet of Frankfurt, however, he was again confronted with difficulties that prevented his immediate departure. It would be but tedious to describe the petty conflicts that continued to require his attention in Germany during the months preceding his departure. Again it is the poet Walther von der Vogelweide who chides the princes for their delaying tactics and bids them permit the King to fulfil his mission to the Holy Land:

> You princes who would gladly be rid of your king,
> Take heed of my advice; I propose nothing foolish.
> If I were you I'd send him a thousand miles away—even to Trani.
> The hero will go on pilgrimage; he who errs in this
> Does so most grievously against both God and Christendom.
> You foes! You should let him have his way and go.
> What if he comes not home again to plague you more?

[1] Ibid. 762–4.

If he remains there, and may God this forfend, you can exult.
If he returns home to us, his friends, then we'll rejoice.
Both sides can thus await good news; and take
    this advice from me.[1]

As the months passed it became apparent that Frederick had no intention of undertaking his expedition to Rome until he felt secure in his far-reaching arrangements for both Germany and Italy. In June he had informed the Pope that he would be unable to reach Rome before the end of September.[2] Although the Diet of Frankfurt had solved several troublesome problems, much remained to be done, especially in Italy, to prepare the way for his departure. It was inevitable that, after his departure from the Kingdom of Sicily in 1212, conditions of near-chaos, not unlike those prevailing during Frederick's minority, would again threaten on the island of Sicily and in Apulia. Hardly had he established himself on the soil of Germany when he took the first steps to avert turbulence in those regions. While holding court at Regensburg in 1213, he authorized Bishop Frederick of Trent as legate general for the whole of Lombardy, the March of Verona, Tuscany, and Romagna, charging him with the restoration of peace and harmony in all the Empire, but specifically in these designated regions.[3]

A few months later, in 1214, he authorized Aldobrandino of Este as military governor in Romagna and as vicar and legate in the whole of Apulia.[4] Upon Aldobrandino's death in the following year, he was succeeded by Bishop Ludolf of Worms who had formerly served as agent of Philip of Swabia in Central Italy.[5] During their lifetime these two representatives of the royal interests (Ludolf died in 1217) were successful in maintaining order, although constantly menaced in their efforts by Dipold of Spoleto, who had been authorized as Otto's representative on the mainland. Only the death of Otto of Brunswick in 1218 made it possible for the Staufen party to regain control. As a measure of security Dipold was arrested and held captive by his son-in-law, James of Severino.[6]

Meanwhile, the departure of Constance and her son to join the King in Germany left the Kingdom of Sicily exposed to the continued depredations by local barons that had existed during the papal regency. Neither Walter of Palear, the Chancellor, in whose care Constance had left the government, nor Cardinal Gregory of the Church of St. Theodore, the papal legate, had been able to maintain order there.

---

[1] For the original see Lachmann-Kraus, *Gedichte Walthers*, 38.
[2] Pressutti, no. 2574, p. 427, 'circa festum beati Michaelis ad se venire proposuisse ut coronetur.'
[3] Huillard-Bréholles, i, part i, 249 ff.
[4] Muratori, *Delle antichità estensi ed italiane*, i. 415.   [5] See above, pp. 51 f.
[6] Richard of San Germano (Muratori, *RIS*, vii), 81.

Although he spent nearly a year on an itinerary which took him through most of the important communes of Northern Italy, Bishop Frederick of Trent achieved but little success, save with the traditional friends of Frederick II, including Cremona, Pavia, and Verona. The Milanese group, including Piacenza, Alessandria, Novara, Vercelli, Como, Tortona, and Crema remained adamant in their opposition.[1] Less than a year later the Bishop was again with the King in Germany; subsequently he departed on a crusade in the Orient from where his death was reported in November 1218.[2]

His successor, Bishop James of Turin, described variously as legate in the whole of Italy and as vicar (*vicarium nostrum*),[3] was even less successful. Only with the arrival of a papal legate, Cardinal Ugolino of Ostia, sent by Honorius III and charged with the special mission of mediating in the conflicts between the cities of Lombardy and Tuscany, was some measure of peace established. However, it was not until November 1218, several months after the death of Emperor Otto, that the Milanese agreed to accept the mediation of the Cardinal.[4]

On 2 December, in the presence of the Archbishop of Milan and the Bishops of Pavia, Cremona, Brescia, Piacenza, Bergamo, Bobbio, and Lodi, the papal legate rendered his decision. The contracting parties were to pledge themselves to live in peace, permanently abandoning all the causes of conflict that had arisen since Frederick's appearance in Lombardy, and to submit all further differences to judicial processes. Each was to liberate all prisoners taken in previous battles.[5] Unfortunately the papal legate had failed to require of the contracting parties a formal recognition of the sovereign authority of the King. Although the Pope officially proclaimed peace between Milan and Cremona on 4 January 1219,[6] Frederick, in the absence of a formal recognition of his sovereign rights, continued to favour the Cremonese and others of that region who supported him.[7] In the course of time, during the year 1220, the remaining Lombard cities, including Milan, agreed reluctantly to recognize the sovereign authority of Frederick. The Milanese were freed from the ban under which they had lived since 1213, and the reconciliation was such that, early in 1221, Frederick could extend his greetings to the *podestà* and the people of Milan as *dilectis fidelibus*.[8] At least for the moment the submission of Milan had its effect also upon the Romagna when the citizens, following the lead of Bologna, made their formal

---

[1] E. Abegg, *Die Politik Mailands in den ersten Jahrzehnten des 13. Jahrhunderts*, 50 ff.

[2] BFW, *Reg.* v, Abt. i, no. 716 ff., and Röhricht, *Beiträge*, ii. 375.

[3] Huillard-Bréholles, i, part ii, 596, 598, 605, 614.

[4] Horoy, ii. 205, and John Codagnellus, *Annales*, 67–8.

[5] *Annales Cremonenses* (*MGH, SS.* xviii), 806; E. Winkelmann, 'Beiträge' (*FzDG* vii, 1867), 308. [6] BFW, *Reg.* v, Abt. ii, no. 6318; *MGH, Epist. Pont.* i.199.

[7] Huillard-Bréholles, i, part ii, 593, 602, 608. [8] Ibid. ii, part i, 126.

submission to the Emperor.[1] The death of Otto of Brunswick and the growing certainty that Frederick II's arrival in Italy was imminent served to make many of the communes of Italy more amenable to a peaceful settlement of their differences. Meanwhile, the Chancellor, Conrad of Metz and Speyer, was successful in pacifying much of Northern Italy. Apart from minor resistance by Faenza, Romagna was completely pacified by the legate.[2]

In Tuscany, where Conrad was charged with the special mission of restoring to the see of Rome the lands of the Countess Matilda, he had but little success. In the absence of an imperial representative from there at the time of the conflict over the throne, the commune of Florence had recognized only the authority of the Count of Tuscany. Moreover, the various communes of Tuscany had appropriated as their own large parts of the lands of Matilda.[3] Although Honorius III had protested at the Chancellor's delay and want of success in completing his mission in Tuscany, he was actually helpless to do so in view of the resistance of the powerful communes.[4]

While the legates of both Frederick II and the Pope were actively engaged in an effort to establish peace among the Lombard and Tuscan cities and to obtain, in advance, the recognition of imperial sovereignty, Frederick was occupied with bestowing privileges and immunities for past favours, or as sureties for his peaceful reception in Italy. In the Diets of Hagenau and Speyer, attended by several Italian bishops and nobles and by ambassadors from Italian communes, he designated the Bishop of Turin and the Marquis of Montferrat as legates in Italy. At the same time he confirmed charters and privileges previously granted during his journey through Italy in 1212, and pledged himself not to bestow his goodwill upon Milan, the traditional enemy of Cremona, without the latter's consent.[5] It was a unique feature of these acts of Frederick that he appeared to be giving notice in advance that, whatever his future policies might be toward the communes, they would be carried out in the interest of, and with the assistance of, a chosen group, notably the friends and allies of Cremona. Save for this one feature, so strikingly apparent in 1219, there is no evidence of a predetermined communal policy. Indeed, it will become increasingly clear that his policy was evolutionary, responding always to his successes or failures in his relations with individual communes, and dictated, in part, by relations between the Lombard League and the Pope.

---

[1] J. Ficker, *Forschungen*, iv. 311–12, no. 270.
[2] *Chronicon Tolosani* (*Documenti di storie italiana: Cronache dei secoli XIII e XIV*), i. 709.
[3] R. Davidsohn, *Geschichte von Florenz*, ii, part i, 74 and 81 f.
[4] Huillard-Bréholles, i, part ii, 815 f.
[5] Ibid. 582 ff. See also E. Jordan, *Les Origines de la domination angevine en Italie*, Introduction, pp. xliv ff.

In the early development of his policy there was a certain flexibility, at times suggesting indecisiveness. Towards the end, particularly after his second excommunication in 1239, there was an unmistakable hardening and a fixed determination to compel the unequivocal submission of the communes to his sovereign authority. The evolution of his policy, therefore, can best be observed in its relation to a series of crucial events from the moment of his arrival in Italy for the imperial coronation, as a result of the Diet of Cremona in 1226 and of the Constitutions of Melfi in 1231, as an aftermath of the victory of Cortenuova in 1237, and finally, after his defeat at Parma in 1248. In the last of these phases it became apparent, as it was apparent to his grandfather in 1183, that the subjugation of the communes of Northern and Central Italy to imperial sovereignty was no longer a possibility—that even emperors are powerless to stem the flood tides of history.

Frederick II's long delay in Augsburg, from the latter part of July until early September, was undoubtedly caused by his desire to obtain full reports from his agents about those regions in Italy through which his expedition was to pass *en route* to Rome. When, at length, he crossed into Italy the army accompanying him was not large.[1] As he completed his final preparations in Augsburg and, accompanied by his Queen, began his leisurely passage into Italy, his court Chancellor, who had preceded him, was effectively engaged in preparing the way for the peaceful journey of his sovereign. Rarely had a German king *en route* to receive the imperial crown pursued a more cautious policy in dealing with the Italian cities. Even the route that Frederick had chosen was such as to prevent possible collision between the sensitive citizenry and the royal troops. In general, he avoided intervening personally in the local conflicts while, at the same time, he employed a free hand in the confirmation of privileges which the cities had traditionally enjoyed within the Empire. It was apparent, however, that where Sicily was concerned he avoided committing himself. Two possible explanations for this caution are: first, that he desired to await final assurance from the Pope with regard to the future of the crown of Sicily, and secondly, and more probably, he was already preparing to end the predominance of the Northern Italian cities in the affairs of the Kingdom.

In the distinction which Frederick made at this time, and later, between imperial Italy and the Kingdom of Sicily it is possible to glimpse something of his future policy. First of all, the focal centres of all his policies were to be in the Kingdom. There his judicial, his administrative, and his economic systems were to take form, capable, however, of

---

[1] *Chronicon Tolosani*, Muratori, *RIS*, new edn., xxviii, part i, 145: 'secum ducens non magnum exercitum.'

ultimate extension throughout the whole of his *imperium*. Two things
he clearly sought, and these had been partially achieved by his Chancellor and other legates or agents: first, he must be assured of peace and
harmony among the perennially warring cities; and secondly, he must
obtain from each of them a formal recognition of his imperial sovereignty.
He had no illusions as to the sensitiveness of these northern communes
when their independence was concerned. The question that confronted
him at this time and throughout the remainder of his reign was: Could
an Emperor of the thirteenth century, whose concept of sovereignty
was derived largely from the imperial system of ancient Rome, induce
the communes, either by persuasion or by force, to abandon their
aspirations for communal independence? Moreover, he was already
well aware that the outcome of his efforts to bring about a reconciliation with the communes was all the more doubtful because of the opposition of the papacy to his concept of the *imperium* and its determination
to support the communes in their resistance. Such was the situation in
Italy as Frederick began his march southwards towards Rome.

Despite his efforts to avoid controversies with the Italian cities, his
unwillingness to commit himself with regard to their future privileges
in Sicily inevitably proved disappointing to the great commercial cities
such as Genoa. In return for the assistance that Genoa had given the
young King on his journey to Germany in 1212, he had promised to
ratify the privileges, concessions, conventions, and gifts which had been
previously granted by his predecessors. Now, however, when in the
castello S. Pietro, near Bologna, he was visited by an embassy from
Genoa seeking confirmation of these promises, he was willing to confirm only those pertaining to the Empire. He offered as an excuse that
he could take action with respect to that which concerned Sicily only
after he had arrived in that Kingdom.[1] The Genoese ambassadors,
angered by Frederick's attitude, abruptly took their leave. Moreover,
they further revealed their dissatisfaction by refusing to send the
customary deputation to the imperial coronation; instead they acquitted
themselves of this courtesy merely through the presentation of gifts.[2]
Henceforth Genoa was to be, except on a few occasions, the enemy of
Frederick II.

If the King pursued a policy of cautious restraint towards the demands
of the Italian cities, he exerted himself to the utmost in his attempt to
satisfy the Pope and the Curia. In his letter to Honorius of 13 September,
only a few days after his entry into Italy, he assured the Pope that he
would accept his counsel as that of a devoted father. Moreover, his
statutes were invariably favourable to the interests of the Church. On

---

[1] *Annales Janvenses (Fonti)*, ii. 168. See also E. Jordan, *Origines*, p. xlvi.
[2] *Annales Janvenses*, loc. cit.

16 September he nullified the acts of the city of Asti which had sought to limit the ecclesiastical authority[1] and, shortly afterwards, extended this statute to include all Italian cities. If he failed to satisfy fully the papal demands with respect to the lands of Matilda it was not for want of genuine effort, as is clear from his document of 30 September 1220, which placed the control of these lands in the hands of the plenipotentiaries of the Roman Church.[2] However, there is some evidence that, despite the efforts of the commune of Florence to maintain control of these lands, the Pope had regained at least sufficient authority there to enable him to make substantial grants to his supporters.[3]

By 4 October while still in Bologna, the King was prepared to send a special embassy to announce his approach to Rome and to arrange for the details of his coronation. Pleading his constant preoccupation with the affairs of Lombardy as an excuse for not taking such action earlier, he now expressed his desire 'to hasten to the feet of Your Holiness'. He assured the Pope of his gratitude for past favours, and ventured the hope that the Holy See would soon 'harvest the fruit from the tree which the Church had planted'.[4]

Unfortunately, no extant document reveals the actual presence of Frederick's embassy with the Pope or describes the negotiations. Only when Honorius sent his own embassy are we made aware, through their instructions, of the nature of the negotiations.[5] They were instructed to formulate in actual laws the substance of certain decrees prepared in advance by the Pope, and to obtain from the King his sanction, under his seal, to the end that, on the day of his coronation in St. Peter's church, they would be promulgated. The embassy was to ascertain from Frederick his attitude with regard to the union of the German and Sicilian Kingdoms and his intentions concerning the crusade. They were to emphasize that the cause of the Christians would be seriously jeopardized if he delayed further in setting out upon his expedition to the Orient. They were to remind him that his definite promises had been violated in that he had not only permitted his son, the King of Sicily, to be elected German King but had also invited the prelates and magnates of Sicily to the imperial coronation, requiring of them a new oath of fealty. These questionable acts gave rise to the suspicion that he now sought to unite the two Kingdoms with the Empire to the detriment of both the Roman see and his own heirs.

Apparently, it was not the intention of the Pope, through these

[1] Huillard-Bréholles, i, part ii, 827 f.
[2] Ibid. 854–5, 856–7.
[3] See, for example, *MGH, Epist. Pont.* i, nos. 150–1, pp. 106–7; and Horoy, iii. 586, 594.
[4] Huillard-Bréholles, i, part ii, 863.
[5] *MGH, Const.* ii, no. 83, pp. 104 ff. See also Huillard-Bréholles, i, part ii, 881.

instructions, to attempt to repudiate the accomplished fact of Henry's election as King of the Germans. It must be assumed that he had accepted this already as essential to Frederick's undertaking the crusading expedition. What now troubled him was the arrival of the Sicilian prelates and magnates in Rome with the evident object of taking the oath to Frederick as his vassals. It was this which, above all, had reawakened the Pope's suspicions concerning the King's future intentions.

From his camp on Monte Mario in the vicinity of Rome Frederick hastened to make a satisfactory reply to the demands of the Pope. Already in September 1220 he had promised to support the Church fully against the heretics of Northern Italy.[1] Accordingly his promises from Monte Mario had to do primarily with the future of Sicily and with his participation in the crusade. He assured the Pope once more that the Empire claimed no jurisdiction over Sicily, that he held it not as the heir of his father or of his paternal ancestors, but solely from his mother's family, who, in turn, held it as a fief from the Church. He further assured the Pope that he would seek neither to take it from the Church nor to unite it with the Empire. He promised to separate completely the administrations of the Empire and the Kingdom, employing only officials of the latter to carry on its work.[2] It is most doubtful whether the Pope was deceived by these assurances of Frederick II. By this time he must have been fully aware how readily the former ward of the Holy See would repudiate his oaths or promises with respect to the Kingdom of Sicily. Concealed behind these promises, now as before, was the firm intention of Frederick II to restore the sovereign authority of his grandfather, Roger II, and of the two Williams, which, in the eyes of the young Emperor Elect, had been ruthlessly and unjustly taken from his mother, Constance of Sicily, when she was powerless to resist the encroachments of the Pope and Curia. Here, as in so many instances in the future, Frederick seems to have appropriated for his own uses the language of the *Dictatus Papae* that was so essential to Gregory VII's interpretation of justice as a papal prerogative: 'that his decree can be annulled by no one, and that he can annul the decree of anyone.'[3] After this formal agreement, however dubious in the eyes of the Pope, nothing remained in the way of the ceremonial coronation, save, perhaps, the lingering doubts of the Pope.

On the morning of 22 November, the last Sunday before Advent, as Frederick II from his camp on Monte Mario turned his gaze towards

---

[1] Huillard-Bréholles, i, part ii, 854.

[2] P. Balan, *Storia di Gregorio IX*, i. 130; Huillard-Bréholles, 'Rouleaux de Cluny' (*Notices et Extraits de la bibliothèque impériale*, xxi, 1865), no. 26. See also the résumé in *MGH, Const.* ii, no. 84, p. 105.

[3] *Dictatus Papae*, art. 18. Also see below, pp. 191 f.

the Eternal City, symbol of his destiny, his thoughts must have been crowded with memories of his turbulent past. In such moments of re-collection it was characteristic of him that when thinking of his 'many laborious struggles' and his first attainment of 'the renown of imperial majesty', it was not the Pope to whom he attributed his triumph but 'the Creator of all things . . . through whom we are guided with desired good fortune to the summit of Empire'.[1]

While there does not exist an eyewitness account of the coronation ceremony of Frederick II but only the brief notices contained in two letters of Honorius III,[2] the actual details can be reconstructed with tolerable accuracy from the *Ordo Coronationis* prepared under Pope Clement V for the coronation of Henry VII in 1312.[3]

From the imperial camp on Monte Mario Frederick II and Queen Constance proceeded towards Rome by way of the Via Triumphalis to the Porta Collina adjacent to the Crescentian Palace. Here they were met by the clergy of the city with crucifixes and censers and conducted in ceremonial procession towards the steps of the church of St. Peter, chanting 'Behold I send my angel before thee . . .'. Before them strode the *praefectus urbis*, bearing a sword, and chamberlains scattering gifts among the populace. On arrival at the open space before the church of St. Peter, Roman senators, now taking their position to the right of the King, guided his horse to the steps of the church. Meanwhile, the Pope with his retinue, emerged in solemn procession from the sacristy and awaited the King at the topmost landing of the stairway. To the right of his throne were the cardinals, bishops, and priests, to the left the cardinal-deacons, and near them various of the lower clergy, magnates, and servants of the papal court.

The King, accompanied by archbishops, bishops, princes, and mag-nates, ascended the steps to the papal throne and reverently kissed the feet of the Pope and offered him a tribute of gold. The King was then embraced by the Pope, who now descended from his throne, and with Frederick on his right and the chief of the deacons on his left, they proceeded to the chapel of Santa Maria in Turribus, where the King took the solemn oath: to be the protector of the Pope, the Roman Church, and their properties in every need. While the Pope, accom-panied by his retinue, went to the altar to pray and then returned to his throne, the King remained in the chapel of Santa Maria in Turri-bus where he was initiated into the brotherhood of the Canons of St. Peter. Now, clad in the vestments of the Emperor, and accompanied by

---

[1] Letter of Frederick (10 Feb. 1221) in Huillard-Bréholles, ii, part i, 123 ff.

[2] Ibid., 52 f. and 82 f.

[3] *MGH, Legum*, ii. 531 ff.; J. Schwarzer, 'Die Ordines der Kaiserkrönung', *FzDG* xxii, 1882), 167–8.

cardinals offering blessings and prayers, he entered the silver gate of St. Peter's and prostrated himself upon the floor while the chief of the deacons pronounced over him an invocation. At the conclusion of this prayer, Frederick arose and advanced to the altar of St. Maurice, where he was anointed by a cardinal, not, as in former times, upon the head with chrism, but on the arms and between the shoulder-blades with ordinary consecrated oil. Although in the Carolingian period the Pope had anointed the Emperor, this had become the privilege of the Bishop of Ostia under the Ottonians.[1] Again the King moved to the altar of St. Peter, where he confessed to the Pope and received from him the kiss of peace. Near the pulpit, where the ceremony continued, the Pope placed upon Frederick's head the spiritual mitre and over that the imperial crown. He then presented him with the sceptre, the imperial orb, and the symbolic temporal sword, while the assembly greeted him with the familiar cry: 'Life and victory to Frederick, the ever glorious, the invincible Emperor of the Romans!' The Emperor now took his place on his throne near the pulpit while his Queen was consecrated as Empress in a similar ceremony. Together the newly crowned monarchs received holy communion from the hands of the Pope. The ceremony was concluded when the Pope bestowed upon each of them the kiss of peace.

The Pope and Emperor left the cathedral, and outside St. Peter's Frederick held the stirrup as the Pope mounted, and, after leading the horse of the Pope a few paces, he mounted his own horse and the two rode together to the church of Santa Maria Transpadina. Here, after a final embrace, each went his separate way, the Pope to the Lateran, and the Emperor to his camp on Monte Mario.

A unique feature of Frederick's stay in Rome had been the absence of the usual conflicts between the German soldiery and the populace. It was obviously with a feeling of profound relief that, a few days later, Honorius wrote to Pelagius, his legate in the Holy Land, that Frederick and his consort had been crowned in Rome with extraordinary alacrity and peacefully.[2] Contemporary chroniclers also were impressed by the absence of the usual antagonism of the citizenry, although they attributed this to fear rather than love.[3]

In accordance with promises made prior to his entrance into Rome, Frederick caused the *Constitutio in Basilica Beati Petri* to be promulgated as laws that were to be valid throughout the Empire.[4] All statutes and

---

[1] J. Schwarzer, 'Die Ordines der Kaiserkrönung' (*FzDG* xxii, 1882), 200.

[2] See Huillard-Bréholles, ii, part i, 82, with false dating corrected by BFW, *Reg.* v, Abt. iii, no. 6409.

[3] Richard of San Germano, 82; *Reineri Annales*, 678: 'plus timore quam amore.'

[4] *MGH, Const.* ii. 106 f.; Huillard-Bréholles, ii, part i, 2 ff. See also G. Fasoli, *Aspetti della apolitica italian di Federico II*, 75 ff.

customs contrary to the freedom of the Church were declared null and void. Taxation either of the Church or of the clergy was forbidden under a penalty of three-fold restitution, and clergymen were not to be summoned before the civil authorities, except with imperial and canonical sanction. Persons remaining under excommunication for a year were to be placed under the imperial ban and all heretics or promulgators of false doctrine were declared outlaws and were to be purged from the land by the civil magistrates. Protection was assured to pilgrims, and shipwrecked property was to be restored to its owner, regardless of local custom to the contrary. The final article of the *Constitutiones* was designed to aid the peasantry, forbidding any encroachment upon their property, and offering protection for their cattle and farming implements.

No less significant than the promulgation of these statutes was Frederick's final act in the coronation ceremonies: the taking of the cross once more—this time from Cardinal Ugolino, later to become Pope Gregory IX. He promised also not only to strengthen the crusading army by March 1221 but to undertake the expedition himself in August of the following year.[1]

As Frederick moved south from Rome he was convinced that the attainment of his lofty position as King of Sicily, King of Germany, and Emperor of the Holy Roman Empire had been made possible only by divine intervention, and that his safe and triumphant return to his native land was 'contrary to the expectations of mankind'.[2] His helplessness through the long years of his minority and his eight years' absence in Germany had exposed the Kingdom of Sicily to the depredations of a host of self-seeking enemies determined to seize every advantage afforded by these conditions.

Particularly destructive to the royal authority had been the regency of the Pope during the years of Frederick's minority. To the Pope and Curia the rightful position of Sicily was not that of an independent sovereign state but a feudal principality subject to the suzerain authority of the Holy See. The regency under Innocent III was administered not as a disinterested guardianship of a sovereign state, but as a protectorate over Church property while awaiting an opportunity for its restoration to papal control.

In the coastal areas of the Kingdom the powerful commercial cities of Northern Italy had firmly entrenched themselves. The city of Syracuse affords a striking example of these encroachments. In this prosperous port and city the dominance of Genoa was virtually undisputed. There the Genoese monopoly of commerce had been maintained under such agents as the corsair, Alaman da Costa, who, after

---

[1] *MGH, Epist. Pont.* i, no. 146, p. 104; Horoy, iii. 573.
[2] *Constitutiones Regni Siciliae*, Huillard-Bréholles, iv, part i, 4.

wresting the city from the Pisans in 1204, brazenly assumed the office of Lord of Syracuse, styling himself in all documents: *by the grace of God, of the King, and of the City of Genoa, Count of Syracuse and Officer of the King.*[1] The Saracens also, once the staunch allies of the Emperor Henry VI, had been in continuous revolt since his death. With their unimpeded access to their fellow Muslims in North Africa they had become a formidable foe of the Staufen restoration and a serious obstacle to the re-establishment of orderly government in the island of Sicily.[2]

The immediate task of the Emperor was to crush the arrogant feudal barons whose presence within the Kingdom offered a threat to an orderly administration. Frederick's expedition to Italy in 1220 to receive the imperial crown awakened many of these barons to the insecurity of their positions, causing them to recognize the necessity of a reconciliation with the Emperor and the procurement of his official recognition of their status. With little knowledge of the character of the Emperor, matured by his eight years in Germany, many barons had assumed that he would readily forgive their past misdeeds and welcome them as vassals. They doubtless hoped also that his crusading pledge would divert his attention from the affairs of the Kingdom, at least until his return from the Holy Land. Moreover, there was always the chance that he would never return. Evidently prompted by such speculations, many had recklessly travelled to Rome to participate in the ceremonies of the coronation.[3] In their first meeting with the Emperor several of these Sicilian magnates recognized too late that this 'boy of Apulia', long the victim of their treasonable usurpations, had become a man endowed with strength and with gifts of statesmanship reminiscent of both his Norman and Staufen forebears. They were made aware that he was returning to the Kingdom fully resolved to erect within it a powerful sovereign state wholly irreconcilable with the chaotic feudal conditions from which they had so long prospered. Chief among his foes in Italy since early childhood were Rainer, Count of Sartiano, Count Thomas of Molise and Celano, and Dipold of Acerra, the bold henchman of the late Otto IV, who had rewarded him with the Duchy of Spoleto. The Tuscan Rainer, formerly an ally of Markward of Anweiler, had later become the supporter of the Pisans in their effort to control the lucrative Sicilian trade.[4] The reconciliation of Pisa with

---

[1] Huillard-Bréholles, i, part i, 172. See also *Annales Janvenses (Fonti)*, ii. 91; Schaube, *Handelsgeschichte*, par. 378, pp. 480 ff.; H. Niese, 'Das Bistum Catania' (*Gött. Nachrichten*, 1913), 55 ff.

[2] M. Amari, *Storia dei musulmani*, iii. 601 ff.

[3] Richard of San Germano, 83; E. Winkelmann, *Kaiser Friedrich II.*, i. 111–12, note 1, lists the magnates whose presence with Frederick is discernible in contemporary documents.

[4] *Annales Janvenses (Fonti)*, ii. 91, 97, relates something of his early achievements with the

Frederick in 1217, and the death of Otto IV in 1218, had left Rainer with no alternative but submission to Frederick in the hope of forgiveness for his past treasonable acts. Without safe conduct, he rashly hastened to Germany in the expectation of effecting the desired reconciliation. But there he was summarily imprisoned by Frederick's orders. Insistent appeals by the Pope for Rainer's release finally induced the King to yield, although only on condition that he surrender the landed estates held by his family in Sicily.[1]

Dipold, long the scourge of Sicily during Frederick's minority, had followed Otto IV to Germany in 1212 when the misfortunes of the latter were crowding upon him. In Germany Dipold was temporarily reconciled with Frederick or, at least, he appears to have been tolerated at the court, where, on 14 February 1213, he witnessed under his original German title as Margrave of Vohburg.[2] Long accustomed to the freedom and the adventurous life afforded by chaotic Sicily, he fled the German court in disguise, making his way to Italy; he returned to his former duchy, Spoleto, where he rejoined his old associates. Upon orders from Frederick II, issued while preparing for his expedition to Italy, Dipold was arrested and held captive by his son-in-law, James of San Severino.[3] Probably in recognition of Dipold's former services to Emperor Henry VI, Frederick was persuaded to grant his release on condition that Dipold's brother, Siegfried, surrender the castles of Cajazzo and Alife in the valley of the Volturno.[4] After thus escaping the drastic punishment which he so well deserved, Dipold was escorted across the Alps into Germany where he seems to have found his future adventures with the Teutonic Knights.[5]

Even before he left Germany, and certainly while he was still in the vicinity of Rome, Frederick's intentions towards the Kingdom of Sicily were apparent. First of all, he was to regain by every available means the lands of the King which had been recklessly dissipated since the death of his mother. And, secondly, he was to seize all castles and all other fortifications essential to the protection of the royal interests and to the crushing of the powerful barons who threatened the unity of the Kingdom.

If Frederick displayed leniency towards Rainer of Sartiano and

Pisans in Syracuse. See also K. Hampe, 'Aus der Kindheit' (*MIöG* xxii, 1901), 596; and F. Baethgen, *Regentschaft*, p. 38, note 2, and pp. 88–9.

[1] *Eracles*, 354; Winkelmann, *Acta*, i. 153 f.

[2] BFW, *Reg.* v, Abt. i, no. 688. He was still at the court of Frederick in the latter part of Mar. 1213 (ibid., no. 695), and probably as late as April of that year (ibid., no. 703).

[3] See above, p. 126.   [4] Richard of San Germano, 93.

[5] See the observations of E. Winkelmann, 'Über die Herkunft Dipolds des Grafen von Acerra und Herzog von Spoleto' (*FzDG* xvi, 1876), 162–3, based upon a passage in the *Chronica Albrici Monachi Trium Fontium*, 879.

Dipold, it can only be assumed that he had exceptional reasons for so doing. For in similar cases, notably that of Thomas of Celano, Count of Molise, he revealed a characteristic severity. Thomas, like his father, had stubbornly supported Otto IV and had continued his opposition to the Staufen heir. Apparently seriously misjudging the temper of the young Emperor, and probably overconfident of the ability of his 1,400 knights to impress him, Count Thomas sent his son to Rome as his representative at the imperial coronation to do homage to Frederick. He probably took this ill-judged step in the conviction that Cardinal Thomas of Capua, one of the most influential of the cardinals, could successfully intercede on his behalf.[1] But Frederick, recognizing the importance of destroying all powerful rivals, turned a deaf ear to pleas for clemency when his powerful foes were concerned. Perceiving that all efforts to obtain a reconciliation were futile, Count Thomas prepared to resist the Emperor with armed force, making ready his castles Bojano and Rocca Mandolfi. From the outset Frederick seems to have been determined to make of Count Thomas of Celano a conspicuous example of his vengeance on his old enemies, thus clearing the way for his new policies in dealing with the Sicilian nobility which he was soon to initiate through the assizes of Capua. After Thomas had been besieged in Celano for three months Frederick agreed to pardon him and his adherents in return for the surrender of the tower and castle of Celano, together with the strongholds Orindole and San Potito. Thomas was compelled to agree to depart on the next passage to the Holy Land and to absent himself from the Kingdom of Sicily for three years, unless recalled by the Emperor. Despite this agreement, the King's Justiciar, Henry of Morra, expelled the citizens of Celano with all their possessions and destroyed the city, except for the church of St. John.[2]

In contrast to his policies in Germany between the years 1212 and 1220 which had been characterized by a yielding of authority to the firmly entrenched princes, in Sicily Frederick now seized the opportunity to restrict similar groups and to force them into a subservient position under the royal power. From the outset, even before his departure from Rome following his coronation, it was apparent that in Sicily he was to move towards a despotic regime, the pattern of his future Empire.

---

[1] For the letter of Thomas of Capua interceding on behalf of Thomas of Celano see Huillard-Bréholles, i, part ii, 928 f.

[2] Ibid., *MGH, Legum*, ii. 250; Huillard-Bréholles, ii, part i, 357 ff. Most of the details are to be found in Richard of San Germano 108–9.

II

SICILY, THE 'MIRROR OF EMPIRE'
REORGANIZATION OF THE KINGDOM

Et ita totas regiones illas iuriditioni et timori suo subdidit.
Richeri Gesta Senoniensis Ecclesiae (MGH, SS. xxv), 302.[1]

IT was in mid December 1220 that Frederick II, on his return to the Kingdom of Sicily, paused in Capua, where for some weeks he was engaged with his jurists and notaries in preparing a body of assizes which provide us with the first clear indication of his future intentions in Apulia and Sicily. His main object in these assizes was to make of the feudal group the nucleus of a military force through which he could restore and consolidate his Kingdom. Where Henry VI had endeavoured to subdue Sicily by the military might of Germany, Frederick II sought to achieve his ends with the aid of indigenous resources. It was characteristic of his statesmanship and a basic feature of his administrative genius that he employed a simple but all-comprehensive formula in the restoration of the sovereign authority in Sicily. This formula appears in the first article of the Capuan assizes and recurs throughout the document, in which he enjoins his subjects to observe strictly all good usages and customs which had obtained in the time of King William. In the XVth article of the assizes Frederick asserted that 'after the death of Henry VI our seal fell into the hands of Markward who, it is said, did much to our prejudice with it—and he is said also to have done likewise with our mother's seal'. Because of this, Frederick now decreed that all privileges granted in the names of the Emperor and Empress were to be surrendered, 'those on this side of the strait by Easter 1221, and those beyond the strait by Whit Sunday (the seventh Sunday after Easter)'. Failure to comply would be punished by the confiscation of the privileges (those that were found to be legitimate were to be regranted under a new seal), and would incur the imperial displeasure. The most important of these assizes, and the most suggestive of Frederick II's aims, was the *de resignandis privilegiis* or the surrender of privileges ostensibly for purposes of official scrutiny and verification. Like most of the early acts of Frederick following his

---

[1] And so he reduced all those parts to his jurisdiction, and to fear of him.

return to Sicily, this assize had its precedent, as he himself pointed out, in 1223. The grandfather of Frederick, Roger II, 'had ordered all grants (*sigilla*) to the Church to be presented for examination'.[1]

How little Frederick felt bound by his own earlier grants of privileges is apparent in the countship of Sora which had been granted by Innocent III, when regent, to his brother Richard Count of Segni and later, in 1215, confirmed by Frederick II. Yet in 1220, in conformity with the assize *de resignandis privilegiis*, he seized this fief as part of the Crown property.[2] Similarly, Stephen, Cardinal of S. Adrian, a nephew of Innocent III, who had long been in possession of Rocca d'Arce, was compelled, after a siege by Count Roger of Aquila, to restore the castle to the Emperor.[3] It is indicative, however, of Frederick's determination to bestow no special favours while regaining control of this Crown property that he compelled his faithful adherent, Roger of Aquila, to surrender Suessa, Teano, and Rocca Dorgone.[4] When admonished by the Pope for these seizures Frederick wrote in justification: 'The Emperor, our father, gave away much of the Kingdom which he ought to have retained, in the expectation of reclaiming it, and, after the death of the Empress many privileges were illegally granted under his seal, as a result of which the greater part of our domain was taken. Therefore, we demanded that all privileges be surrendered into our hands.'[5]

No less important than his seizure of the Crown lands was his wresting of important castles and strongholds from the more powerful barons. It was apparent, even while Frederick was still in the vicinity of Rome, that there was to be a definite pattern in his procedure against the Sicilian and Apulian barons. First, he would reduce the possible threat from the most powerful, including those who were his supporters, by requiring them to surrender their estates, pending a redistribution. In accomplishing this, he would use force, if resistance developed, employing the weaker barons to compel the submission of the more powerful. It is remarkable that within a few months after his return to the Kingdom, he had regained the important castles, Rocca d'Arce, Sorella, Cajazzo, Allifae, Roccamandolfi, Bojano, Foggia, and others. These were to be the centres of his defensive and offensive operations

---

[1] For the assizes see Richard of San Germano, 83–93. Huillard-Bréholles, ii, part i, 365. Concerning the assize *de resignandis privilegiis* see especially P. Scheffer-Boichorst, 'Das Gesetz Kaiser Friedrichs II. etc.' (*Sitzungsberichte der Königlichen Preuss. Akad. der Wissenschaft zu Berlin*, Jahrgang 1900), 132 ff. See also H. Niese, *Die Gesetzgebung der normannischen Dynastie in regnum Siciliae*, 115 f. For this and for many other examples of Norman influence upon the Frederican state see A. Marongiu, 'L'héritage normand de l'état de Fréderic II de Souabe' (*Studi medioevali in onore di Antonio de Stefano*), 341 ff.

[2] Huillard-Bréholles, i, part ii, 427 f.   [3] Richard of San Germano, 93.

[4] Ibid. 88. On Frederick's seizure and administration of castles see especially E. Sthamer, *Die Verwaltung der Kastelle im Königreich Sizilien unter Kaiser Friedrich II.*, 5 ff.

[5] *MGH, Const.* ii, no. 417, pp. 547 f.

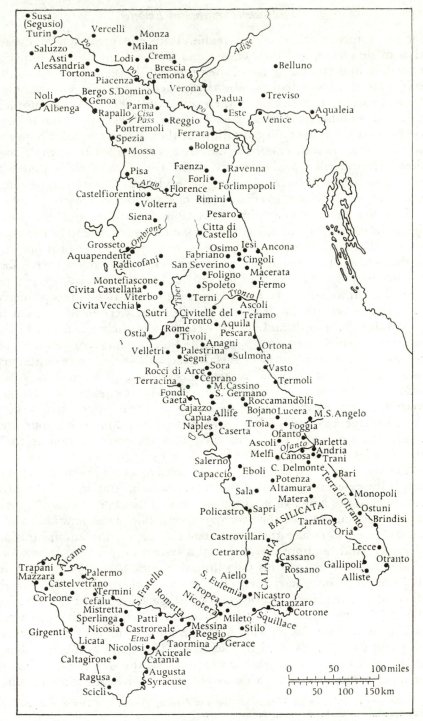

MAP 1. Italian cities and castles mentioned in the text

for the future security of the realm. With the great feudal estates thus made secure, and their castles and fortifications held by imperial castellans and guards, he could then proceed, in the course of time, to subjugate the lesser barons, absorbing them into his ever-expanding bureaucratic system or else, in the event of recalcitrance, seizing their fiefs and sending them into exile. In some instances their lands were confiscated because of alleged failure of their tenants to fulfil required services and, in such cases, the barons were expelled from the Kingdom.[1] Henceforth it was a feature of the Kingdom of Sicily that fiefs were granted exclusively in return for services to the State. The King was overlord of former overlords and of their former vassals.

In order that he might have his domain 'entire and complete' (*plenum et integre*), all cities, fortifications, and castles were to be returned to him. Baronies and the regalia of baronies were to be held only by authorization from the King, and both counts and barons were forbidden to grant any part of, or to diminish, a barony, except by special royal mandate. To ensure against the violation of this principle all privileges emanating from the King's court were to be granted in perpetuity. Both lords and vassals were to hold their tenements in the manner in which they were held in the time of King William, and no services were to be required of vassals except those that were customary under the Norman kings. As a further measure for preserving the feudal estates intact, counts and barons were forbidden to contract marriages, save with the King's consent, and only in conformity with the marriage customs of King William's time. Moreover, sons and daughters, upon the deaths of their parents, were to inherit their patrimonies only in conformity with these early Norman customs.

The assizes of Capua were no less effective as an essential step towards the re-establishment of the central administration and the prerogatives of the King. In addition to the first assize, restoring all good usages and customs of the Norman kings, adequate new laws were promulgated to ensure the maintenance of peace, the administration of justice, and the implementation of a system of taxation. It was forbidden that anyone, on his own initiative, seek to avenge injuries, to make reprisals, or to start a war. Justice was to be sought solely through the courts of the royal magistrates or justiciars. As a further assurance that all justice would be royal justice, both clergy and laymen were forbidden to exercise judicial functions in any manner whatsoever, save when duly authorized by the King. The bearing of arms, sharp knives, and lances, or any other weapon, and the wearing of cuirasses or other armour or arms which were forbidden in the time of King

---

[1] See, for example, the punishment of Roger of Aquila, Thomas of Caserta, and James of San Severino, in Richard of San Germano, 109.

William II were now made punishable offences. It was further ordained that no one was to harbour thieves or other criminals and that anyone apprehended in crime must be handed over to the magistrates for punishment.

Equally important were Frederick's efforts to ensure honesty in the administration of justice. Magistrates and justiciars were required to take oaths that they would perform their duties justly and without fraud. Commandants of castles and the subordinate castellans were to exercise their authority only in conformity with a special royal mandate. Castle servants were not to bear arms when outside the castle or to venture beyond its precincts, save with the consent of the castellan. If the restoration of peace and the maintenance of justice took precedence in Frederick's policies, he concerned himself also with the strengthening of the royal power in other respects. In an effort to check the growth of the independence of municipalities (an independence comparable to that of the Northern Italian communes), he now decreed that *podestàs*, consuls, and rectors were not to be chosen by the cities but, instead, bailiffs were to be appointed by the court. No new markets or other places for trading were to be established, and all trading-places that had come into existence since the deaths of the Emperor Henry VI and the Empress Constance were to be discontinued. What had been ordained in the time of King William concerning the marketing-centres was to be strictly observed. Rigorous royal supervision of all commercial activities was further assured by an assize requiring the closure of all highways, new routes, new ports of entry, customs offices, and other facilities which had been established by anyone or in any manner within the Kingdom since the deaths of Henry VI and the Empress Constance. While, in general, Frederick was well disposed towards all purely commercial activities of the cities, authorizing the annulment of all taxes on commerce levied since the time of King William, he sternly resisted every tendency toward their political independence.

Throughout the Capuan assizes the outstanding characteristic is their dependency upon the earlier assizes of Roger II and his immediate successors. While the initial steps taken at Capua were in themselves imitative, their wisdom lay in the boldness with which they were taken and in the clear recognition by Frederick that they were only initial steps. A more constructive statesmanship was to reveal itself in the years to come, when, employing the assizes of Capua as a nucleus, he expanded them into the remarkable *Liber Augustalis* or *Constitutiones Regni Siciliae* which was to set him apart as the supreme lawgiver of the Middle Ages.[1]

Frederick remained for some months on the mainland, visiting

---

[1] For the promulgation of the *Constitutiones* see below, pp. 242 ff.

Naples, Suessa, Troja, Foggia, Trani, Brindisi, Salerno, and other cities. As he set out from Calabria and crossed over to the island of Sicily in the late spring of 1221, he could feel reassured that on the whole of the mainland, except in the remote valleys of the Apennines, 'everyone had bowed his neck before him'.

At Messina he continued his legislation.[1] In contrast with the assizes of Capua which were concerned chiefly with feudal relations and with the central administration of government, the Messinese legislation had to do with social and criminal matters. The sole source for the substance and phraseology of these laws is the *Chronicle* of Richard of San Germano.

These assizes fall naturally into four main categories: first, against blaspheming by gamblers; second, concerning the distinguishing dress of Jews; third, restraints upon prostitutes; and fourth, the treatment of buffoons and buffoonery. While not forbidding the playing of dice, Frederick sternly forbade blasphemous use of the name of God or the use of disgraceful language, contrary to Christian ideals, which gamblers were wont to employ when losing at dice. For the violation of this law he fixed heavy penalties, rated according to the social status and wealth of the individual concerned. A count found guilty of such blasphemy was subject to banishment from the Kingdom for a period of two years, a baron for three years, and a knight for six years. Non-nobles or burghers were to be penalized by the loss of their tongues, and a professional gambler by the loss of both tongue and right hand. This law applied also to the clergy, even though such restraint were not placed upon them by the canon law. While the subjection of the clergy to this law was primarily intended to emphasize their moral obligation to set a good example for laymen, it reflects also Frederick's insistence that, in matters of criminal justice, the clergy, no less than the laity, were subject to temporal law.

The second of these Messinese laws was enacted in conformity with the Augustinian principle that the just state is essentially a Christian entity and, therefore, could not include non-Christian elements. It required Jews within the Kingdom to wear a distinguishing bluish-grey linen garment and all Jewish men to identify themselves further by the growing of beards.[2] Violators of this law were to suffer confiscation of their entire properties. The poor, or Jews of only moderate wealth, were to be branded on the forehead in consequence of their violations.

---

[1] BFW, *Reg.* v, Abt. i, no. 1325*a*. For the Messinese assizes see Richard of San Germano, 94 ff.

[2] 'Ut eorum (the Jews) quilibet super vestimenta que induet gestet lineum vestimentum clausum undique et tinctum colore celesti.' Ibid. 96.

Reminiscent of ancient Rome were the laws regulating prostitutes and prostitution. For, 'since one diseased sheep often corrupts the entire flock', the public prostitute was forbidden to carry on her vicious profession within the cities. Outside the cities, however, she was permitted to dwell wherever she chose, but as a means of distinguishing her from honest women, she was required to wear a short cape similar to that worn by men. Unless she was wearing this distinguishing garment, she was forbidden to enter cities or villages. As a further measure for isolating prostitutes from the virtuous women of the community, they were excluded from the public baths, save on days especially designated for their use. For reasons not explained Wednesday was designated as the day for the bathing of prostitutes. Violations of this assize were punishable by exclusion from the cities.

Of all the Messinese assizes the most singular is that concerning buffoons (*joculatores*); it decrees that whosoever takes vengeance upon malicious jesters, whether on their person or through their property, is not an offender against the peace, and is not subject to punishment. A probable explanation of this law which would appear to encourage violence against the buffoon and his buffoonery is that it was made in compliance with the wishes of the Pope as a means of checking the circulation of contumacious and insulting *cantilenas* subjecting the clergy to ridicule.[1]

With the promulgation of the Capuan and Messinese assize Frederick could feel for the first time that he was truly sovereign within the Kingdom. As one contemporary chronicler wrote: 'He reduced the Kingdom to his jurisdiction, and to fear of him.'[2]

In marked contrast with Germany, Sicilian laws were promulgated not by the will of the princes and the approval of the King; they were now solely edicts of the King. Under his orders itinerant agents visited the provinces to scrutinize the procedures by which his laws were executed and for the purpose of compelling the surrender or the destruction of castles and other fortified places which had been erected since the time of William II. These agents were also charged with the establishment of royal strongholds necessary for holding the unruly in check.[3]

While it was obviously the intention of Frederick to make his sovereign authority effective over ecclesiastical as well as lay barons, he was compelled to move circumspectly where the former were concerned. In ecclesiastical elections, for example, he was bound by the agreement originally made between the Curia and the Empress Constance,

[1] See B. Capasso, *Sulla storia esterna delle costituzioni del regno di Sicilia*, 12.

[2] *Richeri Gesta Senoniensis Ecclesiae* (*MGH, SS*. xxv), 302.

[3] Richard of San Germano, 110.

and subsequently sanctioned by himself in 1212,[1] prescribing the three steps in the filling of episcopal vacancies: first, the canonical election by the cathedral chapter; second, the agreement of the King; third, the sanctioning of the choice by the Pope. It was an advantage for the King that prior to the actual election he must be informed of the existing vacancy. For in spite of the tenor of the agreement the King was in a position to influence the choice of new bishops. His mere presence in the Kingdom and his ability to grant or to withhold favours from the bishopric made it difficult for the cathedral chapter to act in opposition to his wishes. Frederick did not hesitate to make full use of this opportunity and to exert pressure upon the electing chapter when he felt it advantageous to do so. Within a few months following his arrival in Sicily he was admonished by the Pope for his failure to fulfil his agreement concerning the election of prelates.[2] While this admonition of Honorius III may have caused Frederick to adopt a more cautious policy, he did not abandon his efforts to regain control of the royal domain which had fallen into the hands of the Church, nor did he cease to make his influence felt in episcopal elections.[3] But he could ill afford a serious breach with the Pope at a moment in which, because of his preoccupation with the restoration of order in the Kingdom, he felt compelled to ask for a further postponement of his expedition to the Holy Land. How strongly he felt the need of a conciliatory policy is perhaps best revealed by his order of April 1222 to counts, barons, justiciars, and other officials that they should respect the immunities of the clergy as to taxation, court rights, and services which they had enjoyed in the time of King William.[4] Although far from recognizing the complete independence of the clergy, this grant of privileges, coming as it did at a time when Frederick had already been seriously embarrassed by his crusading pledge, is indicative of his awareness that the Pope and Curia were not without an effective weapon to oppose his alleged encroachments on the freedom of the Church. Indeed, the failure of Frederick to fulfil his promise to undertake a crusade in person in August 1221 placed him at a constant disadvantage in his subsequent negotiations with the Pope and Curia. It is the tragic feature of this whole relationship between the Pope and the Emperor that Honorius and the Curia were not in the least sympathetic towards the rehabilitation of Sicily as a sovereign state. They looked upon it as a feudal principality subject always to the overlordship of the Holy See. To Frederick, on the other hand, it was the supreme goal

---

[1] Huillard-Bréholles, i, part i, 203 f. See above, pp. 80 f.
[2] Ibid. ii, part i, 200 f.
[3] E. Winkelmann, *Friedrich II.*, ii. 142.
[4] Huillard-Bréholles, ii, part i, 239.

of his efforts to make of Sicily a 'mirror' reflecting the image of the future Empire, 'the envy of princes'.[1]

Yet with all his efforts to achieve this cherished goal, he could never escape the insistent proddings of the Pope to undertake the expedition to the Holy Land. It would be erroneous to assume, however, that Frederick wished to rid himself of his crusading obligation or that he now regretted the youthful impulse which, in 1215, had caused him hastily to take the cross. On the contrary, in his letters written during the year 1221, there are numerous evidences of a sincere desire to fulfil his vow. He speaks of the bitterness of heart which he felt in seeing the sacred banner of the cross torn from the Holy Sepulchre, the tomb of the Lord profaned as a sanctuary of the infidel.[2] Moreover, he saw in his crusading effort a means of repaying for having been permitted to achieve the majesty of empire. This success, as he often reiterated, was attributable alone to the Divine Creator, 'through whom we live, move, and have our being'. In gratitude he pledged himself, with all the resources at his command, to cling ever more closely to God. It was, he said, his gratitude that impelled him to take the cross and to call upon the loyal soldiers of the empire 'to take up the weapons of Christian knighthood on behalf of the Church of Christ, your Holy Mother, held wretchedly imprisoned by the infidel'.

It would be but gratuitous misrepresentation to attribute these remarks to hypocrisy or to a deceitful effort to win favour with the Church. As at Aachen in 1215, there is to be found in these letters a sincere expression of gratitude and a generous yielding to the crusading ardour of his era. But in each of them there also appears the unmistakable bitterness and disillusionment born of the recognition that he could not act alone. He appeals for the aid of 'the faithful in all the Empire', and especially in all the cities of Lombardy and Tuscany—indeed, he asks for the aid of the papal legates and of the Pope himself. He has pledged himself to undertake a crusade; he pleads not to be left in the lurch.

In April, before leaving the mainland, Frederick had dispatched the German crusaders under Louis of Bavaria, authorized to act as his representative in the East.[3] But, notwithstanding these evidences of his intention, the Pope, ever suspicious of Frederick's motives, wrote to him some two months before the designated date for his departure saying: 'Many complain that you wish a postponement of your departure.'[4]

---

[1] See his *Novae Constitutiones* (Huillard-Bréholles, iv, part i), 186: 'Ut sit admirantibus omnibus similitudinis speculum, invidia principum, et norma regnorum.'

[2] Huillard-Bréholles, ii, part i, 123–4.

[3] Huillard-Bréholles, iii. 40. That Louis was sent in April is ascertainable from a statement of the *Scholasticus* Oliver. See H. Hoogweg, 'Die Schriften der Kölner Domscholasticus, spätern Bischofs von S. Sabina Oliverius', 283.

[4] Huillard-Bréholles, ii, part i, 190.

Shortly after receiving this letter, Frederick sent forty ships under the command of Walter of Palear, the Chancellor, Admiral Henry of Malta, and Anselm of Justingen.[1] It is apparent that his preoccupation with a crusading expedition during these years and the constant prodding by the Pope and Curia seriously curtailed his success in re-establishing his authority in the Kingdom of Sicily. It is all the more remarkable, therefore, that after the promulgation of the assizes of Capua and Messina he could proceed systematically and successfully towards the rehabilitation of the Kingdom.

Scarcely less important than his subjugation of the feudal group was Frederick's recovery of the Sicilian cities from the powerful maritime communes of Northern Italy, particularly Genoa. In the long years of turbulence in the Kingdom since the death of Henry VI these northern communes had moved, virtually undisturbed, towards a complete dominance of Sicilian cities such as Syracuse. Already during his expedition to Rome for the imperial coronation Frederick had aroused the suspicions of the Genoese as to his future course when he refused to confirm their earlier privileges, offering the excuse that he could take no action prior to his return to the Kingdom.[2] The Capuan assizes, with their several regulations of trade and commerce, left no doubt in the minds of the Genoese that their ascendancy in Sicily was at an end. Not only were their former privileges revoked, but their factory in Palermo, once the palace of Admiral Margarito, was seized. Count Alaman da Costa, since 1204 the Genoese representative in Syracuse, was deprived of his office as 'governor of the city'. William Porcus, 'Admiral of the Kingdom', escaped imprisonment only by precipitous flight.[3] Although in April 1219 Frederick had promised the Pisans full freedom of trade in his Kingdom (*in regnis suis*), mentioning specifically Messina and Palermo as trading centres open to them, when the Pisan *podestà* appeared before him in November for the formal grant, the phraseology of the privilege had been altered to read, 'throughout the whole Empire, by land and water'. No specific mention was made of the Kingdom of Sicily.[4] The term 'per totum imperium' was habitually employed to distinguish the imperial possessions in Italy from the Sicilian Kingdom. Although there is less positive evidence for Frederick's relations with Venice immediately after his arrival in Sicily, there too his policy was shaped by the customs which prevailed in the time of his

---

[1] Richard of San Germano, 98.

[2] An enlightening monograph on Frederick's relations with the maritime cities of the north is H. Chone, *Die Handelsbeziehungen Kaiser Friedrichs II. zu den Seestädten Venedig, Pisa, Genua*; see especially 17 ff.

[3] *Annales Janvenses (Fonti)*, ii. 171.

[4] For the document see Winkelmann, *Acta*, i, no. 232, pp. 213–15. See also Chone, *Handels-beziehungen*, 26.

Norman predecessors. A grant made to the Venetians a decade later, in 1230, for example, permitted for a limited time freedom of exportation from Apulian ports of all merchandise, save grain, in return for the duties which were customary in the time of William II.[1] Other grants of privilege to various cities suggest that Frederick endeavoured to show no favouritism towards any of the great commercial communes of the north. In general he applied the formula which underlay his entire policy of rehabilitation: a return to the norms and standards that prevailed under his Norman predecessors.

The restrictive measures taken against Genoa and the commercial cities of the north made it possible for Frederick to open the way for the future prosperity of Sicilian cities through mercantile activities. Above all, however, he was now in a position to re-establish a royal navy surpassing that of his Norman predecessors. It is remarkable that within a month after his arrival in the Kingdom he could dispatch forty ships with reinforcements to the Holy Land. The rebuilding of a royal fleet was made possible by apportioning the task of providing ships, arms, and men among various cities. Foreign merchants residing within the Kingdom, as well as the clergy, were subjected to taxation in the interests of various special projects of the realm, such as the equipment of galleys sent to aid the crusaders in Damietta.[2] In conformity, however, with his consistent policy aimed at fostering trade and commerce, and as a means of ensuring its continuance in times of crisis, Frederick suspended all port duties during the Saracen war.[3] Moreover, while depriving the maritime cities of all political influence within the Kingdom, Frederick lost no opportunity to encourage the Venetians and others to continue their mercantile activities, in some cases relieving them temporarily from the payment of certain taxes which he continued to require of native citizens.[4] These measures reveal an enlightened commercial policy singularly in contrast with other features of his national economy, notably his efforts to regulate foreign commerce by forbidding the export of precious metals from Sicily and his measures prohibiting the export of grain from the Kingdom until first the royal ships had put to sea.[5]

The immediate effect of these policies was injurious both to the domestic agrarian economy and to the commercial interests of Sicily. One contemporary chronicler, describing the devastating effect of the restrictive measures, wrote: 'As a consequence, provisions and domestic

---

[1] Winkelmann, *Acta*, i, no. 757, p. 604.
[2] Richard of San Germano, 97.
[3] See the application of this policy in E. Winkelmann, 'Bischof Harduin von Cefalù' (*MIöG*, Ergänzungsband), 339. See also H. Chone, *Handelsbeziehungen*, 28.
[4] Richard of San Germano, 96.
[5] *Chronica ignoti monachi Cisterciensis S. Mariae de Ferraria* (*Mon. Storici*, Series I, 1888), 38.

animals were so cheap that it was impossible to obtain for them the cost of production. The Emperor purchased cheaply and sold at a high price.'[1]

Even greater was the damage of Frederick's fiscal policies to the commercial communes of the north, Pisa, Genoa, and Venice. Their lucrative trade in grain exports from Sicily suffered a severe blow. These cities had long been accustomed to look on the Kingdom as a source of this commodity, which provided one of the chief bases for their expanding trade. This advantage was now possessed by the government of Sicily itself and served as an important contributing agent in the redevelopment of a royal merchant marine.[2] Yet, despite these onerous restrictions, the northern communes continued a not insignificant mercantile activity in Sicily through a more limited purchase and export of foodstuffs and the importation of the products of industry and articles of luxury from other ports of the world, notably from Sardinia and from Marseilles and Narbonne in the south of France.[3]

One of Frederick's early achievements in Sicily which was to prove of extraordinary usefulness in his future commercial policy was the re-establishment of a royal navy as well as a merchant marine sufficient to enable him to maintain strict control of the grain trade. For the furthering of his maritime activities he had re-established the old Norman official, the Admiral of the Kingdom, although he limited his duties to maritime activities. After the flight of William Porcus he was succeeded by Count Henry of Malta. Although of Genoese origin, Henry of Malta served the Emperor with loyalty, and it is to be assumed that Frederick must have required of him exceptional guarantees for his future conduct. For, even at this time, the authority of the Admiral of Sicily, although different from that of his Norman predecessors, was to become progressively greater in succeeding years, especially in the years following the Emperor's second excommunication in 1239.[4]

The Admiral's authority extended over the entire Kingdom and he was responsible only to the King. His main function was the supervision

---

[1] *Chronica Santa Maria Ferraria* (*Mon. Storici*, Series I, Naples, 1888), 38. In recognizing the injurious effects of Frederick II's economic policies, J. M. Powell, *Medieval Monarchy and Trade*, 420–524, greatly exaggerates the extent of the damage. Most misleading is his attributing the present-day economic ills of Sicily to the Norman and Hohenstaufen rulers. If any one era is to be held responsible for the economic injury of Southern Italy, it would doubtless be the last half of the nineteenth century. But one would have to review also the entire economic history from the Angevin period.

[2] E. Winkelmann, *Friedrich II.*, i. 143.   [3] Chone, *Handelsbeziehungen*, 32.

[4] Concerning the Admiral see especially W. Cohn, 'Heinrich von Malta' (*Hist. Vierteljahrschr.* xviii, 1917–18), 253 ff. See also L.-R. Ménager, *L'Émirat et les origines de l'amirauté, XIᵉ–XIIIᵉ siècles*.

of the repairs and maintenance of ships, although the Emperor alone could authorize the building of new ships. Only the Admiral was empowered to conduct punitive expeditions against foreign pirates or to commission others to operate against them as his deputies. He was held strictly accountable for the success or failure of such operations. He was also the authorized pirate-in-chief of the Kingdom, directing all 'legitimate' piratical activities and responsible for the protection of persons and property against injuries from alien pirates. To this end, he was empowered to confiscate the property of citizens of offending foreign communes residing in the Kingdom, holding them as security for damages inflicted by their compatriots. In both criminal and civil causes involving members of the maritime services, including duly authorized privateers, he or his deputies were competent to sit in judgement. This extraordinary judicial right was exercised by him during the two weeks prior to the outfitting of the fleet, and during the two weeks following the removal of the armaments from the ships. He exercised extensive authority in the employment and dismissal of subordinate officers, save for those maritime 'counts of the fleet' made hereditary by Frederick's predecessors. Only in the failure of an heir to these hereditary sinecures was the Admiral free to fill a vacancy.

Frederick had now accomplished much toward the reorganization of the Kingdom, but many tasks still remained to be completed before he could feel secure in his achievement. Peace had been generally established on the mainland, but the island of Sicily was still threatened by the hosts of hostile Saracens who had taken possession of much of the mountainous region in the interior, often driving the Christians from the land, seizing their property, and apportioning it among their fellow Muslims.[1] Typical of their depredations was the laying waste of the landed estates of the Archbishop of Monreale.[2] In a series of documents sanctioned by Frederick between July 1220 and 22 March 1221, he restored to the Archbishop the lands that had been seized by the Saracens during the years of turbulence in Sicily and, at the same time, he regranted all the rights which the church of Monreale had previously enjoyed from King William II, the Emperor Henry VI, and the Empress Constance.[3] But such grants were of little importance as long as the Saracens could continue their dominance of the mountainous regions of the interior or maintain unhindered communication with their fellow Muslims in North Africa. Even a strongly fortified region such as Girgenti, which had long served as a refugee centre

[1] M. Amari, *Storia dei musulmani*, iii. 586–7.
[2] See especially the grants of Frederick to the Archbishop, Huillard-Bréholles, i, part i, 184; and Winkelmann, *Acta*, i, nos. 107, 108, pp. 93–5.
[3] Huillard-Bréholles, i, part ii, 800; ibid. ii, part i, 149–52.

for Christians driven from their homes in Sicily, was at last successfully attacked by the Saracens, its bishop taken captive, and its cathedral seized.[1] Such continued depredations compelled him in 1222 to make preparations for a special expedition against their centre of resistance, the castle of Jato (Yato) in the north-west of the island near Alcamo.

In May 1222, at the head of a strong force, Frederick moved upon Jato where the Emir Ben-Abbed had prepared to resist him.[2] By mid June the castle was surrounded and a siege begun. Because of the rock-bound fortifications and the relatively strong force of the emir, a siege rather than a direct attack was advisable. After about two months Ben-Abbed yielded. He was taken captive with his sons and with two Marseillais merchants, alleged traitors; they were hanged in Palermo from a single gibbet.[3] It is related also by the chronicler Abû-al-Fadayl that Abû Ben-Abbed entered Frederick's tent after the capture and, prostrating himself before his captor, pleaded for a reconciliation. Enraged because the emir had mistreated some of his messengers, Frederick tore open the side of his former antagonist with his spur. After leaving him wounded for a week he then hanged him with the two merchants.[4]

By midsummer of 1223 Frederick was again faced with the necessity of a new expedition to the region of Jato.[5] After besieging that and neighbouring strongholds, he succeeded in driving at least a part of the Saracens from their mountain fortifications to the plains below.[6] It was obvious, however, that a decisive defeat of the Saracens could be accomplished only by their removal from their places of concentration and by cutting off their communication with the Saracen settlements in North Africa. Frederick was forced to the realization, as had been his Norman predecessors, that the ultimate security of Sicily against the Saracens was to be achieved only by establishing an effective barrier against invaders from the coastal areas of North Africa. While still in the north-west of the island in the autumn of 1223 at Trapani he dispatched a fleet to the gulf of Gabes (Zerbi); the fleet took posses-sion of the island of the same name, a stronghold of the African sup-

---

[1] G. Picone, *Memorie storiche agrigentine*, vi, part i, Documenti, XI. See also Amari, *Storia*, iii. 604 ff.

[2] Richard of San Germano, 101; *Annales Siculi* (*MGH, SS.* xix), 496.

[3] Ibid.: 'et cepit Benaveth [Benerbeth] [Ben-Abbed] cum filiis suis, et suspendit apud Panormum.' For the hanging of the two merchants see also *Chronica Albrici Monachi Trium Fontium* (*MGH, SS.* xxiii), 894: 'Mirabellum cum duobus filiis et istos duos traditores in uno patibulo suspendit.' See Amari, *Storia*, iii. 612.

[4] See the account of Abû-al-Fadayl Muhammad ali da Hamah (in Amari, 'Estratti del Tarih Mansuri' (*Archivio storico siciliano*, new series, Ann. IX, 1884), 108–9.

[5] Richard of San Germano, 109.

[6] Frederick's letter to Bishop Conrad of Hildesheim (Huillard-Bréholles, ii, part i, 393).

porters of the Sicilian Saracens, and drove out the inhabitants.[1] But the rebellions continued well into the year 1225 and he was compelled to continue the war and to levy new taxes during 1224–5, to meet the necessary expenses for repeated expeditions into the mountainous regions of Sicily. In the next year also he employed the barons and the feudal army to maintain order among the Saracens who continued to make periodic raids from their mountain hide-outs. With the aid of his feudal army he now initiated a plan which in the course of time was to bring peace to the greater part of the Saracen rebels. He removed most of the able-bodied men, an estimated 16,000, and their families to the plains of Apulia where, at first as serfs, they were later assembled as a military colony at Lucera, a few miles north of Foggia.[2] Here, near the site of the great castle which Frederick erected in 1233 to take the place of the old castle of Troja, they lived unmolested in their religious worship and social customs.[3]

In employing this radical solution of a vexing problem Frederick II revealed the rare enlightenment which so often distinguishes him from his contemporaries. His action was probably guided by the memory of his Norman ancestors. For in the security of Lucera, an enclave within a Christian community, the Saracens were again allowed the maximum of freedom and a degree of autonomy under their own officials, *qādīs*, *shaikh*s, and *faqih*s, in return for the payment of a special tax (*jizyah*). Through their skill and industry as farmers and as craftsmen they proved a valuable asset to the Kingdom; even more, they became one of the main supports of the Emperor as a military force, coming in the course of time to serve him with devotion and loyalty. From these colonists also he drew many of his household servants and otherwise employed their skills in a manner that made him, in their eyes, a second 'illustrious and exalted hero', comparable only to the idolized sovereign that the Arab traveller and scholar saw in King Roger II of Sicily.[4] Years later, after Manfred the son of Frederick had succeeded his father, Jamāl-ed-Dīn, ambassador of the Sultan of Egypt and Syria, visited Lucera and was profoundly impressed by the enlightened policy which still prevailed in the governing of the Saracens in the Kingdom of Sicily. He found that they were free to worship as they pleased and otherwise to preserve their native customs. He wrote also of the enlightenment and of the intellectual interests of the Staufen

---

[1] *Annales Siculi* (*MGH, SS*. xix), 496. See also G. La Mantia, 'La Sicilia ed il suo domino nell'Africa settentrionale' (*Archiv. stor. Sic.* xliv, 1922), 154 f.; Amari, *Storia*, iii, 605.

[2] Ibid. 613 f., especially p. 614, note 1. For a comprehensive history of the colony see P. Egidi, 'La colonia saracena di Lucera e la sua distruzione' (*Archiv. stor. per le provincie napoletane*, xxxvi, 1911).

[3] Richard of San Germano, 184.

[4] W. Cohn, *Das Zeitalter der Normannen in Sizilien*, 84.

family which already had established a bond of friendship with the Arab world through Frederick II. Jamāl-ed-Dīn said of Manfred:

When I arrived at his home, I was most honourably received and I was lodged in one of the cities of Apulia. . . . I had many meetings with him and I perceived that he possessed exceptional talents and that he greatly admired the intellectual sciences. He knew by heart the ten *Discourses* (books) of the treatise of Euclid. Near the city where I was lodged was another called Loudjera (Lucera), the inhabitants of which were Muslims, originally of Sicily. There were celebrated the Friday prayers, and the rites of Islam were openly observed. I noted that the principal officers of the Emperor Manfred were Muslims and that in his camp was observed the call to prayers. The city where I lived was five days' journey from Rome. At the moment of my taking leave of the home of the Emperor, the Pope, who is the *caliph of the Franks*, and the King of France were allied for the purpose of attacking Manfred, the Pope having excommunicated him already because of his predilection for Muslims. His brother, Conrad, and his father, Frederick, had also incurred excommunication because of their penchant for Islam.[1]

On more than one occasion Pope Gregory IX complained to the Emperor of the presence of the Saracens of Lucera, charging them with the destruction of Christian churches in order to obtain building materials for their homes.[2] To the papal complaints against the removal of the Saracens from the island to Apulia, Frederick replied that this move not only gave greater security to the churches of Sicily, but it provided an opportunity for the conversion of the Saracens to the Christian faith.[3] Frederick II had, in fact, but little sympathy with the conversion of the Muslims to the Christian faith. A decade was to pass after their establishment in Lucera before he consented to the sending of missionaries among them. As a gesture of goodwill towards Pope Gregory IX, he permitted the entrance of two Dominicans into the colony to seek the conversion of the Saracens.[4] But this generous gesture could give little satisfaction to the Pope and Curia. The pent-up bitterness caused by the presence of the infidel colony manifested itself years later at the Council of Lyons in 1245 when Frederick was charged with leading a number of Saracen rebels from Girgenti and with being responsible for their destroying Christians and violating their wives and daughters.[5] In excommunicating the Emperor at that time, the Pope complained also that Frederick had built a large and strongly fortified city in Christendom, peopling it with Saracens, retain-

---

[1] Jamāl-ed-Dīn is thus quoted in the *Autobiographie a'* Abou 'l-Fidā (*RHC, Hist. or.* i), 170.
[2] Huillard-Bréholles, iv, part i, 405; v, part i, 225.
[3] See especially Frederick's letter of Apr. 1236 (ibid.), 831.
[4] Ibid. iv, part i, 457–8.
[5] Winkelmann, *Acta*, ii, no. 1037, p. 714.

ing their customs and superstitions, and rejecting all Christian counsel and religion.[1]

The failure of the Pope and Curia to appreciate the wisdom of Frederick's solution of the Saracen problem in Sicily serves to emphasize how insuperable was the barrier which lay between an enlightened Emperor and a religious leadership activated not by reason, but by fanaticism and prejudice. Just as Frederick was later to demonstrate a realistic approach to the conflict between Islam and Christianity during the crusade of 1228–9, so in his dealing with the Saracen problem in Sicily he revealed how far he had advanced beyond the narrow dogmatism of his contemporaries. He here displayed the enlightened statesmanship toward non-Christian peoples which in the years to come was to set him apart and to elevate him above the intolerance of his era. Frederick II's drastic solution of the Saracen problem was the last of the steps necessary to the overcoming of the chaotic conditions that had prevailed since the death of the Emperor Henry VI and his Empress Constance. The Kingdom of Sicily was no longer merely a geographical term describing the island and the Apulian mainland. It now assumed the character of a firmly knit sovereign state, held together by the rigorous policies of a capable ruler.

With the completion of these essential steps, Frederick was quick to perceive what his predecessors had failed to see, the need for an intellectual centre other than the royal court and utilizing the diverse cultures of the island and the mainland. To him a basic need of a unified state was a university, firmly controlled by the sovereign authority and equipped to provide thorough training in the learned professions. In his concept of government, always reminiscent of the ancient Roman Empire, the importance of trained jurists, notaries, and other governmental officials was paramount. He was especially aware of the need for such officials trained in accordance with the political philosophy of the Staufens. While, strictly speaking, the University of Naples, established at this time, was not a state university in the modern sense, certainly not the 'first state university', it was, in the fullest meaning of the term, a royal university.[2] As Rashdall has emphasized, there is no parallel in medieval history for such absolute subjection of a university 'in the minutest as well as in the most important matters, to the royal authority'.[3] In his letter of July 1224 Frederick states his object in founding the university: that henceforth in the

---

[1] Matthew Paris, *Chronica majora* (Rolls Series), iv. 435.

[2] In an academic discourse delivered in 1880 by E. Winkelmann, 'Über die ersten Staatsuniversitäten' (Progr. Heidelberg, 1880), 12, he described it as 'die erste von einem Staatsoberhaupte gegründete Universität'. P. H. Denifle, *Die Entstehung der Universitäten des Mittelalters bis 1400*, 452, discusses the fallacy of this description.

[3] *The Universities of Europe of the Middle Ages*, ii. 25.

Kingdom many will become clever and wise, through the acquisition of knowledge and the cultivation of erudition. Like Nicholas of Jamsilla, the Emperor recognized that, since the end of the enlightened era of his Norman predecessors, 'in the Kingdom of Sicily the liberally educated were few or non-existent'.[1]

Frederick expressed the desire in his founding letter that the intellectually hungry might satisfy their longing for learning within the Kingdom itself, and not be compelled to wander in foreign lands. He made it clear also that those who were educated in the university would not go unrewarded in his services.[2] Throughout the letter there are passages indicative of his desire to make use of the ample training provided by the University of Naples for the improvement of the various services of the government. Nor is the letter wanting in passages suggestive of the familiar appeals of a present-day university office of admissions, setting forth the virtues of Naples as the seat of a university and reminding the prospective patrons of the desirability of ¦pursuing knowledge under the observation of parental eyes. While chiefly bureaucratic in its aims,[3] it welcomed foreign students and 'scholars from wheresoever they might come', assuring them of security in their movements within the Kingdom, in their places of lodging, and in their return to their native lands. The invitation to foreign students offered the further temptation of abundant food, of inexpensive living conditions, and of money to be made available to them while in performance of their academic duties. Although emphasizing chiefly the utilitarian studies of grammar and law under distinguished masters, including the learned jurists Roffredo of Benevento and Terrisio of Atina (Pignatelli Terrisius),[4] it made provision also for other disciplines, including philosophy and the natural sciences, under distinguished masters, notably Peter of Hibernia, said to have been the teacher of Thomas Aquinas, and the famous Catalan, Master Arnold.[5]

Lofty as were the aims of Frederick II in establishing the royal University of Naples, it never attained the position of pre-eminence originally hoped for by its founder. Perhaps this failure is attributable in part to the absence of the tradition of learning which formed the foundation for the other medieval universities such as Paris, Bologna, and Oxford. Even more important was its essentially bureaucratic

[1] Muratori, *RIS* viii, cols. 495–6.

[2] Huillard-Bréholles, ii, part i, 451.

[3] C. H. Haskins, *Studies in Medieval Science*, 250. Also the note of Rashdall, *Universities*, ii. 23, note 1.

[4] G. Ferretti, 'Roffredo Epifanio da Benevento' (*Studi medioevali*, iii, 1909), 230–75; F. Torraca, 'Maestro Terrisio de Atina' (*Archiv. stor. napoletano*, xxxvi, 1911), 231–53.

[5] G. Paolucci, *Atti Acc. Palermo*, 3rd series, iv, 1858, p. 44, no. xiv. See especially C. Baeumker, *Petrus de Hibernia*: Sitzungsberichte, Munich, 1920, and H. Grabmann, 'Thomas von Aquino und Petrus von Hibernia' (*Philos. Jahrbuch.* 33, 1920), 347 ff.

character. Its professors were, in fact, officers of the King, employed by him when occasion demanded as active agents of the royal administration. The great universities of Europe were characterized by the autonomous administration of faculties and scholars. Tyranny, even in the most enlightened form, is not conducive to the creative efforts of scholars. Frederick was desirous that the intellectual life of the Kingdom should find its fullest expression at the royal court and, to this end, the administration of the university was placed under the supervision of the royal officials.[1] Thus the university was to become essentially a regional university, designed to serve the needs of a sovereign whose concept of efficient government can best be described as Caesarism or enlightened despotism. To such sovereigns the control of education is thought to be of paramount importance.

[1] Rashdall, *Universities*, ii. 25–6.

III

FREDERICK II, KING OF JERUSALEM

*Li apostoles commanda à l'empereur qu'il passast en le tiere d'Outremer
et fesist son pelerinage, et s'il ne le faisoit, il en tenroit justice.*

Ernoul, 455.[1]

IF Frederick could view with satisfaction his achievements in the
Kingdom of Sicily, he could not fail to recognize also the growing
tension between himself and the Holy See. His concept of sovereignty,
so clearly apparent in his assizes of Capua and Messina, inevitably
involved policies inimical to the Pope and Curia. No less important as a
source of tension was the failure of the Emperor to set out on a crusade
in August 1221, as he had sworn to do at the time of his imperial coronation. For a brief moment the tension was relaxed when the German
crusaders, led by Louis of Bavaria, arrived in Egypt in the late spring
of 1221, and when, shortly afterwards, Frederick sent forty ships under
the command of Admiral Henry of Malta, Walter of Palear, and
Anselm of Justigen to reinforce the crusading army in Syria.[2]

Meanwhile, the ill-starred expedition of Pelagius, the papal legate,
against Cairo, had exposed Frederick to the charge that by delaying his
departure he was responsible for the disaster. For, almost at the moment
of the arrival of Henry of Malta and his associates with reinforcements,
the crusaders, moving up the Nile towards Cairo, had been trapped
in the flooded river by a clever manœuvre of the Egyptian Sultan.
Only the leniency of the Sultan had permitted the helpless crusaders to
escape annihilation. But in return the Christians were compelled to
surrender the city of Damietta which they had recently captured, and
to agree to a truce of eight years' duration, to be broken only 'when a
crowned king from the West' should return to the Holy Land.[3]

The Christian world had been shocked by this catastrophe and Frederick II did not escape the popular censure. His numerous postponements of his expedition were recalled, and his failure to fulfil his vow,
taken years before at Aachen and solemnly renewed at his imperial

---

[1] The Pope required of the Emperor that he cross to the land beyond the sea, and make his
pilgrimage, and if he did not do so he would be liable to punishment.

[2] Huillard-Bréholles, iii. 40; Richard of San Germano, 98.

[3] Röhricht, *Beiträge*, ii. 255; T. C. Van Cleve, 'The Fifth Crusade', *A History of the Crusades*,
ii: *The Later Crusades* (ed. R. L. Wolff *et al.*), 425 ff.

coronation, were now made the subjects for attacks by his critics. This critical reaction is reflected in the poetry of the troubadours, even by those who were often the admirers of the 'open-handed' Emperor. Thus Peirol, who was probably present at the surrender of Damietta on 7 September 1221, wrote:

> Emperor, Damietta awaits you
> and night and day the White Tower weeps
> for your eagle which a vulture has cast down therefrom:
> Cowardly is the eagle that is captured by a vulture!
> Shame is thereby yours, and honour accrues to the Sultan.[1]

Other contemporary critics, more aware of the true cause of the failure, were bitter in their censure of the Pope who had sanctioned the expedition against Cairo, and of Pelagius whose want of military skill had led to the disaster. The troubadour Huon de Saint-Quentin complained:

> They [the Saracens] are in possession of Damietta
> Because of the legate, our enemy,
> And Christians are overtaken by death . . .[2]

Similar also was the complaint of Guillaume le Clerc de Normandie, *Le Besant de Dieu*: 'When the clergy take the function of leading knights, certainly that is against the law. But the clerk should recite aloud from his Scriptures and Psalms and let the knight go to his great battlefields.'[3]

The reaction to the disaster of Damietta is of especial importance as a reflection of the changing attitude in the west towards crusading expeditions. Although the Pope, the Curia, and the crusading preachers continued their insistent appeals for a crusade, employing all propagandist agencies in their efforts, they encountered everywhere a growing resistance. Already in the early thirteenth century a change in attitude towards the crusades was apparent. Frederick II was made well aware of this change when, after his coronation as Emperor, he endeavoured to assemble troops throughout western Europe for his expedition to reclaim the Kingdom of Jerusalem. In April he met the Pope at Veroli where plans for the renewal of the crusading effort were made. Apparently reassured by the results of this conference, the Pope wrote to the legate Pelagius that an agreement had been reached with Frederick who, henceforth, would occupy himself with efforts to recover the Holy Land. He announced also a meeting to take place in Verona in November 1222, to which princes, prelates, and others were being summoned to consider the projected expedition.[4] The meeting, however,

---

[1] See S. C. Aston, *Peirol, Troubadour*, 163, whose translation I have followed; also F. Diez, *Leben und Werke der Troubadours*, 259 and 456.

[2] K. Bartsch and A. Horning, *La Langue et la littérature françaises*, col. 373.

[3] E. Martin, ed. (Halle, 1869), 75. The translation is from P. A. Throop, *Criticism of the Crusade*, 32.   [4] Huillard-Bréholles, ii, part i, 240 ff.

took place not in Verona in 1222, but in Ferentino in March of the following year. There, together with the Pope and Emperor, were also King John of Jerusalem, Hermann of Salza, Grand Master of the Teutonic Order, the Patriarch of Jerusalem, and many other prelates and nobles, although but few princes of the Empire.[1]

Frederick again took the crusading vow and agreed to undertake an expedition to Syria two years later. The death of the Empress during the preceding year made possible also a plan for his marriage to Isabella, daughter of the titular King of Jerusalem and heiress to that kingdom.[2] Henceforth, the conquest of the Orient would be not a papal enterprise, redounding to the glory of the Holy See, but a war of conquest, bringing into the sphere of the Empire the Kingdom of Jerusalem. Once more crusading preachers were dispatched to all parts of Europe, seeking to awaken enthusiasm for a crusade to be led by the Emperor in person. During the succeeding months Frederick had made ready a hundred galleys and some fifty vessels capable of transporting 10,000 foot-soldiers and 1,000 knights. Liberal inducements were offered to all crusaders, including free transportation and provisions.[3]

It was apparent that the efforts of Pope and Emperor evoked but little enthusiasm throughout Europe. King John of Jerusalem, whose close association with the Holy Land gave him unique prestige, travelled widely in France, England, Germany, and Spain seeking to arouse interest in the expedition.[4] Everywhere welcomed as a visitor of special distinction, King John found little enthusiasm for a crusade. However, the King of France, whose death followed closely on the visit of John of Brienne, gave him a large sum of money to aid in financing the war in Syria. But both France and England were so deeply involved in mutual hostilities that participation in a crusade would have been impossible. The King and princes in Spain were engaged in perennial conflict with the Muslims within their own territories. Reports from King John and from Hermann of Salza about conditions in Germany and elsewhere were in agreement that few, if indeed any, in these countries were prepared to take the cross.[5] The widespread apathy, if not the actual hostility towards the crusade, was due in part also to the nature of the preachers sent as propagandists for the enterprise; there

[1] E. Winkelmann, *Friedrich II.*, i. 198; W. Knebel, *Kaiser Friedrich II. und Papst Honorius III.*, 64 ff.

[2] Richard of San Germano, 107.

[3] Huillard-Bréholles, ii, part i, 410.

[4] L. Böhm, *Johann von Brienne, König von Jerusalem und Kaiser von Konstantinopel*, 69 f. See also A. Cartellieri, *Philipp II. August*, iv. 561 f.

[5] Huillard-Bréholles, ii. 412: 'et sic pauci vel nulli sunt qui per omnes provincias illas quas dictus rex dicitur peragrasse, velint se ad Crucis ministerium preparare.'

were complaints that they were generally despised, partly because of their lowly origin and even more because of their want of ecclesiastical dignity and authority.

Faced with these difficulties, Frederick recognized the impossibility of obtaining adequate forces for the undertaking of a crusade in 1225. The Pope also, albeit with reluctance, recognized how seriously this widespread apathy would jeopardize such an expedition. It is probable also that the reports of Conrad, Bishop of Porto, the Pope's special representative in Germany, acquainted Honorius even more fully with the difficulties of a crusading expedition.[1] The presence of the Bishop of Porto and his several aides had, in some measure, created a more favourable sentiment among the German magnates, but their arrival had been delayed too long to influence significantly the recruitment for an expedition in the following year.[2]

Frederick now appealed to the Pope for a postponement, an effort in which he was doubtless supported by King John, Hermann of Salza, and the Patriarch of Jerusalem. Reluctantly Honorius yielded and it was agreed that a conference was to be held at San Germano on 25 July to arrange the conditions under which the postponement would be granted. Present at this conference were many of the foremost prelates and magnates of the Christian world including the Patriarch Gerold of Jerusalem, Cardinal Gualo of St. Martins, the Bishops of Bamberg, Merseberg, Paderborn, and Regensburg, King John of Jerusalem, Reginald of Spoleto, Bernard of Carinthia, and Hermann of Salza, Grand Master of the Teutonic Order, the faithful representative of the Emperor.[3]

The constituent membership of this extraordinary council would in itself suggest the seriousness of Honorius' object in calling it. He had now reached the limit of forbearance. The project upon which he had set his heart had repeatedly failed and, as he had long believed, because of the dilatory tactics of Frederick whose numerous excuses, valid though they may have been, had little significance in the opinion of the zealous Pontiff to whom the recovery of the Holy Land and the dominance of the Church in the East were desiderata to be achieved at any cost. The terms of the agreement now made suggest that Frederick felt compelled to acquiesce temporarily in the interpretation of the *plenitudo potestatis* of the papal office which for the next several decades was to dominate the political philosophy of the Middle Ages. The posision now accepted by the Emperor appeared momentarily to be that of

---

[1] Conrad of Porto was with Hermann of Salza at the Diet of Nürnberg on 23 July 1224. See BFW, *Reg.* v, Abt. i, no. 3930.

[2] See especially the observations of E. Winkelmann, *Friedrich II.*, i. 226 f.

[3] Richard of San Germano, 121.

the wielder of a sword designed to be employed at the behest of the Apostolic See. He pledged himself to set out on a crusade on 15 August 1227 with a thousand knights, maintaining them in the Holy Land for two years. He agreed also to provide ships for the transport of 2,000 armed men with three horses for each, together with their squires and valets. As a guarantee of his good faith, Frederick pledged himself to deposit 100,000 ounces of gold in five instalments in the custody of Herman of Salza, King John of Jerusalem, and the Patriarch Gerold, to be restored to him only after his arrival in Acre, and there to be employed in payment of the expenses of the expedition. In case of his death, or if for other reasons he failed to undertake the expedition, the money thus pledged was to be employed in future efforts to recover the Holy Land. After agreeing to these terms, certainly humiliating to one who saw himself as the heir to the ancient Caesars, Frederick moved to the altar, and there, with his right hand upon the Gospels, he took an oath to depart on the designated date and in conformity with the above agreement. To give greater efficacy to the oath, Reginald of Spoleto also swore 'on the soul of the Emperor', that the terms of the agreement would be executed in good faith and without reservations. He added that the Emperor was prepared to accept excommunication in case of failure.[1]

At first glance it seems incredible that the foremost sovereign of thirteenth-century Europe would thus voluntarily submit to a humiliating bondage which might well carry with it the acknowledgement of the supremacy of the Pope and Curia over the Emperor. Justification for his action can be found only in the firm conviction of the Emperor that he would be able to fulfil the crusading plan successfully, and that, when he had achieved such sovereign authority, the Church could be restricted to its purely spiritual functions within the structure of the state. This concept of the *imperium* was in no sense a concept of Caesaropapism, but rather a limitation of the function of the Church to the care of the spiritual well-being of a World-Christian state. Frederick never lost sight of this aim, which subsequently was to be enunciated in the sonorous rhetoric of his *Liber Augustalis* or *Constitutiones*. Moreover, he must have sensed clearly at this time what later became patent in the pronouncements of the Pope and Curia, that their policies, if unopposed, could result only in the absorption of the *imperium* within the dominion of the Holy See and the irreparable destruction of temporal authority.[1] If, indeed, there is a single episode in the statesmanship of

---

[1] *MGH, Const.* ii, no. 102, pp. 129–31. See also Richard of San Germano, 121.

[2] For a somewhat strained and exaggerated view of the danger see Otto Freiherr von Dungern, 'Constitutional Reorganization and Reform under the Hohenstaufen' (tr. G. Barraclough, *Medieval Germany*), ii. 224 f.

Frederick II in which he recklessly gambled with the imperial office and boldly challenged the aspirations of the Roman See to become the supreme world power, it may well have been this hazardous pledge of the future resources of the Empire for the success or failure of an expedition to the Holy Land.

Harsh as were the terms, and favourable as they were to the interests of the Church, Frederick did not leave the meeting at San Germano empty-handed. He was now the recognized leader of a project which, in the eyes of the Christian world, had failed disastrously under papal leadership. The crusade was now to be an imperial enterprise, freed from the haphazard leadership which had brought nothing but ill for the crusading movements since their inception in the eleventh century, and which had reached its nadir only recently because of the obstinacy of the papal legate at Damietta. Moreover, the successful conquest of the Kingdom of Jerusalem would bring into the purview of the imperial plans the whole of Syria and probably Egypt. Most importantly, the San Germano agreement offered the Emperor additional time in which to complete the consolidation of the Kingdom of Sicily and to regain control of essential regions on the mainland, long defiant of the imperial authority under the auspices of the Milanese.

He was now free also to carry out his marriage with Isabella of Brienne, previously agreed to at Ferentino and which henceforth was to be the basis of his claim to the Kingdom of Jerusalem. Frederick dispatched a squadron, commanded by Admiral Henry of Malta and Bishop James of Patti, to escort his future bride. At Acre representatives of King John, including Guy Lenfant and other Syrian nobles, received the imperial embassy. In the church of the Holy Cross the marriage ring was placed on the finger of Isabella by Bishop James of Patti in the name of his sovereign. In Tyre the Queen received the royal crown, previously worn by her father as titular King and, after fitting ceremonies, she sailed for Italy, accompanied by Balian III of Sidon, Archbishop Simon of Tyre, and other Syrian nobles and ladies. Arriving in Brindisi, Isabella was met by the Emperor and her father, and the formal wedding was celebrated on 9 November 1225.[1]

The marriage of Frederick II to a bride from the ever-mysterious Orient, the land beyond the sea, stirred the imagination of his contemporaries and became the subject of legendary treatment by contemporary poets. Illustrative of this is a singular poem recounting the heroic adventures of Ortnit, obviously a thinly veiled Frederick II, a famous king who ruled over a kingdom which 'had for its name Lamparten

---

[1] For the details of the wedding see 'Relation française du mariage de Frédéric II avec Isabelle de Brienne et ses démêlés avec le roi Jean', Huillard-Bréholles, ii, part ii, 921 ff.

(Lombardy)'.[1] The poet says of Ortnit that he ruled over all Italian lands and that he had conquered the entire country 'from the mountains to the sea' (*von dem birge unz an das mer*). After this noble prince had attained manhood his counsellors, among whom was the Saracen Zacharis, 'the heathen of Apulia', advised him to seek a wife. But such was the grandeur of the young king that it was difficult to find a consort of equal birth. The poet, little concerned with unity of time or with historical accuracy, then introduces an episode of the Fifth Crusade in which Ortnit is made to participate. Aljas, the most noble of the royal counsellors, had told his lord of a heathen monarch named Machorel, a native of Montabur (Mount Tabor), where the crusaders had been repulsed in 1217. This King of Montabur, next to Ortnit himself, was the most noble of sovereigns. More infidels were his subjects than Christians, and he wore the crown of Jerusalem. Tyre (Suders) in Syria was his capital. Thus King John of Brienne, 'the beloved servant of the Pope', is transformed by the poet into a heathen monarch. King Machorel had a daughter who, compared with other women, was as 'beautiful as gold is to lead', but thus far, every man who had sought her hand in marriage had been beheaded by the all-powerful father. This ambitious king, anticipating the death of his wife through whom the crown was inherited, planned to marry his own daughter in order to secure for himself the Kingdom of Jerusalem. Even the ambassadors sent by the monarchs of the world to sue for his daughter's hand had been beheaded. Their heads adorned the battlements of the castle of Montabur. But Ortnit, convinced that only this lovely princess could be a fitting consort, determined to win her by conquest of her father's kingdom. To this end Ortnit hastened to assemble a powerful army. Isabella of Brienne thus becomes a beautiful Saracen princess and her father, titular King of Jerusalem, a would-be incestuous Muslim, lord of the castle of Mount Tabor. The poem reflects the quarrel that developed between John of Brienne and Frederick II shortly after the marriage, when Frederick, contrary to the expectations of his father-in-law, assumed the title King of Jerusalem.

Before setting out for Syria, Ortnit came upon a sleeping dwarf named Albert, who possessed magical powers. After the first unfriendly encounter the dwarf revealed himself as the actual father of Ortnit. He told how the supposed father of the young king, after many years of marriage to the Queen Mother, had despaired of an heir. (Here again the poet finds his inspiration in the birth of Frederick II some

---

[1] *Das deutsche Heldenbuch* (hrsg. von E. Henrici, Berlin und Stuttgart, 1887), 1–24; E. H. Meyer, 'Quellenstudien zur Mittelhochdeutschen Spielmannsdichtung' (*Zeitschr. für deutsches Altertum und deutsche Litteratur*, Neue Folge, vol. 38, 1894), 65 ff.; K. Müllenhoff, 'Das Alter des Ortneit', ibid. 1, 1867), 185 ff., *Ortneit und Wolfdietrich nach der Wiener Piaristenhandschrift* (hrsg. von Dr. J. L. E. von Landhausen: *Bibliothek des Litterarischen Vereins in Stuttgart*, ccxxxix, 1906).

ten years after the marriage of his father, Henry VI, to Constance of Sicily, whose age was such that contemporaries doubted her mother-hood.) The dwarf then relates this story: 'One day the Queen [the mother of Ortnit] sat upon a couch lamenting her fate, whereupon the dwarf entered her apartment and gave her that which she had so long desired' (a recollection of the legend that Constance of Sicily, like the mother of Octavius, had been impregnated by a demon). Ortnit was at first angered and stunned by the dwarf's story, but later, in the presence of his mother, the darkness of his mood lifted and Albert served him henceforth with unchanging loyalty.

Disguised as a merchant, Ortnit sailed to the Orient. Accompanied by Albert, and with a splendid fleet as escort, he entered the harbour of Tyre, guided by the unsuspecting harbour-master. In the belief that the ships were merchant vessels, the gates of the city were per-mitted to remain open and Tyre was quickly captured by Ortnit and his followers during the night. The next morning Ortnit and his army stormed Montabur but failed to gain entrance. In the effort he lost some 5,000 men and was compelled to withdraw across a rivulet where he made his camp in a meadow. (The author here makes use of an episode of the crusade of 1217 when the crusaders began their assault on Mount Tabor from their camp on the rivulet Cresson.) In a second encounter he was again driven back with heavy losses. He would have failed in his effort had not Albert, thanks to his power of making him-self invisible, made his way into the castle and into a chamber where he found the Princess with her mother, weeping and praying to Apollo and Mohammed. Albert informed the unhappy Princess that he had been sent from heaven to take her away to become Queen of Italy. But the Princess replied that she had been born a heathen and must so remain. At last convinced, however, that her father's life could be spared only by her going to King Ortnit, she consented, saying: 'Now take him my gold ring. Say to the Lombard I am favourably disposed towards him. Ask him to withdraw his army from the walls of the castle.' After obeying her command, Albert spirited the Princess from the castle and, defying the pursuit by the infidels, he conducted her safely to King Ortnit. *En route* to Italy she was baptized, after which she became the bride of the King of 'Lamparten'.

Neither the Pope nor John of Brienne could have visualized the possi-bility that Frederick would at once demand direct sovereign control over the newly acquired Kingdom. Whether or not this had been his intention from the outset, or was the result of some difference with John of Brienne, immediately after the formal wedding Frederick pro-claimed himself King of Jerusalem and demanded of his father-in-law that he surrender his titular claims. John of Brienne was stunned by this abrupt and inconsiderate demand.[1]

The two men had long been on the friendliest of terms, and King John had apparently been a welcome guest at the Emperor's court. He had travelled throughout Europe in the interest of Frederick's crusading effort. In the absence of any known cause of difference, it can only be assumed that Frederick, in his conviction that he was divinely ordained to take the crown of Jerusalem, now did what he had planned to do from the moment when the suggestion of the marriage was first made at Ferentino. He thus coldly rejected his father-in-law as a hindrance to his ambitious plans. He moved ruthlessly toward the acquisition of his full sovereign rights, receiving homage from his Syrian nobles, including not only those who had accompanied the Queen but also those who were in Syria.[2] A bitter quarrel ensued, and John of Brienne hastened to Rome to lay his grievances before the Pope.

Like the marriage itself, the quarrel was to become the source of many legends and improbable tales. It was said that Satan had intervened to destroy the friendship of Frederick and John of Brienne, causing the Emperor to neglect his beautiful fifteen-year-old bride. It was said that he had beaten her and that on their wedding night he had deserted her for one of her ladies-in-waiting, a niece of King John, with whom he spent a night of dalliance. Gossip told of how he had imprisoned his Queen and, thereafter, ignored her.[3]

Most, if not all, of these tales can be dismissed as idle gossip, originating in the quarrel of the two men, the causes of which are obscure. Moreover, known facts tend to belie the alleged mistreatment of the Queen. She is known to have accompanied Frederick to Sicily, where, in due course, she gave birth to a son who, in the years to come, claimed the special affection of the Emperor. Also, within a month following the marriage in Brindisi, she participated with the Emperor in conferring privileges upon the Teutonic Order, the Grand Master of which, Hermann of Salza, had played a significant role in negotiating the marriage.[4] The very youthfulness of Isabella of Brienne, still in her early teens, precluded her acting as consort in the way that Constance of Aragon had done. It is noteworthy also that stories of mistreatment of the Queen originated solely with Franco-Syrian, Cypriot, and papal sources friendly to the Briennes.

Despite these misdeeds, or alleged misdeeds, Frederick seems to have been justified on purely legal grounds, and by precedent, in assuming the title of King of Jerusalem and in claiming for himself the prerogatives

[1] Huillard-Bréholles, ii, part ii, 923 f. See also *Eracles*, 358. 'Quant li Johans oi ce, si en fu moult esbahis . . .'
   [2] *Eracles*, 358 f.   [3] *Ernoul*, 451.   [4] Huillard-Bréholles, ii, part i, 536.

appertaining to his Queen. John of Brienne's sole claim was that of regent to his daughter in a kingdom which she inherited from her mother. Morally, on the other hand, there can be no justification for Frederick's action, which was wholly at variance with the understanding of John of Brienne and, accordingly, with the agreement which the Pope and other members of the conference had promoted at Ferentino and San Germano. With ruthless disregard for his father-in-law, Frederick pushed on towards his goal. To Frederick II there could be but one form of success in statesmanship: the attainment of Caesarism, comparable to that of Roman antiquity. To interpret his actions in any other way would be to misjudge and misrepresent his character. There are few instances in his life, after he had attained the imperial crown, of his actions having their origin in compassion or in sentiment. To him his taking of the crown of Jerusalem was destined by God himself who had 'miraculously exalted us above the princes of the earth'.[1]

In Rome, where he had fled after his quarrel with his son-in-law, John of Brienne found sympathy but little immediate aid. Honorius took the Emperor to task for his action, which he characterized as scandalous and injurious to the Emperor's reputation and to the interests of the Holy Land.[2] The attitude of the Pope is further revealed in his studied omission of the title King of Jerusalem, in addressing Frederick. Indeed, it was not until 1231, after the reconciliation of Frederick with Pope Gregory IX, the successor of Honorius, that letters from the papal Chancery to the Emperor included his complete title: *Friderico illustri Romanorum imperatori, semper augusto, Hierusalem et Sicilie regi.*[3]

It is remarkable that, notwithstanding the ill will of the Pope resulting from the mistreatment of John of Brienne, Frederick chose this moment to summon a diet to meet in Cremona at Easter 1226, for the purpose of implementing plans for a crusade, for the extirpation of heresy, and for the restoration of the imperial rights.[4] Evidently he felt that the obligations recently assumed by him at San Germano, giving assurances of his undertaking a crusade, might serve to win the Pope and Curia to a more sympathetic understanding of his announced intention of restoring the imperial rights, all the more so since his plans also included the extirpation of heresy.

For five years, while engaged in the reorganization of the Kingdom of Sicily, he had revealed no aggressive intentions towards either the

---

[1] *MGH, Const.* ii, p. 116, line 34.   [2] Huillard-Bréholles, ii, part i, 597–8.
[3] Ibid. iii. 298.
[4] Richard of San Germano, 125–6; *MGH, Const.* ii, no. 103, p. 644. See also note 2 of Winkelmann, *Kaiser Friedrich*, i. 267, on the extirpation of heresy.

Lombard communes or the Duchy of Spoleto and the March of Ancona, the latter known to be especially coveted by Frederick as a corridor between the Kingdom of Sicily and the imperial possessions in Northern Italy. Thus far, he had satisfied himself with relatively friendly diplomatic negotiations.[1] The vague phraseology which he now employed in summoning the Diet of Cremona, suggests that he himself was as yet uncertain of his future policy. Was he, perhaps, using the Diet as a means of ascertaining just how far he could go, at this time, in formulating a definite policy for the future, all the while concealing his actual intention of demanding, ultimately, the unequivocal submission of the communes to his absolute sovereignty?

It was not mere chance that Cremona was chosen by Frederick II as the meeting-place for the German and Italian princes and prelates. Visitors coming there from either side of the Alps could be comfortably accommodated and, of paramount importance, Cremona was traditionally loyal to the Emperor.[2] Moreover, Cremona was the chief of the Lombard cities hostile to the Milanese group. This hostility had recently been intensified when Frederick granted the Cremonese extraordinary privileges exempting them from punishment for any act committed in Lombardy which would be useful to or redound to the honour of the Emperor and the Empire.[3]

Meanwhile, he ordered the vassals of the Kingdom of Sicily to accompany him to Lombardy, designating Pescara as the place of assembly. Then, leaving his young consort in the castle of Terracina near Salerno, he hastened to Apulia, where he arranged to leave Henry of Morra, the Grand Court Justiciar, as his vicegerent in the Kingdom.[4] Certainly the choice of Cremona as the place of meeting would have aroused the suspicions of the Milanese group of Lombard cities, revealing (as in 1220) his intention to implement his policy, whatever it might be, with the assistance of a group of cities traditionally hostile to the Milanese and their allies. Plans and preparations such as these could have but one effect upon the cities of Central and Northern Italy, always suspicious of the motives of the Hohenstaufen. With the first rumours of the expedition, early in March 1226, plenipotentiaries representing the cities of Milan, Bologna, Brescia, Mantua, Padua, Vicenza, and Treviso met in Mantua where, in conformity with a stipulation of the Peace of Constance of 1183,[5] they re-established the

---

[1] See also E. Jordan, *Origines*, Introduction, pp. xlv ff.

[2] Richard of San Germano, 126. For the Diet see also G. Fasoli, *Aspetti*, 118 ff.

[3] Böhmer, *Acta*, no. 288, p. 254.

[4] Richard of San Germano, 125 ff.

[5] *MGH, Legum*, ii. 177, article 20: 'Item societatem quam nunc habent tenere, et quotiens voluerint, renovare eis liceat.' For the reactions of the Lombard cities see also the excellent treatment by E. Jordan, *Origines*, pp. xlvii ff.

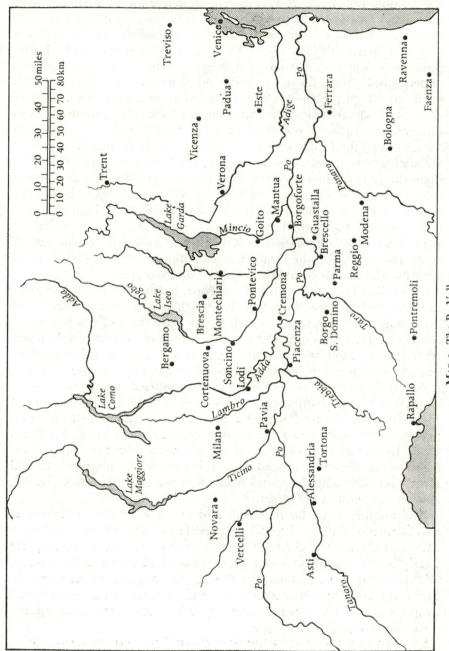

MAP 2. The Po Valley

old Lombard League—it was to remain active for at least the next twenty-five years—and required of the officials and citizens of each commune an annual oath of allegiance to the confederacy.[1] The action of the Lombard cities was doubtless in some measure the result of their consciousness of guilt in encroaching upon regions that were a part of imperial Italy. But a far more significant cause was the marked growth of the sovereign pretensions of these communes during the preceding decades in which the imperial authority had scarcely made itself felt in those regions. Indeed it was during the late twelfth and early thirteenth centuries that the Italian city states, particularly in Lombardy, attained a consciousness of independence and strength that was to characterize them throughout the era of the Renaissance. The decision at Mantua soon attracted other citizens to seek safety in the League. Before the close of the year 1226 Vercelli, Alessandria, Faenza, Lodi, Verona, and Piacenza had joined the original members.[2] Keenly aware of Frederick's recent legislation in Capua, and especially of the law *de resignandis privilegiis*, the Lombard communes were doubtless over-sensitive about their own past privileges and freedoms.

The will of these cities, and of the Pope, to resist Frederick's expedition was further strengthened by Frederick's order for mobilization of his vassals which appeared to include not only those of the Kingdom, but those of the Duchy of Spoleto and the March of Ancona as well. Upon receiving the mobilization order Spoleto and Ancona affirmed their opposition to it unless it was sanctioned by the Pope, contending that these provinces no longer belonged to the Emperor but to the Church. Threatened with punishment unless they complied, they dispatched Frederick's letter to the Pope, who immediately remonstrated with him, taking him severely to task for wanton encroachment upon the Papal State. In no position to engage in a controversy with the Pope, whose assistance he obviously needed in carrying out his Lombard plans, and already at odds with the Curia over other matters, Frederick yielded, though not without resentment.[3]

Still another cause for irritation had arisen since the agreement at San Germano. This was Frederick's persistence in his efforts to influence episcopal elections in Sicily. Traditionally, as Frederick insisted,[4] for nearly 400 years his imperial predecessors had invested the bishops with ring and crozier. Moreover, during the vacancies of bishoprics in Sicily, the lands appertaining thereto had been treated as other feudal properties, and the revenues accruing from vacant episcopal estates,

---

[1] Huillard-Bréholles, ii, part ii, 924 ff.
[2] Ibid. 928 ff.; and F. Güterbock, 'Die Urkunden des Corio' (*Neues Archiv.* xxiii, 1896–7), 215 ff. See also E. Jordan, loc. cit.
[3] Richard of San Germano, 138.
[4] Huillard-Bréholles, ii, part ii, 932–3.

like those of fiefs of minors, became a part of the royal revenues. Often they proved lucrative sources, tempting the King to leave them vacant indefinitely. Five such vacancies existed in 1225—in Aversa, Brindisi, Capua, Conza, and Salerno—and some of them had long been without bishops, much to the irritation of Pope and Curia.

Frederick had also recently imposed a special *collecta*, levied on the clergy as well as the laity, which was regarded as much more onerous than usual. It is reported by Richard of San Germano that the tax levied on the monastery of Monte Cassino was 1,300 ounces of gold.[1] Equally offensive to the clergy was the reactivation of old laws such as that requiring the trial of clerks charged with murder or with treason before royal justices.[2]

In September 1225 Honorius had protested sharply against Frederick's meddling in the affairs of the Church. Shortly afterwards he sent another letter calling attention to the long duration of several episcopal vacancies, declaring that this 'redounded not only to the injury of the property but also to the soul', giving rise to criticism of both the Emperor and the Pope. He then announced that he had filled the vacancies with men of his own choosing, men of discretion and dignity, natives of the King-dom, whose characters were such as to be acceptable to the Emperor. At about the same time vacant abbacies in S. Vicenza on the Volturno and S. Lorenzo in Aversa received new abbots, nominees of the Pope, two monks from the monastery of Monte Cassino.[3] Honorius pursued his independent course still further when, in late December 1225, he rejected two rival candidates for the recently vacated bishopric of Bari and chose his own candidate, Canon Marino Filangieri.[4]

This procedure of the Pope was regarded by Frederick as arbitrary and contrary to agreements originally made with the Empress Con-stance in 1198, and with himself later, giving to the temporal sovereign the right to approve the choice of prelates.[5] Efforts by their respective embassies failed to achieve a reconciliation. The differences between Pope and Emperor were thus intensified at the moment when Frederick was passing through the lands of the Church to reassert his authority over the regions of Italy belonging to the Empire. The hostility that he found there among the Italian cities, together with the ever-growing tension in his relations with the papacy, seriously jeopardized both his efforts to reassert his authority and his crusading plans. For the sake of

---

[1] *Chronica*, 122: 'et tunc loco mutui collecte sunt de terra monasterii Casinensis uncie 1300 per Petrum dominum Ebuli et Nycolaum de Cicala.'

[2] P. Giannone, *Istoria civile del regno di Napoli*, ii: *La politia del regno sotto normanni e svevi*, Lib. XVI, ch. 5.

[3] Richard of San Germano, 122.

[4] F. Ughelli, *Italia sacra* (2nd edn., by Coletti), vii. 885.

[5] Richard of San Germano, 123, 135.

the crusade the Pope had revoked the interdict against Cremona, a city long allied with the Emperor and now the designated meeting-place for a diet.

But there existed now, as before, a bond of sympathy between the cities of the Lombard League and the Pope: their common opposition to the Emperor and his allies. The breaking-point was almost reached in March 1226 when Frederick II, while in Fano, ordered the vassals of Ancona to accompany him to Lombardy, threatening them with punishment if they failed to appear. He was thus encroaching on the Papal State, a matter on which the papacy was extremely sensitive. Already in 1222 the dispute over the Duchy of Spoleto and the March of Ancona, possessions which Frederick in his more helpless years had been compelled to surrender, had led to serious differences with the Pope and Curia. At that time Frederick's imperial legate, Gunzelin of Wolfen-büttel, in an effort to regain these territories for the Emperor, had driven out the papal officials. He had so roused popular resentment that Frederick was compelled to disclaim all responsibility for his legate's actions and to forbid him to undertake measures in opposition to the Apostolic See in future.[1] The Pope, however, was convinced, despite his protests of innocence, that Frederick himself had initiated the legate's actions.[2] Much as the Emperor coveted these regions which separated the imperial holdings in Italy, it is most improbable that he would have sanctioned at this time any action on the part of his legate that could have led to an irrevocable breach with the Pope.[3]

Nevertheless, the Pope and Curia had long been suspicious of the motives of the Emperor, and any action taken by him or by any of his adherents in Ancona or Spoleto would have been regarded by them as a sign of his aggressive intentions. The Pope did not dispute Frederick's right to provision his troops while passing through the Papal State *en route* to Cremona, where preparations for a crusade were to be made. It had been clearly established in the *Golden Bull of Eger* in 1213 that only for the purpose of receiving the imperial crown, or when summoned because of some need of the Church, was the Emperor to pass through or to obtain provisions from these lands of the Church.[4] At this time, therefore, the Pope assured Frederick that in consideration of the crusading plans the request for this privilege would have been granted. What the Pope did oppose was the employment of Sicilian forces within

---

[1] BFW, *Reg.* v, Abt. i, nos. 1410–17; and Ficker, *Forschungen*, ii. 435 ff. See also D. Waley, *Papal State*, 126 f.

[2] Winkelmann, *Acta*, ii. 718.

[3] The observation of Ficker, loc. cit., that any actions, if initiated by Frederick, 'sich aus einem entschiedenen Bruch mit der Kirche ergeben mussten. . . . Ein eigenmächtiges Vorgehen seiner Beamten und Anhänger ist da auch nicht gerade unwahrscheinlich.'

[4] *MGH, Const.* ii. 59. See also Migne, *PL* 217, 301 f.

the Empire in a manner which threatened the interests of the Church, and Frederick's treatment of the lands of the Church as if they were imperial fiefs, obliged to provide military service at his command. Frederick's apparent assumption that he had an independent right, without the consent of the Pope, to act in this way evoked from Honorius the bitter remark: 'You speak of yourself frequently as *advocatus* [steward] of the Church. Keep in mind, however, that this means nothing other than protector of the Church.'[1] One thing of significance emerges from this episode: Frederick II, despite his promises, did not regard the separation of Central Italy from the Empire as irrevocable.

Meanwhile, Frederick's irritation at the action of the Pope in filling the vacant bishoprics and abbacies without consulting him called forth a protest in which he revealed all the pent-up grievances, real or imaginary, which he had harboured against the papacy since his childhood. Unfortunately, this letter is lost, but its contents can be reconstructed with tolerable accuracy from the reply of Honorius III, who answered the complaints seriatim, and from a later manifesto of Frederick, following his excommunication by Gregory IX in 1227. He charged the Pope with violating the agreement that gave the Emperor the right to approve or disapprove of candidates elected to the vacant bishoprics. He complained of the ingratitude of Pope and Curia, citing his devotion to the interests of the Holy See, contrary to the advice of the princes. He insisted upon his past obedience to the Church, which he described as more sincere than that of his predecessors. With special bitterness he charged the Pope and Curia with sending enemies of the King into Apulia; with elevating Otto of Brunswick to the German throne, thus robbing him in his infancy of his birthright. Recalling the chaotic years during his minority, he asserted that the Pope and Curia had been concerned not with the interests of the papal ward but solely with the advantages to be obtained by the Church at the expense of the Kingdom. Finally, he complained that the Pope had provided protection for Apulian rebels who had defied the authority of the King.

The reply of Honorius to these and other charges, even more than Frederick's letter, reveals the resentment of the papacy towards him. Rarely had the papal Chancery produced a letter more richly adorned with rhetorical locutions, with more cutting satire, with more bitter irony, than that which it now prepared in reply to Frederick. 'If our letter has caused astonishment to you', the reply began, 'certainly yours has evoked greater astonishment in us. You say in effect that, contrary to the expectations of everyone, and to the advice of princes, if we may use your words, you have devoted yourself to our interests

---

[1] *MGH, Epist. Pont.* i, no. 296, p. 216; Huillard-Bréholles, ii, part i, 589 f.

and have been more obedient than your predecessors. The facts disprove each of these statements. If you will but compare your own actions towards the Church with those of other emperors of your family, you will find but few in which you take precedence . . . You accuse the Church of sending your enemies into Apulia under the pretext of protecting your interests; and of elevating Otto to the throne of your ancestors. What else could the Pope have done on your behalf, helpless and abandoned as you were? How can you invoke such charges against the Church which, next to God, was so considerate of your safety? What have you done for the Church—what can the Church hope for from you?' Honorius then reminded Frederick that the crown of Germany was not hereditary, but elective, and that Philip of Swabia had been unable to obtain it for his nephew, whereupon the princes of Germany elected Otto.

It is an extraordinary feature of this letter that Honorius pretends to be entirely oblivious of the role of his predecessor in attempting to force the election of Otto IV. After thus delineating these and many other shortcomings of Frederick, the Pope reminded him of the desire of the Holy See to mediate between John of Brienne and himself, insisting upon the injuriousness of their differences to the reputation of the Emperor.[1]

With regard to the crusade, the letter continues: 'You complain that we are placing heavy burdens upon you, and that we will not lift a finger to aid you, forgetting that you took the cross in Germany voluntarily, forgetting that in this business the Church has borne not a light burden in tithes, forgetting that through the preaching of our colleagues and others, many powerful and noble men, great and small, have taken the cross.' The letter then insists: 'In all our dealing with you we have had in mind your interests rather than our own. Yet, forgetting the words of you and your mother, and the arrangements of the holy fathers, you complain about the election of these prelates.' It deals also with the alleged encroachments of the papacy in the election of the bishops, reminding the Emperor that the manner of choice would indeed 'be most chaotic if the judgement of the Apostolic See was dependent upon your arbitrary action. Never would we elevate unworthy persons. But you must not permit your suspicions to extend too far. Do not forget that we, on our part, have far more complaints against you because of your violations of the freedom of the Church.'

The letter then ventures to state the intentions of Frederick: 'After casting aside the bishops, the pillars of the Church, you anticipate subjugation of the lesser clergy all the more easily.' The Emperor was reminded that 'the hand of the Lord has not yet become so weak that

[1] *MGH, Epist. Pont.* i, no. 296, pp. 216–22; Huillard-Bréholles, ii, part i, 588 ff., and iii. 37 ff.

it is unable to destroy the haughty and to humble the arrogance of the mighty. In the lustrous moment of success, therefore, do not depart from the humility which you displayed in adversity.'

It was the habit of Frederick II to think of the Kingdom of Sicily as it was in the days of his Norman ancestors: an independent sovereignty little troubled by the temporal intervention of the Pope. As he contemplated this letter it was apparent that the Pope and Curia had emerged as antagonists unjustly placing themselves in the way of the restoration of the Kingdom. They had, as Frederick believed, failed to protect his legitimate interests in his childhood. It was they who had wrested from his helpless mother numerous concessions that made it impossible for him to regain certain features of his sovereignty. It was they who would now willingly prevent the rehabilitation of the Kingdom, by forcing him, because of his youthful pledge at Aachen, to undertake a crusade before his authority had been re-established in Sicily and Apulia, and before the traditional imperial rights were recognized again in Central and Northern Italy. Indeed, it not infrequently appears in the course of this bitter exchange of letters that the interests of Pope and Curia were far less devoted to the crusade than to finding in the Emperor's anticipated absence an opportunity for checking the growth of his sovereign power.

PART IV

FREDERICK II AS CRUSADER

I

PRELIMINARY TO THE CRUSADE
THE RECALCITRANT LOMBARDS

Iue volgra, si dieus o volgues
Acsem cobrat Suria,
E'l pros emperaire agues
Cobrada Lombardia . . .

Piere Cardinal (C. A. F. Mahn, *Die Werke der Troubadours*), ii. 239.[1]

F EW events in the life of Frederick II offer greater possibilities for misrepresentation than his expedition into Lombardy in 1226. What, indeed, was his motive in undertaking this expedition, which from the outset showed so little likelihood of any desirable results? Was it his belief, perhaps, that his recent success in restoring order in the Kingdom of Sicily had so impressed the cities of the north that they would now voluntarily submit or show a more conciliatory attitude? The natural assumption is that his object was precisely what he stated in his letter: the reformation of the political status of the Empire (*reformatione status Imperii*). Certainly, this was the obvious and logical next step in a plan which contemplated first the establishment of the imperial dominance in Sicily, then in Italy, and finally, in Germany. In Central and Northern Italy he could thus secure a bridge between the Kingdoms of Sicily and Germany.[2] But was he so little aware of the political strength of the Lombard communes or of the particularistic sentiment among their citizens as to assume that their progress toward independence could be checked?[3] On the contrary,

---

[1]
  Would, if it please God,
  That we could have conquered Syria
  And that the worthy Emperor
  Could have recovered Lombardy.

[2] E. Abegg, *Die Politik Mailands in den ersten Jahrzehnten des 13. Jahrhunderts*, 99. See above, p. 101.

[3] Concerning the tendencies within these cities, especially during the first quarter of the thirteenth century, see E. Salzer, *Über die Anfänge der Signorie in Oberitalien* (*Hist. Studien*, Heft 14, 1900), 37 ff. See also Davidsohn, *Forschungen*, iv. 8 ff.; and idem, *Geschichte von Florenz*, ii. 29 ff. For Bologna see A. Hessel, *Geschichte der Stadt Bologna* (*Hist. Studien*, Heft 76, 1910), 33 ff.

he seems to have sensed fully the extent of the growth of this spirit of independence, recognizing that in a leading city such as Milan it must be crushed at any cost if, in the end, he was to realize the establishment of the Caesarian authority which was the goal of his every endeavour. It can hardly be doubted that, since his eight years' stay in Germany, Frederick had perceived that the goal of universal empire was to be attained only if first the Roman Church and the Lombard cities could be integrated within the fabric of the Empire in such manner that temporal sovereignty would rest solely in the hands of the Emperor. So too his years of experience since his imperial coronation in 1220 had revealed to him how essential it was that Italy and, indeed, Rome itself should become the centre of the restored Empire. It was this that he visualized when, in calling the Diet of Cremona, he mentioned as one of its purposes 'the restoration of imperial rights' or, as he phrased it in a letter to the *podestà* and people of Viterbo, 'jura imperii in statum optimum reformare'.[1] It is apparent throughout his reign that his concept of supreme temporal authority could brook no rivalry, even from the Holy See—that the eradication of such rivalry was, in fact, a *sine qua non* in the attainment of his goal. Likewise he regarded as incompatible with his concept of imperial sovereignty the unlimited autonomy of the communes. It is most improbable, however, that he contemplated at this time, as the members of the Lombard League feared, the subjugation of the communes of Northern and Central Italy, comparable to that already achieved in the Kingdom of Sicily. Nor is it probable that it was his intention at this time to initiate the regime which his later successes in 1236–8 made it possible for him to impose. It was only after the recovery of Vicenza, Padua, Treviso, and other regions, that he was in a position to impose an imperial administrative system compatible with his concept of empire.[2] Like his Norman predecessors, he was keenly aware of regional and ethnical differences. The machinery of government that he employed in Sicily, in Central and Northern Italy, or in Germany would always be adaptable to local characteristics while at the same time ensuring a firm imperial control. Milan and its allies continued as the most immediate barrier to the realization of his aim in Northern Italy, while Cremona and its allies offered a promising medium, now, as later, through which the pretensions of the Milanese and their allies could be checked. Frederick had no illusions as to the potentialities of the communes. He sympathized with and endeavoured to promote their economic development, but he was determined to check their political aspirations. Unlimited autonomy of these communes implied not only defiance of the Emperor

---

[1] Huillard-Bréholles, ii, part ii, 548.
[2] See below, p. 400, and E. Jordan, *Origines*, Introduction, pp. L ff.

but it meant also the ignoring of the traditional rights of the bishops in these cities, many of which had been usurped already.[1]

The superior resources of Milan, its numerous instruments of power, its consciousness of its own traditional strength and dignity, in contrast with other cities—all of these made it expedient, if not imperative, for smaller cities, not traditionally associated with Cremona, to seek refuge in the Lombard League, dominated by the Milanese. It was difficult for Milan to forget, as for other Lombard cities to ignore, the role of the proud city of St. Ambrose in the early years of triumphant Christianity when the Roman emperors:

> Holding in the left hand the golden orb
> Which symbolizes rule over kingdoms,
> In the right hand the sceptre of empire,
> In the manner of Julius, Octavianus, and Tiberius;
> Are supported on one side by the Roman Pope,
> On the other by Archbishop Ambrose.[2]

The communal or corporate ideal had taken possession of the imagination of the Northern and Central Italian communes. Their opposition to any form of external sovereignty was such as to ensure their will to resist the Emperor and, if need be, the Pope also. They were allies of the Pope only in so far as they recognized in him a powerful support in their resistance to the Emperor. Cremona, on the other hand, was traditionally bound to the Hohenstaufen emperor. This bond had been strengthened by a generous gift which the Countess Matilda of Tuscany had bestowed upon Cremona, including not only the city of Crema but also the so-called insula Fulcherii, between the Adda and Serio rivers. This gift became a source of continuous discord between Milan and Cremona, driving Cremona into the arms of the Emperor for protection.[3]

Expediency might well have dictated a reconciliation with the Lombard League in 1226, when its assistance could have been invaluable in Frederick's conflict with the Pope. There is reason to assume that, after the death of Otto IV in 1218, he could have obtained

---

[1] Huillard-Bréholles, ii, part ii, 704: 'ac relevare libertatem ecclesiasticam que ibidem multipliciter asserebatur oppressa.'

[2] *Benzonis Episcopi Albensis ad Henricum IV. Imp. Lib. I (MGH, SS.* xi), 602:

> Portans in sinistra aureum pomum,
> Quod significat monarchiam regnorum,
> In dextera vero sceptrum imperii
> De more Iulii, Octaviani, et Tiberii;
> Quem sustentant ex una parte papa Romanus,
> Ex altera parte archipontifex Ambrosianus . . .

[3] *Sicardi Episcopi Cremonensis, Cronica (MGH, SS.* xxxi), 162. See also Ficker, *Forschungen,* ii. 200, par. 301; Böhmer, *Acta,* no. 109, p. 101, for the grant: 'fideli nostro Tinto Cremonensi qui dicitur Mussa de Gatta.' See Stumpf, no. 3876.

the support of the Milanese.[1] A *rapprochement* would have been of doubtful value, leading inevitably to the alienation of Cremona while also convicting Frederick of ingratitude towards the most faithful of his supporters. His moral obligation to support Cremona was further strengthened when in August 1212, at Mantua, he had pledged himself to honour the former grant of Crema and the insula Fulcherii to Cremona and also had it 'sworn on his soul' that when he became Emperor he would protect the city in the holding of this grant.[2]

The approach of Frederick towards Lombardy in 1226, although with only a small army,[3] gave rise to rumours throughout Northern Italy of the fabulously large resources said to be available to him for the subjugation of the Lombards. Contemporaries spoke of riches greater than any since Charles the Great, of the abundant wealth of Sicily and Apulia.[4] The coming of the Emperor was hailed by others, both cities and magnates, with pleasurable anticipation. One Ghibelline chronicler reports: 'Just as out of season fish-spawn in a dried up river bed are revitalized when the water flows in again, so also the cities and magnates who in days of old had enjoyed the favour of his imperial majesty, hastened to join him once more when they were made aware of his imminence.'[5]

After a brief pause in Rimini, Frederick's first stop in imperial Italy, he proceeded about 22 April to Ravenna where, during the succeeding weeks, he was joined by some of the German prelates and princes.[6] Frederick's long delay in Ravenna is doubtless to be explained by the hostility of the Lombard League, which made it advisable to await the arrival of reinforcements from Germany that had been ordered to Lombardy under the leadership of his son, King Henry (VII).[7]

Aware of Frederick's order to his son to cross the Alps into Lombardy, representatives of the Lombard League assembled in a castle near Verona on 20 May, where they initiated a series of new measures intended to ensure the fullest possible co-operation of its members. They forbade all intercourse with cities not affiliated with the League and enjoined individual cities not to carry on correspondence with the Emperor or to communicate with him orally.[8] It was apparently at this

---

[1] Abegg, *Die Politik Mailands*, 99.

[2] Böhmer, *Acta*, 772; Ficker, *Forschungen*, ii, no. 373, p. 419.

[3] *Breve chronicon de rebus Siculis*, 897.

[4] *Chronica Albrici Monachi Trium Fontium* (*MGH, SS.* xxiii), 919; *Annales S. Justinae Patavini* (*MGH, SS.* xix), 152.

[5] *Annales Placentini Gibellini* (*MGH, SS.* xviii), 469.

[6] *Breve chronicon de rebus Siculis*, 897; *Cronica Reinhardsbrunnensis* (*MGH, SS.* xxx, part ii), 603–4.

[7] Richard of San Germano, 136.

[8] *Series instrumentorum super renovatione Societatis Lombardiae* (Huillard-Bréholles, ii, part ii, additamenta), 929 f.; and B. Corio, *Historia di Milano* (Venice, 1554), 89 f.

time also that the League made provision for blocking the passage of
the German King into Italy, an extreme measure, taken, it was said,
when the Emperor refused to confirm the treaty of Constance of 1183,
the Magna Carta of their regalian rights, until first the hostile cities
submitted unconditionally.[1] The determination to resist the Emperor
with every possible means is further indicated by what appears to have
been an invitation to John of Brienne, the estranged father-in-law of
the Emperor, to become their military leader. In any case John was
invited to Faventia (Faenza) at this time and was received there with
honour and entertained liberally.[2] If this was the object of his visit, and
the reason for the liberality of his hosts, John apparently refused whatever offer was made, probably out of consideration for the future interests of his daughter. It was only after her death and during Frederick's
absence in Syria that, at the behest of Gregory IX, John of Brienne assumed command of the papal forces in an attempt to wrest control of
the Kingdom of Sicily from the Emperor.[3]

It seems incredible that Frederick made no serious effort to oppose
the League by force and that his son Henry (VII), after waiting helplessly for six weeks near Trent, was but little disposed to join forces
with his father. The explanation is perhaps to be found in the kind of
troops accompanying him. His followers were chiefly mounted and
could enter Italy only through the narrow passes where the support of
foot soldiers was essential because of the nature of the terrain. Accordingly a contemporary poet wrote of Henry's coming:

> Though amply provided with troops
> But, I believe, not with infantry,
> He hastened to cross the mountains
> And to assist his father
> In the latter's evil designs.[4]

Reasons for the failure to take aggressive action may lie also in
Frederick's desire to avoid open conflict with the Lombard cities at this
time. It would otherwise be difficult to find justification for his patient
waiting for several weeks in Ravenna where, with some recently arrived
German princes, who had reached Italy by circuitous routes, he passed
the days, not in military preparations, but indulging his favourite
pastime, hunting with dogs and falcons. Meanwhile, the troops accompanying him on the expedition from Sicily were idly encamped in the

---

[1] *Chronicon Tolosani* (*Documenti di storia italiana: Cronache dei secoli XIII e XIV*, i), 719;
Muratori, *RIS*, new edn. xxviii, part i, 156.

[2] Muratori, *RIS* xxviii, part 1, 154: '. . . venit Faventiam; quem Faventini honorabiliter
recipere, [et] ei in omnibus largissime dederunt expensas . . .' See also *Ernoul*, 452 f.

[3] See below, pp. 211 ff.

[4] *Carmen Placentini De colloquio celebrato ab imperatore cum Cremonensibus et Parmensibus in loco
Burgi sancti Dompnini* (*MGH, SS.* xviii), 440, lines 16 ff. See also *Chronica regia Coloniensis*, 258.

vicinity of Faenza. The inactivity of Frederick and the effective blocking
of the Veronese pass to his son Henry served to embolden the League
and to stiffen its resistance to all reasonable conciliatory approaches.
When, at length, Frederick left Ravenna and when some of his troops
moved from their camp near Faenza, they were to witness something
of the hostility and arrogance of members of the League. Frederick
himself, abandoning his intention to negotiate personally with the
Bolognese, departed hastily in the direction of Cremona in order 'to
pass the city of Bologna at once and peacefully'. His troops, among
whom were some Germans, were met by open hostility in the vicinity
of both Faenza and Bologna. In Faenza a knight, mistaken by the
citizens for Frederick, was slain.[1]

On 14 May Frederick was reinforced by troops from the friendly
cities of Cremona, Parma, Reggio, and Modena, who escorted him to
Modena; his troops from Bologna and Faenza arrived there on the
following day. Proceeding then via Reggio, he reached Parma on 18
May. By this time he must have recognized the futility of his Lombard
expedition. His army had suffered greatly from the harassments of the
Lombards, and while in Parma he received news of the defection of the
city of Bergamo to the Lombard League.[2]

It was doubtless these incidents with the Lombard cities that determined Frederick to make a special effort to gain the support of the Pope.
He chose the most obvious approach, that of emphasizing his obligation to lead a crusade and the importance of removing all hindrances to
that enterprise. An opportunity presented itself in the recent arrival at
his court of Conrad of Urach, Cardinal of Porto, who had served the
Pope as special legate in Germany for matters pertaining to the crusade.
The initial step in this new approach was to send the Cardinal, accompanied by Hermann of Salza, Conrad of Hildesheim, the Archbishop of
Milan, and others, to negotiate with the leaders of the League and with
the more influential of the Lombard prelates. The immediate object of
the negotiations seems to have been to facilitate the entrance of King
Henry with his German following, emphasizing their role as crusaders.[3]
But by this time the arrogance of the League and their growing contempt
for the military weakness of the Emperor led them to impose conditions
which they themselves must have recognized as wholly unacceptable.[4]
The cities of the Lombard League agreed not to molest the Diet in so
far as it concerned itself with the crusade, provided the Emperor would

[1] *Cronica Reinhardsbrunnensis*, 604; *Chronicon Tolosani*, 718; Muratori (*RIS* xxviii, part i), 155,
note 5; *Annales Placentini Gibellini* (*MGH, SS.* xviii), 469: 'indubitanter credentes quod esset
imperator.'
[2] *Annales Bergomates* (*MGH, SS.* xviii), 810.
[3] BFW, *Reg.* v, Abt. i, no. 1620a.
[4] For details of the conditions see Huillard-Bréholles, ii, part ii, 609–12.

first release the major portion of the armed forces, contending that these forces were not necessary for the arrangements of a crusade. King Henry, still in Trent, was to be allowed passage with 1,200 mounted men. They demanded also that the Emperor formally recognize the League as reactivated in conformity with the Peace of Constance. The Emperor was to pledge himself not to proclaim the imperial ban during his sojourn in Italy.

The prestige of the Emperor has suffered immeasurably as a result of the contemptuous treatment by the cities of the Lombard League. His only advantage from these negotiations was the publicizing of the Diet of Cremona as intended primarily to further the crusading effort. It was through this that he had succeeded in enlisting the support of the bishops at his court who, in their manifesto of 16 June 1226, represented Frederick as coming into Italy 'peacefully through cities and highways, intending injury or trouble to none'. In the same document the bishops were zealous in their defence of the rights of the Emperor, describing him as the supreme law-giver who could not be prevented from the execution of his laws. They stated further that he claimed nothing more than the rights enjoyed by his predecessors. They concluded, therefore, that the demands made by the Lombard cities were impossible because they were dishonourable.[1]

This shifting of responsibility for the failure of the Diet by representing it as injurious to the crusading effort was, if nothing else, a clever diplomatic move in Frederick's relations with the Pope and Curia. Bishop Conrad of Hildesheim, the special legate of the Emperor in Italy charged with matters pertaining to the crusade, was now justified (and unanimously supported by the bishops at the court of Frederick) in proceeding against the cities of the League in accordance with the intentions of the papal mandate.[2] Before the actual imposition of the ban the Bishop of Hildesheim granted a delay to terminate by 24 June 1226, a date designated by the Emperor as terminal for the submission.[3] It is doubtful whether the Emperor expected the submission of the hostile cities, but he had obtained a striking advantage in that he had driven a wedge between the League and the Pope.

On 19 June Frederick began the evacuation of his court at Parma, sending his cooks in advance to Borgo San Donnino, and on 22 June he himself followed with his army.[4] A short time before, apparently about the middle of June, King Henry, after six weeks of idleness in the

---

[1] Ibid. 610. For the propagandist nature of the manifesto of the bishops see O. Vehse, *Die ämtliche Propaganda in der Staatskunst Kaiser Friedrichs II.*, 13 ff.

[2] Huillard-Bréholles, ii, part ii, 612: 'secundum formam mandati apostolici sententiando procedere contra eos de jure poterat et debebat.'

[3] Ibid. 643.

[4] *Cronica Reinhardsbrunnensis*, 605.

vicinity of Trent, began his homeward march.[1] His departure was marked by the burning of the city of Trent, whether by accident or by a deliberate incendiary act on the part of the withdrawing troops or camp-followers is not known. It was perhaps inevitable that contemporary Italian chroniclers saw in the burning only the latter, while German chroniclers saw in it either an accidental or coincidental catastrophe.[2]

But the date stipulated for the submission of the League came and passed without the appearance of the representatives of the cities before the Emperor. Probably in the belief, however, that the departure of King Henry and his troops might have altered the attitude of the League, Frederick was persuaded to permit the Patriarch of Jerusalem to attempt to reopen the negotiations.[3] The meeting took place at Marcaria, where at first the negotiations appeared to be making some progress, but the Milanese group persisted in offering proposals that were unacceptable. Again the negotiations failed and the ambassadors returned to the court on 10 July.[4]

The Emperor's expedition had been a disastrous failure. His prestige was seriously damaged throughout the world of Christendom. Whatever plans he had for the future of imperial Italy must necessarily be postponed to an indefinite future when, after completing his expedition to the Holy Land, he could devote his undivided attention to the restoration of his imperial authority in Italy. In retrospect it is apparent that these events of 1226 in Lombardy indicate already that the progress of the communes towards independence had advanced too far to be effectively checked by any resources available to a thirteenth-century Emperor. The grandiose ideas dominating the thinking of Frederick II were doomed to failure where Italy and Rome were concerned. Although Frederick apparently did not fully comprehend the magnitude of this failure or its portents for the future, it must have been a sadder and wiser Emperor who, on 18 July 1226, turned his back on Lombardy and began his return march to the Kingdom of Sicily.[5]

---

[1] He was still in Trent on 11 June and on 15 August he was in Ulm on the upper Danube: BFW, *Reg.* v, Abt. i, nos. 4008–10.

[2] *Chronica regia Coloniensis*, 258: 'in quorum discessu Tridentum civitas casuali incendio concrematur.' Richard of San Germano (Muratori, *RIS* vii), 138.

[3] Huillard-Bréholles, ii, part ii, 644.

[4] The *Carmen Placentini* (*MGH, SS.* xviii), 442, says of this meeting:

> Nichil fecit cum nuntiis,
> Quos tradere mendatiis
> Nisus est. Hec ut viderunt,
> Ad propria redierunt
> Decimo de Julio.

[5] His last extant document from Borgo San Donnino is dated 18 July 1226. See BFW, *Reg.* v, Abt. i, no. 1663.

This Lombard experience of 1226 is of the greatest consequence in that it marks a turning-point in the attitude of Frederick II towards the Pope and Curia. Throughout his earlier years in Sicily and in Germany, despite temporary differences, he revered the Pope and honoured the papal office as the spiritual vicar of God upon earth. Henceforth, a progressive change in his attitude is apparent in which he comes more and more to regard the Pope, not as a bona-fide spiritual leader, but as a temporal rival demanding supervisory rights over all states and all temporal policies.

On his homeward march an unfortunate incident further endangered his relations with Honorius III and threatened for the moment to alienate the Pope and Curia completely. The incident originated in the questionable activities of a Tuscan imperial vassal, Tancred of Campiglia, whose fief was adjacent to papal territory. Tancred was accused of intercepting messages and imprisoning the messengers of the Pope *en route* both to and from Rome. These messages were said to have been turned over to Reginald, Duke of Spoleto, the imperial legate in Tuscany, which gave rise to the suspicion that the Emperor himself was aware of this interference. Because of the long conflict between Pope and Emperor over the Duchy of Spoleto, Honorius believed this practice was associated with a scheme to restore the Duchy to imperial control. In an angry letter of 21 July 1226, which must have reached Frederick while he was passing through Tuscany or Spoleto, the Pope emphasized his disbelief that this practice could have been carried on without the Emperor's knowledge and contrary to his wishes. The suspicions of the Pope are all the more plausible in that Frederick at this time bestowed upon Tancred of Campiglia the castles of Faghina and Balni with all their appurtenances, as in the time of Frederick Barbarossa and Henry VI.[1] It is probable that this letter, together with another which reached Frederick about a month later, caused a sudden about-face on his part. The second letter may well have been regarded as an ultimatum demanding pointedly whether or not Frederick would accept in good faith 'that which Brother Leonardus [the papal ambassador] proposes to you . . .'.[2]

At the end of August Frederick sent the Pope a most conciliatory letter in which, after setting forth the injuries that the imperial dignity and the honour of the Empire had suffered at the hands of the Lombards, he agreed, in the interest of the crusade, to leave the mediation of the conflict between the Lombards and himself in the hands of the Pope and cardinals. There is, however, an implication in one passage of this letter that the Pope was not blameless in the failure of the Diet

[1] Huillard-Bréholles, ii, part ii, 633, 674. See also *MGH, Epist. Pont.* i, no. 306, pp. 233–4.
[2] Ibid., no. 307, p. 234.

of Cremona. 'In what measure', Frederick wrote, 'the interests of God himself were injured, in what measure the honour of the Roman Church, as well as that of ourselves and of the Empire, was disparaged, your Holiness will be able readily to perceive.'[1]

Frederick's willingness to abide by the papal mediation must have seemed to the Pope as sincere as it was miraculous. At the same time Honorius could not fail to recognize the difficulties inherent in his office as mediator. His cautious approach is apparent in his letter to the rectors of the League and in another letter addressed to the Bishops of Piacenza, Lodi, and Parma, urging them to co-operate in his efforts.[2] A few weeks later (1 October 1226) Frederick also gave assurance that he would make provision for the equipment and transportation for not only the numbers of crusaders designated in the San Germano Agreement but for all crusaders without distinction. He also gave assurance that ample ships would be in readiness at the designated ports and at the time agreed upon at San Germano.[3]

In the course of time the rectors of the League agreed to send plenipotentiaries to negotiate with the Emperor.[4] The negotiations in Rome progressed with remarkable speed and on 8 December 1226 an agreement was concluded.[5] Guided by this general agreement, the Pope formulated his judgement which he submitted to the Emperor and the cities of the League on 5 January 1227.[6] In substance, the papal judgement was as follows: The Emperor was to promise both for himself and for his son to pardon the alleged wrongs that he had suffered at the hands of the cities of the League. Both they and the Emperor were to free all prisoners and restore their property. Bans published against the rebellious cities, including the imperial edict closing the University of Bologna, were to be nullified. Both sides were to agree to eschew future ill will, to forget their past animosities, and to indulge in no further injurious acts. In other matters the papal judgement established the *status quo ante bellum*. Imperial ordinances against heretics, the harbourers of heretics, and the promoters of heresy were to be strictly enforced, without prejudice, however, to the ordinances of the cities. All statutes contrary to the liberties of the Church and the clergy were to be revoked. *Podestàs*, consuls, and rectors were to bind themselves by oath to the

---

[1] Huillard-Bréholles, ii, part ii, 677.

[2] *MGH, Epist. Pont.* i, nos. 309–10, pp. 235–6.

[3] See his letter to Master Arnold, crusading preacher in Germany, Huillard-Bréholles, ii, part ii, 678–80. Later, Pope Gregory IX referred to these promises in his encyclical letter preferring charges against Frederick. See ibid. iii. 26–7.

[4] *MGH, Epist. Pont.* i, no. 319, pp. 240 ff.

[5] Galvanus Flamma, *Chronica* (Muratori, *RIS* xi), col. 669; *Annales Placentini Guelfi* (*MGH, SS.* xviii), 443; John Codagnellus, *Annales*, 84; Richard of San Germano, 139.

[6] *MGH, Epist. Pont.* i, no. 327, pp. 246 ff. For other correspondence of the Pope with the League see ibid., nos. 328, 329, 330.

strict enforcement of the above articles. With respect to the crusade, the communes were to levy and maintain at their own expense 400 mounted troops for use by the Emperor in the Holy Land for a period of two years.

Although certainly not pleased with this judgement, Frederick presented his formal acceptance in a letter dated 1 February 1227.[1] The rectors, however, did not accept the terms promptly. Although they had far more reason to be satisfied with them than Frederick, they procrastinated in giving their approval, offering the flimsy excuse that the document had fallen into the water during its transmission and had become nearly illegible. Accordingly, they requested further delay. The reply of Honorius reveals the intensity of his bitterness and resentment. He dismissed their excuse as subterfuge, considering it a clumsy artifice for seeking to evade unequivocal acceptance, and accused them of wanton injury to the Roman Church, the Emperor, and to Christ himself, whose business—the crusade—was thus impeded. He angrily denied the requested delay, charging them to fulfil their obligations and to support the expedition to the Holy Land so that the Emperor could have no further reason to postpone his departure. Moreover, if they persisted in defying the Lord God and the Pope, he would be compelled to call upon the resources of Heaven and earth to chastise them.[2] But it was not until 26 March, a week after the death of Honorius III, that the Lombards submitted their formal acceptance.[3]

The one consolation of the dying Pope was, perhaps, his belief that a *rapprochement* between the Emperor and the Lombards was now in sight. It had apparently been in anticipation of this that he made a last appeal to Frederick for a reconciliation with John of Brienne. On 27 January, Honorius had named the former titular King as governor of the *patrimonium* between Radificone and Rome, with the exception of the March of Ancona, the Duchy of Spoleto, Reati, and Sabina.[4] In his letter to the Emperor he wrote: 'To whom more faithful would it be possible to entrust the Kingdom of Jerusalem? Who would be more welcome to the faithful living there? Who is more terrifying to the infidels? Who is more useful to the business of the Holy Land?'[5]

There is some evidence that a partial reconciliation may have been achieved when, towards the close of 1227, the father of Isabella of Brienne, 'moved by natural piety', expressed his willingness to release to Frederick the 50,000 silver marks given him by Philip Augustus to be employed in the recovery of the Holy Land.[6] This temporary reconciliation or

[1] *MGH, Const.* ii. 143–4. [2] *MGH, Epist. Pont.* i, no. 342, pp. 259–60.
[3] Huillard-Bréholles, iii. 5; *MGH, Epist. Pont.* i, no. 344, p. 263.
[4] Ibid. i, no. 339, pp. 257 f.
[5] Ibid. i, no. 338, p. 256 f.; Huillard-Bréholles, ii, part ii, 708–9.
[6] *Ex Chronici Turonensi* (*RHGF* xviii), 318.

attempted reconciliation was, at most, of brief duration, for, after the death of Isabella of Brienne, her father became an active leader of papal troops seeking to wrest the Kingdom of Sicily from Frederick's control.

Pope Honorius III had died on 18 March 1227, and on the following day Ugolino of Ostia and Velletra, a nephew of the late Innocent III, was chosen by the cardinals as Pope, taking the name of Gregory the Ninth.[1] Despite the intimacy of the new Pope with his predecessor, they represent contrasting types in temperament and in methods of procedure. To Honorius III a conciliatory policy invariably took precedence over harshness and obstinacy. He sought always to avoid conflict, to live in peace, trusting hopefully that the cherished goal of his pontificate, a successful crusade to the Holy Land, could at last be achieved. Gregory IX, on the other hand, knew little of conciliation or of patience. From the moment of his election he anticipated the impending conflict with the Emperor, whose good faith with respect to the crusade he had long doubted. It is often apparent also that to Gregory the crusade *per se* was far less important than it had been to Honorius III. It was, indeed, secondary to a much more ambitious goal: the complete triumph of the papacy over the Empire in the struggle for predominance in Christendom (the *societas Christiana*). His long and varied experience as cardinal, extending over a period of twenty-eight years, and his many diplomatic missions in the interests of the Holy See had enabled Gregory, as few other men of his time, accurately to appraise the aims and purposes of the Staufen Emperor. For him the moment had arrived when every instrument available to the Church must be resolutely employed to wrest from an ambitious temporal ruler the pretended sovereignty of the world. If his kinsman, Innocent III, had pointed the way to the full realization of the potentialities of papal authority, Gregory IX, master of the canon law that he was, travelled the route toward that end with boldness and sure-footedness.

Distinguished among canon lawyers of his era, patron of learning, skilful judge of men, masterful leader, he surrounded himself with men of like mind and temperament: Cardinals Godfrey of Castigilione of Milan, Sinibald Fiesco from Genoa, Rinaldo Conti of Anagni. These and others among his intimates belonged to that class of priest of whom Roger Bacon said: 'for every theologian among the cardinals there were twenty canon lawyers.'

Although an intimate friend and ardent admirer of St. Francis of Assisi and the first active protector of both the young Francis and his Order, Gregory's interest seems to have been less in the simple piety and practical virtues of the Order than in its usefulness in his struggle against widespread heresy. Indeed, the outstanding feature of his pontifi-

---

[1] *Vita Gregorii IX* (Muratori, *RIS* iii), cols. 575 ff.; also in *Liber Censuum*, ii. 19.

cate was his continuous conflict against heresy as shown by his numerous decretals on the subject, which contributed so greatly to the suppression of the Waldensians and the Cathari, and which led ultimately to the centralized papal Inquisition in various regions of Europe.

One is impressed inevitably by a certain ambivalence in the character of Gregory IX, a man of sincere piety, of exceptional learning, and friend and protector of the universities. His unquestionable virtues were often subordinated to what he accepted without qualification as the material as well as the spiritual interests of the Church. Vigorous in mind as in body, Gregory appeared impervious to the assault of senility. Indefatigable in the pursuit of his aims, he was incapable of acknowledging defeat. His eloquence was thought by his admirers to be comparable to that of Cicero. He wrote as he spoke with fiery zeal, employing all the rhetorical adornments of the fashionable Capuan school of rhetoricians. His policies, born always of his extreme views of papal authority, were pursued with obstinacy and inflexibility. Honorius III had leaned heavily upon Gregory who, as Cardinal of Ostia and Velletri, had served him well. In a letter of January 1217, during the early years of his pontificate, Honorius had described the Cardinal 'as a man after our own heart, acceptable to God and to man, forceful in word and deed, a distinguished member of the Church enjoying our confidence in all things—among all our brothers most esteemed by us'.[1]

At the time of Ugolino's elevation to the papal office the concept of the Pope as the Vicar of Christ had become fixed in both theology and canon law. The hierocratic organization of society, conceived to be the *societas Christiana*, was thought to be necessarily subject to the government of the head of the Church, no longer merely the successor of St. Peter, but, through him, Vicar of Christ, the King of Kings, and the Lord of Lords. To Gregory IX and his canonistic contemporaries, the Pope was truly a monarch, the source of all governmental authority.[2] Accordingly, no obligation of the Vicar of Christ was greater than that of controlling the use of the temporal sword, the sword for the punishment of evil-doers, to be wielded at the Pope's bidding by the temporal sovereign. Gregory IX accepted unequivocally the opinion expressed long before by St. Bernard of Clairvaux that, although the temporal ruler was entrusted by the Pope with the material sword, it was not to be drawn from its sheath by his own hand.[3] If Gregory IX and his

---

[1] *MGH, Epist. Pont.* i, no. 12, p. 10. The conclusion of M. Maccarrone, *Potestas directa e Potestas indirecta nel teologi del XII e XIII sècolo* (*Misc. hist. pont.* 18, 1954), 27 ff., that the *potestas directa* developed only gradually in canonical thinking during the last half of the thirteenth century fails to place sufficient emphasis upon its development under Gregory IX.

[2] See also W. Ullmann, *The Growth of Papal Government*, 283, 419; and A. M. Stickler, '*Imperator vicarius Papae*' (*MIöG* lxii, 1954), 165–212.

[3] Ullmann, op. cit. 431, note 1.

immediate successors were ruthless in their efforts to protect this God-given authority it was not for reasons of selfish ambition or greed, but rather in their deeply ingrained conviction as theologians and canon lawyers that it was their supreme obligation to do so, even though, at times, sacrificing their pastoral duties while struggling to maintain their supreme authority.

To Gregory IX it was a cause of acute anguish and, ultimately, of all-pervading hatred that the former ward of Pope Innocent III, who had shown such docility towards his guardian during his childhood, now stood defiantly against the Holy See. Even more, he looked upon Frederick as the champion of a form of Caesarism determined to restore to the Holy Roman Emperor and to the King of Sicily the full sovereign rights of the pre-Constantinian emperors. Frederick, on his side, had no illusions as to the intentions of Gregory IX, depicted by imperial propagandists as boasting openly of his unlimited power. A propagandist diatribe, certainly written vindictively and unsupported by the prevailing contemporary opinion, describes Pope Gregory seated with companions at his bountiful table, buoyed in spirit by an abundance of wine, discoursing upon the future world dominance of the papacy. On such occasions he is said to have visualized the subjugation of the Empire to the papal will. He is depicted as imagining the Pope, seated upon his throne, surrounded by the assembled kings and princes of the earth bearing rich gifts and, at his bidding, leading armies destined to augment and to protect the far-flung papal realm.[1] Whatever exaggeration may appear in unfriendly characterizations such as this, Gregory IX anticipated at this time the scene of opulence and splendour which was to be briefly realized in the great jubilee of the year 1300, in the pontificate of Pope Boniface VIII.

Gregory IX, like most of the canonists influenced by doctrines that had become crystallized during the thirteenth century and, even more, by the hierocratic ideology as developed earlier by John of Salisbury, held that 'each of the swords was given to the Church, but one of them is wielded by the Church, and the other is ordered by the Church to be wielded.'[2] As the staunch supporter of St. Francis of Assisi and a friend of the Minorite Order as a whole, it was to be expected that Gregory IX would share something of their simple piety and their deep consciousness of the needs of humanity. Far from that, he saw in the Minorites useful agents in the achievement of his God-ordained goal, the supreme

---

[1] Huillard-Bréholles, v, part i, 311: 'Tunc tibi Romanorum subest imperium; tunc adferunt tibi munera reges terre; tunc vinum mirabiles facit exercitus; tunc tibi serviunt omnes gentium nationes.'

[2] *MGH, Epist. Pont.* i, no. 672, p. 568. See John of Salisbury, *Polycraticus*, Bk. IV, ch. iii. It is obvious also that Gregory IX was influenced by similar remarks of Bernard of Clairvaux, *De Consideratione*, IV, 3, col. 776.

authority of the Pope in temporal as in spiritual things. He did not hesitate to employ them in the most unworthy roles in his conflict with the Emperor. He pursued his policy towards papal world dominion with all available temporal as well as with all ecclesiastical weapons. To the mind of Gregory IX his conduct towards the Emperor could not be judged as either immoral or unethical. He saw himself as the guardian of a sacred trust, the Vicar of Christ seeking to preserve the *societas Christiana* from the ruthless encroachments of an evil and ambitious temporal sovereign. His methods of accomplishing this were unrelated to the standards of conduct common to mankind. They were subject only to the judgement of God whose representative upon earth he believed himself to be. It was not the immediate events of 1227 that gave rise to his implacable opposition to Frederick II. It was the cumulative grievances of the entire Hohenstaufen era which now, under the brilliant direction of the most skilled of the Staufen, threatened to engulf the Christian state. Gregory saw in Frederick's long-standing obligation to undertake a crusade the supreme opportunity for crippling, if not destroying, the Hohenstaufen menace. He perceived clearly that the crucial step was the annihilation of Frederick II.

Whereas Honorius III pretended to pursue a middle course between the Lombard League and the Emperor, Gregory IX made no effort to conceal his alliance with the communes. The agreement to which the League had reluctantly subscribed before the death of Honorius III was still wanting the signature of the Marquis of Montferrat and several Lombard cities. Ignoring these deficiencies, Gregory forwarded to the Emperor, not the entire agreement, but an imperfect abstract, oblivious of the inevitable suspicion that such action would arouse, that a secret understanding existed between the Curia and the Lombard League. This suspicion was ultimately confirmed when the 400 troops, pledged by the communes for Frederick's use in the Holy Land, never made their appearance.[1]

---

[1] Röhricht, *Beiträge*, i. 17; and note 91, p. 63.

II

FREDERICK II TURNS BACK
HIS EXCOMMUNICATION

Daz kriuce man für sünde gap
z'erloesen daz, vil hêre grap:
daz wil man nû mit banne wern,
wie sol man nû die sêle ernern?

Freidank, *Bescheidenheit* (ed. Sandvoss), 119.[1]

As Gregory IX found it expedient to favour the Lombards, so he found it opportune to prod Frederick to accomplish his crusading expedition. His first letter to the Emperor, dated 23 March 1227, was a thinly veiled threat. He admonished Frederick faithfully to fulfil his vow, while warning him: 'Beware lest you place each of us in a position from which, even with the best will, we perchance cannot easily extricate you.' He was apparently already so firmly convinced of the Emperor's intention to violate his pledge that he made no effort to conceal his suspicion.[2] Contrary to the papal expectations, however, the preparations of the Emperor had moved forward rapidly since January 1227, and they were of a nature to leave little doubt of his sincerity of purpose.

In the place of zealous priests, the chief agents of recruitment in the past, Frederick now attracted his crusading army with generous promises or with extensive grants of money and estates. Far beyond the obligations that he had assumed at San Germano, he offered free provisions and transportation to all crusaders, kings, princes, prelates, and simple knights and squires.[3] It was with such offers that he obtained the support of princes and magnates, including the Duke of Limburg, the Count of Urach, and some 700 Thuringian and Austrian knights. Even with these generous offers, the number of effective troops assembled at the port of embarkation was small. Certainly swarms of lowly pilgrims gathered there, but these were untrained as warriors, often pious old men and women impelled by religious zeal, or others moved by the

---

[1] The cross was given that one might be redeemed from sin,
     As was also the Holy Sepulchre.
     Now that one is denied these by the ban
     How can one save one's soul?

[2] *MGH, Epist. Pont.* i, no. 343, pp. 261–2. See also Huillard-Bréholles, iii. 3.

[3] Huillard-Bréholles, iii. 39 ff.; Röhricht, *Beiträge*, 18–19.

spirit of adventure. Typical of these were the pilgrims from England, who, although described by a monkish chronicler as 'tried men', are said to have pledged themselves as crusaders, impelled by the miraculous apparition of a cross in the sky.[1]

Obtaining money to meet the crusading expenses was the all-important problem. Frederick had obligated himself at San Germano to raise huge sums for the purpose of building the necessary ships and for meeting other expenses. These sums had to be raised mainly by the imposition of new crusading taxes, mostly levied upon the great monastic foundations. Monte Cassino is said on one occasion to have provided 450 ounces of gold.[2] It is a remarkable tribute to the soundness of the national economy of the Kingdom of Sicily that Frederick was able to meet promptly the instalment payments that had been required of him by the agreement of San Germano. Mercenaries were obtained from whatever sources were available. Some 250 knights formerly in the service of the Pope were now included among the mercenaries of the Emperor.[3] This body of 250 troops, together with 700 levied in Thuringia and 100 in the immediate following of the Emperor, provided a force superior in numbers to the 1,000 troops for which he had pledged himself at San Germano.[4]

During the summer of 1227 the masses of pilgrims coming from all regions of Europe streamed into Brindisi, the designated port of embarkation.[5] It would be idle to estimate their numbers. Contemporary chroniclers speak either in general terms or else with obvious exaggeration.[6] Doubtless because of Frederick's generous promise to provide transportation for all crusaders, many indigent and idle put in their appearance at Brindisi. The route via Barletta southward through Bari was thronged by those who had chosen to travel overland. As the human flood-tide was reached at midsummer, inevitable disease, aggravated by the intense heat, by insanitary living conditions, and by the un-accustomed way of life, attacked large numbers of the pilgrims. Many succumbed to the plague and others, terrified by the sight of disease and death, hastily returned home, leaving numerous empty transports in the harbour. The more hardy awaited the completion of preparations and, in early September, many of them sailed for Syria.[7]

---

[1] Roger of Wendover, iv. 144. See also *Annales Monasterii de Waverleia* (Rolls Series), 303.

[2] Richard of San Germano, 146.

[3] J. Mikulla, *Der Söldner in den Heeren Kaiser Friedrichs II.*, 28; E. Kestner, *Der Kreuzzug Friedrichs II.*, 26–7.

[4] Huillard-Bréholles, iii. 45. See also T. C. Van Cleve, 'The Crusade of Frederick II' (*A History of the Crusades*, ii: *The Later Crusades*, ed. R. L. Wolff), 447.

[5] John Codagnellus, 85.

[6] See, for example, *Cronica Reinhardsbrunnensis* (*MGH, SS.* xxx, part i), 609; Roger of Wendover, iii. 149; *Annales Monasterii de Waverleia* (Rolls Series), 303.

[7] Huillard-Bréholles, iii. 43.

Before embarking Frederick and the Landgrave of Thuringia had been attacked by the plague and, while *en route* southwards, the Landgrave died. Meanwhile the condition of Frederick had worsened and he resolved to disembark and to await recovery, announcing his intention of resuming the journey the next May. In order that the expedition as a whole might not be delayed, he placed twenty galleys at the disposal of the Master of the German Order and the Patriarch, designating Duke Henry of Limburg as his deputy in command of the crusaders, pending his own arrival in Syria.[1] Frederick then hastened to Pozzuoli, near Naples, a resort long famous for its health-giving mineral baths. After some weeks devoted to recuperation, he proceeded to Capua, remaining in the general vicinity of that city during the latter part of November.[2]

After his decision temporarily to forgo the voyage, he sent an embassy to Rome to explain the circumstances of his return from Otranto. But the Pope, in no mood to hear even valid excuses, refused to receive his embassy. On 29 September 1227 Gregory proclaimed the ban. There is no evidence that the Pope made the slightest effort to ascertain the truth or falsity of the Emperor's reported illness, although contemporary sources are generally agreed that he was too ill to continue the voyage.[3] The failure of Gregory to investigate, his unseemly haste in pronouncing the ban, and his various denunciations of the Emperor suggest that he had no interest in ascertaining the truth. He appears rather to have seized this propitious moment for the destruction of a formidable rival. Moreover, his continued attitude of unreasonableness suggests the probability that he was far more pleased with the turn of events than he would have been if Frederick had been successful in his expedition. His encyclical letter in which he set forth the specific charges against Frederick[4] was necessarily devoted primarily to the Emperor's repeated postponements and his ultimate failure to undertake the expedition. In singular contrast with this, his letter to the Emperor at the end of October 1227,[5] setting forth the reasons for proclaiming the ban, was concerned not so much with the failure of the crusade as with Frederick's alleged encroachments upon the suzerain rights of the Holy See in Sicily. In this letter the Pope dwelt especially upon the oppression of the Church and the persecution of the counts and others who had feudal obligations towards the Holy See. Above all, he complained that the clergy throughout the Kingdom of Sicily, notwithstanding that Frederick held it merely as a fief from the Church, had suffered many wrongs.

[1] Richard of San Germano, 147; Huillard-Bréholles, iii. 44.
[2] BFW, *Reg.* v, Abt. i, nos. 1711 ff.
[3] *Breve chronicon de rebus Siculis*, 897: 'Et superveniente infirmitate transire non potuit.' *Eracles*, 364: 'maladie prist al empereor par quoi il ne se pot metre en mer.' See also Huillard-Bréholles, iii. 44.
[4] Huillard-Bréholles, iii. 23–30.
[5] Ibid. 32–4.

Some prelates, he declared, had been sent into exile, the churches, hospices, and other religious foundations despoiled. Still avoiding the issue for which, ostensibly, the Emperor was excommunicated, the Pope then continues: 'We can no longer tolerate these acts or, with good conscience withhold our punishment. It profiteth a man nought if he gain the whole world to the detriment of his soul.' He then assured the Emperor of his readiness to restore him to favour if he would but return to the way of justice. Otherwise, 'we shall proceed accordingly as God and justice dictate'. But, vaguely concealed beneath these remarks about Sicily was the demand that Gregory was actually making of his rival: the abandonment of all sovereign claims to Sicily and the unqualified recognition of the feudal lordship of the Holy See. In return for this he would revoke the ban.

To the Christian world Gregory spoke in different language. His charges against the Emperor were set forth in an encyclical letter of 10 October 1227, which was all-comprehensive, exaggerated, and cleverly misleading.[1] He recalled how Frederick, the orphaned infant, had been taken into the protection of the Church 'as if from his mother's womb' (*quasi a matris utero excepit*), nourished on the milk of the Church, rescued by her from the hands of his would-be murderers, educated and protected in her strong arms until he attained his maturity. The Church, he said, had thought to find in this child 'a rod and staff' for its support. It had elevated him first to the dignity of King and then to the lofty imperial office. Gregory then related how Frederick, after being summoned to Germany to receive the crown, 'voluntarily and without advice, unknown to the Holy See', had taken the cross. Later he had suggested excommunication for himself and for others who wantonly failed to fulfil their pledges at a specified time. But, in violation of these pledges, he had asked for numerous postponements, even after having renewed his crusading vow in the basilica of St. Peter following his imperial coronation. Gregory reviewed also the history of Ferentino and San Germano and of Frederick's marriage to the heiress of the Kingdom of Jerusalem. With especial bitterness he told of the Emperor's voluntary agreement to suffer excommunication if, within two years, he did not sail with 1,000 knights to be maintained in the Holy Land at his own expense for two years. He reviewed also the other promises of the Emperor: his agreement to provide gold to be held until his arrival in Syria; to outfit 100 transports and 50 galleys. Gregory turned then to the assembling of the crusaders in Brindisi, charging the Emperor with wanton neglect; with responsibility for the sickness and death of large numbers of the assembled pilgrims. 'He delayed the Christian army', says Gregory, 'in the summer heat in an insalubrious climate until many

[1] Huillard-Bréholles, iii. 23 ff.

died, not only a great part of the common pilgrims, but not a few nobles and magnates, from pestilence, from thirst, and from many other afflictions.' The Pope mourned especially the deaths of the Bishop of Augsburg and the Landgrave of Thuringia. Of Frederick's failure to depart, he says: 'He, however, contemptuous of all promises . . . was allured by the customary pleasures of his Kingdom, making a frivolous pretence of illness.' In conclusion Gregory summarized the specific reasons for Frederick's excommunication: 'He did not cross the sea at the prescribed time . . . he did not lead there the 1,000 soldiers to be maintained at his expense for two years. He did not transmit the pre-arranged sum of money.' Failing in the faithful fulfilment of these articles of his agreement, Frederick, in the language of the Pope, 'entangled himself voluntarily in the meshes of the aforesaid excommunication'.[1]

But some of these charges were patently false and, in large measure, they justify the observation of a contemporary that the action of the Pope was 'instigated by the devil' (*papa diabolo instigante*).[2] It is true that the Emperor had not departed at the appointed time. Had Gregory limited himself to this single charge he would have been, in a strictly legal sense, justified in proclaiming the excommunication. Morally and humanely speaking, he was guilty of inexcusable harshness and of incredible callousness in demanding the punctual departure of a leader whose serious illness appears to have been amply vouched for by companions whose reliability can hardly be questioned. Contemporary evidence leaves no reasonable doubt that the Emperor, like the Landgrave of Thuringia, who succumbed on 11 September, was seriously ill.[3] As to the other charges, the Emperor had in fact enlisted the services of more than the 1,000 troops required by the terms of the agreement and had paid regularly the instalments of the 100,000 ounces of gold that he had pledged.[4]

Even less justifiable was Gregory's charge that the Emperor, in choosing the port of Brindisi, situated as it was in a 'foul and deadly climate', was responsible for the sickness and death of so many crusaders. Brindisi had been regularly chosen by crusaders as one of the most appropriate ports of embarkation. Innocent III and the prelates and princes in arranging the details of the Fifth Crusade during the Fourth Lateran Council had designated both Brindisi and Messina as ports of departure.[5] There can be no adequate reason to assume that Frederick

---

[1] 'Sed in his tribus articulis manifeste deficiens in excommunicationis descripte laqueum ultroneus se ingessit . . .' Huillard-Bréholles, iii. 29.
[2] *Notae Sancti Emmerami* (*MGH, SS.* xvii), 573.
[3] See above, p. 196, note 3.
[4] Huillard-Bréholles, iii. 45.
[5] F. Hurter, *Innozenz III*, ii. 693; A. Luchaire, *Innocent III: Le Concile de Latran*, 55 f.

had ever pledged himself to feed or to transport the hordes of common pilgrims such as many of those who jammed the roads to Brindisi in 1227. His promises were obviously intended to apply solely to crusaders, of whatever degree, capable of bearing arms or otherwise performing essential duties of a military expedition. One can only conclude, therefore, that these charges reveal every evidence of wanton misrepresentation intended to prejudice public opinion and to derogate the Emperor in the eyes of all Christians. Under the pressure of this ill will of the world of Christendom, Frederick might be expected to submit unqualifiedly to the papal demands, above all to the stipulations of the Curia regarding Sicily. From the Pope's letter to the Emperor, so singularly in contrast with his encyclical, this was the unmistakable *quid pro quo* for the lifting of the ban. That the Pope was guilty of misrepresentation is further suggested by his making use in 1239, at the time of the second excommunication of Frederick, of the wholly unsupported gossip that Frederick had poisoned the Landgrave of Thuringia.[1] It would be difficult to conceive of any loss among the Emperor's close associates on this expedition that could have provided a greater cause of grief than the death of his most capable lieutenant and faithful friend.

In replying to these charges in a letter addressed to 'crusaders everywhere',[1] Frederick revealed a studied restraint, in marked contrast with the irresponsible attack of the Pope. His reply is characterized by moderation, calmness, and sincerity of tone. He wrote:

We speak reluctantly, but we cannot dissemble that which we have too long kept silent: that the hopes which have deceived many have perhaps deceived us also. We appear to be approaching the end of time in which love is seen to grow cold not only in its branches but in its roots. For, not only does people rise against people, not only does kingdom menace kingdom, not only do pestilence and famine fill the hearts of the living with terror, but charity itself, by which both heaven and earth are ruled, is threatened not just in its streams, but at its very source. The Roman Empire, ordained of Divine Providence as defender of the Christian faith, is seriously threatened not by the lowest but by those whom it honours and whom it had considered as fathers . . . what can we do when the Vicar of Christ, the successor of the blessed Peter, in whom we had placed our trust, viciously and unworthily attacks our person, and seems totally devoted to exciting hatred against us?

Frederick then appealed to all Christendom to hear the provocations suffered by him at the hands of the Church, 'our stepmother' (*matris*

[1] Huillard-Bréholles, v, part i, 329.
[2] Huillard-Bréholles, iii 37 ff.: 'universis crucesignatis.'

Ecclesie in filium novercantis). He answered seriatim the papal charges
against him, employing the arguments noted above.[1]

His self-defence, however, was ignored by Gregory, who simply dismissed it by refusing to receive the imperial ambassadors.[2] In short,
Frederick must first appeal to the Pope as a penitent sinner, submitting
helplessly to demands that would completely nullify his claims to the
sovereignty over Sicily. By accepting the Pope's terms Frederick would
have recognized precisely those claims that the thirteenth-century
canonists, of which Gregory was an articulate member, persistently
made with respect to the *plenitudo potestatis* of the papal office.[3]

Acutely aware of the extreme claims of the Curia and conscious of the
obstinacy of Gregory IX in pressing home his advantage, Frederick now
determined to enlist the support of the monarchs of Europe, especially
the Kings of England and France, in opposing what he believed to be an
insatiable lust for temporal power by the Pope. The letters addressed to
these Kings are more than the fulminations of an angry Emperor; they
are in fact the beginning of a series of such letters extending over the
next two decades in which Frederick II, as the foremost sovereign of
Europe, sought to arouse the temporal rulers to a consciousness of the
dangerous encroachments of the papacy. They are in every respect
prophetic of the rising storm of protest which a half-century later was
to overwhelm Boniface VIII. To the King of England Frederick wrote:
'Has not the King of England seen his father, King John, held in excommunication until both he and his Kingdom were made tributary?'
He called attention to the Count of Toulouse and other princes whose
persons and whose lands the Curia endeavoured to keep under excommunication and the interdict until they were reduced to subserviency. Frederick wrote also of the abuses of simony, of usury, and of
various exactions made by the Church of Rome by which the whole
Christian world was infected. He scoffed at the honeyed words of the
clergy, 'insatiable leeches, their language sweeter than honey, softer than
oil'. He reminded the barons of England how King John had been
described in the bulls of Innocent III as the obstinate enemy of the
Church. But, when the King submitted his person and his Kingdom to
the Holy See that same Pope, insensitive to shame and contemptuous of
the fear of God, crushed those whom he had imperilled. He warned
against the traps set by the prelates in which they sought to ensnare one
and all, to extort money, to oppress the free, to disturb the peace of the
world: 'Disguised in sheep's clothing, these ravenous wolves send legates

---

[1] See above, pp. 198 ff.

[2] Huillard-Bréholles, iii. 44: 'nuntios nostros recipere noluit nec audire.'

[3] Concerning these extreme views of the thirteenth- and fourteenth-century canonists see
especially J. Rivière, *Le Problème de l'Église et de l'État au temps de Philippe le Bel*, 58 ff. See also
W. Ullmann, *Medieval Papalism*, 151–3, 163, 187, 195.

hither and thither to excommunicate, to suspend, to punish—not as sowers of seed, that is the Word of God, but to extort money, to harvest and reap that which they did not sow.' Frederick then turned to a theme that from now on was ever-recurrent in his thinking and writing: the departure of the Church from the simplicity of its founders. Like the Franciscans and Dominicans and, in the spirit of the seer of Calabria, Joachim of Floris, he conjured up a picture of the simplicity, even of the poverty, of the primitive Church so abundantly demonstrated in the lives of the saints. 'No man', he said, 'can erect the Church on a foundation other than that laid by the Lord Jesus himself.' He concludes his letter with an appeal to the princes of the earth to unite and take measures against this avarice, this evil, admonishing them 'to look to your own house when that of your neighbour is on fire'.[1]

Alone of the sovereigns of his era, Frederick II thought he recognized in the thinking of Gregory IX what he believed a serious distortion of the theory long before attributed to Pope Gelasius I: 'The spiritual and temporal powers are entrusted to two different orders, each drawing its authority from God, each supreme in its own sphere and independent within its own sphere from the others.'[2] In every act of Gregory IX Frederick saw the emerging of a theory far removed from the so-called Gelasian theory, comparable to that of Bernard of Clairvaux, and more daring than that of Innocent III. To the mind of Frederick, the Emperor and Pope shared a common responsibility for the maintenance of peace upon earth, for the eradication of heresies, for the subjugation of rebellions, and for the crusades against the infidel.[3] It is a remarkable feature of the thinking of Frederick II that from the humiliating obligations forced upon him at San Germano, so degrading to the imperial dignity, he came to regard the Pope as a positive enemy of the Christian faith. This attitude was intensified by each new conflict until, in the full bitterness of his frustration, he exclaimed: 'From him in whom all men hope to find salvation of body and soul comes evil example, deceit, and wrongdoing.'[4]

After the excommunication, as Frederick proceeded with his plans for a new expedition in May, the fleet which had sailed in August must have arrived in Syria not later than early October. Soon afterwards the twenty galleys, dispatched by Frederick from Otranto, arrived. In the absence of 'the crowned king from the west' mentioned in the Treaty of Damietta in 1221, Duke Henry of Limburg, although authorized as

---

[1] Matthew Paris, *Chronica majora*, iii. 153: 'Tunc tua res agitur, paries cum proximus ardet.'
[2] Gelasius, *Epistolae*, viii (Mansi, *Sacrorum Conciliorum Collectio*), 31. See also Migne, *PL* 59, cols. 41 ff.; and R. W. and A. J. Carlyle, *Mediaeval Political Theory*, i. 175–6, 184–93.
[3] This concept is most fully and maturely presented in a letter of Frederick to the cardinals in 1239: Huillard-Bréholles, v, part i, 348 ff.
[4] Ibid., part ii, 706.

imperial deputy, was faced with a difficult decision. The morale of the
crusaders deteriorated constantly through the effects of illness and
uncertainty as to their future usefulness. The unthinking masses
of pilgrims clamoured for aggressive action. Many, discouraged by
the failure of the Emperor to sail, had already returned home. The
statement of the Pope, however, that 40,000 had returned may be dismissed as an exaggeration.[1] Disinterested sources leave no doubt that
large numbers of those who had sailed from Brindisi returned home.
Duke Henry's decision to break the truce and to move against the
Muslims before the arrival of Frederick the following May was doubtless a desperate step to check the disintegration of the crusading force.
The German troops, no less than the masses of the pilgrims, wanted
either to attack or to return home. Fortunately, Duke Henry was able
to find temporary employment for many of the discouraged crusaders in the much-needed restoration of Caesarea and Jaffa. While this
fortifying of the two port cities was clearly in violation of the treaty, it
did not stir the Arabs to attack. The sudden death of al-Muʿaẓẓam,
Governor of Damascus, contributed to the immediate safety of the
crusaders. Taking advantage of this opportunity, French crusaders
seized and attempted to reclaim the whole of the city of Sidon, half of
which had long been in possession of the Muslims. At the same time
the Germans began the reconstruction of Montfort (Qalʿat al-Qurain)
near Acre, later to become headquarters for the Teutonic Order in
Syria.[2]

The failure of the Muslims to offer active resistance to these encroachments is to be explained by the unrest in Syria and Egypt. The sons and
heirs of the late Sultan of Egypt, al-ʿĀdil, had long been involved in
bitter family feuds which seriously threatened the peace of the Muslim
world. The chief rivals were al-Kāmil, Sultan of Egypt since his father's
death, and his brother al-Muʿaẓẓam, Governor of Damascus. By 1225
this rivalry had attained such intensity that al-Kāmil was persuaded
that his brother threatened the sultanate itself. This danger was all the
more alarming because al-Muʿaẓẓam had formed an alliance with
Jelāl-ad-Din, Shah of Khorezm, a region extending from the lower
Oxus across the steppes westwards to the Caspian Sea, traditionally
hostile to the Aiyūbid sovereigns. In desperate fear, al-Kāmil, forgetting
for the moment the threat from the crusaders, and more concerned with
the preservation of his Egyptian realm than with the retention of Jerusalem, appealed to Frederick II for assistance. The Egyptian historian,

---

[1] See the letter of Gregory quoting the Patriarch of Jerusalem in Matthew Paris, *Chronica
majora*, iii. 128. For this and for the full account of the Crusade see T. C. Van Cleve, 'The
Crusade of Frederick II' (loc. cit.), 447 ff.

[2] *Ernoul*, 459.

Maqrīzī, relates that in the year 1226 'Malek al-Kāmil sent the Emir
Fakhr-ad-Dīn to the Emperor, "King of the Franks", to ask him to
come to Acre, promising him many cities of Palestine which belonged
to the Muslims if he would attack al-Mu'aẓẓam.'[1] These negotiations,
begun in 1226, appear to have been carried on throughout 1227, probably by Thomas of Acerra as the Emperor's *bailli* in Syria. Some time
in 1227 also Frederick sent one of his most trusted counsellors, Bishop
Berard of Palermo, who, in the company of Thomas of Acerra, visited
the court of al-Kāmil; after a ceremonious reception and an exchange
of gifts they continued their journey to Damascus to open negotiations
with al-Mu'aẓẓam. But here they were rudely dismissed with the curt
response: 'Say to your master that I am not like certain others and that
I have nothing for him but my sword.' Apparently in the autumn of
1227 al-Kāmil again sent Fakhr-ad-Dīn to the Kingdom of Sicily.[2] It
may be conjectured that it was on this visit that he was knighted by
Frederick II. Whether at this time or subsequently, during the negotiations in Syria, he received the insignia of which the chronicler Joinville
later said: 'On his banner, which was barred, he bore on one bar the
arms of the Emperor who had knighted him.'[3]

As these preparations of the Emperor advanced through his agents
in Syria and Egypt he was occupied with efforts to justify himself to the
people throughout the West. In addition to his letter addressed to 'all
crusaders', he sent Roffrido of Benevento as his special envoy to Rome.
'With the consent of the Senate and the people of Rome', Roffrido read
publicly the Emperor's justification for the delay in his departure for the
Orient.[4]

The conciliatory mission of Abbot Roffrido had been most favourably
received and had won some sympathy for the imperial cause. A friendly
atmosphere had been created during the preceding year when the
Emperor had generously supplied the famine-stricken city with food.
Moreover, opposition to the Pope developed around several powerful
families, chiefly the Frangipani. During the Easter festivities, when the
ban was again proclaimed in the Basilica of St. Peter and the Pope
denounced the Emperor, the bitter resentment of the congregation was
stirred to the point of eruption, Infuriated, the congregation turned
against the Pope with the irresponsible violence of a frenzied mob,

---

[1] Maqrīzī, *Hist. d'Égypte* (tr. E. Blochet, *ROL* ix, 1901), 509–10. See also Badr-ad-Dīn al-
'Ainī (*RHC, Hist. or.* ii), 185 f. The diplomatic relations mentioned above have been dealt
with in an article by E. Blochet, 'Relations diplomatiques des Hohenstaufen avec les sultans
d'Égypte' (*Rev. Historique*, lxxx, 1902), 53 ff. For the conflicts of al-Kāmil and his kinsmen see
H. L. Gottschalk, *Al-Malik al-Kāmil von Ägypten und seine Zeit* (Wiesbaden, 1958).

[2] For these events see first Maqrīzī (*ROL* ix, 1901), 511, and then Badr-ad-Dīn al-'Ainī
(*RHC, Hist. or.* iii), 186 f., and Richard of San Germano, 146.

[3] Joinville, *Hist.* (ed. Natalis Wailly), 109–10.   [4] Richard of San Germano, 149.

driving him from the basilica and pursuing him through the streets.
Gregory fled helplessly, first to Viterbo, and later to a more secure refuge
in Perugia.[1] Nevertheless, from his place of refuge the Pope continued
his efforts to prevent the successful accomplishment of the crusade. It
was said by contemporaries that crusaders passing through Lombardy
en route to join the Emperor were robbed by order of the Pope.[2] As a
further hindrance to Frederick's crusading efforts, Gregory also ordered
the clergy of Sicily to pay no taxes levied by the Emperor for the projected expedition.[3] Already he had ordered them to place under the
interdict all places in which the Emperor sojourned, branding as heretics
those who refused obedience to his order.[4] Notwithstanding the Pope's
unrelenting opposition, Frederick continued to push forward his crusading plans during the early months of 1228.

On 26 April 1228 the young Empress, Isabella of Brienne, died
following the birth of her son, Conrad. In defiance of the interdict
recently proclaimed by the Pope, Frederick ordered solemn requiem
services to be celebrated for her throughout the Kingdom.[5] The enemies
of the Emperor, never at a loss to propagate the most insidious falsehoods
respecting his brutality, declared that the Empress had been beaten by
the Emperor and had finally perished in prison.[6] The fallacy of this
accusation is, if for no other reason, established by the fact that
the death of Isabella of Brienne, through whom Frederick claimed the
Kingdom of Jerusalem, actually weakened his position as far as the
Kingdom was concerned. Moreover, there exists no contemporary corroborative evidence for what appears to have been merely one of many
malicious charges.

The death of Isabella of Brienne, however, may well have made it
less difficult for her father, the titular King John, to take up arms against
his son-in-law as leader of the papal forces. Already the Pope had begun
preparations for armed opposition to Frederick in the Kingdom of
Sicily and had provided considerable sums of money for the enlisting
of mercenaries in Tuscany and Lombardy.[2] As the time for Frederick's
departure in May 1228 drew near, he could have had no doubt that
during his absence his enemies in the West, instigated and financed by
Gregory IX, would join in a common effort to destroy his prestige and
to wrest from him both the Sicilian and the imperial crowns. It is noteworthy that no sooner had the Pope received word of the Emperor's
actual departure than he sent a legate into Germany charged with the

---

[1] Richard of San Germano, 150; *Annales Sancti Rudberti Salisburgenses* (*MGH, SS.* ix), 784.
[2] *Burchardi Chronicon* (*MGH, SS.* xxiii), 383.
[3] Richard of San Germano, 150.
[4] Huillard-Bréholles, iii. 54.
[5] Piero della Vigna, *Epist.*, Lib. IV, no. 2, vol. ii, p. 6.
[6] Malespini, *Historia Fiorentina* (Muratori, *RIS* viii), col. 959. See also *Ernoul*, 453.

mission of arranging for the election of a rival king in Germany.[1] The chronicler of Cologne relates that the Pope sent to Germany and Denmark as legate Cardinal Otto of St. Nicholas 'to do injury to the Emperor and to this end to seek the counsel of Duke Otto of Lüneburg. But the latter advised against undertaking anything against the Emperor.' Another contemporary asserts that the object of Cardinal Otto was to contrive to bring about the election of a new king.[2]

The successful accomplishment of the crusade had now become a political necessity to the Emperor—the only means by which he could demonstrate to the princes and people of Christendom the sincerity of his motives. With a confidence hardly warranted by the precarious situation in which he found himself, and in the face of the resistance that the Pope was now able to evoke, the Emperor completed his preparations. It was probably while celebrating Easter in Barletta, towards the end of March 1228, that Frederick received intelligence of the death of al-Muʿazzam, Sultan of Damascus, which had taken place the previous November.[3] The arrival of this news may explain also the haste in which Frederick, in early April 1228, sent 500 troops to the Orient under the leadership of Richard Filangieri as reinforcements.[4]

While at first sight the death of the bitterest of his Aiyūbid foes might appear to Frederick as propitious for his future plans, he must have recognized also that it removed a chief cause of al-Kāmil's anxiety. Would the Sultan of Egypt, once so eager for the assistance of Frederick, now welcome him to Syria or easily surrender Jerusalem into his hands? The heir of al-Muʿazzam was his son Malek an-Nāsir Dā'ūd, a boy only twelve years of age, not a formidable rival to the Sultan of Egypt. The news of al-Muʿazzam's death, however, must have given added stimulus to Frederick's preparations for his departure. It was imperative that he act speedily before conditions in Syria were stabilized and a united resistance to the crusaders made possible. It is the irony of the whole conflict between Emperor and Pope that conditions had never been more favourable for the reconquest of the Kingdom of Jerusalem than they were in the spring of 1228. Yet, moved by what he conceived to be the interest of the Church, the Pope was relentless in his efforts to prevent Frederick's departure. It had never been more apparent than at this time that his true interests were not in a crusade but in the ruin of

---

[1] *Chronica regia Coloniensis*, 260–1.

[2] Conrad of Fabaria, *Casus S. Galli* (*MGH, SS.* ii), 181.

[3] As to the date of al-Muʿazzam's death see E. Winkelmann, *Friedrich II.*, ii, p. 11, note 4, and E. Kestner, *Kreuzzug Friedrichs II.*, p. 34, note 2. *Eracles*, 365, places the death of al-Muʿazzam as coinciding with the arrival of the crusaders in Sidon. The Arabic sources, however, are agreed that his death took place in early November. The long delay before news of his death reached the West may be accounted for by the fact that the next passage of ships from Syria would normally take place in the spring.

[4] Richard of San Germano, 150.

the Emperor at whatever sacrifice. As Frederick had long believed, Gregory was concealing from the Christian world his real motives.[1]

Convinced that reconciliation with Gregory IX was unattainable, save at the price of complete humiliation to himself and dishonour to the imperial office, Frederick determined to take his departure for the Holy Land. The birth of his son Conrad on 25 April and the death of Isabella of Brienne ten days later necessitated a rearrangement of the line of succession. Early in May he had summoned the spiritual and temporal princes and magnates to Barletta. There it was decided that his son Henry, King of Germany, was to succeed to the imperial throne and to the throne of Sicily. In the event of Henry's death and the absence of direct heirs, the hereditary family estate of Swabia was to fall to young Conrad. Reginald, son of the former Duke of Spoleto, was named vicegerent in the Kingdom of Sicily and imperial vicar in the March of Ancona and in the lands of Matilda. As at the Diet of Capua in 1220, it was decreed and approved by the oaths of the princes and magnates that peace should be maintained throughout the Kingdom as under the last of the Norman kings in 1198.[2]

The birth of Conrad and the death of the Empress caused Frederick to delay his departure until June. During this interval he took other security measures, apparently necessitated by new activities on the part of Gregory, to protect the borders of his Kingdom. In a manifesto to the 'faithful of the Empire' he authorized the plenary powers of Reginald of Spoleto in Ancona and in the lands of Matilda, assuring the inhabitants that these regions would remain under the jurisdiction of the Empire.[3] As revealed in a letter on the eve of his departure in June 1228, Frederick now made a last-minute effort to persuade the Pope to lift the ban, since he was actually *en route* to the Holy Land, 'in the service of Jesus Christ'. But this final effort was futile. The only result of a visit to the Pope by Bishop Albert of Magdeburg and two Sicilian justiciars was to confirm the Emperor in his suspicion that the Pope was preparing to foment rebellion against him.[4]

On 28 June Frederick, accompanied by the Archbishops of Palermo, Reggio, Capua, and Bari, and the commander of the fleet, Admiral Henry of Malta, set sail from Brindisi. The forces accompanying him were not numerous. The main body of the crusaders had sailed in August of the preceding year and additional reinforcements had followed in April 1228.[5] Even with these, however, the number of effective troops

[1] See, for example, Frederick's letter of Apr. 1228, addressed to 'consilio et communi Cesenensi' (Huillard-Bréholles, iii), 57–60.

[2] Richard of San Germano, 151.

[3] Huillard-Bréholles, iii. 65–6, 68.   [4] Ibid. iii. 72.

[5] *Breve chronicon de rebus Siculis*, 898; Richard of San Germano, 151. See also the letter of the Pope: Huillard-Bréholles, iii. 495.

available to the Emperor was inadequate for any sustained military effort.

To Gregory IX the defiant departure of Frederick in total disregard of the papal ban was as disturbing as it was unexpected. Upon receiving confirmation of the sailing from Brindisi the Pope could only say of it, 'without penance and without absolution . . . and without anyone's knowing for certain whither he sailed'. To his faithful subjects the Emperor had written on the eve of his departure: 'With Christ as our leader we have just left Brindisi for Syria, sailing swiftly before favourable winds.'[1] Whatever doubts Gregory IX may have had as to 'whither the Emperor had sailed', we are most fully informed by a contemporary, who obviously accompanied the expedition, as to the details of the day-by-day voyage. On 28–9 June the ships sailed from Brindisi to Otranto, thence on 30 June to the island of Fano (Atthanos); 1 July, to the island of Corfu; 2 July, to Porto Guiscardo on the coast of Cephalonia, one of the Ionian Islands; 4 July, to Modoni (Methoni) on the south-western tip of the peninsula of Greece; 5 July, to Portocaglie, not far from Cape Matapan; 6 July, to the island of Cerigo; 7–8 July in Suda Bay on the north coast of Crete. Then, navigating leisurely along the coast of Crete, the expedition paused for a day and night at Candia (Erakleion); 12 July, in the open sea again to the island of Rhodes until 15 July; then, sailing along the coast of Asia Minor, the crusaders arrived at Phenika (Phimea) on 16 July, where, attracted by the abundant supply of fresh water, they rested during 16–17 July. At length, sailing for the island of Cyprus, they landed at Limoso (Limassol) on 21 July, after a voyage of twenty-four days.[2]

---

[1] For the Pope's letter see *MGH, Epist. Pont.* i, no. 831, p. 731; for Frederick's letter, Huillard-Bréholles, iii. 73.   [2] *Breve chronicon de rebus Siculis*, 898 f.

III

FREDERICK II, DIPLOMAT OR CRUSADER?

Got die stat erloeset hât,
an der des glouben fröude stât.
waz bedurfen sünder mêre
wan 'z grap und kriuces êre?

Freidank, *Bescheidenheit* (ed. Sandvoss),
p. 121, lines 7 ff.[1]

A. THE KINGDOM OF SICILY DURING FREDERICK'S ABSENCE

FREDERICK II's defiance of the papal authority, his determination to proceed on his expedition to the Holy Land although an excommunicate, placed the Pope and Curia in a delicate position. Could the Vicar of Christ and St. Peter be thus defied by a temporal sovereign? Could such defiance go unpunished? Obviously, contempt for the authority of the Pope must be restrained by every available means, if the prestige of Rome was to be maintained. Not only must the Kingdom of Sicily be taken from Frederick, but he must be made to forfeit also the crowns of Germany and the Empire, yielding place to some willing servant of the papacy. Once more the imperial crown, a symbol of subserviency, must be given, as in the days of Innocent III, to a papal creature. Plans, long in the making, could now be set in motion. Accordingly, subjects of the Emperor in both Germany and Sicily were freed from their oaths of allegiance by papal decree. But in Germany papal interference with the freedom of election was accepted even less in the spirit of obedience than in years before when the heir of Henry VI was set aside by order of Innocent III and the crown transferred to the Welf, Otto IV. The princes of Germany, both temporal and spiritual, gave little heed to the ban through which Pope Gregory IX endeavoured to destroy both the Emperor and his son. On the contrary, they revealed unmistakably their loyalty, or perhaps their gratitude, to the Emperor in return for the many valuable privileges which he had bestowed upon them.

Conditions were different in Italy where, only a few months before, the Lombard League, led by the implacable city of Milan, and aided and abetted by the Pope, had defied the imperial authority by every

[1] For a translation of these lines see below, p. 220.

means at their command. The absence of the Emperor from his Kingdom, while engaged in his crusade in the Holy Land, offered to the Pope
and the Lombards a unique opportunity to strengthen their opposition
to him through an offensive and defensive alliance. A secret understanding was known, even in Germany, to exist between the Pope and the
Lombard League, and was given at least passing notice by more than
one contemporary chronicler in entries such as: 'Lombardy and Tuscany
conspired with the Pope against the Emperor' or 'the Pope, the Lombards,
and the Duke of Bavaria, Louis, united in opposition to the Emperor'.[1]
This secret understanding was strengthened further when the Pope
informed the members of the League that, in their interest, he was prepared to begin negotiations for an agreement pledging them mutually
to opposing the common foe.[2]

In Tuscany the Emperor's position was less seriously threatened,
chiefly because of numerous rivalries among Tuscan cities themselves.
Some of these, notably Siena, although wavering at times, remained
loyal to the Emperor. But papal legates were active in these cities, seeking by threat or persuasion to win their allegiance to the Pope.[3] As was
to be expected, the dissolution of the oath of allegiance to the Emperor
that had failed so signally in Germany was not without success in Italy.
On 31 July 1228, at Perugia, Pope Gregory proclaimed the dissolution
of the oath in the Sicilian Kingdom, an action several times repeated in
various letters. He accompanied this also with a threat of excommunication of all who participated in an attack against lands of the Roman
Church and against those who aided in the usurpation of the spiritual
or temporal rights of the Holy See.[4] Frederick's regent, Reginald of
Spoleto, could not have regarded this action by the Pope as other than
a declaration of war. With the object, therefore, of forestalling any
initial advantage of the papal army, Reginald immediately invaded the
March of Ancona and the Duchy of Spoleto in the autumn of 1228.
Before this, however, his activities in Ancona had already evoked from
the Pope the accusation that he was manifestly hostile to the interests
of the Holy See. At the same time Gregory had demanded of Reginald
submission and reparation within eight days, admonishing him that
failure to comply would be met with excommunication and the inter-
diction of regions in which he sojourned.[5] That Gregory should thus

---

[1] See, for example, *Annales Sancti Rudberti Salisburgenses* (*MGH, SS.* ix), 784; *Annales Scheftlarienses maiores* (*MGH, SS.* xvii), 339.
[2] *MGH, Epist. Pont.* i, no. 395, p. 313; Huillard-Bréholles, iii. 145 f.
[3] These legatine activities in Tuscany have been described in detail by E. Winkelmann, *Friedrich II.*, ii. 27 ff. See also R. Davidsohn, *Geschichte von Florenz*, ii, part 1, 150 f.
[4] *MGH, Epist. Pont.* i, no. 831, p. 731.
[5] Ibid. i, no. 375, pp. 291 ff. For Reginald's invasion see especially J. F. Ficker, 'Der Einfall Reinalds von Spoleto in den Kirchenstaat' (*MIöG* iv, 1883), 351 ff.

grant Reginald a period of eight days in which to give satisfaction for his alleged misdeeds suggests the precarious situation in which the Pope found himself. For already Reginald, as an associate of the excommunicated Emperor, was automatically under the ban in accordance with the Pope's proclamation from Perugia on 31 July. Obviously, Gregory was playing for time, hoping by means of a threat directed immediately at the imperial regent to persuade him to withdraw from the territory claimed by the Pope. Gregory had failed to find the anticipated support from the northern cities, including the Lombard League, which were now harassed by disruptive differences among their own members, especially among the cities of the upper Po valley.[1]

While not repudiating their alliance with the Pope, they were compelled to delay sending their pledged mounted troops to aid the papal army. It was not until mid January 1229 that some of these troops were made available.[2] Irritated and impatient as a result of the delay, Gregory now sought other ways and means of carrying on war against Reginald. His most pressing need was money; he satisfied this by means of heavy exactions from the British Isles and, to a lesser degree, by levying tithes in France, Sweden, and Denmark. England, as a feudal dependency of the Holy See, proved most fruitful as a source of revenue. There Master Stephen, the papal chaplain, as agent of the Pope, was authorized to apply the most rigorous pressure, including excommunication, against those who resisted the exactions. In compliance with a demand from Master Stephen, the King convoked a council at Westminster, summoning archbishops, bishops, abbots, priors, templars, hospitallers, earls, barons, rectors of churches, and all who held from him, to hear the reading of the Pope's letter. The requirement of the Pope was a familiar one: a tenth part of all movable property from clergymen and laymen alike. After the reading of the letter Master Stephen addressed the gathering, emphasizing the honour and the advantages which they would derive from generous giving. His audience was but little moved by his remarks but, unfortunately, the King had already promised the Pope the desired aid and could offer no comfort to the earls, barons, and the laity in general, who protested vehemently that they would not pay the required sums. The prelates, however, more vulnerable to papal threats, felt obliged to yield. As a contemporary chronicler reports, 'the prelates having no other recourse, took the chalices, goblets, and other sacred vessels from the churches, selling some and placing others in pawn.' In concluding his account, the same chronicler says that when the whole amount was collected and transmitted to the Pope, 'he distributed it so liberally to John of Brienne and

---

[1] See, for example, *Annales Janvenses* (*Fonti*), ii. 37 ff.

[2] Savioli, *Annali bolognesi*, iii, part 1, 69; and John Codagnellus, *Annales*, 87 f.

other leaders of the army, as to cause serious injury to the Emperor for, in his absence, they destroyed his towns and castles'.[1]

By measures such as these the Pope was able to find necessary resources for levying and maintaining troops. He employed two armies, consisting of men recruited from the Papal State and mercenaries from France, England, and Spain. One of the armies was commanded by John of Brienne and Cardinal John Colonna. Its mission during the first phase of the conquest was to oppose the movements of Reginald on the Italian mainland. The second army, consisting chiefly of troops from the Patrimony and bearing the papal insignia, a key, was sent into the Kingdom under the command of Pandulf, a papal chaplain, Counts Thomas and Roger of Celano, and other Sicilian nobles who had been expelled from the Kingdom by the Emperor.[2] Contemporary chroniclers were quick to assume that John of Brienne, ignoring the interests of his grandson Conrad, had seized the opportunity offered by the absence of the Emperor to further the claims of his nephew, Walter, son of Sibylla and the late Count Walter I of Brienne.[3]

The first army achieved some success on the mainland, driving Reginald from the Duchy of Spoleto and the March of Ancona where the imperial cause was supported by several cities and where Reginald had taken possession of the region as far north as Macerata.[4] The second army in its first operations had but little success. It did succeed in crossing the border of the Kingdom on 18 January 1229, where for a time it was held in check by the forces of the Grand Justiciar, Henry of Morra. Later, in the following March, Morra was finally routed, part of his troops withdrawing to San Germano and part, including the Justiciar himself, retreating to Monte Cassino. The moral effect of the defeat and flight of the imperial Justiciar was most injurious, causing several cities and strongholds, including Monte Cassino, San Germano, and Rocco Janula, to defect to the papal party. The imperial forces were thus compelled to flee secretly during the night to Capua, where they were reassembled by the Justiciar. This unexpected success of the papal army compelled Reginald of Spoleto to withdraw from the March of Ancona in an effort to unite with the remnants of Henry of Morra's army in Capua. But he found all roads blocked by enemy troops and only with difficulty moved his forces as far as Sulmona. It was apparently during these temporary successes of the papal army that Gregory sent into the field, presumably to aid if not to replace, his chaplain, Pandulf,

---

[1] Roger of Wendover, iv. 202–3.

[2] Richard of San Germano, 152; see also *Vita Gregorii IX* (Muratori, *RIS* iii), 577; (*Liber Censuum*, ii), 21.

[3] *Chronica Albrici Monachi Trium Fontium* (*MGH, SS.* xxiii), 925.

[4] Richard of San Germano, loc. cit.: 'usque Maceratam Cesaris imperio subiugarat.'

Cardinal Pelagius of Albano, whose ineptitude had contributed so greatly to the Damietta disaster a few years before.[1]

The reverses of the imperial troops in the Terra di Lavoro and the withdrawal of Reginald of Spoleto from the March of Ancona were especially serious in that they opened the way to the papal troops for the conquest of Apulia. Nearly half of the mainland provinces were now in their hands. It is all the more remarkable, therefore, that the papal troops did not drive deep into Apulia and so complete the plan of John of Brienne to take possession of the harbours of that region in order to facilitate the capture of the Emperor in the event of his sudden return from the Orient. Meanwhile, Thomas of Acerra who had arrived in the Kingdom after a rapid voyage from Syria, hearing of the progress of the conflict in Apulia and evidently believing that John of Brienne had completed his plans, wrote to the Emperor: 'I beg of you . . . to take precautions for your safety and your honour. Your enemy, John of Brienne, has garrisoned all ports on this side of the sea with numerous armed spies in order that you, in the event of an incautious return voyage, may be easily taken captive.'[2] Other loyal subjects also warned the Emperor of the growing dangers in his Kingdom, telling of the fall of San Germano, of the enemy's pressing on towards Capua, and of the defection of several cities and castles to the papal party.[3] Undoubtedly this defection of hitherto loyal cities was due to the widely circulated rumours of the Emperor's imprisonment or death.[4] In the Emperor's absence also the Saracens in the mountainous regions of Sicily south and south-west of Palermo again revolted.[5]

Gregory IX must have been too well informed about events in Syria to give credence to the rumour of Frederick's death. Yet he did not scruple to make the fullest possible use of it for propagandist purposes. Indeed, contemporaries suspected that the Pope himself was responsible for the rumour.[6] The Pope was all the more disposed to employ such deceit because he was convinced that victory in Sicily was now assured. In the event of Frederick's return he would find that, as vassal of the Holy See, his authority in Sicily had been invalidated—that regions once held by him had now reverted to the Church.[7] In the language of a

---

[1] Richard of San Germano, 154–5.

[2] Huillard-Bréholles, iii. 112; Roger of Wendover, iv. 182–4.

[3] See the fragment of MS. 8314, 3, printed in the Additamenta of Huillard-Bréholles, iii. 487–8.

[4] *Burchardi Chronicon* (*MGH, SS.* xxiii), 383: 'famam fecit in Apulia divulgari, imperatorem esse mortuum. Quocirca civitates, quae adhuc adhaerebant imperatori, disponebant se tradere sub dominio papae . . .'; *Sächsische Weltchronik*, 248: 'De wile dat de keiser over mere was, gewan eme de paves af siner stede unde siner burge vele, wante he let predegen dat de keiserd ot were.'   [5] Abū-l-Fidā (*Archivic stor. Sic.* N.S., ix, 1884), 123.

[6] *Burchardi Chronicon* (*MGH, SS.* xxiii), 383. See also *Breve chronicon de rebus Siculis*, 902–3.

[7] See Gregory's letter of 7 Sept. 1229 (*MGH, Epist. Pont.* i), no. 402, p. 322.

contemporary it was the intention of Gregory IX 'to expel him [Frederick] from his exalted station and in his place to elevate some peaceful and obedient son'.[1]

As the success of the papal army mounted in the Kingdom, the Pope abandoned his earlier plans and found in Sicily an opportunity for the direct extension of his sovereignty into that region. Henceforth barons, as well as the cities, were to recognize the Pope as their immediate overlord. While granting to individual cities extensive privileges, including the right to choose their *podestàs*, consuls, rectors, or other officials, and freedom from customs duties, he claimed for the Holy See the same taxes that had formerly been claimed under the imperial administration.[2]

The victories of the papal armies and the confident implementation of new administrative measures in captured cities or regions might well have given rise to the conviction that the cause of the Emperor was lost. Thomas of Acerra witnessed these signs of the papal triumph and wrote to Frederick that John of Brienne had been heard to remark that 'there is no emperor other than myself'.[3]

B. FREDERICK REGAINS THE KINGDOM OF JERUSALEM

For almost a full year, from 28 June 1228 until 10 June 1229, Frederick was in the Orient, thus affording the Pope an opportunity to pursue his hostile activities in both Germany and Italy. Frederick's first task was to obtain the submission of the Kingdom of Cyprus to the imperial sovereignty. The heir to the Cypriot throne, young Henry of Lusignan, a boy of nine, whose father had done homage to Emperor Henry VI, was regarded by Frederick as an imperial ward. On his arrival at Limassol the Emperor was met by Marshal Richard Filangieri, who had sailed with reinforcements the preceding April, and by numerous Cypriot nobles.[4] He was respectfully received by the Cypriots, including the *bailli* of the Kingdom, John of Ibelin, Lord of Beirut. But Frederick's singular lack of tact in handling the delicate question of his right as overlord alienated many of the barons, whom, together with John of Ibelin, he invited to a banquet. Although several of the friends of Ibelin, sensing danger in the doubtful cordiality of the Emperor, sought to dissuade him from accepting the invitation, he is reported to have replied 'that he would rather be captured or put to death and to suffer whatever God had in store for him than permit that anyone should be able to say that

---

[1] Roger of Wendover, iv. 182.
[2] This policy is apparent in Gregory's letters to his legate, Pelagius, and to various cities (*MGH, Epist. Pont.* i. no. 386, p. 305; 388, 307; 392, 310; 394, 312; 401–2, 321).
[3] Roger of Wendover, iv. 182.   [4] *Breve chronicon de rebus Siculis*, 900.

through him or his family, or through the people on this side of the sea, the service to God or the conquest of the Kingdom of Jerusalem was delayed or hindered'.[1] John of Ibelin attended the banquet, and upon the completion of the last course he was confronted with two demands from the Emperor: first, 'that you surrender to me the city of Beirut, for you do not have it or hold it justly'; second, 'that you refund to me all that the bailliage of Cyprus and the regalia thereof has yielded since the death of King Hugh; that is, the revenue for ten years, for that is my right according to German usage'.

With commendable courage John of Ibelin defended his right to Beirut as a fief received from his sister and Amaury of Jerusalem in exchange for the constableship. He then challenged the Emperor to prove that he held the fief illegally, offering to furnish proof of his rightful claim in the court of the Kingdom of Jerusalem. As to the revenues from the bailliage of Cyprus and its regalia, he continued: 'I have had none whatsoever and my brother had nothing save the annoyance and the labour as the governor of the Kingdom.' Then, to the dismay of all present, the lord of Beirut concluded: 'Be assured that for the fear of death or of prison I will do nothing more unless the judgement of the good and loyal court requires me to do so.'[2] Although a reconciliation was later effected, this episode and the weeks of tension that succeeded served as an unfortunate introduction of the Emperor to his subjects in the Orient.

Leaving *baillis* to administer the Cypriot cities, Frederick sailed from Famagusta on 2 September, accompanied by his young ward, Henry of Luisignan, John of Ibelin, and many Cypriot barons, reaching the port of Acre on 7 September.[3] Conditions in Syria were not suitable for a successful crusade. The effective troops remaining there were not numerous. Roger of Wendover, apparently employing an eyewitness report, says that on the Emperor's arrival 'he found the army under the leadership of the Duke of Limburg, the Patriarch of Jerusalem, the Archbishops of Nazareth, Caesarea, and Narbonne, the English Bishops of Winchester and Exeter, the masters of the Hospital, the Knights Templar, and the Teutonic Hospitallers, who united under their command about 800 pilgrim knights and about 10,000 foot soldiers gathered from various parts of the world.'[4] The number of troops accompanying Frederick was not large—a few thousand at most. While it is impossible from the loosely employed figures of the contemporary sources to make an accurate estimate of the total resources in armed

---

[1] Philip of Novare, *Mémoires* (ed. C. Kohler), 13–14. See also J. L. Lamonte, *The Wars of Frederick II*, etc., 75 ff.   [2] *Mémoires*, 16–17.

[3] Ibid. 23; *Eracles*, 369; *Breve chronicon de rebus Siculis*, 900 f.

[4] *Flores Historiarum*, iv. 175.

troops, it is apparent that the numbers were inadequate for any large-scale military effort. From the outset Frederick must have been aware that whatever success was to be achieved would come, not from warfare, but from diplomacy.

On his arrival in Syria he was at first received with enthusiasm by the clergy, the Templars, and others, although there is probably exaggeration in the contemporary account that 'the Templars and Hospitallers, upon his arrival, fell upon their knees and adored him, kissing his knees'.[1] In the light of their later attitude of open hostility, it can only be assumed that these knights were guilty of hypocrisy at a moment when they hoped the Emperor's coming might serve their interests, or else that the chronicler, desiring to depict a scene of Christian solidarity and brotherly love, purposely exaggerated the friendliness of the reception. A more accurate account appears to be that of Philip of Novare who says simply: 'the Emperor was very well received in Syria and all did homage to him. He left Tyre and went to the city of Acre and was received there with honour.'[2] It is most improbable that the crusaders who thus received him could have been unaware of the extent of the breach between the Emperor and the Pope. It is to be assumed, however, that already they anticipated a more conciliatory attitude on the part of the Pope, now that Frederick had actually arrived in Syria. If the clergy denied him the kiss of peace and refused to break bread with him as an excommunicate, this was not so much a display of hostility as a formality in keeping with the practices of the Church. Anxiously they hoped for his early absolution and beseeched Frederick to seek at once for a reconciliation with the Pope so that the crusading effort might prosper. They could not have been aware of how far the Pope had moved already in his effort to destroy the Emperor. Frederick recognized, despite most serious misgivings, that expediency demanded a serious effort towards conciliation. As his emissaries to Rome he chose the Archbishop of Bari, long a staunch supporter of the Emperor, and Count Henry of Malta, Admiral of the Sicilian fleet. At the same time he named Reginald of Spoleto, his deputy in Sicily, as minister plenipotentiary to negotiate with the Pope. He could not have known at this stage to what extent Reginald had evoked the opposition of Pope and Curia by his invasion of the Duchy of Spoleto and the March of Ancona. Meanwhile, a letter of Gregory to the Patriarch of Jerusalem and the grand masters of the knightly orders admonishing them to have no part in Frederick's activities in Syria informed them also of the alleged misdeeds of Reginald of Spoleto.[3]

---

[1] Ibid. 174.　　　　　　　　　　　　　　　　　　　　　　[2] *Mémoires*, 23.

[3] Huillard-Bréholles, iii. 82 f.; Richard of San Germano (*MGH, SS.* xix), 354; *Eracles*, 370; *Ernoul*, 462.

Bewildered by this extraordinary conduct of the Pope, the crusaders, including the knightly orders, were at a loss as to procedure in their relations with the Emperor. The Teutonic Order, under the guidance of Hermann of Salza its Master, continued its loyal support of the Emperor. Opposing Frederick, however, with a bitterness and vindictiveness surpassing even that of the Pope, was the Patriarch Gerold who, although well aware that the illness which had led to Frederick's excommunication had been a real one, now became the Pope's chief agent in persecuting him. This impossible situation caused Frederick to approve an arrangement whereby the nominal command of various units of the expedition was given to men who were his faithful friends, although free from the taint of excommunication: Hermann of Salza, Richard Filangieri, under whose command reinforcements had been sent to Syria, and Eudes of Montbéliard, Constable of Syria.[1]

It was fortunate that al-Kāmil was in no position, despite the death of his brother al-Muʿaẓẓam, to offer effective resistance to the Emperor. As a man of exceptional honour and integrity it is apparent that he desired to avoid a conflict with Frederick, who had come to Syria partly as a result of the Sultan's invitation. Immediately after the death of al-Muʿaẓẓam, al-Kāmil had hastened from Egypt with the object of seizing the lands of his brother, including Jerusalem, now claimed by an-Nāṣir, the twelve-year-old heir of the late governor of Damascus. Thus threatened with dispossession, an-Nāṣir appealed to another uncle, al-Ashraf, Governor of Kelat, for aid. But al-Ashraf found it more expedient to support his brother al-Kāmil. The brothers proceeded to lay siege to the city of Damascus and to make other plans for the disposal of former possessions of al-Muʿaẓẓam. They were still engaged in this family squabble during Frederick's stay in Syria between September 1228 and May 1229.[2] Under these circumstances the presence of the Emperor at Acre was, in the language of an Arabic chronicler, 'like an arrow in a wound'.[3] Al-Kāmil's possession of Jerusalem, however, now placed him in a much better position for bargaining with the Emperor than he had been a few months before when he had appealed for aid against al-Muʿaẓẓam. While still at Recardine, the site of his encampment near Acre, Frederick sent Thomas of Acerra and Balian of Sidon as his emissaries to Nablus to inform the Sultan of his arrival. They were commissioned, of course, to request of the Sultan the fulfilment of his promise to surrender Jerusalem. The emissaries were received with

---

[1] Schirrmacher, *Friedrich II.*, ii. 183, erroneously attributed the appointment of these men to the Pope. For a criticism of this and for a more plausible interpretation see E. Kestner, *Kreuzzug*, 43, note 2.

[2] For the activities of al-Kāmil and his brother al-Ashraf in relation to an-Nāṣir see Abū-l-Fidā (*RHC, Hist. or.* i), 103; Abū-Shāmah (ibid. v), 190 f.

[3] Abū-l-Fidā, loc. cit.

courtesy and valuable gifts were exchanged, although al-Kāmil remained non-committal with respect to Jerusalem, permitting them to depart without a satisfactory answer.[1]

During the remainder of the year 1228 embassies were several times exchanged but without tangible results. The most fruitful of these parleys were between Frederick and his friend, formerly his guest in the Kingdom of Sicily, Fakhr-ad-Dīn. It was at this time that the Emperor, skilled as he was in the Arabic tongue and in the knowledge of the sciences, favourably impressed the Arabic ambassador and thus, indirectly, the Sultan himself. The contemporary Egyptian historian Maqrīzī relates that Frederick sent several difficult questions pertaining to the science of mathematics to the Sultan, who gave them to men of great learning for appropriate answers. This scholarly exchange appears to have succeeded where other methods failed.[2] It was these exchanges with various Muslims that gave rise to the suspicions of many Christians and evoked from Gerold, Patriarch of Jerusalem, bitter complaints about the Emperor's conduct. But even more damaging to Frederick was his alleged enjoyment of the exotic entertainment of the Arab world. In a letter to the Pope, Gerold wrote: 'It is with the greatest shame and disgrace that we report to you that it is said the Sultan, hearing of the Emperor's enjoyment of living in the manner of the Saracens, sent to him singing girls and jugglers, persons who were not only of ill repute but unworthy even to be mentioned among Christians.'[3] Tales of Frederick's predilection for Saracen ways of life make their appearance also in the writings of contemporary Western chroniclers who tell of his feasting with Saracens in his palace, and of his introducing 'Christian dancing women to perform before them and, as it was said, they [the Saracens] had cohabited with them.'[4] The Swabian poet Freidank, who had accompanied Frederick on his crusade, expressed his sorrow that the diplomatic relations were secret and that they had been carried on in a bartering spirit. He complained of the tedious negotiating, comparing the Sultan and the Emperor to two misers who, in attempting to divide equally three pieces of gold, were never able to reach an agreement.[5]

But Frederick had reason to cultivate the goodwill of the Sultan, though the process might be tedious. Under existing conditions it would

---

[1] *Eracles*, 369 f. [2] *Hist. d'Égypte* (*ROL* ix), 528 f.
[3] Huillard-Bréholles, iii. 104 f. [4] Roger of Wendover, iv. 198.
[5] *Bescheidenheit*, 119:

> Vilkarc und Samkarc
> solten teilen drî marc:
> Vilkarc woltez bezzer hân,
> Samkarc woltez ime niht lân;
> der strît ist ungescheiden
> under den kargen beiden.

have been inexpedient for either the Sultan or the Emperor to carry on negotiations openly. To the Sultan the presence of the Emperor, although as an invited guest, became more embarrassing with each passing day, now that the reason for inviting him no longer existed. Frederick's position was even more difficult in the face of open opposition from the Pope, the Patriarch Gerold, and many leading crusaders. Towards Frederick's original embassy the Sultan had been evasive and he had returned them to the Emperor with gifts of varicoloured silks and other rich and exotic presents from the Orient. When Frederick again sent Balian of Sidon and Thomas of Acerra to the recent headquarters of al-Kāmil at Nablus and they asked for an audience they were told that he was on his way to Gaza (Gadres) and that he desired them to go away 'for he wished to remove himself from the Emperor and his parleys'.[1] Obviously, the predicament of the Sultan was serious, but as a man of honour he recognized that it was of his own making. The Emperor also appreciated the difficulties of al-Kāmil, and so he ignored the curt dismissal of his emissaries, believing that patience and persistence could obtain the desired end.[2] It was at this time that Frederick moved the crusading army from Recardine to Jaffa where the fortifications had been under repair since the arrival of Duke Henry of Limburg the preceding autumn. In making preparations for this march the Templars and the Knights of St. John created further difficulty as serious as it was ludicrous. Announcing that they could not associate with an excommunicate, their leaders, Peter of Montaigu, Grand Master of the Templars, and Bertrand Thessy, Master of the Hospitallers, ordered their troops to follow the Emperor at a distance of a day's journey. As the possibility of an attack by the Muslims became more imminent in the vicinity of Arsuf, Frederick, responding to pleas of some of the pilgrims, induced the Templars and Hospitallers to join the main body by agreeing that henceforth orders would be promulgated 'in the name of God and Christianity without naming the Emperor'.[3] In this manner the army moved without serious incident into Jaffa. Shortly after their arrival Frederick received reports of the activities of John of Brienne and other leaders of the papal forces in the vicinity of San Germano and of the defection of many Sicilian cities to the Pope. He therefore appealed to his loyal subjects to stand fast and at the same time ordered the Admiral of the fleet, Henry of Malta, to send twenty galleys to Syria by the following Easter.[4]

Continued delay in the Orient might now cost the Emperor both his Kingdom of Sicily and the imperial crown. If, however, he departed without accomplishing his mission in the Holy Land his prestige

---

[1] *Eracles*, 372: 'et ce faisoit il por esloigner l'empereor et ses paroles.'   [2] Ibid.
[3] Ibid. 373: 'le ban de Deu et de la Crestienté sanz nomer l'empereor.'   [4] Ibid.

throughout Christendom would be destroyed. The winter and early spring of 1229 could well be decisive as to his future. A letter supposedly written at this time by Frederick to the Sultan and quoted by an Arabic source, whether or not authentic, reveals how desperately Frederick desired to bring the expedition to a successful conclusion:

I am your friend. You must be aware that I am supreme among all the princes of the West. It is you who caused me to come here. The kings and the pope know of my expedition. If I return without having obtained something, I shall lose all respect in their eyes. After all, is not the city of Jerusalem the place of birth of the Christian religion? Have you not destroyed it? It now stands in direst need. Give it back to me in the condition in which it is so that upon my return home I may hold up my head among kings. I renounce in advance all advantages which I might obtain from it.[1]

Although the authenticity of this letter may be questioned and suspected of being an Arab invention, its contents are in substance similar to a remark of Frederick to his friend Fakhr-ad-Dīn that 'if he had not feared injury to his honour he would not have demanded so great a sacrifice of the Sultan'.[2]

Al-Kāmil's recognition of his obligation to Frederick and his own difficulties arising from the siege of Damascus compelled him at length to yield to the insistent demands of the Emperor. Maqrīzī says of this agreement: 'That treaty was the result of the ill-conceived action of al-Kāmil in negotiations with the King of the Franks and of the fear which embarrassed him that he would not be able to resist the attack of the sovereign of Damascus. That is why he acceded to the terms.' Whatever may have induced the Sultan finally to agree to the terms of peace, it is apparent that Frederick's friendship with Fakhr-ad-Dīn, 'son of the sheikh of sheikhs', was of the utmost usefulness in the final outcome of the negotiations. He is known to have visited the Emperor many times in the course of the negotiations.[3] Muslim historians are in agreement that the treaty was a great misfortune for which al-Kāmil merited the severest censure. One of them described it as 'that baleful event, one of the most disastrous for Islam'.[4]

Unfortunately, no authentic copy of the treaty is extant. Its contents must be reconstructed from various Arabic sources, from passages in the letters of the Patriarch Gerold, of Hermann of Salza and, especially, from a letter of Frederick II to the King of England. It was perhaps inevitable that these accounts would vary somewhat in details.[5] As

---

[1] M. Michaud, *Bibliothèque des Croisades*, iv. 429 f. The reference to the 'destruction' of Jerusalem doubtless refers to the razing of the walls by al-Muʿaẓẓam during the Damietta crusade.   [2] Maqrīzī, *Hist. d'Égypte*, 525–6.   [3] Ibid. 525.

[4] Badr-ad-Dīn al-ʿAinī (*RHC, Hist. or.* ii, part i), 187.

[5] For the various versions of the treaty see Huillard-Bréholles, iii. 86 ff., 90 ff. The letter of Frederick to Henry III of England is to be found in full in Roger of Wendover, iv. 191.

finally concluded on 18 February 1229 the terms of the treaty were: The
Sultan agreed to the surrender of Jerusalem, including the Holy
Sepulchre, save that the Muslims were to retain Al-Ḥaram ash-Sharīf,
the enclosure containing the Mosque of Omar and the Temple of
Solomon (Qubbat aṣ-Ṣakhrah). Christians were to have access to the
Temple for prayer and the Muslims, in return, were permitted access to
Bethlehem although the town itself was ceded to Frederick, together
with a strip of territory between Jerusalem and Bethlehem. Nazareth,
Sidon, Tibnin (Turon), Jaffa, and Acre, dominating the coast, were
granted to the Christians.

Some contradictions exist as to the rights of the Christians to fortify
Jerusalem. Although in his letter to the King of England, Frederick
states that 'we are allowed to rebuild the city of Jerusalem in as good a
state as it has ever been, and also the castles of Jaffa, Caesarea, Sidon,
and the castle of St. Mary of the Teutonic Order which the brothers of
that order have begun to build in the mountainous district of Acre . . .',[1]
Muslim sources dispute this, saying: 'the Emperor could not rebuild the
fortified enclosure.'[2]

There was to be an exchange of prisoners, a *qāḍī* was permitted to
dwell within the city of Jerusalem to represent the interests of the
Muslims there, and non-resident pilgrims were to be given protection
during their sojourns in the city. Finally, a ten-year truce was agreed to.
The obvious weakness of the treaty was its want of general sanction by
the peoples involved. It was not a treaty between states but between
two men both of whom were capable of a tolerance and friendliness
towards the opposing side which their followers did not share. Among
the crusaders only the German and Sicilian followers of Frederick were
favourably disposed to the terms, while the Knights of St. John, the
Patriarch of Jerusalem, and others strongly opposed them. Those who
were closest to the Emperor could not comprehend what more he could
have obtained. The lines of the poet Freidank, himself a crusader, may
be taken to express the prevailing sentiment of his German compatriots:

> God has delivered the city,
> In which the joy of the faith resides.
> What more can sinners desire
> Than the sepulchre and the glorious cross?

---

[1] Roger of Wendover, iv. 191 f.   [2] Maqrīzī, *Hist. d'Égypte*, 525.

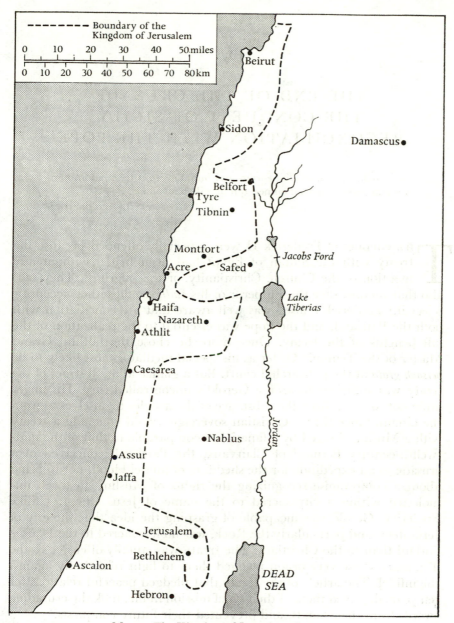

Boundary of the
Kingdom of Jerusalem

| 0 | 10 | 20 | 30 | 40 | 50 miles |

| 0 | 10 | 20 | 30 | 40 | 50 | 60 | 70 | 80 km |

Beirut

Sidon

Damascus

Belfort
Tyre
Tibnin

Montfort
Acre ● Safed

Jacobs Ford

Lake
Tiberias

Haifa
Nazareth
Athlit

Caesarea

Jordan

Nablus

Assur
Jaffa

Jerusalem
Bethlehem

Ascalon

Hebron

DEAD
SEA

MAP 3. The Kingdom of Jerusalem after 1229

IV

THE END OF THE CRUSADE
THE CONQUEST OF SICILY
RECONCILIATION WITH THE POPE

Et venient ad te curvi filii eorum, qui humiliaverunt te, et adorabunt
vestigia pedum tuorum omnes, qui detrahebant tibi . . .

Isaias 60 : 14.[1]

THE enemies of Frederick II were especially offended because the
treaty with the Sultan of Egypt had been made 'without any
mention of the Church, Christianity, or the pilgrims'. They said
also that no one, save the Emperor or his *bailli*, could either accept or
reject it.[1] Frederick himself was well aware that a reconciliation with
both the Patriarch and the Pope was essential to the realization of the
full benefits of the treaty. Once more he chose the faithful Grand
Master of the Teutonic Order as his special mediator most likely to be
persona grata at the patriarchal court. But a glance at an abstract of the
treaty was sufficient to arouse Gerold's uncontrolled fury. His anger
arose not so much from the substance of the articles themselves as from
the circumstance that a Christian sovereign would conclude a treaty
with a Muslim. Moved by a fanaticism comparable to that of the mid-
twelfth-century Bernard of Clairvaux, the Patriarch conceived of a
crusade as an expedition for the shedding of infidel blood, not to bring
about a compromise recognizing the rights of Muslims to dwell unmolested within a city sacred to the name of Jesus Christ. Unlike
Frederick, Gerold was incapable of grasping the idea that the city of
Jerusalem, and particularly the Rock, was no less sacred to the Islamic
faithful than to the Christians. The treaty was equally offensive to the
Templars whose very origin pledged them to fight relentlessly against
the infidel. The article of the treaty that pledged peaceful relations for
ten years deprived them of their chief mission in life, took the crusading
swords from their hands, and prevented their future conquests.[3]

The Patriarch and the Templars felt keenly that Frederick had ignored

---

[1] The sons also of them that afflicted thee shall come bending unto thee; and all they that
despised thee shall bow themselves down at the soles of thy feet (Isaiah 60 : 14).

[2] Complaint of the Patriarch Gerold to the Pope (Huillard-Bréholles, iii), 102 ff.

[3] BFW, *Reg.* v, Abt. i, *Einleitung*, p. xxxvii.

their interests. In his letter of 26 March 1229 to the Pope describing Frederick's activities in Syria, Gerold depicted him as the enemy of the Church, as its betrayer. He turned a deaf ear to all pleas of Hermann of Salza for a reconciliation. Henceforth, the irate Patriarch had but one end in view, the destruction of Frederick II and all his works. Above all, the Emperor must be prevented from making a triumphal entry into the city of Jerusalem. The crusading army must be forbidden by threat of excommunication to follow him there. The city itself must be placed under the interdict. Post-haste, he dispatched the Archbishop of Caesarea to the army to carry out the necessary restraining orders. But he arrived too late. The Emperor had moved with most of the pilgrims into the city of Jerusalem on 17 March. There the representatives of the Sultan awaited his coming, prepared to make the formal surrender. Frederick lost no time. He told of his arrival in a letter to King Henry III of England:

On the seventeenth day of the month of March in the second indiction, which was the sabbath, with all the pilgrims who with us had followed Christ, the son of God, faithfully, we entered the Holy City of Jerusalem, and there as Catholic Emperor, on the next day, after worshipping at the Sepulchre of the Lord, we wore the crown which God the Omnipotent, through his special grace, provided for us from his majestic throne . . .[1]

Thus on 18 March 1229 Frederick II, an excommunicate, advanced to the altar of the Church of the Holy Sepulchre and simply and without consecration took the crown from the altar and placed it upon his own head.[2]

Immediately after the coronation, and after he left the church, an address of Frederick II was read by Hermann of Salza, first in Latin and then in German. From the letter of Hermann of Salza it is possible to reconstruct the substance of this address. Frederick told how he had taken the cross at Aachen and how, by numerous obstacles, he had been delayed in the fulfilment of his vow. He expressed his forgiveness of the Pope for frequently admonishing him because of his delays and for proclaiming the ban against him. For, 'in no other way', said Frederick, 'could the Pope avoid the slanderous abuse of mankind or avert disgrace'. He excused the Pope also for his continued opposition to him after he had crossed the sea 'because the report was spread abroad that the Emperor had gathered an army, not to reconquer the Holy Land, but to oppose the Church'. Had the Pope known of Frederick's true intentions he would not have written letters to oppose him, but to support him. Frederick then expressed his belief that the Pope would have been thoroughly displeased had he known how many in Palestine

---

[1] Roger of Wendover, iv. 192–3.
[2] Hermann of Salza's letter to the Pope (*MGH, Const.* ii), 167.

were working to the injury of the whole Christian people (*que nocuerunt toti populo Christiano*). As to the future, Frederick stated his intention to do everything that would redound 'to the honour of God, the Christian Church, and the Empire, so that his sincere desire for peace would be apparent to all'. He concluded his address with an assurance of his humility, saying that he did not wish to exalt himself but rather to bow before the Most High 'in the measure that He has placed me as His Vicar upon earth'.[1] Frederick was justly proud of his achievement. Why should not the whole of Christendom rejoice with him? As he wrote to King Henry III of England: 'In these few days, by a miracle, rather than by valour, that undertaking has been achieved which for a long time numerous princes and various rulers of the world . . . have not been able to accomplish by force.'[2]

Although thwarted in his effort to prevent the triumphal entry of Frederick and the pilgrims into Jerusalem, the Bishop of Caesarea, who arrived on 19 March, proceeded to place the city of Jerusalem under the interdict. His action succeeded only in stirring the anger and resentment of the pilgrims who, after achieving the goal for which they had left their homes, were denied access as faithful Christians to the Holy Sepulchre. The Bishop himself was embarrassed and apparently bewildered by what must have seemed to him an unwarranted procedure. When the Emperor, provoked by the Bishop's mission, summoned him to give an account of his actions, he failed to appear.[3]

If the Patriarch of Jerusalem and the Pope were bitter in their denunciations of Frederick for the compromise agreement with the Muslims, so also the Arab world was unanimous in denouncing it. The inhabitants of Jerusalem wept on hearing the order to evacuate the city. 'They were desolate upon seeing the city pass from their control and they sharply criticized the conduct of al-Kāmil, adjudging him unworthy.' One of the Arabic poets wrote: 'How sad it is for us to see Jerusalem fall in ruins, and the star of its splendour wane and disappear.'[4] Ibn-al-Athīr in his *Al-Kāmil fī-t-ta'rīkh* relates that, upon the surrender of Jerusalem, 'a profound and painful emotion seized the Muslims who were humiliated and grieved beyond the power of expression'.[5]

Despite the deep chagrin and sorrow of the Arabs over the loss of Jerusalem, the personality of Frederick II impressed them profoundly during his sojourn among them. They were obviously disappointed in his physical appearance, and one of them wrote: 'He is ruddy and bald; he has weak eyesight; if he had been a slave, one would not have paid

---

[1] *MGH, Const.* ii. 167–8.
[2] Roger of Wendover, iv. 189 f.
[3] *MGH, Const.* ii. 168. See also W. Jacobs, *Patriarch Gerold von Jerusalem*, 37.
[4] Badr-ad-Dīn al-'Ainī (*RHC, Hist. or.* ii, part i), 190.
[5] Ibn-al-Athīr (*RHC, Hist. or.* ii, part i), 176.

200 drachmas for him. His conversation reveals that he does not believe in the Christian religion. When he spoke of it, it was to ridicule it.' The same source relates also that the Emperor made no effort to prevent the Muslims who accompanied him from participating in the midday prayer. It was both astonishing and pleasing to the Muslims, as the author relates, that there was in Frederick's retinue a Sicilian Muslim who had been the Emperor's tutor in Arabic logic.[1] When the Emperor arrived to take over the city of Jerusalem he was accompanied by the Emir Shams-ad-Dīn, *qāḍī* of Nablus, as official escort. When the *qāḍī*, desiring that the Emperor be in no wise offended by his fellow Muslims, ordered the muezzins not to make their customary call to prayers, Frederick took the *qāḍī* to task, saying, 'you have done wrong; why do you deprive yourself because of me of your normal obligation, of your law, of your religion?' On another occasion he is said to have reprimanded a priest who entered the mosque of Omar carrying a Bible in his hand, saying that he had agreed that the Muslims were to be protected against insults in their mosques and that they were not to be molested during their religious ceremonies. He is said to have reminded the priest that 'it was through the grace of the Sultan that he has restored to us our churches—let us not abuse it'.[2] The characteristics of Frederick which appealed most to the Arabs were his cultural interests, especially his knowledge of the mathematical sciences and philosophy. The *qāḍī*, Djemāl ad-Din-Ibn Quacel, who on one occasion visited the Kingdom of Sicily as ambassador, said of Frederick II: 'He was distinguished among all the kings of the Franks for his talents and for his taste for philosophy, logic, and medicine; he had an appreciation of the Muslims since he had been reared in Sicily where the majority of the inhabitants profess Islam.'[3] It was Frederick's intimate Muslim friend, Fakhr-ad-Dīn, as ambassador of the Sultan, who paid the Emperor the highest tribute: 'since the time of Alexander there has been no prince in Christendom such as he [Frederick], not only because of his great power, but also on account of the skill with which he dared to oppose the Pope, their khalif, to move against him, and to put him to flight.'[4]

Frederick's stay in the city of Jerusalem was brief. Further disquieting news from the Kingdom of Sicily had reached him early in March. When, therefore, the city had actually been surrendered into his hands

[1] Presumed to have been Ibn-al-Djusi (Ibn-Giouzi). See also Amari, *Storia dei Musulmani*, iii (old edn.), p. 701, note 1 (new edn., 1937, p. 720, note 2): 'Ibn-al-Gawzl'.

[2] Maqrīzī, *Hist. d'Égypte*, pp. 526-7. See also Ibn-al-Athīr (*RHC, Hist. or.* ii, part i), 193-4.

[3] Abū-l-Fidā (*RHC, Hist. or.* i), 104.

[4] M. Amari, 'Estratti del Tarih Mansuri' (*Archivio stor. Siciliano*, new series, Ann. IX, 1884), 123. See also his note 2 in which Amari interprets, 'e muove [in armi] contro di esso e [tel] caccia via', as applying to the flight of the Pope from the Church of St. Peter during the angry uprising of the Romans. See above, p. 203 f.

he recognized that he must return with the least possible delay to his Kingdom. Before departing, however, he left behind him a number of knights from the crusading army to guard the city.[1] Frederick had given assurance to the King of England that 'before we take leave of the city of Jerusalem, we have decided splendidly to rebuild its towers and its walls and we intend so to arrange affairs that there shall be no less care and industry displayed there in our absence than if we were present in person'.[2] The knights left behind and charged with the work of reconstruction were probably from the Teutonic Order, the most devoted of Frederick's supporters.[3]

Despite their earlier opposition to the imperial plans, the Templars and Hospitallers appear to have volunteered in a last-minute statement to aid in the reconstruction.[4] This sudden about-face cannot rightly be interpreted as a conciliatory gesture but appears rather to coincide with the belated recognition by both the Orders and the Patriarch Gerold that the achievement of Frederick II was something which might be made to redound to their own advantage, especially after the Emperor's departure which they believed to be imminent.[5] Gerold, describing these events, depicts Frederick as abruptly taking his leave of the Templars and as riding away so rapidly from Jerusalem in the direction of Jaffa that those in his company were scarcely able to keep up with him. From Jaffa he proceeded to Acre where, as he was well aware, he must face the most bitter resistance to his plans from the unyielding Patriarch. While previously Gerold had refused to recognize any of the achievements of Frederick, now he determined to claim them for the papal party. With the money that the King of France had left for the conquest of Jerusalem[6] he planned to equip troops and, on the departure of the Emperor, to take possession of Jerusalem in the name of the Pope. In this enterprise the Templars were to be his allies. When he learnt of Gerold's intention Frederick demanded an explanation. But the Patriarch shielded himself by offering the excuse that the troops were to be employed against the Sultan of Damascus, who had not agreed to the treaty. When the Emperor ordered him to desist, Gerold replied that he could not obey orders from an excommunicate without endangering his soul. Faced with this obstinate resistance, Frederick summoned the pilgrims and the inhabitants of Acre, together with the prelates and

---

[1] Gregory IX, in a letter of 26 Feb. 1231, mentions these knights: 'militibus peregrinis quos ipse duxerat . . .' (*MGH, Epist. Pont.* i), 345.

[2] Roger of Wendover, iv. 193.

[3] Huillard-Bréholles, iii. 98, and the letter referred to above, p. 224, note 1.

[4] See the letter of Gerold to 'all faithful Christians', Huillard-Bréholles, iii. 137.

[5] See on this also the conflicting views of E. Kestner, *Kreuzzug*, 64, and E. Winkelmann, *Friedrich II.*, ii. 129, note 2.

[6] See above, p. 160.

other members of the clergy, to an assembly at which he gave expression to his grievances against the Patriarch and the Templars. Philip of Novare gives a brief account of the gathering: 'At Acre the Emperor assembled his followers and had all the people of the city come there, and many Pisans were there who were quite well disposed towards him. He addressed them and told them what he desired; and in his address he complained much of the Temple.'[1] In his manifesto addressed to all Christians[2] the Patriarch summarized the remarks of the Emperor, emphasizing especially his punitive measures. Not only did Frederick condemn the Templars as traitors, but he ordered all knights who had been enlisted to oppose him to leave the city, authorizing his *bailli*, Thomas of Acerra, to inflict corporal punishment upon those who refused. When this measure proved inadequate he ordered the closing of the gates of the city to all persons hostile to him, including the Templars. He then placed his troops strategically throughout the city in stations which would provide access to the homes of the Patriarch and the Templars. If we may accept the account of the irate Gerold, even the churches were occupied by the Emperor's troops. Preaching friars venturing to incite disobedience among the people were ordered to be seized and soundly thrashed.

Meanwhile, the Emperor, hard-pressed as he was by the activities of John of Brienne and other leaders of the papal troops against the Kingdom of Sicily, was in no position to remain in Acre to crush the growing opposition. Further negotiations were made impossible by the Patriarch's unreasoning obstinacy. After shipping or destroying all available arms, to prevent their being made use of by the Patriarch and the Templars, Frederick embarked with his following on 1 May 1227. As his *baillis* in Syria he named Balian of Sidon and Garnier l'Aleman (Werner of Egisheim), an Alsatian.[3] Also, before his departure, he leased the *baillage* of Cyprus for a period of three years to five *baillis*: Amaury Barlais, Amaury of Bethsan, Gauvain of Chinchi, William of Revet, and Hugh of Gibelet (Jubail). A garrison was left behind to protect the imperial interests in Acre and the Teutonic Order was given possession of the stronghold, Qal'at al-Qurain (Montfort), dominating the city of Acre.[4] Cypriot sources, unfriendly to the Emperor, relate that as he was on his way to his ship in the early morning, while passing along the street of the butchers, Frederick was pursued by people ill disposed towards him, who 'pelted him with tripe and with bits of meat most

[1] *Mémoires*, 24–5. See also Lamonte, *The Wars of Frederick II*, pp. 90–1.
[2] Huillard-Bréholles, iii. 138.
[3] Philip of Novare, *Mémoires*, 25.
[4] Most of these arrangements are described in *Eracles*, 375, and by Philip of Novare, *Mémoires*, 25. For his grants to the Teutonic Order see Huillard-Bréholles, iii. 117 f.: 'et castro novo, quod dicitur Montfort.'

scurrilously'.[1] This somewhat incredible tale is related only by chroniclers who supported the Cypriots, particularly the Ibelins, and owes its origin most probably to a desire to derogate the Emperor while praising John of Ibelin, Lord of Beirut. The latter, together with Eudes of Montbéliard, Constable of Jerusalem, is said to have hurried to the spot and to have driven away with blows those who had been throwing things at the Emperor. Accompanying Frederick on his voyage were his young ward Henry, King of Cyprus, and the Marquis of Montferrat. They paused on the island of Cyprus 'at Limassol, and there established the aforementioned King Henry and gave him to wife one of his cousins, the daughter of the Marquis of Montferrat'.[1]

After a voyage of extraordinary speed for that time, Frederick landed in his Kingdom at Brindisi on 10 June. His unexpected arrival, the report of which apparently did not reach Rome until a month lates, may well have been something of a shock to the Pope, who was not wholly free of guilt in spreading the rumour of the Emperor's death.[2] The news of Frederick's return spread rapidly throughout Sicily, and from Barletta he issued his appeal to his loyal followers for support. The response was immediate and enthusiastic. Thomas of Acerra, who had arrived before the Emperor, took command of the large numbers of troops in Capua and was joined shortly afterwards by Frederick himself. Loyal troops assembled from all parts of the Kingdom, and German crusaders, returning from the expedition to Syria, joined the Sicilian forces before proceeding homewards. Now that he had an army of sufficient size, Frederick began the reconquest of his Kingdom. Success after success attended his efforts and, before the end of the year 1229, he was again in full possession of his Kingdom. Dependent as they were on mercenary troops, the leaders of the papal armies found themselves unable to meet the heavy expenses of the conquest. It is said that Cardinal John Colonna, leader of one of the papal armies, was compelled at times to satisfy his mercenaries from his private resources. Towards the end of the summer of 1229 the want of funds was so acute that the Cardinal was compelled to take leave of his army and hasten to the Pope at Perugia to seek ways and means of providing for the mercenary army. The Cardinal was reimbursed for his generous sacrifices whed the Pope, in July 1232, arranged for repayment through a merchant of Siena.[3] No less important than the want of funds was the effect of Frederick's safe return. Many who had readily enlisted in the papal armies in the belief that the Emperor was dead now showed little

---

[1] Philip of Novare, *Mémoires*, 25.

[2] For the date of Frederick's arrival see *Breve chronicon de rebus Siculis*, 902. For the Pope's alleged guilt in spreading the rumour of Frederick's death see above, p. 212, note 6.

[3] BFW, *Reg.* v, Abt. iv, 13104.

interest in that service. Large numbers of the Lombards withdrew to their homes while the papal troops remaining in the Kingdom were demoralized, causing a speedy withdrawal across the Volturno. Richard of San Germano wrote that, with the spread of the news 'that Caesar had come from Syria to Apulia, the papal army began to dissolve because of fear'.[1] In a letter to his friend Fakhr-ad-Dīn Frederick told how, upon his arrival at Brindisi, he found that John of Brienne and the Lombards had entered his Kingdom. With the spread of the report of his return the invading army, filled with terror and confusion, fled across the Volturno.[2]

From Capua, which for some time John of Brienne and Pelagius had been besieging, and from which they had withdrawn as far as Teano upon receiving intelligence of his approach, Frederick sought to cut their line of retreat. With this in view he made a thrust through Alife and Venafro, but the enemy forces had retreated with too great speed to be overtaken. At this time Frederick believed the retreat had been ordered by the Pope and had so stated in a letter to Fakhr-ad-Dīn. It is of interest to observe that in a subsequent letter to his Arab friend he corrected this statement.[3] This large-scale retreat must have been most distressing to the Pope, carrying with it his hopes for triumph over his foe, profound humiliation, and the loss of papal prestige. How disastrous the military effort was is perhaps best revealed by the withdrawal of the former titular King of Jerusalem from the joint leadership of the papal army. The unfortunate Brienne, a competent military leader, was again to witness the collapse of a military enterprise in the company of the ill-starred Pelagius who had brought disaster to the crusaders at Damietta. It could have been only with profound disillusionment that he now sought safety from the pursuing Emperor in his native Champagne. In the words of a contemporary, 'John of Brienne, a declared enemy of the Emperor, fearing capture, fled to his native soil of Gaul'.[4] Already the disastrous flight of the 'Key Soldiers' was indicative of the extent of the fiasco of the papal effort to wrest the Kingdom of Sicily from Frederick II. By the last week of October 1229 the papal troops had disappeared beyond the borders of the Kingdom. The forces of the Emperor entered the border city of Sora which had been in possession of a papal garrison. The city itself he burned, although the castle of Sorella on the outskirts still remained in possession of an enemy garrison when Frederick

---

[1] *Chronica*, 157.

[2] The letter is translated from the Arabic by M. Amari, 'Estratti del Tarih Mansuri' (*Arch. stor. Sicil.* ix, 1884), 119 ff. See especially p. 121: 'Quando poi noi scrivemmo e inviammo messaggi a significare ch'eravamo ritornati sani e salvi, cominciarono i nostri nemici a turbarsi; entrò negli animi loro il terrore e la confusione; [in fine] voltarono le spalle retraendosi disordinati a due giornate di cammino.'   [3] *Ibid.*

[4] Roger of Wendover, iv. 209. *Eracles*, 379: 'et s'en ala en France li rois Johan.'

returned to Apulia.[1] The punishment inflicted upon Sora indicates the violence of the Emperor's wrath towards those who deserted him in time of need. It is related that 'those of his adversaries who were taken prisoners in the castles were either flayed alive or hanged from the gibbet'.[2] It is somewhat surprising that so little is said of Frederick's acts of vengeance by contemporary chroniclers. It may well be that such acts were accepted as a matter of course in that age and were accorded only passing notice. Thus Richard of San Germano, speaking of William of Sora who surrendered the castles of Trajetto and Sujo to the enemy, states simply that he was hanged, along with others, outside the city of Sora. Necessarily refraining from capital punishment where the clergy were concerned, the Emperor took his revenge upon them for their disloyalty by seizing their property and placing it under royal administration.[3]

Frederick did not carry the war beyond his own borders. When he had successfully driven the enemy from the Kingdom he ended his northward drive, although it lay well within his power to utilize this favourable moment for incorporating into the Kingdom both the Duchy of Spoleto and the March of Ancona, thus linking the Kingdom with the imperial possessions to the north. But the time for this was inopportune. His future plans required most of all a conciliatory policy towards the Pope and Curia. In a world of Christendom that still saw in the papacy the heart and centre of its faith, the focal point of its social order, there was nothing to be gained by what might well be regarded as irresponsibility. So far, in his conflict with Gregory IX he occupied the position of the injured party. Unquestionably, the Pope's conquest of the Kingdom of Sicily in the absence of Frederick had established him as the aggressor against a sovereign who had sacrificed much and taken extraordinary risks to serve the interests of the Christian world. Frederick now badly needed the goodwill of Christendom. Peace with the Pope was good policy. But, though the Pope was defeated, he was determined that Frederick should not too easily enjoy the fruits of victory. Even in the most critical moments of his pontificate Gregory IX at no time lost sight of the advantages that he possessed over the temporal rulers of the earth. Frederick, perhaps more than any of his contemporary sovereigns, was aware of the significance in the eyes of Christendom of the Pope as Vicar of Christ. Accordingly, there is no moment in the career of Frederick II when his need for self-restraint was greater. The German princes, so deeply indebted to him

---

[1] Richard of San Germano, 163.
[2] Roger of Wendover, iv. 209. See also *Chronica Albrici Monachi Trium Fontium* (*MGH, SS.* xxiii), 925.
[3] Richard of San Germano, 156–63.

for their unique position, could now be employed to good advantage as mediators between himself and the Holy See. It was the loyal and indefatigable Hermann of Salza, aided by Thomas of Capua, Cardinal Priest of St. Sabina, who made the successful preliminary approaches to the Pope and Curia. Fortunately there were several among the cardinals who were convinced of the errors of Gregory's policies and who, in a crisis such as then existed, could make their influence felt. Moreover, by assuming responsibility for the good faith of the Emperor, as they had done on more than one occasion in the past, the German princes at last prevailed upon the Pope to permit Frederick to make his peace. Although the Pope yielded, it was all too apparent that the actual removal of the ban was a deep humiliation to him. For a man of Gregory's unfailing singleness of purpose such a step must have seemed to him a repudiation of all that he had worked for since his elevation to the papal throne. Having yielded, however, on the question of the ban, the ultimate victory was, in a large sense, his. At first sight it appears incredible that Frederick II, so completely the military victor, could now, in return for the removal of the ban, yield much of what he had tenaciously clung to in the past. Indeed, as the negotiations proceeded, Frederick's insistent desire for penance must have strengthened the belief of the Pope that every advantage was on his side, that he could impose upon the Emperor whatever demands he desired. The negotiations, begun in San Germano, were of long duration: it was not until 23 July 1230 that they were finally concluded in Ceprano in the presence of numerous spiritual and temporal princes.

The most significant of the concessions made by Frederick were to demands repeatedly made by both Honorius III and Gregory IX in the past. Henceforth the Sicilian clergy were to be exempt from temporal jurisdiction and from general taxation. Episcopal elections were to be free and the right of royal sanction was henceforth excluded. Frederick was to give satisfaction for the properties which he had confiscated after his return from Syria, from Templars, Hospitallers, and other ecclesiastical persons. In addition various lay personages whose property had been taken or who had been driven from their estates were to be recompensed for their losses. At first sight these terms appear to have been severe blows to the concept of sovereignty of Frederick II and serious departures from the traditional ideals of the Norman kings and the Hohenstaufen emperors. But was this a second Canossa? Or was it, in truth, merely a further reminder to Frederick of what he had long been aware: that the ultimate aim of the Pope was the elimination of him as King and Emperor? In assessing the significance of these concessions there is always the likelihood of measuring them in terms of modernity—not as concessions peculiarly related to the thirteenth century.

Frederick's world outlook, it is true, far transcended that of his own era, but he rarely lost sight of the fact that a politically successful statesman cannot appear to act beyond the limits that the world outlook of his era will permit. At Ceprano, as at Eger in 1213, and in Frankfurt in 1220, Frederick yielded to what he recognized as the one universally accepted institution of Christendom, the papal hierarchy. There is much truth in Hampe's comparison of Frederick's conflict with the Church with the fight of Hercules with the Hydra, 'the body of the Hydra always sprouted a new head'.[1] Conditions in 1229–30 were not yet suitable for pressing home Frederick's plans for the future realization of imperial sovereignty. His concessions at San Germano were in no sense an abandonment of these plans; they represent merely the imperial recognition of the necessity of marking time.

Not only must Frederick have time to re-establish and strengthen his hold in the Kingdom of Sicily, but he must face once more the serious problems imposed by the opposition of Lombardy to his plans. It can hardly be doubted that while the Lombard cities remained powerful enough to maintain their position as individual states, each exercising virtually unrestricted authority, the prospect for the re-establishment of a Roman Empire comparable in its sovereign rights to that of antiquity was remote. Moreover, as long as these cities of Lombardy maintained an offensive and defensive alliance with the papacy the chances of successfully opposing them were small. If, on the other hand, Frederick could win either of these allies to the support of his plans, the possibility of eliminating the other could be entertained. His policy for the moment, therefore, was directed towards *rapprochement* with the Holy See and, ultimately, the driving of a permanent wedge between these traditional allies. In the concept of Empire which now governed his policies the co-operation of Church and State was imperative. How closely Frederick was to identify these two institutions in the future will appear most strikingly in his *Liber Augustalis* or *Constitutiones* which he was to promulgate shortly after his reconciliation with the Pope in 1230.

It is noteworthy also that the extent of the concessions made by Frederick at Ceprano can easily be exaggerated. Questions such as the freedom of elections and the immunity of the clergy to general taxation had long existed as subjects of contention between the popes and emperors. The surrender of the right of imperial sanction of the choice of prelates was not as serious a weakening of the sovereignty of the King of Sicily as at first appears. It is most unlikely that a canonical election would normally be made in the face of the hostility of a powerful king and emperor. Certainly a cathedral chapter in Sicily would endeavour,

---

[1] K. Hampe, 'Kritische Bemerkungen zur Kirchenpolitik der Stauferzeit' (*Hist. Zeitschr.* 93, 1904), 425.

in so far as it was possible, to choose for its bishop a candidate whose relationships with the monarch might be expected to produce the best conditions for the bishopric. The restoration of confiscated property of the knightly orders and of lay nobles who had offended the monarch was, in fact, merely a return to the *status quo ante bellum* and was not, therefore, a serious encroachment upon royal sovereignty. The one thing that Frederick II needed most in 1230 in order to give validity and permanence to his achievement in the Orient and to give him freedom of action in the future organization of his Empire was the lifting of the ban. This he achieved in his peace settlement with the Pope. It could not have been other than astonishing to the world of Christendom that a King and Emperor who only a short time before had been depicted by Gregory IX as having 'eaten and drunk with Saracens', as being a 'blasphemer and a disciple of Muhammad', had now become, 'the beloved son of the Church'.

PART V

FREDERICK II, TYRANT OF SICILY

FREDERICK II'S *LIBER AUGUSTALIS* *JUSTITIA*

In hoc enim gloria regis extollitur et servatur, ut in quiete pacis populum dirigat et in iusticie vigore conservet.

MGH, Const. ii, no. 200, p. 267.[1]

IN September 1230 when Frederick II visited Pope Gregory IX at Anagni and 'this great priest and this mightiest of emperors feasted together for three days in the palace of the Supreme Pontiff',[2] he could for the first time since his coronation feel free to devote himself wholeheartedly to the establishment of his authority as King and Emperor in Sicily and Germany. No longer would he be subjected to insistent pressure by the Pope and Curia to fulfil his crusading vow; no longer would his title as King of Jerusalem be denied him. However temporary his arrangements in Germany may have been upon his departure from there following his eight years' residence; however humiliating his expedition into Lombardy in 1226; however subservient to Pope and Curia he may have felt compelled to appear, he could now move confidently, albeit circumspectly, towards his ultimate goal of Caesarism. The twenty years between 1230 and 1250 were to be the years of Frederick's matured statesmanship, the years witnessing his greatness as legislator, as administrator, as poet, philosopher, and scientist—above all, as the patron of a unique cultural revival.

Rarely in the history of the Western world has there been a more obstinate challenge to statesmanship than that which was now presented to Frederick II in his task of drawing together the reins of an Empire that extended from northern Germany to the Kingdom of Jerusalem; from Northern Italy, through Apulia and Sicily. How far was it possible in the thirteenth century to give unity and coherence to such an empire? To what extent could the sporadic manifestations of a cultural renaissance be made to express themselves as the common achievements of widely diversified peoples? In what measure could these heterogeneous peoples be consolidated under the unifying force of a universal law,

---

[1] For in this the renown of the King is exalted and preserved: that he governs the people in the tranquillity of peace and shields them by the force of justice.

[2] Roger of Wendover, iv. 216.

embodying concepts of justice akin to those of Roman antiquity? And, most difficult of all, could Frederick, by force or by reason, induce the Church to accept the principle that, by the grace of Divine Providence, the Emperor is arbiter between divine and human law—that he is, in matters of justice, what the Pope is in matters of faith? Already this concept of the immediacy of the Emperor's relation to God had been expressed in a letter of Frederick, written while he was in Syria, to the King of England shortly after his taking the crown of Jerusalem. 'We, as Catholic Emperor,' he wrote, 'wore the crown which Almighty God provided for us from the throne of his majesty when of his special grace, he exalted us on high among the princes of the world.'[1]

What Frederick had so sorely needed during his eight years in Germany in order to make possible the solidification of the disparate principalities—a compact family estate comparable to that of the Capetian Île de France—he now possessed in relation to the Empire as a whole in his hereditary Kingdom of Sicily. Here were his own people, accepting him not only as their hereditary monarch, heir to the Norman sovereignty, but as such by divine ordination. Supported by the loyalty of large elements of his Sicilian subjects and by what he conceived to be the gracious hand of God, the unique personality of Frederick II was to express itself in creating in Sicily the image of what was ultimately to be his World Empire. Here was the nucleus of his far-flung authority which he was to exercise in the future, comparable in dignity to that of the ancient Caesars. Despite the heterogeneous population, whether Greek, Arabic, Lombardic, Roman, or Norman, all had known but little of governments other than absolutist. All, with the exception of the Arabs, acknowledged the Christian faith, which, despite differences between Roman and Greek Catholicism, was a unifying force that could be used effectively by an enlightened sovereign. Already a uniform administrative system, a composite of Greek, Arabic, Lombardic, Roman, and Norman institutions, had been more or less perfected by the Norman-Sicilian rulers. Culturally also an amalgamation of formerly dissident elements was in progress and was capable of unlimited development when guided by a perceptive and understanding sovereign. In short, in a constituency accustomed to obedience the task of unification and consolidation which lay before Frederick II was one that he alone could accomplish. Under the existing conditions, the key to a successful achievement of this task was absolute sovereignty.

Certainly it was from his Norman ancestors that he derived his concept of kingship, that the function of the King is, above all, to establish and maintain peace, to punish wrong-doing, and to correct injustice.[2]

---

[1] Roger of Wendover, iv. 192–3.
[2] R. Gregorio, *Considerazioni sopra la storia di Sicilia*, p. xix; R. Pirri, *Sicilia sacra*, i. 393.

Like his Norman predecessors, he held fast to the principle that in matters of legislation the King is supreme, receiving from God the sole authority to make, to unmake, and to promulgate laws.[1] Theoretically also, Frederick II followed the Norman kings in asserting that a function of the kingship is the maintenance of the well-being of the Church, to protect and to augment its possessions.[2] In practice, however, his actions towards the Church and clergy were in sharp contrast with those of Roger II and the two Williams. The difference derives largely from the fact that at the Norman court there existed an intimate association of the King and the clergy. Throughout the Norman era the ecclesiastical princes exercised a preponderant influence at the court, both as counsellors and as ministers.[3] The policy of Frederick II, on the other hand, suggests always a tendency towards greater secularization of government officials. After his imperial coronation and his return to the Kingdom of Sicily he dissociated the clergy, save in a few instances, from participation in the government, replacing them with lawyers.[4]

The principal organ through which Frederick II exercised his sovereign authority, the *curia regis*, was strikingly similar to the Norman *curia* as to function, but widely different in constituency. True, most of the old official titles continued to appear among the personnel of Frederick's court, including Grand Justiciar and Justiciar, Grand Chamberlain and judges; seneschals and constables, dapifers or stewards, logothetes, and marshals. But the functions of these officials, often ill defined during the Norman era, were well defined in Frederick's court as to duties and as to the relations with one another. In short, the bureaucratic system took hold so that the reins, firmly held by the King, reached out through successions of officials, high and low, to the most subordinate of functionaries.

In wielding his sovereign authority through this vast hierarchy, Frederick II possessed both the talents and the compelling urge essential to the successful achievement of his ends. Master of several languages, he was free of the provincialism which was likely to prevail among the thirteenth-century monarchs of the West. Schooled in Arabic philosophy and Byzantine statecraft, and accustomed to associate with Greeks and Saracens, as well as Normans, French, Italians, and Germans, he was singularly free of all social and religious prejudices towards non-Christian peoples. As he revealed during his expedition to Syria and in his treatment of the Muslims in Lucera, he possessed the qualities inherent in the truly cultivated man of any era: a sincere and deep

[1] See the Assizes of the Kingdom of Sicily in the Appendix of F. Brandileone, *Il diritto romano nelle leggi normanne e sveve del Regno di Sicilia*, 96.

[2] See especially the two documents of William I and William II respectively, in K. A. Kehr, *Urkunden*, 433, 440.

[3] F. Chalandon, *Domination*, 617.   [4] See below, p. 240.

appreciation of the cultural potentialities of mankind, regardless of race or nationality. With these qualities, he was equipped, as no other monarch of his era, to undertake the building of an empire. Physically indefatigable, mentally alert, and always articulate, he moved easily and confidently towards the human destiny which Dante, reflecting the wisdom of Aristotle, represented as apprehension through *potential intellect*. Frederick II seems never to have doubted that there are eras in history in which tyranny or enlightened despotism is not only justifiable but necessary. Roman law, never absent from a Hohenstaufen court, provided ample theoretical support for his absolutism; the Arabic states, intimately observed by him during his crusade, revealed to him the bureaucratic agencies through which the theory of absolutism could be applied in practice to an unlimited sovereignty.[1] Just as he conceived of his temporal authority as ordained of God and independent of the restraints of the Pope, so he regarded his 'Order of Justice' as resting, not upon a foundation of clerical and feudal officialdom, but upon a group of lay jurists schooled in ancient Roman administrative, legislative, and judicial processes. The Byzantine heritage of Sicily, with its pattern of sovereignty in which all the reins of government were joined and tightly held in the hands of a central hierarchy, served in part to create an atmosphere thoroughly congenial to the political ideals of Frederick II. Since the arrival of the Hautevilles in Apulia and Sicily the monarchs of this venturesome family had understood how to adapt both the Byzantine and Arabic bureaucratic systems to the institutions of the West. Frederick II could improve upon this effort by virtue of the knowledge of a host of attendant jurists, products of the revival of Roman law of the twelfth and thirteenth centuries, through which the concept of the sacredness of the imperial office was strengthened and widely disseminated.

Just as Frederick could say of Alsace in its relation to other regions of Germany that it was the land 'which among all others of our patrimony we hold most dear', so he could say of the Kingdom of Sicily in its relation to the Empire as a whole:

Though . . . the many nations who breathe under our rule in a desirable state of peace are a constant source of concern for us, we are led by a special affection to think assiduously on how the native population of our Kingdom of Sicily, which demands a more special attention, and which is the most brilliant of all our possessions, may so flourish in honourable peace that it may be increased as in the times of Caesar Augustus.[2]

On many occasions he visualized in this most admirable of his hereditary

---

[1] See especially the development of this concept by F. Kampers, *Kaiser Friedrich II. Der Wegbereiter der Renaissance*, 36.

[2] Winkelmann, *Acta*, i, no. 799, p. 622.

possessions a renewed prosperity comparable to that of the time of Caesar Augustus. This land of his birth was 'the apple of his eye', 'a haven during storms', 'a garden of pleasure in the midst of thorns'.[1]

With amazing success Frederick had accomplished the preliminary steps in the rehabilitation of the Sicilian Kingdom shortly after his coronation as Emperor. But his preoccupation with the imperial interests in Lombardy and with the preparations for the pledged crusade had made it impossible to push to completion the work of reorganization. Throughout his reign the basic plan for the future Empire was never to change: first Sicily, then Central and Northern Italy, and finally Germany were to be brought within the framework of the *imperium*.[2] It is in the recognition of this as the basic plan that is to be found the significance of his assizes of Capua and Messina, of his summoning the Diet of Cremona in 1226, of his persistent efforts to regain control of the Duchy of Spoleto and the March of Ancona, of his first and second Lombard expeditions, of his determination to crush the Lombard League, of his expedition to Germany in 1235 and, finally, of his belief in the necessity of possessing the city of Rome itself as the centre of empire. This was the plan that Frederick conceived as realistic even when, speaking idealistically, he visualized the *imperium* as embracing the earth, and himself as *pater imperii, imperii auctor, imperialis rector*.[3]

Frederick never ceased to enunciate the principle that God caused a mere human creature, possessing no superiority to other men, save the dignity of his office, to be elevated as ruler of mankind. He was no less convinced that disobedience to the imperial will was a form of heresy which must be punished as treasonable. Thus he condemned as heretics those who claimed obedience only to God. For, like those who refused submission to the Church, they denied obedience to the man ordained of God to rule the world. Following the traditional doctrine of Christendom, he held that all things must be subordinate to a higher power: the Empire to the Emperor who, in turn, like the Pope, is subject only to God.

In an extraordinary letter, addressed to 'doctoribus et scolaribus' of the University of Bologna, Frederick asserted that all authority of the imperial government had been placed by God in the hands of one individual in order that it might not be lessened by division.[4] Those who oppose this are guilty of denying divine arrangements and may be legitimately punished. Frederick saw himself as seated upon a temporal throne of God, as if he himself were God, having power to alter existing

---

[1] See ibid., no. 811, p. 630; no. 935, p. 710; Huillard-Bréholles, vi, part ii, 569.

[2] See K. Klingelhöfer, *Reichsgesetze*, p. 25 and note 3. Also see above, pp. 101 and 179.

[3] *MGH, Const.* ii. 323, line 7; 365, line 8.

[4] A. Gaudenzi, 'La costituzione di Federico II che interdice lo Studio Bolognese' (*Archivio stor. italiano*, 5th series, 42, 1908), 356.

laws and to change conditions of the era in which he lived. The Emperor
was in all temporal things what the Pope was in all things spiritual:
each in his peculiar sphere was God's vicar upon earth.[1] In contrast
with his grandfather and his father, who venerated the laws of Constantine, Justinian, Valentinian, Charlemagne, and Louis the Pious as
'divine oracles',[2] Frederick II looked beyond them to Caesar Augustus
as his guide and mentor in his effort to restore peace and tranquillity
upon earth.[3] Indeed, there is much in the writings of Frederick II to
suggest that the shades of difference between grandfather and grandson
may be due to the greater influence of Caesar Augustus upon the thinking of the latter. To his Sicilian subjects there was nothing incongruous
in Frederick's references to himself as *magnificus* and *Caesar* or in his
exaltation of himself by implication in referring to *magnificus ille Julius
primus Caesar*.[4]

With concepts such as these, which had tended to crystallize during
the ten years since his imperial coronation, Frederick now approached
his great task as lawgiver in his *Constitutiones* or *Liber Augustalis*, promulgated in August 1231. This remarkable document, so revealing of
the genius of Frederick II, owes its greatness not to originality—for it
was not original—but rather to its selectivity, its clarity, and, above all,
to its comprehensiveness. Although Lombard features are discernible
here and there throughout the *Constitutiones*, and Norman influences are
ever present, the paramount influence, directly or indirectly, is Roman.
Its contents can be traced to three main sources: to the preliminary laws
promulgated at Capua and Messina during the first years after his
imperial coronation; to the laws and ordinances of his Norman ancestors
as Kings of Sicily; and finally, to the *novella* made necessary by the
normal changes in the customary procedures of a people in a prosperous
and dynamic state. The latter group derives naturally from the dictum
of Frederick II that whosoever wears the imperial crown is competent
to change the laws and the conditions of the era. In general, it may be
said of this group of laws that they often resulted from the application
of Roman law principles, thanks to the participation of Bolognese jurists
and to the vague procedural remnants of the customary practices of
both Lombards and Normans. What, indeed, were these old Norman
laws and customs which the assizes were intended to restore? To what
extent could the new customs and the new conditions be brought within
the purview of this earlier legislation? These questions he sought to

---

[1] The following passage in a document of Frederick II is especially relevant, Winkelmann,
Acta, ii, no. 1035, p. 711: 'cumque haberet cornu potestatis ac os loquens ingentia, putavit,
quod posset mutare leges et tempore.'

[2] *MGH, Const.* i. 322.

[3] See especially Winkelmann, *Acta*, i, no. 283, p. 257, and below, pp. 245 ff.

[4] Huillard-Bréholles, vi, part i, 28.

resolve by a process singularly reminiscent of the procedures of his Norman cousins in England: inquests similar to those employed in the compilation of Domesday Book, obtaining the sworn testimony of local men. From each province Frederick ordered that four prudent elderly men be chosen and summoned to testify concerning traditional laws and procedures in their respective provinces in the time of the Norman kings.[1] It was from the testimony of these men that many of the laws promulgated in the *Liber Augustalis* or *Constitutiones* were assembled and compiled. Frederick could truly say of them that they had been codified, not without abundant advice and much deliberation, and on the authority of the *Lex Regia*, the citizens (*Quirites*) had transferred to the *princeps* of Rome the right to make and to execute the laws.[2]

He perceived that the laws of his Norman predecessors, especially the codification of Roger II, were a composite of ancient Roman, Byzantine, and Arabic laws.[3] These collections or codifications became the bases for Frederick's legislation. Like his juristic advisers, he looked upon law as having its origin in the necessary temporal relationships of men—not in supernatural sources. But, if the laws of Frederick appeared to have their origin in precedent, they became, when embodied in his *Constitutiones*, royal laws, subject to change only by the will of the sovereign. Frederick did not share the medieval opinion that law is a permanent structure or that immemorial custom is capable of embodying all questions of human relationships, requiring only that the appropriate law be sought and found. What Frederick's jurists derived from these precedents in 1231 at Melfi 'did not take the form of precedents but of royal laws'.[4] Frederick himself, no less than his learned legal advisers, held firmly to the conviction that the Emperor 'receives his inspiration from heavenly reflection'. He was the creator, not the 'finder of law' in the accepted medieval sense—he was the 'maker or creator of new law'. Frederick II conceived of his unique position as legislator precisely as did the medieval publicist, John of Viterbo, author of the treatise 'De Regimine Civitatum': 'God subjected the laws to the Emperor and gave him as a living law to men.'[5]

The processes through which the *Constitutiones* came into existence are reminiscent of the great achievement of Justinian and his able jurists such as Tribonian. Few monarchs have been as well served by

---

[1] Winkelmann, *Acta* (*an.* 1230), i, no. 761, p. 605.

[2] Huillard-Bréholles, iv, part i, 33.

[3] For the collection of laws of Roger II, found without title in 1856 by John Merkel, and for the later transcription of William II, known as the *Assiza regum regni Sicilie*, see E. Caspar, *Roger II*, 237 ff. As to the retention of previously existing customary laws see ibid. 242 f.

[4] H. Niese, *Gesetzgebung*, 8–9.

[5] John of Viterbo, 'De Regimine Civitatum' (ed. C. Salvemini: *Bibliotheca Juridica Medii Aevi*, iii), 128.

capable jurists as was Frederick II. It may perhaps never be determined beyond all doubt which of the several jurists was to Frederick II what Tribonian was to Justinian. There appears to be no adequate reason to minimize or to dispute the statement attributed to the Emperor in the closing sentences of the *Constitutiones* that he had ordered 'Master Piero della Vigna, Justice of our Superior Court,' to codify these laws.[1] The role of Piero della Vigna in the actual administration of the government in the succeeding years and his manifold activities in the political and cultural life of the court appear to set him apart as the most likely of the jurists to be entrusted with this task.

It would be erroneous, however, to describe the *Constitutiones* or *Liber Augustalis* as merely a codification. Although consisting in part of previously unwritten customary laws and procedures of the realm, these were now greatly expanded and, above all, subjected to a process of Romanization. In many instances Roman law was cleverly introduced in place of the old Norman and Lombard laws. Less important, although by no means negligible, was the influence of the canon law, abstracted largely from a Roman-canonical law book which had made its appearance a short time before in Bologna.[2] The opposition of the Pope to what he called the 'unjust laws' (*leges iniquas*) arose not from the spirit of the laws but rather from the underlying principle that the Emperor was competent to change traditional laws and to alter existing customs and conditions. Most of all, the Pope must have resented Frederick's departure from the concept of justice which Gregory VII had long ago repeatedly emphasized as the peculiar responsibility of the Pope who, as Christ's Vicar on earth, is the 'debitor justiciae in omnibus qui in Christo sunt—curia totius Christianitatis'.[3]

The Emperor's competence to change and even to create law in the interest of justice upon earth is nowhere better illustrated than in the restrictive measures he imposed. He accepted natural law as a creation of God, as an emanation from universal law which, once promulgated, could not be altered by God himself. Accordingly, without equivocation, and without reference to the prohibition of clerical involvement as promulgated by the Fourth Lateran Council, or to the hesitant arguments of the canonists, Frederick repudiated quite independently the trial by ordeal. As to the ordeal by fire, he held that it defied natural law, that the natural heat of red-hot iron could not 'become lukewarm or cold without the intervention of a natural cause'. Similarly, he

[1] Huillard-Bréholles, iv, part i, 176.

[2] H. Niese, 'Zur Geschichte des geistigen Lebens am Hofe Kaiser Friedrichs II.' (*Hist. Zeitschr.* 108, 1912), 534–5.

[3] It is estimated that Gregory VII employed *Justitia* in this sense some 200 times. See E. Bernheim, 'Politische Begriffe des Mittelalters im Lichte der Anschauungen Augustins' (*DZfG*, Neue Folge 1, 1896–7), 7.

repudiated the lingering belief that 'because of a seared conscience the element of cold water will not receive the guilty'.[1] It was this defiance of traditional concepts of law and justice—this assumption of God-like sovereign authority—this professed determination to rule as God's plenipotentiary upon earth, that led the Pope to make the bitter complaint that 'in his Kingdom none dares to move hand or foot save with his consent'.[2] In his concept of his office the Emperor alone was the source of all temporal justice and justice was the author of peace. There is in this concept the ever-present inspiration of the Augustan Empire, the vision which Virgil beheld with the coming of Octavianus: 'the great cycle of eras is born anew. Now comes the Virgin (Justitia), the reign of Saturn returns; now from high heaven a new generation descends.'[3]

Frederick saw in himself the servant of the newly returned *Justitia*. The importance that he attached to the imperial office as the arm of justice was apparent already at the moment of his return to Sicily in 1220, and is inherent in the assizes of Capua and Messina. Even more it permeates the *Liber Augustalis* or *Constitutiones*. When he considered them appropriate, he utilized many of the penalties imposed by Roger II and William II for such criminal acts as falsification of documents, the sale, possession, or use of poisons intended to affect the mind of the victim or to cause his death.[4] While retaining essentially the old laws concerning pandering, adultery, compulsory prostitution, arson, perjury, blasphemy, and other such crimes, he often imposed more severe penalties for these misdeeds. Thus mutilation by the amputation of the nose, the hand, or the tongue was prescribed for panders, perjurers, and blasphemers.[5] Whether in the adoption of old punishments or in the imposition of new, Frederick acted in the profound conviction that his legislation was sustained by Divine Providence through whom he derived his competence to arrange all human relationships.

From the outset the administrative system of Frederick II was centred in the Grand High Court Justiciars and in the Justiciars of the provinces. Already, in 1221, the office of *magnae curiae magister justiciarius* had assumed great importance when Pope Honorius III complained that Walter, Count of Catrone, then holding that office, had encroached

---

[1] See especially W. von den Steinen, *Das Kaisertum Friedrichs des Zweiten nach den Anschauungen seiner Staatsbriefe*, no. 9, p. 37. For an excellent account of papal and canonistic thinking leading up to the Canon of 1215 against ordeals see J. W. Baldwin, 'The Intellectual Preparation for the Canon of 1215 against Ordeals' (*Speculum*, xxxvi, 1961), 613 ff.

[2] *MGH, Epist. Pont.* i, no. 601, p. 648: 'ubi nullus manum vel pedem absque ipsius movet imperio.'

[3] *Ecloga* iv.

[4] *Constitutiones*, Huillard-Bréholles, iv, part i, 164–78.

[5] Ibid. 172, 173, 175.

upon the *patrimonium* by taking hostile action against the city of Rieti.[1] In most of the officials of the court of Frederick II there was a certain continuity from the Norman era. This was strikingly true of the office of Justiciar (*justiciarius*). It was after the reorganization of the Sicilian constitution under Roger II, in 1140, that the Justiciar assumed a more or less definite role in the *curia regis*.[2] Even then, however, Roger II himself usually presided at sessions of the *curia* when he was, in fact, his own Grand Justiciar. It was in the practice of delegating royal officials to various provinces with orders to make specific inquests that the office of Justiciar had its origin.[3] Originally, such officials seem to have been charged primarily with jurisdiction in criminal cases and in certain civil cases involving fiefs, but before the close of the reign of Roger II the Justiciar was, in fact, the viceroy of the King, authorized to dispose of any royal business[4] that the King might designate.

In course of time the Kingdom was divided into jurisdictional regions (*justitiae*), each with its Justiciar or, apparently in some instances, Justiciars.[5] It was during the reigns of Roger's successors, William I and William II, that the Grand Justiciar of the Royal Court assumed his position as chief of the judicial personnel of the *curia regis*.[6] In addition to the *magistri justiciarii magne regie curie* or Grand Justiciars of the Royal Court, there were also during the Norman era the *magistri justiciarii* of the provinces, and below them the simple *justiciarii* and *iudices*.

The judicial system of Frederick II was, in large measure, a continuation of the Norman. The differences appear, not in the personnel of the Justiciary, but rather in the ever-expanding judicial business. As the royal administration developed between 1220 and 1239, and as the threat to the Kingdom and the Empire increased during the conflict between Frederick II and the Pope, the organization of the Justiciary became more rigid. More and more its control tended to centre in the royal court. Formerly the Grand Justiciar had exercised his functions while moving about the Kingdom. In 1239 he became a more constant member of the royal court. Some of his former functions were assumed by the two Master Justiciars, each governing one of the great subdivisions of the Kingdom, although directly responsible to the Grand High Court Justiciar, who, in turn, was directly responsible to the Emperor. The Justiciary, like all other departments of the government, now fell within the framework of a close-knit hierarchical organization. A Grand Justiciar such as Henry of Morra with the full title Master Justiciar of the Great Imperial Court (*magne imperialis curie magister*

---

[1] Horoy, iii. 863. [2] E. Caspar, *Roger II*, 308 ff.
[3] Chalandon, *Domination*, 646 ff.
[4] Ibid. 679, 681, and K. A. Kehr, *Urkunden*, no. 14, p. 431.
[5] *Romoaldi Annales* (*MGH*, *SS*. xix), 423.
[6] Caspar, *Roger II*, loc. cit. See also W. Behring, 'Sicilianische Studien', i. 14.

justiciarius) was, at least nominally, regarded as having jurisdiction over the whole Empire. In actuality his authority appears to have extended only over the Kingdom of Sicily and imperial Italy. Below him were, first, two Master Justiciars and, subordinate to them, the Justiciars of the provinces. How completely this hierarchical organization had developed by the last decade of Frederick's life is apparent in an order, promulgated probably in 1244, requiring that all petitions, whether from the Empire or Kingdom, be presented to the Grand Master Justiciar of the Imperial Court.[1] Here, as in other instances, where such phrases as *tam de imperio quam de regno* are employed, *de imperio* appears to have applied to the imperial possessions on the mainland of Italy in contrast with the Kingdom.[2] The full significance of that office came to be recognized during the long tenure of Henry of Morra, who occupied it for twenty years after 1223. During those two decades he appeared not only in a judicial capacity but as regent of the Kingdom and as trusted imperial plenipotentiary.[3] The importance that the Emperor attached to the Justiciar of the Imperial Court, the Master Justiciars of the two sub-divisions of the Kingdom, and the Justiciars of the provinces is to be seen in the regulations governing such officials, first in the *Liber Augustalis* as it appeared in 1231, and subsequently as it was modified in 1239–40 and in 1244.[4] In each of these modifications the authority of the Justiciar was increased and the dignity of his office enhanced.[5]

While these articles of the *Constitutiones* applied primarily to the *magne imperialis curie magister justiciarius* and to the two Master Justiciars of the grand sub-divisions of the Kingdom, they appear to have applied also by implication to Justiciars of whatever degree. Above all, the Justiciar must be the 'mirror of justice', an 'example to others'. The dignity which the Emperor bestowed upon this office is emphasized in an article of the *Liber Augustalis* decreeing that 'when at any time the Master Justiciar visits a city, there to hold court with our judges, the Justiciar of the provinces, who may by chance be present, shall maintain silence, as the lesser light is dimmed when it is overtaken by the greater'.[6] The authority of the Grand Master Justiciar was greatly extended in 1244,

---

[1] Huillard-Bréholles, vi, part i, 160: 'Praecipimus offerri magistro justitiario omnes petitiones tam de imperio quam de regno tam de justitia quam de gratia.' On the probable date of this see Ficker, *Forschungen*, i, par. 202, note 4, p. 363; and par. 206 and notes.

[2] Huillard-Bréholles, Introduction, p. cxxxviii, note 1.

[3] A monograph including a sketch of Henry of Morra by M. Ohlig, *Studien zum Beamtentum Friedrichs II. in Reichsitalien von 1237–1250* (Diss., Frankfurt, 1936), has eluded my every effort to obtain it either in the original or in copy.

[4] See *Constitutiones*, Book I, Title XL, part ii, and Title XLI (Huillard-Bréholles, iv, part i), 47, 49–50, 182 f.; and ibid. vi, part i, 158.

[5] See H. Niese, *Gesetzgebung*, 168–9.

[6] *Constitutiones*, Title XLI, Huillard-Bréholles, iv, part i, 50.

when he was charged with the reparation of injuries, abuses, extortions, etc., of all inferior Justiciars; with the restoration of property which had been wrongfully seized, and with the release of persons unjustly held prisoners. Moreover, he was at that time permitted to exercise these functions without the necessity of consulting the Emperor. He was assisted in these duties by four accompanying justices who appear to have been appointed for life.[1]

The officials assigned to govern each of the two great sub-divisions of the Kingdom bore the dual title of Captain and Master Justiciar. Their jurisdiction extended over the provinces which lay within their respective sub-divisions. Their functions, broadly defined, were: to make known the imperial decrees throughout the provinces; to hold or to expedite the holding of courts on regularly assigned days; to take cognizance of all serious offences involving counts, barons, and other personages of rank. As their titles indicate, their functions were political and military as well as judicial. Normally, their courts were held twice annually for the adjudication of major crimes and grievances. They also possessed appellate jurisdiction over the provincial Justiciars. The Master Justiciar represented the Emperor, save in cases involving treason and certain other crimes against the crown. In a large sense, he supervised all royal officials within his sub-division, including royal procurators, castellans, etc. As early as 1220 Matthew Gentile served as Captain and Master Justiciar for Apulia and the Terra di Lavoro[2] and was succeeded in this office in 1221 by Thomas of Acerra.[3] In March of 1221 the new office of Grand Master Justiciar of the Imperial Court was established.[4] At that time also five judges (later four) were associated with him as *magne imperialis curie iudices*.[5]

The similarity of titles indicates that the judicial functions of the Superior Justices of the High Court and those of the Grand Master Justiciar cannot be too narrowly separated when purely judicial functions are concerned. At times, in the absence of the Grand Master Justiciar, the *magne imperialis curie iudices* appear to have performed his judicial functions.[6] The close association of the two offices becomes increasingly apparent during the frequent absences of the Grand Master

[1] Huillard-Bréholles, vi, part i, 156 ff., especially 158.

[2] E. Winkelmann, 'Zur Geschichte Kaiser Friedrichs II. in den Jahren 1239 bis 1241' (*FzDG* xii, 1872), 558. See also Huillard-Bréholles, ii, part i, 597, note 1, and 168, note 1.

[3] Richard of San Germano, *an.* 1221, 94.

[4] H. Niese, 'Normannische und staufische Urkunden' (*QF* ix, 1906), 250 f.: 'Richerius Melfiensis episcopus imperialis aule familiaris et magne curie magister iustitiarius.'

[5] Ibid. See also W. E. Heupel, *Der sizilische Grosshof unter Kaiser Friedrich II.*, 84, 139 ff., for the pertinent documents.

[6] See, for example, a document drawn up in favour of Thomas of Santa Maria de Luco, in which the decision was rendered by Simon of Tocco, Peter of San Germano, and Henry of Tocco, *magne imperialis curie judices*: Huillard-Bréholles, ii, part i, 431–3.

Justiciar from the court on missions which were not connected with judicial matters.[1]

It was not until 1239 that the two great sub-divisions of the Kingdom of Sicily were placed regularly under the jurisdiction of each of the two Master Justiciars, who assumed in their respective sub-divisions many of the functions previously exercised by the Master Justiciar of the Kingdom. The provincial Justiciars, while subject to the constant supervision of the Master Justiciars, were, like their superiors, responsible to the Emperor. They too exercised administrative as well as judicial functions and, towards the end of Frederick's reign, they commanded the imperial troops within their provinces. They were subject to constant supervision in all their activities, and every precaution was taken to detect and prevent abuse of office. The local Justiciars could not be residents of the provinces in which they served, and were rarely permitted longer than one year's tenure in office within the same province, although there were some notable exceptions to this rule.[2]

The provincial Justiciars were not permitted to enter into contracts, to be betrothed, or to marry within their respective provinces during their tenure. Like other holders of benefices from the Emperor, they could marry only with his consent. Neither the Justiciar nor his sons could hold property within the province, nor could they engage in any form of profiteering. They must be content solely with the emoluments of their offices. Lest they be tempted to enter clandestinely into profitable enterprises or to show favouritism toward local residents, they were forbidden to accept any form of hospitality when holding court in any part of their provinces.[3]

The Justiciars, rarely lawyers themselves, were accompanied by trained jurists when on judicial missions. Just as the Grand Master Justiciar of the Imperial Court was attended by four Justices of the High Court, so also the Master Justiciars of the royal sub-divisions each had his accompanying judge or judges. Large cities, such as Naples, Messina, and Capua, usually had five resident judges and seven notaries, while the smaller towns each had three judges and six notaries. The provincial Justiciars were aided also in their purely judicial functions by one judge and one notary. Like the Justiciars of whatever degree, the judges and notaries were royal appointees. Ecclesiastics were strictly barred from all justiciarships, ostensibly because the office involved, at times, the *jus sanguinis*, although long before this time bishops had constantly

---

[1] Heupel, *Grosshof*, 88–9.

[2] Huillard-Bréholles, Introduction, p. cdxv, note 2, compiled from the *Chronica* of Richard of San Germano.

[3] *Constitutiones* (Huillard-Bréholles, iv, part i), 187, 189–91.

exercised this function.[1] A more plausible explanation of the exclusion of the clergy from this office is to be found in Frederick's tendency to secularize all the activities of government that he considered temporal functions and therefore sharply differentiated from spiritual functions by the will of Divine Providence.

[1] *Constitutiones* (Huillard-Bréholles, iv, part i), 187 ff.

II

THE KINGDOM OF SICILY
DESPOTIC BUREAUCRACY

Nec ob hoc solum quod altius sedeant reges et Cesares ab aliis distinguntur,
sed quod profundius videant et virtuosius operentur.

Letter of Frederick II to his son (Huillard-Bréholles, v, part i, 274).[1]

THE most striking feature of the *Liber Augustalis* or *Constitutiones* is
its emphasis upon the ultimate authority of the royal court, the
heart and centre of which was the Emperor. Repeatedly in royal
documents, as in the *Constitutiones*, the *plenitudo potestatis* of the Emperor
is emphasized.[2] As with so many other features of the royal court of
Frederick II, this was but a continuation of the absolutism in the
Norman-Sicilian concept of sovereignty, originally introduced by Roger
II and continued through the reigns of the two Williams. This is apparent in the development of the Justiciary, the Camera or fiscal and
economic department, and in the Chancery. It is in the latter department that Frederick II made the earliest and most radical departure
from the Norman pattern, but only after his imperial coronation and
after his return to the Kingdom of Sicily. The full significance of this
change can be understood only in contrast with the Norman system
from which it was derived and from which it deviated.

The pattern of the Norman-Sicilian Chancery was created by Guarin,
the first of the royal Chancellors of King Roger II. It remained substantially unchanged until the year following Frederick II's return to
Sicily, 1221. Originally the Arch-Chaplain (*magister cappellanus*), Guarin
seems to have combined the duties of that office with the Chancellorship. As Chancellor he immediately assumed a position of authority
which made him, in some respects, the *alter ego* of the King.[3] His duties
were manifold and variable, although it is probable that his extraordinary power was derived chiefly from his preponderant influence in

---

[1] Kings and Emperors are not distinguished from other men merely because they are
seated more loftily, but because they comprehend more fully and act more worthily.

[2] *MGH, Const.* ii, no. 156, p. 192: 'Teneamus et simus in *potestatis plenitudine constituti*.' See
also ibid. 359.

[3] K. A. Kehr, *Urkunden*, 72–5; Pirri, *Sicilia Sacra*, i. 525; Caspar, *Regesten*, no. 72: 'Guarinus
Magister cappellanus, cancellarius.'

shaping royal diplomas, mandates, privileges, disposition of petitions, and other documents inherent in the authority of an absolute monarch.

Even greater, perhaps, was the power and influence of Admiral Maio who, beginning his official duties as archivist (*scrinarius*), became Vice-Chancellor in 1151 and Chancellor during the last years of Roger II.[1] Like his predecessor, Guarin, and his several successors, he was at times governor, commander of expeditionary forces, administrative official, and, next to the King himself, the responsible executive for both internal and external affairs. He continued as Chancellor under William I where he was, as he has been justly described, 'in some ways the actual sovereign'.[2] Subsequently, he was rewarded with the title of Emir of Emirs (*ammiratus ammiratorum*), traditionally the most important official among the courtiers of the Norman conquerors of Sicily.[3]

The development of the Chancery and of the extraordinary prestige and power of the Chancellor was further extended under the youthful Frenchman, Stephen Perche, who, as the court favourite of Margarita, the Queen Regent of young William II, was given unlimited authority until finally overthrown by a group of courtiers hostile to the foreigner's influence.[4] It was said of Stephen that a short time after his elevation as Chancellor he won the confidence of the Queen so completely that he ruled the Kingdom as he desired.[5] While exercising extraordinary political power, Stephen Perche made few significant changes in the characteristics of royal diplomas, although he introduced some innovations in the procedure of the notaries in the Chancery.[6]

It is obvious that because of their many and varied duties the Chancellors, who were frequently absent from the court for long periods, were not in a position to be other than general directors of the activities of the Chancery, although it is apparent during the chancellorship of each of them that they maintained a firm hold upon its personnel and its proceedings. The actual implementation of diplomas, privileges, mandates, etc., devolved upon a chief notary, or protonotary, and his lesser aides.[7]

If we may believe the strongly partisan account of the so-called Falcandus, it was Matthew of Salerno ('Ajello') who led the conspiracy against Stephen Perche and who, although only a *magister notarius* at the time, coveted the chancellorship.[8] Serving as Vice-Chancellor from 1170 to 1189 during the reign of William II, Matthew was made Chancellor

---

[1] K. A. Kehr, *Urkunden*, 49–50.

[2] Chalandon, *Domination*, ii. 177: 'en quelque sorte le véritable souverain.'

[3] See especially *Romoaldi Annales* (*MGH, SS.* xix), 427.

[4] For his career and influence at the court see Chalandon, *Domination*, ii. 320 ff., and K. A. Kehr, *Urkunden*, 84 ff. The basic source is Falcandus, *Historia* (*Fonti*), especially 110 ff.

[5] *Romoaldi Annales* (*MGH, SS.* xix), 436.

[6] For his political power see Amari, *Storia dei Musulmani*, iii. 497. See also K. A. Kehr, op. cit. 85.

[7] K. A. Kehr, *Urkunden*, 96–9.

[8] *Historia*, 69.

in 1190 by Tancred of Lecce shortly after the election of the latter by the Nationalist or Sicilian party, in opposition to Henry VI and Constance.[1] Despite his hostility to Stephen Perche and his criticisms of the operation of the Chancery, Matthew's influence, like that of his predecessor, was chiefly political, with but slight impact upon the internal operation of the Chancery.

The transition, therefore, from the Norman to the Hohenstaufen era, only a few months after Matthew's death, seems to have had little effect on the Chancery. Moreover, numbers of Sicilian magnates and bishops well disposed towards the Hohenstaufen were associated with Henry VI from the beginning of his conquest. Among these was Walter of Palear, Bishop of Troia, who appears as witness to imperial documents in 1192, together with Markward of Anweiler and other German and Sicilian magnates and bishops.[2]

It is not known in what capacity Walter served at the court of Henry VI during the years between the first and second Sicilian expeditions. But shortly after Henry's return and successful conquest of the Kingdom, Walter appears as Sicilian Chancellor in the following association with Conrad of Hildesheim, Frederick's German Chancellor and representative in Sicily: 'Ego Corradus dei gratia imperialis aule cancellarius una cum domino Gualterio regni Sicilie cancellario recognovi.'[3] It may be assumed, therefore, that the office of chancellor and the Chancery itself during the lifetime of Constance and during the regency of Innocent III continued much as they had been in the Norman era. It was typical of Conrad that he was disposed to make the fullest possible use of knowledgeable Norman-Sicilian officials, such as Eugene of Palermo with whom he formed a close personal and official association in 1196, and who was especially active in the operation of the Camera during the early months of Henry VI's reign.[4] Walter of Palear, like Eugene of Palermo, seems to have been given the utmost freedom in the exercise of his office as Chancellor, not only during the brief vicegerency of the Empress Constance but also during the regency of Innocent III. Subsequently also, until shortly after Frederick's coronation as Emperor and his return to Sicily, when he dispensed with the chancellorship, Walter continued in that office. After the departure of Walter of Palear from the court in 1221, the royal seal was entrusted to John, Abbot of Casamara, although the position of the abbot was relatively insignificant at the court.[5] This was indicative of the new order of administration in

---

[1] K. A. Kehr, op. cit. 62. See above, pp. 5–6.
[2] Stumpf, iii (Acta imperii adhuc inedita), nos. 407 and 410.
[3] Ibid., no. 421.
[4] For this association see especially E. Jamison, *Admiral Eugenius*, 151 ff.
[5] Huillard-Bréholles, ii, part i, 260. See also H. M. Schaller, 'Die staufische Hofkapelle im Königreich Sizilien' (*Deutsches Archiv*, xi, 1954–5), 486 ff.

which the King, assuming an absolute authority, could brook no rivalry from a formerly influential nobleman such as Walter of Palear.[1] Henceforth, the King would act not through a Chancellor, but through a Chancery, the notaries of which were responsible directly to the King. Moreover, the members of the former Council, chiefly nobles and prelates during the early years of Frederick's reign, were now, with but few exceptions, replaced by jurists or by juristically educated notaries who acted as counsellors. This reorganization was in conformity with the Emperor's policy of reducing to a minimum the influence of the clergy and nobility and the creation of an officialdom of laymen wholly dependent upon the will of the sovereign.[2] It was characteristic of the states of western Europe during this era that their sovereigns permitted the office of Chancellor to remain vacant, while the Chancery itself continued to function through its notaries.[3] From the time of Frederick II's return to Sicily in 1220 the term *cancellaria* appears almost consistently instead of *cancellarius*. In Germany the office of Chancellor continued after its disappearance in Sicily.

The change in the Chancery at the imperial court in Sicily is to be seen in the activities of a group of counsellors (chiefly jurists) who, as intimates of the Emperor, were often authorized to carry out mandates of his which formerly would have been dealt with by the Chancellor. These counsellors can best be described as *relatores* (proposers or movers), a term employed as early as the Carolingian era to designate court officials to whom, in their capacity as referendaries, letters and petitions addressed to the Emperor were referred for appropriate action.[4] More and more these *relatores* (*ad hoc* chancellors), often specialists in certain fields of administration, assumed the function of the Chancellor. Under Frederick II they became the chief agency for liaison between the Emperor and the numerous notaries who constituted the department of the Chancery. It was the *relator* who must ascertain the will or who

---

[1] See, above, the several chapters concerned with Frederick's minority for the power of Walter as Chancellor. For Frederick II's absolutism see A. Manongiu, 'Note federiciane' (*Studi medievali*, new series, 1952), 292–324.

[2] V. Samanek, *Kronrat und Reichsherrschaft im 13. und 14. Jahrhundert*, 2. See also H. Bresslau, *Handbuch der Urkundenlehre für Deutschland und Italien*, i. 431. It is to be noted, however, that court chaplains continued as active officials especially as ambassadors (see H. M. Schaller, op. cit. 491, 492).

[3] H. W. Klewitz, 'Cancellaria' (*Deutsches Archiv* i, 1937), 73–4. That this change in the various states of Europe was in keeping with the new conception of the state has been shown by A. Brackmann, 'Die Wandlung der Staatsanschauungen im Zeitalter Kaiser Friedrichs I.' (*Hist. Zeitschr.* 145, 1931), 1 ff.

[4] Du Cange, *Glossarium Mediae et Infimae Latinitatis* (10 vols., Paris, 1883–7), vii. 106, quotes a passage from *Capitulis Caroli M.*, Lib. 2, cap. 26: 'Et quando aliquis ad nos necessitatis causa reclamaverit, ad eos possimus Relatorum querelas ad definiendum remittere.' See *MGH, Legum*, i, *Hludowici et Hlotharii Capitularia, Ansegisi Capitularium*, Liber II, 296, lines 10–14.

shared the *conscientia* of the Emperor, and it was he who must assume responsibility for action in conformity with the Emperor's wishes.[1] In years of great activity, such as the decade following Frederick's second excommunication in 1239, eighteen such officials appear from time to time with special commissions to implement the imperial orders through the notaries of the Chancery.[2] Usually *relatores* thus commissioned were also chiefs or members of the various court offices, i.e. judges, proto-notaries, chamberlains. At times also provincial officials, temporarily at the court, might serve as *relatores*. Most conspicuous, however, as officials serving in this capacity were men such as Thaddeus of Suessa or Piero della Vigna who were especially mentioned by the Emperor as counsellors. Frequently employed also as *relatores* in the imperial Register of 1239–40 were Master Albert of Catania, William of Tocca, and, most frequently of all, Richard of Trajetto. Often imperial docu-ments implemented by these officials were accompanied by notations indicating both the *relator* responsible for its preparation and the notary who drafted it: *De mandato imperiali facto per judicem T. de Suessa scripsit Jacobus Bantra.*[3] That these men enjoyed the special confidence of the Emperor is apparent both in the number and in the variety of subjects in which they were privy to the imperial *conscientia* and with which their letters of reply (*litterae responsales*) and letters close dealt. It has been estimated that during 1239–40 the notary Richard of Trajetto was mentioned 60 times, more or less, as *relator*; Piero della Vigna about 150 times; and Thaddeus of Suessa some 75 times.[4]

Many of the letters prepared by these men are replies to inquiries by local Justiciars, regional chamberlains, procurators, or other judicial or financial officials. They are of especial interest in revealing how closely the Emperor observed all branch departments of the far-flung adminis-trative and judicial business of his Kingdom. Close scrutiny of these letters as well as of royal mandates, often sent out as letters close, sug-gests also the growing importance of Piero della Vigna at the court of Frederick II. It is at once apparent that many of the most delicate questions arising between the Emperor and the Church were generally referred to him for consideration and reply.[5] Further evidence of the Emperor's reliance upon Piero della Vigna is to be found in letters of reply and in royal mandates concerned with high treason, the choice of

[1] V. Samanek, *Kronrat*, 29–30. See also Winkelmann, *Acta*, i, no. 924, p. 701: 'de quibus si ad vestrum spectat officium, nostram conscientiam consultatis.'

[2] W. Heupel, *Der sizilische Grosshof*, 7. See also V. Samanek, *Kronrat*, 28.

[3] Huillard-Bréholles, v, part i, 451 f.

[4] This estimate of W. Heupel, *Grosshof*, 8–9, differs somewhat from that of V. Samanek, *Kronrat*, 28, but in no wise detracts from the exceptional activity of these men.

[5] This has been previously noted by W. Heupel, *Grosshof*, 9, and is to be seen in several typical letters in Huillard-Bréholles, v, part i, 435, 437, 439, 474, 518, 524, and numerous others.

ambassadors, especially for oriental courts, and with questions pertaining to Frederick's most cherished project, the University of Naples.[1] In certain matters of special importance Piero della Vigna, Thaddeus of Suessa, and Richard of Trajetto acted conjointly as *relatores* in the preparation of a royal mandate. This was especially true in times of great crises such as the year 1240 when the Emperor ordered the Justiciars of the provinces to enlist mercenaries to be employed in an expedition against the Lombards.[2] How little Frederick concerned himself with social position or class in choosing his *relatores* is to be seen in this frequent association of Richard of Trajetto, a notary, on a plane of equality with the two Justices of the Superior Court. This is perhaps best illustrated by Johannes Maurus who, although a Moor, rose from slave to Chamberlain (*camerarius*). He appears on more than one occasion as the author of letters of reply and royal mandates having to do with expenditure of royal funds.[3]

The governmental reorganization which took place as a result of the promulgation of the *Liber Augustalis* tended, with the passing of time, to establish a tightly organized bureaucratic system in which officials, high or low, never ceased to be conscious of the immediate influence of the royal court. The administration of justice, the levying and collecting of taxes, the waging of war, the control of the fiscal system, the initiation of new laws and ordinances—all these were functions of the central government, the *curia regis*. While most of the departments of government had originated in the twelfth century under Roger II or the two Williams, it was Frederick II who defined the functions of each in its relation to the others and so organized all of them that they operated constantly as the direct agents of the King. As one traces the development of this bureaucracy through the years between 1231 and 1250 it appears as a gradually perfected pyramidal structure, the base of which became perfectly articulated with the apex, the seat of the King and Emperor. Any effort, therefore, to describe the royal court in detail must make allowance always for an evolutionary development reaching its nearest perfect form in the last decade of Frederick's life. The second excommunication of the Emperor in 1239 and his deposition at the Council of Lyons in 1244 compelled him to extend and to consolidate his sovereign authority. As these changes occur, however, one ideal is never lost sight of: the ultimate centralization of administration, justice, and legislation in the hands of the Emperor who, in his own person, was the animating force that imparted life and vigour to every agency and to every official throughout the Kingdom.

The first significant changes in the manner of administration resulted

[1] Heupel, loc. cit.   [2] Huillard-Bréholles, v, part ii, 924.
[3] See, for example, ibid. v, part i, 486–7, 492.

from the increased business of the court imposed by the assizes of Capua and Messina. What was begun in these assizes was carried further towards the ultimate goal of Caesarism in 1231 at Melfi, in 1239, following Frederick's second excommunication, when he felt free to include within his jurisdiction the lands of the Church, and in 1247 after the conspiracy against his life. The final step towards complete hierarchical rule was taken when vicars-general, established throughout the provinces of Italy and Sicily, were chosen primarily because of their close relationship with the Emperor—with but few exceptions from sons and sons-in-law. After the promulgation of the *Liber Augustalis* in 1231, the trend towards secularization became more pronounced. While this trend was, in some measure, the most revolutionary feature of the Hohenstaufen era as a whole, its realization in the political sphere was so complete under Frederick II as to make of it the most striking characteristic of his reign. Indeed this political change is but a single manifestation of what has been aptly described as 'a spiritual revolution of immeasurable importance which amounted in essence to a secularization of the whole of human life'.[1]

It would perhaps not too greatly distort Frederick's concept of the *imperium* to describe it as comprehending the *ecclesia* as the body comprehends the soul. The temporal administration, therefore, of the Empire, the determining of that which is just or unjust, including measures necessary for the safeguarding of the Church, was the task of the supreme temporal sovereign, the Emperor. To Frederick II in the thirteenth century, as to Dante in the fourteenth, there was nothing incongruous in the concept of a world-monarch who was directly responsible to God and yet who was, at the same time, obedient to the Pope in spiritual things. While such convictions as these might evoke from contemporaries the charge of heresy, Frederick regarded himself as incapable of heresy where his sovereignty was concerned, because he owed obedience to God only and was the temporal agent of God upon earth. He expressed his concept of his unique position in a letter to his friend Fakhr-ad-Dīn, written after his return from the crusade, in which he described himself as 'protector of the Roman Pontiff, defender of the religion of the Messiah'.[2]

Even more incompatible with the thinking of the Pope and Curia, indeed, with Christian thought traditional in the Middle Ages, was Frederick's theory of sovereignty as set forth in the preamble of the *Liber Augustalis*. In substance this theory was: After the world was created by Divine Providence, man, in the image of God, with soul and body,

[1] A. Brackmann, 'The National State' (Barraclough, *Medieval Germany*, ii), 297–8.
[2] M. Amari, 'Estratti del Tarih Mansuri' (*Arch. stor. siciliano*, new series, Ann. IX, 1884), 120: '. . . sostegno del pontefice di Roma, aiutator della religione del Messia.'

and but little inferior to the angels, was called into being. This creature of God was made sovereign over the earth, crowned with the diadem of honour and glory. He was provided with a companion, a woman, from his own body. They were endowed with pre-eminence over all other creatures, which, in the beginning, made them immortal. But, because of their violation of the first law, they destroyed the precious gift of immortality. So that their species might not perish, however, their seed became fruitful and their mortal progeny spread over and dominated the earth, although inheriting from their sinful parents the punishment meted out to the transgressor. Plagued by this mortal sin, men came to hate one another and, contrary to the law of nature, they divided and disputed their common possessions, thus falling into deadly strife. Unbridled wickedness prevailed among them until, moved by the very urgency of their condition, and through divine inspiration, they chose princes to rule over them and to put an end to their strife. These chosen rulers were given power over life and death and, as vicars, through the grace of God, they were empowered to adjudicate and to give to each that which was due. God also commanded these princes to safeguard the Christian Church, the mother of the community of mankind, against its enemies and against heretics, in order that the people might enjoy the blessings of peace and justice. It was to this end, so the preamble continues, that Frederick himself, contrary to the expectations of mankind, was elevated above all the princes of the earth, to the supreme office of Roman Emperor.[1]

It is at once apparent that Frederick departed abruptly and boldly from the traditional doctrine of the Church that princes were established as a punishment for man's sinfulness. In its place he substituted a doctrine of *necessity* which men are made to comprehend through divine inspiration: 'and so the necessity of things, no less than the inspiration of Divine Providence, gave rise to the rulers of the people, empowered to restrain the licence of evil-doers.'[2] Implicit in the whole of the preamble to the *Liber Augustalis* or *Constitutiones* is the idea expressed a generation later by St. Thomas Aquinas: 'Gratia non tollit naturam sed perficit.'[3] Frederick's conception also of the role of the ruler in this society born of necessity anticipates the later thinking of St. Thomas. Before humanity can enjoy eternal salvation man must first be restored to his state of pristine innocence. But this is to be accomplished only when justice is made to prevail upon earth, and only the prince is the fountain of justice. It was the often-reiterated conviction of Frederick II

---

[1] *Constitutiones*, Huillard-Bréholles, iv, part i, 3–5.
[2] 'Sicque ipsa rerum necessitate cogente nec minus divine provisionis instinctu, principes gentium sunt creati per quos posset licentia scelerum coerceri.' Ibid. 3.
[3] 'Grace does not abolish nature but perfects it.'

that the glory of the kingship comes from the princely guiding of the people 'in the tranquillity of peace and the protecting of them by the force of justice'.[1] It was precisely this thought that St. Thomas also expressed as to the ultimate aim of mankind, i.e. the attainment of complete blessedness (*perfecta beatitudo*). But this was something to be attained only in a future life, although preparation must be made for it during man's terrestrial existence. This was possible only through the *pax terrena*, the securing of which St. Thomas regarded as the function of the prince, made possible as an expression of God's providence.

It may always be debatable whether or not Frederick's concepts of a sovereign state and of sovereignty had their origin in the purely practical demands with which he was faced, and in remnants of old laws still extant, or were the inevitable outcome of his metaphysical ideas. It may be questioned also whether or not Frederick, as a practical statesman, left to his counsellors, especially to Piero della Vigna, the task of giving to his state a philosophical justification.[2] The probable answer to each of these questions is that Piero della Vigna, as so often during his long service to the Emperor, was merely giving expression to a political philosophy or, indeed, to a metaphysical system, which was the common property of the two men. For there would seem to be here marked evidence of the intellectual intimacy which caused Dante to ascribe to Piero della Vigna the words: 'I am he that held both keys to the heart of Frederick, and I turned them, locking and unlocking so smoothly that I excluded from his secret thoughts almost every man.'[3]

The coexistence of God and necessity as activating or originating forces in the emergence of sovereign authority was not, in the thinking of Frederick, discordant or incongruous. He saw them as complementary to each other, as the soul is to the body. For, in the concept of Frederick, the necessity of things does not exist without God, nor can it exert its influence without his incentive. Thus marriage was introduced because of the necessity for procreation, but only through the consent of the heavenly will.[4] Through specific laws, however, governing the institution of marriage or other social institutions within the Kingdom, Frederick 'as the vital and animated law upon earth' had no doubts as to his right to regulate them.[5]

Frederick II assumed a commanding position among a small group of men of the thirteenth century whose insistent search for the natural

---

[1] *MGH, Const.* ii. 267: 'ut in quiete pacis populum dirigat et in justicie vigore conservet.'

[2] See the remarks of K. Hampe, 'Das neueste Lebensbild Kaiser Friedrichs II.' (*Hist. Zeitschr.* 146, 1932), 457.

[3] *Inferno*, XIII, lines 58 ff.

[4] *MGH, Const.* ii, no. 188, p. 230.

[5] Huillard-Bréholles, iii. 469 and 231 note 1: 'viva et animata lex in terris'; 'dominus imperator qui est animata lex in terris . . .'

causes of all things, whether animate or inanimate, gradually pointed the way for the human intellect to escape from its preoccupation with the miraculous. In an age rigorously disciplined in the acceptance of the supernatural and miraculous as adequate explanations of phenomena, Frederick moved boldly across the restrictive boundaries delineated by the Church. He thus made possible a concept of government based upon laws that were adaptable to a changing world and capable of creating an environment of terrestrial peace without impinging upon the spiritual province of the clergy. Frederick's *Constitutiones* possesses a dynamic quality, often anticipating the political philosophy of both Dante and St. Thomas Aquinas. Like St. Thomas, Frederick conceived it to be the function of a king 'to preside over all human activities and to direct them in virtue of his own power and authority'.[1] Although perceiving that a king must direct human activities in virtue of his own authority, St. Thomas, as a cleric, was unable to escape the traditional doctrine of the Church that 'he who has charge of supreme ends, i.e. the attainment of the blessed life which is promised in heaven, must take precedence over those who are concerned with aims subordinate to these ends'.[2] Dante, however, layman that he was, clarified the theory of sovereignty which Frederick II and his juristic counsellors obviously anticipated. Thus Dante says: 'Therefore man had need of two guides for his life: whereof one is the Supreme Pontiff, to lead mankind to eternal life . . . and the other is the Emperor, to guide mankind to happiness in the world, in accordance with the teaching of philosophy. . . . It is therefore clear that the authority of temporal monarchy comes down, with no intermediate will, from the fountain of universal authority. . . .'[3]

This theory of the two powers had been lucidly set forth by Frederick II in his letter to the cardinals in 1239 defending his orthodoxy and protesting the right of Gregory IX, 'since he was not a true pontiff', to bind and loose. It is in this letter that he presents his own interpretation of the doctrine of the 'two luminaries' in opposition to that held by the canonists of the thirteenth century: 'God, at the creation of the world,' Frederick insisted, 'had placed two lights in the firmament, a large one and a smaller one, the large one to preside over the day, the smaller one, over the night. But these two are independent of each other, so that one never disturbs the other, although one communicates light to the other.'[4] Cognizant also, as they undoubtedly were, of the political philosophy of Otto of Freising, as well as of the Roman law, Frederick and his legal advisers at no time lost sight of the fact that the Empire pre-existed the

---

[1] *De Regimine Principum*, Book I, ch. xv.

[2] '. . . qui de ultimo fine curam habet, praeesse debet his, qui curam habent de ordinatis ad finem . . .' Ibid. loc. cit.

[3] *De Monarchia*, Book III, ch. 16. From the translation of F. J. Church, 1879.

[4] Huillard-Bréholles, v, part i, 348.

Roman Church. Otto of Freising had written: 'When the sovereignty of the Romans had progressed to its best state and to the loftiest peak of empire, he [God] willed that his Son, Christ, should take flesh.'[1]

As was habitual in the Middle Ages, Frederick II conceived of the *imperium* in a two-fold sense: on the one hand, it was the whole of the Christian world; figuratively, however, it embraced the earth; it was 'the empire, vast in extent and limited in its breadth only by the boundaries of the earth'.[2] Strictly speaking, there existed in Frederick's thinking no hard-and-fast separation of Church and State, of *imperium* and *ecclesia*. As he expressed it in a letter to Pope Gregory IX in 1232, *ecclesia* and *imperium* are descriptive of two manifestations of the same society of men, one of these a healing balm, the other a cutting sword, but each having its origin in divine authority.[3]

As the years went by the conviction grew in the mind of Frederick II that the imperial office, thus made illustrious by the reflected glory of God, had become the peculiar possession of the Hohenstaufen. In a letter to the King and the nobility of France written in 1247 he complained that Gregory IX had once irresponsibly excommunicated him and that Pope Innocent IV, at the Council of Lyons, had offered various kings and princes the imperial dignity and 'our Kingdom', which had been acquired by the Staufen 'and made illustrious by the blood of our fathers and consecrated by their sepulchres and statues'.[4] Thus the *Fortuna Caesarea* had come to be lodged within the Staufen family, making of its members, as occupants of the imperial throne, a part of world destiny, 'the divine offspring of the blood of the Caesars'. But, since necessity and the inspiration of Providence gave to the prince supremacy over other men, the Roman Emperor, who rules also by virtue of his election by the German princes, does so through more than earthly power. The German princes had recognized this more than temporal right when, in electing Conrad, the son of Frederick II, as King of the Romans they exercised their electoral authority through 'the grace of the Supreme King'.[5]

This insistence upon the sanctioning of the imperial authority by God, and the association of the ideas of world monarchy with God, imparted to the Emperor such an aura of dignity that it was said of him that 'he wished to seat himself upon the throne of God as if he were God'.[6] He saw in himself the acme of universal authority, the heir of the omnipotence of the ancient Caesars. God led and guided him in each victory

---

[1] *Chron.*, Lib. V, 4, p. 189. See also ibid., Lib. III, Prologue, p. 132.

[2] Winkelmann, *Acta*, i. 315.   [3] Huillard-Bréholles, iv, part i, 409 f.

[4] See Huillard-Bréholles, vi, part i, 514; and the slightly different text in C. Höfler, *Kaiser Friedrich II.*, 418.

[5] *MGH, Const.* ii. 441: 'inspirante nobis tam salubre consilium gratia summi Regis . . .'

[6] Winkelmann, *Acta*, ii, no. 1037, p. 711: 'quasi deus esset, in cathedra dei sedere voluit.'

and made his fortune complete. God held him aloof from dangers and permitted him to foresee them.[1] In his insistence upon his nearness to Divine Providence Frederick at no time disputed the spiritual function of the Pope. As he repeatedly emphasized: God 'has decreed that the machine of the world is to be governed, not by the priesthood alone, but by the royal and the priestly authority together'.[2] It was from such concepts of the sacredness of his office that Frederick derived the meaning of empire, the five-fold mission devolving upon him who holds the title, Augustus: to care for the Empire; to protect its honour; to augment its laws; to extend its boundaries; to enrich its faith.[3]

To Frederick II the responsibility of the Emperor for maintaining peace was in no sense limited. Like his predecessors of antiquity, he conceived of the *imperium* as embracing the entire earth. 'Our reins', he once wrote to the Romans, 'extend to the outermost limits of the earth. ... Rome shall yield to us, because the earth serves us, the sea obeys us, and at our nod all desires are fulfilled.'[4] Piero della Vigna wrote of the Emperor: 'Truly the earth and the sea honour him, and fittingly the air praises him to whom the world looks as Emperor.' Piero said of him: He is 'the friend of peace, the patron of charity, the maker of laws, the conservator of justice, the authority governing the world in its permanent arrangement'. He declared that it was of him that Ezekiel (17 : 3), said: 'A great eagle with great wings, long winged, full of feathers, which had divers colours.'[5]

Throughout the Middle Ages there was a certain vagueness as to the relationship existing between the Emperor and the kings of the emerging states of Europe. In addressing his immediate subjects Frederick spoke without restraint of the boundless authority of the Emperor, by virtue of whose breath the whole world lives. In a letter to his German subjects he reminded them also of the greatness and majesty of the Empire in virtue of which they held the sovereignty of the world.[6]

In contrast with these exaggerated claims, there is a marked restraint in Frederick's letters to princes outside his immediate royal and imperial authority. In a letter to the King of England about the Tatar invasion he wrote: 'We cannot remain silent on a matter which concerns not only the Roman Empire . . . but also all the kingdoms of the world that practise Christian worship.'[7] In another letter, to his brother-in-law Richard of Cornwall about the wrongs which he had suffered at the

---

[1] Matthew Paris, *Chronica majora*, iii. 631.   [2] Ibid. iv. 129.
[3] See, for example, the *Prooemium* to *Constitutiones* (Huillard-Bréholles, iv, part i), 3–4. See also von den Steinen, *Kaisertum*, 24–7.
[4] Huillard-Bréholles, vi, part i, 145; Piero della Vigna, *Epist.* ii. 8.
[5] Huillard-Bréholles, *Pierre*, no. 107, p. 425.
[6] *MGH, Const.* ii. 267; ibid. 224. See also ibid., no. 197, p. 263.
[7] Matthew Paris, *Chronica majora*, iv. 112.

hands of the popes, he wrote: 'not more to our injury than to all kings and princes.' He was equally circumspect when, in the same letter, he said: 'It is true, it begins with us, but it will end with some other kings and princes . . . kings, therefore, defend the justice of your own cause in ours.'[1]

Already in Frederick's time the concept of a universal *imperium* was much disputed. The Emperor himself appears to have employed this all-comprehending concept of the *imperium* in a more or less idealistic or figurative sense. Certainly the last half of the thirteenth century witnessed the general acceptance of the opinion that the kings of Europe were wholly independent of imperial authority.[2] The restrained remarks of the Emperor when addressing the King of France and the King of England and their obvious feeling of independence leave no doubt that it had become a mutually accepted principle 'that the French cannot make laws for the Empire, or the Emperor for the King of France'.[3] Whatever may have been the hopes and expectations of Frederick for the future of his *imperium*, the *Liber Augustalis* or *Constitutiones* was, in fact, an effective instrument only in the Kingdom of Sicily, albeit a Sicily which Frederick saw as the model of a future Empire.

---

[1] Ibid. iii. 588–9.   [2] Carlyle, *Mediaeval Political Theory*, v. 145.   [3] Ibid. 146.

III

THE FISCAL ADMINISTRATION OF
THE KINGDOM OF SICILY
SOURCES OF REVENUE

Imperialis excellentie solium tunc augetur cum retinendo que donat
et donando que retinet . . .

Huillard-Bréholles, iv, part. i, 485.[1]

THE emphasis which Frederick II placed upon justice as the all-
dominant function of the Emperor made it inevitable that his
judicial system would be first to fall within the framework of his
hierarchical regime. Hardly less important, however, was the *camera*
which, as a highly specialized department of the *curia regis*, had gradually emerged during the thirteenth century. Although at first wanting
the close-knit hierarchical organization that characterized the judiciary,
there was a perceptible unity in the *camera*, the fiscal and business centre
of the royal court. Like the Justiciary and the Chancery, the Camera
was a direct descendant of the Norman-Sicilian system. Its differences
in the Frederican court stemmed chiefly from the expansion and greater
complexity of the imperial regime, from the changes in the social and
economic structure of the state, especially in the feudal society, from
the changed status of the municipalities, and from the greatly expanded
political and economic relations with the outside world. Yet, in its
broad outlines the financial administration, including the office of the
magister camerarius palatii (the Grand Chamberlain of the Palace or of the
Royal Court), the *dohana de secretis*, and the *dohana baronum*, was a
continuation of that of Roger II as it had developed toward the middle
of the twelfth century and as it was expanded by his successors, the two
Williams.[2]

[1] The rule of the imperial excellence is then increased when it bestows for the purpose
of conserving and when it conserves for the purpose of bestowing.

[2] The following description is based on Falcandus, *Historia (Fonti)*, 48–50, 109; Cusa, *I
Diplomi greci ed arabi di Sicilia*, 489–90, 564, 622, 626: C. A. Garufi, 'Sull'ordinamento amministrativo normanno in Sicilia: exhiquier o diwan?' (*Archivio stor. italiano*, 5th series, i. xxvii),
17, 19, 20 f., 26–7, 40, and 227–63; Pirri, *Sicilia sacra*, i. 384, ii. 1017; Kehr, *Urkunden*,
282 ff.; Amari, *Storia*, iii. 327. See also E. Jamison, 'The Norman Administration of Apulia
and Capua' (*Papers of the British School at Rome*, vi, 1913), 413 ff., and Chalandon, *Domination*,
647 ff.

The chief official of the Norman-Sicilian *camera*, the *magister camerarius palatii* or Grand Chamberlain of the Palace, was the dominant figure in the hierarchical organization of the financial administration. Under him were the two branches of the treasury: the *dohana de secretis* and the *dohana baronum*. The former, in addition to being the supervisor of all employees of the *camera*, was concerned chiefly with tenures and services due to the Crown. He was responsible for the list of villains bestowed by the King in the granting of a domain. In general, he dealt with all economic rights of the King in relation to the royal domains. The *dohana baronum* was concerned with all business of the feudal group, the registration of the names of vassals and the record of services due to the King, the number of knights, sergeants, etc., to be provided by each feudal holding.[1]

The functions of both the *dohana de secretis* and the *dohana baronum* varied within the framework of their respective departments. They might be arbitrational, judicial, or auditorial. This may best be observed through the activities of Eugene of Palermo, an official of long experience, who at different times occupied each of these offices. At one time he might be seen in Salerno auditing the accounts of a provincial *bailli*, at another, occupied with judicial business, hearing a suit concerning the wrongful occupancy of land belonging to the state.[2]

The hierarchical organization of the Camera extended from the office of the Grand Chamberlain of the Palace down to the provincial *magistri camerarii* who were concerned with all business pertaining to the royal revenue within their respective provinces, including supervision of lesser functionaries.

The usefulness of the Grand Chamberlain (*magister camerarius palatii*) and of the cameral organization as a whole was fully realized during the tenures of two occupants of that office, Richard, designated as *Ricardus camerarius* or *camerarius imperialis aule*, and Johannes Maurus, a Moorish slave who rose to become Chamberlain.[3] Of obscure origin, Richard held the office of Chamberlain during the crucial year of 1212, when Frederick journeyed to Germany to receive the crown. He continued to witness as *camerarius* until 1234. He died in 1239, when he was succeeded by Johannes Maurus,[4] who continued as *camerarius* until after the death of Frederick II. It was during his tenure that the office attained its complete hierarchical organization and became the most

---

[1] The most satisfactory treatment of the *dohana baronum* is that of Garufi, op. cit. 20 ff.

[2] For these and other duties of the *magister duanae de secretis* and *magister baronum* see especially E. Jamison, *Admiral Eugenius*, 70–1.

[3] Winkelmann, *Acta*, i. 262; Huillard-Bréholles, v, part ii, 720. See also Nicholas of Jamsilla, *Historia* (Muratori, *RIS* viii), col. 522.

[4] Huillard-Bréholles, Introduction, p. cxlvii; and the passage in Kehr, 'Thomas von Gaeta' (*QF* viii, 1905), 44.

important department of Frederick's administrative system. Moreover, it was destined to exercise a perceptible influence on the corresponding departments of the governments of modern Europe. The activities of the *camera* of the palace during his regime can be generally summarized as follows. It dealt especially with the intimate affairs of the royal household; with periodic reports from the provincial Chamberlains; with orders directed to the *magistri procuratores* and *secreti* or tax-collectors of imperial Italy, Apulia, Calabria, and the island of Sicily. Below the Grand Chamberlain or *camerarius imperialis*, and responsible to him, were various court officials, often appearing as *relatores*, more or less specialists in fiscal and household affairs which were under the supervision of the *camera*. As *relatores* they were charged with answering inquiries from regional or provincial *camerarii* or other subordinate officials throughout the provinces, and with drawing up royal mandates pertaining to expenditures authorized by the Emperor.[1]

The several tasks assigned to the court officials who, as *relatores* or as *ad hoc* Chancellors, were frequently associated with the Chamberlain are ascertainable from documents prepared by them with the assistance of notaries. The most noteworthy of this group of officials is Master Roger Camera; he, like Johannes Maurus, dealt frequently with the provincial *procuratores*, *secreti*, and other local officials, with expenditures for the imperial falconers, keepers of the zoo, the stud, and the imperial foresters. While the functions of Roger Camera were of such nature as to suggest a marked similarity to those of a royal or imperial steward or *bailli*, he performed them under the direction of the Chamberlain, Johannes Maurus.[2] Other *relatores*, also subordinate to the Imperial or Royal Chamberlain, were charged with supplying and managing the royal kitchen. For example, orders issued from the *camera* by one John of Palermo as *relator*, and addressed to the *procurator* of the Terra di Lavoro, had as their object the procuring of fish, wine, and other comestibles for the royal table.[3] Further activities of the *camera* are to be noted in some eighty letters prepared upon the orders of Albert of Catania as *relator* and concerned with loans from merchants of Rome, Siena, Parma, and other cities.

The regional or provincial administration was under a *magister camerarius* or a *secretus* as, for example, the frequently addressed *secretus* of Messina or the *camerarius* of the Terra di Lavoro. Their hierarchical ranking followed much the same pattern as the *magister justiciarius* in those sub-divisions.[4] The term *secretus* is an abbreviation of the original title

    [1] Huillard-Bréholles, v, part i, 477, 483, 486–7, 492, etc.
    [2] Ibid. 486; Heupel, *Grosshof*, 12, makes the plausible conjecture that Roger Camera belonged to the Camera family and his name was not derived from the office.
    [3] Ibid. 14.
    [4] Huillard-Bréholles, v, part ii, 603 ff.; and his Introduction, p. cdxvi, especially note 4.

doanarius de secretis et magister questorum. There was also another important financial official, the *magister procurator*, whose function originally seems to have been limited to the lands of the royal domain. There were times, however, when his activities closely coincided with those of the provincial *magister camerarius* and also when the two offices were occupied by the same individual.[1]

Just as the Master Justiciar supervised the work of the inferior judges in police matters, the Master Chamberlain was responsible for the adjudication of civil causes. Also within the jurisdiction of these officials was the superintendence of the imperial estates, the collection of customs, and other taxes. The Master Chamberlain not only nominated other civil officials within his area, but was also responsible for their proper performance. He was arbiter in many civil causes, notably in redressing damages to private persons inflicted by lesser imperial officials such as harbour-masters and supervisors of royal warehouses. He took cognizance also of causes involving the lesser fiefs, except those which were a part of the royal domain. The *Liber Augustalis* continued the functions of the *baillis* much as they had been established by Frederick's Norman predecessors.[2] They were appointed not by the Emperor but by the Master Chamberlain of the province or region in which they functioned. Like other officials concerned with the financial administration, the *baillis* were held to strict accountability and, in the event of proved malfeasance in office, they were subjected to the severest penalties. After payments were made for the various services within their jurisdiction the receipts from all authorized sources were sent to the royal *camera* where they were guarded by three treasurers, usually in the castle of San Salvatore in Naples. The financial administration throughout the Kingdom received the over-all supervision of courts of reckoning, *ratione curiae*. Unlike the supreme imperial court, this court of reckoning was mobile and was usually made up of a small number of officials, the *schola ratiocini*, who established themselves in a centrally located city until the completion of their assigned mission. Such a court was that which Frederick ordered to be established at Monopoli for the purpose of revising the accounts of the fiscal officials of the provinces of Bari and Otranto.[3]

During the last decade of Frederick's reign, when constantly hard pressed for funds for carrying on his struggle against the Italian cities of the north, he gave the court of reckoning a more regular, if not permanent, organization. In May 1240 he appointed four commissioners (subsequently changed to three) to constitute a court of reckoning to sit at Melfi. This court, similar in some respects to the English court of

[1] Ibid., Introduction, p. cxxvii, and iv, part i, 210.
[2] Ibid., iv, part i, 37–44; 202–4. [3] Ibid. 216 ff.

exchequer, was authorized to review accounts of all fiscal officials. Its function included the checking of current accounts and a re-examination of all reckonings of financial officials since the imperial coronation in 1220. It was charged with ascertaining what might still be due to the imperial treasury and, in case of deficits, it was authorized to compel the defaulting officials to make restitution.[1] This rigorous financial organization was made possible both by Frederick's departure from (or, more accurately, his radical modification of) the Sicilian feudal regime and by the application of methods derived from the Arabs.[2]

It becomes apparent as one follows the development of Frederick II's financial system that the key to its success was the efficient functioning of the provincial officials. The organization of the provincial government under both the *magister camerarius* and the *magister justiciarius* became much more rigid during the last twelve years of Frederick's reign, notably in 1240, following his second excommunication, and in 1246, after the conspiracy against his life. As in the central government there was a marked tendency towards greater precision. This is to be seen in the fixing of the number of Justiciars and Chamberlains at not more than one to each province, and in the assignment to each of a fixed number of judges and notaries. The cities also were subjected to a more regular administrative organization, usually with one bailii and one judge to arrange the legal proceedings and three judges to dispose of the cases involved. Exceptions were made for more important cities, including Naples, Messina, and Capua where there were five judges and eight notaries, made necessary because of the greater bulk of legal business, contracts, deeds, etc.[3]

These and other changes were directed towards a greater efficiency in the administration made imperative by the increased pressure from the conflict with the papacy, the determination of the Emperor to

---

[1] Huillard-Bréholles, v, part ii, 967–8. See also iv, part i, 219, note 1; and BFW, *Reg.* v, Abt. i, nos. 3079, 3080.

[2] See F. Kampers, *Wegbereiter*, 37. It is not the place here to review the conflicting opinions as to the origin of the Norman-Sicilian exchequer, i.e. whether Norman-French, in imitation of the English exchequer, or Arabic. See, for example, R. Gregorio, *Considerazioni sopra la storia di Sicilia*, i, 2nd ed., 1873, ch. vi, 257–66, who advanced the Norman-French theory, and who has been supported both by Stubbs and Freeman. The theory of Arabic origin is to be found in Amari, 'Sulla data degli sponsali di Arrigo VI con Constanza la erède del trono di Sicilia e sui divani dell'azienda normanna in Palermo' (*Atti della R. Acad. dei Lincei*, 3rd series, ii, 1877), 18 ff. Whatever the origin of the Norman-Sicilian exchequer may have been, there can be little doubt that Frederick's entire fiscal system owed much to Arabic influences. See also Garufi, 'Sull'ordinamento amministrativo normanno in Sicilia' (*Arch. stor. ital.*, 5th series, xxvii, 1901), 225–63.

[3] See first Huillard-Bréholles, iv, part i, 187, and then, A. Caruso, 'Le leggi di Federico II pubblicate a Barletta nel mese di ottobre del 1246' (*Studi in onore di Riccardo Filangieri* (Naples, 1959), 221–2. See also idem, 'Indagini sulla legislazione di Federico II di Svevia per il Regno di Sicilia — Le leggi pubblicate a Foggia nell'aprile 1240' (*Arch. stor. pugliese*, iv, 1951), 41 ff.

compel the submission of the Lombard communes, and (after 1246) the need for greater security against internal conspiracies.

The necessity for maintaining an almost continuously active army imposed a heavy demand upon the treasury. Although the regular income of the Sicilian crown exceeded that of other European monarchies, Frederick was compelled to alter and to expand the prevalent system of taxation and, certainly in imitation of the Arabs, to broaden the base of the direct tax as well as to augment the state income by employing a widely extended indirect taxation. After his return from his crusade in 1229, Frederick extended his taxation to cover all commodities which came within the purview of his monopolistic system. In the same way he was probably influenced by the Arabic system of tolls or customs levied at the Sicilian ports upon merchants exporting or importing goods.

A singular document contained in the *Chronica* of Richard of San Germano reveals the desire of Frederick to do away with exceptional taxes which had been imposed during the regency. In this, he decreed that citizens were no longer to be taxed for merchandise which they exported or imported, at a rate different from that which was customary under the Norman kings, his predecessors. Moreover, the old rate was re-established on apples, nuts, and various fruits, grass for cattle, beer, the sales tax on livestock, fees for weights and measures, tuna fish, anchovies, flax, cotton, and leather. This document, however, is chiefly of interest in revealing Frederick's idea of what taxation should be. In actuality it applied only to the year of momentary peace in 1231–2, following Frederick's reconciliation with the Pope; unfortunately, he was soon compelled to abandon this generous policy because of new demands on the treasury. It is noteworthy, however, that afterwards the new tax laws almost invariably included an apology. A typical note of this kind was the explanation that the new tax was levied only because the honour of the Empire required it and because his faithful subjects would never permit such a need for funds.[1] Most of these new or extraordinary taxes, including harbour dues, fees for grazing, fishing, and taxes on iron, steel, salt, and numerous other commodities, were collected annually.

The tax system rested fundamentally on the income from extensive crown lands, in the various provinces, supervised generally by royal procurators.[2] Feudal incidents were levied, normally, only under four conditions or on four occasions: when the sovereign raised an army for the defence of the realm; at the time of a coronation; when the King's

---

[1] Richard of San Germano, 183; Piero della Vigna, *Epist.* ii. 38.
[2] *Constitutiones speciales super magistris procuratoribus*, Huillard-Bréholles, iv, part i, 207 ff., Lib. I, Titt. LXXXVI, LXXXVII, LXXXVIII, XC.

son was knighted; when his daughter was married. These were the traditional feudal taxes to which Frederick's subjects, like those of western Europe as a whole, had long been accustomed. After 1229, when Frederick was engaged in driving the papal armies from his Kingdom, he levied the so-called *collecta*, a general tax demanded of all his subjects, including the clergy, as an emergency measure. What had formerly been infrequently collected now became a frequent, if not a regular, imposition. Against the complaints of the clergy that such taxation was illegal when applied to *res ecclesiasticae* or spiritualities, Frederick defended his actions on the ground that temporalities, i.e. lands held feudally by the Church, were taxable.[1] Shortly before his death Frederick himself recognized that he had permitted the *collecta* to become an abuse. In his testament he expressed the desire, 'that men of our Kingdom shall be free and exempt from all general taxes as they were accustomed to be in the time of King William II, our kinsman'.[2]

Frederick's rigorous regulation of trade and commerce, both import and export, while hindering, did not destroy the commercial activities which had long flourished in Sicily. After the initial impact of the assizes regulating the activities of foreign cities, especially the Lombard communes, in the Kingdom of Sicily, both foreign and domestic trade again revived and became important features of the national economy. Strict supervision of all aspects of trade, through tariffs, custom duties, and various fees, also provided a substantial source of the royal revenue. As a means of controlling these tariffs, Frederick established a system of *fondachi* or warehouses in which both native and foreign merchants were required to store their merchandise pending the levying of the tariff (*jus dohanae*), about 3 per cent of the sale price, and the warehouse tax (*jus fundici*), about 3½ per cent of the sale price.[3] There were also certain incidental fees, including landing and harbour dues. These regulations were applicable alike to imports and exports. Not only in the old ports, but in the newly designated harbours, Garigliano, Vietri, Pescara, St. Cataldo, Catrone, Agosta, Trapani, and Heraclea, where new facilities were provided, both customs and warehouse officers were established.[4] Lodgings for travelling merchants, previously maintained by private enterprise, became under Frederick II state monopolies and were maintained in each of the warehouses. In order that the maximum revenue might be raised from these accommodations, fees were demanded for beds, lights, wood, and straw.[5] Stationed in the warehouses also were

---

[1] H. J. Pybus, 'Frederick II and the Sicilian Church' (*The Cambridge Historical Journal*, iii, 1929), 159–60.

[2] *MGH, Const.* ii, no. 274, p. 386.

[3] Winkelmann, *Acta*, i, nos. 790, 792, 795, pp. 615–19. See also M. Garcia-Pelayo, *Frederico de Suábia e o nascimento do estado moderno* (tr. A. de Castro), 73.

[4] Huillard-Bréholles, v, part i, 418 ff.   [5] Richard of San Germano, 183.

vehicles, available for a substantial fee for the transportation of merchandise.

The meticulous administration of the *dogana* (*dohanae*) and the *fondachi* was assured by the two officials, the master of customs (*magister dohanae*) and the master of the warehouse (*magister fundicarius*), who served as checks upon each other. Indeed it was a unique feature of the hierarchical organization of the *camera* that all officials subordinate to it, from the *magister camerarius* of the imperial court, through the *magistri camerarii* of the provinces, the *magistri procuratores*, the *magistri fundicarii*, and all the lesser agents subject to their control, served as mutual checks upon one another.

The entire governmental organization of the Sicilian state was designed to provide the royal treasury with the maximum income. It is understandable, therefore, that in times of peace Frederick endeavoured to remove all serious obstacles to mercantile activities. Characteristic of this policy was a mutual ten-year agreement in April 1231 with the Sultan of Tunis, Abu-Zacharia, which, in addition to releasing all prisoners held by each, provided for reciprocal trading privileges.[1] There is some evidence also that Frederick contemplated similar agreements with India and Egypt. The English chronicler Matthew Paris states that Frederick 'was the friend and co-partner of all the sultans of the East in commercial enterprises; so that, on his account, merchants travelled by land and by sea to India'.[2] The Egyptian historian Maqrīzī relates that Frederick, during his negotiations with al-Kāmil while in Syria, sought to obtain an agreement for trade with Alexandria. While no evidence is extant that such an agreement was actually consummated, a vigorous trade with Egypt continued throughout Frederick II's reign.

The early measures taken in 1220–1 to regain control of the cities of Sicily from the powerful northern communes had been especially disastrous to the Genoese, whose dominance of the city and port of Syracuse had given them an extraordinary trading advantage in the Kingdom. Repeated efforts on the part of the Genoese to persuade the Emperor to modify his restrictive policies proved futile.[3] Bitterly as they resented this imposition as well as the seizure of their warehouse in Palermo and the removal of Count Alaman from his assumed position as 'governor', they had no recourse save to accommodate themselves to the changed conditions. The removal of the Genoese from the most favoured position which they had so long enjoyed was sufficient notice

[1] *MGH, Const.* ii, no. 153, pp. 187 ff.

[2] *Cronica*, v. 217. See also Maqrīzī, *Hist. d'Égypte* (*ROL* ix), 520; Amari, *Storia*, ii. 266; L. de Mas-Latrie, *Traités de paix avec les Arabes d'Afrique septentrionale*, Introduction, 82 ff. and 122 ff.

[3] *Annales Janvenses* (*Fonti*, ii), 171.

to other northern communes that they were now faced with a powerful and uncompromising competitor in their commercial activities. These communes continued to trade throughout the Kingdom, but only with the one assurance that duties which they were compelled to pay would be no higher than in the time of King William II.

It is a striking illustration of Frederick's interest in the promotion of trade that he made exceptions to these rigorous prohibitory laws where favoured individuals were concerned. Genoese colonists within the Kingdom and, in some cases, influential families in Genoa known to be friendly to the Emperor were able to obtain letters of safe-conduct both for themselves and for their merchandise. Other merchants from the interior of Lombardy, from cities such as Piacenza and Asti, were also granted special privileges in various parts of the Kingdom. Usually there was in these exceptions, especially in the case of Genoa, a recognition of self-interest on the part of the Emperor, who habitually chose his admirals from Genoese families such as the Spinolas and the de Maris. In 1239, for example, his Admiral of the Sicilian fleet was Nicolas Spinola who, after his death, was succeeded in that office by Ansaldus de Mari.[1]

Other cities that had been traditionally less involved with the Kingdom prior to Frederick's return in 1220 accommodated themselves more easily to his policies. The Pisans, habitually friendly towards the emperors, whether Welf or Staufen, found it necessary to reassess their relations with Frederick II after the death of Otto of Brunswick. The best they could obtain in negotiation in 1219 was assurance of protection within the Kingdom of Sicily, notably in Messina and Palermo, for trade and commerce. They failed to obtain, however, what they most desired, exemption from custom duties.[2] Moreover, further negotiations in November 1221, during which they endeavoured to obtain a renewal of port privileges, achieved nothing other than the resanctioning of their rights and privileges within the Empire (*per totum imperium*).[3] Despite restrictions depriving them of custom-free trading privileges, the Pisans continued a not insignificant trade with the Kingdom of Sicily, maintaining warehouses in the harbours of Messina and Naples.[4] Other Tuscan merchants, notably from Siena and Florence, shared in this trade and commerce.[5] Especially favoured were the occasional merchants from Rome, who could trade free of duties.[6] The treaty of Frederick with Venice, 20 September 1220, like those with Genoa and Pisa, granted

---

[1] Huillard-Bréholles, v, part i, 577; Winkelmann, *Acta*, i, no. 861.
[2] Ibid. no. 160, p. 137.   [3] Ibid. no. 232, p. 213.
[4] R. Davidsohn, *Forschungen*, ii. 305 f., nos. 2324, 2327.
[5] In addition to the above citation see Blancard, *Documents inédits sur le commerce de Marseille*, i, nos. 17, 115; ii, no. 627.
[6] Winkelmann, *Acta*, i, no. 793, p. 619.

security of trade and freedom from duties in the Empire, but not in the Kingdom of Sicily. The phrase 'regnum nostrum' employed in the treaty applies solely to imperial Italy.[1] For the Venetians, as for the other cities of the north trading with the Kingdom of Sicily, the agreement of 1175, made by King William II, continued as the basis for the levying of duties.[2] Even more than the other great commercial communes of the mainland, Venice was dependent upon the grain trade with Apulia and Sicily. It was possible, therefore, for Frederick to employ this export trade as a means of influencing the Venetian attitude towards the Lombard League. Thus in 1230, when he granted the Genoese the privilege of importing and exporting merchandise free of duty, and required no tax of them other than that which was customary under William II, he granted a more restricted privilege to Venice. The Venetian privilege provided that 'until the next festival of St. Peter [29 June], all Venetian merchants who live within the Kingdom or who enter it should be permitted to export cheese, oil, meat, and all merchandise, with the exception of grain, from the Apulian ports without opposition, and only such tax was to be levied as was customary in the time of William II'.[3] The exclusion of grain, upon which the Venetians were so dependent, would seem to imply a punitive measure, although it may have been merely a precaution taken to ensure that the grain supply would be adequate for local needs. It is not improbable also that this limited privilege was tentative, pending the final formulation of policy in the *Liber Augustalis* or *Constitutiones* which was promulgated the following year. In September of that year, in response to an inquiry made by harbour officials at Trani and Barletta, Frederick replied that 'the Venetians were to pay the custom duties, as before, and the warehouse fee in accordance with the current statute'.[4] Some evidence of indecision with respect to Venice suggests that he may have postponed the formulation of a definite trade policy until after his visit to that city in March 1232, during which he endeavoured to win the support of the commercially minded Venetians through trade concessions.[5]

It was only after 1236 that the Venetians openly opposed the imperial policies in Lombardy—a change in attitude which was brought about when the *podestà* of Milan, a son of the Doge of Venice, was taken captive by the imperial troops. Relations were further strained when,

---

[1] *MGH, Const.* ii. 93 ff. In opposition to Winkelmann and other earlier historians, I follow H. Chone, *Handelsbeziehungen*, 132 ff. (*Anhang*) in the interpretation of 'regnum nostrum'.

[2] Winkelmann, *Acta*, i, no. 757, p. 604: 'quod olim felici tempore regis Guillelmi secundi . . . solvere consueverunt.'   [3] Ibid.

[4] Ibid., no. 792, p. 619.

[5] H. Chone, *Handelsbeziehungen*, 55, says of Frederick's policy: 'Er wusste welche Anziehungskraft ein grosser Handelsvorteil für sie besass.'

in 1238, the Venetians entered into a mutual defence treaty with the Genoese, pledging themselves to support the Pope. In the long run, however, economic self-interest outweighed other considerations, and, in 1245, the Venetians were induced, through clever diplomacy, to re-establish friendly trade relations temporarily with the Kingdom of Sicily. An unexpected opportunity for Frederick's conciliatory diplomacy arose in 1245 when Venetian ambassadors returning from the Council of Lyons were taken captive by the Count of Savoy. Friendly intervention by Frederick procured their release. Visiting the court of the Emperor to express their gratitude, they found a friendly reception, including a formal address of welcome by the Emperor, which prepared the way for the restoration of trade.[1]

Like Venice, the Adriatic city of Ravenna also participated in the trade with the Kingdom of Sicily, chiefly in grain and other foodstuffs. The importance of this trade is apparent in the agreement of Venice with Ravenna in 1234 not to hinder the importation into their harbours of certain specified commodities, including wines, oil, fish, cheese, and figs, from the March of Ancona and from Apulia.[2] On the opposite shore of the Adriatic the city of Ragusa (the modern Dubrovnik), under Venetian suzerainty in the thirteenth century, also shared in the Apulian commerce. An agreement in May 1223 between Venice and Ragusa stipulated that 'from the merchandise of the Kingdom of Sicily and Apulia the inhabitants of Ragusa shall pay a fortieth part to the commune of Venice'. At the same time Ragusan merchants were pledged 'not to attempt to visit the Kingdom if the Venetians were forbidden to do so'.[3] There were times also during the hostilities between the Kingdom and Venice, notably in 1240, when Frederick sought to establish trade relations not only with Ragusa, but with Spalato (Split), Zara, Almissa, and other cities along the Dalmatian coast.[4] These efforts of the Emperor were not without success. While shipping in Adriatic waters was at times seriously interrupted, there are many instances of friendly relations between merchants of the Kingdom and the inhabitants of the cities of the Dalmatian coast. Subsequently, after the temporary re-establishment of peace between Frederick and the Venetians, cities such as Zara shared in the trading advantages provided by the treaty.[5]

[1] Martino da Canal, *La Cronique des Veniciens* (ed. A. Zon in *Arch. stor. ital.*, series I, viii, 1845), 404 ff., Chone, op. cit., 119 f.

[2] A. S. Minotto, *Acta et Diplomata e Tabulario Veneto*, iii. 34. See also W. Lenel, *Die Entstehung der Vorherrschaft Venedigs in der Adria*, 47.

[3] G. Tafel and G. Thomas, *Urkunden zur älteren Handels- und Staatsgeschichte der Republik Venedig*, ii. 311: *Fontes rerum Austriacarum*, xiii. See also C. Jireček, *Die Bedeutung von Ragusa in der Handelsgeschichte des Mittelalters*.

[4] Huillard-Bréholles, v, part ii, 781.

[5] Ljubić, *Monumenta spectantia historiam Slavorum meridionalium*, i, p. 79, no. 101.

The Sicilian Kingdom also had trade relations with western cities outside Italy, but contemporary sources supply few details of the nature and extent of this commerce. The proximity of the port of Marseilles to the western coast of Italy had long before brought the two regions into close commercial relationships. A privilege granted to the Massaliots by Frederick Barbarossa in 1164, and renewed in May 1222 between Frederick II and Peter, Bishop of Marseilles, remained the basis for trade between the Kingdom and the city until 1233. Certainly from 1233 to the end of Frederick's reign active trade relations continued between Marseilles and the Kingdom of Sicily. The port of Marseilles was especially useful to the Genoese and to the merchants of southern France during periods when it was difficult or impossible to trade directly with Sicilian ports. By means of limited partnerships or through the establishment of a *Société en commandite* (a limited liability company) with Massaliot merchants, various foreign merchants were able to carry on a profitable trade with Sicily. The Emperor himself is known to have made purchases for his art collections from Massaliot merchants. There was an active export trade via Marseilles to Messina and Naples in textiles from cities and towns of southern France and from northern cities, including Arras, Châlons, Louviers, and Provins.[1]

At no time did Frederick attempt to set up a government monopoly for the grain trade, although, as the Crown was the chief exporting agency of the Kingdom, his policies often seemed essentially monopolistic.[2] Not only did he control the quality of the grain yield of the royal estates that he had authorized to be cultivated under the supervision of the procurators, but he also fixed the amount of the yield of the royal fiefs (*domania*) payable by the occupants. Thus on 12 July 1231 he established that for grain, vegetables, flax, and hemp a twelfth part of the harvest was to be delivered to the royal warehouses, in return for which the tenants were to be released from further direct taxes.[3] It was also the privilege of the Emperor to purchase private supplies of grain for export, all the more lucrative to him because it was tax free. (All grain exported by private individuals was subject to taxation either in kind or in money. All merchandise, export or import, transported across the borders of the Kingdom was subject to tolls and duties.[4])

In establishing control over the trade and commerce of the Kingdom

---

[1] For records of this trade via Marseilles see L. Blancard, *Les Notules commerciales d'Amalric* (*Doc. inédits sur le commerce de Marseille*), nos. 556, 582, 702. See also Schaube, *Handelsgeschichte*, 498–9.

[2] The statement of Schaube, *Handelsgeschichte*, 505, is a judicious estimate of Frederick's policy with respect to the grain trade: 'Ein Getreidehandelsmonopol hat er zu keiner Zeit, auch für den Ausfuhrhandel nicht, eingeführt; wohl aber war die Krone die bei weitem grösste Getreideexportfirma des Königreichs.'

[3] Winkelmann, *Acta*, i. 615.   [4] Ibid. 616.

and over its economic activities as a whole, Frederick also gave consideration to the non-Christian inhabitants, the Jews and the Muslims. In addition to the land tax determined through assessments, there was in each province a special capitation tax levied on Muslims and Jews who, like Christians in Muslim countries, were regarded as aliens, although enjoying some freedom of movement and legal standing. Frederick displayed towards Jews and Muslims a broad spirit of tolerance as long as they were obedient to the imperial laws. He placed Jews, Muslims, and other aliens, under the immediate protection of the Crown.[1] As non-citizens the Arabs were subject to taxation for their protection and could be made available as mercenary soldiers in the imperial army. The Jews, while distinguishable from Christians by their beards and by their dress, were protected in some of their non-Christian practices such as usury 'because it is well known that they are not under the laws of the blessed Fathers'.[2] Frederick was aware of the value of the Jews in augmenting the royal treasure. Just as the Saracens at Lucera proved of great use to the Emperor, so also certain Jewish monopolies were made profitable to the state. Thus in 1231 Frederick (to his own advantage) granted the Jews of Trani the right to buy and sell silk throughout the Kingdom of Sicily; at about the same time they were granted monopolistic rights in the dye industry in the entire Kingdom. Jews were employed also in the administration of the textile industry, as well as in the administration of the salt and iron monopolies. Two Jewish agents, Jacob de Magistro Milo and Ursu de Fusco, are mentioned in documents as imperial agents in that capacity.[3] Carefully administered state monopolies became remunerative sources of royal revenue. In conformity with his monopolistic policies, Frederick reorganized the system of tolls and custom duties: all tolls and duties, including those formerly collected by various lords, were now transferred to the royal administration. The new rates were declared effective on 12 August 1231.[4]

One of the Emperor's greatest advantages lay in the fact that he owned and operated a fleet of merchant ships. It was through this that he came nearest to a monopoly in grain. In the spring of 1240, when badly in need of money, he profited from a serious famine in Tunis to fill the royal treasury. A certain Angelo Frisario, a harbour-master of Sicily, discovered that Genoese merchants, aware of a Tunisian grain shortage, had been supplied with funds by the King of Tunis for the purchase of unlimited grain supplies in the Kingdom of Sicily. Trans-

[1] *Constitutiones*, Lib. I, Tit. XXVII, Huillard-Bréholles, iv, part i, 28–9.
[2] Ibid., Lib. I, Tit. VI, Huillard-Bréholles, iv, part i, 11.
[3] Winkelmann, *Acta*, i, no. 773, pp. 609–10; Richard of San Germano, 176.
[4] Winkelmann, *Acta*, i. 616.

porting the grain in their own ships to the Tunisian market, the Genoese were selling it at an enormous profit. Upon hearing of this, Frederick sent an order to the Admiral of the fleet to the effect that no ship in Sicily was to be loaded with grain until after the imperial ships were loaded and put to sea, thus enabling him to reach the market ahead of his competitors. Meanwhile he dispatched an Arabic-speaking ambassador to a designated Tunisian port to receive the ships and to arrange for the sale of their cargo. Despite this apparently high-handed procedure, Frederick had stipulated in his original order that privately owned ships, bound for Tunis, that had already loaded their cargoes and paid the harbour fee were to be allowed to proceed.[1] This venture is said to have earned a gross total of some 40,000 ounces of gold for the royal treasury and to have yielded a profit of 100 per cent.[2] The policy of the Emperor in regulating the grain export was essentially opportunist; it was the necessity of the moment that dictated his policy. In contrast, his treatment of iron, steel, salt, and dye was frankly monopolistic after 1231.[3]

As early as 1222 Frederick established within the Kingdom a uniform coinage. At that time he also pledged all subjects in cities, towns, and castles to employ only the newly coined *denarius* in their financial transactions. Six reliable men (*sex bonorum hominum*) were sworn to ensure the strict enforcement of this pledge in each region.[4] This was the initial step towards rescuing the coinage from the chaotic condition into which it had fallen during the years of Frederick's minority and during the eight years of his absence in Germany. Even before that time, the generally enlightened King Roger II was said to have withdrawn the superior currency from circulation, issuing in its stead an ersatz coin containing a heavy alloy of copper.[5]

From time to time Frederick had other coins minted in silver or copper. Most important of his gold coins were his *Augustales*, first issued in 1231. Perfect in design and workmanship, these coins reflect the influence of antiquity. They symbolized, as no other tangible articles could, Frederick's concept of the meaning of temporal sovereignty. In contrast with earlier coins bearing the image of the Saviour or some other Christian symbol as assurance of their honest value, the *Augustales* bore on one side the image of Frederick II, ordained of God as Vicar upon earth and authentic successor of the divine Caesars. On the opposite side was the imperial eagle, partially encircled by the name

[1] Huillard-Bréholles, v, part ii, 687, 780, 782, 793.
[2] H. Chone, *Handelsbeziehungen*, p. 96 and note 3.
[3] Richard of San Germano, 170; also *Constitutiones* (Huillard-Bréholles, iv, part i), 211.
[4] Richard of San Germano, 103; M. Garcia-Pelayo, *Nascimento do Estado Moderno*, 73 f.
[5] See B. de Falco, *Chronicon* (ed. Del Re, *Cronisti e scrittori sincroni napoletani*), i. 251–2.

FRIDI . . . RICUS. Although inspired by, if not modelled upon that of Caesar Augustus, Frederick's eagle presents certain significant variations. It retains the three-quarter profile of the body and the backward turn of the head of the Augustan eagle, while revealing also definite influence of the heraldic eagle of the late Roman and medieval eras: the elongated head, the beak of exaggerated proportions, the sharply voluted wings, and the heavily chiselled scale-like feathers so characteristic of the heraldic eagles of the Middle Ages.[1] The *Augustales* are far more than expressions of Frederick's aesthetic sense. They are suggestive of the concept of *imperium* so eloquently expressed in the preamble of the *Liber Augustalis* or *Constitutiones* which made its appearance in the same year. More than all else this coin, so reminiscent of the grandeur of ancient Rome, was probably intended to be symbolic of the *Fortuna Caesarea* which Frederick confidently believed to be the unique spirit that exalted and sustained the Roman Emperor as the sovereign of the world.

In the course of time Frederick took over the control of the banking and exchange agencies throughout the Sicilian Kingdom which had formerly been privately maintained. A first step in this direction was taken in 1220 as he passed through San Germano after his coronation. Here he assumed control of the exchange of money, long in the hands of the church of Cassino which had held it as a concession from the Emperor Henry VI.[2] Henceforth, the control of the exchange banks and other centres of banking was granted as a concession in return for substantial sums of money, thus becoming one of the many new sources of the royal revenue. Frederick exercised the greatest possible care in the choice of the money-changers (*campsores*), charging them especially with the obligation of protecting the monetary interests of foreigners sojourning in the Kingdom. A letter from the royal Chancery in December 1239 instructed the recipient official that pilgrims who had been compelled to delay their embarkation in Messina because of rough weather were to be safeguarded against extortion by the appointment of *campsores* and other trusted men to advise and protect them.[3]

Mutually beneficial to merchants, both foreign and domestic, as well as to the royal administrative system, were Frederick's regulations establishing uniform weights and measures under strict governmental supervision, and with severe penalties inflicted upon those who failed to make use of the new standard.[4]

[1] See first, the thorough study of the coin by E. Kantorowicz, *Friedrich II., Ergänzungsband*, Exkurs 1, p. 255; then J. Deér, 'Adler aus der Zeit Friedrichs II: *victrix aquila*' (P. Schramm, *Kaiser Friedrichs II. Herrschaftszeichen*), 97 ff.

[2] Richard of San Germano, 83.

[3] Huillard-Bréholles, v, part i, 586: *Litterae responsales ad Johannem Cioffum.*

[4] Richard of San Germano, 176.

The control of the economic activities of the Kingdom was extended also to include the markets and fairs. Here the basic policy, as enunciated at Capua in 1221, was that of Frederick's Norman predecessors, especially of King William II. All usurpations of market privileges during the chaotic years since the death of Emperor Henry VI and the Empress Constance (*post obitum parentium nostrorum*) were invalidated and only such were permitted to continue their activities as had existed in the time of King William II.[1] Further regulations concerning fairs on the mainland of Italy were promulgated in 1234 when the Emperor, holding a general court at Messina, decreed that fairs were to be held successively in several districts of the Kingdom during the spring and summer months.[2] That such periodic fairs were not held in the larger cities of the mainland, i.e. Naples, Gaeta, Brindisi, or the island cities of Messina and Palermo, is probably to be explained by the existence in these cities of large permanent markets.

Frederick II had little or no conception of a system of free enterprise in the modern connotation of that term. His policies, with but few exceptions, originated in the immediate needs of the state. From the moment of his return to Sicily following his coronation, his assizes and decrees regulating trade and commerce, whether domestic or foreign, including also tolls and tariffs, markets and fairs, and coinage, aimed at the creation of a centrally controlled economic system which could be made to produce income for the royal treasury. Nothing was left to chance or to indirection. Waste of effort or inappropriate methods of agriculture or of industry were intolerable in Frederick's system. He was indefatigable in his efforts to increase agricultural productivity and to foster an efficient animal husbandry. Improvement of the soil claimed his attention no less than commerce. His interest in scientific methods led him to a personal investigation of such matters as agronomy,[3] ways of improving the breeding of cattle, horses, and sheep, and methods of improving the production of dyes, such as indigo and henna. His interest in increasing and improving the general productivity of the Kingdom led him to encourage horticultural experiments, efforts to increase the production of date palms, raw silk, sugar cane, and other commodities.[4] In 1231 he issued an edict for Apulia and other parts of the Kingdom ordering that steps be taken to exterminate a species of destructive locust (*ad destruendam pestem brucorum*), and fixing a penalty for those who neglected to do so.[5] He was no less concerned with the

[1] Ibid. 90: 'et ea que tempore regis Guillelmi facta fuerunt precipimus firmiter observari . . .' [2] Ibid. 187.

[3] For his interest in soil selectivity, types of soil, etc. see especially A. de Stefano, *Frederick II e le correnti spirituali del suo tempo*, 106.

[4] See especially his order to the *secretus* of Palermo, 28 Nov. 1239 (Huillard-Bréholles, v, part i), 535–6; and ibid. 571–4. [5] Richard of San Germano, 174.

laziness and ineptitude of his subjects as hindrances to prosperous agriculture. On at least one occasion the *magister justiciarius* of the Terra di Bari was ordered to admonish all within his jurisdiction to cultivate their fields more industriously lest there be a want of provisions.[1]

---

[1] Winkelmann, *Acta*, i, no. 816, p. 633.

PART VI

FREDERICK II
PATRON OF THE ARTS
AND SCIENCES

I

THE NORMAN CULTURAL HERITAGE
OF THE SICILIAN COURT OF
FREDERICK II

O votive puer, renovandi temporis etas,
Ex hinc Rogerius, hinc Fredericus eris,
Maior habendus avis, fato meliore creatus
Qui bene vix natus cum patre vincis avos.

Liber ad Honorem Augusti (Fonti), p. 95, lines 1376–80.[1]

WHEN Frederick II returned to his native Apulia in 1220 he arrived with a clear appreciation that his primary task was the restoration of the administrative, the judicial, and the economic systems, for without these the Kingdom would sink into anarchy. He was equally aware that the cultural life must be revived in the pattern of the twelfth-century achievements of his Norman ancestors, King Roger II and the two Williams. Indeed, his cultural policies, like his administrative and judicial policies, received their stimulus from his Norman predecessors. It was a unique feature of Sicily and Apulia that they had long been the seats of different peoples and various cultures, each of which, despite its proximity to the others, had retained its integrity. On the island of Sicily the Arabs had long been predominant, a fact which the Norman conquerors recognized and wisely employed to their own advantage. Present there also were Latin and Byzantine elements. In the province of Messina in particular there was a large Greek element among the population. It was there that King Manfred, son and successor of Frederick II, found the Greek scholar Bartholomeo, who at the King's request translated Aristotles' *Ethics* from the Greek into Latin. As late as the sixteenth and early seventeenth centuries the majority of the Messinese continued to employ the Greek language.[2]

[1] O promised boy, the life of an age renewed,
Hence you will be Roger, hence, Frederick.
Held greater than your forebears
And born for a better fate,
Soon after birth, together with your father
You will surpass your ancestors.

[2] M. Crusius, *Turco-Graeciae libri octo*, 538; O. Hartwig, *Zentralblatt für Bibliothekswesen*, iii, 1886, 184, 224.

The regions of the Italian mainland most deeply influenced by the Greeks were the Calabrian peninsula, the Terra d'Otranto, and the Basilicata along the Gulf of Taranto. One of the most dense concentrations of Greeks during the eras of the Normans and the Hohenstaufen was along the Aspromonte ridge, east of Reggio di Calabria. In 1217 this entire region was Greek-speaking. Equally important as a centre of Greek concentration was the Terra d'Otranto, south of Lecce and including the cultural centres of Gallipoli and Alliste. Here in several villages the speaking of Greek has continued to the present day.[1] It was the monasteries of the Terra d'Otranto that were, after 1220, to give the court of Frederick II a renewed contact with Byzantine culture. Among the many Basilian monasteries of that region St. Nicola di Casole was pre-eminent. Founded in 1099, it owed its earliest privileges to its Norman benefactors, first to Bohemund I, and later to King Roger II and the two Williams, and, in the thirteenth century, to Frederick II. Throughout its history it was noted for its collection of Greek and Latin manuscripts and as a flourishing literary centre. As Calabria was distinguished as a centre of Byzantine art and architecture, so the Terra d'Otranto was pre-eminent in belles-lettres.[2] It was not the policy of the Norman kings to molest these several cultures or to try to change the habits and customs of the various peoples, except perhaps where religion was concerned. They desired merely to create an effective sovereign authority within the Kingdom, providing public security, while focusing the attention of the central government upon matters pertaining to the state as a whole. Roger II was chiefly concerned, once his sovereign authority was made secure, with the restoration of the vigorous cultural and intellectual life which had obtained in the respective regions of the Byzantine and Arabic dominance.[3] Local officials in the Kingdom were little changed except where changes were essential in order to integrate them closely and uniformly with the central government. Moreover, the Norman Kings found the Muslim officials particularly useful in the financial administration and in the navy. Royal diplomas and other documents were prepared in Greek, Latin, or Arabic, accordingly as they were directed to one or another of these nationalities.[4] It was only after the successful conquest of these regions by the Normans that the impact of the cultures of Northern Italy,

---

[1] G. Rohlfs, *Das Fortleben des antiken Griechentums in Unteritalien*, especially, 7 ff., and idem, *Griechen und Romanen in Unteritalien*, especially 4 ff. and 87 f. See also A. Guillou, 'Inchiesta sulla popolazione greca della Sicilia e della Calabria nel Medioeva' (*Rivista stor. ital.*, 75, 1963), 53–68.

[2] P. Batiffol, *L'Abbaye de Rossano*, pp. xxviii ff. See also below, p. 300 f., for the Greek scholars and poets from St. Nicola di Casole in Frederick's court circle.

[3] E. Caspar, *Roger II*, 448. See also R. S. Lopez, 'The Norman Conquest of Sicily' (*A History of the Crusades*, i, *The First Hundred Years*, ed. M. W. Baldwin *et al.*), 66 f.

[4] F. Chalandon, *Domination*, ii. 710 ff.

France, and England made itself felt effectively there. Apart from the Basilian monasteries of Calabria and the Terra d'Otranto, for which the extant sources are meagre, three places in Southern Italy and Sicily, Salerno, Monte Cassino, and the Sicilian court at Palermo, provided exceptional opportunities for the reception and the dissemination of the cultural influences of the Orient and of western Europe.

The dominance of Salerno in medical studies is perhaps sufficiently explained by its favourable geographical position, and this may also account for the fact that it was fully established as a school of medicine long before the great universities such as Bologna, Paris, and Oxford came into existence. It should not be overlooked that Salerno had been renowned since antiquity as a health resort, possessing a salubrious climate and with easy access to the famed mineral baths of the area, such as the near-by Pozzuoli. The school of Salerno was unquestionably of Latin origin; it continued inconspicuously during the barbarian invasions and became famous as a medical school in the ninth and tenth centuries with a concept of medicine quite unlike that of Western Christendom generally.[1]

Monte Cassino also was favoured from the days of its foundation as a focal centre for 'the continuity of tradition between the ancient and the modern world'.[2] If it were possible to accept without qualifications the account of Peter the Deacon, librarian and chronicler of the monastery, we should have to conclude that the relations of Monte Cassino with Constantinople began with its foundation. Unfortunately, this alleged early relationship derives solely from documents which Peter himself forged. There is, in fact, no positively established relationship before the end of the ninth century.[3] With the coming of the Normans the Sicilian court, as a convenient meeting-point of north, south, east, and west, became an active centre for translating from Arabic and Greek and a place where scientific and literary works were written in Arabic and Greek as well as in Latin.[4]

With the ending of the Norman era, and because of the turbulence which prevailed thereafter for several decades, the cultural activities of Sicily were carried on chiefly by scholars in the Basilian libraries of Calabria and the Terra d'Otranto that had been patronized and protected by the Norman kings. Subsequently, many features of the renewed intellectual activity at the court of Frederick II after 1220 were to

---

[1] S. De Renzi, *Collectio salernitana*, i. 116–18 and 121.

[2] H. Bloch, *Monte Cassino, Byzantium, and the West in the Earlier Middle Ages* (*Dumbarton Oaks Papers*, no. 3, 1946), 165 ff.

[3] See first *Chronica Monasterii Casinensis* (*MGH, SS.* vii), 839, and then E. Caspar, *Petrus Diaconus und die Monte Cassineser Fälschungen*, 170 ff., and L. T. White, Jr., *Latin Monasticism in Norman Sicily*, 10.

[4] C. Haskins, *Renaissance of the Twelfth Century*, 59–60.

receive their stimulus from the Greek scholars who had pursued their scholarly interests inconspicuously during the seemingly sterile period following the death of William II. This inconspicuousness, together with the paucity of extant sources relating to these monasteries, compels a greater emphasis than might otherwise be justified upon Monte Cassino and Salerno as the chief cultural and intellectual centres of Southern Italy during the eleventh and twelfth centuries.

The individual to whom most credit is due for the ascendancy of Monte Cassino during the eleventh century was its learned Abbot, Desiderius, scion of a noble Lombard family of Benevento. His devotion to a religious life had begun in the cloisters of his native city. It was only in 1058 that he was chosen as Abbot of Monte Cassino. Although of Lombard origin, he was essentially Byzantine in his cultural tastes and interests, even though a political opponent of the Byzantine Empire. From the outset this penchant for the Byzantine was apparent in his efforts to beautify the monastery, taking Byzantine art and architecture as his models. These features of Byzantine building, so sedulously fostered by Desiderius, culminated in what has been aptly described as 'an international style of the twelfth century'.[1]

Even more important for the cultural history of the West was the Abbot's interest in the liberal arts and his zeal in promoting scientific studies among the monks attracted to the monastery. In this also his hostility to the Byzantine Empire as a political influence was subordinated to his humanistic and scientific interests. Monks from the East were generously welcomed by him and it was with them that many of the scholarly achievements of the monastery originated. Desiderius was especially active in enriching the library with historical, scientific, and literary works. Associated with him in this was Leo of Ostia, librarian and chronicler, to whom we are indebted for the *Chronica Monasterii Casinensis*, which was later continued, at the request of Abbot Reginald, by Peter the Deacon during the eventful years from 1130 to 1137.[2]

Foremost among the scholarly monks in Monte Cassino was the young nobleman Alfanus, from the princely house of Salerno. Persuaded by his intimate friend Desiderius to become a monk, Alfanus quickly acquired status among the regular clergy, first by a pilgrimage to Jerusalem, and, upon his return, by his election as Archbishop of Salerno.[3] Like many of his Arabic and Greek contemporaries, Alfanus was both physician and poet. Apart from his priestly capacity, he is noteworthy for his role in the history of medicine and as an eleventh-

---

[1] W. Koehler, 'Byzantine Art in the West' (*Dumbarton Oaks Papers*, no. 1, 1941), 76, 79.

[2] M. Manitius, *Geschichte der lateinischen Literatur des Mittelalters*, part iii, 75 ff. and 546 ff.

[3] For the life of Alfanus see especially Manitius, op. cit., part ii, 618–37; M. Schipa, 'Alfano I' (*Archivio di Salerno*); H. Bloch, *Monte Cassino*, 218 ff. The chief original source is Peter the Deacon, *De Viris Illustribus Casinensis Coenobii* (Migne, *PL.* 173), ch. xix, cols. 1050 f.

century votary of belles-lettres. A contemporary physician, Constantine Africanus, dedicated a translation of a work on diseases of the stomach to Alfanus. A manuscript entitled *Tractatus Alfani Salernitanensis de quibusdam questionibus medicinalibus* bears further testimony to his medical scholarship.[1] The fact that his *De pulsu* was based upon a Byzantine work rather than upon the more widely known work of Galen is an interesting illustration of his Byzantine connections. It was probably also through his Byzantine associations that he became interested in translating Nemesius' work *On Human Nature*, esteemed for its knowledge of physiology and Greek and Roman anthropology.[2]

It was after his elevation as Archbishop of Salerno that Alfanus revealed his exceptional skill as a poet and became known to his contemporaries as a master of prosody. Although written in Latin, his poetry, both in form and content, is suggestive of that of the thirteenth-century poets of St. Nicola di Casole who were members of the court circle of Frederick II. Much of it is personal in content, reflecting the interests and activities of his era, yet it is also rich in spiritual sentiment. Some of his poems are in praise of the heroic deeds of various members of the princely family of Salerno, Gisulf, Guido, and Gaimar, 'whose deeds of valour resounded throughout the world'. He also sang the praises of the city of Salerno, which he described as more powerful than the city of Rome, for in Salerno the science of medicine was so perfected that no sickness flourished there.[3]

As if anticipating the thinking of the Popes and canonists of the thirteenth century, Alfanus, in his poem *ad Hildebrandum archidiaconum romanum*, extolled the theocratic system of Hildebrand, who was later to become Pope Gregory VII. He contrasted the statesmanship of the Pope with that of the emperors of antiquity; indeed, Gregory is represented as surpassing them because of his gentler methods. Rome with all its grandeur continues head of the world (*caput mundi*), with the Pope occupying the throne of the ancient Caesars. Alfanus concedes that the heroic emperors of antiquity did much for the 'Fatherland', but it was not given to them to enjoy their sovereign authority in enduring peace. It was Gregory who established the eternal sovereignty of the Roman Church. Boundless as was his admiration for Roman antiquity, Alfanus was conscious of no incongruity when he envisaged a renewed Roman Empire ruled by the successors of St. Peter.[4]

---

[1] Manitius, op. cit. 619.

[2] See especially H. Bloch, op. cit. 219–20 and note 195.

[3] M. Schipa, op. cit. 37 ff. Schipa offers an analysis of several of the poems. See especially the poem *ad Guidonem fratrem principes salernitani*, 39 ff., in which Alfanus says of Salerno:

Tum medicinali tantum florebat in arte,
Posset ut hic nullus langor habere locum.

[4] For pertinent passages of the poem see Schipa, 'Alfano I,' 36 ff. See also P. E. Schramm,

Again, his attachment to the Rome of antiquity is vividly set forth in his *Vita et agon sanctorum XII fratrum martyrum*, concerned with the saintly lives of twelve brothers who were martyred in Benevento in the third century during the reign of Maximian. The significance of the poem lies, not in its main theme, but in its wealth of antique lore. Nothing else so well illustrates the continuity of ancient traditions at Monte Cassino as the abundant knowledge of and sympathetic appreciation of antique institutions, mythology, geography, and astrology that are revealed by Alfanus in this and other poems. Indeed, he is comparable in this to the Basilian poets at the court of Frederick II who sought to preserve the continuity of the traditions and culture of antiquity.[1] Certainly no literary figure in medieval Europe had so nearly achieved in both the form and content of his works a spiritual union with classical antiquity.

It was Alfanus who was responsible for bringing the Saracen physician Constantine Africanus from Carthage to Salerno and Monte Cassino.[2] The extravagant praise of Constantine by Peter the Deacon is responsible for the several legends which arose during the Middle Ages about his learning and his influence upon the development of the medical sciences in the West. This ardent monkish chronicler credited Constantine not only with great learning in grammar, logic, geometry, arithmetic, astronomy, and physics, but also in all the lore of the Chaldeans, the Arabs, the Persians, the Saracens, the Egyptians, and the Indians, the result of his thirty years as resident and student in Africa.[3] While there can be no doubt of the importance of Constantine in furthering the study of medicine at Salerno through his translations from Arabic and Greek medical writings, he was in no sense responsible for the earliest translations of Galen and Hippocrates. Early in the eleventh century medical treatises were being written at Salerno, and both Galen and Hippocrates had appeared in Latin translations in the sixth century.[4] If it appears surprising that Frederick II, a century later, was at first indifferent to the achievements of Salerno and its contributions to medical studies, the explanation may be found in part in his preoccupation with the University of Naples, but even more, in the abundance of translations from the Arabic and Greek sources originating from

Kaiser, Rom et Renovatio, part i, 248–9; and H. Bloch, *Monte Cassino*, 218 ff. Useful also is the work of G. Falco, 'Un vescovo poet del sec XI: Alfano di Salerno' (*Arch. della R. Società Romana di stor. pat.* 35, 1912), 439 ff., 462, 466 ff.

[1] See below, p. 301 f. and Manitius, op. cit. 622, 631 f.

[2] See Peter the Deacon, *Liber De Viris Illustribus Casinensis* (Migne, *PL* 173), ch. xxiii, cols. 1033–4, for the main facts of Constantine's life. The most detailed and critical survey of his life is R. Creuz, 'Der Arzt Constantinus Africanus von Montekassino' (*Studien und Mitteilungen zur Geschichte des Benediktinerordens und seiner Zweige*, xlvii, 1929), 1–44.

[3] Peter the Deacon, *Chronica* (*MGH, SS.* vii), 728.

[4] See Cassiodorus, *De Institutione Divinarum Litterarum* (Migne, *PL* 70), col. 1146.

Spain and Sicily in the thirteenth century. It is noteworthy, however, that in 1231 Frederick II brought the school of Salerno within the purview of his paternalistic control, regulating the issuing of medical licences, and placing the administration of the school largely under the jurisdiction of the court.[1]

Alfanus died during the year 1085, while Desiderius, much against his will, was chosen by the cardinals to succeed Gregory VII. He took the name Victor III, although the turbulence in Rome and within the ranks of the clergy delayed his consecration until 1087; shortly afterwards he died. In the early years of his conquest Robert Guiscard, by his marriage with Sykelgaita, sister of Gisulf of the princely house of Salerno, and through his friendship with Desiderius, had established relationships with the city of Salerno and with Monte Cassino that were to endure, with but few interruptions, until Roger II became king, uniting the southern mainland with the island and making of the royal court itself the cultural centre of the Kingdom.

The passing of the great trio of Monte Cassino and the era of near-chaos on the mainland which followed the death of Robert Guiscard checked temporarily the intellectual and literary ascendancy of both Salerno and Monte Cassino. As the governments of the sons of Robert Guiscard weakened on the mainland, Roger, the youngest son of Tancred of Hauteville, successfully tightened his hold on the island. Known as the 'Great Count of Sicily', he laid the foundation of the monarchy which his son, Roger II, was to govern so effectively. Whereas Robert Guiscard on the southern mainland of Italy had concerned himself primarily with the subjugation of the Lombards and Greeks, Count Roger I of Sicily was inaugurating a policy of tolerance towards the Greeks and the predominant Saracen population which was to associate them culturally, administratively, and militarily with the Norman sovereigns who succeeded him.[2]

Count Roger I died in 1101, leaving his infant son as his successor and his widow, Countess Adelaide, as regent during her son's minority. Unfortunately, we have little information from contemporary sources about the events of her regency. Such evidence as we have leaves no doubt that Adelaide's trials and tribulations were many. Singularly enough, her most serious difficulties came not from the Saracens but from arrogant barons, hoping to profit from the inevitable weakness of the central government following the death of the Great Count. Fortunately, the wise rule of the latter had attached many of the barons to the Hauteville family and, with their protection, the second Count Roger succeeded to the countship under the regency of his mother. By

---

[1] Huillard-Bréholles, iv, part i, 235–7: *De medicis*.
[2] See especially E. Caspar, *Roger II*, 8 ff.; and F. Chalandon, *Domination*, i. 330 ff.

1130 the young Count had completely dominated not merely the island of Sicily but Southern Italy as well, and, on Christmas Day of that year, amidst pageantry of oriental splendour, he was crowned king in Palermo.[1]

It was characteristic of Roger II that he created a splendid court in Palermo where he surrounded himself with men devoted, like himself, to cultural pursuits. It is here that we can see the archetype of Frederick II's court. The most intimate of Roger II's associates and advisers were the Arab geographer, Edrisi, the Calabrian Greek theologian and homilist, Theophanes Cerameus, and the Greek scholar and translator, Doxapater.[2]

The greater part of the life of Edrisi, who died in his sixty-sixth year, was spent in the service of Roger II. The intellectual intimacy between him and his sovereign foreshadows the relations of Frederick II with Michael Scot. He is a remarkable example of the way in which the Norman-Sicilian kings utilized the skills of the conquered Muslims while making loyal supporters of them. Roger II found in this learned Arab not merely a loyal panegyrist, but one whose extensive travels and critical knowledge of the scientific achievements of the ancient Greeks and of his own people enabled him to construct an extraordinary map, engraved on silver, with a descriptive text. Just as later Frederick II refused to be bound by the generally accepted statements of Aristotle, substituting, instead, his own observations, so Edrisi, in accordance with King Roger's instructions, moved well beyond the Ptolemaic system, which was the foundation of his map, by including also knowledge gained from his own travels and observations and from the reports of Arabic geographers.[3] The methods of Edrisi, if they were not the model for Frederick II in writing his treatise on falconry, were strikingly similar. Frederick II summoned to his court men from distant lands who were skilled in the art of falconry and other bird and animal lore. From these he exacted 'whatever they knew best and, committing to memory their sayings and practices, he verified and compiled the desired information'.[4] Edrisi's work did not introduce a perfected cartography, nor did it greatly advance the science of geography as a whole, but it contains an astonishing body of information concerning

[1] E. Caspar, op. cit. 96; Chalandon, op. cit. ii. 9. See also the very useful article of H. Wieruszowski, 'Roger II of Sicily, *Rex-Tyrannus*, in Twelfth-Century Political Thought' (*Speculum*, xxxviii, 1963), 46 ff.

[2] M. T. Mandalari, 'Enrico Aristippo, Arcidiacono di Catania, nella vita culturale e politica del sec. XII' (*Bolletino storico Catanese*, anno I–II, 1936–XIV–1937–XV, 1938–XVI), 89.

[3] See especially Amari and Schiaperelli (trans.), *L'Italia descritta nel Libro del Re Ruggero*, 4–8.

[4] For Frederick's methods see his *De Arte Venandi cum Avibus* (ed. C. A. Willemsen, 1942), Prologue.

history and natural history, flora, and fauna, and throws much light upon the peoples of Western Europe and elsewhere in the twelfth century. The map and the descriptions of the regions of the earth undoubtedly left much to be desired. Yet, notwithstanding many inaccuracies, the geographical investigations of Roger II and Edrisi marked a notable advance in scientific method.[1]

No less important than the geographical work itself is the character portrayal of Roger II in Edrisi's dedicatory remarks. Of the King he said:

With superior intellect he unites goodness. To these are added also firm resolution, keen understanding, depth of spirit, imperturbable poise, perceptiveness, and a just outlook and competence in all his undertakings, revealing superior intelligence. . . . He dispatches with ease the most intricate affairs. He dominates the whole range of his sovereignty. His sleep is as the awakening of other men; his judgements are the most accurate; his generosity is like the inexhaustible sea and the torrential rains. I can neither enumerate his knowledge of the exact sciences, nor set bounds to his wisdom.[2]

Another member of Roger's learned circle, the Greek theologian and court preacher, Theophanes, was equally flattering. Famed for the simplicity and naturalness, and, above all, for the eloquence of his homilies, Theophanes probably reached the heights of eloquence on Palm Sunday 1140, when, preaching before the King and a distinguished audience he prefaced his sermon by a tribute to the King.

How shall my sermon do justice [he asked] to both the noblest of feasts and the royal name? I fear and tremble, anxiety overwhelms me, I am drenched in sweat, reverence fills me, my soul trembles, my mind wavers, my heart throbs, my voice fails me in fear lest my words may be as salt water to the ears of the King and I can draw none fitting. . . . O King, your God-given triumphs, your virtues, and your deeds of fame will be in other eras and by other men appraised and shall be extolled again and again as long as the ocean is bounded by the land![3]

The importance of Theophanes at the court of Roger II derives not so much from his eloquence or his literary contributions; it is to be found rather in his close association with a Norman king whose tolerance towards Arabs and Greeks and appreciation of their cultural gifts set him apart from his contemporaries. This association is important also in that it established a precedent which became the guiding principle of Roger's grandson, the Emperor Frederick II of Hohenstaufen. King Roger's

---

[1] E. Caspar, *Roger II*, 447–58.

[2] Amari, *Bibliotheca Arabo-Sicula, versione italiana*, i. 33. See also Caspar, op. cit. 443, and Amari, *Bibliotheca*, ii. 429.

[3] P. Francesco Scorso (ed.), *Théophane de Taormine, Homiliae in Evangelia dominicalia et festa totius anni*, Homilia xxvi. 183–4.

understanding of Greek, like his scientific interests and knowledge, is all the more extraordinary in that we are so little informed as to his tutors at the court of his father, the Great Count, or of his mother, the Countess Adelaide.

It was at the bidding of Roger II that another learned Greek, Nilus Doxapater, wrote in 1143 his *History of the Five Patriarchates*, in which he endeavoured to demonstrate that 'Rome was a see of the same order as the other Patriarchal sees of Christendom'.[1] In this work he developed the thesis, later revived by the Greek poets at the court of Frederick II and so inimical to the Church of Rome, that, since Rome ceased to be an imperial city because it fell under the bondage of the barbarians, it lost its imperial dignity and its precedence. This is undoubtedly the Doxapater, or Doxopatrios, who is said to have translated the prophecies of the Erythraean Sibyl from the Chaldean and whose work was subsequently translated into Latin by Admiral Eugene of Palermo, his younger contemporary at the Norman-Sicilian court.[2]

Tolerant as were the Norman kings towards the Greek Church, it was but natural that they should endeavour, when possible, to further the interests of the Church of Rome.[3] After the Normans were firmly established in power in the twelfth century, Latin influences inevitably became more pronounced through contacts with Northern Italy and with France and England. At first a gradual process, Latinization rapidly increased during the later decades of the century. In some measure this is attributable to the influx of Lombard colonists who entered Southern Italy in such numbers as to excite the wonder of contemporaries. The chronicler Hugo Falcandus relates that in 1168 the Lombard cities alone offered the royal Chancellor, Stephen Perche, the Archbishop of Palermo, some 20,000 soldiers. It has been plausibly estimated that the colonists may well have numbered at least 100,000.[4] Certainly the influx of large numbers of Northern Italians would tend to neutralize the dominant oriental influence of the Byzantine and Arabic elements, making possible a more active Latinization of all ethnic groups within the Sicilian Kingdom. Although they desired this Latinization, the Norman kings utilized as fully as possible the superior culture of each of these peoples. Hugo Falcandus could truthfully say of Roger II that 'he

---

[1] G. von Parthey, *Hierocles Synecdemus et notitiae Graecae episcopatuum. Accedunt Nili Doxapatrii notitia partriarchatuum*, 265 ff. See also E. Jamison, *Admiral Eugenius*, 26 ff.

[2] E. Jamison, *Admiral Eugenius*, 21 ff. See also C. Alexandre, *Oracula Sibyllina*, ii. 291–4; and O. Holder-Egger, 'Italienische Prophetieen' (*Neues Archiv*, xv, 1889–90), 141–78, especially 155. Pertinent also are L. Sternbach, 'Eugenius von Palermo' (*Byzantinische Zeitschr.* xi, 1902), 406 ff.; and S. G. Mercati, 'È stato trovato il testo greco della Sibilla Tiburtina', *Mélanges Henri Grégoire I*, 473–81.

[3] L. T. White, Jr., *Latin Monasticism*, 46.

[4] See Falcandus, *Historia* (*Fonti*), 155, and L. T. White, Jr., *Latin Monasticism*, 60. Professor White has emphasized that the term 'Lombard' meant simply 'mainlanders'.

informed himself, with the utmost diligence of the customs of other kings and peoples, to the end that he could adopt all that he considered good and useful'.[1] Evidence of this is to be found chiefly in court circles where all these cultures appeared together. Among the royal officials were Normans, French, Italians, Greeks, and Arabs.[2] It is difficult to determine to what extent an exchange of the various cultures took place among the masses of the people although the fact that many inhabitants of the Kingdom could make use of several languages made possible the fusion of the best elements of each.[3]

The preponderance of Greek and Arabic influences continued for some time, causing a marked contrast between Southern Italy and Sicily and the north of Europe. During the Norman era, however, the influence of the north is increasingly apparent in court circles, just as the Norman-Sicilian influence made itself felt in all the countries of Western Europe. It was in the fields of law and medicine that Italy was to surpass and to influence the countries of the north, while theology and poetry continued the main cultural preoccupations of France and, to a lesser extent, of England and Germany. The intellectual and cultural reawakening of Italy was greatly stimulated by schools which were established for laymen of the merchant class. Their object was to produce individuals capable of carrying on correspondence essential to the expanding mercantile activities of the Italian cities. No less important to these mercantile interests were representatives trained in law. Lawyers and notaries became the most literate members of society. It was inevitable that the literary interests of these laymen would find expression in forms associated with their professions; the authors of juristic treatises, letters, and municipal chronicles were generally notaries or, in some instances, municipal judges.[4] Despite the observation of Master Buoncompagno, the thirteenth-century *dictator* and mentor of literary style, that 'merchants in their letters do not require an ornate phraseology', the study of rhetoric was considered essential to the development of documentary and epistolary styles.[5]

---

[1] Falcandus, *Historia*, 6.

[2] The presence of Arab secretaries in the royal chancery, H. Niese, 'Zur Geschichte', 478, note 1, has been established through his analysis of a pictorial illustration in the manuscript of Pietro da Eboli, *Liber in Honorem Augusti*, Tav. VII, 124.

[3] The cultural exchange in the mid twelfth century has been described by P. Batiffol, *L'Abbaye de Rossano*, 85 ff. As to the Byzantine influence on the culture and civilization of Southern Italy see J. Gay, *L'Italie méridionale et l'empire byzantin*, ii. 592–8.

[4] F. Novati, *L'influsso del pensiero Latino sopra la civiltà Italiana del medio evo*, pp. 232 ff., and idem, 'Rapports littéraires de l'Italie et de la France' (*Académie des Inscriptions et Belles Lettres: Comptes Rendus des Séances de l'Année*, 1910), 169 ff., C. Hegel, *Geschichte der Städteverfassung der Zeit der römischen Herrschaft bis zum Ausgang des zwölften Jahrhunderts*, ii. 210 f., Schmeidler, *Italienische Geschichtsschreiber des XII. und XIII. Jahrhunderts*, 38 and 87.

[5] See the remark of Buoncompagno, *Epistole mercatorum*: 'Mercatores in suis epistolis verborum ornatum non requirunt.'

Throughout the twelfth and thirteenth centuries numerous textbooks with such titles as *Precepta Dictaminis, Summae Dictaminum* were widely used. In the thirteenth century this stylistic interest reached the height of its development in the bombastic treatise *Buoncompagnus*, so called from its egotistical author, Master Buoncompagno, professor of rhetoric at Bologna, who proclaimed himself superior to Cicero.[1] But even though jurists and notaries educated at Bologna appeared at the Norman court during the twelfth century, the predominant cultural influences at court were of Greek and Arabic origin.[2]

It would be erroneous, however, to over-emphasize the absence of Latin cultural influences from the north upon the courts of Messina and Palermo. From the time of the Great Count, Roger I, the influence of the Normans and the French gradually made itself felt. The most striking example of early northern influence was that of France and England; it came mainly from officials of the royal court. Although King Roger attracted to his court men of talent from every land, he showed a preference for the French and English.[3] During the greater part of the reign of Roger II an Englishman, Robert Selby, was Chancellor, certainly from July 1137 to October 1151. It is not improbable that Thomas Brown, so intimately associated with the court circle after 1137, went to Sicily at the same time as Robert Selby, probably as the latter's protégé. After the disgrace and murder in 1160 of Admiral Maio who had long dominated the Chancery, and the imprisonment of his successor, Henry Aristippus, the direction of the Chancery passed to an Englishman, Richard Palmer, described by Falcandus as 'vir literatissimus et eloquens'.[4]

The most notable French official was Count Stephen of Perche; he was made Chancellor in 1166 and subsequently, in November 1167, was elected Archbishop of Palermo. The importance of the French and the Anglo-Normans as chancellors and as other officials lies not so much in the influence which they had on the form of official documents of kings and nobles, but in their effect on literary style. Even where the French language was employed, the forms of official acts continued to be modelled upon Greek and Lombard charters.[5] Frequent visits of Western Europeans would inevitably exercise considerable influence

---

[1] Concerning him see G. Bertoni, *Il Duecento*, 148; K. Sutter, *Aus Leben und Schriften des Magisters Buoncompagno*, especially 3–15. For the many treatises of this kind in the Middle Ages see the various works of L. von Rockinger, especially *Über Formelbücher vom dreizehnten bis zum sechzehnten Jahrhundert als Rechtsgeschichte*, 'Über ars dictandi und die summae dictaminis in Italien' (*Sb. Bayer. A.* i, 1861), 98–151.

[2] F. Giunta, *Bizantini e Bizantinismo*, 147 ff.

[3] C. H. Haskins, 'England and Sicily in the Twelfth Century' (*EHR* xxvi, 1911), 433 ff., 641 ff.; K. A. Kehr, *Urkunden*, 49.

[4] *Liber de Regno Sicilie (Fonti)*, 6; see also Kehr, *Urkunden*, 83.

[5] Ibid. 84 ff.

upon the literature and general culture of Sicily. When Bishop Stubbs, in his preface to the *Chronica* of Roger of Hoveden, says of Peter of Blois that he 'was the intimate friend of both Henry II and William the Good', one can hardly doubt that Peter's cultural attributes, especially his superior Latin style, evoked their admiration. Less striking, but deserving notice, was the influence of William, the brother of Peter, who, although Abbot of a Calabrian monastery, devoted himself to the writing of prose and poetry, including tragedy and comedy.[1] An example of French influence upon Sicilian Latin prose style was the *Historia Sicula* of Gaufred Malaterra, who was probably of Norman origin, and, like many of his contemporaries, attracted to Sicily by the triumphs of Count Roger I, the hero of his *Historia*.[2]

The most splendid period of Norman-Sicilian scholarship was during the last years of Roger II's reign and under his successors, the two Williams. The period was distinguished especially by the achievements of Henry Aristippus and Eugene of Palermo. It had been plausibly conjectured that Henry Aristippus may have been the tutor of Roger's sons, William, later to become King William I, and Henry, who died while still a youth. It is possible, however, that the tutor or tutors of the young princes may have come from the monastery of St. Nicola di Casole, which was patronized by King Roger, or from other centres of learning in the Byzantine areas of the south of Italy. The interest of Henry Aristippus and his associates in the study of Platonic philosophy may have been inspired by the philosophical studies of the school of Chartres. This conjecture is made the more plausible by recent studies which have revealed some evidence that Aristippus was of Norman origin.[3] Whether of Norman or of Greek origin, Henry Aristippus bears witness to the continuity of the Byzantine culture. Long after the Norman conquest of Apulia and Sicily the scholars of Southern Italy continued their associations with Constantinople.[4] The Greek Scholarios, who lived between 1050 and 1130, was notable as a collector. His testament reveals that his library contained more than 300 manuscripts which he bequeathed to the monastery of S. Salvatore di Bordonaro near Messina where, as a Basilian monk, he died.[5] As we have seen, however, such

---

[1] *Histoire littéraire de la France*, xv. 412 ff., 414 ff.; W. Clötta, *Komödie und Tragödie im Mittelalter: Beiträge zur Literaturgeschichte des Mittelalters und der Renaissance*, i. 76–8. See also Manitius, *Geschichte*, ii, 3, pp. 1021 ff.

[2] For the *Historia* see Muratori, *RIS*, new edn., v, part i, pp. iv–vii.

[3] E. Jamison, *Admiral Eugenius*, pp. xviii–xx.

[4] P. Batiffol, *L'Abbaye de Rossano*, 79–105: 'Origines de la Libraire du Patir'.

[5] F. Lo Parco, 'Scolario-Saba bibliofilo italiota, vissuto tra l'XI e il XII secolo e la biblioteca del monastero basiliano del SS. Salvatore di Bordonaro pressa Messina' (*Atti della R. Accademia di archeologia, lettere e belle arti* [*Società Reale*] *di Napoli*, N.S., i, 1910), 207 ff., J. L. Heiberg (review), 'Francesco Lo Parco. Scolaria-Saba bibliofilo italiota' (*Byzant. Zeitschr.* xxii, 1913).

manuscript collections were not at all unusual and were probably accessible to Henry Aristippus and his contemporaries at the royal court.

The chief contemporary source for the life of Henry Aristippus is the
Liber de regno Sicilie by the so-called Hugo Falcandus. Unfortunately,
this work leaves us completely in the dark as to his origin. Most convincing of his non-Sicilian origin is the generally accepted observation
that he possessed an excellent knowledge of Latin, while his Greek was
elementary. The statement of Hugo Falcandus that Aristippus was
'mansuetissimi virum ingenii et tam latinis quam grecis litteris eruditum',
obviously makes no distinction as to his skill in the use of the two
languages.[1] One is disposed, however, to accept the opinion that the
superiority of his Latin is indicative of his non-Greek origin and the
further observation 'that no original writings of his in Greek are extant,
but only his preface in a distinguished Latin style'. Moreover, as Miss
Jamison has emphasized, Aristippus is merely a nickname and has no
relevance as to his nationality.[2]

In 1154, two years after the death of King Roger II, Henry Aristippus
was made archdeacon of Catania; some years later he was member of
an embassy sent by King William I to Constantinople. It was about this
time also that he made the translations from Plato that established his
fame as translator, the *Meno* (*c.* 1154) and the *Phaedo* (*c.* 1156), the
latter while with the army at the siege of Benevento.[3] As a result of
his mission to Constantinople, Aristippus obtained a manuscript of
Ptolemy's *Almagest*, a gift of the Byzantine Emperor to King William.
His interest in Greek philosophy and science carried him beyond his
Platonic studies to the translating of the fourth book of Aristotle's
Meteorologica and the *De Vita Philosophorum* of Diogenes Laertius.[4]

After the murder of the Emir or Admiral Maio, former Chancellor,
Henry Aristippus succeeded to the vacant office, not with the title of
chancellor, but as acting admiral or, more accurately, as chief minister.[5]
He did not long enjoy the power and the prestige of that office, for, like
his great predecessor, he became involved in the political intrigues and
conflicts of the court and, falling under the King's displeasure as a suspected member of an alleged treasonable conspiracy, he died in prison
in 1162.[6]

More versatile than Henry Aristippus, and probably the most distinguished translator and literary figure of twelfth-century Sicily, was

---

[1] Ed. G. B. Siragusa (*Fonti*), 44.

[2] *Admiral Eugenius*, p. xix; see also L. Minio-Paluello (ed.), *Phaedo, Interprete Henrico Aristippo*
(*Plato Latinus*), Preface, ix, note 1.

[3] Ibid. 90. See also Mandalari, 'Enrico Aristippo' (*Bolletino storico Catanese*, I–II, 1939), 96;
V. Rose, 'Die Lücke im Diogenes Laërtius' (*Hermes*, i, 1866), 376.

[4] Mandalari, op. cit. 108. See also L. Minio-Paluello, *Phaedo*, Preface, p. ix, note 1, and
Jamison, op. cit., p. xvii and note 1.

[5] Falcandus, op. cit. 44.　　　　　　　　　　　　　　　[6] Mandalari, op. cit. 121 f.

Admiral Eugene of Palermo. Member of a family long associated with the official life of Sicily, he was active in diplomatic missions between West and East. He was employed almost continuously throughout the reigns of the two Williams, Tancred, the Emperor Henry VI, and during the vicegerency of the Empress Constance in the absence of the Emperor in Germany.[1] Eugene's long career as public official, marking him always as a personage of unusual distinction, lends much weight to the contention that he was probably the author of various historical works, notably the *Historia* of the so-called Hugo Falcandus and the *Epistola ad Petrum* which appeared either anonymously or under pseudonyms.[2] He first came into prominence as translator when he participated, probably as 'expositor', with the anonymous translator of Ptolemy's *Almagest*, which had been brought from Constantinople by Henry Aristippus. Described by the anonymous translator of the *Almagest* as 'fully expert in Greek as in Arabic, and not ignorant of Latin',[3] Eugene was interested also in Euclid's *Data* and *Catoptica* and in the *Mechanics* or *Physica Elementa* of Proclus. The wide range of Admiral Eugene's interests is illustrated by his translation of the so-called *Prophecy of the Erythraean Sibyl*. This prophecy, allegedly made in the time of King Priam and translated from the Chaldean into Greek by Nilus Doxapater, was translated from Greek into Latin by Admiral Eugene.[4]

Another work of oriental origin with which the name of Admiral Eugene is associated is the ancient Arabic (originally Sanskrit) collection of tales, *Kalīlah wa Dimna*, sometimes known also as *A Mirror of Princes*. It is best described as a book of animal fables, depicting the manner in which princes should rule their subjects. In the last quarter of the eleventh century it was translated into Greek at the command of Alexius Commenus and it was apparently in this form that it was edited and revised by Eugene of Palermo.[5]

The Norman-Sicilian court officials, like higher clergy and monks of Sicily and Southern Italy (for example, Alfanus, Romuald of Salerno, and the monks of Calabria and the Terra d'Otranto), cultivated the art of poetic composition. In this Eugene of Palermo was no exception. If no other evidence existed of the Byzantinization of Southern Italy in the twelfth century, the Greek poems of Admiral Eugene would suffice.[6]

[1] The most thorough treatment of Eugene is E. Jamison, *Admiral Eugenius*. See especially 35, 51, 60–1, 106. Useful, although with some inaccuracies, is C. Cipolla, 'Ricerche su Eugenio L'Emiro' (*Archivio stor. siciliano*, 3rd series, 1, 1946.)

[2] See the highly plausible arguments of E. Jamison, op. cit., part ii.

[3] See the text of the preface to the anonymous translation in C. H. Haskins, *Medieval Science*, 191–3.

[4] See above, p. 292, note 2.

[5] See first K. Krumbacher, *Byzantinische Literatur*, 895–7; and then E. Jamison, *Admiral Eugenius*, 8–21, especially 19–20.

[6] For the poetry of Eugene see L. Sternbach, 'Eugenios von Palermo' (*Byzant. Zeitschr.* xi,

It has been appropriately suggested by Miss Jamison that the poems of Eugene of Palermo can be classified under five categories: epigrams, chiefly of religious subjects; vices and virtues, illustrated by both Biblical and classical subjects; poems devoted to nature and natural phenomena; verse letters addressed to various personages; and episodes from the life of Eugene.[1]

It is perhaps inevitable in studying the life of a man of the stature of Admiral Eugene, whose activities spanned more than the last half of the twelfth century, that one may be tempted to go further in exploring his importance in the cultural history of his era, as well as his influence upon the future of Western culture. Indeed, it would be enough if we recognized him primarily for his studies and his translations in mathematics, as the author of numerous Greek verses, and as the 'transmitter of two curious bits of Oriental Literature'. It is remarkable, therefore, that more recent studies have emphasized his creativeness in methods of fiscal administration in the Kingdom of Sicily; his contributions to natural history through his close and accurate observations of natural phenomena, whether the water-lily or the common housefly; his transmission of physiognomic lore, as well as physical science; his assimilation and transmission of Platonic political theory; and, finally, his probable authorship of contemporary works of history, including the *Epistola ad Petrum*, the *Liber de Regno Sicilie*, and parts of the *Chronica S. Mariae de Ferraria*.[2]

As a youth Eugene of Palermo had witnessed the transition of Sicily and Apulia into the Norman monarchy. In his old age he saw the destruction of that monarchy by the Hohenstaufen and, before his death in 1202, he witnessed the beginning of the period of chaos during the minority of Frederick II and the temporary cessation of the intellectual, literary, and scientific activity which, having its auspicious beginning in the eleventh century, culminated in a twelfth-century renaissance in Sicily.

1902), 406–51; K. Horne, 'Metrische und Textkritische Bemerkungen zu den Gedichten des Eugenios von Palermo' (ibid. xiv, 1905), 461–78, and continued in xvi (1907), xvii (1968), and xx (1911).

[1] *Admiral Eugenius*, 6 ff.
[2] E. Jamison, *Admiral Eugenius*, Epilogue, 314. I would add, however, that Miss Jamison's attribution of some of these historical works to Eugene of Palermo is still open to question.

II

THE PURSUIT OF LEARNING AT THE COURT OF FREDERICK II

Intentio vero nostra est manifestare in hoc libro . . . ea, que sunt, sicut sunt.

Frederick II, *De Arte Venandi cum Avibus*, Prologue.[1]

THE pursuit of learning at the court of Frederick II has frequently been misrepresented by placing a too literal interpretation upon the remark of Nicholas of Jamsilla, a thirteenth-century chronicler, that, at the time of Frederick's arrival, there were few or no scholars in Sicily.[2] Had Nicholas simply noted the absence of scientific endeavour comparable to that of Henry Aristippus and Eugene of Palermo at the Norman-Sicilian court he would have been more accurate. He seems to have been unaware that in the monastic libraries of Calabria, the Basilicata, and the Terra d'Otranto there were great collections of manuscripts, both Greek and Latin, and devoted scholars who had continued with their pursuits even during the years of turbulence since the end of the Norman era. Shortly after Frederick's return following his coronation as Emperor, several of these learned Greeks, notably from the monastery of St. Nicola di Casole, in the Terra d'Otranto, appeared at Frederick's court as secretaries, translators, and in other official capacities.[3] Their main interest was literary, the cultivation of the art of poetry. How many others may have continued their scholarly and literary pursuits in the obscurity of the monasteries we do not know. But it is remarkable that those who entered the service of the court cultivated the art of poetry in a manner often reminiscent of Alfanus at Monte Cassino and Eugene of Palermo at the Norman-Sicilian court. Like their predecessors, they were steeped in the lore and traditions of antiquity.

Much more apt is the further observation of Nicholas of Jamsilla, that it was one of Frederick's tasks, by means of liberal inducements, to attract learned men from other regions. In such invitations he gave no

---

[1] It is our intention in this book to set forth the things that are as they are.
[2] Muratori, *RIS* viii, col. 496.
[3] See especially Gigante, *Poeti italobizantini del secolo XIII: Collana di studi greci*, xxii. 8 ff.

thought to differences in religion or racial origin. Some of those invited were Christians, many were Jews or Muslims, all were devoted to the pursuit of learning and belles-lettres. When, for various reasons, it was impracticable to have them present in person, he engaged them in learned correspondence, seeking their opinions upon a great variety of subjects, especially in the sciences and mathematics.

The original patron of St. Nicola di Casole had been the Norman, Bohemond of Taranto, son of Robert Guiscard; the Norman counts and kings of Sicily had continued this patronage. Frederick II had gratefully accepted it as an obligation of his Norman cultural heritage.[1] It may well be assumed that the superior education of King Roger II is attributable in part to the influence of the scholars of St. Nicola di Casole. Moreover, there is every reason to assume that the rich store of learning from the Byzantine libraries of Southern Italy, not only that of St. Nicola di Casole, but of others in the Terra d'Otranto, Calabria, and the Basilicata, continued to flow into the court of Frederick II as it had into the courts of Roger II and the two Williams. The mingling of the Basilian scholars at the court with those of Arabic or Western origin and the obvious welcome extended to them by Frederick II, emphasizes his awareness of the continuity of intellectual and literary activities from the Norman-Sicilian era. As protégés of the learned Abbot Nectarios of St. Nicola di Casole, these Greek poets and scholars had long had access to the monastery's rare collections of antique manuscripts thought to be among the best in the Byzantine libraries of Southern Italy.

Frederick II's intellectual interests and the cultural preoccupations of his court were in no sense isolated phenomena. The similarity of his interests, his tastes, and even his capabilities, to those of his grandfather, Roger II, are always discernible. Such differences as existed were often the result of environment. Frederick II, from his earliest infancy, was almost continuously in the midst of Arab cultural influences, more removed from the ideals of both Monte Cassino and Salerno with which the Normans, in the early days of their conquests, had been in intimate contact. Differences in temperament and personality account for the catholicity of Frederick's interests as contrasted with the more limited activities of his Norman predecessors. The differences must be explained in part by Frederick's good fortune in being able to build upon a solid cultural foundation erected by his predecessors, although it had been neglected for several decades.

If he resembled his Norman predecessors in their common interest in learning, and differed from them chiefly by virtue of the greater intensity and variety of his cultural activities, the difference is much more

---

[1] P. Batiffol, *L'Abbaye de Rossano*, pp. xxviii ff.

pronounced when he is contrasted with the contemporary sovereigns of Europe as a whole. The mere literary interests were shared by other monarchs, but Frederick's patronage of the natural sciences and mathematics, coupled with his habitual association with men distinguished by their achievements in these sciences, including many whose religions and customs differed from his own, gives him a unique position in cultural history. His tolerance towards other religions and other peoples is illustrated by his acceptance of the Basilian scholars to whom he permitted complete freedom of thought, even when they opposed the pretensions of the Popes and the Roman Church. Thus the Calabrian poet, George of Gallipoli, a Greek Ghibelline at Frederick's court, affected to see in him a sovereign comparable to Zeus, destined to crush the temporal pretensions of the Bishop of Rome and to restore the dignity of the Eternal City and the grandeur of the ancient Empire. George of Gallipoli's heroes were Job, Ahab, Aaron, and David, but he clothed them with attributes little different from those of the Greek and Roman gods. Less skilled in the art of poetry than Alfanus and Eugene of Palermo, he was deeply devoted to Frederick II, whom he eulogized as a 'tower of light'. His poetry often suggests his role as imperial propagandist, a characterization borne out by his verses of reproach addressed to the unfaithful city of Parma in 1247.

Another Greek official at the court of Frederick II, often serving as amanuensis for correspondence addressed to the Greek sovereigns, Michael Comnenus and John Vatatzes, was John of Otranto. He too directed a scornful poem to the unfaithful Parmesans; in it he predicted their destruction at which even the name of their city would be obliterated, giving place to Frederick's triumphant siege-city, Victoria. He depicted the degradation of the treasonable citizens, shorn of their liberties and reduced to servitude. Also of note was John's son, Nicholas of Otranto, an epigrammatist and member of the secretariat of the imperial court.

Another Italo-Byzantine poet whose interests in classical antiquity were not unlike those of Frederick II was John Grasso, unique as a tragic poet. Thoroughly steeped in classical tradition, he is aptly described as having achieved 'a symbiosis of pagan motifs and Christian sensibility'.[1] Conspicuous among his poems evoking the spirit of antiquity is his *Lament of Hecuba at the Fall of Troy*; although crudely constructed, at times it surpasses Euripides in the horror of its tragic episodes. The importance of John Grasso is to be found not in the perfection of his verse form or, indeed, in his power of dramatization. His poetry is of interest because of its wealth of classical lore—a Greek Christian in Italy nostalgic for the glories of ancient Greece. He, like

---

[1] M. Gigante, *Poeti italobizantini del secolo XIII*, xxii. 11–12.

his Italo-Byzantine contemporaries, bears witness to the continuity of Greek culture in the Frederican era in Sicily.[1]

Frederick II was interested in the literary achievements of these men as he was in those of the Latin and vernacular poets in his court. But the most distinguishing feature of his reign was his patronage of and his participation in the philosophical, the mathematical, and the scientific pursuits of his court circle. His similarity to his maternal grandfather has been noted already, but whereas Roger II's chief interests were in geography, to which, with the aid of Edrisi, he applied a scientific approach, Frederick II applied the scientific method to a variety of pursuits.

It is unfortunate for the history of science in the West that the Greek monks in the Basilian monasteries such as that of St. Nicola di Casole, eager as they were to transport scholarly works from Constantinople and other places in the Orient, had no deep interest in the writings of Aristotle or other works in philosophy, mathematics, and the sciences. Why had they not continued the same interest that impelled Henry Aristippus to bring from Constantinople the *Almagest* of Ptolemy and to begin a translation of Aristotle's *Meteorologica*, or that caused Eugene of Palermo to translate the *Optica* of Ptolemy and to display more than a casual interest in other mathematical works of the Greeks? The answer apparently is that, while the linguistic ability to make such translations obviously existed in the various Basilian monasteries, the moving force in scientific activities was not to be found in the monasteries but in the courts of enlightened sovereigns such as Roger II and the Williams. This explanation becomes more plausible when, only a short time after Frederick's arrival in Sicily, evidences of scientific interest and activity reappeared, especially between 1220 and 1232. Quite early in his imperial reign he caused the works of both Aristotle and ibn-Rushd (Averroës) to be translated and sent copies of the translations to the professors and students of the universities of Bologna and Paris. His covering letter is a remarkable document, revealing with extraordinary clarity the intellectual characteristics of Frederick II.[2] In his opening remarks he notes that from his youth he had been eager for knowledge and had always esteemed it, 'inhaling tirelessly its sweet perfumes'. He then tells how he had had various works of antiquity collected and

---

[1] For the poets mentioned see A. M. Bandini, *Catalogus codicum mss. Bibliothecae Mediceae Laurentianae*, i. 23–30. For a general survey of these poets see K. Krumbacher, *Gesch. d. Byzant. Lit.* 768 ff. See also J. N. Sola, 'De Codice Laurentiano, X plutei V. (*Byzant. Zeitschr.* xx, 1911), 373 ff., and M. Gigante, op. cit., for analyses of their poems.

[2] For the letter see Huillard-Bréholles, iv, part i, 383 ff. I am, of course, aware that this letter has been attributed by several scholars to Manfred rather than to Frederick II. The evidence, however, is not conclusive. Internal evidence suggests that Frederick rather than his son was the author.

translated for his own use but, because the noble possession of knowledge is not weakened when shared with others and disseminated, but is made even more fruitful and more enduring, it ought to be made available to others. He continues:

> Therefore we will not conceal those fruits, gathered with so great effort, nor can we find satisfaction in thinking of them as our own property unless first we share with others so great a good. . . . You men of learning, who cleverly draw fresh water from ancient reservoirs, thus extending the refreshing cup to thirsty lips, have prior claim. Therefore deign to accept these books as a gift from your friend, the Emperor, and, at his request and through the kindness of your hearts, make known to him what you discover as a result of your researches. We believe it to be useful and of value to us to provide the opportunity for our subjects to enlighten themselves, because, well informed, they will more readily do what is right and, leaning upon the staff of knowledge, they will provide better for themselves and for the Fatherland.

Apart from Frederick's intimate acquaintance with the Arabs of Sicily, his greater reliance upon Arab and Jewish scholars rather than Greek arose from the extraordinary impact of Averroës' translations and interpretations of Aristotle upon him and upon the learned members of his court. To a large extent Averroës must be credited with giving to the West in the twelfth and thirteenth centuries a far more accurate concept of Aristotle than had been available in the early Middle Ages. Averroës himself seems to have made an extraordinary appeal to the Western mind. It is often apparent that it was not Aristotle but Averroës who rekindled the fires of philosophical controversy among the Scholastics. Moreover, it was in the twelfth century, not many years before the advent of Frederick II as Sicilian King, that translations from the Arabic into Latin began in Spain, especially in Toledo. The opening years of the thirteenth century saw the Graeco-Arabic culture of Spain infiltrating the world of Western Christendom and leading to a substitution of an Arabic Aristotelianism for the limited and imperfect Boethian tradition. If the court of Frederick II participated more abundantly in this than did the courts of other European monarchs it is to be explained by the environment of a Sicilian-Arabic culture which had been cultivated by the Norman kings and revitalized by the dynamic personality of Frederick II. It was his predilection for Arabic philosophy that evoked the frequent charges of heresy against him, charges which were insistently pressed at the Council of Lyons at the time of his deposition by Pope Innocent IV.[1] Further ground for these charges was undoubtedly

---

[1] See below, pp. 486 f. and 489 f. As to the influence of Averroës on Western Christian thought as a whole, see M. Grabmann, *Der lateinische Averroismus des 13. Jahrhunderts und seine Stellung zur christlichen Weltanschauung* (*Sb. B. A.*, Jahrgang 1931, Heft iii). See also H. A. Wolfson, 'The Twice-Revealed Averroës' (*Speculum*, xxxvi, 1961), 373 ff.

provided by his intimate association with Muslim scholars such as his Arab tutor in logic who accompanied him on his crusade in 1228, and by his frequent correspondence with Arabs and Jews in Spain and else-where. Arabic sources invariably express either amazement or pleasure at finding a Christian who was not only tolerant of Islam but also ex-pressed admiration for it, and at the same time was capable of observ-ing the shortcomings of his fellow Christians.[1] A revealing feature of Frederick's intellectual outlook, which must have been most disturbing to the pious, was his statement in the book of falconry: 'Our work is to present things that are as they are.'

To the medieval mind, quickened by its intellectual and artistic interests, Frederick II gave a new and powerful impulse, broadening its vision, severing its restrictive bonds, brushing aside the obstacles which had held it in restraint for a thousand years. Some of his contemporaries were more than vaguely aware of these qualities of the Emperor. Thus one of them exclaimed: 'O fortunate Emperor, truly I believe if ever there could be a man who, by virtue of knowledge, could transcend death itself that you would be that one!'[2] Even more extravagant was the praise of Master Henry of Avranches, an itinerant poet, sometime resi-dent at the court of Frederick. To him the Emperor was comparable to Robert Guiscard who checked the power of Rome; to David who stopped the Philistines; to Charlemagne who conquered idolatry; to Caesar who conquered all. Even more lavishly the same poet praised Frederick for his intellectual qualities—for his inquisitiveness. It was not enough that he ruled an Empire. He must explore for himself the secrets of knowledge. It was this restless inquisitiveness that caused him to choose as his companions at court the ablest of scholars: comparable to Plato for logic; to Cicero for rhetoric; to Donatus for grammar; to Euclid for geometry; to Pythagoras for music; to Ptolemy for astrology.[3]

As we have seen, the Greek cultural activity in Southern Italy and in some regions of the island of Sicily continued its inconspicuous develop-ment in various monasteries during the turbulent period of Frederick II's minority. In contrast, the Arabs of Sicily, so influential in the era of the Norman kings and under the Emperor Henry VI, appear to have deteriorated culturally during the papal regency and, thereafter, until long after Frederick II's return to Sicily in 1220. Unwilling to accept the governing regimes of that turbulent period, they devoted their energies to futile revolts, isolating themselves more and more in the

---

[1] Amari, *Bibliotheca Arabo-Sicula*, ii. 254; M. Steinschneider, *Die hebräischen Übersetzungen des Mittelalters*, 3 ff.; R. Straus, *Die Juden im Königreich Sizilien unter Normannen und Staufen*, 81 ff., especially 84–5.

[2] C. H. Haskins, *Studies in Medieval Science*, 294, for the Latin text of this tribute.

[3] E. Winkelmann, 'Drei Gedichte Heinrichs von Avranches an Kaiser Friedrich II.' (*FzDG* xviii, 1878), 482 ff.; especially 491.

mountain fastnesses, while their cultural influence was sharply curtailed. Even under Frederick II's friendly encouragement it did not regain its former position. Continued revolts of the Arabic population until their segregation in the Saracen colony of Lucera further impaired their chance of a return to a position of influence at the court. There is some evidence of a revival of intellectual and artistic activity among the Saracens of Lucera which might well have regained its former influence had it not been for the abrupt ending of the Hohenstaufen authority in Sicily following the death of Frederick II in 1250 and that of Manfred a few years later.[1] As Amari pointed out long ago, Frederick II was not the first but the second of the 'two baptized sultans' on the Sicilian throne.[2] In so far as circumstances permitted, this 'second baptized sultan' followed the policies of the first in dealing with the Saracen people. Moreover, even in Palermo during the turbulent years of the regency, some Saracens continued to live, and it was probably from them, although we do not know in what manner, that Frederick II received his earliest training in the Arabic language and philosophy.

Arabic influence at the court of Frederick II became increasingly important as his reign progressed. Several native Saracens were active as government officials from the early years of Frederick's arrival. After 1239 Johannes Maurus, a Muslim, the royal Chamberlain, was one of the most trusted of Frederick's officials. Diplomatic correspondence with Arabic states, however, was generally prepared by scholars learned in the Arabic language, although not of Arabic origin. The most active of them were Obert Fallamonaca, *magister duanae secretus*, and Master Theodore of Antioch, philosopher and court astrologer.[3] It may be conjectured also from the numerous criticisms of Frederick by the Popes for his intimacy with Saracens that among them were frequent visitors to, if not regular members of, the court circle.

It was this very quality of cosmopolitanism, together with his intellectual honesty—his insistent search for truth as opposed to tradition—that was so clearly expressed in Frederick's alleged remark: 'One should accept as truth only that which is proved by the force of reason and by nature.' Suspicion of his orthodoxy was increased as a result of his correspondence relating to various intellectual problems with Muslims and Jews and his acceptance of gifts such as that sent him by Sultan Ashraf of Damascus in 1232 and described by a contemporary as 'a planetarium, constructed with admirable skill, on which were figures of the sun and

---

[1] See especially P. Egidi, 'La colonia saracena di Lucera e sua distruzione' (*Archiv. Stor. per le provincie napoletane*, xxxvi, 1911), 597 ff.

[2] *Storia dei Musulmani*, iii. 372.

[3] See, for example, the documents in S. Cusa, *I diplomi greci ed arabi della Sicilia*, ii. 676, no. xv, and pp. 743–4. For Master Theodore see Amari, iii. 710–13; Ch. V. Langlois, *La Connaissance de la nature et du monde*, 203.

moon indicating the hours of the day and night in the course of their determined movements'. No less astonishing, and certainly more displeasing to many of his contemporaries, was Frederick's learned correspondence with Sultan al-Kāmil concerning intricate problems of algebra and geometry. This correspondence also led to Frederick's acquaintance with a learned sheikh, Alem-ed-Dīn-Hanéfi, to whom he subsequently addressed various questions on astronomy and mathematics.[1]

The most intimate of Frederick's guides in his scientific pursuits was Michael Scot who is credited by Roger Bacon with introducing the Arabo-Aristotelian philosophy to the West. Unfortunately, many facts in the life of Michael Scot are not available. It is known that he was of Scottish origin, although his birth can be placed only approximately, some time during the last quarter of the twelfth century. There seems to be little doubt that his death occurred in 1236, during the Emperor's preparations for the reopening of the war against the Lombards. In one of the poems addressed to Frederick II in that year Henry of Avranches refers to Michael's death. He is described as 'scrutinizer of the stars, augur, and soothsayer: another Apollo who, as a diviner of fates, yielded to fate'.[2] Pope Honorius III in 1224, in a letter to the Archbishop of Canterbury, recommends Michael as a man of learning, and some three years later (April 1227) Pope Gregory IX describes him as one who 'had pursued learning since boyhood'. Pope Gregory also mentions Michael's knowledge of Hebrew and Arabic.[3] There are no other contemporary references to his education.

Some time before 1217 Michael Scot went to Spain, completing in that year also his translation of al-Bitrūjī's (Alpetragius') *Kitāb al-Hay'ah*, the configuration of the heavenly bodies or, as it is sometimes called in its Latin translation, *De verificatione motuum coelestium*,[4] a work that was to have a profound influence upon Western European thought concerning the planets. The work of al-Bitrūjī, embodying, as it did, the Aristotelian theory of homocentric spheres, reopened the ancient conflict, long known to the Greeks and Arabs, between the astronomy of Ptolemy and the physics of Aristotle.[5] The profound influence of this and other translations of Michael Scot on thirteenth-century scholars is reflected in the remark of Roger Bacon, who wrote: 'The philosophy

---

[1] See the encyclical of Gregory IX, 21 July 1239 (Huillard-Bréholles, v, part i), 340; *Chronica regia Coloniensis*, 263; P. K. Hitti, *History of the Arabs* (London, 1940), 610; E. Blochet, 'Les Relations diplomatiques des Hohenstaufen avec les Sultans d'Égypte' (*Rev. Historique*, lxxx, 1902), 60; Maqrīzī, *Histoire d'Égypte*, 528 ff.; and 'Estratti Tarih Mansuri', 119.

[2] Pressutti, no. 4682; and Auvray, *Registres de Grégoire IX*, no. 61.

[3] Winkelmann, 'Drei Gedichte', p. 486, lines 58–9, 84.

[4] A. Jourdain, *Recherches critiques sur l'âge et l'origine des traductions latines d'Aristote*, 133.

[5] See P. Duhem, *Le Système du monde* (1958 impression), iii. 214 f., P. K. Hitti, *History of the Arabs*, 572.

took on a new development among the Latins when Michael Scot appeared bearing certain parts of the *Natural Philosophy* and *Metaphysics* of Aristotle and his scholarly translation of the Arabic commentaries.' Bacon's phraseology has at times been interpreted as introducing the 'new Aristotle' into Western Europe for the first time. What we really have here is a recognition by Bacon that the translations of Arabic versions of the Greek philosophers and scientists gave a new impulse to the study of them. A literal translation would seem to imply that, since Michael Scot appeared with his translations of the Arabic version of Aristotle, together with his commentaries, the philosophy of Aristotle has been magnified among the Latins (*magnificata est philosophia Aristotelis*).[1] But if Bacon thus praised Michael Scot in these seemingly extravagant terms he was also Michael's severest critic, asserting that he, Gerard of Cremona, Hermann the German, and William Flemming were ignorant of the languages from which they were translating and of the sciences which they were endeavouring to translate.[2]

Between 1224 and 1227 Michael Scot enjoyed the favour and encouragement of both Honorius III and Gregory IX, who must have been fully aware of the importance of his work as a stimulus to the study of the authentic Aristotle. It was Frederick II, however, who was to become the true patron of Michael, probably as early as 1220, certainly after 1227, when he was regularly at the imperial court until his death in 1236. Meanwhile, he had become acquainted with Leonardo of Pisa (Leonardo Fibonacci), who dedicated his *Liber Abaci* to him in 1228.[3] At the court of Frederick II Michael Scot was usually mentioned as Frederick's astrologer.[1] Some time before 1232 he dedicated to Frederick his translation of *Abbreviatio de Animalibus*, and probably about the same time he dedicated his three works on astrology to him. Frederick's interest in astrology was largely stimulated by the writings of Michael Scot. He undoubtedly shared the views of the latter set forth in the preface to Michael's *Introduction to Astrology* that 'the signs and planets are not first movers or first causes, and do not of themselves confer aught of good or evil, but by their motion do indicate something of truth concerning every body produced in this corruptible world'. It was the learned Scot also who introduced Frederick to the mysteries of physiognomy through the writing of a singular textbook on that subject, his *Physiognomia*, dedicated to the Emperor. In his introduction to this work Michael Scot relates to the Emperor how, through knowledge of physiognomy, he could read in the countenances or detect in the tones

[1] L. Thorndike, in his *History of Magic and Experimental Science*, ii. 312 ff., has called attention to the frequent misuse of this passage in Roger Bacon. For the passage see *Opus majus* (ed. Bridges), i. 10 f. and 55. [2] *Compendium* (Rolls Series), 471.

[3] *Scritti di Leonardo Pisano* (ed. B. Boncompagni), i. 1, and ii. 253.

[4] Salimbene, *Cronica*, 512: 'Michaelis Scoti, qui fuit astrologus Friderici.'

of voices the true sentiments of his counsellors, their virtues and their vices, their innermost thoughts.[1] The disposition of the Emperor to rely upon these physiognomic indications became more pronounced in the later years of his life. The suspicion inevitably arises that this may provide the explanation for the cruel punishments inflicted by him upon such counsellors as his long-faithful protonotary and logothete, Piero della Vigna.[2]

Frederick's interests in astrology, although heightened by Arabic influences, were in no sense attributable to them alone. They sprang from Frederick's own intellectual curiosity, a quality revealed in the meticulous observations in his book on falconry. It was wholly in conformity with the intellectual outlook of the age that he accepted astrology as no less scientific than astronomy. In this he followed the ancient Roman emperors and, like them, he would undertake no important enterprise without first consulting the stars. It was said that he would not enter the city of Florence because he believed that an astrologer had predicted he would suffer death there. Unfortunately, he ascertained too late that the destined place of his death was not Florence but Fiorentino. Obedient to the astrological teachings of Michael Scot and other astrologers, Frederick II regarded the exact moment of conception in human generation as of paramount importance. For at that moment, he believed, the foetus receives each of the determining influences that will shape its future history. A remarkable example of Frederick's acceptance of the influence of astrology on human destiny was his postponement of his cohabitation with his young spouse, Isabella of England, because a court astrologer had ascertained that the stars were not propitious for successful coitus.[3] After Frederick's defeat at Parma his enemies found special reason for exultation in that 'this disciple of Beelzebub and Ashtaroth' had been accompanied into battle by a host of astrologers and magicians whose predictions were based upon serious miscalculations.[4] In his belief in astrology Frederick was merely continuing in the footsteps of his Norman predecessors. Astrology had been recognized officially in Sicily, certainly by King William II, and probably earlier. The Sicilian poet Pietro da Eboli provides evidence that an Arab was court astrologer at the time of William's death.[5]

[1] See the edition of this work by R. Foerster, *Scriptores Physiognomonici Graeci et Latini*, p. xxiii; and A. H. Querfeld, *Michael Scot und seine Schrift De Secretis Naturae*, 20–3 and 26.

[2] See below, pp. 520 ff.

[3] See the following for evidences of Frederick's acceptance of astrological teachings: Saba Malespini, *Historia Fiorentina* (Muratori, *RIS* viii), col. 788; Matthew Paris, *Chronica majora*, iii. 324; L. Thorndike, *History of Magic*, ii. 328–9.

[4] Albert of Beham (ed. Höfler), 128.

[5] For the twelfth-century acceptance of astrology see T. O. Wedel, 'The Mediaeval Attitude toward Astrology' (*Yale Studies in English*, lx, 1920), 60. See also Pietro da Eboli, *Liber ad Honorem Augusti* (*Fonti*), Tav. III, note 3, p. 121.

It is an illustration not only of the restless intellectual curiosity of Frederick II but also of his admiration for the scholarship of Michael Scot that he submitted to him a list of questions pertaining to various natural and supernatural phenomena. He inquired about the creation of the earth, its support in space; the numbers of the stars in the heavens, and of their respective distances from one another. He inquired about the heaven in which God sits upon his throne and of the angels and saints who attended him there. With the curiosity of medieval man which later appeared so strikingly in Dante, Frederick asked his learned companion as to the locations of hell and purgatory, and of the heavenly paradise: 'Whether under or on or above the earth [or above or in the abysses]', and of the nature of the saints who dwell there. In the world of natural science, he inquired about the dimensions of the earth and its substance; the nature of the water of the sea, of fresh-water springs, and of the brackish waters; about winds and volcanic eruptions.[1]

Several years after the death of Michael Scot, apparently about 1240, Frederick addressed a similar list of questions to scholars of various Muslim countries. One such list, addressed to a celebrated Arab philosopher, ibn-Sab'īn, has been preserved, together with the answers, in an Oxford manuscript entitled *Questions siciliennes*. This list as well as a further one addressed some years later to the learned Spanish Jew, Juda ben Solomon Cohen, author of an encyclopedia of philosophy, was concerned chiefly with such subjects as: the age of the universe; various metaphysical and theological questions; the value and the number of the categories; and, again, the nature of the soul.[2]

Michael Scot's instruction of Frederick appears at times to have been intended to guide him away from the magic and secret arts. Thus Michael distinguishes between what he calls *mathesis*, the true mathematics, or the true learning, and *matesis*, meaning divination or false mathematics, the art of magic. Michael Scot is here employing an ancient distinction, well known in the early Middle Ages.[3] But, despite Michael's appreciation of the distinction between the true and the false sciences, he was not wanting in knowledge of the false sciences and often gives the impression that he was one of their votaries. It can be plausibly assumed that he was Frederick's guide and mentor in these as well as in the legitimate pursuit of knowledge.

[1] For the Latin text of Frederick's inquiry see C. H. Haskins, *Medieval Science*, 292–5, and for the English translation, ibid. 266–7.

[2] See especially M. Amari, 'Questions philosophiques addressées aux savants musulmans par l'empereur Frédéric II' (*Journal asiatique ou Recueil de mémoires d'extraits et de notices relatifs à l'histoire . . . des peuples orientaux*, 5th series, i, 1870), 240 ff. See also E. Renan, *Averroës et l'averroïsme: Œuvres complètes*, (final ed.), iii. 225 ff., and, more recently, P. K. Hitti, *History of the Arabs*, 587.

[3] Roger Bacon, *Opus majus* (ed. Bridges), i. 239: 'Sed vocabulum falsae mathematicae sine aspiratione scribi . . .'

Although much praised by his contemporaries for his great learning, Michael Scot perhaps deserves less credit for the advancement of true science than his fellow astrologer, Master Theodore of Antioch, who was described in the prologue of the medieval French *Livre de Sidrach*, as 'Todre le philosophe'. The great Leonardo of Pisa called Theodore 'the supreme philosopher of the imperial court' because of his skill in Aristotelian philosophy and mathematics.[1] His less scholarly but highly important functions at the court were that of amanuensis in the writing of official correspondence in the Arabic language and, at times, that of serving as diplomatic agent or royal messenger to Arabic-speaking sovereigns.[2] He seems to have served as court confectioner also: in a letter to Piero della Vigna, while giving his signature as 'Theodore philosophus', he informs his friend that he is sending him a box of sugar of violet (*zucaro violaceo*).[3] When Frederick II was writing his book on falconry Theodore played an important part by translating Arabic works on the subject; one of the best-known of these was *De Scientia Venandi per Aves*, by the Arab falconer, Moamyn, which Theodore translated into Latin. It is an interesting commentary on Frederick's own skill in the Arabic language that he is said to have corrected Theodore's translation during the siege of Faenza in 1240–1.[4] Theodore was also the author of a work on hygiene, derived largely from the *Secretum Secretorum* of the Pseudo-Aristotle.[5]

With the coming of Michael Scot, Theodore of Antioch, and other philosophers and translators to the court of Frederick II there is a marked increase in both the quality and the quantity of scientific works. By 1230 the influence of the Hispano-Arabic science upon Sicilian scholars had noticeably increased and, as Niese has remarked, this explains 'why "Sicilian" translations won an influence comparable to the Spanish' while at the same time causing an 'intensification of scientific efforts in Sicily'.[6]

There is perhaps in the constant designation of Michael Scot and Theodore as Frederick's astrologers an implication that his chief interests were in the dubious pseudo-secret sciences. But his insatiable intellectual curiosity carried him also into the world of pure mathematics. Frederick often went outside the scholarly circle of his court in an effort to expand his knowledge. It was thus that he became acquainted

---

[1] See Ch. V. Langlois, *La Connaissance de la nature et du monde*, 203, and *Scritti di Leonardo Pisano*, ii. 247–9.

[2] See Huillard-Bréholles, v, part i, 556; part ii, 630, 727, 745, 750 ff.

[3] Huillard-Bréholles, *Pierre*, 347–8.

[4] See the passage quoted by Haskins from MS. 1461, fo. 73, Biblioteca Angelica: 'et correptus est per ipsum imperatorum tempore obsidionis Fayentie' (*Medieval Science*, 318).

[5] K. Sudhoff (ed.), *Archiv. für Geschichte der Medizin* (hrsg. von d. Puschmann-Stiftung, ix, 1915), 4.

[6] 'Zur Geschichte', 505.

with Leonardo of Pisa, the foremost mathematician of his era who, in the early years of the thirteenth century, wrote the most important of his works, the *Liber Abaci*, recognized as 'the first complete and systematic explanation of the Hindu-Arabic numerals by a Christian writer'.[1] Leonardo was not a permanent resident of the Frederican court, but he was intimately associated with several of its members and was presented to the Emperor himself by John of Palermo, with whom he participated before the court circle in learned discussions of arithmetic and geometry.[2] Leonardo had a profound knowledge of Euclid's work on geometry and Heron's *Metrica*. It is thought that his *Practica Geometriae*, containing a great variety of theorems, may have been based upon Euclid's lost book, although it is obviously original in part.[3]

It is from four works of Leonardo of Pisa, the *Liber Abaci*, the *Practica Geometriae*, the *Liber Quadratorum*, and the *Flos*, a letter to Magister Theodorus, that we derive our knowledge of his mathematical skill and some knowledge of the man. More than any of the regular members of the learned court circle Leonardo enables us to measure the intellectual interests and mathematical competence of Frederick II.

In any effort to reconstruct the learned court circle one is inevitably baffled by the loss of the imperial Register, except for a few months of the year 1239–40. Occasional references, however, in contemporary chronicles to the numbers of persons accompanying Frederick on his expeditions, such as the astrologers, the magicians, and soothsayers, who are said to have been with him at the siege of Parma, or the Arab tutor mentioned as accompanying him on his crusade, lead to the suspicion that others may have been important members of the court circle as scholars and translators.[4] To the enemies of Frederick II such as Albert of Beham, who ridiculed the activities of the 'astrologers and magicians' at the siege of Parma, there was probably little distinction to be drawn between scientists and charlatans if they were seen in the company of Frederick II.

As to translations made either at the court or by outsiders at the command of Frederick II, there was unquestionably a renewed activity

---

[1] See G. Sarton, op. cit. ii. 611; M. Cantor, *Vorlesungen über Geschichte der Mathematik*, vol. ii, ch. 41: 'Leonardo von Pisa und sein *Liber Abaci*', and ch. 42: 'Die übrigen Schriften des Leonardo von Pisa'. See also S. Günther, *Geschichte der Mathematik*, vol. i, ch. 15.

[2] *Scritti di Leonardo di Pisa*, ii. 253.

[3] R. B. McClenon, 'Leonardo of Pisa and his *Liber Quadratorum*' (*The American Mathematical Monthly*, xxvi, 1920), 2. See also R. C. Archibald, *Euclid's Book on Divisions of Figures; with a Restoration based on Woepeke's Text and on the* Practica Geometriae *of Leonardo Pisano*.

[4] See for example Albert of Beham (ed. Höfler), 128:

> Amisit astrologos et magos et vates.
> Beelzebub et Astharoth, privatos penates,
> Tenebrarum consulens per quos potestates
> Spreverat ecclesiam et mundi magnates.

resulting from the influence of the Toledo group upon the Sicilians. It is apparent also that scholars elsewhere in Europe were, by the middle and latter half of the thirteenth century, making use of Toletan translations from the Arabic and were acquainted also with those of Sicilian scholars. Roger Bacon cites specifically the translations of Michael Scot.[1] It is difficult to estimate the influence of these Sicilian Aristotelian transla-tions and treatises, although it is probable that translations made at the court of Frederick II improved in some measure the current versions of Aristotle, including the *Physics* and *Metaphysics*. The importance of the Sicilian translators, however, is not in their being the first to translate or to disseminate Latin translations of the Arabic versions of the works of Greek antiquity. Rather, their importance is to be found in the variety of works they translated from the Arabic and in the more or less original treatises on a variety of scientific subjects in which they em-ployed both Greek and Arabic sources, supplementing them by their own observations.

A striking example is the work of Jordan Ruffo, a Calabrian marshal of the Emperor, on veterinary science; it is based, in part, on Greek sources but is written largely from the author's personal experience and incorporates also many valuable suggestions from Frederick II.[2] It is known that this work was undertaken at the order of Frederick II and was written under his personal supervision until his death, which pre-ceded that of Jordan Ruffo by nearly two years. It was the first compre-hensive treatise in the West on the medical treatment of horses and was to become the basis for numerous similar treatises during succeeding centuries. It is perhaps correctly described as *Liber Marescalchiae* and contains seventy-six chapters covering every known or suspected disease and injury of horses, as well as their proper care and training. On its completion in 1252 it was dedicated to the memory of Frederick II.[3]

It is paradoxical that the Italo-Byzantinian scholars at the court of Frederick II were skilled in the Greek language but ignorant of science, while such scholars as Michael Scot knew little or no Greek and trans-lated, instead, from the Arabic into Latin, accomplishing this only with the aid of interpreters (usually Jewish). One striking example of direct translation from the Arabic was the *Liber magistri Moamin falconerii*, a treatise on hunting translated into Latin by Theodore of Antioch with-out the assistance of an interpreter.[4] Generally, Jews, attracted to Sicily from Spain and Provence, were employed as interpreters in translating

---

[1] *Opus Majus* (ed. Bridges), i. 55; and ii. 10, 11, 85 note 1.

[2] See the Introduction of J. G. Schneider's edition, *Friderici II imperatoris de arte venandi cum avibus*, vol. i, p. xv.

[3] L. Moulé, *Histoire de la médecine vétérinaire*, ii, especially 25–30.

[4] H. Werth, 'Altfranzösische Jagdlehrbücher nebst Handschriften-Bibliographie der abendländischen Jagdliteratur überhaupt' (*Zeitschr. für romanische Philologie*, xxii, 1898), 177.

both from Arabic and Hebrew. The most noteworthy of these Jewish translators and a frequent collaborator with and interpreter for Michael Scot was the Provençal Jacob ben Anatoli, referred to by his contemporaries as Jacob Anatoli, who arrived at the court of Frederick about 1231. Neither the date of his birth nor that of his death is known, although he probably died in about 1256. Not only was he famous as a Talmudic scholar but he was learned also in philosophy and astronomy. He was a skilful translator from Arabic into Hebrew, and probably from Hebrew into Latin. In virtually all the Aristotelian and Averroistic translations of Michael Scot Jacob Anatoli was his collaborator; he praised Michael for his intellectual honesty. At the same time he paid his respects to Frederick II as 'a lover of learning who was my patron. May God grant him his blessing to the end that he may be elevated above all kings, and may the Messiah come during his reign!'[1] It has been plausibly conjectured that this Jacob Anatoli is the same as the Jew, Andreas, mentioned by Roger Bacon as aiding Michael Scot in his translations.[2]

Among Frederick's Jewish correspondents and occasional visitors to the court was the Spanish Jeuda or Jehuda ben Solomon Ha-Kohen, perhaps more familiarly known as Juda ben Solomon Cohen. He was born in Toledo in the second decade of the thirteenth century, probably in 1219, and as early as 1237 he was in learned correspondence with Frederick II's 'Philosopher'—presumably Theodore, since Michael Scot had died at least a year before. Ten years later he was the guest of the Emperor at the court in Tuscany. Frederick's interest in Jewish and Arabic philosophy and mathematics is perhaps a sufficient explanation of his correspondence and subsequent meeting with Juda ben Solomon Cohen.

Frederick's interest in the *Dalālat al-Ḥā'irīn* or *Guide for the Perplexed*, a work completed before the close of the twelfth century and designed to reconcile Jewish theology with Arabic Aristotelianism, led to correspondence and subsequent meetings with Moses ben Salomon of Salerno, a noted commentator on Maimonides. Both Frederick and his court circle seem to have become acquainted with Maimonides largely through him. Together with Nicholas Peglia of Giovinazzo, founder of the Dominican monastery of Trani, Moses ben Salomon is credited with translating *The Guide of the Perplexed* at the command of the Emperor.[3]

The mingling of the Orient and Occident at the Sicilian court is nowhere better illustrated than in Frederick II's own work, *De Arte*

[1] E. Renan, 'Les Rabbins français' (*Hist. Littéraire de la France*, xxvi), 580 ff.; especially 583, 585.
[2] H. Graetz, *Geschichte der Juden*, vii. 472. See also the English ed. (Philadelphia, 1891–8), iii. 566–7; and Renan, loc. cit.
[3] Straus, *Die Juden im Königreich*, 79, 86; Steinschneider, *Übersetzungen*, 1–3 and 433.

Venandi cum Avibus. In this work one feels that all Frederick's scholarly efforts, the results of his correspondence and learned discussions with men from all corners of the earth, found their ultimate repository.[1] One of the most striking features of the book is its evidence of Frederick's intimate knowledge of the pertinent works of Aristotle, particularly the *Liber Animalium*, including the three treatises: *De Animalibus Historia*, *De Partibus Animalium*, and *De Generatione Animalium*. It is generally apparent also that his references to these works are to the translations known to have been made by Michael Scot. But Frederick's own experience and observations soon led him to distrust many of the findings of Aristotle. Indeed, if there were a single moment during the Middle Ages of which it could be said: Here begins the habit of thinking based upon a determination to see the world of nature as it is, it would be when the greatest of the thirteenth-century sovereigns boldly defied the prevailing acceptance of Aristotle as infallible. In his preface to the *De Arte Venandi* he says: 'We discovered by hard-won experience that the deductions of Aristotle, whom we followed when they appealed to our reason, were not entirely to be relied upon.' It is little wonder that Pope Gregory IX quickly perceived the dangers inherent in the dawn of an age of reason—a new era in which the enlightened scholars of Christendom would accept, in questions pertaining to the earth and to nature, only that which is provable by reason.[2]

Frederick again stresses the importance of first-hand investigation of natural phenomena in his preface: 'There is another reason why we did not follow the Prince of Philosophers: he was ignorant of the practice of falconry . . . In his work, the *Liber Animalium*, we find many quotations from other authors whose statements he did not verify and who, in their turn, were not speaking from experience. Entire conviction of the truth never follows mere hearsay.'[3] As these remarks indicate, Frederick did not ignore theoretical considerations but his emphasis was always on the factual. His treatment of the technique of hunting with birds, therefore, is based upon his own observations, although he obviously made some use of works written during the late twelfth and early thirteenth centuries; these included the writings of Daude de Pradas (in the Provençal dialect), the Latin works of the so-called Dancus, and a treatise by a certain William, falconer of King Roger II of Sicily—all widely known to Western hunters.[4]

[1] The best and the most recent edition of the *De Arte Venandi* is that of C. A. Willemsen. I have made constant use also of the splendid work of C. A. Wood and F. M. Fyfe, *The Art of Falconry, being De Arte Venandi of Frederick II of Hohenstaufen* (1955).

[2] See the assertion of the Pope, Huillard-Bréholles, v, part i, 340. Kantorowicz, *Kaiser Friedrich II.*, 336 describes the *De Arte Venandi* as a 'Wendepunkt im abendländischen Denken'.

[3] See the Preface as translated by C. A. Wood and F. M. Fyfe, op. cit. 4.

[4] For these works see H. Werth, 'Altfranzösische Jagdlehrbücher' (*Zeitschr. für romanische*

The sections of the book dealing with the anatomical structure of birds and their habits and habitats, derive, in part, from Aristotle's *Liber Animalium* and from various Arabic treatises, although not without careful verifications and, in numerous instances, with disagreements. Among the Arabic sources was of course the work of Frederick's own falconer—Moamyn's *De Scientia Venandi per Aves*, which had been translated into Latin under Frederick's direct supervision by Theodore the Philosopher.

While Frederick's *De Arte Venandi* reveals the thorough acquaintance of its author with the existing works on falconry, it is a work of great originality, and reflects the scientific method of its author and his keen critical faculties. It reflects too the extraordinary and many-sided personality of Frederick II as nothing else does, save perhaps his *Liber Augustalis*. It was characteristic of his curious habits of mind that he says in the introduction: 'Certain branches of the art have, it is true, been explored by various other persons in the practice alone . . . but with a lamentable want of mastery of the general topic.'[1] Like many other achievements of Frederick II, the *De Arte Venandi* marks a significant break with the prevailing methods and ideals of scholarship. Always it reflects the dominant maxim: 'Our intention in this book is to set forth . . . those things that are as they are.' How closely Frederick adhered to this expressed intention is revealed in his sketches of birds which, by virtue of their accuracy of anatomical detail, often suggest a meticulousness comparable to that of the anatomical drawings of Leonardo da Vinci. Whether Frederick himself made the drawings personally—and certainly as one skilled in drawing he was capable of doing so—or whether he left them to others, it is apparent that he insisted upon complete accuracy of detail. The *De Arte Venandi* is far more than a hunting-book. It is, in fact, a scientific treatise of the first order, employing the methods of modern science and rejecting all hypotheses which could not stand the test of positive proof. It is not only a study of the various species of birds, with detailed anatomical comparisons and contrasts and intricate delineations of the mechanics of flying, but it is also a treatise on zoography and on the habits of birds.[2]

Frederick's experimental interests revealed themselves also in his hunting with beasts of prey, hunting-leopards, or cheetahs. On more

---

Philologie, xii, 1898), 178 ff.; see also C. H. Haskins, *Medieval Science*, ch. xii, pp. 346 ff. For the text of the Daude see *Le Livre du roi Dancus: Texte français inédit du XIIIe siècle suivi d'un Traité de Fauconnerie également inédit d'après Albert le Grand avec une notice et des notes*, H. Martin-Dairvault, 30 ff.

[1] Quoted from C. A. Wood and F. M. Fyfe, *The Art of Falconry*, 3.

[2] These features of Frederick's work have been especially well treated by F. Kampers, *Wegbereiter*, 72 ff. See also A. Nitschke, 'Friedrich II. Ein Ritter des hohen Mittelalters, *Hist. Zeitschr.* 194, 1962), 13–26.

than one occasion his orders, emanating from the royal Chancery, gave instructions to various of his animal custodians to move his cheetahs to some specified hunting-preserve.[1]

Akin to Frederick's interest in hunting with birds and beasts was his admiration for horses, first acquired as a small boy when he became noted for his exceptional skill in horsemanship.[2] But his interest in horses went far beyond superficial considerations, impelling him to a scientific study. As we have seen, it was at his command that Jordan Ruffo prepared a treatise on hippiatry. In it he observes that he had profited from the advice of the Emperor, who was expert in the care of horses.

Frederick's interest in birds and beasts extended beyond domestic species or those which could be made useful in war or in hunting. His menagerie, which at times accompanied him on his expeditions, excited the wonder of European contemporaries. The ubiquitous chronicler Salimbene tells of the Emperor sending elephants, dromedaries, camels, leopards, gyrfalcons, and hawks into Lombardy, and how these had passed through the city of Parma. And, as if fearful that his narrative might appear incredible, he adds: 'As I have seen with my own eyes.' Matthew Paris, the English chronicler, sharing the astonishment of his contemporaries, relates that the Earl of Cornwall, brother-in-law of the Emperor, while passing through Italy, saw one of these elephants in Cremona. The *Annales Placentini Gibellini* relates also that one of the imperial elephants died in Cremona in 1248 and tells of the credulous people who expected its bones, after burial, to be transformed into ivory. On Frederick's visit to Germany in 1236 he was accompanied by his menagerie. A contemporary chronicler was especially impressed by the multitude of camels which passed through the city of Colmar.[3] A giraffe, a gift from the Sultan of Egypt, is said to have been the first to appear in Europe since Roman times.[4] If Frederick's interests were often directed towards the world of birds and beasts, he was no less concerned with humanity. This concern reveals itself especially in his efforts to improve the science of medicine and personal hygiene. One of the best-known poems of Pietro da Eboli, in praise of the baths of Puzzuoli, was dedicated to Frederick, some time between 1212 and 1221, apparently as a tribute to his interest in the science of medicine.[5] Similarly Master Theodore, court philosopher, dedicated his treatise on hygiene to

---

[1] See, for example, Huillard-Bréholles, v, part ii, 619, 733, 817.

[2] See above, p. 63.

[3] Salimbene, *Cron.* (*MGH, SS.* xxxii), 92; Matthew Paris, *Chronica majora*, iv. 166; *Annales Placentini Gibellini* (*MGH, SS.* xviii), 496; *Annales Colmarienses* (*MGH, SS.* xvii), 189.

[4] See the notes of M. Michaud, *Bibliothèque des Croisades*, iv. 436.

[5] G. B. Siragusa's preface to the *Liber ad Honorem Augusti di Pietro da Eboli* (*Fonti*), pp. xviii ff. and Ries (*MIöG* xxxii, 1911), 576 ff. See also Huillard-Bréholles, 'Notice sur le véritable auteur du poème "De balneis Puteolanis"', especially 344.

Frederick II.[1] The preventive measures drawn up by Adam of Cremona (*Regimen iter agentium vel peregrinantium*) for the safeguarding of the health of Frederick's crusading army resemble to a certain extent the precautionary instructions issued to modern Western armies bound for the East.[2] Frederick's attention to personal cleanliness where he himself was concerned was contrary to the standards of contemporaries, who saw only obstinate sinfulness and vanity in his frequent Sunday baths.[3]

Even more inimical to his contemporaries were the experiments that Frederick made with the intention of extending his knowledge of the characteristics of the human species. It was inevitable that an age accustomed to accept established authority with regard to all things, human or divine, would be scandalized by his alleged methods in carrying out these experiments. There is unquestionably considerable exaggeration in the contemporary reports of these activities, although Frederick's intellectual urge to ascertain the truth appears often to have carried him beyond the bounds of propriety. Certainly subject to suspicion are the tales related by Salimbene which often appear to have their origin in hostile propagandist sources. Such is the story of Frederick's ordering a man to be securely enclosed in a wine-cask when endeavouring to prove that the soul, thus confined, dies with the body. Salimbene saw in this act of Frederick an attempt to justify the Epicurean doctrine, which he attributes solely to the prophet Isaiah: 'Let us eat and drink for tomorrow we die.' It was Salimbene also who told the story of 'Nicholas the Fish', condemned by his mother's curse to live an amphibious life. The Emperor is said to have ordered the unfortunate Nicholas to dive twice in succession to the bottom of Charybdis to fetch a sunken golden chalice in an attempt to test the capacity of the human body to withstand the pressure of water at a great depth—an experiment which ended in the death of the reluctant Nicholas. It is related also that, in an effort to discover what language men would naturally speak if reared in complete seclusion and denied the hearing of all spoken words, he caused new-born infants to be reared by foster-mothers who were 'to suckle and bathe them but in no wise to speak to them'. For, as Salimbene relates, 'he desired to know whether or not they would speak Hebrew, which is the original language, or Greek, Latin, or Arabic, or the language of the parents from whom they were born. . . . But the infants died.' Frederick is said also to have attempted to

---

[1] See the edition by Sudhoff (*Archiv für Geschichte der Medizin*, ix), 4.

[2] F. Hönger, *Ärztliche Verhaltungsmassregeln auf dem Heerzug ins Heilige Land für Kaiser Friedrich II. geschrieben von Adam von Cremona*; see especially the list of subjects treated (pp. 1–5) and the address to Emperor Frederick Roger (p. 96).

[3] *Johannes Vitodurani Chron.* (*MGH, Scriptores, nova series*, 3), 10: 'Fertur insuper, quod frequenter balneis usus fuerit diebus dominicis. Per hoc patet, quod precepta Dei et festa et sacramenta ecclesie irrita censuit et inania.'

determine the effect of sleep and of exercise upon the digestive system. He is alleged to have ordered two men to be disembowelled, one after sleeping and the other after exercising, in order to determine by means of a post-mortem examination how their respective digestive processes had been affected.[1] Salimbene himself, however, appears to have been doubtful of the accuracy of these tales, remarking that he could relate many others which he had heard, save that it disgusted him to tell of such foolishness. One can only conclude that, if excessive cruelty accompanied Frederick's efforts in experimentation, it was because he lived in an age when cruelty was not uncommon, appearing at times as an attribute of piety. The significant feature of all this is that Frederick II had the will to seek for truth by means of experimentation in those realms of thought where passive acceptance was the established order of the day.

[1] Salimbene, *Cron.* (*MGH, SS.* xxxii), 350–3. For 'Nicholas the Fish' see also Franciscus Pipinus, *Chron.* (Muratori, *RIS* ix), col. 669.

III

ANTECEDENTS OF THE SICILIAN LITERARY STYLE AND THE ADVENT OF THE 'SICILIAN SCHOOL' OF POETRY

Vivat igitur, vivat sancti Friderici nomen in populo, succrescat in ipsum fervor devotionis a subditis, et fidei meritum mater ipsa fidelitas in exemplum subjectionis inflammet.

> Eulogy of Frederick II by Piero della Vigna (Huillard-Bréholles, *Pierre*, 425–6).[1]

THE profusion of Arabic and Byzantine elements in the culture of the Norman court of Frederick II's twelfth-century forebears seems at first glance to have overshadowed the influence of Northern Italy and of France. A casual visitor might have failed to observe at the court of the Norman kings the characteristics common to the courts of the West such as those of England and France. For in Sicily he would have seen the King wearing a crown of Byzantine design, royal robes adorned with Arabic symbols, ceremonials of Byzantine origin, a royal bodyguard of Muslims, palaces teeming with Arabic and Greek servants and oriental functionaries.[2] Upon closer observation, however, the visitor would have seen relatively inconspicuous signs of northern influence, chiefly from France and Bologna. From the former were linguistic influences in the royal Chancery; from the latter were juristic principles destined in time to dominate Sicilian law and procedure. Already in the time of Roger II there was present at the Norman court a small group of jurists, expounding Roman and canon law as taught in the Bolognese schools. As in England, under the contemporary Angevin king, Henry II, so also in Sicily during the middle and last half of the twelfth century, both Roman and canon law flourished. The assizes of Ariano, promulgated in 1140 by Roger II, bear witness to the depth of this penetration of the jurisprudence of Northern Italy. So also the formulas of royal

---

[1] May the name of the saintly Frederick endure among the people! May the warmth of that devotion to him be strengthened among the subjects! And may loyalty, the mother of faith itself, so influence that faith that it will become a pattern of obedience!

[2] Throughout the work of Hugo Falcandus, *La Historia o Liber de Regno Sicilie (Fonti)*, are to be found striking evidences of this predominant oriental influence at the Sicilian court. See also F. Chalandon, *Domination*, ii. 738 ff.

documents, not unlike those emanating from the papal Chancery, gradually assumed the stamp of Bolognese influence.[1]

The Bolognese culture that moved southward into the Sicilian Kingdom was not only juristic. Although in general its votaries were the legalistically educated court and provincial officials, various influences had broadened their intellectual and artistic interests; as aspiring young lawyers, seeking outlets for their talents in the practical commercial enterprises of Italy they had become devotees of belles-lettres. Bologna had numerous students from France and from other regions of Western Europe. Many of them, interested primarily in Roman law, in philosophy, or in canon law, were drawn, perhaps unwittingly, towards literature for its own sake. Well before the end of the twelfth century, interest in literary style was widespread among Bolognese students. As Hans Niese has emphasized: 'It is significant for the development of Latin poetry that in Bologna at this time the textbook of poetics of the Anglo-Norman Godfrey of Vinsauf made its appearance.'[2] As some of these students drifted southwards to seek employment at the Norman-Sicilian court they carried with them their interests in belles-lettres. The earliest examples of a conscious preoccupation with literary style are to be found in oratory and in the epistolary genre as practised in Bologna and among officials of the Lombard cities who had acquired their skills either directly or indirectly from the Bolognese teachers. In the Italian communes practical considerations provided the initial stimulus for the revival of oratory and a stylistic interest in letter-writing. Ability to speak fluently and to write with refinement of phrase came to be regarded as essential attributes of the successful *podestà* and other communal officials.[3] The inaugural address of the *podestà* was prepared with meticulous consideration for literary style, richly adorned with passages from the Old and New Testaments, from Cicero, 'who above all was honoured here', from Ovid, and from the *Corpus juris civilis*.[4] Striking examples of the model texts employed in the practice of literary style in thirteenth-century Italy were the various writings of Albertano of Brescia, a lawyer and soldier who was taken prisoner by Frederick II during the siege of Brescia in 1238.[5] Among his writings were *De arte loquendi et tacendi*, *De amore et dilectione Dei*,

---

[1] H. Niese, *Die Gesetzgebung der normannischen Dynastie in Regnum Siciliae*, 37 ff., 44 ff., and 129 ff.; and E. Caspar, *Roger II*, 242 and 245 ff.

[2] 'Zur Geschichte', 519. See also E. Faral, *Les Poétiques du XIIe siècle*, 194 ff.

[3] F. Herter, *Die Podestaliteratur Italiens im 12. und 13. Jahrhundert*, 8 ff.

[4] Ibid. 17 ff. and 21 ff. By far the most complete treatment of source material is L. von Rockinger, *Briefsteller und Formelbücher des XI. bis XIV. Jahrhunderts*.

[5] The chief source for Albertano's life is *Jacobi Malvecii Chronicon Bixomum* (Muratori, *RIS* xiv), col. 907, which describes him as 'vir praecipuus, sapientia plenus'. Albertano's *Liber Consolationis et Consilii* has been edited by T. Sundby under the auspices of the Chaucer Society, 1873.

and *Liber Consolationis et Consilii,* works later translated into Italian and widely used as stylistic models. They consisted chiefly of rhetorical selections or, as the Italians called them, *fiore di rettorica,* moral maxims, gathered somewhat indiscriminately from antique and Christian sources. Albertano has been repeatedly criticized for the jumbled and disorganized nature of his collection of maxims.[1] Such criticisms, although just in part, tend to minimize the importance of these collections in shaping the literary styles of both the Latin and vernacular writings of the thirteenth and fourteenth centuries. Well before the thirteenth century these stylistic influences of the north were apparent in the Sicilian Kingdom, where the French language as well as the French Latin style were rapidly becoming indispensable to the officials of the royal court.[2] French influence was especially important in shaping the oratorical and epistolary styles. A glance at the *Epistola ad Petrum,* a product of the bitter debate over the choice of a successor to the Sicilian throne following the death of William II, leaves no doubt that its author was schooled in the Bolognese rhetoric which, in turn, was derived in part from the French. Indeed, it is not improbable that the so-called Falcandus, alleged author of the *Epistola* and the *Liber de Regno Sicilie,* a notary of the royal Chancery, was himself a product of the Bolognese school and may well have been of French origin.[3]

Both the oratorical and the epistolary genres continued to be cultivated, much in the style of these early examples, at the court of Frederick II. The Emperor himself, deeply sensitive to style, is known to have delivered more or less formal addresses on several occasions, particularly in moments of crisis in his conflicts with the Pope and Curia. Philip of Novare, in his *Mémoires,* relates that 'at Acre the Emperor assembled his men and had all the people of the city come there . . . He addressed them and stated that which he desired; and in his address he complained much of the Temple.'[4] The English chronicler Roger of Wendover relates also that after the Emperor, at that time an excommunicate, had placed the crown of Jerusalem on his own head in the Church of the Holy Sepulchre, 'he sat there on the patriarchal throne and made a speech to the people excusing his evil deed and charged that the Roman church proceeded unjustly against him'.[5] A more reliable report of this incident given by Hermann of Salza, Master of the Teutonic Order,

---

[1] Bertoni, *Il Duecento,* 228. For criticism of him see G. Tiraboschi, *Storia della Letteratura Italiana,* iv, part 1, 272 ff.

[2] Bertoni, *Duecento,* 32.

[3] B. Schmeidler, *Italienische Geschichtsschreiber,* 79. See, however, the excellent summary of the various opinions concerning his origin in E. Jamison, *Eugenius,* 198 ff. For Miss Jamison's plausible attribution of the *Epistola* and the *Historia* to Eugenius see above, p. 297.

[4] Quoted from J. L. Lamonte, *The Wars of Frederick II against the Ibelins,* 90–1. See Philip Novare, *Mémoires* (ed. Kohler), par. XLIII, pp. 24 ff.

[5] *Flores Hist.* iv. 198.

a participant in the proceedings in Jerusalem, states merely that the Emperor called upon Hermann to read his address to the people in both Latin and German. It is more in keeping with oriental customs, which were already influencing Frederick, that he left the speech-making to a trusted *aide*. Particularly in his later years, as his concept of the dignity of the royal office developed, he did not usually address the people himself but 'commanded his logothete to speak'.[1] It was in this capacity that, in the last years of Frederick II's reign, Piero della Vigna so abundantly justified his characterization as 'the mouthpiece of the King'. The logothete at the court of Frederick, as described by the chronicler Salimbene, was 'one who makes speeches in public and presents to the people the edicts of the Emperor or other princes'.[2] On the eve of his second excommunication in 1239, while at Padua, Frederick is said to have spoken to the assembled citizens, but it was his High Court Justice, later logothete, Piero della Vigna, who made the eloquent defence of the Emperor against the papal charges.[3] The one occasion on which Frederick personally assumed the full duties of a public orator in his own defence was during the Christmas festivities at Pisa, when in an effort to refute the persistent charges of heresy, he delivered an eloquent plea for a peaceful reconciliation with the Pope.[4]

Frederick's admiration for the oratorical skill of others is best illustrated on the occasion of the funeral of his first-born son, Henry (VII), whose rebellion against his father had led to his humiliating deposition and, later, to what was apparently his suicide. A Minorite brother, Lucas of Bitonto, delivered the funeral oration, choosing as his text 'Arripuit Abraham gladium, ut immolaret filium suum' (Genesis 22: 10), not without implicating the Emperor as responsible for his son's act. Frederick, far from taking offence, was so moved by the beauty of the passages commending the attribute of justice that he expressed a desire for the oration.[5]

The oratorical and epistolary styles cultivated at the court of Frederick II were akin to the prose composition of Albertano and others from whom the Bolognese jurists had learned the *ars dictaminis*. At the time of Frederick's return to the Kingdom of Sicily in 1220 large numbers of students from Southern Italy had pursued or were pursuing their studies in Bologna.[6] A work of unquestionable influence in shaping literary style at the court of Frederick II, and one which illustrates the interrelationship of Bologna and Naples, was the *Dedignomion, summa*

---

[1] See F. Schneider, 'Toskanische Studien', part iii (*QF* xii, 1909), 54.
[2] *Cronica*, 343.   [3] Below, pp. 428 ff.   [4] Below, p. 441.
[5] Salimbene, *Cronica*, 88.
[6] H. Niese, 'Zur Geschichte', 520–1, note 3, has compiled a partial list of these students.

derivationum or *Speculum artis grammatice* of Walter Ascoli, probably the 'Gaulterius' who was professor of grammar at the University of Naples.[1]

The diplomatic correspondence from the papal court also had a direct influence upon the style cultivated in the Chancery at Frederick's court. Numerous examples of this highly ornate style are to be seen in the letters of Cardinal Thomas and Reginald of Capua whose styles can best be described as characteristic of the Capuan school.[2] The innumerable letters of Innocent III as well as his speeches and sermons reflect the so-called Capuan style, while bearing witness also to the careful cultivation of a definite style within the papal Chancery. Frederick II recognized this style as offering a desirable model for the royal Chancery. Both he and his contemporaries in the papal Curia considered the rhetorical letter as essential to the successful pursuit of diplomacy.[3] How assiduously the epistolary art was cultivated as a form of literature is to be seen in a variety of collections of letters of that era—often fanciful and satirical, or merely bizarre. Such, for example, were the exchanges of letters between Soul and Body, between Life and Death, between the Creator and the Universe, etc. A unique example of this style of whimsical letter-writing is given by Terrisio of Atina, who depicted a celebration by the wild animals of Apulia in gratitude for the Emperor's proclamation of a closed season for hunting.[4]

The influence of Piero della Vigna and Roffredo of Benevento, the Bolognese jurist and teacher of law, in shaping the curriculum of the University of Naples would alone have assured the continuation of the Bolognese tradition there in the teaching of law, grammar, and rhetoric.[5] These subjects were obviously taught in conformity with the long-established models of Bologna. Students of law, educated in the new university and later employed in the Sicilian Chancery or elsewhere in the royal government, made use of the style of their northern

---

[1] C. H. Haskins, 'Magister Gaulterius Esculanus' (*Mélanges Ferdinand Lot*), 245 ff., has dealt fully with the writings of Gaulterius.

[2] For striking examples of Reginald's style see K. Hampe, 'Aus der Kindheit Kaiser Friedrichs II.' (*MIöG* xxii, 1901), 529 ff.; idem, *Mitteilungen aus der Capuaner Briefsammlung* (*Sb. H. Ak.* 1910), nos. 13 (I, II) and 14 (IV). See also K. Hampe and R. Hennesthal, 'Die Reimser Briefsammlung in cod. 1275 d. Reimser Stadtbibliothek' (*Neues Archiv*, 47, 1927–8), 518–50; and *Hist. Vierteljahrschr.* iv, 1901, 164 f. and 179 f. See also the enlightening article of E. Heller, 'Zur Frage des kurialen Stileinflusses in der sizilischen Kanzlei Friedrichs II.' (*Deutsches Archiv*, xix, 1963), 434 ff.

[3] See Frederick's statement (Winkelmann, *Acta*, i, no. 286); and H. Niese, 'Zur Geschichte', 531.

[4] See C. H. Haskins, *Medieval Culture*, 135 ff.; K. Hampe and R. Hennesthal, op. cit. 524: *Universis animalibus eadem lege viventibus fere bestie de regno Apulie gressus elegere tuciores.* This letter has been edited by Wattenbach (*Sb. Ber. Ak.*, 1892), 91–123.

[5] See H. Rashdall, *Universities*, ii. 123, note 1. Pertinent also are the *Lettres de Nicolas de Rocca à un Maître Pierre* (probably Pierre de Hibernia), 'à qui il demande la permission de faire un cours public sur l'art épistolaire', in Huillard-Bréholles, *Pierre*, nos. 84, 85, pp. 381 ff.

contemporaries. Moreover, the northern influence is apparent in both the official imperial correspondence and the *Liber Augustalis* or *Constitutiones*. Such writings reveal also the characteristics of Piero della Vigna and his disciples, many of whom had acquired their literary styles under his guidance in the Chancery of Frederick's court.[1]

Active as were the officials of the court of Frederick II in the revival of Latin prose and in the cultivation of a literary style reflecting that of Roman antiquity, there was little attention given in the court circles to historical writing or to biographies recording the achievements of Frederick II. The one notable exception to this generalization was a work by Bishop Mainardino of Imola, long lost, but partially incorporated in the fifteenth-century *Compendio dell'istoria del regno di Napoli* of Pandulf Collenuccio (Collenutio). Much of the subject matter of the *Compendio* could have been obtained only from a contemporary of the Emperor and from one who was intimately acquainted with court life.[2] It was the greatest of misfortunes to the reputation of Frederick II that there was not at his court a skilled biographer like Einhard, Guillaume le Breton, Otto of Freising, or Joinville. Most of the contemporary chronicles of his deeds are coloured by hatred, by deep-seated and irrational prejudices, by envy, or by purposeful misrepresentation originating with the papal and Guelph chroniclers. Such accounts have served not only to accentuate his faults, actual or alleged, but to distort or conceal his extraordinary virtues. As Karl Hampe has observed in his brilliant discourse, *Kaiser Friedrich II. in der Auffassung der Nachwelt*, the collective judgements of the Guelph chroniclers have given him the predominant characteristics of godlessness and superstitiousness, covetousness and cruelty, ingratitude, arrogance, and ostentatiousness.[3] Only the faithful protonotary and logothete, Piero della Vigna, thanks to his numerous letters and other writings, has revealed, often incidentally, the true attributes of his great sovereign. The absence of historical writings from the works of the Sicilian courtiers and officials is all the more surprising in view of Frederick's interest in and encouragement of all forms of Latin writings, as attested by the numerous books dedicated to him. He is known also, even in his boyhood, to have been an avid student of history.[4]

Absent also from the literary contributions of the Frederican court were long Latin poems such as the *Pantheon* of Godfrey of Viterbo and

---

[1] K. Hampe, *Beiträge zur Geschichte der letzten Staufer: Heinrich von Isernia*, 34; idem, *Konradin*, 68 ff.; and Huillard-Bréholles, *Pierre*, 55 f., 59 ff.

[2] F. Güterbock, 'Friedrich II., das verlorene Geschichtswerk Mainardinos' (*Neues Archiv*, xxx, 1904–5), 37–83, not only offers many plausible examples of Collenuccio's probable use of Mainardino, but thinks also that Tristan Calco in his *Mediolanensis Historiae patriae* (Milan, 1627) drew heavily upon the same contemporary source.

[3] See especially p. 10.   [4] Above, p. 63.

the *Liber ad Honorem Augusti* of Pietro da Eboli, imitations of Virgil and Ovid, designed to eulogize or to recount the deeds of Emperor Henry VI, father of Frederick II. Instead, we find scattered bits of Latin verse, often mingled with the prose writings of chroniclers such as Richard of San Germano, the legal writings of Roffredo of Benevento, and the letters of Piero della Vigna. A long poem by Pietro da Eboli, dedicated to young Frederick, was designed not so much to honour the Staufen heir as to extol the virtues of the baths of Pozzuoli.

It is surprising also that there was little or no interest in the genre so popular in northern Europe, the Goliardic or poetry of vagrancy. It may be assumed that the jurists at the court were little attracted to verse forms and subjects so greatly at variance with the classical models, and that the noble courtiers, votaries of the more refined lyric poetry, had no taste for the rollicking versification of the Goliards. Although sharing an interest in satirical poetry with the Goliards, Piero della Vigna, on a loftier plane, directed his satirical shafts in more conventional poetic forms, choosing as his themes the greed and covetousness of the prelates and the machinations of the begging friars. It was in this vein that he lamented the absence of humility among leaders of the Church. No longer were leaders sought as the successors of the fisherman Peter, but instead, rulers not unlike Constantine were demanded.[1]

Although the superior literary skill of Piero della Vigna is to be observed chiefly in his epistolary writings and in the sonorous prologue of the *Liber Augustalis* or *Constitutiones*, he was distinguished also for his Latin verse. His poetic style, like that of his epistolary and oratorical writings, bears clearly the stamp of northern influence, while it often surpasses the models of his Bolognese or Capuan predecessors. It was this extraordinary man, contemptuously described by Salimbene as originating in the Kingdom of Apulia, 'natione vilis', and who as a student at Bologna was said to have been compelled to beg for the necessities of life, that was destined to guide the faltering steps of the court circle in the refinements of literary styles, whether oratorical, epistolary, or in the writing of Latin and vernacular poetry. It is a distinguishing feature of Piero's Latin writings of whatever genre that they reflect the influence of classical styles, at least as these styles had been copied by the Latin writers of France. It was under his guidance that the prose style, earlier popularized in Italy by Buoncompagno,[2] reached the peak of its popularity in the Kingdom of Sicily. A host of disciples now appeared who, like Piero della Vigna and Buoncompagno,

---

[1] See the satirical verses of Piero della Vigna among the 'Pièces justificatives' in Huillard-Bréholles, *Pierre*, 402–17, especially p. 403.

[2] See F. Novati, *Freschi e mini del Dugento*, 309 ff.; idem, *Storia letteraria d'Italia*, 464–5; and G. Bertoni, *Il Duecento*, 147 ff.

'spoke obscurely and in the grand manner'.[1] Typical of Piero's literary disciples were Nicholas of Rocca, an indefatigable letter-writer of the Frederican court circle, and Teresio of Atina, a professor at the University of Naples.[2]

This growing sensitiveness to literary form within the Sicilian court circle was stimulated by the many-sided interests of Frederick II. He was much more than a patron of belles-lettres; he was an actual participant in the literary pursuits of his court. His early linguistic interests, including his interest in Latin which he doubtless acquired from his childhood tutors such as William Franciscus,[3] continued throughout his life. There is little reason to doubt that he spoke Italian, German, Latin, French, and Arabic, or that he wrote with some fluency in all these languages, with the probable exception of German.[4] There is evidence to warrant the assumption that he was skilled also in the use of the Greek language, although here it is difficult to distinguish between his skill and that of his several amanuenses.[5] There is no surviving evidence that Frederick wrote Latin poetry, although he was certainly adept in the writing of Latin prose. It was doubtless Piero della Vigna or the notaries of Frederick's Chancery who were responsible for what Pope Gregory IX described as *dictatoris facunditas* in referring to the Emperor's letters.[6]

The literary efforts in Latin prose and poetry thus far described were the products of the juristically educated officials of the Sicilian court. Far more important in the history of belles-lettres was the Italian poetry emanating chiefly from the nobility at the court. It is of this poetry that Dante said: 'And from the fact that the royal throne was Sicily it came to pass that whatever our predecessors wrote in the vulgar tongue was called Sicilian; and this name we also retain, nor will our successors be able to change it.'[7]

This genre had made its appearance long before in Provence among the troubadours, certainly as early as the mid eleventh century, and

---

[1] Odofridus, quoted by H. Kantorowicz, 'Über die dem Petrus de Vineis zugeschrieberen "Arenge"' (*MIöG* xxx, 1909), p. 653, note 1.

[2] Examples of their letters are to be seen in Huillard-Bréholles, *Pierre*, 'Pièces Justificatives', nos. 73–5, 76–83, 84, 85, 86, 87–93, and others. See especially Teresio's eulogistic letter to the students and professors of Bologna on the death of Master 'Bene', a professor of grammar, ibid., no. 6, pp. 300ff.   [3] Above, pp. 46 f. and 50.

[4] As to his ability to speak these languages, see C. Jourdain, *Recherches critiques sur l'âge et l'origine des traductions latines d'Aristote*, 1963, 153. Evidence to the contrary presented by J. M. Powell (*Speculum*, xxxviii, 1963), 481 ff., is insufficient; heads of states do not make translations of official documents, even when they know the language in which they are written.

[5] N. Festa, 'Le lettre greche di Federigo II' (*Arch. stor. ital.*, 5th series, xiii, 1887), 1 ff. See also G. Wolff, *Vier griechische Briefe Kaiser Friedrichs des Zweiten*, 6–7.

[6] Huillard-Bréholles, iv, part i, 444.

[7] *De Vulgari Eloquentia*, Book I, ch. xii. The translation here, as elsewhere, is that of the Temple Classics (reprinted, 1934), 39.

had penetrated into northern France through the trouvères during the last quarter of the century. In the mid twelfth century it entered Germany and was much in evidence at the brilliant diet of Frederick Barbarossa in Mainz in 1184, among both visiting French troubadours and native German minnesingers.[1] Almost simultaneously with the establishment of the court epic in Germany came the lyrics of the minnesingers, achieving their perfected form with Walther von der Vogelweide whose verses reflect his intimate association with the Hohenstaufen sovereigns, Henry VI, Philip of Swabia, and Frederick II. During his eight years in Germany (1212–20) Frederick II became well acquainted with the poetry of both the troubadours and the minnesingers. German lyricists other than Walther with whom he had some association were Diepold of Hohenburg, Gottfried of Neifen, Burkart of Hohenfels, and Otto of Botenlauben.[2]

It was during his first residence in Germany also that the troubadours Guillaume de Figueira and Aimeric de Peguilhan praised him for his generosity.[3] The commercial and political ties between North-western Italy and Southern France had provided an easy entrée for the wandering troubadours into Italy before the close of the twelfth century. Their influence was widely felt in the knightly court circles and in the communes by the opening of the thirteenth century.[4] Well known at the Northern Italian courts were Pierre Vidal, Rambaut de Vaqueiras, and Gauceln Faidit. They were especially welcomed at the courts of the Marquis of Montferrat and Albert Malaspina, who were themselves inspired to similar poetic efforts.[5] Already well known to Frederick before his return to Sicily in 1220, these poets of the north were welcome visitors at his court. Whether the establishment of the Sicilian school of poetry was the result of direct contact with Provence or of the influence of the Provençal poetry of Northern Italy, it was rapidly popularized at the court of Frederick II. There can be no doubt that some of the *canzoni* of the Frederican circle are definite imitations of Provençal originals.[2] It is highly probable that Piero della Vigna (who, like his sovereign, was a devotee of the lyric) acquired his taste for Provençal poetry while a student at Bologna. This probability gives more than a little weight to the argument that one of the chief sources of Sicilian lyric poetry was Northern France whence the style had spread through

---

[1] F. Koch, *Geschichte deutscher Dichtung*, 50. See also W. von Giesebrecht, *Kaiserzeit*, v. 65.

[2] C. A. Willemsen, *Kaiser Friedrich II. und sein Dichterkreis*, 14.

[3] Above, pp. 84 ff.

[4] T. Casini, *Geschichte der italienischen Literatur* (tr. from the Italian by H. Schneegans in G. Gröber, *Grundriss der romanischen Philologie*, ii, part ii), 15 ff.

[5] Ibid. 13 ff. See also G. Bertoni, *Il Duecento*, 'La poesia provenzale nell'Italia superiore', 7 ff.

[6] E. Wilkins, 'The Derivation of the Canzone' (*Modern Philology*, xii, 1915), 527.

Italy via Bologna.[1] It is perhaps futile, however, to seek to establish any one of these suggested sources as predominant or as exclusive in shaping the Sicilian-Italian lyric poetry. In its substance it was unquestionably influenced directly by the Provençal.

No European court was more fully exposed to the various literary influences than that of Frederick II after Frederick's return to Sicily from Germany in 1220 and following his imperial coronation. No other sovereign was more eager to welcome them. As Dante observed, 'those who were of noble heart and endowed with graces strove to attach themselves to the majesty of such great princes (Frederick II and Manfred); so that, in their time, whatever the best Italians attempted first appeared at the court of these mighty sovereigns.'[2] Both the Emperor and the most influential of his court officials were fully acquainted with the poetry of Northern France, of Provence, and with that of the minnesingers. It would be most singular if the poetry which they themselves wrote and which they so generously patronized did not reflect in substance and in form the influence of each of these regions. Because of the cosmopolitan character of the Frederican circle and the Emperor's own receptiveness to new ideas, it may be safely concluded that all these sources shared in shaping the vernacular poetry of Sicily: that in substance it drew heavily from both Provence and Northern France and that 'the technique of the *canzone* was, in large measure, derived from that of the Minnesong'.[3] The men who constituted the literary circle of Frederick's court were influential in many realms of Sicilian life. Unlike the poets at the court of Frederick Barbarossa and Henry VI, who were generally known only as poets, those who surrounded Frederick II came largely from the most active and highest officials of the government.

The many-sidedness of Frederick's talents, his known patronage of men of letters and science, and, above all, Dante's tribute to him have perhaps led to an over-insistence upon the actual authorship of several poems in the Italian language. While his authorship of at least four of these poems is probable—it is most plausibly established with respect to the *canzone* of which the opening line is 'De la mia disianza'—positive proof is wanting.[4]

---

[1] This explanation was offered by E. Monaci in his 'Elementi francesi nella più antica lirica italiana' (*Scritti di storia di filologia e d'arte*, 1907), 237; and by G. Bertoni, 'L'iniziazione francese nei poeti meridionali della scuola siciliana' (*Festschrift Camille Chabineau*, Erlangen, 1907), 819. See also idem, 'Lirica francese e poesia romanzesca nell'Italia di Sud' (*Storia letteraria d'Italia*, 1910), 23 ff.　　　　　　　　[2] *De Vulgari Eloquentia*, Book I, ch. xii.

[3] See especially the carefully considered conclusions of E. Wilkins, 'The Derivation of the Canzone' (*Mod. Philology*, xii, 1915), 549 ff. See also C. Battisti, 'La poesia aulica siciliana e la corte di Federico II' (*Arch. stor. pugliese*, xiii, 1960), for its comparison with the German lyrics.

[4] See the judicious treatment of this question by H. H. Thornton in *Speculum*, i, 1926

Frederick II's significance in the Sicilian school of poetry does not rest upon established proof of actual authorship of any of the numerous lyric poems emanating from the Sicilian court. Far more important was his sensitiveness to beauty and to artistic excellence in any form and his recognition and encouragement of the vulgar tongue as a medium for the development of a great literature. Perhaps even more important was his desire to surround himself with men whose literary tastes enabled them to create a 'Sicilian poetry' of singular beauty so that, in time, other European monarchs were incited to emulate his example.[1] Intimately associated with him in this achievement were his sons Manfred, Frederick of Antioch, Enzio of Sardinia, and his grandson, Conradin, as well as a host of noblemen and royal officials, including among others, Roger of Amico, Reginald and James of Aquino, James of Lentini, Guido Colona, and, above all, Piero della Vigna. Henry (VII), the first-born of Frederick's sons, although absent from Sicily and from the court circle, is thought to have shared the literary interests of his father and brothers. It is known that he was surrounded by numerous minnesingers who have been credited with 'building the bridge to the classical German Volkslied'.[2]

Although there is no extant example of lyric verse attributable to Henry (VII), there is a singular figure of speech in one of the last *canzoni* of the troubadour Gaucelm Faidit that he addressed to his mistress, Marie de Ventadour, which suggests Henry's preoccupation with lyric poetry. The troubadour here compares the changing moods of a poet to those of an unnamed German king—obviously Henry (VII), who, when conquered and imprisoned by the Emperor, sang as his arms were stripped away—even as he saw the wheel of fortune turn—and then wept at eventide.[3]

As one contemplates these years of brilliant creativeness under

87–100, 398–409; ii, 1927, 463–9. On the other hand, C. A. Willemsen, in his excellent monograph, *Kaiser Friedrich II. und sein Dichterkreis*, although hesitant, appears to be less cautious in attributing at least two, and probably three, of these Sicilian lyrics to Frederick (see p. 15, and then the two poems on pp. 45–7). See also the critical edition of the poems by B. Panvini, 'La scuola poetica siciliana' (*Archivum Romanicum*, xliii, 1963), 139 ff.

[1] For a list of the poets at his court see E. F. Langley, 'The Early Sicilian Poets' (*Publications of the Modern Language Association of America*, xxviii, new series, XXI, 1913), 468–73.

[2] As quoted by C. A. Willemsen, *Dichterkreis*, 18.

[3] F. Diez, *Leben und Werke der Troubadours*, 306–7:

> Al semblan del rei ties,
> Quant l'ac vencut l'emperaire,
> E il fez tirar, quant l'ac pres,
> Sa careta e son arnes,
> Don el cantav' al maltraire
> Vesen la roda virar,
> E'l ser plorav' al manjar —
> Cant, on plus ai malanansa.

Hohenstaufen patronage, especially at the court of Frederick II between
the years 1220 and 1250, it becomes ever more apparent that this was
a crucial moment in cultural history—a moment when the lay intellect
and the lay response to the beauty of an untrammelled artistry came
close to emancipating themselves from ignorance and bigotry. Here,
indeed, was a manifestation of the capacity of the human spirit to
obtain what Dante, a generation later, termed the true goal of mankind:
'apprehension by means of the potential intellect' (*apprehensio per intel-
lectum possibilem*).[1] Frederick II did not conceive of man's 'potential
intellect' as limited either to speculative thinking or to the attainment
of political wisdom. Certainly he recognized, as did the percipient
Florentine, that 'there are things to be done which are regulated by
political wisdom, and things to be made, which are regulated by art'.[2]

The adoption of the native *volgare* by the Sicilian poets rather than
the Provençal, so long preferred by the poets of the north of Italy, is
doubtless adequately explained, as Gaspary has suggested, by the
greater difficulty at the court of Frederick in acquiring fluency in the
employment of a foreign tongue.[3] The themes of the 'Sicilian lyrics'
were those of the troubadours, reflecting the same ideas, the same
imagery as the Provençal poetry. But, as Casini has remarked, this
poetry 'had already grown old and monotonous when it came to Italy
. . . and, because of its chivalrous-feudal content, did not fit into the
spirit of the more bourgeois and practical society upon which the Hohenstaufen was based'.[4] Indeed, it is difficult to visualize the juristically
trained officials of the Sicilian court or the nobility of the court circle,
unaccustomed as they were to the chivalry peculiar to Provence,
treating the themes of Provençal lyric poetry with the spontaneity and
the warmth of feeling characteristic of the original troubadours. The
Emperor himself, surrounded by his oriental harems, accustomed to
segregate his wives in isolated castles under the watchful eyes of eunuchs,
appears somewhat incongruous in his role as a troubadour. One thinks
also of the unhappy Queen of Sardinia, wife of Frederick's talented son,
Enzio, languishing in her island castle, little better than a servant to
her lord and master. To the chivalrous knight of Provence, owing
homage and fealty to his lord, there was nothing inconsistent or alien
in the role of suppliant for his lady's love. For she, like the feudal
overlord, stood high above the humble suitor. To this lowly vassal,
aware of his own unworthiness, it was perhaps natural to pour forth
his anguished heart in lyric strain. To him it was not merely affectation

---

[1] *Monarchia*, Book I, ch. iii, line 36.
[2] Ibid., lines 56 ff.
[3] *Geschichte der italienischen Literatur*, 56; Eng. tr. by H. Oelsner, 55.
[4] 'Sizilianische Dichterschule' (Gröber, *Grundriss*, ii), 15.

that the cruelty of his adored but high-born mistress could wring from him bitter tears or provoke him to such confessions as:

> At sight of her I tremble with fear
> as a leaf shakes in the wind

or

> Good lady, I ask nothing of you save
> that you take me as your servant.

Even less consonant to the poet of the imperial court must have been the acknowledgement of his lady's scorn for him. He could not easily imagine himself near death when love went unrequited, nor could he feel that love of her could so exalt him that he could ascend to the loftier social peak upon which she was wont to dwell. In short, one can never escape the conviction that the lyric poetry of the Frederican court was at best a technically skilful imitation of an alien art, often flawless in form, but wanting in warmth and sincerity. The words do not ring true in one of the poems attributed to Frederick II when the poet says:

> Fate compels me to love you and to obey your will

or

> A day will be to me as a thousand years,
> O lady, that will return me once more to you.[1]

'Sicilian' lyric poetry cannot be said to have produced great works of art which reflect the authentic spirit of the Sicilian Kingdom as Provençal poetry mirrors the very image of its native land. The importance of 'Sicilian' poetry lies, rather, in the creation of a metrical form that could, in time, produce an authentic native poetry. As Dante observed a few decades later, this so-called 'Sicilian' language produced a 'courtly and curial vernacular language in Italy . . . which belongs to all the towns in Italy but does not appear to belong to any one of them, and by which all the municipal dialects of the Italians are measured'.[2] Here, indeed, is the beginning of a literary tradition which revealed its full potentialities in the poetry of Dante and Petrarch when they perfected the *volgare* as the true medium for poetic expression in their native land. However uncertain it may be whether or not there existed a lyric poetry in the Italian tongue prior to the Frederician era, and whether or not the idea of writing in the vernacular originated

---

[1] H. H. Thornton, 'Poems Ascribed to Frederick II and "Rex Fredericus"' (*Speculum*, i), 91 and 94:

> . . . fui dato in voi amando
> ed in vostro volere.

> Ed e' mi pare mille anni la dia
> ched io ritorni a voi, madonna mia . .

[2] *De Vulgari Eloquentia*, Book I, ch. xvi.

elsewhere in Italy, there can be no doubt that the 'Sicilian' was the oldest active school of poetry.[1]

It is perhaps natural to exaggerate the importance of the 'Sicilian School' of poetry and to insist unduly upon Frederick II's being one of the first Italian poets. In this, as in so many other realms of his restless activity, Frederick's greatness lies in his extraordinary capacity to remove the traditional restraints which, under less enlightened sovereigns, held in check intellectual and artistic development. His desire always to see things as they are led him to an appreciation of the vulgar tongue, and to his bold effort to give to it a place of honour and dignity in the cultural life of Italy. Dante and many of his contemporaries were aware that the Sicilian literary language was actually not Sicilian. Rather, they saw it as a fused language, like Chaucer's Middle English, a courtly speech which, although starting in the south, 'came more and more to resemble the dialects of Central Italy, and particularly the Tuscan type'.[2]

[1] H. Niese, 'Zur Geschichte', 512.
[2] K. Vossler, *Mediaeval Culture*, ii. 69.

10. A wax impression of a cameo from a relief of the head of Frederick II, said to
have been modelled from a plaster cast of the head before it was severed from the
statue above the portal of the bridge-tower of Capua. See p. 341.2

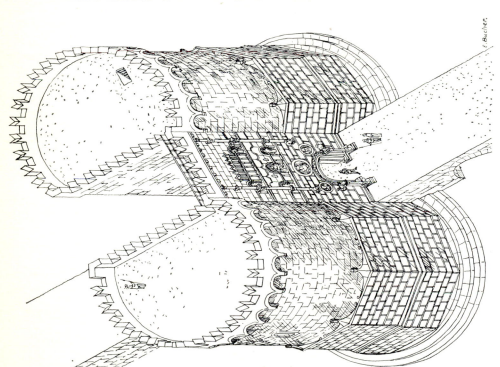

E.Bucher.

9. Bird's-eye view of a conjectural reconstruction of the portal and

8. An Arab astrologer at the Norman-Sicilian court (third from left). See pp. 308–9

7. In the second archway from the left, a Saracen notary at the Norman-Sicilian court. At the extreme right Matthew 'd'Ajello' is depicted writing to Tancred. See p. 293 and note 2

Below: The poet Pietro presents his *Liber ad Honorem Augusti* to the Emperor

4. Head of Frederick II in profile
(Photographed from his gold coin, the *Augustalis*)

6. The eagle of Frederick II's gold coin, the
Augustalis. See pp. 277–8

5. Crown, found in
the sarcophagus of
the Empress Constance
in Palermo. See p. 67

3. Henry VI, attended by Fortune, Virtue, and Justice, occupies the throne in Palermo. See p. 9

Serenissim' imparoz henr' fabaria nemes nuaos ab urbe pang receptt

Nuncu panozmu

trisstis uxoz tanered

ſ cu popa nobili ẏ triipho glorofo aucust' igredtt' panormu

2. Henry VI, at Salerno, receives the ambassadors from Palermo. Queen Sibylla weeping near the castle window as she loses her crown. Below: Triumphal entry of Henry VI into Palermo. See pp. 8–9

11. Attempted reconstruction of the façade of the bridge-towers and portal of Capua, showing the arrangement of the busts and statues according to C. A. Willemsen's interpretation. See pp. 342 f.

CAESARIS IMPERIO REGNI CUSTODIA FIO. QUAM
MISEROS FACIO QUOS VARIARE SCIO

INTRENT SECURI QUI QUAERUNT VIVERE PURI   INFIDUS EXCLUDI TIMEAT VEL CARCERE TRUDI

12. Probable arrangement of the head and busts in the circular niches beneath the seated statue of
Frederick II. The female head is believed to symbolize *Justitia*, while the two busts below are believed
to represent the imperial justices, Piero della Vigna below and to the right of Justitia, and Thaddeus
of Suessa to the left. See p. 343

F. I.

13. Sketch of a part of Castel del Monte, showing the portal, the Gothic windows, and the octagonal towers at the corners of the main structure
See pp. 344 f.

14. At top: Distant view of Castel del Monte. Below: Details of the portal. The steps on either side have been covered by debris. See pp. 344 f.

16. Equestrian statue at the entrance of the Georgian choir of Bamberg Cathedral

15. The mutilated remnants of what appears to have been an equestrian statue in the Castel del Monte suggesting a marked resemblance to illustration 16. See p. 345

17. Reliquary, constructed from a chalice and a crown by order of Frederick II for the skull
St. Elizabeth of Thuringia, now in the State Museum in Stockholm. See pp. 387 f.

IV

FREDERICK II, PATRON OF ART

L'antiche mura, ch'ancor teme et ama
E trema 'l mondo, quando si remembra
Del tempo andato e'n dietro si rivolve . . .
　　　　　　　Petrarca, *Rime*, liii.[1]

FREDERICK has been appropriately described as a forerunner of
the Renaissance, in that he was both a 'discoverer of nature' and
a patron of the burgeoning literary and artistic activities of the
thirteenth century. But this description, like phrases such as 'the first
modern man' or 'the first European', is patently misleading because of
its exclusiveness; it fails to emphasize sufficiently the stimulus given
to these activities by Frederick's Norman and Hohenstaufen forebears.
We have already seen something of the Norman cultural heritage at the
Sicilian court. It is sometimes overlooked, however, that in Germany
at the height of Frederick Barbarossa's reign, 'the *virtù* of Rome,
purified, enriched, untrammelled, firmly established, influenced art
in language and in image'.[2] With Frederick II these influences, both
Norman-Sicilian and German, continued. Architecture, sculpture,
painting, no less than science and belles-lettres, were all preoccupations
of Frederick II. A contemporary observed also that he was proficient
in all mechanical arts.[3] His *De Arte Venandi cum Avibus*, with its multitude
of flawlessly drawn sketches, the variety of pleasing architectural
innovations in his castles and residential palaces, some of which were
known to have been designed by the Emperor, bear testimony to his
artistic skill and judgement.[4] Unfortunately, time and vandalism have
spared none of the paintings executed at his command. As in music and
the dance, we have only the observations of contemporaries or near-
contemporaries as to his tastes and interest in painting. Franciscus
Pipinus, a fourteenth-century chronicler, has left a description of a painting in a Neapolitan palace, made at Frederick's orders, which appears

[1] 　　　　The ancient walls, which still with awe and love
　　　　The world admires, when it recalls
　　　　The days gone by and turns to look behind . . .
[2] F. Kampers, *Wegbereiter*, 74.
[3] *Ricobaldi Ferrariensis Historia* (Muratori, *RIS* ix), col. 132.
[4] Richard of San Germano, 132.

to have evoked the chronicler's interest by its symbolism rather than by its aesthetic qualities.[1] The description, obviously made while the composition was still intact, suggests that it was intended to depict the Emperor in his favourite role, the personification of *Justitia*. Frederick was represented as seated upon a lofty throne pointing his finger towards Piero della Vigna, seated below him. In the foreground were kneeling subjects, appealing for justice. The accompanying inscription read:

> Caesar amor legum, Friderice piissime regum,
> Causarum telas nostrasque resolvere querelas.[2]

Below this was the Emperor's reply:

> Pro vestra lite censorem juris adite:
> Hic est: jura dabit vel per me danda rogabit.
> Vinee cognomen Petrus, judex est sibi nomen.[3]

How skilfully this symbolic painting was executed in the technical or aesthetic sense we do not know. It is to be assumed that in this, as in the numerous sculptural remnants, Frederick demanded the best possible— the best in imitation of the antique. He was here being depicted in the role which he conceived the chief function and the *raison d'être* of the imperial office: arbiter of justice in all temporal things—the God-ordained agent of justice on earth even as the Pope was vicar of God 'in matters of heavenly grace'.

From other contemporary or near-contemporary sources we know also that non-religious paintings were not uncommon in palatial buildings of thirteenth-century Sicily. Often our information about such paintings is derived indirectly from contemporary correspondence, which is less concerned with the description of artistic subjects than with official business or religious transactions. An example is a letter of Pope Innocent III, written in 1204, in which he complains of a painting in the palace of the Bishop of Troja depicting the city of Foggia. The concern of the Pope was not for the painting as a work of art, but as an affront to the citizens of Foggia, in that the existence of such a painting in the palace of the Bishop of Troja was intended to imply, despite documentary evidence to the contrary, that the jurisdiction of the bishopric, in temporal as in spiritual matters, extended over their city.[4] There are references to other paintings, executed before

---

[1] *Chronica* (Muratori, *RIS* ix), col. 660.
[2]   Caesar, guardian of laws, Frederick, most pious of kings,
        Adjudicate our suits and resolve our complaints.   (Ibid.)
[3]   For the just settlement of your lawsuits look to him:
        He will do justice or request me to render it.
        Vigna is his family name—he is called Peter, the Judge.
[4] *Epist.* VII, cli, col. 446.

1230, in a monastic church of the Teutonic Order in Andria, a favourite city of Frederick II.[1]

In painting, as in literature, the plastic arts, and architecture, the tastes of Frederick II were influenced by the northern European, the Byzantine, and the native Sicilian styles, but always present was his effort—often groping—to recapture the antique spirit. While this was doubtless most nearly achieved in sculpture by Nicholas of Cicala in Frederick's magnificent triumphal gate at Capua, the effort is no less apparent in other arts. As if in anticipation of his successors, the despots of the Italian city-states of the fourteenth and fifteenth centuries, Frederick's appreciation of the beautiful, particularly his penchant for *objets d'art* of antiquity, caused him to sponsor various archaeological projects. The best known of these was his authorization of a contemporary scholar to excavate in the surroundings of the newly founded (1232) city of Augusta near the site of the ancient Megara Hyblaea, in the expectation of discovering important artistic works of antiquity.[2]

At times Frederick's zeal for objects of art carried him beyond the bounds of propriety when, in the manner of emperors before and since, he seized as his own artistic creations which he saw during his various expeditions. He did not hesitate to carry away some antique columns from the Church of San Michele in Ravenna to be incorporated in one of his palaces. One might well employ with reference to him the language of Einhard, who said of Charlemagne: 'Since he could not procure marble columns elsewhere for the building of it, he had them brought from Rome and Ravenna.'[3] With the nonchalance not infrequently to be found in zealous collectors, on one of his expeditions into the *patrimonium* Frederick carried away to Lucera a group of bronze statuettes depicting men and beasts. The chronicler Richard of San Germano states that among the treasures taken by the Emperor from the ancient monastery were a reredos of gold and another of silver, also a much-prized statuette of the Virgin, and that some of these were never returned.[4] Objects thus obtained were usually placed in the various imperial collections, together with precious Latin, French, and Arabic manuscripts. Such treasures were sometimes purchased also for the Emperor from Venetian, Provençal, or other merchants. These transactions were carefully recorded in the imperial Register, authorizing that the necessary payments be made. There is the record of the purchase of an onyx piece and other objects from a Provençal merchant at a cost of 1,230 ounces of gold.[5] As with so many of his other interests

---

[1] See R. d'Urso, *Storia della città di Andria*, 70–1.
[2] Huillard-Bréholles, v, part ii, 825.
[3] *RHGF* v. 99. See also F. J. Biehringer, *Kaiser Friedrich II.*, 369.
[4] *Chronica*, 211.
[5] Huillard-Bréholles, v, part i, 478.

that were later emulated by the princes of Europe, Frederick's art collections of Capua and Naples set a fashion assiduously copied by sovereigns throughout the era of the Renaissance.

Contemporary chroniclers tell of Frederick's fondness for music and the dance and of his maintenance of a group of singers for service in the palace chapel in Palermo. He is said to have preferred the simple Gregorian chants which he caused to replace the Greek chants, long widely employed in the kingdom of Sicily.[1] He was an admirer also of the exotic music and dances of the Orient with which he entertained his guests in his residential palaces at Foggia and elsewhere. The English chronicler Matthew Paris relates that during a visit of Richard of Cornwall, brother of the Empress Isabella, to the court of Frederick II on his return from a crusade in 1241, he was entertained with various games, a variety of musical instruments, and by court jugglers and dancers. Earl Richard was especially delighted by the performance of two Saracen girls standing upon large balls which they moved rhythmically to music while singing and gracefully pirouetting, beating their cymbals and castanets.[2] Frederick's preoccupation with lyric poetry was closely associated with his appreciation for music, which Salimbene noted in his remark that the Emperor 'could sing and he knows how to compose *cantilenas* and music'.[3]

Frederick's official correspondence reveals that even under the urgent pressure of his imperial duties he sought diversion in the dance. A letter of the year 1240 reminds the *secretus* of Messina that, 'as you have written us, you have found a Saracen dancer who comes from Aquitaine, and who knows how to do many kinds of dances, and that you have taken care to retain him for our court. We desire that you send him to us at once.'[4] Interests such as these, although common a century and a half later among the princes of Europe, indicate how far the cultural tastes of Frederick II had advanced beyond those of his thirteenth-century contemporaries. In contemplating the varied interests of the Sicilian court circle, in philosophy, in the sciences and mathematics, in literature and the fine arts, it is difficult to avoid the conclusion that, humanistically speaking, the Renaissance had already begun.

Of all the interests of Frederick II none so graphically illustrate the blending of the best of the medieval with the ancient as architecture and sculpture. Frederick's restless spirit found its chief aesthetic expression in architecture and sculpture. The well-known dictum of Nietzsche applies to Frederick II with just as much force as to the emperors

[1] R. Pirri, *Sicilia sacra*, ii. 1359.
[2] *Chron. majora*, iv. 147.
[3] *Cronica*, 34–9.
[4] Huillard-Bréholles, v, part ii, 721. R. Gregorio, *Rerum Arabicarum, quae ad historiam Siculam spectant, ampla collectio*, Preface, p. xi.

of Roman antiquity: 'In architecture pride triumphs over the force of gravity, the will to power manifests itself; architecture is a kind of power-eloquence achieved by forms.'[1] Although inheriting from his Norman ancestors many magnificent palaces of Arabic and Arabo-Byzantine styles, Frederick was the creator of a palatial architectural style peculiarly his own. On the mainland of Italy some eighteen of his castles are known to have existed.[2] No longer did he follow the models of the pleasure palaces of Messina, of the inviting retreats of Linaria and Aetna, of Parco, or of La Favara, later known as Castello de Mare Dolce, built in the mid twelfth century for King Roger II at the foot of Mount Grifone and long a favourite residence of the Norman kings.[3] Ibn Djubayr wrote of the Norman castles near Palermo: 'The King's palaces are disposed around the higher parts, like pearls encircling a woman's full throat.'[4] In contrast with these, Frederick's castles were simpler and more severe, yet never wanting in elegance of design and décor. At the same time they often differed considerably from the structures of Northern Europe.

One of the earliest of his castles, that of Foggia, was begun in 1223, some three years after his return to Sicily from Germany. Although situated in the midst of an extensive limestone plain, it provided easy access to the royal forest and hunting preserve, the Incoronata[5] (*Bosco della Incoronata*). An additional reason for the choice of this site was no doubt its strategic location adjacent to those regions of Italy so bitterly contested between the Pope and Emperor.[6] The castle of Foggia was primarily a residential palace, one of several in the now relatively barren Capitanata which in the thirteenth century had many allurements for Frederick II. Little of the original structure remains to bear witness to the splendour of this royal residence which the Emperor visited frequently and for longer periods than he spent elsewhere.[7] Only the

---

[1] F. Nietzsche, 'Götzen-Dämmerung oder wie manmit dem Hammer philosophiert' (*Gesammelte Werke*, xvii. 115). For the various types of Hohenstaufen castle see H. Hahn *et al.*, *Hohenstaufenburgen in Süditalien* (Ingelheim, 1961).

[2] G. Dehio, 'Die Kunst Unteritaliens' (*Hist. Zeitschr*. 95, 1905), 196–7.

[3] For the Norman-Sicilian castles see E. Caspar, *Roger II*, 465–70. Highly useful also is the work of F. J. Biehringer, *Kaiser Friedrich II.*, part iii: 'Die Bauten Kaiser Friedrichs II.' For an over-all survey of Frederick's architecture see G. Agnello, 'L'architettura militare, civile e religiosa nell'età sveva' (*Arch. stor. pugilese*, xiii, 1960).

[4] Amari, *Biblioteca arabo-sicula*, i. 160. The translation is that of R. J. C. Broadhurst, *The Travels of Ibn Jubayr*, 348.

[5] See C. Perifano, *Cenni storici di Foggia*, ch. V, 'Foggia nell'epoca degli svevi', 64 ff., especially p. 70.

[6] See first A. Haseloff, *Die Bauten der Hohenstaufen in Unteritalien*, i. 45 ff., and then Huillard-Bréholles, *Recherches sur les monuments des Normands et de la maison de Souabe dans l'Italie méridionale*, Pl. XVIII, and idem, *Hist. Dip.*, Introduction, p. dxlvii.

[7] He himself says in a letter: 'Cum solatiis nostris Capitanate provinciam frequentius visitemus et magis quam in aliis provinciis . . . trahimus ibidem . . .' Huillard-Bréholles, v, part ii, 943. See also A. Haseloff, op. cit. i. 45 ff., 52 ff.

arch of the doorway remains with its richly carved imposts surmounted by images of the imperial eagle with outspread wings upon pedestals from which the arch springs. The arch, some eight feet in width at its base, is of beautiful design, reflecting in some of its intricate leaf-like ornamentations the influence of the antique. The mason responsible for the work, Bartholomew of Foggia, a master craftsman, apparently executed it in conformity with plans drawn by the Emperor himself. It is apparent that the designer of Foggia, like his successor, Nicholas of Pisa, employed models of ancient origin. It is unfortunate that we do not have contemporary evidence of Frederick's intimate association with sculptors, painters, and architects; we seek in vain in the realm of art for a Michael Scot, a Leonard of Pisa, a 'Todre, le philosophe', or a Piero della Vigna. Perhaps it may be assumed from the passage cited above that Frederick himself was sufficiently skilled in the mechanical, as in the fine arts, to design his castles and sculptural ornaments with his own hand—that he was, in the words of Bertaux, 'the actual sculptor'.[1] The elaborate inscription above the arch carries the implication of the Emperor's participation in its design:

SIC CESAR FIERI JUSSIT OPUS ISTUD
BARTHOLOMEUS SIC CONSTRUXIT ILLUD.[2]

It has been plausibly suggested that the inscription or, more accurately, the two inscriptions, commemorate two achievements: the erection of the arch and the building of the entire structure.[3] The continuation of the inscription reads:

ANNO AB INCARNATIONE MCCXXIII
MENSE JUNII XI INDICTIONE, REGNANTE
DOMINO NOSTRO FREDERICO IMPERATORE
ROMANORUM SEMPER AUGUSTO ANNO III
ET REGE SICILIE ANNO XXVI, HOC OPUS
FELICITER INCEPTUM EST PREPHATO
    DOMINO PRECIPIENTE
HOC FIERI JUSSIT FREDERICUS CAESAR URBS SIT
FOGIA REGALIS SEDES INCLITA IMPERIALIS.[4]

---

[1] É. Bertaux, *L'Art dans l'Italie meridionale*, 717.
[2]   Thus [or in this manner] Caesar ordered this work to be constructed.
      Bartholomew constructed it accordingly.
[3] Huillard-Bréholles, Introduction, p. dxlviii.
[4] For the inscription see H. W. Schulz, *Denkmäler der Kunst des Mittelalters in Unteritalien*, i. 208.

In the year of the incarnation MCCXXIII, the eleventh indiction, in the month of June, being the third year of our lord Frederick always august as emperor of the Romans, and his twenty-sixth as king of Sicily, this work was auspiciously begun by order of the said lord. The Emperor Frederick ordered this to be built that the city of Foggia might become the illustrious royal seat of the empire.

After the collapse of the palace in 1543, the original arch was incorporated into the front wall of a newly constructed building on the same site. Other remnants of the palace were stored in a municipal building where they have long remained, a fragmentary but significant memorial to the artistic taste of Frederick II.

It was eleven years later, in 1234, that Frederick ordered the construction of the triumphal portal, later known as the Castel del Torre, a strongly fortified bridge-tower guarding the Via Appia where it crosses the Volturno at Capua.[1] The remark of the chronicler, 'quod ipsa manu propria consignavit', could imply that Frederick merely gave his personal orders for the construction of the portal, although it may well be interpreted in the literal sense that he himself designed it.[2] Various orders issued by Frederick during 1239–40 for marble necessary for the arch between the towers flanking the bridge and for roofing the towers, 'in order that they might not be injured by the rain', reveal that the construction continued through those years.[3] The building is variously described as *castellum, turris pontis*, or simply as *turris*. Because of the ruined condition of the original structure we are dependent upon descriptions by several individuals who saw it in the last half of the thirteenth century or between then and its demolition in the sixteenth century. The oldest description is that of Andrew of Hungary, an eyewitness of the capture of the city by Charles of Anjou as the result of the defeat of Manfred in 1266.[4] He was impressed by the great size of the towers, by their strength and beauty and, even more, by their cost, which he estimated at 20,000 ounces of purest gold (*viginti milibus unciarum auri purissimi*). He was no less impressed by the statue of Frederick II, which he described as an 'eternal and imperishable memorial', arms extended and two fingers pointing as if threatening the passers-by with the warning inscribed below:

> CESARIS IMPERIO REGNI CUSTODIA FIO.
> QUAM MISEROS FACIO QUOS VARIARE SCIO.
> INTRENT SECURI QUI QUAERUNT VIVERE PURI
> INFIDUS EXCLUDI TIMEAT VEL CARCERE TRUDI.[5]

[1] Richard of San Germano, 188.

[2] Concerning the building see the thorough study of C. A. Willemsen, *Kaiser Friedrichs II. Triumphtor zu Kapua*, 7 ff. and also the work of C. Shearer, *The Renaissance of Architecture in Southern Italy*, 1 ff.

[3] Huillard-Bréholles, v, part i, 513, part ii, 673, 880.

[4] *Andreae Ungari Descriptio Victoriae a Karlo com. Reportatae* (*MGH, SS*. xxvi), 571. See also C. von Fabriczy, 'Zur Kunstgeschichte der Hohenstaufenzeit' (*Zeitschr. für bildende Kunst*, xiv, 1879), 180–9; 209–22; especially 183 ff.

[5]   At the command of Caesar I stand as protector of the kingdom.
      How wretched I make those whom I know to be false.
      They who seek to live undefiled may safely enter.
      Let the faithless fear to be kept out or perish in prison.
                    Andreae Descriptio, loc. cit.

Several decades later, in 1330, the learned lawyer Lucantonio of Penna mentioned the portal in his *Commentary on the Justinian Code*, describing not only the statue of Frederick II with its accompanying verse but also the busts (*imagines*) of 'two judges', perhaps erroneously identified as Thaddeus of Suessa and Piero della Vigna, below the statue of Frederick, one at his left, the other at his right, an inscription in verse above each.[1] Antoninus, Archbishop of Florence (1389–1454), tells in his *Cronica tripartita* of two amazing towers on the river near Capua.[2] Bartholomeo Fazio (d. 1465), court historian of King Alfonzo I of Naples, mentions in his description of the capture of Capua by the condottiere Braccio of Montone in 1421, the 'excellence of the workmanship in free-stone [ashlaring] of the two square towers'. He states also that the city of Capua was protected by two strongholds, one opposite the city, the other at the exit of the bridge.[3] As Fabriczy has pointed out, the latter is obviously the one to which the two towers belonged, while the former was in the encircling wall of the city and was probably completed after Frederick's time.[4]

A detailed description of the strongholds, although not of the sculpture of the portal, is included in a fifteenth-century biography of this same Braccio of Montone by Giovanni Antonio Campano, Bishop of Teramo. He tells of 'the two splendid and best fortified towers of Italy', and continues with an elaborate description of the two strongholds. Capua, he says, 'is almost surrounded on three sides by the river Volturno so that at many points the river serves as a wall'. He was especially impressed by the strategic location and by the massiveness of the fortifications with their walls of extraordinary thickness, constructed of blocks of marble the joints of which were cemented, not with mortar, but with melted lead. As double assurance against assaults by battering-rams, trebuchets, mangonels, and other siege machines, a second wall of quarried stone surrounded the main structure. High above the aperture of the great portal was a splendid cubicle or apartment (*regium cubiculum*), containing marble statues or busts and antique carvings. Each of the towers was surrounded also by a well-fortified, crown-like bulwark or rampart (*propugnacula*), and the two were joined by a wooden bridge. A subterranean cistern or reservoir was accessible by means of a single passage to be used by the garrison in the event of an emergency.

---

[1] Lucas de Penna, *Commentaria in tres posteriores Libros Codicis Justiniani*, Lib. X, Tit. 40, lex 4, p. 446. For the inscription see also *Gesta Romanorum*, liv; Thomasso de Masi, *Memorie degli auranci*, iv. 192; and P. della Valle, *Lettere sanesi sopra le belle arti*, i. 198 ff.

[2] *Chronica*, part iv, Tit. 19, ch. 6, part. i, p. 127. See also C. Fabriczy, loc. cit.

[3] 'Una contra urbem, altera ad exitum pontis sita.' B. Facii or Fazio (Facius), *De rebus gestis ab Alphonso primo Neapolitanorum rege*, Lib. II, pp. 22 ff., and the earlier edition (Lyons, 1562), 41.

[4] Op. cit. 184.

The author emphasizes also the massiveness of the tower foundations, which he describes as equalling in depth the height of the outer structure.[1]

Further details of the triumphal bridge-tower are supplied by a sixteenth-century chronicler, Scipio Sannelli, a Capuan, who wrote a history of his native city down to the year 1571, later continued by his nephew Alessandro Pellagrino.[2] In this work, written shortly before the demolition of the building, Sannelli states that in the year 1247 Frederick had a splendid marble portal constructed between the towers with various artistic ornaments. In the upper part he placed the several admirable statues which subsequently were found in the ruins of Capua; somewhat below these was placed his own statue with a crown upon its head and above it the inscription previously mentioned in the chronicle of Andrew of Hungary. Sannelli describes the arch of the great portal as adorned with sculptured figures in polished white marble depicting the trophies and the victories of the Emperor. He continues: 'In our day all this is in ruins; only the statue of Frederick now stands, since recently the senate of Capua has had it restored with its inscription near the bridge-gate.'

But even this sixteenth-century description leaves much to be desired. The statue of Frederick II, obviously intended as the focal centre of the statuary group, had been seriously mutilated and the decision of the Capuan council to preserve it as an 'antique memorial' could not accurately restore its original characteristics. It was this restored statue, however, which the Neapolitan historian, Daniele, saw and described.[3] At that time the more than life-size statue, although seriously mutilated, still revealed a youthful monarch seated upon his throne and sufficiently intact to permit Daniele to note the superior workmanship of the sculptor and to recognize that it had been chiselled in the manner of a beautiful antique original.[4] Unfortunately the statue was further mutilated shortly after Daniele's description, its head removed and destroyed or lost, and its sculptured ornamentation injured. In this condition the torso of the statue remains to the present day. Daniele is said to have made a plaster cast of the head, before its final mutilation and this, in turn, was copied for a cameo setting of a ring.[5] Here the Emperor is portrayed as unmistakably youthful and wearing a light crown.[6]

---

[1] *Joannis Antoni Campani Opera: de rebus gestis Andreae Brachii Perusini*, Lib. VI (Muratori, *RIS* xix), col. 365. See also Fabriczy, loc. cit.

[2] Fabriczy, op. cit., pp. 85 ff.

[3] P. della Valle, *Lettere sanesi*, i. 200–1.

[4] Ibid.; Fabriczy, 'Kunstgeschichte', 215.

[5] See also F. von Raumer, *Hohenstaufen*, iii. 283; and É. Bertaux, *L'Art dans l'Italie méridionale*, 716 and fig. 269, p. 600.

[6] See especially C. A. Willemsen, *Triumphtor*, 34, and his several notes, 91.

Frederick's features are finely chiselled, indeed so much so as to suggest an idealization rather than an attempt at faithful portrayal. The countenance is scornfully arrogant, expressive of the majestic pride of a sovereign deeply conscious of the exalted—almost God-like—position which he conceived of himself as occupying upon earth. In the eyes of his contemporaries he stood aloof. His closest associates, the men who best exemplified his sovereign authority, Piero della Vigna and Thaddeus of Suessa, looked upon him as a man apart—'not super-human but superior-human'. It was this quality that made itself felt to an early observer of this 'eternal and imperishable memorial'.

For many years, indeed until quite recently, this broken statue of Frederick II afforded the sole remnant of what obviously had been a splendid array of sculptured figures adorning the façade of the triumphal arch of Capua. Discoveries in recent years have brought to light other statues and busts in niches above the great portal which, probably since the sixteenth century, had been hidden by mortar and rubble. Of especial interest is the head of a woman almost three times larger than life size, which Sannelli believed to be a symbol of the 'fidelity of Capua' (*Fedeltà di Capua*), an idealistic personification of the city that 'constantly and above all others remained faithful to the Emperor'.[1] These more recent discoveries, together with the statue of the Emperor, not only serve to emphasize the extent of the antique influence but also reveal a skill in workmanship which suggests that already in thirteenth-century Apulia the practice of working from antique models was not unknown and that it may have spread from that region to Central Italy. Indeed, the evidence is most convincing that Nicholas of Pisa, who is described by Vasari as perfecting his sculptural skill by copying the reliefs of antique sarcophagi, was of Apulian origin, and may have had direct connection with the sculptors employed by Frederick II.[2]

These more recent discoveries have made it possible to conjecture a plausible reconstruction and to interpret the probable meaning of the sculptural arrangement above the great portal.[3] The statue of Frederick II, much more than an 'eternal and imperishable memorial' in the sense of a physical likeness, appears rather to be a part of an ensemble of statues and busts intended, collectively, to represent his concept of the imperial majesty, the imperial spirit as it reveals itself in the exalted judge of all temporal things—not the Emperor as a physical being, but as the personification of all that *Justitia* implies. Accordingly, the colossal head of the woman, apparently originally attached to her bust

[1] Fabriczy, op. cit., 216. See also C. A. Willemsen, *Triumphtor*, 44–8.

[2] R. Davidsohn, *Forschungen*, iv. 530–5. See also Baron Heinrich von Geymüller, *Die Anfänge der Architektur der Renaissance in Italien*, 12 ff., and J. A. Crowe and C. B. Cavalcaselle, *A New History of Painting in Italy*, 106 f.

[3] See C. A. Willemsen, *Triumphtor*, 61–75, and his *Abbildungen*, nos. 105–7.

adorned by an imperial eagle against her exposed breast, did not occupy the loftiest niche above the portal, nor was she intended to depict the 'loyalty of Capua' as Sannelli conjectured. Instead, the more plausible conjecture of C. A. Willemsen suggests that she was intended to personify the *Justitia Caesaris*, so frequently mentioned in the official documents of Frederick II. It was she who was represented as saying:

At the command of Caesar I stand as protector of the kingdom.
How wretched I make them whom I know to be false![1]

The busts of the two men, uncovered from the rubble, seem to have occupied two round niches below and on either side of Justitia, the one on the right of the gateway, generally identified as Piero della Vigna, and the one on the left, as Thaddeus of Suessa. It was they, as imperial justices, who were represented as delivering the admonitions inscribed in the perimeters of the circular niches. The inscription in the niche on the left as once faces the portal reads:

They who seek to live undefiled may safely enter.

The inscription on the right of the portal was an admonition to the faithless:

Let the faithless fear to be shut out or to die in prison.

In smaller niches to the right and left of the Emperor's statue were two figures and, directly above them, two others, all without accompanying inscriptions. It is obvious, however, that they also are symbolic and may, as Willemsen has plausibly conjectured, represent the attributes of Justice, either Reason, Foresight, Necessity, Law, or else, Wisdom, Clemency, Prudence, Piety.[2] Although this interpretation of the statuary of the splendid Capuan portal is necessarily conjectural it is in keeping with the known character of the Emperor. He was the Emperor, the arbiter of temporal justice with all the awe-inspiring implications of the word. It is this that was represented in the Capuan gate—it was this that he sought to depict as 'eternal and imperishable'. Here in sculpture was set forth the conception of the *imperium* which he had so often defined: 'to guard the realm, to protect its honour, to augment its privileges, to extend its boundaries, to reward the faithful.'[3]

No less expressive of Frederick II's aloofness, his conception of himself as superior by virtue of his office, is another of his singular archi-

[1] In addition to Willemsen, see also P. Schramm, *Kaiser Friedrichs II. Herrschaftszeichen*, 127 ff., and C. Shearer, op. cit. 85 ff.

[2] See Willemsen, loc. cit., and P. Schramm, *Herrschaftszeichen*, 129. For the attributes of Justice see A. Gaudenzi, 'I. Tempio della Giustizia a Ravenna e a Bologna' (*Mélanges Fitting*, 1908), ii. 719.

[3] See, for example, the several citations of W. von den Steinen, *Das Kaisertum Friedrichs des Zweiten*, 61, 79 ff. See above, p. 262.

tectural achievements, the Castel del Monte. This unique structure
rises almost defiantly from the highest point of the Apulian plateau,
some 1,700 feet above sea level. In the district of the Murge, nine or
ten miles from the city of Andria, the castle occupies the site of the Haut
Mont or Mont Hardi of Frederick's Norman predecessors, long recognized as an exceptional strategic position.[1] As it now stands, the castle
gives the impression of isolation, bleak and forbidding in aspect; and
yet, as one approaches it, no matter from which direction, its apparent
isolation assumes a majestic loneliness. It impresses especially by its
unique design and by what, originally, was superb craftsmanship as
can still be seen in the flawless articulation of its masonry. It was constructed almost simultaneously with the triumphal bridge-tower of
Capua and, in some measure, reflects the same predilection for the
antique. Documents from the royal Chancery indicate that its construction had advanced only slightly in 1240.[2] It was completed during the
following five or six years, probably in 1246, when the Emperor is
thought to have resided there for a short time.[3] Structurally, Castel
del Monte bears no resemblance to other buildings in Apulia or
elsewhere; it has no precedent in military architecture. The plan is
that of a vast octagon with the addition of an octagonal tower at each
of the corners of the main structure. The walls are constructed of
cream-coloured blocks of freestone and joined with such precision as
to suggest that originally, when free from erosion, the joints must have
been barely perceptible. The edges of the roof and the crowns of the
towers have crumbled and fallen away, although most of the mural
structure remains intact. The somewhat monotonous surface of the
walls is relieved only by scattered slits or loopholes designed for military
purposes. Water drains extending from the roof appear to have con-
verged in an octagonal marble basin in the centre of the inner court.[4]
The sole entrance to the castle is a huge portal, facing eastward, of
such size as to fill much of the space between two of the octagonal
towers. Leading to it are twin stairways, and on each side it is flanked
by pilasters topped by capitals of modified Corinthian design. Above
it is a triangular tympanum recessed within the framework of the
cornices of the pediment surmounting a secondary arch below. This
tympanum retains only vague traces of original decorative figures,

[1] See especially R. d'Urso, *Città di Andria*, 50 ff. My description of the castle is based in
part upon two visits but greatly supplemented by the thorough study of C. A. Willemsen in
his copiously illustrated booklet, *Castel del Monte*. See also Bertaux, *L'Art dans l'Italie méridionale*,
719 ff., and D. Salazaro, *Notizie storiche sul Palazzo di Federico II a Castel del Monte*, 1–12.

[2] See the document in Huillard-Bréholles, v, part i, 697, which refers to the castle as
'Sanctum Mariam de Monte'.

[3] Huillard-Bréholles, Introduction, p. dl, note 2.

[4] An eighteenth-century sketch, perhaps of questionable authenticity, is the source of this
conjecture. See G. Dehio, 'Die Kunst Unteritaliens' (*Hist. Zeitschr.* 95, 1905), 200.

probably reliefs of Frederick and his son Manfred.[1] The entire design of the great portal suggests, unmistakably, the influence of antique models, although the rigidity of some of the ornamentation continues the medieval tradition. The Gothic influence is especially marked in the pointed arch of the doorway and in the columns on either side with their delicate capitals surmounted by images of the Hohenstaufen lions. The Gothic is emphasized also in the window immediately above the pediment which, in contrast, is of classical design, as if again accentuating Frederick's concept of his own era as a continuation of that of the antique Caesars. To the modern observer contemplating this extraordinary portal there is a distinct meeting of ancient and medieval characteristic of the cultural and intellectual outlook of Frederick II.

Elsewhere, on each of the remaining seven walls between the octagonal towers are two Gothic windows, one directly above the other, to provide light for the rooms of the lower and upper floors. The windows of the lower floor, severely plain, are bordered by a simple band or ribbon of red breccia, while the upper windows are more elaborately designed and ornamented with slender columns supporting a simple plate tracery in the head of the arch. The structure, when viewed as a whole, reflects the many-sidedness of the imperial taste, combining features of the antique, the Cistercian gothic, and the Apulian Romanesque.

Eight rooms on the lower floor, trapezoidal in shape, surround the inner octagonal court, with which several of them have direct access, through arched portals varying in design. All but two are connected by narrow passages with the octagonal rooms of the towers, three of which contain winding stairways leading to the upper floor. The remaining five contain small cubicles, wash-rooms, water-closets, or storage compartments. The three portals leading to the inner court are of relatively simple design. Above one of these is the mutilated remnant of what appears to have been an equestrian statue surmounted by the fragments of a baldachin. This, together with the posture of the torso and the elevation of the right arm, as they are still faintly distinguishable, suggests a marked resemblance to the equestrian statue at the entrance of the Georgian choir of Bamberg Cathedral.[2] Another sculptured relief on a wall of this inner court, so badly mutilated as to be almost indistinguishable, appears to have depicted a hunting scene reminiscent of an antique bas-relief.

The eight rooms of the upper floor reflect the sensitiveness of Frederick II to interior décor as well as his love of creature comfort. In

---

[1] Willemsen, *Castel del Monte*, 7, 9, and also D. Salazaro, *Notizie storiche sul palazzo*, 1–12.

[2] G. Dehio, *Geschichte der deutschen Kunst*, i. 333 ff., and the *Abbildungen* to vol. i, fig. 454, p. 409. See also C. A. Willemsen, *Castel del Monte*, 37.

contrast to the gloom of the lower rooms, those of the upper floor are lighted by means of the large mullioned Gothic windows, below each of which is a window-seat, accessible by means of several marble steps. The few imperfect remnants of the original interior decoration suggest that it combined features of Byzantine, Gothic, and Romanesque. Here were once-colourful marble columns, mosaic floors, walls of white marble and reddish breccia. The groined vaults of the ceilings are supported by clustered columns or by pilasters, usually surmounted by richly adorned capitals of varying designs with ribs radiating to the ornamented apexes of the ceilings. To what extent other decorative features may have been employed in the interior decorating can only be conjectured. But Frederick's known use of oriental finery and the habitual use of exotic fabrics and *objets d'art* by his Norman ancestors permit the assumption that the interiors, particularly those of the upper chambers, were elaborately decorated.

Few known works of art or architecture of the Middle Ages reflect as vividly the tastes and the ideals of the patrons who inspired them as do these two structures, the bridge-tower of Capua and the Castel del Monte. Like Frederick's *De Arte Venandi cum Avibus*, these splendid structures are the affirmation of Frederick's nostalgic yearning for the majesty of the emperors of ancient Rome and an expression of his insatiable urge to artistic creativeness. In his artistic, as in his scientific and literary pursuits, Frederick II was often compelled, for want of leisure, to find the fulfilment of his desires vicariously in the men of genius and talent attached to his court. But these men—whether the Scotsman, Michael, the Tuscan, Leonardo, the Jew, Juda ben Solomon, or the Saracen, Fakhr-ad-Dīn—far from resenting or minimizing Frederick's philosophical, mathematical, or literary and artistic efforts, recognized in him not merely a sovereign patron, but an intellectual co-worker, activated by a spiritual urge which, in all ages and in all regions of the civilized world, has elevated the scholar and the artist above the common level of mankind.

PART VII

FREDERICK RETURNS TO
GERMANY

I

THE GERMAN REGENCY AND THE SUCCESSION OF HENRY (VII)

> Nos enim sumus dominus et imperator imperii; per nos enim et de mandato nostro reverentia debetur eidem . . .
>
> Letter of Frederick II to the Citizens of Worms, 1235 (Huillard-Bréholles, iv, part i, 529).[1]

THE departure of Frederick II from Germany in 1220, and his preoccupation with the Kingdom of Sicily and Lombardy, compelled him to leave the government of Germany in other hands. His son, Henry (VII), then in his ninth year, could not be expected to succeed to the kingship for several years. Moreover, as pledged crusader, hard pressed by the Pope and Curia to fulfil his crusading vow, Frederick was most unlikely to make an early return to Germany. It was of the utmost importance that a competent regency be appointed.

Frederick's experience during the eight years in Germany had revealed to him that his chief reliance must be on the ecclesiastical princes, 'the pillars of the Kingdom'. It was inevitable that the regent and guardian of his son should be chosen from that class. Of these princes, the one most endowed with the abilities requisite for that office was Engelbert, Archbishop of Cologne.[2] It was not until Frederick II had entered the Kingdom of Sicily after his coronation as Emperor that Engelbert was officially designated as regent.[3]

As Archbishop of Cologne since 1216, Engelbert had revealed his loyalty to the Staufen cause by subduing all hostile elements within his province. In the language of a contemporary, Caesar of Heisterbach: 'No one was so powerful that he dared to pillage the lands of his enemy in the Duchy and the Archdiocese of Engelbert. He curbed the arrogance of the counts and other nobles and rulers so that it was not necessary for him to destroy any castle or to devastate any region.' More

---

[1] For we are lord and emperor of the empire; it is through us and by our command that reverence is owed to him [Henry (VII)] . . .

[2] For Engelbert's life see Caesar of Heisterbach (Böhmer, *Fontes*, ii); J. Ficker, *Engelbert der Heilige, Erzbischof von Köln und Reichsverweser*; K. Langosch, *Caesarius von Heisterbach, Leben, Le den und Wunder des heiligen Erzbischofs Engelbert von Köln*; H. Foerster, *Engelbert von Berg, der Heilige* (Elberfeld, 1925).

[3] Caesar of Heisterbach, *Vita* (Böhmer, *Fontes*, ii), 299 ff.

by cleverness than by war he subdued all the lords, so that the lines of Ovid appear to have been intended for him: 'who sorrows when he is compelled to be severe.'[1] Not only in Cologne but also in other cities, notably Soest, he exercised greater authority than any of his predecessors; but, says his biographer, 'he had the mouth of a lamb and the heart of a lion'. As Archbishop of Cologne he had regained much of the property which his predecessors had lost through shiftlessness or through weakness, although (his biographer felt compelled to add), 'I think he would not have achieved much by litigation and by judicial proceedings had he not possessed vigour of mind and a strong army.' His appearances at court were attended by such splendour and dignity that he was thought to be superior to all other princes. As member of their estate he was indefatigable in his efforts to protect their interests against the growing spirit of independence among the cities. Yet, despite this, the merchants are said to have 'praised and honoured him and to have thanked God because he had bestowed such power upon the Archbishop'. Engelbert was known also as the protector of the oppressed, 'the hammer against tyrants'. This same contemporary, always the panegyrist, describes the Archbishop as 'generous, humble, reverent, and courteous'. He then adds, 'although my lord is considered worldly, he is not as he appears outwardly'.[2]

Notwithstanding these qualities of wisdom, virtue, and mildness, the doughty Archbishop felt compelled to maintain an elaborate bodyguard as protection against his enemies among the nobility. It would have been impossible for Frederick to find a more capable guardian for the interests of his son or a more capable regent of the German Kingdom. In no sense, however, was Engelbert entrusted with unlimited authority. He was to rule with the advice and consent of the royal council and with the assistance of the Chancellor, Bishop Conrad of Metz and Speyer, who, as trusted representative of Frederick II, returned to Germany from his mission in Italy in 1221.

The immediate personal care of the young King was, for a time at least, entrusted to Swabian *ministeriales*, officials of the Staufen household who had risen to positions of extraordinary influence during and since the time of Frederick Barbarossa. Among the earliest of these tutors of the King was Werner of Boland; after his death he was succeeded by Gerhard of Dietz.[3] Although Engelbert was officially appointed as guardian, there can be no doubt that the actual education of the royal lad was left to these Swabian officials. Subsequently, when the breach

---

[1] *Ex Ponto*, II. ii. 123.

[2] K. Langosch, *Caesarius*, 38–42.

[3] *Gesta Treverorum Continuatio Quarta* (*MGH, SS.* xxiv), 399; *Sächsische Weltchronik* (*MGH, Deutsch. Chron.* ii), 243.

between Henry (VII) and his father became irremediable, it was these Swabian intimates who were largely responsible for his policies which so obstinately clashed with those of the Emperor. Prominent among these *ministeriales* were the *Truchsess* or Grand Master of the Royal Household, Eberhard of Waldburg, and Henry of Tanne, Provost of the Cathedral of Constance, as protonotary. Another close companion of the royal boy was the dapifer or steward, Conrad of Winterstettin, who, after accompanying Frederick to Italy in 1220, returned to Germany with Conrad of Metz and Speyer in 1221.[1] This group of *ministeriales* at times wielded an influence on the policies of Henry (VII) comparable to that of the ecclesiastical princes who constituted the Council. The temporal princes played only an insignificant role in the government. This divided authority, often the result of usurpations by the *ministeriales*, led to numerous differences between them and the regency and, ultimately, brought catastrophe to the young King.

The problems facing the German government had to do chiefly with maintaining the public peace and with the territorial expansion towards the north-east. Especially in Saxony, there appeared at the beginning of the regency serious causes of unrest, originating in the choice of a new Bishop of Hildesheim. In 1220 Bishop Siegfried resigned and, in July of the next year, the cathedral chapter chose as his successor the *scholasticus* of Mainz, Master Conrad, who, like his well-known contemporary, Oliver, *scholasticus* of Cologne, had attracted favourable attention as a crusading preacher in Germany.[2] The *ministeriales*, who had a remote claim to participate in the election of a new bishop, although they had rarely made use of it, now strongly opposed the appointment of the *scholasticus*. Upon Conrad's arrival at the royal court to receive the regalia, representatives sent by the *ministeriales* endeavoured to prevent the investiture. When, therefore, the quarrel appeared to be developing into a serious defiance of the regency's authority, and the King himself had agreed to the investiture, Engelbert, knowing that the Pope approved, proclaimed a general peace for the whole of Saxony in the name of the King. This shrewd move by the regent received an immediate pledge of support from the important princes of Saxony, both ecclesiastical and temporal. Some months later Pope Honorius III praised these princes, including not only the Bishops of Halberstadt and Hildesheim, but also the Duke of Saxony, the Count of Anhalt, and the *ministeriales* of Magdeburg, for their part in the 'preservation of peace in your territories'.[3]

While this was but one of the many internal problems faced by the

---

[1] Winkelmann, *Acta*, ii. 682.
[2] *Chronicon Hildesheimense* (*MGH, SS.* vii), 860.
[3] Huillard-Bréholles, ii, part ii, 723 ff. See also *MGH, Epist. Pont.* i. 141.

regency, it is not only typical but also the most serious. Generally speaking, the independence of the individual principalities was such, thanks to the numerous concessions confirmed to them prior to Frederick's departure in 1220, that most of the internal problems were concerned with petty local quarrels. Petty as many of them were, however, they might well have weakened the central authority, had it not been for the firm hand of the regent. Moreover, when King Henry attained his majority and took over the government of the Kingdom in person, his frequent intervention in the settlement of these local problems contributed to the growing hostility of the princes towards him. Ultimately also, Henry's efforts to curb the authority of the ecclesiastical princes, contrary to the policies of his father, contributed to Frederick's decision to depose his son.

Far more important to the future history of Germany were the external problems that faced the government during the regency, especially the relations of Germany with the ambitious Kingdom of Denmark under the regime of King Waldemar II. During his long conflict with his Welf opponent Otto IV, Frederick II, greatly in need of assistance in the north of the Kingdom, had, with the concurrence of the princes, concluded a treaty with Waldemar, recognizing the claims of the Danish King to the region between the Elbe and the Elde rivers which the Danes had conquered in 1201.[1] The German counts of that region had been compelled, reluctantly, to submit to the Danish overlordship. One of these vassals, Henry, Count of Schwerin, felt that he had suffered much damage under the Danish suzerainty. Every effort to obtain redress for alleged wrongs had resulted only in subjecting him to the ill will of his overlord. An opportunity for revenge arose in the spring of the year 1223 when King Waldemar, with his eldest son and a small following, was hunting in the island forest of Lyo where they were greeted in an apparently friendly manner by the Count. But, after feasting and drinking with them until almost dawn, and when the King and his son were asleep in their tent, Count Henry, with his men, entered and took them prisoners, seizing also a rich booty from the royal ship which was moored near by. The prisoners were bound and carried away to Dannenberg Castle in Lüneburg.[2]

Few events in Germany during the years of the regency made a more profound impression than this imprisonment of a powerful king by a mere count, for Waldemar, despite the smallness of Denmark, had created a formidable fleet and army which he had employed with extraordinary skill and foresight.[3] As head of the regency, Engelbert

[1] See above, pp. 164 ff.
[2] *Holsteinische Reimchronik* (*MGH, Deutsch. Chron.* ii), 620 ff.
[3] H. von Sybel, 'Deutschland und Dänemark' (*Hist. Zeitschr.* 12, 1852), 11.

could not remain aloof from this incident which had stirred the whole of Europe. The person of a king had been wronged, and by a count of the German Kingdom. Together with King Henry, Engelbert hastened to Nordhausen and there, with the Count of Schwerin, bargained for the release of the important prisoners into the hands of the royal government.[1] A tentative agreement was reached according to which the Count of Schwerin was to receive a substantial sum of silver marks and King Waldemar, after agreeing to yield all territory south of the Eider to its former possessors, was to be released to the royal authorities. It is to be assumed that Engelbert fully approved of this settlement since, on 26 September of the same year (1223), he granted to 'his dear friend, the Count, in recognition of the many services which he had performed for him in Saxony', a yearly supply of fifteen tuns of precious Rhine wine.[2] But, before Engelbert could conclude the final terms of the settlement with Waldemar, both the Pope and the Emperor intervened. Pope Honorius III, denouncing Henry of Schwerin as a common rebel, demanded that he be punished by the most extreme penalties for his crime 'against God and the Roman Church'.[3]

About the same time also the Pope told Engelbert to require of the Count of Schwerin that 'within a month from receiving the letters we have sent him on this matter he restore King Waldemar and his son to complete liberty and permit them to go freely with no obstacle of any kind'. If he refused to obey, the Count and all who were associated with him in his wrongdoing were to be excommunicated and the diocese placed under the interdict. The outraged Pope wrote also to the Emperor demanding that the royal prisoners be given their freedom, declaring that no king in the world would be safe if such acts of violence were permitted to go unpunished.[4] The Emperor, however, was as little disposed to act on the papal protest as he was to accept the Nordhausen agreement between Engelbert and King Waldemar. His objection may well have been that it was 'too much German and too little imperial'.[5]

Accordingly he took the negotiations from the hands of the regent and appointed instead a special commission, described as *nuntii imperii*, headed by Hermann of Salza, Grand Master of the Teutonic Order. This commission proceeded to Dannenberg where it met the Count of Schwerin and his associates and the Danish representatives, headed by Count Albert of Orlamünde. As a concession to the Pope, it was agreed first of all that Waldemar was to undertake a crusade to the Holy Land, actually in fulfilment of an earlier promise. He was to set out in August

---

[1] *Chronica regia Coloniensis*, p. 253; *Sächsische Weltchronik* (*MGH, Deutsch. Chron.* ii), 244.
[2] See the full account of this in von Sybel, loc. cit.
[3] Horoy, iv. 446.   [4] *MGH, Epist. Pont.* i. 166–8.
[5] H. von Sybel, op. cit. 17.

1226 with a hundred ships and to accomplish his crusade during the summer of 1227. If, for any cause, he was delayed, he was to pledge to the agents of the King of Jerusalem 20,000 marks of silver to be paid in August 1227. In addition, Waldemar was to give security for himself and for his successors for the Northalbingen region (Ditmarsh), and to surrender the rights which he had obtained during the throne conflict between Otto IV and Frederick II. The ransom of the King was fixed at 45,000 marks of silver.[1] Obviously, the agreement had been accepted by the Danes merely as a means of freeing the King and his son. Almost immediately after the release of King Waldemar II, preparations were begun to regain by force what had been lost. Meanwhile, the Germans, recognizing that their eastern colonial efforts would be of no avail if Waldemar succeeded in regaining his position on the Baltic, made a determined effort to resist. The princes, temporal and spiritual alike, whose territories were threatened by the ambitious Danish King, assembled all available manpower for the decisive conflict. Counts Adolf of Holstein, Henry of Schwerin, and other nobles, as well as the cities of Hamburg and Lübeck, participated in the assembling of the army of resistance. North of Segeberg, in an open plain near the village of Barnhövde, the encounter at length took place on 22 July 1227. The Danes were overwhelmingly defeated and lost for ever the dominant position which they had gained on the Baltic.[2]

The intervention of Frederick II in the affairs of Germany at this time, despite his preoccupation with Sicily and with preparations for a crusade, is indicative of the role which he was to retain for himself in the future. At no time did he cease to regard his son Henry (VII), although the latter was duly crowned King of the Romans, as subordinate to the Emperor. Moreover, the transfer of the negotiations from the regent, Engelbert, was in no sense a repudiation of the Archbishop's authority as the Emperor's agent. On the contrary, it was merely a recognition by Frederick that Engelbert, as Archbishop of Cologne and as regent, could not connive at the obvious wrongdoing of Count Henry of Schwerin, no matter how advantageous the results of his actions might be for Kingdom and Empire. For Frederick II the whole affair was an opportunity to reassert the imperial authority in the region of the Baltic.

In general, the relations between the Emperor and his regent in Germany were harmonious. The only significant difference arose over a matter of foreign policy. Frederick, indebted as he was to the King

---

[1] The essential terms of the agreement are to be found in the *Chronica regia Coloniensis*, 254, although not without errors.

[2] *Sächsische Weltchronik* (*MGH, Deutsch. Chron.* ii), 24–77; *Annales Stadenses* (*MGH, SS.* xvi), 359.

of France for his support during the throne conflict, desired to continue
the alliance originally formed with Philip Augustus. In November 1226
King Louis VIII sent an embassy to Sicily to negotiate with the
Emperor for the renewal of the treaty made between Philip Augustus
and Frederick II in 1212 at Maxey-sur-Vaise near Vaucouleurs.[1] The
new treaty of 1224 was even more binding than the earlier one. The
contracting parties agreed to form no alliance with the King of England or with his heirs. They mutually agreed also to give no aid to or
to harbour rebels, enemies, or outlaws of the other.

Meanwhile, Archbishop Engelbert, faithful to the traditions of
Cologne, desired to institute close political and economic ties with
England. Soon after the death of Philip Augustus it seemed to Engelbert
that the moment had come for severing the alliance with France which
had served as a barrier to a *rapprochement* with England. Accordingly,
he dispatched an embassy to the King of England with a plan for a
diplomatic marriage between young Henry (VII) and Isabella, sister
of the English King, Henry III. His plan went even further, suggesting
a marriage alliance between the English King and a daughter of the
Duke of Austria.[2] On the other hand, Frederick II was determined
not only to continue the alliance with the King of France, his 'brother
and friend', but to push through the marriage of his son Henry to
Margaret, eldest daughter of the Duke of Austria, despite the support
of Engelbert's plan by the German princes (their support had been
obtained at the Diet of Ulm in January 1224). Accordingly, in conformity with the Emperor's wishes, the marriage of Henry (VII) and
Margaret of Austria was celebrated at Nuremberg on 25 November
1225.[3] Engelbert, who had never ceased to seek to further his own plans
for an English alliance, did not live to witness the celebration of the
marriage of his ward. Two weeks before this event the Archbishop was
murdered by a relative as the result of a private quarrel.[4] During the
following year Louis, Duke of Bavaria, was chosen by the Emperor to
succeed Engelbert as regent and as guardian of Henry (VII).[5]

The regency of Louis presented a striking contrast to that of the
powerful and energetic Engelbert of Cologne. The fundamental difference arose from the dominant personality of the Archbishop, one of
the most conspicuous examples of the half-temporal, half-spiritual
princes of thirteenth-century Germany. Where Engelbert often pursued

---

[1] See above, pp. 262 ff. See also A. Cartellieri, *Philipp II Augustus*, iv. 332, and, for the
instrument itself, Guillelmus Armoricus, *De Gestis Philippi* (*RHGF* xvii), 85, note b.
[2] See the letter of Walter, Bishop of Carlisle, to Henry III (Huillard-Bréholles, ii), 833;
Rymer, *Foedera*, i. 275. See also A. W. Leeper, *A History of Medieval Austria* (Oxford, 1941), 302.
[3] *Cronica Reinhardsbrunnensis* (*MGH, SS*. xxx), 603.
[4] Caesar of Heisterbach, *Vita*, Bk. II, chs. i ff.; *Chronica regia Coloniensis*, 255.
[5] *Cronica Reinhardsbrunnensis* (*MGH, SS*. xxx), 605.

a policy of virtual independence, Louis of Bavaria, with few exceptions, acted *de plenitudine concilii nostri*.[1] Equally significant during his regency was the growing influence of the Swabian *ministeriales*, especially that of the two branches of the Tanne family, the Waldburgs and the Winterstettins. During the last years of Louis's regency his documents indicate a gradual disappearance of some of the more powerful ecclesiastical princes from the court and a temporary increase in the influence of a small group of temporal princes. The most influential of these was Leopold of Austria, father-in-law of Henry (VII), until his voluntary withdrawal from the court in 1228.

The absence of the strong hand of Engelbert resulted also in the outbreak of many local feuds in various regions of the Kingdom of Germany, which seriously threatened the royal authority. It had been one of the features of Engelbert's regency that he had prevented these petty local conflicts from seriously involving the regency. Unrest developed in Germany, especially following the death of the Count Palatinate, Henry of Saxony, and the succession of his son, Otto of Lüneberg. It is a remarkable feature of these years, however, that the excommunication of Frederick II in 1227 had little effect on the loyalty of most of the German princes to the Emperor. Meanwhile, the persistent tendency of young King Henry to slight or to ignore Louis of Bavaria heightened the feeling of insecurity throughout the Kingdom. During the year 1228 a rumour was spread abroad that Louis of Bavaria and other princes were unfaithful to the royal interests. The King himself seems to have been convinced that Louis had been in secret communication with the Pope and others who were known to be plotting the destruction of the Staufen family, following the excommunication of Frederick.[2] The rumour appeared all the more plausible when Cardinal Otto of St. Nicholas arrived in Germany as legate of the Pope with the intention of doing injury to the Emperor, and to this end, conferred with Otto, Duke of Lüneburg.[3] The machinations of the papal legate afforded Henry (VII) an excuse to do what he had long contemplated: assume control of the German government and free himself from further interference by the regent. In making this decision, however, he alienated not only Duke Louis of Bavaria, but also his father-in-law, Leopold of Austria. Both these princes now absented themselves from the royal court after September 1228, although the definitive break seems to have taken place some time during the Christmas festivities at Hagenau.[4]

---

[1] See examples in Huillard-Bréholles, ii, part ii, 879, 882, 908; iii. 376, and many others.
[2] *Notae Sancti Emmerammi* (*MGH, SS.* xvii), 576; *Annales Scheftlarienses maiores* (*MGH, SS.* xvii), 338.
[3] *Chronica regia Coloniensis*, 260–1.
[4] *Annales Scheftlarienses maiores* (*MGH, SS.* xvii), 338.

The independent rule of Henry (VII) was jeopardized from the out-set, not only by the intrigues of the papal legate Otto, but even more by the open hostility of the Duke of Bavaria. The young King sought valiantly to protect the imperial interests in Germany during his father's absence in the Holy Land, although, as the sequel to his efforts will reveal, they often gave rise to actions which were contrary to the policies of his father. Fortunately, for the time being, Louis of Bavaria found little support among the German princes and nobles. It is remarkable that the King did not immediately undertake a punitive expedition against the Duke; but he did not do so until late August 1229, when, 'with a large army, King Henry invaded the territory of the Duke along the Danube'. On 27 August he compelled Louis to accept an armistice and, subsequently, a treaty of peace in which the Duke pledged his future loyalty.[1]

Meanwhile, the papal legate, having failed to obtain the consent of the Duke of Brunswick to oppose the Staufen interests or to find an acceptable anti-king, was compelled to content himself with the organiza-tion of a faction to support the interests of the Pope against the King and Emperor. He achieved his greatest success among the begging friars who, recently established in Germany, at first found little sym-pathy among the ecclesiastical princes. The royal documents continue to bear witness to the loyalty of the great majority of ecclesiastical princes to the Staufen interests during the Emperor's absence in Syria and during the conflict with the Pope after his return. Despite their growing discontent with King Henry, from whose court they often absented themselves, their attitude towards Frederick II was, with rare exceptions, consistently loyal. The most striking feature of the period of self-government of Henry (VII) at this time was the extra-ordinary influence exerted by the Swabian *ministeriales* at the court. Where formerly they had functioned chiefly as court officials, carrying out the policies of the regent and his council of ecclesiastical princes, they now became advisers of the King. The Waldburgs and the Winterstettins in particular were responsible for many of the policies that alienated the once-powerful ecclesiastical princes and contributed to the break of Henry (VII) with his father. Meanwhile, Frederick's negotiations with the Pope after his successful reconquest of the King-dom of Sicily drew the German princes once more into close association with the Emperor. It was their mediation during the summer of 1230 that succeeded in bringing about a reconciliation of the Pope and Emperor.[2]

---

[1] Ibid. 339. See also Henry's letter (Huillard-Bréholles, iv, part ii), 683.

[2] *Burchardi Chronicon* (*MGH, SS.* xxiii), 383. See also C. Rodenberg, 'Die Vorverhandlungen zum Frieden von S. Germano' (*Neues Archiv*, 1892–3, xviii), 203, and the extracts from the letter of Thomas of Capua, 182 ff.

Relations between Henry (VII) and the German princes deteriorated rapidly from the moment he assumed independent authority in the Kingdom. Just as Frederick II, during his eight years in Germany, had been faced with the growing independence of these princes, so Henry was compelled to witness the weakening of the royal authority through their obstinate demands for greater autonomy. Again like his father, the young King could not ignore the rapidly developing municipalities which, with their ever-expanding commercial interests, were outgrowing the restrictive governments of their princely overlords. Unlike his father, however, Henry did not feel deeply obligated to the princes for his crown. Frederick had constantly found himself indebted to them for their assistance during his residence in Germany between 1212 and 1220, not only for their aid in maintaining peace but also for aid in winning the imperial crown. Where he had regarded them as 'pillars of the realm', his son found them only hindrances to his power. Almost the last official act of Frederick II before his departure for Rome in 1220 was to grant privileges to the ecclesiastical princes in return for their election of his son as King. If Henry was aware of this, he dismissed it as a misfortune which now resulted in the restricted exercise of his royal authority. Indeed every step of Frederick II towards obtaining the imperial crown had served to weaken the position of his son and successor as German King. Even now, in 1229–30, Frederick obligated himself still further to the princes, both temporal and spiritual, by permitting them to serve as his mediators with the Pope. He was in no position to ignore whatever further demands they might make for new and far-reaching privileges. Thus Henry (VII) found himself once more the victim of his father's policies.

Moreover, Henry, in contrast with Frederick II, was nationally or particularistically minded rather than imperialistic. Always he appears as the champion of centralized authority in Germany. Obviously, this attitude led to his several efforts to stay the independent tendencies of the principalities which showed persistent signs of becoming states within the state. At the same time he was more disposed to favour the cities in their efforts to liberate themselves from the dominance of their princely overlords. Henry's determination to free himself from restraints imposed by the princes became even more pronounced as his self-confidence increased after his successful expedition against Louis of Bavaria in 1229, and after his equally successful opposition to the papal intrigues in Germany during his father's excommunication and absence in the Holy Land. By 1230 he openly opposed the two troublesome policies of his father: that of yielding to the demands of the territorial princes, and the curbing of the efforts of the communes to attain their independence. Illustrative of Henry's more liberal policies towards the cities were his grants of privileges to Liège, Verdun, Nimwegen, and other cities.[1] Temporarily he could pursue this liberal policy with impunity during the absence of many of the princes in Italy as intermediaries between the Emperor and Pope. The day of reckoning, however, could not be long postponed; Henry must soon face powerful ecclesiastical princes in whose territories so many of the larger cities were located.[2]

On their return from Italy after the peace of San Germano, the princes, obviously with the support of the Emperor, lost little time in compelling Henry to revoke the extensive privileges which he had granted to the cities. It was under this pressure that between 20 January 1230 and 1 May 1231, during a diet at Worms, laws were promulgated strengthening the authority of the princes over their cities. These restrictive measures forbade the cities to establish communes, to promulgate codes of laws, to form brotherhoods, or to enter into any kind of confederacy. More significant was the victory of the princes in the promulgation of the *Constitutio in Favorem Principum* of 1 May 1231, which safeguarded their privileges in minutest detail,[3] a document which later the Emperor also felt obliged to confirm.

Theoretically, Henry's policies, aimed as they were at curtailing the independence of the principalities and at strengthening the economic potentialities of the communes, were sound. The paradox of this clash of interests between Emperor and King is that Henry was pursuing precisely the same policy with regard to the cities that Frederick himself had vainly attempted to follow during his early years in Germany. It is obvious that Frederick had abandoned his liberal policy towards the cities only because he recognized that the support of the territorial princes was essential to the achievement of his imperial goal. While he had usually received some kind of fair exchange, some *quid pro quo*, for his concessions, Henry was now compelled to sacrifice sovereignty itself. The *Constitutio* of 1231 was not merely a grant of privilege, it was a signing away of sovereign authority, and so irreparably damaging to the central administration and to the judicial authority of the King. It is doubtful whether Henry (VII) was aware, as his father was, of the political dangers inherent in the granting of too great independence to the communes. Frederick's experience in Italy, especially in Lombardy and Tuscany, had left him no illusions as to the aspirations or the determination of the freedom-loving communes.

While these differences of outlook between father and son were an important contributing factor in the growing unrest in Germany, other

---

[1] Huillard-Bréholles, iii. 331, note 2, 425 ff.
[2] See especially E. Franzel, *König Heinrich (VII)*, 130 ff.
[3] *MGH, Const.* ii. 413 f., 418 ff.

causes were also present; symptoms of this unrest had appeared at the moment of Henry's break with Louis of Bavaria and Leopold of Austria, his father-in-law. Henry wanted also to divorce his wife, Margaret of Austria, and to marry Agnes, the daughter of Ottokar I, King of Bohemia.[1] Most of all, however, the tension between Frederick and his son was heightened by their failure to agree as to the actual status of the King in relation to the Emperor. Was Henry king, in fact, or was he an imperial vicar, subject always to the will of the Emperor? There came a time when Henry made it clear that he regarded himself as an independent German king and that he was growing more and more restive under his father's restraints. Frederick, on the other hand, especially after his return from the Holy Land and his successful reconquest of Sicily, displayed an ever-increasing tendency to establish his imperial authority. He saw in his son merely a provincial governor responsible for the scrupulous implementation of his imperial policies where Germany was concerned. Well aware of his son's attitude, Frederick, after making peace with the Pope, determined to clarify the respective positions of Emperor and King. When he had last seen his son Henry, he was still a boy, and Frederick seems to have failed to comprehend the effects of years of separation and of the growing self-confidence of a youth upon attaining his mature years. Preoccupation with the affairs of Sicily and of Northern Italy necessarily postponed any final agreement with his son at this time. The unsettled conditions in Lombardy now claimed his special attention. As conditions worsened there he made known his intentions to convene a diet in Ravenna for the purpose of restoring order.[2] That city had been chosen as a meeting-place upon the advice of the Pope, and the date agreed upon was 1 November 1231. A special letter of Frederick summoned the Diet, the object of which was 'to restore the universal peace of the Empire and to dispose affairs in Italy to a state of prosperity and peace'. In another letter he bade the Milanese to refrain from further aggression against the Piedmontese, assuring them that, in agreement with the Pope, he was coming into Lombardy for the purpose of establishing enduring friendly relationships.[3] Such appeals, however, served only to revive the old suspicions as to the actual motives of the Emperor. Once more the Milanese group of cities moved to re-establish the Lombard League. In a meeting of their representatives in Bologna on 26 October 1231 it was resolved to assemble an army of some 3,000 mounted troops, 10,000 foot soldiers, and 1,500 bowmen. The members of the League

---

[1] Conrad of Fabaria, *Casus S. Galli* (*MGH, SS.* ii), 180; *Annales Wormatienses* (*MGH, SS.* xvii), 43.

[2] Huillard-Bréholles, iii. 282.

[3] Ibid. iv, part i, 266 f., and Piero della Vigna, *Epist.* ii. 16.

appealed to the Pope also for assurance that the Emperor would not be accompanied by an army during his stay in Ravenna.[1]

In view of the hostile attitude of the Lombard League, it is not improbable that the Emperor, long before arriving in Ravenna, had recognized that the diet must necessarily turn its attention primarily to conditions in Germany and, for the moment at least, leave in abeyance the restoration of 'prosperity and peace' in Italy. This undoubtedly is the explanation for the small following which accompanied him to Ravenna. Meanwhile, the Lombard League, as in 1226, blocked the passes of the Alps to prevent the entrance of the Germans into Italy.[2]

Henry (VII), now resolved upon an independent policy, chose to ignore the summons of his father to the Diet of Ravenna and betook himself in December to the royal palace in Hagenau, where he remained throughout the Christmas festivities.[3] The summons seems to have applied solely to the King and princes whose presence was desired at the Diet of Ravenna. But the hostility of the Lombard League compelled the postponement of the formal opening of the Diet until Christmas. Some German princes succeeded in crossing the barriers in disguise (*occulte venerant ad tapinum*). When, at length, the Diet of Ravenna was actually assembled, its activities were limited largely to punitive measures against the Lombard League for continuing to bar the Alpine passes and to the settlement of a dispute with the Genoese. At a meeting held in mid January (1232) in the palace of the Archbishop of Ravenna the recalcitrant Lombard cities were again placed under imperial outlawry. At the same time Frederick also took punitive measures against the city of Genoa which, in defiance of the Emperor's orders, had chosen a Milanese as *podestà*. Despite the protests and excuses of the Genoese, the Emperor held firmly to his pronouncement against such elections, thus alienating the Genoese, who insisted upon the right of freedom of election. The unyielding attitude of the Emperor caused great unrest among the citizens of Genoa, some desiring to join the League. Others, however, favoured the Emperor, and the city, in a final showdown, abstained from allying with the League.[4]

After pronouncing the ban against the Lombard League, Frederick summoned a new diet to be held in Aquileia, again ordering his son to be present.[5] Because of his determination to prolong his absence from the Kingdom of Sicily he also designated as his representatives there Count Thomas of Acerra as Captain and Military Leader and the Grand Justiciar, Henry of Morra, as head of the Civil administration.[6]

---

[1] John Codagnellus, *Annales*, 109.
[2] *Annales Sancti Rudberti Salisburgenses (MGH, SS.* ix), 785; *Annales Janvenses (Fonti,* iii), 59.
[3] BFW, *Reg.* v, Abt. i, nos. 4221–3.
[4] *Annales Janvenses (Fonti,* iii), 59–60, 63.   [5] John Codagnellus, *Annales,* 110f.
[6] Richard of San Germano, 177 (Jan. 1232).

Henry (VII) seems to have contemplated absenting himself also from the Diet in Aquileia. There can be little doubt that already he was considering open revolt against the Emperor. He could not have been ignorant of the unfavourable reaction of the princes as well as of the Emperor to his ignoring the summons to Ravenna, since it is known that some of the *ministeriales* with whom he was most intimate had returned to Germany after attending the Diet.[1] It was during this time that, having alienated many of the princes, he relied almost exclusively on the *ministeriales*. A privilege of his to the city of Worms of mid March 1232 states that 'the most exalted Lord Emperor, our father, made over to and committed to our authority the country of Germany without restrictions'.[2] This was clearly in defiance of the Emperor and it completely ignored the legislation of the princes at Worms during the preceding May. It was probably the influence of the Chancellor, Bishop Siegfried of Regensburg, and of the royal steward Werner of Boland, who had returned from Ravenna in March, that caused a change in the attitude of the young King. The Chancellor had previously been urged (by the Pope and the German princes of the Diet) to use all his influence to prevent the King from opposing his father.[3]

Meanwhile, Frederick II, with many princes and magnates, set out about 7 March from Ravenna by the sea route to Aquileia. He also visited Venice where he entered into an agreement with the Doge and Council providing for freedom of trade between Venice and the Kingdom of Sicily.[4] It was not until the second week of May 1232 that he was joined in Aquileia by King Henry and some German princes.[5] It is indicative of the strained relations between father and son that Henry was assigned quarters in Cividale del Friuli, a few miles north of Aquileia. The Emperor was in no mood to deal leniently with his son, and it was only after the intercession of the princes that he refrained from inflicting rigorous punishment upon young Henry.[6] The oath which he required of Henry shows how little confidence the Emperor had in his son's intentions. The text of the oath has not survived, but in a letter to Pope Gregory IX, dated 10 April 1233, Henry repeated the essential articles. He pledged himself in no wise to injure the person, the lands, the honour, or the dignity of his father. He also agreed under oath to dismiss all hostile advisers and to accept deposition and excommunication voluntarily if he failed to live up to his promise. But the Emperor demanded even more. The King was compelled to request the

---

[1] Huillard-Bréholles, iv, part ii, 558.   [2] Ibid. 564.
[3] BFW, *Reg.* v, Abt. iii, 6877.
[4] See above, p. 273.
[5] *Chronica regia Coloniensis*, 263; *Annales Placentini Gibellini* (*MGH, SS.* xviii), 470.
[6] The relations of Henry (VII) and Frederick have been dealt with in detail by P. Reinhold, *Die Empörung König Heinrichs (VII) gegen seinen Vater*.

princes of Germany to stand surety for his future conduct.[1] Such was the outcome of this meeting between father and son—the first in ten years. It is inconceivable that the King, Hohenstaufen that he was, possessed of a will of his own, as he had so abundantly demonstrated before leaving Germany, could have accepted these terms save with profound humiliation. Further events were soon to reveal the impermanence of a reconciliation which, if accepted at face value, could have resulted only in crushing the spirit of an active and ambitious sovereign.

But, if the German princes intervened on behalf of the young King in his quarrel with the Emperor, they seized the opportunity also for pressing home their own demands for greater freedom. They had greatly influenced the agenda of the Diet, which consisted chiefly of complaints against the independent tendencies of the German cities. Essentially their demands were for the imperial sanctioning of the all-comprehensive laws that had been promulgated at Worms the previous May.[2] Most of the privileges granted were not new. The significance of the *Constitutio in Favorem Principum*, sanctioned at this time by Frederick II, is that it collected and codified previous scattered laws and privileges that opposed the independence of the cities. What the ecclesiastical princes hoped for, and actually what they achieved at Aquileia, was the nullification of all laws and privileges of the cities previously granted by various emperors, kings, archbishops, and bishops. Like the *Confoederatio* of 1220, the *Constitutio* of 1231–2 was aimed at giving to the ecclesiastical princes complete supervision over all local legislation and all local administration, nullifying all statutes made by burghers or by guilds contrary to the wishes of the bishops. Moreover, all officials and functionaries of whatever degree, not previously authorized by the bishops, were to be dismissed and all guilds disbanded. Only the coinages of the respective princes were to pass as legal tender. Much more comprehensive than its counterpart in the *Confoederatio* of 1220 was the section in the *Constitutio* concerning the right of fortification and the erection of buildings in the territory of a prince or bishop. The new statue of 1231–2 included the significant concession by the Emperor that 'no new castles or cities shall be erected by us [i.e. Emperor or King], or by anyone else to the prejudice of the princes'. Thus the young King's obstinate resistance to the powerful ecclesiastical princes had made it possible for them to exact from the Emperor a sovereign right which previously Frederick II had safeguarded. The King of Germany and the Emperor were virtually excluded from the independent principalities. It is noteworthy also that in the *Confoederatio* of 1220 only the

---

[1] Huillard-Bréholles, iv, part ii, 952–3, and part i, 325–6.
[2] *MGH, Const.* ii, no. 171, pp. 211–13, and no. 304, pp. 418 ff.

ecclesiastical princes and the King were concerned; in the *Constitutio* or *Statutum* a third party, the temporal princes, was included. A feature of the *Constitutio* was its weakening of the status of the cities which, as independent and prosperous communities allied with the central government, could have provided a formidable medium for curbing the growing sovereignty of the principalities.[1]

These restrictions, however, in no way applied to the royal or imperial cities of Germany. Indirectly, they proved an advantage to the latter, leaving them free to continue their more or less unimpeded development. The royal government continued as before to promote trade, to grant mercantile privileges, to aid in the building of walls and highways, despite complaints from the princes that this policy was injurious to their interests and contrary to the principles of the *Constitutio*.[2] Frederick's decision at this time, certainly made most reluctantly, to favour the princes and to extend to them an even greater independence than before, proved fateful for the future history of Germany, placing a final stamp of approval upon a movement already sanctioned by his predecessors: the substitution of a confederation of principalities for monarchy, feudal decentralization for the unity of a kingdom.[3]

[1] H. Mitteis, *Der Staat des hohen Mittelalters*, 400ff.
[2] See, for example, *MGH, Const.* ii, no. 324.
[3] See also K. Hampe, *Kaisergeschichte*, 289, and P. Kirn, 'Die Verdienste der staufischen Kaiser um das Deutsche Reich' (*Hist. Zeitschr.* 164, 1941), 269ff.

II

HENRY (VII) IN REBELLION AGAINST THE EMPEROR

Novit vero ille qui nihil ignorat et qui scrutator cordium est et rerum,
. . . quod postquam a tenera etate recessimus . . . nunquam aliquid eorum
fecimus ex certa scientia vel ex animo que deberent paterno affectui
displicere aut etiam que offendere possent imperatoriam majestatem.

> Letter of Henry (VII) to the Pope (Huillard-Bréholles,
> iv, part ii, 686)[1]

THE meeting in Aquileia could have given but little satisfaction either to Frederick II or to his son. The nature of the guarantees exacted from Henry and from the German princes suggests how little confidence the Emperor had in the permanence of the reconciliation, while the depth of the humiliation of the young King could lead only to an inextinguishable resentment towards his father. Temporarily their relationship appeared to have been improved. Frederick's preoccupation with the affairs of Lombardy probably explains his noninterference in Germany between 1232 and 1234. The few imperial documents relating to Germany during these years suggest, superficially, a want of interest or lack of concern with affairs north of the Alps. Henry (VII) also seems for the moment to have yielded to the full participation of the German princes in the government of the Kingdom. Indicative of this was the activity of several powerful and influential ecclesiastical and temporal princes in the Diet of Frankfurt in August 1232. Again, the princes appeared with him at Hagenau where he had summoned the bishops, counts, and barons of Alsace in May or June of the following year. So too in July 1233 large numbers of princes complied with the royal summons to Mainz.[2] There appears in the co-operative spirit in which the King and princes proceeded in the vexing problem of heretical persecution at Mainz some evidence that Henry now recognized the council of princes as essential to the successful administration of the royal government. Also the large numbers of

---

[1] He who is ignorant of naught and the scrutinizer of hearts and deeds knows that since our departure from childhood we have done nothing wittingly, either in thought or in deed, that could displease paternal affection or offend imperial majesty.

[2] Huillard-Bréholles, iv, part ii, 579; *Annales Marbacenses*, 95; *Chronica regia Coloniensis*, 265.

privileges and safe conducts granted at this time by the central government to churches, monasteries, and other spiritual establishments, as well as to princes and minor nobles, are evidences of the King's co-operation with the princes and of the increase in his prestige among influential circles in Germany. It has been observed also that the intercourse of all classes with the royal court was as active as it had been during the regency of Engelbert of Cologne.[1]

During these years there is little or no evidence of a preponderant influence of the *ministeriales* at the royal court. A more striking example of Henry's apparent reconciliation with the princely class was his friendliness towards the Bishop and the citizens of Strassburg, whom he had so bitterly opposed during the sojourn there of the papal legate, Otto of St. Nicholas, a few years before.[2]

Despite these several instances of Henry's acquiescence in the will of his father, there is no evidence suggesting that he no longer resented the humiliation to which he had been subjected in Aquileia. Even when he accepted his princely advisers in place of his more intimate friends among the Swabian *ministeriales* he could not escape the conviction that he was constantly under the surveillance of an essentially unfriendly group. It is hardly to be doubted that, at least surreptitiously, he continued to seek the counsel of his more congenial associates. He clung steadfastly to the conviction that his formal election as German King carried with it the inherent implication of independent authority. The old tension between the ecclesiastical princes and the cities persisted and might at any moment involve the King in decisions which would reveal the conflict between the royal and imperial policies.

It was most unfortunate that just at this time heresies, spreading throughout Europe, often in epidemic proportions, made their appearance in various regions of Germany, contributing to the unrest which endangered the peaceful relationships of the King, both with the Pope and the Emperor. It is not the place here to treat these different heresies in detail, but rather to emphasize how, individually and collectively, they were considered by both the Pope and Emperor as dangerous and disturbing influences in the established social order, the *societas christiana*. As heresies increased in Germany and in Italy during the decade following the imperial coronation, measures of repression and persecution inevitably became more severe. This was contemporaneous with the establishment and growth of the mendicant orders in Germany during the regency of Engelbert, the Archbishop of Cologne, and with the more aggressive policies of Ugolino Conti of Segni as protector of the Orders, first as Cardinal and, subsequently, as Pope Gregory IX.

---

[1] J. Rohden, 'Der Sturz Heinrichs (VII.)' (*FzDG* xxii, 1882), 356.
[2] Huillard-Bréholles, iv, part ii, 604–5.

It has been justly observed, however, that widespread persecution of heretics by the Dominicans in Germany, even after 1232, when they became active agents of the Inquisition, cannot be substantiated, and that it is an exaggeration to speak of persecutions of heretics in the whole of Germany. On the contrary, the extreme persecutions, those instigated and authorized by Conrad of Marburg, were limited almost exclusively to the diocese of Mainz.[1]

The uncompromising policies of severity of Frederick II towards heresy, one of the chief causes of friction between himself and his son Henry (VII), can be understood only in the light of Frederick's often-expressed belief in the necessity for the preservation of the indissoluble union between the Roman Church and himself; for, no matter how antagonistic he was towards individual Popes or, indeed, towards the papacy, he never lost sight of the importance of the Roman Church in the perpetuation of the Empire.[2] The policy of Frederick II with regard to heresy was to receive its supreme test by virtue of the activities of Conrad of Marburg and his associates as agents of the Inquisition in Germany. On the one hand, there was an almost fanatical devotion to the religious austerity evoked by the hatred of heresy and, on the other, a rising resentment at the reckless exercise of authority by the inquisitors.

A tragic devotee to Conrad's religious ideas was Elizabeth, widow of Louis of Thuringia, who, as the companion of Frederick II on the ill-fated crusade of 1227, had died of the plague while sailing from Brindisi to Otranto. The widowed Landgravine, daughter of the King of Hungary, had been taken while still a child from her native land, to be reared in the luxurious Thuringian court, pending her marriage to young Louis, the heir to the principality, only to be left alone in a foreign land, in the unfriendly atmosphere of the Wartburg palace, when her husband departed on a crusade, never to return. Already fascinated by the Franciscan ideal of poverty and pathologically inclined towards self-abnegation (as were many of her contemporaries), she yielded completely to the influence of her confessor, the harsh and unbending priest, Conrad of Marburg. Gladly she submitted to the whip of her fanatical confessor, thus strengthening her belief in the emptiness of all temporal things, while sharing the suffering of Christ in her anticipation of heavenly bliss. By the austerity of her life, her more than child-like piety, her affectation of a life of poverty, and her unquestioning trust in Jesus, she became, in the eyes of her contemporaries, a symbol of

---

[1] L. Förg, *Die Ketzerverfolgung in Deutschland unter Gregor IX.*, 70 ff. See also Caesar of Heisterbach, *Vita* (Böhmer, *Fontes*, ii), ch. ix, and K. Langosch, *Caesarius*, 49 ff.

[2] Huillard-Bréholles, i, part ii, 749: 'ad conservandum inter nos et Romanam Ecclesiam indissolubile vinculum.'

Christian saintliness. Her early death, in her twenty-fourth year, undoubtedly heightened this aura and led to her early canonization in 1235, only a short time after her death.[1]

It was this over-zealous priest who was authorized as early as 1227 by Pope Gregory IX to enlist the aid of a few appropriate companions for the purpose of conducting investigations of all alleged heretics. At that time Gregory praised Conrad for the meticulous care and the zeal with which he ferreted out heresies 'in patribus Teutonie'.[2] In 1231 Conrad's authority was further extended when he, his chosen companions, and the preaching friars were entrusted with the actual conduct of inquisitions, independently of the bishops who previously had been responsible for such proceedings.[3] It was after his investiture with this independent authority that Conrad began his cruel and unnatural punishments of alleged heretics, stimulated by the religious unrest in the Rhineland which swept that region of Germany simultaneously with the 'great Halleluja' in the March of Treviso in Italy, led by the Dominican friar, John of Vicenza.[4]

Inherent in the authorization of Conrad and his associates were the seeds of discord between the bishops and these more or less independent inquisitors. Moreover, the zeal of Conrad was such that, once authorized, his measures were as rigorous as they were unwarranted. Fanatic that he was, Conrad did not seek proof of heresy against those who were maliciously accused, but accepted as evidence any accusation or denunciation, seizing all suspects and consigning them, often as the result of false testimony, to be burned alive. As long as his irresponsible acts were confined to the lower classes he remained immune to the restraints of bishops or lay princes. When, however, his unbridled zeal carried him into the ranks of the nobility, involving Count Henry of Sayn and others of his class, widespread unrest resulted.[5] Powerful opposition now developed throughout Germany into a determined effort to check the

---

[1] For the life of St. Elizabeth and the activities of Conrad of Marburg see: H. Mielke, *Die heilige Elisabeth* (Sammlung genienständlicher Vorträge, N.F. Serie 6, Heft 125), especially pp. 30 ff., K. Wenck, *Die heilige Elisabeth*; P. Braun, *Beichtvater d. heiligen Elisabeth und deutscher Inquisitor, Konrad von Marburg* (Beiträge zur hessischen Kirchengeschichte, iv, 1909–11), 253; A. Hauck, *Kirchengeschichte*, iv. 925 ff., and his sketch of the pertinent sources, note 1; J. Ancelet-Hustache, *Sainte Élisabeth de Hongrie*. Notwithstanding its erotic implications, the work of E. Busse-Wilson, *Das Leben der heiligen Elisabeth von Thüringia*, is useful in setting forth a more plausible interpretation of Elizabeth's asceticism. In opposition, however, see W. Mauerer, 'Zum Verständnis der heiligen Elisabeth von Thuringia' (*Zeitschr. für Kirchengeschichte*, lxv, 1934–5), 16–64.

[2] *MGH, Epist. Pont.* i, no. 362, p. 277.

[3] Winkelmann, *Acta*, i, no. 624, p. 499.

[4] Dealt with at length by C. Sutter, *Johann von Vicenza und die italienische Friedenbewegung im Jahre 1233*.

[5] *Chronica regia Coloniensis*, 264. See also A. Hauck, *Kirchengeschichte*, vol. iv, 1st and 2nd edns., p. 883, notes 1 and 2; 3rd and 4th edns., p. 918, notes 1 and 2; he has assembled the pertinent sources.

irresponsible persecutions. The Archbishops of Mainz and Trier, together with men from all classes, appealed to the King to intervene and to check the activities of Conrad of Marburg and his associates. In conformity with the wishes of Henry (VII), a synod was held in Mainz on 25 July 1233 which dealt not only with the appeal of the accused Count of Sayn but with the whole question of the inquisition. The Synod sent an embassy to the Pope to set before him the numerous complaints and to appeal for measures of relief. At first the Pope was disturbed by these reports but further developments in Germany caused him to alter his plan of action. Conrad of Marburg, greatly incensed at the proceedings in Mainz and at the hostility of the bishops, left the city with the intention of returning to Marburg. While on his way he was murdered on 30 July 1233. The news of this murder so angered Pope Gregory that he destroyed the document which he had prepared for the embassy from the Synod of Mainz.[1] The Pope, obviously blinded by his intense hatred and fear of heresy, failed to grasp the seriousness of the unrest in Germany. Meanwhile, on 11 February 1234, during a diet at Frankfurt, King Henry, exasperated by the fanatical persecutions, used intemperate language in condemning all such activities, even going so far as to accuse the Bishop of Hildesheim of preaching a crusade against heretics. The Bishop had undoubtedly shown poor judgement in bestowing the emblem of the cross upon those who actively opposed heresy, contrary to the traditional use of the cross as an emblem to be worn only by those who fought the infidel.[2]

The role of Henry (VII) throughout this deplorable episode can only be characterized as highly commendable, revealing the superior enlightenment that one habitually associates with his father. It is all the more lamentable, therefore, that a sovereign such as Frederick II, whose general cultural level was so far above the bigotry common to his era, could, for reasons of political expediency, sanction laws against heresy so far below the level of enlightenment revealed in the laws of Henry (VII), promulgated on 11 February 1234. The explanation is to be found, not in bigotry, but rather in Frederick's concept of *ecclesia* and *imperium* as coincidental, made so by the wisdom of Divine Providence, so that defiance of the authority inherent in either of these was heresy. Thus in his *Liber Augustalis* he said of heretics: 'they wish to unstitch the seamless coat of Our Lord . . . We decree that they be delivered to the flames in the sight of the people.'[3] However praiseworthy the

---

[1] *Annales Wormatienses* (*MGH, SS.* xvii), 40; *Gesta Treverorum Continuatio Quarta* (*MGH, SS.* xxiv), 402; *Chronica regia Coloniensis*, 265; *Chronica Albrici Trium Fontium* (*MGH, SS.* xxiii), 931 f., *MGH, Epist. Pont.* i, nos. 451, 453, 454.

[2] *Annales Erphordenses* (*MGH, SS.* xvi), 28; *Gesta Treverorum* (*MGH, SS.* xxiv), 402; *Sächsische Weltchronik* (*MGH, Deutsch. Chron.* ii), 250.

[3] Huillard-Bréholles, iv, part i, 5–7. Ibid., part ii, 635 ff., for the laws of Henry (VII).

enlightened procedure of Henry (VII) was, he had acted contrary to the approved policies of both Pope and Emperor. Even though his policy concerning heresy might not in itself have provoked a conflict with his father, he further compromised his position by antagonizing certain German princes whose friendship was at that time of the utmost usefulness to the Emperor.

In 1233 Henry assembled an army of some 6,000 troops with which he invaded the territory of Otto II of Bavaria, who had recently succeeded his father, Louis, the former guardian of Henry (VII). Perhaps the invasion was induced by hostile acts of Otto, inspired by the prevalent gossip that the Emperor had instigated the murder of the late Duke. Henry (VII) in his manifesto of 2 September 1234 defended his invasion of Bavaria by saying that it had been undertaken in the service of his father.[1] The expedition had been arranged at the Diet of Mainz to which many princes had been summoned to consider the question of heresy, and must have been undertaken with the full knowledge, if not the approval, of them. A contemporary, in describing the expedition into Bavaria, says of it: 'The King, with many princes and a large army, entered Bavaria with the object of destroying the Duke, but through the mediation of the Archbishop of Salzburg peace was made, and Otto gave his young son to the king as hostage.'[2]

But the Duke of Bavaria was not the only prince offended at this time by Henry (VII). With the advice of some (at least) of the princes, he had also undertaken a punitive expedition against several Swabian nobles and *ministeriales*, friends of the Emperor, including Counts Conrad and Godfrey of Hohenlohe and the Margrave of Baden, because of their alleged acts of violence. He had destroyed their castles, levied fines against them, and demanded hostages as security for their future conduct.[3] The princes, considering themselves unjustly treated, hastened to Italy where, in a meeting with the Emperor, they convinced him of their loyalty and obtained his support in opposition to his son. Frederick II, again revealing an unyielding hostility towards his son, ordered him to restore the destroyed castles at his own expense, to release the hostages, and to remit the fines which he had levied against the princes.[4] Meanwhile, Henry had sent his own ambassadors, the Archbishop of Mainz and the Bishop of Bamberg, to the Emperor to defend the measures which he had taken against the princes. The ambassadors were charged also with the mission of seeking to persuade the Emperor to revoke his orders with regard to the restoration of the castles and

[1] Conrad of Fabaria, *Casus S. Galli* (*MGH, SS.* ii), 181: *Chronica regia Coloniensis*, 265; *Annales Marbacenses*, 95.

[2] *Annales S. Rudberti Salisburgenses* (*MGH, SS.* ix), 785.

[3] Huillard-Bréholles, iv, part ii, 683–4.

[4] *Annales Marbacenses*, 96.

the remission of the fines. They failed, however, to alter the decision.[1] But Henry continued his efforts to justify his position. In a manifesto he presented an elaborate apologia for his past actions. He told how, with the aid of the princes, he had maintained law and order in the Kingdom. He complained also that his father, instead of approving his energetic actions, had willingly lent his ear to hostile tale-bearers and how, at length, Frederick had induced the Pope to excommunicate him. Of the embassy which he had sent to the Emperor, he said that he had desired, through it, to be reassured that he was not excluded from his father's affection. Meanwhile, he had appealed to the princes upon whom, above all, the Emperor depended, to support him by their counsel, and to prevail upon the Emperor to do nothing which would impugn the honour of the King. The letter closed with the asssurance that, since childhood, he had committed no act intentionally which could displease or offend the Emperor.[2]

In seeking to analyse the true causes of this singular relationship between Frederick II and his son, it is apparent that contemporary sources are inadequate in revealing them. Had Frederick II already determined to depose his first-born in favour of his younger son, Conrad, for whom he had a deep affection? Or, was he convinced from evidence not available to us that his son Henry was plotting against him, as the Duke of Bavaria is said to have suspected? Or, again, was Frederick suspicious that Henry's particularistic policies in Germany might, in time, become a serious obstacle to his own imperial plans? Had Henry (VII) been too long away from his father's influence to be able to grasp the vast imperialistic aims which had become the motivation of all Frederick's policies? Definitive answers to these questions are impossible in that they involve too many unknown and unfathomable elements. Fundamentally, the position which Henry (VII), as duly elected King of the Romans, was compelled to assume in relation to the Emperor was impossible. It subjected Germany to the wills of two sovereigns with opposing concepts of their missions. How fully Henry (VII) was aware of this and how bitterly he resented it, we have seen already. His position was made doubly difficult also in that German princes, who had reason to fear the immediate presence of a king in their midst, were more disposed to look with favour upon the government of an emperor who was far away and who was unlikely to make frequent appearances in Germany. Suspicious as he was of his son's motives, it was not difficult for these princes to convince the Emperor that Henry was plotting against him. There is some evidence also that the King, conscious of his guilt which Otto of Bavaria is said to have

[1] *Annales Scheftlarienses Maiores* (*MGH, SS.* xvii), 340. See also note 3, p. 370.
[2] Huillard-Bréholles, iv, part ii, 686.

uncovered, had acted in desperation when he sent his own ambassadors to the Emperor in order to counteract this accusation and to protest his innocence. But scarcely had his embassy departed for Italy when, in an assembly of bishops, *ministeriales*, and burghers at Boppard, the King is said to have accepted the evil advice that he oppose his father. Through entreaty and through bribery he is said to have sought support for a rebellion, not without some success.

Despite the initial enthusiasm of a few such supporters at Boppard, the King was not widely successful in winning the support of the princes. Among ecclesiastical princes who revealed some interest in his rebellious plans were the Bishops of Augsburg and Würzburg, and the recently elected Bishop of Worms. The Abbot of Fulda also is known to have joined the partisans of the King. Other supporters consisted of a motley group: disgruntled Swabian *ministeriales* and a few of the lesser nobility from that region.[1] The temporal princes, with the exception of the Duke of Austria and Styria, remained loyal to the Emperor. Pledges exacted by Henry from the Rhineland cities and from the cities of Alsace, especially, that they would support him against all opposition, with no exceptions, proved of little value in the end, even though he demanded hostages as security.[2] Most of these cities found it expedient, at least for the moment, to comply with the King's demands. Only the city of Worms steadfastly refused to desert the Emperor, despite the support of Henry by Landolf, the recently elected Bishop of Worms. Although Henry resorted to rigorous measures, proclaiming the ban of outlawry against the citizens, and laying siege to the city with some 5,000 troops, the embattled inhabitants, resorting indiscriminately to bribery and to prayer, held out until the Emperor's arrival.[3]

Henry's vacillation at this time and his various acts, apparently committed in desperation, may well be explained by his knowledge of the Emperor's determination to destroy him. He was certainly aware that in the summer of 1234 Frederick, accompanied by his young son Conrad, had visited Pope Gregory IX at Rieti.[4] Ostensibly, Frederick had made this visit for the purpose of offering his assistance to the Pope against the rebellious Romans who had compelled him to flee the city and take refuge in Rieti. In one of those periodic outbreaks not uncommon in the late Middle Ages, the citizens of Rome were seeking to throw off the papal dominance, demanding the right to elect the Senate, to coin money, to impose taxes, and to abolish the immunity of the clergy to civil authority. Above all, as Roman citizens, they claimed

---

[1] *Chronica regia Coloniensis*, 266. See also Nitzsch, 'Staufische Studien' (*Hist. Zeitschr.* 3, 1843), 394.

[2] *Annales Marbacenses*, 96.

[3] *Annales Wormatienses*, 43–4.

[4] Richard of San Germano, 188. *Breve chronicon de rebus Siculis*, 905.

as privileges immunity from the papal excommunication and interdict.[1]
Towards the end of May 1234 the hostility of the citizens was such that
the Pope, with all the cardinals, fled to Rieti. On a similar occasion
earlier, the Pope had appealed for aid, but, because of his preoccupation with affairs in Sicily, the Emperor had been unable or unwilling
to comply with the request. Now, however, in need of the friendly support of the Pope both in dealing with his rebellious son in Germany and
in the settlement of his differences with the Lombard cities, he grasped
this opportunity to serve the Pope, recalling, somewhat belatedly and
with questionable sincerity, his role as *advocatus* of the Church.[2] Obviously, Gregory and the Curia were suspicious of his offer. This suspicion was somewhat allayed when Frederick offered his six-year-old son
Conrad as security for his honourable intentions.[3]

Subsequent events leave little room for doubt that Frederick's sudden
interest in protecting the Pope and Curia was intimately related
to his desire for their support in the deposition of his son Henry (VII).
Doubtless the chief reason for Frederick's taking his son with him
to Rieti was to introduce him to the Pope as future German King, for
the one issue upon which Gregory IX and the Emperor were fully in
agreement was that Henry (VII) must be deposed. The offer of young
Conrad as hostage proved sufficient to satisfy the Pope, and the boy
was returned to the Kingdom.[4] The proceedings at Rieti could have
taken place only because of the need of Pope and Emperor for mutual
support. Frederick's initiative in hastening there was, in fact, a shrewd
diplomatic move, giving tangible expression to his oft-repeated designation of himself as 'protector of the Church'.

It is significant that the agreement between Pope and Emperor took
place prior to Henry (VII)'s most serious act of desperation, an alliance
with the Milanese and the Lombard League, which provided justification
for the belief that he was determined to oppose his father with every
possible means. It was not until February 1235 that he went even
further in seeking foreign allies, when he sent the Bishop of Würzburg
and Henry of Neiffen to the King of France, Louis IX, in a vain effort to
find support.[5] Henry had long recognized that the Pope and Curia were
unalterably hostile to him, if for no other reason than that it had been
his indefatigable efforts that had shattered the mission of the papal
legate, Otto of St. Nicholas, sent into Germany during the Emperor's
crusade with the mission of destroying both the Emperor and his son.

---

[1] Roger of Wendover, *Flores*, 322. See also Gregorovius, *Geschichte der Stadt Rom* (4th edn.
Stuttgart, 1892), v. 164 ff.; also (tr. A. Hamilton, London, 1897), v. 170 ff.

[2] Huillard-Bréholles, iv, part i, 422 and 472. See also *Vita Gregorii IX* (*Liber Censuum*,
ii), 25.

[3] Huillard-Bréholles, v, part i, 298.

[4] Richard of San Germano, 188.

[5] *Annales Marbacenses*, 96.

Indeed, it is impossible to find any evidence of friendliness on the part of Gregory towards Henry (VII) from the moment of his assumption of an independent role in the government of Germany. It is not improbable that this hostility on the part of both Pope and Curia originated even earlier in that they had always resented his election as King of the Romans. In their opinion Frederick had permitted the election to take place in defiance of his earlier promise and contrary to the repeatedly expressed objections of the Pope—a procedure which they had reluctantly tolerated but which they had never approved.

On 5 July 1234, months before the 'day of Boppard', Gregory had issued instructions for the excommunication of Henry and, thereafter, no longer recognized him as king, referring to him only as 'the son of the Emperor'.[1] The deposition of Henry (VII) as King of Germany might well offer further advantages to the Pope and Curia who, in the coming years, would find less opposition from a regency for the six-year-old Conrad than from an active, ambitious, and determined king such as Henry had shown himself to be. This change might also have been considered as a means of preventing the continued union of Kingdom and Empire.[2] From the moment of the alliance of Frederick II and Pope Gregory IX the fate of Henry (VII) seems to have been irrevocably determined. With the irresistible combined resources of papacy and Empire against him, and with but feeble support in Germany, he himself must have recognized that resistance was futile. This became all the more apparent when, in mid March 1235, the Pope sternly warned the German princes of the serious consequence of supporting 'the son of the Emperor', at the same time dissolving all oaths taken to Henry in opposition to his father.[3] Obviously, the Pope's instructions for the excommunication of Henry must have been issued before he was aware of the alliance of the Milanese and the King, for Gregory now found himself in the position of supporting the Emperor against the Lombard cities, his only dependable allies.

How closely the Pope had associated himself with the Emperor's plans is again apparent in his role in arranging the marriage alliance between Frederick II and the Princess Isabella, sister of Henry III of England, which was to be consummated during the Emperor's projected visit to Germany.[4] This marriage, initiating a diplomatic change diametrically opposed to the policy Frederick had pursued since his invitation to accept the German crown in 1212, was intended primarily as a concession to Cologne and as a gesture of final reconciliation with

---

[1] Huillard-Bréholles, iv, part i, 473–6.

[2] J. Rohden, 'Der Sturz Heinrichs' (*FzDG* xxii, 1882), 386; O. Lorenz, 'Kaiser Friedrich II.' (*Hist. Zeitschr.* 11, 1851), 327.

[3] Huillard-Bréholles, iv, part i, 530.

[4] Ibid. 515, 537. See also E. Kantorowicz, 'Petrus de Vinea in England' (*MöIG* li, 1937).

the Welfs. It thus achieved what Engelbert of Cologne had so ardently sought while serving as regent and guardian of young King Henry, although with the difference that Frederick now assumed the role that Engelbert had intended for King Henry. Both Pope and Emperor were aware of the possible dangers of this diplomatic revolution and it was this that caused Gregory to reassure the French King that it should in no wise arouse his suspicions. Frederick II also, in a letter to the French King, gave his assurance that his projected marriage would not alter their long-standing friendship.[1]

While there is no evidence indicating that the Pope had an ulterior motive in promoting this marriage, it might well have been considered as advantageous to him, in that it would leave the King of France freer to support the Pope in any further conflict with Frederick II. Actually, however, Frederick's alliance with the Pope at Rieti proved more advantageous to him than it was profitable to the Church. Some years later (1239), in a moment of bitterness the Pope told how Frederick had 'hastened, although not summoned', to Rieti and there, in all humility, had promised to defend the Church to the utmost of his ability. 'And then', the Pope continued, 'he shamefully fled before the enemies of the Church.' And this, continued the Pope, Frederick had done despite the benefits bestowed upon him by the Holy See, which, among other things, 'had supported him against his son Henry'.[2] But this judgement of the Pope is unnecessarily harsh. Certainly Frederick's sudden departure for Sicily while the siege was still in progress casts doubt upon the sincerity of his motives; it should not be overlooked, however, that the troops which he left to continue the siege forced the Romans to make peace.[3]

From Foggia Frederick explained in a letter to the Pope that his hasty return to the Kingdom of Sicily had been unavoidable and that it was not his intention to leave the Church unprotected. He stated further that he had made war against the Romans solely as protector of the Church and that in so doing he had sacrificed some excellent men. Accordingly, he was not opposed to any peace which would be satisfactory to the Church, although he advised against an unsatisfactory peace, certainly implying his intention to return if necessary.[4] Upon the receipt of this letter, Gregory authorized an embassy to conclude peace with the Romans and on 12 May he gave his consent to the terms which

---

[1] Huillard-Bréholles, iv, part i, 537 and 539.

[2] See Gregory's letter to the Archbishop of Canterbury, 21 June 1239 (Huillard-Bréholles, v, part i, 327 ff., 333).

[3] See, for example, *Albrici Monachi Trium Fontium Chronica* (*MGH, SS.* xxiii), 936; *Sächsische Weltchronik* (*MGH, Deutsch. Chron.* ii), 250.

[4] Huillard-Bréholles, iv, part i, 535. See also another letter of Frederick to the Pope written at the time he left the siege (Winkelmann, *Acta*, i, no. 334, p. 296).

they had arranged. A few days later, on the 16th, the Romans confirmed their acceptance of the terms and agreed to endeavour to conclude peace with the Emperor and with others who had aided the Pope.[1] While the entire conflict with the Romans confirms what had so frequently been apparent—that Frederick II was not especially distinguished as a military leader—it does not justify the charge of Gregory IX years later that 'he shamefully fled before the enemies of the Church'.

There can be no doubt that the protracted siege of Rispampani had seriously delayed Frederick's preparations for his expedition to Germany. Already in 1234 his intention to visit Germany was well known and in July he had written to the Archbishop of Trier that he would summon a diet to be held in Frankfurt on the next St. John's Day (24 June 1235). Early in the year 1235 he wrote to the citizens of Worms, thanking them for their steadfast loyalty to him in resisting the efforts of his son, and informing them of his imminent journey to Germany.[2] At the beginning of the year he ordered a general tax or *collecta* throughout the Kingdom of Sicily to ensure an ample treasure for the expenses of the expedition. Sometime between 8 and 18 April, in a diet at Fano, a regency to rule the Kingdom of Sicily during his absence was created, consisting of the Grand Justiciar, Henry of Morra, Thomas, Count of Acerra, the former captain of the Kingdom, and three prelates, the Archbishops Berard of Palermo, James of Capua, and Bishop Peter of Ravella.[3]

---

[1] *MGH, Epist. Pont.* i. 521. See also Richard of San Germano, 190.

[2] Böhmer, *Acta*, no. 303, p. 267; Huillard-Bréholles, iv, part i, 527–8.

[3] Richard of San Germano, 189. See also E. Winkelmann, 'Zur Geschichte', 526, and his *Beilage*, 522 ff.

III

DEPOSITION OF HENRY VII
THE ADVENT OF A NEW EMPRESS

> Volvitur orbe suo fortuna, revertitur ad se:
> Sic stat in ambiguo, quod firmius esse putatur.
> Cassibus imbutus nudus cadit et resolutus.
> Est, fuit, et non est; venit, fuit, et nichil est,
> Dum redit in nichilum, quod fuit ante nichil.
>
> Conrad of Fabaria, *Casus S. Galli* (*MGH, SS.* ii), 179.[1]

EARLY in May 1235 Frederick II, accompanied by his son Conrad, the Grand Master of the Teutonic order, Hermann of Salza, and a small following set sail from Rimini for Cividale Friuli, well supplied with funds for the expenses of his expedition to Germany. So great was Frederick's confidence in the loyalty of the Germans that he took with him no army. Each day as he proceeded from Friuli through Austria and into Germany via Nürnberg, where he was in mid June, princes and cities sent embassies to greet him and to express their pleasure at his arrival.[2] The Emperor had deceived his son by taking the route through Styria and Austria. Many of Henry's troops were still engaged in the futile siege of Worms when the Emperor made his entrance into Germany. As the princes and nobles hastened in ever-increasing numbers to join the Emperor, the young King must have recognized the seriousness of his situation. Many of his followers deserted him as they sensed his inevitable doom. When the hopelessness of his position became all too apparent, he yielded to the advice of some of the princes and placed himself at the mercy of the Emperor. Frederick wrote of these things in a letter to his faithful adherents in Lombardy:

[1] The wheel of Fortune rotates, returning
  whence it started;
Thus stands in doubt that which was
  deemed permanent.
Caught in the toils, it falls, naked and void.
It is, it was, it is not; it came, it was, and
  it is nothing.
Then it returns to nothing, that which was nothing
  before.

[2] Richard of San Germano, 190; *Breve chronicon de rebus Siculis*, 905; *Chronica regia Coloniensis*, 266; *Sächsische Weltchronik* (*MGH, Deutsch. Chron.* ii), 250; *Annales Marbacenses*, 96.

how at Regensburg, with many princes, nobles, and *ministeriales* from various parts of Germany, as well as from his Swabian Duchy, he provided for the public peace and how, while there, he had received a favourable reply concerning his future bride, the sister of the King of England. He told also how his son, deserted by his former followers, at first shut himself in the castle of Trifels and then, reconsidering, sent an embassy to Nürnberg pleading for a reconciliation and promising to obey all the Emperor's commands.[1] Frederick then sent Hermann of Salza to conduct the penitent youth to him.[2] Accompanied by numerous princes, with chariots bedecked with gold and silver and draped with purple and fine linen, Frederick proceeded to Wimpfen. Accompanying him also were his Saracen body-guard, many Ethiopian servants, camels and dromedaries, leopards and apes, other exotic beasts, and his closely guarded treasure-chest. Thither also came the unfortunate young King with a small escort and cast himself at his father's feet, pleading for mercy, but found little of the spirit of forgiveness in his unrelenting parent. Yielding to the intervention of various princes, the Emperor postponed his decision as to his son's punishment until his arrival in Worms, placing Henry under guard until that time.[3]

On 4 July the Emperor made his ceremonial entrance into the city of Worms, which was festively adorned for the long-hoped-for reception. Among the twelve bishops awaiting his arrival was the Bishop-Elect, Landolf of Worms, who, despite the loyalty of the city to the Emperor, had recently sided with Henry. Angered by his presence, Frederick ordered the Bishop from his sight, compelling him to leave the city.[4]

At Worms Henry was again conducted to the irate Emperor before whom he prostrated himself in bitter humiliation. Then in the presence of the assembled princes, he was compelled to lie, despised and unnoticed, for a long time until some princes, more compassionate than the unforgiving father, interceded in his behalf. He was ordered to renew his unconditional submission, to relinquish all claims to the German throne, and to surrender the castle of Trifels, the repository of the royal insignia. Now, probably because of the hopelessness of his situation, he seems to have regained something of his old pride and he defiantly refused to accept the terms. It is this tragic moment that the troubadour, Gaucelm Faidit, with pardonable poetic licence, immortalized when he said of this young King: 'vanquished and imprisoned

[1] *Gesta Treverorum Continuatio Quarta* (*MGH, SS.* xxiv), 403; *Chronicon Ebersheimense* (*MGH, SS.* xxiii), 453; *Sächsische Weltchronik* (*MGH, Deutsch. Chron.* ii), 250; Huillard-Bréholles, iv, part ii, 945 f.

[2] *Annales Marbacenses*, 97.

[3] *Continuatio Funiacensis et Eberbacensis* (*MGH, SS.* xxii), 348.

[4] *Annales Wormatienses*, 44.

. . . he sang as his arms were stripped away—even as the wheel of fortune turned—but wept at eventide.' The desolate Prince was given over to the surveillance of his bitter foe, Duke Otto of Bavaria, by whom he was held in prison at Heidelberg. Henceforth he played no further part in German history. His future was one of continued imprisonment until his tragic end. Later he was removed to Alerheim whence, after many months, he was taken for greater security to Rocca San Felice near Melfi, where he remained for several years. Twice more he was moved, first to Nicastro and then, after six years, he is said to have been summoned to his father's court, probably with the intention of granting him forgiveness. But Henry, anticipating no such relenting, and convinced that his father's aim was to order his execution, took advantage of a favourable moment as he rode with his guards across a bridge near Mortorano and drove his horse into the abyss below. Only one contemporary source, the *Chronicle* of Richard of San Germano, contradicts this account of the death of Henry (VII), saying that he died of natural causes at Mortorano.[1]

Although at the time of his son's deposition Frederick II revealed no evidence of sentiment, years later, upon receiving the report of Henry's death, Frederick wrote, in a letter to the barons, prelates, and citizens of the Kingdom of Sicily: 'Paternal grief over the death of my first-born son triumphs over the decree of the austere judge and forces a flood of tears from the depth of my heart, which the recollection of wrongs suffered and stern justice, until now, have restrained.' He then ordered that masses for the repose of his son's soul be celebrated throughout the Kingdom and that all customary funeral rites be observed. He expressed the desire that all of his faithful subjects who were accustomed to share his good fortune should now participate in his grief. It is characteristic of Frederick's outlook on life and of his exalted concept of his imperial office, in which inexorable justice must be made to triumph even over the deepest sentiments of mankind, that he was profoundly moved by the funeral oration delivered over his son's body, in that he, the Emperor, was likened unto Abraham who hesitated not at all to prepare to sacrifice his first-born son.[2]

With the imprisonment of Henry and his removal from Germany the revolt collapsed. A few of the worst offenders among the King's associates, Egeno of Urach-Freiburg, Henry of Neifen, and Anselm of Justingen, continued for a time as trouble-makers, especially in Swabia. Although receiving appeals for aid from faithful adherents in that region, Frederick did not personally intervene. At length in a general

---

[1] See first *Continuatio Eberbacensis* (*MGH, SS.* xxii), 348; and then, *Benvenuti Imolensis Comment. in Dantis Comoed.* (Muratori, *Antiq.* i), 1054. See also Richard of San Germano 213.

[2] See above, pp. 245 f., and Piero della Vigna, *Epist.* iv. 1.

amnesty the remnants of Henry's partisans were granted full pardon. Their reconciliation is attested by their signatures on various documents from the royal Chancery.[1] Towards the former recalcitrant Bishops, Hermann of Würzburg, Conrad of Speyer, and Landolf of Worms, whose disloyalty had especially angered the Emperor, he appeared at first to be unrelenting. Only when they were summoned to Rome to appear before the Pope, and were exonerated by him, did Frederick yield to a reconciliation.[2]

Whatever sorrow or feeling of guilt Frederick II may have experienced at Worms over the degradation of his son was soon eclipsed by the anticipation of his own marriage to Isabella of England. Of all the arrangements agreed to between the Emperor and the Pope at Rieti or afterwards, this marriage was, from the point of view of Gregory IX and the Curia, the most to be desired. Just as Innocent III had fostered the alliance between Frederick and Philip Augustus prior to the battle of Bouvines in his own interest, so now Gregory IX saw an even greater advantage in a reconciliation of the Staufen and the English King. This alliance would have the further advantage of ending definitely the ancient feud between Hohenstaufen and Welf.

During the pre-nuptial negotiations Piero della Vigna and his associate ambassador to the English court, after obtaining consent to the marriage, had asked permission to see the intended bride, who was fetched from the Tower of London for their inspection. In her twentieth year at that time, the Princess delighted the ambassadors not by her beauty alone, but equally by 'her virgin modesty' and by 'her regal dress and bearing'. The ambassador eagerly confirmed the marriage agreement by oath 'on the soul of the Emperor', presenting her with a ring in token of the betrothal. Satisfied with the more than favourable report of his embassy, Frederick, shortly after Easter, sent the Archbishop of Cologne and a group of noblemen to escort the future empress to Germany. After a last solemn festival held before the Latin Gate near Westminster, the Princess and her ladies-in-waiting set out with the escort on the journey to Germany. On 11 May 1235, the party set sail from Sandwich and, after a voyage of three days and nights, they entered the mouth of the Rhine. At Antwerp they were met by a German escort and by numerous clergy from near-by districts, together with musicians with their instruments, all of whom accompanied the prospective bride with all kinds of nuptial rejoicings to Cologne. There the citizens had made elaborate preparations for her reception. The principal streets were gaily decorated and the balconies were filled

---

[1] See Huillard-Bréholles, iv, part ii, 732–3, 817–18.
[2] *Annales Wormatienses*, 45. See also the letter of Pope Gregory IX (Huillard-Bréholles, iv, part ii), 842.

with noble ladies who eagerly awaited the moment when the Princess, removing her head-dress, permitted all 'to get a look at her'. Upon seeing her they had nothing but praise 'for her beauty and for her humility'. Following the festivities in the city of Cologne the Princess was taken to a quiet abode outside the city where, for the next six weeks, she awaited the instructions of the Emperor.

After a journey of seven days from Cologne, Princess Isabella and her retinue arrived in Worms where she was received by the Emperor, who was 'delighted with her beyond measure'. The marriage was solemnized on 20 July. The English nobles who had accompanied the Princess were released from their mission, and with numerous costly and exotic gifts for the royal brother-in-law, including three hunting-leopards or cheetahs, they returned to England.[1] It was said that the Emperor, in conformity with the advice of his astrologers, refrained from consummating the marriage on the first night, but awaited a more propitious time on the following morning. Then, with the supreme confidence which he had in his astrologers, he dismissed his consort to the care of her ladies-in-waiting, admonishing her to 'take good care of yourself for you now bear in your womb a son!' Thus the beautiful Isabella, like her predecessor Isabella of Brienne, was sent away to the cloistered isolation of an imperial castle to await the fulfil-ment of the destiny assigned her by her imperial spouse.[2]

Certainly there is some evidence that a son, Jordanus, was born in the year 1236, and died shortly afterwards, but the only son of Frederick II and Isabella of England whose birth can be firmly established was a second Henry, born in 1238, and named after his uncle, Henry III, the King of England.[3]

In Mainz, where the Emperor had gone after the marriage festivities of Worms, one of his first acts was his meeting with Otto of Brunswick, nephew of the late Otto IV, and grandson of the once-powerful Henry the Lion. Before the assembled magnates, Otto, with hands clasping those of the Emperor above the Holy Cross of the Empire, pledged himself to obey in good faith 'all of our mandates . . . taking care that never would he injure the Empire, or, at the instigation of anyone, assail our honour'. In return for this unqualified submission Otto was to receive as imperial fiefs Lüneburg with all its castles and appur-tenances, Brunswick, and other lands of the Welf family, with the title of hereditary Duke, to descend through both the male and the female lines. In addition, Otto was to receive henceforth the tithes of

---

[1] Roger of Wendover, *Flores*, iv. 333–9; Matthew Paris, *Chronica majora*, iii. 324; *Chronica regia Coloniensis*, 266.
[2] Matthew Paris, loc. cit.
[3] Rocco Pirri, *Chronologia Regum Siciliae*, 50.

Goslar, previously ceded to his father by Philip of Swabia.[1] Of this day, notable in so many respects in the history of medieval Germany, the chronicler of Cologne could say: 'The Emperor ordained that the day be recorded in all the annals of the Empire because, with the princes assenting, the Roman empire was increased by the creation of a new prince.'[2]

But the Diet of Mainz was no less notable for another event which took place there during Frederick's memorable visit. This was the promulgation of the body of laws designed to establish and maintain the public peace. It is a striking feature of these new laws that they were published in the German language as well as in the customary Latin. This circumstance has at times led to a somewhat over-zealous effort to establish the German text as the original and the Latin as merely a translation. As previously argued by H. von Voltelini, it is most unlikely that the chancery in drafting these laws would have abandoned the Latin language, which was habitually employed in similar legislation. This in no sense detracts from the significance of a nearly simultaneous promulgation of the laws in German.[3] This publication of the laws in the German language is, in some measure, symbolic of the significance of this brilliant gathering, so reminiscent of a similar diet held by Frederick Barbarossa in 1184, in which a new spirit of German unity appeared to be born. Like his grandfather in 1184, Frederick II in 1235 stood out as an independent sovereign at the height of his power. His position at Mainz was in striking contrast to that which he occupied in 1220, when, immediately before his departure for Rome to receive the imperial crown, he felt compelled to yield to the princely pressure by agreeing to the *Confoederatio cum principibus ecclesiasticis*, which in so great measure recognized the independent position of the ecclesiastical princes. At Mainz in 1235 his powerful personality dominated the proceedings. The *Constitutio Pacis* or *Mainzer Landfriede* was, indeed, a constitution, the work of a triumphant Emperor who had just forced to submission his rebellious son, strengthened his diplomatic ties by his marriage with the sister of an English King, made peace with the Welfs, and created a new duchy in Germany. The moment was propitious for the introduction of constitutional reforms in unsettled Germany.

Roughly, the *Constitutio Pacis* is divided into two parts. The first fourteen articles or chapters deal with the re-establishment of the

---

[1] Huillard-Bréholles, iv, part ii, 754–7.

[2] *Chronica regia Coloniensis*, 267.

[3] 'Die deutsche Fassung des Mainzer Landfriedens' (*Zeitschr. des hist. Vereins für Steiermark*, xxvi, 1931: *Festschrift für Luschin von Ebengreuth*), 73 ff. See also H. Steinacker, 'Der lateinische Entwurf zum Mainzer Landfrieden König Heinrichs (VII) von 1234' (*MöIG* xlvi, 1932), 188. For the support of German as the original language employed see K. Zeumer, in *Neues Archiv*, xxviii, 1902–3, 435 ff.

public peace and its future maintenance, while the remaining fifteen are concerned chiefly with criminal jurisprudence.[1] Significant among the former are the protection of the jurisdiction of the bishops within their respective dioceses; the fixing of the responsibility of the *advocatus* or steward in relation to church property; the punishment of violators of a sworn armistice; the compelling of princes to abide by the customs of their principalities; prohibition of self-vindication; abolition of un-just dues and taxes; regulation of mintage rights and rights of trans-portation. The *Constitutio Pacis*, like the *Liber Augustalis* in the Kingdom of Sicily, is not significant primarily for its innovations, but rather for its revitalization of laws which had fallen into abeyance. Above all, it was reinforced by the strength of an all-powerful Emperor, one that at no time allowed it to be overlooked that he was, by election and by divine ordination, the supreme legislator upon earth. One thinks of Frederick's experience with his recalcitrant son when he promulgated a new law (Article XV), the substance of which was:

Whatsoever son shall violently eject his father from his castles or other property, or shall attack the same with fire or with plundering, or plot with his father's enemies, taking an oath, vulgarly known as *verderprusse*, to attack his honour or seek his injury or destruction, shall forfeit all inheritance, and shall be adjudged as perpetually deprived of his fiefs and his personal posses-sions. Neither his father nor any judge shall be able to reinstate him.[2]

Reminiscent of the *Liber Augustalis* was the establishment in Germany of an imperial Grand Justiciar, 'a man of free condition, who shall hold office for at least a year'. He was to preside at court every day, save holidays, rendering justice in all complaints, 'excepting those concerning princes or other persons of high degree', which were speci-fically reserved for the Emperor. Like his Sicilian counterpart, the Grand Justiciar must be a layman, immune to the influence of bribery or to subornation in any form whatsoever—incapable of adjudicating save in what he knows or believes, in good conscience and in good faith, to be just and without fraud and without deceit.

Here, indeed, appears to be more than a faint suggestion of Frederick's future intentions with respect to Germany. In this moment of triumph, contrasting so sharply with his early experiences in the land of his Staufen forebears, he seemed to envisage the day when, after the secure conquest of Northern Italy, he could at last successfully turn his atten-tion to the incorporation of Germany within the framework of his World Empire. It is perhaps not an exaggeration of the significance of this 'Proclamation of Mainz' to characterize it as 'a preliminary

---

[1] H. Mitteis, 'Zum Mainzer Reichslandfrieden von 1235' (*ZfRG, Germ. Abteilung*, lxii, 1942), 32; for the Latin text see *MGH, Const.* ii, no. 196, pp. 241 ff.

[2] Ibid., pp. 244–5.

regulation, as in Sicily the Capuan Proclamation had been the fore-runner of the great Constitution of Melfi'.[1]

It was at this time that the itinerant poet Henry of Avranches, so often the eloquent eulogist of Frederick II, urged him to follow the example of Pope Gregory IX who had recently codified the canon law, and to have prepared a codification of the civil laws. For, says the poet, 'It is not a great task and you would merit eternal fame. You would not have to do the work in minute detail. On the contrary it would suffice to eliminate the superfluous.' He reminded the Emperor that so great was the inundation of the superfluous laws that a child would have become an old man before he could read through all of them.[2]

But the poet, always perceptive of the genius of the great Emperor, was not alone in this desire. The acceptance of the project by the assembled princes at Mainz suggests that such a codification was widely recognized as desirable. Frederick was well aware, however, that the time had not yet arrived when Germany could be brought firmly under the control of the imperial sovereignty in the manner of Sicily. It was doubtless sufficient to him for the time being that during his visit to Germany in 1235, especially in the favourable environment of Mainz, he could hopefully visualize the possibility of a unification of the German principalities under a strong central administration—an important step towards its ultimate incorporation in the Empire. If, in the end, this project could not be realized, the failure must be attributed not to inherent weaknesses of the plan in Germany itself, but rather to the inability of Frederick to check the inevitable independence of the Lombard cities. For without this a unification of the Kingdom of Sicily, Central and Northern Italy, and Germany could not be achieved. Frederick's death fifteen years later without a successful conquest of Lombardy left Germany a prey to the ever-expanding authority of a multitude of independent principalities. The final failure of Frederick's imperial plans in the mid thirteenth century sealed the fate of German unification just as it shattered the Hohenstaufen dream of World Empire.

It was in consideration of his ultimate plans that Frederick devoted himself assiduously to obtaining sufficient military support to compel the submission of the Lombard communes. He felt so confident of this that in August 1235 he wrote to the Pope that at Mainz the princes had

---

[1] E. Kantorowicz, *Kaiser Friedrich II.*, 376–7 (English edn., 1931, 411).
[2] E. Winkelmann, 'Drei Gedichte' (*FzDG* xviii, 1878), 490:

> Est labor exiguus, famamque mereberis illo
> Perpetuam; nec habebis opus suplere minuta,
> Immo sufficiet resecare superflua, quorum
> Vix homo diluvium toto percurreret evo;
> Ante senectutem leges vix perleget infans.

pledged themselves to undertake an expedition against the Lombards.[1]
Certainly not the least important object of the Diet of Mainz was to
'promote the honour of the Empire' by re-establishing its right to
Lombardy and to encourage the princes to defeat its adversaries by
force of arms, for this, as he sought to assure them, was their rightful
heritage.[2] For a year he deliberated with the princes over ways and
means by which this expedition was to be accomplished, claiming for
this purpose the full aid of Germany.[3] But, despite his efforts and, notwithstanding the promises of the princes, he had but little success in
obtaining the desired support. The first contingent of troops dispatched to Verona under the leadership of Gerhard of Arnstein
numbered no more than 500. They were to await the arrival of the
Emperor with the anticipated large army.[4] Although the prestige of
the Emperor in Germany was never before or afterwards as great as it
was during his visit in 1235, there was but little comprehension of his
imperialistic plans. The enthusiasm that his visit evoked during the
Diet of Mainz, and in other assemblies of princes and nobles, was not
so much because of his imperial office but in recognition of his German
sovereignty. For even though he received but a meagre following for
his military expedition to Italy, he moved triumphantly from place to
place in Germany, revealing himself not only as the magnificent
Emperor but, much more, in his favourite role of supreme judge upon
earth. What, indeed, could more fully represent him as the agent of
Justitia herself than an incident which took place in Hagenau during
the winter of 1235–6? Here he was called to pass judgement in an
alleged ritual murder of a Christian boy by the Jews of that region.
Few of his actions during the second visit to Germany attracted more
widespread attention than this, the repercussions of which extended
far beyond the borders of that country. From the outset Frederick's
procedure was unique. After first creating a commission of princes,
magnates, nobles, and clergy to consider the truth or the fallacy of the
charges, he was forced to the conclusion that, because of their conflicting
views, they could not give him adequate advice. He then appealed to
various sovereigns of the Western world to send to his court as many
Jewish converts to Christianity as possible who were learned in the
Hebraic law. These men, having been once of the Jewish faith, would
reveal what they knew. It is known from the reply of King Henry III of
England that an imperial marshal did appear at the English court with
this request. There he was honourably received and astonished the

---

[1] Huillard-Bréholles, *Rouleaux de Cluny*, no. 95.
[2] *Annales Scheftlarienses* (*MGH, SS.* xvii), 340, and *Chronica regia Coloniensis*, 267. See also
E. Jordan, *Origines*, Intro., p. li; *MGH, Const.* ii. 239f.
[3] Huillard-Bréholles, iv, part ii, 759 f., 889 f., 896 f., 901 ff.
[4] *Chronica regia Coloniensis*, 268.

King and courtiers by the 'hitherto unheard-of occurrence which has recently taken place in your country'. Henry replied that he was sending two discreet, recently baptized Jews who were willing to comply with the Emperor's requests.[1] When at length the desired neophytes appeared at the imperial court, they pursued their inquiry with the utmost diligence. They were then called before the Emperor who questioned them as to whether or not Jews could be induced to commit such a crime. Their reply, although obviously in agreement with the preconceived opinion of Frederick, was certainly disconcerting to his less rational contemporaries. The reply was emphatic that Hebrew scriptures forbade the sacrificial shedding of human blood—that both the Bereshith and the Talmud imposed heavy penalties against persons guilty of blood sacrifices. In conformity with the report of this group, whose investigation Frederick had followed closely, the *Privilegium et Sententia in Favorem Iudaeorum* was drawn up and promulgated in July 1236. It forbade all persons, laymen or ecclesiastics of high or low degree, on any occasion whatsoever, to make such charges against the Jews.[2]

The procedure, with the ensuing grant of protection to the Jews, was so at variance with the prevailing concepts of the era that it was received with dissatisfaction by many Christians.[3] But Frederick's effort to establish the facts in the case, as opposed to ill-founded gossip, was not without influence on the age in which he lived. A decade later Pope Innocent IV instructed the bishops of Germany to protect the Jews there who had been robbed and persecuted by both temporal and ecclesiastical magnates on the pretext that during the Easter festivities they had put Christian boys to death. He emphasized further, in language similar to that of Frederick's commission of neophytes, that such deeds by the Jews would be contrary to their laws.[4] Thus Frederick's arch-enemy, who hounded him relentlessly until his death, had recognized that Frederick II was, indeed, the image of *Justitia*, the avenging force in the world of Christendom, if not divinely ordained, nevertheless competent, by virtue of superior intelligence, to establish peace and order upon earth.

It was no less astonishing to contemporaries, who were wont to regard Frederick II as atheistic and scornful of things Christian, when in May 1236, while in Marburg, he visited the shrine of Elizabeth of Thuringia. What impulse impelled him to this extraordinary display of piety we do not know. Perhaps its explanation must be sought in the same source that had impelled him two decades before at Aachen to

---

[1] See the letter of Henry, Huillard-Bréholles, iv, part ii, 809–10.   [2] Ibid. 275.
[3] *Richeri Gesta Senoniensis* (*MGH, SS.* xxv), 324.
[4] *MGH, Epist. Pont.* ii, no. 409, pp. 297 ff.

take the cross. Or could it have been some intimate bond of friendship with the late Landgrave of Thuringia, husband of Elizabeth, who had died of the plague in 1227, when in the company of the Emperor, *en route* to the Holy Land? Or must the explanation be sought in a sincere expression of pious sentiment, a phenomenon not wholly alien to the habitually impious? Or, was it but a part of a well-calculated plan to impress the Pope whose recently formed alliance with the Emperor was so desirable for Frederick's future plans in Lombardy? An expedition such as Frederick contemplated, ostensibly against the Lombard League, might well be suspected of having as its ultimate object the subjugation of the whole of Italy to the imperial authority. If possible, therefore, Frederick must prevent the renewal of the papal ban. While the motives of men are rarely discernible, save through conjecture, Frederick II's complete devotion to his ideal of Empire was such that any action of his which could move him towards the realization of that ideal would have been taken without consideration of its sincerity or insincerity. For just as Gregory IX and his successor, Innocent IV, permitted no consideration of the scrupulous or the unscrupulous to stand in the way of their concepts of papal omnipotence, so Frederick, in his concept of World Empire, accepted the doctrine that the end justifies the means. It is idle to seek for concepts of ethical conduct in the modern sense among Popes or Emperors of the thirteenth century. In short, it is most difficult to visualize Frederick II in the role of the pious pilgrim humbly worshipping at the shrine of a saint whose earthly existence had been cast in the mould of Franciscan poverty and humility.

It was in early May 1236 that the recently canonized Elizabeth received her royal burial and translation to her saintly shrine. A great throng had assembled for the brilliant occasion. A contemporary chronicler estimated the number, with characteristic medieval exaggeration, at twelve-hundred thousand (*duodecies centum milia hominum promiscui sexus*) men and women. Among the notables in attendance were the Archbishops of Mainz, Trier, and Bremen, numerous bishops, the Landgrave of Thuringia, Henry, and the children of Elizabeth, Hermann and Sophia. Into the midst of this vast assembly came the Emperor, wearing his royal crown and imperial vestments. Advancing to the sarcophagus, he lifted the first stone with his own hands.[1]

Removed from its original place of repose, the body of the saint was placed in an oaken coffin plated with gold and adorned with graven figures in silver and inlaid with precious stones. Two contemporary sources give further details of the Emperor's part in the ceremony. One of these relates that before the body was translated to its splendid

---

[1] *Chronica regia Coloniensis*, 268.

sarcophagus 'the head of the saintly Elizabeth was separated from the body in order that it might not inspire a sense of horror at being seen. Also Minorite brothers separated the flesh and hair from the skull with a small knife. The Emperor then placed a crown of gold and precious stones upon her head as token of his devotion to the saintly Landgravine.'[1] Another chronicler adds that, at the time of the translation, Frederick made an offering to the Saint of a *cifum* or chalice from which he was wont to drink, and in which the skull was now enshrined.[2] A recent study of this *cifum*, now a museum piece, indicates that the original chalice had been considerably enlarged at the time of the translation by the addition of a calotte so that it became a head-reliquary of sufficient size to accommodate a crowned skull.[3]

Whatever the motive that impelled this display of piety towards his saintly kinswoman (and the kinship was most remote), there can be little doubt that Frederick made the most of the occasion to impress the multitude of onlookers with the sincerity of his piety. No less ostentatious was a communication of Frederick, addressed shortly after the translation to the Order-General of the Minorites, Elias of Cortona. This is a shining example of the euphuistic rhetoric so popular in the imperial Chancery of the mid thirteenth century. The obvious care with which it was written leaves little doubt that it was intended to be widely circulated. Resolved into simpler language, this letter is intended to convey the idea that Frederick, because of the late Landgrave, his second cousin, who was married to the holy Elizabeth, felt himself drawn to her by sincere affection (*affectione sincera*) and, in the splendour of his majesty, he did not shrink from participating in the beatification of the royal lady. But not merely the bond of consanguinity impelled him to honour the saint, but pious devotion (*sancta devotio*) as well.[4] Perhaps, as he fulfilled this act of piety, he was not unmindful of the last moments of his friend, the loyal young Landgrave of Thuringia, at Brindisi and Otranto when together they had been stricken by the plague and when the less fortunate Louis succumbed. For the third time, as at Aachen in 1215, and at the sarcophagus of his first Empress, Constance of Sicily, in Palermo, Frederick yielded to an emotional impulse which appeared alien to his character. Just as at Aachen in 1215, when he signalized his elevation to the German throne by taking the cross, so now at Marburg, on the eve of his departure for Italy, he signalized his plans for the further expansion of his sovereign authority by a similar gesture of piety.

---

[1] P. Schramm, *Kaiser Friedrichs II. Herrschaftszeichen*, 28. See also Montalambert, *Life of Elizabeth*, ii. 246–7.　　　[2] *Richeri Gesta Senoniensis* (*MGH, SS.* xxv), 320.
[3] See the contribution of O. Källström, 'Das Reliquiar in Stockholm mit den von Friedrich gestifteten Kronen und seinem "Becher"' (Schramm, loc. cit.). Section B of this article, by Schramm, is pertinent.　　　[4] Källström, loc. cit.

PART VIII

FREDERICK'S SECOND EXPEDITION
AGAINST THE LOMBARDS

I

FROM VICENZA TO CORTENUOVA

*Exultet jam romani imperii culmen, et pro tanti victoria principis
mundus gaudeat universus.*

Letter of Piero della Vigna (Huillard-Bréholles, v, part i), 137.[1]

AFTER participating in the translation of the body of the saintly
Elizabeth of Thuringia, Frederick devoted himself actively to the
preparations for the Lombard expedition. During these last
months in Germany, in the spring and summer of 1236, he came to
recognize how fragile was his alliance with the Pope, now that his
son had been deposed. The Pope had been manœuvred into a position
wholly at variance with that which he was accustomed to occupy in
relation to the Lombards. It was to be expected that he would endeavour
by every possible means to extricate himself. It is most improbable that
he would have considered sacrificing permanently his alliance with the
cities whose attitude towards the imperialistic ambitions of Frederick
II coincided with his own. It was essential, therefore, that the Pope
continue his role as mediator while awaiting an opportunity to
prevent an actual imperial invasion. He himself sought to create this
opportunity during the Diet of Mainz by attempting to persuade the
German princes to refuse to support the hostile measures of Frederick
against the Lombards. When this effort failed and the German princes
were found to be sympathetic to the imperial design, Gregory appealed
directly to Frederick through a series of letters seeking to dissuade him
from carrying out his military plans.[2]

For Frederick it was highly useful to have the Pope, for the time being,
in a neutral position. Accordingly, he declared himself ready to accept
the continued mediation of Gregory, although he made his acceptance
conditional by requiring that the mediation attain its ends by Christmas
1235, and by demanding that the Lombards increase the fine of 20,000
marks, originally levied against them for damages inflicted by their

---

[1] Now let the head of the Roman Empire exult, and for the victory of so great a prince let
the whole world be joyful.

[2] See first, the Pope's letter (Huillard-Bréholles, iv), 735; and Frederick's letter (*Rouleaux
de Cluny*, no. 95, Aug. 1235); and then *MGH, Epist. Pont.* i. 557 ff.; and Huillard-Bréholles,
iv, part ii, 771, 870, 914, etc.

alliance with his son Henry, to 30,000 marks.[1] In case of failure of the cities to comply with these terms, they were to be excommunicated by the Pope. Frederick must have recognized that it was most unlikely, if not impossible, that the Lombards would agree to these or any other terms. It is to be assumed, therefore, that he had already abandoned hope for a peaceful settlement of the Lombard question and that his acceptance of the Pope's mediation was a diplomatic manœuvre rather than a bona-fide consent. He recognized the importance of appearing in the best light possible. If, in the end, the negotiations failed, it would be the Lombards, and not the Emperor, who were responsible for the failure. But the Pope was not deceived by this seemingly accommodating spirit on the part of the Emperor. In a letter of 22 September 1235 to Hermann of Salza, Gregory hinted at evil influences and warned of probable serious consequences if Frederick should undertake a conquest before the mediation was completed. Although conscious of the difficulties of his position as mediator, the Pope continued his efforts, appealing to the Emperor to send plenipotentiaries to Rome by 1 December for the purpose of negotiating with the Lombards. A similar appeal to the rectors of the cities of the Lombard League and to the papal legate in Lombardy, the Patriarch of Antioch, dated 26 September 1235, while expressing sympathy for the Lombards because of the brief time allotted them by the Emperor, also warned them of the dangers of continued delay.[2] Neither the Pope nor the Emperor could have been surprised at the reaction of the Lombard cities to this warning. On 7 November they renewed the Lombard League in accordance with the old form, this time, however, including the city of Ferrara.[3]

In late October or early November Hermann of Salza, the imperial plenipotentiary, had arrived in Italy.[4] Meanwhile, Frederick was active in restoring peace and order in Germany while awaiting reports from his plenipotentiaries in Italy. Both in Augsburg and in Hagenau, where he spent the greater part of the winter of 1235–6, he was occupied with the punishment of various disturbers of the public peace. The most serious problem claiming his attention during these final months of his residence in Germany was the need to pacify the turbulent Duke Frederick II of Austria, the last of the Babenbergs, son and successor of the late Leopold 'the Glorious', who had died in 1230.[5] From the outset this quarrelsome young prince had shown little disposition for

---

[1] Huillard-Bréholles, iv, part ii, 876–7. For the fine originally levied see ibid., part i, 351.

[2] *MGH, Epist. Pont.* i. 556–7 and 559–60.

[3] Huillard-Bréholles, iv, part ii, 797: 'secundum antiquum modum et formam.'

[4] E. Winkelmann, 'Eine nothwendige Berichtigung zu Gunsten Gregors IX. etc'. (*FzDG* vi, 1866), 631, note 1.

[5] See A. Ficker, *Herzog Friedrich II. der letzte Babenberger.*

friendliness towards the Emperor. He had ignored the summonses to attend both the Diet of Ravenna and the meeting of the princes in Aquileia. The Emperor complained bitterly of the Duke's conduct, saying: 'We invited him to the Diet at Ravenna and promised to receive him with paternal affection, but, although a neighbour, he refused to come ... Likewise he refused in childish manner our summons to Aquileia which we attributed to the foolishness of his youth.' Moreover, in the conflict of the Emperor with his son Henry (VII), Duke Frederick had taken a more than questionable position. As the Emperor made his way to Germany, and was on the border of Styria at Neumarkt (Nówy Targ), Duke Frederick demanded 2,000 marks to assist him in a war which at that time he was waging against Hungary and Bohemia—a demand, of course, which the Emperor refused.[1] Also, after the submission of King Henry, one of his chief associates in the revolt, Anselm of Justingen, found a safe refuge at the court of Duke Frederick of Austria. For these and for other reasons the Duke was summoned to the Diet of Augsburg to account for his recalcitrance. But again he ignored the summons. Although these and numerous other charges against the Duke were laid before the Diet, the Archbishop of Salzburg, as intermediary, succeeded in obtaining a new terminus for his appearance, this time at a proposed meeting of the princes at Hagenau. Once more the Duke failed to appear and it was at last agreed that a peaceful settlement with him was impossible. In June 1236, at Augsburg, he was formally declared an outlaw and his lands forfeit.[2]

The Emperor now determined to depose the Duke, delegating the punishment to his rivals and near neighbours, the King of Bohemia, the Duke of Bavaria, the Margrave of Brandenburg, and the Bishops of Bamberg and Passau. At the same time he concluded an alliance with these princes, agreeing not to make peace or to conclude an armistice with Duke Frederick, save with their consent.[3] But, despite this threat from his enemies, Duke Frederick prepared to resist with all the resources at his command. Save for Wiener-Neustadt and Linz, however, his cities as well as his *ministeriales* deserted him. When, at length, in the autumn of 1236, his enemies actually invaded his territories there was no recourse for him other than to yield or to seek the shelter of the impregnable walls of Wiener-Neustadt. For the moment the invaders were unopposed and even Vienna opened its gates to become the seat of an imperial governor, Conrad, Burgrave of Nürnberg.

---

[1] *MGH, Const.* ii. 269 ff.
[2] Huillard-Bréholles, iv, part ii, 855 ff.; Hermann Altahensis, *Annales* (*MGH, SS.* xvii), 392.
[3] *MGH, Const.* ii. 273.

After delegating these several princes to undertake the Austrian conquest, Frederick continued to make preparations for his expedition into Lombardy. Towards the end of April 1236 he sent Gebhard of Arnstein with 500 knights in advance to Verona where, despite opposition from the Pope and his supporters, Ezzelino of Romano had gained control. It was the intention of Frederick to join Gebhard at an early date.[1]

These preparations made by the Emperor in the spring and summer of 1236 caused the Pope great anxiety. He now protested vigorously to Frederick, insisting that the Lombard expedition would coincide with the expiration of the truce with the Saracens and would thus occasion further postponement of the projected crusade. Whatever considerations of diplomacy had restrained him in the past, Frederick now revealed his impatience with the efforts of the Pope to impede his plans. Early in May 1236 he answered the Pope's protest in a manner that left no doubt as to his intentions:

Italy is my heritage, and this is known to the whole world. It would be ambitious and evil to covet the property of others while relinquishing my own, all the more so because the arrogance of the Italians, especially of the Milanese . . . has provoked me. Moreover, I am a Christian, and however unworthy a servant of Christ, am prepared to vanquish the enemies of the cross. But since so many heresies not only exist but flourish in Italy, and the weeds are beginning to smother the wheat in the Italian cities, especially in Milan, to wage war against the Saracens, while leaving these [heresies] unpunished would be to treat the wound where the steel has entered with superficial remedies, causing an ugly scar, not a cure. . . . I have determined to apply the wealth of this country to avenge the Crucified One. For Italy has abundant arms, horses, and wealth, as everyone knows.[2]

No less enlightening as to the ultimate aims of Frederick with regard to Italy is a letter written about the same time summoning representatives of the cities north of Rome to a diet to be held in Piacenza on 25 July of the same year to discuss the Holy Land and the reformation of the Empire and the establishment of peaceful and just conditions in that region.[3] The summoning of a diet, to be held at Piacenza with the object of realizing these imperial ideals, immediately evoked from Gregory IX a hostile response. His first act was to appoint as his legate in Lombardy, not the Patriarch of Antioch, as desired by Frederick II, but a native Piacentine, Cardinal Bishop James of Palestrina, known to be opposed to the policies of Frederick. In a letter of 10 June directed to both the Emperor and his diplomatic representative, Hermann of Salza, Gregory warned against listening to disparaging

---

[1] *Chronica regia Coloniensis*, 268 f. See also F. Stieve, *Ezzelino von Romano*, 31.
[2] Matthew Paris, *Chronica majora*, iii. 375.   [3] *MGH, Const.* ii. 268.

remarks about the Cardinal, and described him as one who could be relied upon to safeguard the honour of the Church and Empire.[1] The Cardinal Bishop of Palestrina, apparently in the belief that he was carrying out the actual intention of the Pope, immediately assumed a partisan attitude by inducing the city of Piacenza to desert the Emperor and to subject itself to a rector of Venetian origin, William of Andito, thus making it impossible for the diet to be held in that city. How bitterly Frederick II resented this procedure on the part of the Pope and his agent is revealed in letters not only to the Pope, but also to the Kings of England and France; in these he contended that he was constrained to support the rights of the Empire against the Lombards all the more because their attacks against his imperial majesty were indirectly attacks against the Church. He insisted in one of these letters: 'We firmly avow, although it must be apparent, that no other motive dictates our action than that of taking up the cause of the Crucified One.'[2] In his letter to the King of France Frederick gave assurance of his intention to lead a powerful army to the Holy Land, to the glory of God and the Empire, when the discord in Italy was brought to an end.

The Pope's reply to Frederick's protest against the appointment of the Cardinal of Palestrina bears witness to the breach between Gregory and the Emperor, henceforth increasingly hostile and irreconcilable. Not only did he defend the actions of the Cardinal, but he reminded the Emperor of a long series of provocations which the Roman Church has suffered from him: the oppression of the churches of Italy; Frederick's seizure of the Civita Castellana in the vicinity of Viterbo. Above all, he reminded the Emperor that it was not within his province 'to pry into the secrets of our conscience whose judge is in heaven'. Then he made the declaration so prophetic of the papal concept of *plenitudo potestatis* which was to prevail in the last decades of the thirteenth century: 'The Apostolic See to whose judgement the whole earth is subject is itself subject alone to the judgement of God.'[3] The remainder of Gregory's letter was an elaboration of this theory of omnipotence. He evoked the so-called Donation of Constantine, by which Constantine the Great, as the sole sovereign of the world by virtue of the consent of the senate and the people of Rome, was said to have conferred upon the Vicar of the Prince of the Apostles, not merely sovereignty over the city of Rome, but over the whole of the Roman Empire in the West, both in spiritual things and over the souls of men. Accordingly, it was the Apostolic See that, by virtue of divine authority

---

[1] *MGH, Epist. Pont.* i. 589 f.

[2] Huillard-Bréholles, iv, part ii, 872 ff. See especially p. 879. The letter to the Pope is not extant, but its contents are known from the papal reply (ibid. 914).

[3] Ibid. 919.

had transferred the Empire to the Germans in the person of the Great Charles. In so doing, however, the Pope surrendered nothing of his jurisdiction, retaining also possession of the temporal sword which he conferred 'upon your predecessors and upon you'.

The entire tone of this remarkable letter leaves no doubt that Gregory was now disposed to shift the ground of the conflict from the Lombard question to the broader issue of world dominance. Acceptance of this extreme papal doctrine would have acknowledged the Pope as the sole arbiter of all disputes over the contested regions of Italy, leaving the Emperor helpless in his effort to punish the cities of the Lombard League for what he conceived to be an act of treason in conspiring with his son Henry against the imperial authority. Gregory IX recognized in Frederick II an antagonist of such potentialities that only by his complete elimination could the Holy See hope to attain supremacy. For it was nothing less than this that the Curia, under the impact of the theories of the extreme canonists of the thirteenth century, had come to accept as its rightful heritage from the Prince of the Apostles by virtue of the arrangements of Christ himself. Henceforth, both Pope and Emperor were well aware that the conflict for World Empire had entered its final stage in which it was to be determined which of these rival claimants to supremacy would emerge triumphant. The Lombard question might appear to the world as the source of friction, but it was, in fact, only a secondary feature of the larger and crucial issue.

As to the cities of the Lombard League, they had no desire to subject themselves either to the Emperor or to the Pope. If they were habitually allied with the papacy it was not through desire to support the concept of authority expounded in the letter of Gregory IX, but merely to serve their own interests through the assistance of a useful ally. They were unwilling to yield even the smallest part of what they conceived their rights or what they had obtained either from Frederick II or from his predecessors. They had attained a position of strength from which they no longer regarded the Peace of Constance as an irrevocable representation of their rights, but rather as an indication of the inevitable course which they must follow. To the cities of the League other Lombard cities such as Cremona, unwilling to join with them in opposing the Emperor, were outlaws, subject to plunder and to persecution. Moreover, the Cremonese group of Lombard cities were all the more bitterly opposed by the League because of their alliance with Ezzelino of Romano, the most powerful of Frederick II's allies in Italy.[1]

---

[1] See especially F. Stieve, *Ezzelino*, 29 ff. Recent studies, supplementing earlier ones, are articles by G. Fasoli, R. Manselli, C. G. Mor, M. Boni, E. Raimondi, and P. Toschi, in *Studi Ezzeliniani* (Rome, 1963).

Just as the cities of Northern Italy, following either Milan or Cremona, took sides with one or the other of the great antagonists, Pope or Emperor, so also the few remaining powerful princes took sides in accordance with their personal interests. Most conspicuous among such princes were Azzo of Este and Ezzelino of Romano. Since 1220, when Frederick visited Rome to receive the imperial crown, Azzo of Este had been closely allied with him; he received from the newly crowned Emperor in 1221 the confirmation of his feudal holdings. This friendly relationship continued until 1228, when Azzo described himself as 'by the grace of God, the Pope, and the Emperor, Margrave of Ancona and Este'.[1] Only after the break between Gregory IX and the Emperor became irrevocable in 1228 did Azzo align himself with the papal party. This is attributable in part to his obligation to the Pope as his feudal overlord, but, even more, to his traditional opposition to Ezzelino of Romano, the staunch supporter of the Emperor. Thereafter the whole of Northern Italy fell prey to violent civil conflicts in which these ruthless adversaries were leading figures. These conflicts reached the height of their bitterness in 1236, when Azzo of Este was chosen *podestà* of Vicenza.[2]

It was in the midst of these depredations of Azzo and his allies that Ezzelino appealed to Frederick II, who was still in Germany, for aid. In reply, Frederick informed him through Gebhard of Arnstein, who had earlier entered Verona with the vanguard of the German troops, of his projected expedition into Italy. In June the Emperor was in Augsburg where, in the near-by Lechfeld, he was assembling his forces for the Lombard expedition.[3] The unexpected course of events in Austria had occasioned some anxiety over the Emperor's projected departure from Germany. Shortly after he had delegated the safe-guarding of Austria to a group of princes, the young Duke, aided by Count Albert IV of Bogen, in a sudden sally from Wiener-Neustadt routed the troops of Conrad, the imperial governor, although they outnumbered his own force ten to one, and captured the Bishops of Passau and Freising.[4] Many princes now exerted pressure upon Frederick not to employ the whole of his forces against the Lombards until the rebellious Duke of Austria had been compelled to submit. Reluctantly he consented to divide his forces. In a letter to Gebhard of Arnstein, who awaited his arrival in Verona, he wrote that he would not delay the Lombard expedition but would send a part of his forces against the Duke of Austria and would himself proceed with a larger

[1] Muratori, *Antiq.* i. 335–6: 'Azzo Dei et Apostolica et Imperiali gratia Anconitanus et Estensis Marchio.'
[2] Nicholas Smeregus, *Annales Civitatis Vincentiae* (Muratori, *RIS*, new edn., viii, part 5), 5.
[3] *Chronica regia Coloniensis*, 269.
[4] *Continuatio Sancrucensis Secunda* (*MGH, SS.* ix), 638–9.

force to Italy.[1] At about the same time Frederick named Ezzelino as his special representative with full authority in Vicenza. Thereupon, Azzo officially proclaimed that whosoever in any way entered into an alliance with the Emperor, or even mentioned his name, would be liable to the death penalty.

But in the midst of preparations for his departure to Italy, Frederick found increasing reasons to doubt the wisdom of dividing his assembled forces. While the Germans generally were sympathetic with the object of his expedition into Lombardy and agreed that Italy, as a part of the Holy Roman Empire, must be regained, many of them felt that this should be achieved through the resources of Apulia and Sicily and the cities of Northern Italy loyal to the Emperor.[2] The numbers assembled on the Lechfeld fell far short of expectations and, when divided, left only a small detachment to accompany the Emperor. In May, with an optimism which was soon found to be unjustified, Frederick had written to his subjects in the Kingdom of Sicily that, inasmuch as the Germans would provide him with a substantial army, he would not need to call upon the Sicilians for military aid. He would, however, be compelled to ask of them considerable sums of money in order to crush the rebels completely.[3] This letter was obviously designed to prepare the loyal Sicilian subjects for a *collecta* which in the following March was levied throughout the Kingdom.[4] The 500 knights led by Gebhard of Arnstein had reached Verona on 16 May 1236, where they proved of the utmost usefulness in reinforcing the hard-pressed troops of Ezzelino of Romano. The main army, led by the Emperor, set out from Augsburg on 24 July, numbering only about 1,000 mounted troops. It is to be assumed that two squires accompanied each knight thus bringing the total to at least 3,000. In addition there was an unknown number, probably not large, of foot soldiers.[5] On 12 August Frederick had reached Trent where he was met by Gebhard of Arnstein, Ezzelino, and Alberigo of Romano. Four days later they proceeded together to Verona where the Emperor was received with great honour.[6]

After resting his army at Vacaldo, south of Verona, for several days, Frederick crossed the Mincio *en route* to Cremona without being attacked by the Milanese or their allies.[7] While the Emperor proceeded

---

[1] *Annales Placentini Gibellini* (*MGH, SS.* xviii), 474.

[2] *Cronica Dominorum Ecelini et Alberici fratrum de Romano* (Muratori, *RIS*, new edn., vii, part 4), 37; *Chronica di Antonio Godi* (Muratori, *RIS*, new edn., viii, part 2), 12.

[3] Huillard-Bréholles, iv, part ii, 931.   [4] Richard of San Germano, 193.

[5] *Chronica regia Coloniensis*, 269. See also R. Manselli, 'Ezzelino da Romano nella politica italiana del sec. XIII' (*Studi Ezzeliniani*, 1963), 48 ff.

[6] *Annales Veronenses* (Muratori, *RIS* viii, col. 629); ibid. (*MGH, SS.* xix), 10. See also 'Fragmentum de prima Friderici secundi, Romanorum imperatoris, in Lombardos expeditione' (Huillard-Bréholles, iv), part ii, 948.

[7] Ibid.; *Rolandini Patavini, Chronica Marchie Trivixane*, Lib. III.

on his way towards Cremona, Ezzelino, now encamped near the Mincio, received intelligence of the enemy's presence at Ripalto on the
Adige. He hastily planned a manœuvre whereby he hoped to immobilize
the forces of Azzo in the vicinity of Ripalto and, at the same time, to
form a protective shield for Verona. After destroying a near-by bridge
with the object of impeding or preventing the further progress of Azzo's
forces in the direction of Verona, he established contact with friendly
elements in the city of Vicenza, preparatory to a projected attack on
the city. Then, after devoting two weeks to undermining the loyalty of
Azzo's following in that region, he notified the Emperor that all was in
readiness for the attack. After a forced march Frederick appeared
suddenly with his army near the camp of the enemy on the Adige.
This unexpected approach of the Emperor and his army so terrified
the troops from some of the Lombard cities allied with Azzo that they
fled in wild disorder. The combined forces of Frederick and Ezzelino
then moved rapidly towards Vicenza. When the citizens refused to
open the gates, German troops, who had mounted the walls during the
night of 1 November, succeeded in gaining access and plundered and
burned most of the city (*fere totam incendit*) before Ezzelino succeeded in
checking their depredations. In the eyes of one contemporary chronicler
the defiant city had suffered a merited punishment:

> As you deserve, Vicenza, you are consumed by fire;
> You will submit to the just authority of Caesar.[1]

It was shortly after the capture of Vicenza that Frederick, while
walking in a field with Ezzelino, is reported to have said to him: 'I
wish to demonstrate in what manner you must establish firmly your
authority and your leadership in the city.' Then, taking in his hand his
sword, he cut down the long blades of grass.[2] When at length order was
restored in the city Frederick dealt leniently with the citizens, save
those who, like the tall blades of grass, appeared to be a menace. To
most of the inhabitants he restored their possessions. He placed over
them an imperial *podestà*.[3] It was just at this time that the Emperor

---

(Muratori, *RIS*, new edn., viii, part 1), 47 f. See also *Annales Placentini Gibellini* (*MGH, SS.*
xviii), 474.

[1] Richard of San Germano (*MGH, SS.* xix), 374:

> Pro meritis dignis Vincentia te cremat ignis;
> Subderis imperio Cesaris ingenio.

The chief sources for the operation of Ezzelino are: Maurisius, *Cronica Dominorum Eccelini*
(Muratori, *RIS*, new edn., vii, part 4), 39; *Cronica S. Petri Erfordensis* (*MGH, SS.* xxx, part 1),
393; Antonio Godi, *Cronica* (Muratori, *RIS*, new edn., viii, part 2), 12; see also the fragmentary account of Frederick's expedition (Huillard-Bréholles, iv, part ii), 948-9.

[2] Antonio Godi, *Cronica* (Muratori, *RIS*, new edn., viii, part 2), 13.

[3] Maurisius, *Cronica*, loc. cit.

found it necessary to hasten back to Germany where the Duke of Austria continued to be a serious threat to the imperial authority.[1]

The capture of Vicenza opened the way for the surrender of other cities. Ferrara, under the leadership of Salinguerra, surrendered voluntarily, and during February 1237, Ezzelino and Gebhard of Arnstein succeeded in occupying Padua while also gaining some advantages in the March of Treviso. South of the March Ezzelino had reached a peaceful settlement with the Paduans and was permitted to take possession of the city, agreeing to release all prisoners, to pardon all offenders, and to preserve the traditional liberties of the city. On 25 February he made his triumphal entry. It is said that upon entering he removed his iron helmet, leaned sideways from his saddle, and kissed the gatepost of the Porta Torresella. But this singular gesture proved to be no kiss of peace. Soon the nobles and magnates were to witness how well their new lord had learned the lesson of successful despotism from the demonstration of Frederick II in the garden of Vicenza. Such was Ezzelino's cruelty that a conspiracy was formed against him, the object of which was to open the gates of the city secretly to Azzo of Este. But the cunning of Ezzelino detected the conspiracy well in advance and Azzo, upon his arrival, only narrowly escaped capture, leaving most of his following as captives in the prisons of Ezzelino.[2]

Before continuing his operations in Italy Frederick had apparently determined that Austria must first be brought firmly under the imperial authority. His hasty return to Germany is to be attributed also to his desire to obtain the promise of the German princes to elect his son Conrad as King of the Romans. While the German princes had been successful in wresting the cities of Austria, including Vienna, from Duke Frederick, he continued successfully to defy them from his fortified castle of Neustadt. From this stronghold he dominated the right bank of the Danube and the frontiers of Styria, although the Duchy itself had, for the most part, submitted to the imperial authority. Many of the Austrian nobility and the citizens of Vienna, long weary of the tyranny of the Duke, appealed to the Emperor to strengthen his hold over the Duchy. Accordingly, Frederick now determined to take over the government of Austria as if that region were a part of the Hohenstaufen patrimony.[3]

---

[1] *Rolandini Patavini Chronica* (Muratori, *RIS*, new edn., viii, part 1), 48. See also *Annales Bergomates* (*MGH, SS.* xviii), 810, which places the Emperor's departure in November: 'circa festum sancti Andreae [30 November] rediit in Alemaniam ad coadunandum exercitum, Vicentia iam capta.'

[2] *Cronica Dominorum Ecelini et Alberici Fratrum de Romano* (Muratori, *RIS*, new edn., viii, part 4), 41; *Rolandini Patavini Cronica* (Muratori, *RIS*, new edn., viii, part 1), 53, also in *MGH, SS.* xix. 64.

[3] For the Austrian expedition of Frederick see A. Ficker, *Herzog Friedrich II. der letzte Babenberger*, 47 ff. See also *Monumenta Raitenhaselacensia* (*Monumenta Boica*, iii), 134.

As he moved on to Vienna he must have considered this a most propitious time to extend his ambitious plans. He regarded Duke Frederick of Austria as a rebel and an outlaw, thus forfeiting all claims to Austria and the March of Styria. Moreover, with no direct heir to lay claim to these regions, they could become key positions for the imperial control of central Europe. The Emperor's gratification at this opportunity for the extension of his authority is reflected in the several privileges which at this time he bestowed upon his faithful subjects in Styria and Austria in April 1237. Because the inhabitants of Styria had loyally supported him, he decreed that the March was never again to fall under the dominance of an Austrian prince, or of any other prince, save by request of the citizens. Various laws were promulgated also designed to do away with the grievances which the subjects had suffered under the rule of Duke Frederick. Henceforth, judgements were to be pronounced only in accordance with the customary laws of the regions in which the litigants lived. If anyone holding a fief died intestate, the next of kin, whether male or female, could inherit the fief. Trial by battle was abolished and proof by witnesses alone would serve henceforth to determine guilt. Serfs seeking refuge in cities could not be harboured there, save with the consent of the estates, and no new coinage was to be permitted.[1]

Frederick also bestowed a number of privileges upon the city of Vienna. Most meaningful as an indication of his future plan was his initial statement: 'We have taken the city and citizens under the government of ourselves and of the Empire perpetually and irrevocably.' Just as in the *Liber Augustalis* in Sicily, so in these privileges, he reaffirmed earlier laws, especially those granted in 1221 by Leopold 'the Glorious' to his Viennese subjects.[2] Frederick retained for himself and his successors the right to nominate annually the city judge, granting to the municipal council an advisory role. The judge was not permitted, however, to levy any kind of tax or fine, even with the Emperor's consent, unless approved by the citizens. Military service for the citizens was forbidden for a period longer than between sunrise and sunset. Both civil and criminal causes involving citizens were to be tried by the citizens themselves, save in cases involving *lèse-majesté* and high treason. An obvious concession to prevailing religious ideas was the exclusion of Jews from all public offices in order that they might not oppress Christians. Instead of ordeal by battle a citizen was permitted to undergo the seven-fold compurgation. 'Desiring also that appropriate

---

[1] For the complete document see Huillard-Bréholles, v, part i, 61–5. See also A. Ficker, *Herzog Friedrich*, 66–8 and, more recently, H. Hantsch, *Geschichte Österreichs*, i. 105 ff.

[2] For the text of the *Leopoldinum* see Huillard-Bréholles, v, part i, 55 ff.; see also *Urkundenbuch zur Geschichte der Babenberger in Österreich*, ii, no. 237, pp. 56 ff.

provision be made for study, to the end that wisdom may be incul-
cated in the people and the ignorant youth instructed', he provided
for the appointment of a schoolmaster.[1]

Although suggestive of the ultimate aims of Frederick II with
regard to Austria and the March of Styria, his arrangements of 1237
did not long endure. The Duke of Austria, after successfully maintaining his hold on the castle of Neustadt for six months, emerged shortly
after Frederick II's departure in April, took vengeance upon many of
his enemies, and succeeded in carrying on a defensive war for the next
several years. By the summer of 1245 he had regained control of
virtually all his former possessions. Unfortunately, Bishop Eckbert of
Bamberg, who had been designated as governor, died. His successors
generally proved too weak to oppose the Duke effectively, and gradually
while the Emperor was preoccupied with the Lombard conflict for
the next years Duke Frederick built up his strength sufficiently to offer
a formidable resistance to the imperial plans. In the end Frederick II
found it expedient to seek the quarrelsome Duke as an ally. After the
death in 1241 of his third wife, Isabella of England, the Emperor
sought the hand of Gertrude, the niece of Duke Frederick, hoping
thereby to attain peacefully what he had been unable to achieve by
force.[2]

Before returning to the Lombard conflict, however, Frederick II had
accomplished one of the objects of his visit to Germany, the election of
his son Conrad as King of the Romans. Almost simultaneously with
the Emperor's entry into Vienna in January 1237, Conrad had crossed
the Danube to join his father. Undoubtedly Frederick's temporary
success in Styria and Austria had facilitated his obtaining the consent
of the German princes to the choice of his son. That there was still some
opposition to the election is suggested by a statement of a contemporary
chronicler that Conrad had arrived with a large group of associates
with whom he spent 'three months in idleness, dissipation, and drunken-
ness, accomplishing nothing useful'.[3] Without corroborative evidence,
however, this appears to be merely a gratuitous expression of disappro-
bation. Towards the end of February 1237, while still in Austria,
Frederick succeeded in having his son chosen as King of the Romans
by the German princes. Under the agreement with the princes, Conrad
was to be designated as 'King of the Romans and our future Emperor
after his father's death'. Frederick evidently sought in this manner to

---

[1] Huillard-Bréholles, v, part i, 57.

[2] See below, p. 481. For the history of Austria following the Emperor's return to Italy see
H. Hantsch, *Geschichte Österreichs*, 106 ff. See also G. Juritsch, *Geschichte der Babenberger und
ihrer Länder*, 563 ff.

[3] *Continuatio Sancrucensis* (*MGH, SS.* ix), 639. The election has been dealt with in detail by
K. G. Hugelmann, *Die Wahl Konrads IV. zu Wien i. Jahr 1237*.

prevent a repetition of the claims of his son Henry (VII) to the right to rule independently.[1]

The election was noteworthy in several respects. Not only was it brought about without consulting the Pope, but it was achieved by the princes alone as electors, and in such manner that it was evidently intended to emphasize the right of election as solely a princely privilege. In a letter Frederick II described the election as having been accomplished by the German princes in their right as successors of the Conscript Fathers:

For, in the beginning of the city of Rome, after the memorable defeat of the Trojans and the destruction of their celebrated city, the highest power of the Kingdom and the right of creating emperors resided in the Conscript Fathers of the new city. Because, however, of the continuous and successive expansions of the Empire, the pinnacle of such great fortune could not remain within a single city even though, in contrast with others, it was the most noble. But after the authority of the Empire, by virtue of transmigration, had extended even to the most remote regions, it finally came permanently to reside in the German princes, for reasons no less wise than necessary, to the end that the Emperor might spring from those who could provide for the Empire's prosperity and its security.[2]

In the month of April 1237, at the urgent insistence of Hermann of Salza, Frederick consented to the reopening of the negotiations with the Pope and the Lombards. While *en route* from Austria to Bavaria he authorized Hermann, together with Justice Piero della Vigna, to negotiate concerning the Lombard question.[3] The urgency of this renewal of negotiations arose from the activities of the recently appointed papal legates in Lombardy, the March of Treviso, Romanola, and Venetia, Cardinal Bishop Reginald of Ostia and the Cardinal Priest Thomas of S. Sabina, who had been sent into those regions in place of the objectionable James of Palestrina with the ostensible mission of making peace.[4] In the spring of 1237 also Pope Gregory called upon the Lombard cities to send representatives to Mantua. In consultation with the cardinal legates ways and means were to be sought for making peace with the Emperor. They were to endeavour to ascertain also how preparations for the relief of the Holy Land could be better implemented.

It is most improbable that Frederick anticipated a successful outcome

---

[1] *MGH, Const.* ii, no. 329, p. 441: 'eligentes ipsum ibidem in Romanorum regem, et in futurum imperatorem nostrum post obitum patris habendum.' See also H. Bloch, *Die staufischen Kaiserwahlen und die Entstehung des Kurfürstentums*, 332 f.

[2] *MGH, Const.* ii, loc. cit.

[3] Richard of San Germano, 193.

[4] Huillard-Bréholles, iv, part ii, 925: 'ut ibi pacem reformare procurent'. See also the letter of Pope Gregory, *MGH, Epist. Pont.* i, no. 704, p. 605.

of the mission of his ambassadors. Despite the necessity of abandoning the Mantuan meeting, Frederick's ambassadors insisted that it be held in Brescia instead, and that Lombard representatives be summoned to appear there not later than 25 July 1237. The legates, however, in telling the Pope of the postponement of the meeting, also painted a lurid picture of the conditions which they found in Lombardy, dwelling especially upon the sad plight of the prisoners held by the Emperor: how they were threatened by fire and sword, their hands cut off, how not even children and widows were spared, and how no respect was shown for sacred things.[1] It was probably more than idle suspicion, therefore, that made the Emperor doubt the sincerity of the cardinals as peacemakers. When at length a meeting with them took place the proposals for a peaceful settlement were: the Lombard League was to be dissolved, not again to be revived, and all members released from their obligations. The formerly hostile cities were to provide troops to be employed by the Emperor on a crusade, and to restore to him all rights pertaining to the Empire. Citizens who had been banished from Piacenza were to be permitted to return.[2]

Whether or not the attitude of the cardinal legates contributed to the failure, the attempted negotiations proved futile. It is not unlikely that a letter of Piero della Vigna set forth the true cause of the failure when he wrote to the Archbishop of Capua: 'Our skiff is tossed about between Scylla and Charybdis, between the machinations of the cardinals and the Lombards.'[3] Hermann of Salza revealed the dissatisfaction of the Emperor, who was still in Germany, with the attempt to achieve peace through negotiations when he wrote to the cardinals: 'Caesar with a victorious army is *en route* for Lombardy.' He told them also of the dissatisfaction of the princes of Germany and of their demands that the Lombards be subjugated, 'not by conciliation, but by the shedding of blood as the outraged *imperium* requires'.[4]

The Emperor, meanwhile, having disposed satisfactorily of his affairs in Germany, set out in August 1237 for his return to Italy, arriving in Mantua on 12 September. His army was not large, but was rapidly augmented by forces from the Ghibelline cities, Verona, Pavia, Parma, Cremona, Reggio, Ferrara, and Modena, together with the mounted troops of Ezzelino. Also 10,000 Saracen troops had been ordered up from Lucera. The Emperor again made his camp on the banks of the Mincio at Goito in the diocese of Mantua.[5] In contrast with his earlier expedition, his combined forces were now so great as

[1] *MGH, Epist. Pont.* i, no. 704, p. 610.
[2] *Annales Placentini Gibellini* (*MGH, SS.* xviii), 476.
[3] Piero della Vigna, *Epist.* iii. 29.
[4] Huillard-Bréholles, v, part i, 93 f.
[5] *Annales Veronenses* (*MGH, SS.* xix), 10, *Annales Placentini Gibellini* (*MGH, SS.* xviii), 476.

to cause anxiety in the regions through which he passed. Many of his former foes hastened to make peace. As one stronghold after another fell into the hands of the Emperor (incuding Goito, where he established his camp, Montechiaro, and others on the route to Cremona),[1] the fear of the cities increased. They followed the movements of the Emperor closely, although refusing to give battle in the open fields.

The Pope also, no less alarmed for the papal interests than were the cities for their own, endeavoured to reopen negotiations with the Emperor. It was a last desperate attempt when on 2 November 1237 Gregory again appealed to Frederick to devote his military efforts to a crusade, emphasizing especially the need of support for the French crusaders with ships, supplies, the use of harbours and other facilities within the Kingdom of Sicily.[2] But the appeal, probably futile in any case, was too late. The Milanese and their allies were now fully armed and were busily engaged in gathering reinforcements.[3]

By mid November the Lombard troops had constructed a well-nigh impregnable camp not far from Ponte Vico on swampy terrain formed by a tributary stream and the river Oglio. Their location enabled them not only to withstand the assaults of the enemy but also to cover the city of Brescia. But Frederick manœuvred his troops in such manner as to give the impression that it was his intention to withdraw to Cremona, some thirty miles south, for the winter. The enemy, observing these movements and convinced of his intention to go into winter quarters, now felt free to emerge from their stronghold. They had failed to observe, however, that Frederick had retained a considerable force, including his Saracen cavalry, which he planned to employ in an intercepting movement if and when the Lombard forces, using the bridges up-stream, attempted to cross the river in the direction of Milan. At Soncino he awaited the next movement of the enemy forces. After two days they began to evacuate their swampy stronghold and to cross the Oglio near Cortenuova. Upon receiving intelligence of this movement, Frederick broke camp on 27 November, sending an advance-guard well forward of the main body to observe the enemy. Coming upon a detachment of enemy troops the advance-guard engaged with them, routing them after about an hour's fighting. The enemy fell back as far as the position of the *carroccio* or standard-chariot of the Milanese, nearly two miles from Cortenuova. Meanwhile, the Emperor, coming up from Soncino with the main body of his army, received a report of the engagement of his advance-guard. Fearing for the fate of this relatively small detachment, he hastened to its relief

---

[1] *Chronica regia Coloniensis*, 271. See also *Annales Placentini Gibellini* (*MGH, SS.* xviii), 476–7, and F. Stieve, *Ezzelino*, 37–8.

[2] Huillard-Bréholles, v, part i, 126–8.   [3] Piero della Vigna, *Epist.* ii. 3, 35, 50.

only to find that the encounter had ended. The road was blocked by the dead and dying men and horses of the enemy. With the Emperor's arrival the battle was resumed near the *carroccio*. The mounted troops and the foot soldiers of the Lombards were in closely massed formation, prepared for a last-ditch resistance. In a desperate effort they succeeded

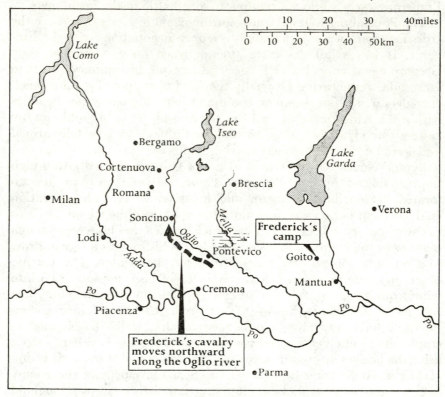

MAP 4. Site of the battle of Cortenuova

in holding their position until darkness forced the cessation of battle. The imperial forces, however, spent the night in an alert position, removing their swords but retaining their armour on their bodies. With the coming of the dawn it was discovered that the enemy had withdrawn. They had evacuated the castle of Cortenuova, leaving behind their pack-train and a part of the *carroccio*, carrying with them only its upper portion including the cross. In the speed of their flight, however, even this was later abandoned because of the difficulty of transporting it over roads flooded by heavy rains. Many of the Lombards had failed to make their escape and large numbers, including the *podestà* of Milan, Pietro Tiepolo, son of the Doge of Venice, were taken prisoner.[1]

---

[1] *Annales Placentini Gibellini* (*MGH, SS.* xviii), 476 ff.; Matthew Paris, *Chronica majora,*

As to the numbers captured or slain, Frederick said, in concluding his letter to his brother-in-law, the Earl of Cornwall: 'It is estimated that nearly ten thousand men were taken or slain, among whom fell many nobles and leaders of the Milanese faction.' From the conflicting contemporary sources it is impossible to make an accurate computation of the numbers of the opposing forces, particularly of the slain and captured. It appears highly probable that the number of imperial troops at the outset did not exceed 25,000, while those of the Lombards numbered less than 20,000. There is some reason to assume also that on the morning of the actual encounter the numbers engaged on each side were considerably less, probably about 19,000 imperial troops and some 16,000 Milanese and their allies.[1] The rejoicing of the imperial party at the outcome of the battle knew no bounds, moving the Emperor and others to write lengthy and ornate letters which serve as indispensable sources for the details of the battle. Among the most notable of these are the above-mentioned letter of Frederick to Richard of Cornwall and another to the Archbishop of York.[2] Even more striking is an encyclical letter of Piero della Vigna, the High Court Justice, addressed to the faithful of the Empire, of which the following passages are typical: 'But who can describe the perils of that day? Who can tell of the heaps of the enemy dead? Who can count the multitude of the captured?' In describing the prowess of the Emperor and his German troops, Piero wrote: 'Then Caesar, in advance of all his soldiers, gave proof of his matchless valour, and his Germans bathed their swords in the crimson blood.'[3]

After the battle of Cortenuova Frederick made his triumphal entry into the city of Cremona. The celebration of the victory was reminiscent of the triumphs of the Emperors of ancient Rome. In the procession were numerous prisoners of war, their leaders following in chains. The *carroccio* of the Milanese, now the symbol of their degradation, was dragged along by the Emperor's elephant, the centre of interest to the spectators. On the back of the elephant was mounted a wooden tower from the pinnacle of which floated the imperial banner; at its base lay the banner of the enemy. The *carroccio* was shorn of its emblem of honour, its standard lowered and trailing in the dust. The chief of the Guelfs, Pietro Tiepolo, *podestà* of Milan, a rope round his neck and his hands manacled with heavy chains, was bound to the front of the

iii. 443 (Frederick's letter to the Earl of Cornwall). The battle has been dealt with by K. Hadank, *Die Schlacht bei Cortenuova*.

[1] I have found no more plausible computation than that made many years ago by C. W. von Funck, *Geschichte Kaiser Friedrichs des Zweiten* (1792), 204–5. See also J. Mikulla, *Der Söldner in den Heeren Kaiser Friedrichs II.*, 36 ff.

[2] Huillard-Bréholles, v, part i, 134 ff.

[3] Ibid. 138–9.

triumphal chariot. The gaily decorated streets were filled with singing and rejoicing throngs and above the din of the procession the blasts of the trumpets heralded the approach of the Emperor.[1]

The celebration of the victory of Cortenuova was in every respect a reflection of Frederick II's concept of himself as the successor of the ancient Caesars. Even the battle in which, above the din and clatter, was heard the imperial war-cry '*Miles, Roma! Miles, Imperator!*' echoed the spirit of Roman antiquity. Few incidents in the life of Frederick reveal more clearly his insistent efforts to restore to the Middle Ages the glory that was ancient Rome's. The triumphal procession through the streets of the friendly Cremona was meticulously staged in accordance with the ancient pattern as described by medieval chroniclers such as Sicard of Cremona, who, in his *Mitra* or *De Officiis Ecclesiasticis Summa*, depicted in detail a typical *Triumphus* of the ancient Caesars, and in accordance with the well-defined technical phraseology pertaining to the *Triumphus* in the *Etymologies* of Isidore of Seville.[2]

News of the victory at Cortenuova, announced to the Pope and Curia in a jubilant letter of Piero della Vigna, occasioned them profound sorrow. The Pope is said to have been saddened 'even unto death' (*usque ad mortem doluit*) when the *carroccio* of the Milanese was presented to the Roman magistrates in a gesture emphasizing the imperial office as a heritage from the ancient Caesars:

> Therefore, O city, may you be mindful of those former triumphs
> Offered to you by the Kings who waged war![3]

In defiance of the papal resistance the senate had the *carroccio* placed in the Capitol, mounted on five marble columns with the following inscription:

> RECEIVE, O ROME, AS AN ETERNAL
> ORNAMENT OF THE CITY, THIS CARROCCIO,
> THE GIFT OF THE AUGUST EMPEROR, FREDERICK II!

---

[1] The most detailed description of the Emperor's triumphal entry is that of Piero della Vigna, *Epist.* ii. 35. Brief descriptions are those of *Chronica regia Coloniensis*, 271–2, and *Andreae Danduli Chronicon* (Muratori, *RIS*, new edn. xii), 350. For the elephant and its caparisoned wooden tower see Salimbene, *Cronica* (*MGH, SS.* xxxii), 94. *Alberti Milioli Notarii Regini Liber de Temporibus* (*MGH, SS.* xxxi), 512, describes the elephant as having on its back a well-armed *carroccio*. For the humiliation of Pietro Tiepolo see H. Kretschmayr, *Geschichte von Venedig*, ii. 43 ff.

[2] For Sicard's description see Migne, *PL* 213, col. 82. See also *Isidori Hispalensis Episcopi Etymologiarum sive Originum Libri XX* (ed. W. M. Lindsay), vol. ii, Books XVIII, ii: 'De Triumphis', Book XIX, xxiv: 'Toga . . . Trabea'. P. E. Schramm, *Kaiser, Rom et Renovatio*, part ii, 39–40.

[3] For the reaction of the Pope see *Annales Placentini Gibellini* (*MGH, SS.* xviii), 478. For the verse accompanying the *carroccio* see Huillard-Bréholles, v, 163, note 1:

> Ergo triumphorum Urbs potes memor esse priorum
> Quos tibi mittebant reges qui bella gerebant!

CAPTURED THROUGH THE DEFEAT OF MILAN,
IT COMES AS A GLORIOUS SPOIL OF VICTORY
TO PROCLAIM THE EMPEROR'S TRIUMPH.
LET IT STAND IN THE CITY IT IS SENT TO HONOUR,
A REMINDER OF THE OPPROBRIUM OF THE ENEMY.
VENERATION FOR THE CITY IMPELLED HIM TO SEND IT.[1]

---

[1] Muratori, *Antiq.*, ii. 491–2:

CAESARIS AUGUSTI FRIDERICI ROMA SECUNDI
DONA TENE, CURRUM, PERPES IN URBE DECUS.
HIC MEDIOLANI CAPTUS DE STRAGE TRIUMPHOS
CAESARIS UT REFERAT, INCLITA PRAEDA VENIT.
HOSTIS IN OPPROBRIUM PENDEBIT IN URBIS HONOREM
MICTITUR. HUNC URBIS MICTERE JUSSIT AMOR.

II

CONTINUED CONQUEST OF THE LOMBARD COMMUNES

Urbs cecidit, de qua, si quicquam dicere dignum
Moliar, hoc potero dicere: 'Roma fuit!'
Non tamen annorum series, non flamma, nec ensis
Ad plenum potuit hoc abolere decus.

> Hildebert of Lavardin (in Jean-Barthélemy Hauréau, *Les Mélanges
> poétiques d'Hildebert de Lavardin*, Paris, 1882), xxxvii, lines 19 ff.[1]

A NY uncertainty there may have been as to the ultimate aims of
Frederick II ceased to exist after the fall of Vicenza and his defeat of the Milanese and their allies at Cortenuova. Even before
he left Germany more than a suggestion of his ambitious plans was
implicit in his letter to Pope Gregory IX claiming Italy as 'my heritage'.
His intentions at that time seem to have encompassed far more than
the mere punishment of the arrogant Lombard communes. The Pope
himself must have sensed an ominous change in the attitude of his
great antagonist. Not Verona, not Vicenza, not even Milan, was the
coveted goal of his conquering expedition—but Rome, the Eternal
City, restored as the centre of the renewed Empire of antiquity. In
this moment which brought him so near to the realization of the dignity of the *imperium* of the Caesars, he wrote to the citizens of Rome:

All powerful reason and nature which rules over kings make it our duty,
in this moment of triumph, to extol the fame of the city which our predecessors exalted by the splendour of their triumphs and, in appropriate language
we acknowledge our obligation. For if indeed the triumph is associated with
the inevitable nature of its origin, we would not be able to exalt the imperial
office unless first we extol the honour of the city which we recognize as the
source of our *imperium* . . . Accept, therefore, O Quirites, with gratitude the
triumph of your Emperor! From this may your fondest hope be realized
because, since we love to conform to the customs of antiquity, we aspire to
the restoration of the ancient nobility of the city.[2]

---

[1]   The city fell, of which, if I labour to say something worthy of her,
            I shall be able to say this: "She was Rome!"
     But neither the passing years,
            nor fire, nor sword,
     Could destroy its grandeur completely.

[2] Huillard-Bréholles, v, part i, 161-3.

In contrast with the rejoicing of Frederick II and the citizens of Cremona, the defeat at Cortenuova filled the Milanese with black despair. A contemporary chronicler relates that the citizens, 'raising their heels against God', suspended the crucifixes upside down in their churches, polluted the altars with unmentionable filth, expelled the clergy, ate flesh on fast-days and during Lent. For the moment the cities of the Lombard League were demoralized. On 12 December Lodi submitted to the Emperor almost without a show of resistance. The city of Milan, recognized leader of the rebellious cities, surrounded by the enemy, deprived of communication with many of her allies, was dangerously weakened. Bridges had been broken and highways made impassable so that necessary provisions were often wanting. Of this widespread demoralization Matthew Paris wrote: 'Many surrendered themselves and their cities, humbled by the example of others.'[1] In Lodi, where he spent the greater part of December 1237, Frederick continued his preparations for his chief immediate objective, an attack against the city of Milan, planned for the following spring. From there also early in the year 1238 he ordered a heavy *collecta* to be levied throughout the Kingdom of Sicily.[2]

Milan, now deserted by many of her old allies in the League, and threatened by other cities formerly oppressed by her, felt compelled to appeal to the Emperor for a peaceful settlement. Early in December a Minorite brother, Leo, accompanied by several nobles and citizens of Milan, repaired to the imperial camp with generous peace proposals. Some differences exist among contemporary sources as to the details of these proposals, but, in general, they appear to have contained the following: recognition of the Emperor as their legitimate sovereign; the surrender or destruction of their banners or else payment of a considerable sum of gold and silver as compensation for past damages; the providing of 10,000 troops annually to be employed by the Emperor in the Holy Land. In return they required of the Emperor that he forget their past differences and that he permit them to retain their traditional privileges. 'But', says a contemporary chronicler, 'the lord Emperor refused all these offers, obstinately demanding that the citizens, together with the city and property, surrender themselves voluntarily to his will.' The Milanese stoutly rejected this demand to which they are said to have replied: 'We fear your savagery, having learned by experience. We would rather die by the sword or spear behind our shields than by treachery, starvation, or the flames.'[3] In vain those who were

---

[1] Matthew Paris, *Chronica majora*, iii. 409–10.
[2] Richard of San Germano, 193.
[3] Matthew Paris, *Chronica majora*, iii. 496; *Thomae Tusci Gesta* (*MGH, SS.* xxii), 513: 'ut omnem voluntatem suam de civitate posset facere et personis.'

closest to the Emperor endeavoured to persuade him to pursue a more conciliatory policy. The chronicler Salimbene tells of the intercession of one of Frederick's natural daughters, Violante, the Countess of Caserta. She is said to have asked the Emperor: 'Why do you plunge into another war with the Lombards, since already you have everything in your Kingdom in which human life could take delight?' Frederick is said to have replied: 'I am aware Countess that what you say is true, but I have now gone so far that I cannot turn back save with dishonour.'[1] In this reply there is much more than mere arrogance and obstinacy inspired by the events of the moment. To Frederick II with his concept of the *imperium*, the God-given supreme authority upon earth, there could be no turning back—only a pressing forward until, at length, the goal was attained: supremacy in all temporal things within the Empire. Frederick II was too well aware of the potentialities of the Lombard cities, especially of the most powerful of these, Milan, to have any doubts that, despite evidences of submission, this was a crucial conflict, a struggle to determine the future sovereignty over Italy. He had to crush the temporal authority of the papacy and the Lombard communes, the two things which prevented his restoration of imperial authority. The Milanese offer of submission, compensation, and military aid for the conquest of the Holy Land was worthless, unless the commune and all its allies had yielded unconditionally to the imperial authority.

In this moment of his ascending fortunes Frederick II seems to have lost something of the caution which had habitually characterized his relations with both the Pope and the communes. He obviously regarded the unwillingness of Milan to yield unconditionally as a temporary decision, likely to be altered under the pressure which he now believed himself to be in a position to apply. During these months of triumph in 1236–8 he was convinced that at last he had found favourable conditions in which to implement the administrative and judicial systems which had gradually evolved since his imperial coronation. Vicenza, Padua, Treviso, Mantua, Lodi, and the greater part of the Piedmont had now yielded to the conquests of his captains. What he achieved in these regions was to be the pattern not only of his future reign, but of that of his successors, both Hohenstaufen and Angevin. The key to his reorganization was centralization, to be implemented through a hierarchical organization, centring in the person of the Emperor and his Curia Regis and extending downward through vicar-generalships to the *podestàs* of each city, subject always to the despotic authority of the Emperor. The system would be still further perfected when the officials of both the vicariates and the individual cities were of Sicilian origin

---

[1] *Cronica*, 303.

and fully acquainted with the hierarchical organization as it had operated in the Kingdom. The final stage of its development would be attained when Frederick's sons and sons-in-law occupied the more important vicar-generalships.[1] The communes, now becoming imperial cities, would necessarily surrender their autonomy and the right of free election of their magistrates. The high court of the Kingdom would extend its jurisdiction to the imperial vicariates throughout the conquered regions of Italy.[2]

Seen in retrospect, the dynamic historical force of the thirteenth century—communal movement—was far too vigorous to be successfully checked by the resources at the command of the Emperor. Had it been possible for Frederick II to raise and to maintain a standing army, conscious of its obligation to a unified and solidified Empire, he could have forced the permanent submission of the ambitious communes. But with decentralization widespread in much of the Empire, and with the spirit of independence rampant both in the principalities of Germany and in the communes of Italy, the future could offer to Frederick only a continuous series of wars against a hydra-headed monster. No sooner would he achieve a momentary victory over one or several of these, comparable to that at Cortenuova, than he must again assemble his forces to crush another, leaving the previously conquered cities or principalities to recover their strength and their resources for the renewal of the conflict. In a large sense, the inevitable failure of the vast concept of Empire of Frederick II was presaged in his recognition at this time that he had gone too far to be able to turn back, save with dishonour. Even if he had displayed a conciliatory spirit, as did his grandfather after the misfortune of Legnano, the result could have been nothing more than a temporary pacification. The victory of Cortenuova had given a new, albeit an unwarranted, stimulus to Frederick's Caesarian ambitions, evoking in him a reckless optimism. He envisaged himself as delivering a crushing blow, first to the recalcitrant Lombard cities, and then to the Roman papacy, if it persisted in its opposition to his destined goal: the restoration of the Empire with its heart and centre in its ancient abode, the Eternal City of Rome. In order to attain this goal he must overcome, on the one hand, the will of the Milanese and their allies to resist to the last ditch and, on the other hand, the thoroughly aroused Pope and Curia, who were willing for the moment to subordinate the spiritual leadership of Christendom to the task of gaining pre-eminence in the temporal sovereignty of the world.

[1] See below, pp. 445, 449 ff.
[2] See also E. Jordan, *Origines*, Introduction, 7, li, lv, and Ficker, *Forschungen*, ii, par. 416, pp. 530 ff.

It is a plausible assumption that it was under the influence of this optimistic outlook, and probably while in Verona in early April 1238, that Frederick wrote enthusiastically to the people and senate of Rome concerning his plans to elevate the city once more to its ancient dignity (*in statu dignitatis antique*). He mentioned also his intention to bestow upon the magistrates and citizens various official positions of honour in the imperial administration.[1]

In the vicinity of Verona during April 1238 Frederick II busied himself with the gathering of troops for his projected attack of the Milanese and their allies. Cremona and Reggio provided him with considerable numbers of mercenaries, both mounted troops and foot-soldiers.[2] In June the Count of Acerra and the Grand Justiciar, Henry of Morra, arrived with troops, money, and supplies from the Kingdom of Sicily. Various Christian countries, including France, Spain, England, Hungary, and Greece, provided him with troops, often mere adventurers, restless and predatory men. From England also came a hundred knights, led by Henry of Trubleville, sent by the King of England who also supplied the Emperor with substantial sums of money.[3] In late June or early July also a large and well-equipped army from Germany, accompanied by young Conrad, entered Italy via the valley of the Adige. The Saracen troops from the Kingdom of Sicily were also summoned to the north once more, bringing with them pack animals, mules, camels, and dromedaries.

Because of the dominant position of Milan in relation to the Lombard cities, it would at first glance appear desirable to centre the attack directly upon that city. Its capture and the punishment of its traditionally hostile citizens would certainly have brought to an end the resistance of its allies. But Frederick recognized the difficulties and hazards of such an undertaking, well aware of Milan's superior resources, the strength of its fortifications, and the prowess of its citizens in resisting such attacks. Brescia, on the other hand, the most dependable ally and second only to Milan as a rallying point for resistance to the Emperor, was less well fortified. Perhaps decisive also was the

---

[1] Huillard-Bréholles, v, part ii, 761. The dating of this letter has long been the subject of controversy: thus Huillard-Bréholles, v. 761, fixes the date as 1240, while Winkelmann (*FzDG* xii, 1872), p. 287, note 1, prefers 1239; *BFW*, *Reg.* v, Abt. i, no. 2199, places it in Oct. 1236. More tenable is the conclusion of Gregorovius, *Geschichte der Stadt Rom* (4th edn.), v. 197–8, note 4, that the letter was written in 1238, a date which has been most plausibly established by Kantorowicz in his *Friedrich der Zweite*, ii. 283 ff.

[2] For his recruiting at this time and for the arrival of troops from Sicily and elsewhere see especially *Annales Placentini Gibellini* (*MGH*, *SS.* xviii), 479; and *Memorial Potestatum Regiensium Gestorumque iis Temporibus a 1154–1290 auctore anonymo Regiensi* (Muratori, *RIS* viii), col. 197; *Chronica Brixienses* (ibid., xiv), col. 910. Concerning Frederick's political and military situation in Northern Italy after Cortenuova see R. Cessi, 'Dopo Cortenuova' (*Archivio storico pugliese*, xiii, 1960), 77–90.

[3] Matthew Paris, *Chronica majora*, iii. 485.

advice of Ezzelino of Romano, who, doubtless for reasons of personal ambition, strongly urged that Brescia be taken before the assault be made upon Milan. On 11 July 1238 the siege was begun. The main camp of the imperial army lay between the river Mella and the city of Brescia. In preparation for the attack the Emperor had ordered the most formidable siege-machines known to thirteenth-century warfare: siege-towers, trebuchets, mangonels, *ballistae*, and battering-rams. Conditions appeared to be most favourable for a victorious siege, promising even greater fame to the Emperor than the battle of Cortenuova. But ill prepared as the Brescians seem to have been, they were fortunate in taking captive a Spanish military engineer, one Calamandrinus, who had been procured by Ezzelino as engineer to aid the imperial forces in the attack of the city. Quickly recognizing the usefulness of their captive for the construction of much-needed defences, the Brescians rewarded him with not only a home but also a wife in return for his services in preparing the defences of the city. As the siege continued this fortunate capture of a capable engineer contributed decisively to the ultimate success of the Brescians.[1]

But even more, the besieged, conscious of the Emperor's hatred of their city as the intimate associate of Milan, and expecting only the most extreme punishment in the event of their capture, resisted the attack with the utmost determination. Surprised and angered at this obstinate resistance of the citizens, who had defied the assaults of his machines and killed many of his troops, Frederick resorted to a device which was long to remain a blemish on his memory. In order to protect the remaining siege-towers from the *ballistae* of the Brescians he bound prisoners, many of whom had been taken captive in the battle of Cortenuova, in positions where they would be exposed to the projectiles of the besieged, in the expectation that in consideration for their kinsmen among the prisoners, the Brescians would desist from further use of their destructive weapons. As a retaliatory measure, however, the Brescians suspended imperial prisoners in front of the enemy battering-rams which were breaching their walls. But the most effective of the defensive measures of the besieged were their frequent sorties against the enemy; in most of these they had been repulsed, but not without inflicting some losses upon the enemy. In early October, on an unusually dark night, they made such a sortie into the enemy camp, surprising the German troops. Penetrating deep into the lines and finding the enemy troops sleeping in their tents, gorged with wine (*multo gravati vino somnoque*), they inflicted heavy losses upon them. It is said that the invading detachments penetrated almost to the quarters of the Emperor. Frederick had wasted more than two months in an

---

[1] *Annales Placentini Gibellini*, 479.

unsuccessful siege which had brought only humiliation to his forces. Unseasonable weather with storms and continuous rains had increased the difficulties of the operation. Most of all, the morale of his motley troops had been shattered. The successful sally of the Brescians served as a decisive blow. The Emperor burned his siege-machines and abandoned the operation, withdrawing to the friendly city of Cremona.[1] He dismissed the Ghibelline troops that had joined him from the various Italian cities, retaining only part of the feudal army from Germany.

How greatly Frederick II had exaggerated the importance of his victory at Cortenuova, how nebulous were his dreams of a restored Empire, became all too apparent as he abandoned the siege of the city which was to have been the first step towards the crushing of Milan and the Lombard League. The fear which he had inspired among the more timid of the Lombard cities was now dissipated. The *émigrés* from Brescia and elsewhere, who had relied on the success of the imperial arms to restore them to their native cities, were discouraged. Many of them, anticipating continuous exile, requested of the Emperor new homes and lands in the Kingdom of Sicily. In response to this request he gave them the former Saracen city of Corleone and the surrounding territory where, during the year 1238–9, a Lombard colony was established.[2] The failure of Frederick II was much more than a temporary defeat. It was soon apparent that it marked a turning-point in his conflict with the Lombards and the papacy. Milan, Bologna, and Piacenza were soon once more on the offensive. The Pope, who had affected a hands-off policy while the siege of Brescia was in progress, now again assumed an attitude of open sympathy for the Lombard cause as well as an unmistakable hostility to the Emperor. As early as August 1238 he took a step which was an open declaration of war by sending into Lombardy one of the most implacable of Frederick's foes, Gregory of Montelongo, authorized first merely as courier or *missus* (*nuntius*), but later named as legate of the Pope. Under whatever title he carried out his mission in Lombardy, this skilled intriguer and capable military leader was to offer, henceforth, the most formidable opposition to the plans of Frederick II.[3] He was to achieve among the cities of the Lombard League a unity and solidarity which prior to this time had never been attained. Not since his alliance with Frederick

---

[1] The chief source is *Annales Placentini Gibellini*, 480. See also *Chron. Estense* (Muratori, *RIS*, new edn.), xv, pt. 3, 15; *Annales S. Justinae Patavini* (*MGH, SS.* xix), 156: 'Et ita eodem anno imperator obsedit Brixiam a medio Julio usque ad festum sancti Michaelis'; *Chronica Brixienses* (Muratori, *RIS*, xiv), col. 912; *Alberti Milioli Notarii Regini Liber de Temporibus* (*MGH, SS.* xxxi), 513. See also E. Jordan, *Origines*, p. lxxi.

[2] T. Fazzello, *De Rebus Siculis Decades Duae* (Palermo, 1558), 265.

[3] For his activities see especially H. Frankfurth, *Gregorius de Montelongo*, 12 ff.; and the more recent article of G. Marchetti Longhi, 'La legazione in Lombardia di Gregorio da Monte Longo' (*Archivio Soc. Rom.* xxxvi, 1913), 225 ff., especially pp. 261 ff.

in opposition to King Henry (VII) of Germany had the Pope felt freer to assume the role in which he now appeared, that of leader of resistance to the Emperor. Throughout the siege of Brescia, although aware of the Pope's attitude, Frederick continued his efforts to negotiate with Gregory in Rome whither the latter had recently returned after one of his numerous forced sojourns in Anagni.[1]

Yet, while these negotiations were in progress, Frederick did not hesitate to take a step which could only result in the most bitter opposition from the Pope. He arranged the marriage of his natural son Enzio to Adelasia, heiress to several provinces of the Kingdom of Sardinia. The opposition of the Pope to this marriage, which he considered as having for its object the absorption of Sardinia into the Empire, had its origin in a dubious claim of the Church to the island. This claim was based originally on the forgery, the so-called Donation of Constantine and, subsequently, on the alleged renewal in the Donation of Louis the Pious. There had been little or no opposition to this claim throughout the early Middle Ages. As late as 1219 Frederick II had pledged himself, in so far as possible, to defend and to aid the Church in retaining Sicily, Corsica, Sardinia, and other jurisdictions of the Holy See.[2] But long before this somewhat perfunctory promise was made by Frederick II at Hagenau, Sardinia had become the object of conflicting claims between Genoa and Pisa. Apparently ignoring papal claims, or else considering them moribund, Frederick Barbarossa, on 17 April 1165, with the consent of the German princes, had conferred the sovereignty over Sardinia upon Pisa.[3] At that time, however, the Genoese refused to abandon their claim and war continued periodically between the two powerful commercial rivals, Pisa and Genoa, for the possession of the island. Two Pisans, Ubald and Lambert Visconti, armed a considerable fleet and launched an attack upon the Genoese, who, meanwhile, had recognized the overlordship of the Holy See in Sardinia. Upon the death of Lambert Visconti, Ubald succeeded to the sovereignty over several Sardinian provinces. Other districts or provinces of the island, notably Gallura and Logudoro, were held by Adelasia who, shortly afterwards, was married to Ubald Visconti, thus uniting most of the provinces. In 1237, in a reconciliation between the Pope and Ubald, both he and Adelasia agreed to swear fealty to the Pope as overlord of Sardinia. Moreover, under the terms of the agreement, the provinces held by Adelasia were to revert to the possession of the Holy See in the event of her death without heir.[4]

---

[1] Richard of San Germano, 198.
[2] *MGH, Const.* ii, no. 65, pp. 77ff.
[3] Stumpf, no. 4042; *Annales Pisani* (*MGH, SS.* xix), 252. See also W. von Giesebrecht, *Kaiserzeit,* v. 486; and vi. 449.
[4] Muratori, *Antiq.* vi. 19–20.

Shortly after this agreement had been made Ubald died and Frederick II seized this opportunity to extend the imperial influence over the island. He negotiated a marriage alliance between his young son Enzio, who had recently attained his majority and had been knighted by his father, and the widowed Adelasia.[1] But Pope Gregory IX, no less eager to ensure the rights of the Holy See in the island, had other plans. In a letter consoling Adelasia on the loss of 'so noble a husband', he reminded her of the expediency of a remarriage and generously offered his services in seeking a suitable spouse.[2] Perhaps for reasons of delicacy, the Pope forebore at this time mentioning the name of the prospective groom, although shortly afterwards in another letter he revealed to the young widow that his choice was a man faithful to the Holy See.[3] In this second letter he threatened her with excommunication if she married anyone 'who might do injury to the rights of the Church'. But despite such threats, Adelasia made her own decision and in October she was married to Enzio.[4]

Gregory IX vigorously protested against the marriage for which he blamed Frederick II. In his excommunication of the Emperor shortly afterwards the Sardinian affair was among the chief complaints drawn up by the Curia. But Frederick stoutly supported his own claims to the island much as his grandfather, Frederick Barbarossa, had done in 1165. After asserting that Sardinia had belonged to the Empire since antiquity, he said: 'I have sworn, as now the world knows, to restore the scattered Empire, and this I shall accomplish with unremitting effort.'[5]

Already determined to oppose the Emperor with all available resources, the Pope's indignation towards him was redoubled. An opportunity for revenge soon arose. Chagrined by his failure at Brescia, Frederick had turned to the commune of Genoa for aid in his effort to gain control of north-western Italy. Shortly after abandoning the siege of Brescia he sent an embassy to Genoa to obtain from the council the oath of fealty of the commune. Upon the insistence of several citizens that a matter of such great importance should be placed before the whole body of citizens, the *podestà* summoned a popular assembly to be held in the church of San Lorenzo. Here the demands of the Emperor were read. The *podestà*, who favoured the Guelf faction, in a fiery address warned the citizens of the heavy burdens which would be thrust upon them under the imperial regime and told them of the tyrannous acts of the Emperor in various parts of the Empire. Moved by this

[1] *Annales Placentini Gibellini*, 480.
[2] *MGH, Epist. Pont.* i. 624.
[3] Ibid., p. 629: 'nobilem virum Guefum de Porcaria, apostolice sedis filium et fidelium.'
[4] Richard of San Germano, 198.
[5] Matthew Paris, *Chronica majora*, iii. 527.

address and the obvious agreement of the citizens, the council dismissed the imperial embassy with an official refusal to submit.[1] The Pope lost no time in taking advantage of this favourable state of affairs in Genoa. In a well-equipped galley he sent his own embassy there for the purpose of bringing about peaceful relations and also to secure a reconciliation and alliance between Genoa and Venice. As a result of the papal effort the two republics signed a treaty on 30 November 1238 that was to continue for nine years, during which they agreed to act jointly against all who disobeyed the spiritual authority of the Pope.[2] They agreed also to act jointly against any corsair or enemy who made unsafe the sea routes between Genoa and Venice or between Sardinia and Genoa. During a voyage the ships of each were to display both Genoese and Venetian flags, their own on the right, the other's on the left. All differences arising between the two were to be resolved by the Pope. Finally they agreed that during the next nine years no *rapprochement* of any kind with the Emperor would be made save with the consent of the Pope.[3]

But Gregory was not satisfied with merely a defensive alliance. He aimed at a more comprehensive plan, an offensive alliance of the two great sea powers which ultimately could result in the conquest of the Kingdom of Sicily. He succeeded first in winning the support of Genoa for the plan when, on 26 July 1239, an agreement was reached with that city enlisting its services in the conquest of the Kingdom of Sicily.[4] This agreement was of little value, however, without the participation of Venice. Moreover, it was stipulated in the Genoese treaty that Genoa would not be bound by the aforesaid terms if the commune of Venice did not enter into a similar agreement with the Pope and the Roman Church. It was not until 23 September that the Venetians, after much hesitation, accepted the terms, the most important of which were: each of the cities agreed to arm twenty-five galleys for the conquest of Sicily, the Pope providing half of the cost; as compensation, they agreed also to transport 500 or 600 mounted troops, 4,000 foot soldiers, and 1,000 slingers which the Pope would supply; if the war continued for more than six months and the Emperor was not checked in Lombardy, the contracting cities were to equip eight galleys at their own expense. Above all, the contracting parties were, under no circumstances, to make peace with the Emperor, save by mutual consent. The Genoese were to receive as a fief the city of Syracuse, which they had long dominated prior to Frederick's return to Sicily in 1220, and

---

[1] *Annales Janvenses (Fonti,* iii), 87–8.

[2] *Andreae Danduli Chronicon* (Muratori, *RIS,* new edn., xii, part 1), 296. See also Winkelmann, *Acta,* ii. 690; and Kretschmayr, *Venedig,* ii. 44 ff.

[3] Winkelmann, *Acta,* ii. 689; *Annales Janvenses (Fonti,* iii), 88 ff.

[4] Ibid., and BFW, *Reg.* v, Abt. iv, 13293.

the Venetians were to receive Barletta and Salpi on the Adriatic coast. This alliance proved a serious blow to the imperial plans both commercially and strategically by virtue of the future control of both the Adriatic and the Tyrrhenian seas by the Emperor's enemies.[1]

It was at this time also that the enemies of Frederick, encouraged by the growing tension between him and the Pope, sought to accomplish his ruin in the eyes of the Christian world by character assassination. Superior as he was intellectually and culturally to the age in which he lived, Frederick was especially vulnerable to the propagandist abuse and disparagement by the bigots and hirelings of the Guelf party. None was more skilled in the art of character assassination than the papal chaplain and biographer of Pope Innocent IV, Nicholas of Carbio, who depicted Frederick II as the vilest of men, alleging that, in his contempt for religion, he had converted a holy altar in an Apulian church into a privy and that in several places where there were churches consecrated to the service of God, he had constructed houses of prostitution. Moreover, Nicholas of Carbio continued his poisonous attacks by charging that Frederick, not content with the prostitution of young women and girls, indulged 'in a vice disgraceful even to think about or to mention, and most evil to practise. For he broadcast his crime, that of Sodom, openly, not attempting to conceal it'.[2] That such accusations, the facile weapons of character assassination in all ages, are to be dismissed as slanderous falsifications is perhaps sufficiently established in that such practices are psychologically contradictory to Frederick's well-known habits of life. As pointed out by one of his early biographers, 'The excessive love of Frederick for women appears, on the contrary, in contradiction to the vicious habit of pederasty, and even in the Orient, the manners of which this prince is reproached with adopting, the two passions are usually mutually exclusive.'[3]

To his unscrupulous critics Frederick's contempt for the authoritarianism of his era—his disposition to accept as truth only that which could be rationally explained—was regarded as perhaps even more damning than his alleged unnatural sins. Thus he was accused of scoffing at the holy mystery of the Eucharist. 'How long', he is said to have exclaimed when witnessing the holy communion administered to the dying, 'how long will this hocus-pocus continue!' He was said also to have scoffed at the Virgin birth, saying of it: 'They are complete fools who believe God could be born of a Virgin' . . . supporting this heresy by the fallacy that 'no one can be born whose conception

---

[1] See first Winkelmann, *Acta*, ii. 689; and then H. Chone, *Handelsbeziehungen*, 82 ff.; and Huillard-Bréholles, v, part i, 390–4.

[2] Nicholas of Carbio, *Vita Innocentii IV* (ed. J. Paguotti, *Archivio della R. Soc. Rom. di Storia Patria, xxi*, 1898), 102 ff.

[3] Huillard-Bréholles, *Hist. Dip.*, Introduction, p. cxcii.

was not preceded by coitus between a man and a woman', and that 'one ought not to believe anything, save that which can be proven by nature and by the force of reason'. His critics took special delight in quoting the gossip, which found its way into several contemporary chronicles, that Frederick had said: 'There had been three impostors or deceivers (*baratores sive quillatores*) in the world, Moses, Christ, and Muhammad; and thus he exalted Muhammad by associating him with Moses and Christ.'[1] In a letter addressed to the Archbishop of Canterbury late in May 1239 Gregory incorporated many of these bits of unsupported gossip with the intention of convincing the British, who were not easily persuaded as to the accuracy of these charges, that Frederick II, in addition to his encroachments upon the papal territories, was both monster and blasphemer.[2]

When viewed against the background of Frederick's professions of faith to be found in one form or another in his voluminous letters, his laws, his addresses and other writings, it is impossible to accept the vicious and unwarranted propaganda. In many respects the accusations are reminiscent of the extravagant charges employed by Gregory IX in his denunciations of Frederick for his failure to fulfil his pledge in 1227 to go on a crusade, and for fulfilling it in 1228 against the will of the Pope. At the time Gregory hesitated not at all to make use of the most irresponsible gossip to injure Frederick, and yet this same Pope, who had previously heaped charges of viciousness, infidelity, and blasphemy upon him, addressed him after the peace of San Germano with equal exaggeration, and probably with equal insincerity. Frederick consistently and energetically supported the principle of the independence of the temporal authority in its relations with the spiritual, a principle which was to be ardently defended a generation later by Dante in his *De Monarchia*.[3] To the Popes and Curia of the thirteenth century this doctrine was incompatible with their cherished concept of papal *plenitudo potestatis*. In support of their concept of supreme authority, both Gregory IX and his immediate successor, Innocent IV, believed they were justified in employing every available weapon, scrupulous or unscrupulous, in destroying their antagonists.

The alleged sacrilegious remarks with regard to the 'three impostors', often assumed to have originated solely with Simon of Tournay at the beginning of the thirteenth century, were actually copied from various

---

[1] The chief sources for his alleged blasphemies are *Chronica Albrici Trium Fontium* (*MGH, SS.* xxiii), 944; Matthew Paris, *Chronica majora*, iii. 607; 'Vie de Grégoire IX' (*Le Liber Censuum*, ii. 33). [2] Matthew Paris, op. cit. iii. 590–608.

[3] See especially *De Monarchia*, Book III, and Dante's remark in ch. iv, lines 103 ff.: 'Sic ergo dico, quod regnum temporale non recipit esse a spirituali, nec virtutem quae est ejus auctoritas, nec etiam operationem simpliciter; sed bene ab eo recipit, ut virtuosius operetur per lucem gratiae, quam in coelo Deus et in terra benedictio summi Pontificis infundit illi.'

chronicles, including those of Giraldus Cambrensis and Albericus of Troisfontaines, and cleverly rearranged by propagandists of the papal court.[1]

As this tense relationship was developing between the Pope and the Emperor, Frederick was pushing forward his preparations for the renewal of the war with Milan. It was of the utmost importance to prevent the Pope from proclaiming the ban of excommunication against him. The Christian world, long accustomed to acknowledge the spiritual supremacy of the Pope, would, in the event of an actual break with the Emperor, throw the weight of its sympathy on the side of the Church. Whatever Frederick's personal feelings towards Gregory IX, he must convince the world of Christendom that his antagonism was directed not against the papacy, but solely against the person of Gregory IX. Accordingly, in a remarkable letter written from Padua on 10 March 1239, he made a direct appeal to the College of Cardinals, as the 'successors of the Apostles', placing them on an equality with the Pope.[2] He said of the cardinals: 'You who are the candles of the Church, placed on a hill, not under a bushel, may, by your good works, give light to the house.' In his efforts to prevent independent action by the Pope in the event of excommunication he advanced the opinion that 'you are thought to share equal participation in whatever he who presides over the See of Peter proposes as law or promulgates officially'.[3] In consideration of this coequality, he pleaded with the cardinals to check the proceedings of the Supreme Pontiff which, for evident reasons, the world recognized as unjust as they were gratuitous (*voluntarios*). This concept of coequality was not unique. It had been strongly advanced in the late eleventh century by a group of cardinals who asserted unqualifiedly that they 'shared in the divinely ordained authority of the Roman See'.[4] This opinion was, of course, to be actively revived during the conflict between Philip the Fair and Boniface VIII at the close of the thirteenth century, and was to play a significant part throughout the conciliar movement. At that time also John of Paris went even further in ascribing to the cardinals actual superiority over the pope when he advanced the argument that, while a general council is thought to be the appropriate authority to depose a pope, the College of Cardinals is competent to do so.[5]

[1] See especially the enlightening observations of K. Hampe in his review of E. Kantorowicz, *Friedrich II. (Hist. Zeitschr.*, 146, 1932), 470 ff. See also note 1, p. 421 above.

[2] Huillard-Bréholles, v, part i, 282: '. . . vos Apostolorum statuit successores ut Petro pro omnibus ministrante, vos qui estis candelabra Ecclesie supra montem . . .'

[3] 'Cum ad singula que presidens Sedi Petri proponit statuere vel denuncianda decrevit equa participatio vos admittat.' Ibid. 282–3.

[4] B. Tierney, *Foundations of the Conciliar Theory*, 70. See also J. B. Sägmüller, *Die Tätigkeit und Stellung der Kardinäle bis Papst Boniface VIII.*, 12 ff.

[5] *De Potestate Regia et Papali* (ed. J. Leclercq, Paris, 1942), 254: 'Credo tamen quod simpli-

At the Council of Lyons, Pope Innocent IV said: 'He [Frederick] did not hesitate to oppose even the Pope with his slander and his persecution.' The chief papal propagandist, Cardinal Rainer, in a scurrilous attack upon the Emperor, obviously intended to influence the proceedings of the Council of Lyons, charged that Frederick, in a letter to the cardinals, had threatened to murder both the Pope and the cardinals supporting him if he, the Emperor, should be excommunicated.[1] The offending letter of Frederick which had given rise both to the papal charge and to the more extreme accusation of the propagandist was one which Frederick had addressed to the cardinals on 10 March 1239. In it he asserted: 'If the Holy Father is disposed to injure us so seriously, then we must, because of the injustice inflicted upon us, give consideration to resorting to measures of retaliation which the Emperor is wont to employ.' And then he continued the alleged threat with the additional statement: 'Although we are favourably disposed to promote the honour and security of all of you, yet we cannot with equanimity ignore the offences of injurious ones, and if we cannot stop these in their beginnings, it shall be lawful for us to counter injuries with injuries which we shall not be able to undo.'[2] But, if there was in this letter a word or phrase which might be construed by the papal propagandists as a threat against the life of the Pope, another letter of the Emperor addressed to the cardinals immediately after the first was most conciliatory.[3]

He began by reminding them that 'so far we have devoted ourselves to the honour of God and to the Holy Roman Church, our mother . . . and we consider ourselves as her son and special guardian, whose holy mysteries we worship with Catholic conviction and honour with all our heart and soul'. In addition to his earnest desire to obtain the support of the cardinals, it appears most probable that in this second letter Frederick was seeking to refute the current gossip concerning his infidelity and his contempt for the mysteries of the Church. 'We do not hesitate', he continued, 'to offer to you who are placed as luminaries upon a mountain, as lights in the world, and as the hinges of the faith governing the house of God, the token of our devotion.' He assured the cardinals further that he had always been and was still prepared to offer the same devotion to the Pope himself if, in so doing, he could safeguard the rights, the honour, and the dignity of the Empire, of himself, and of his faithful adherents in the Empire and in the Kingdom. Because of the aggressive and unjust acts of Pope Gregory IX, he

citer sufficeret ad depositionem huiusmodi collegium cardinalium, quia ex quo consensus eorum facit papam loco ecclesie, videtur similiter quod possit eum deponere . . .'
[1] F. Graefe, *Die Publizistik in der letzten Epoche Kaiser Friedrichs II.*, 109 ff., 130.
[2] Huillard-Bréholles, v, part i, 282; see also Matthew Paris, *Chronica majora*, iii. 549 f.
[3] *MGH, Const.* ii, no. 214, pp. 289–90.

concluded, he had placed his trust in the cardinals and, through them, in a future Pope and in a General Council which was to consist of German princes and the kings and princes of Christendom as a whole. Frederick thus introduced into the papal-imperial conflict, or, perhaps more accurately, into the temporal-spiritual conflict, the concept of the supremacy of a General Council as opposed to the autocracy of the Pope, a concept that was to obtain widespread support during the conflict between Pope Boniface VIII and Philip the Fair of France and throughout the conciliar movement. Here, as in so many of the activities of Frederick II, the weakness of his position lay in the circumstance that his thinking was so far in advance of the era in which he lived. Had he been able in the year 1239 to obtain the intellectual and moral support that made possible the triumph of Philip the Fair over Boniface VIII at the turn of the century, the papal office might have been compelled to assume its appropriate position as the spiritual leader of Christendom, while abandoning its disastrous pretensions to temporal authority which had so long made impossible the operation of orderly temporal government in the Western world. In contemplating these decades of strife, involving Innocent III, Honorius III, Gregory IX, and Innocent IV in the perennial conflicts with the Hohenstaufen, one is constantly reminded of the observation made years later by Marsilio of Padua that 'the singular cause which, in the past, has given rise to civil discord or intranquillity in principalities and communities, and which will likewise continue in other states hereafter (unless it is checked): the belief, the desire, and the effort by means of which the Roman Bishop and his clerical associates, in particular, aim to seize each secular sovereignty (*principatus*) and possess excessive temporal wealth.'[1]

---

[1] *Defensor Pacis* (ed. C. W. Previté-Orton), Dicto III, cap. 1.

PART IX

THE RIVALRY FOR EMPIRE
FREDERICK II *v.* GREGORY IX

I

THE SECOND EXCOMMUNICATION OF FREDERICK II

Credo quod Gregorius qui dictus est nonus
Fuit apostolicus vir, sanctus et bonus,
Sed per mundi climata strepit ejus sonnus
Quod ad guerras fuerat semper nimis pronus.

From the satirical verses of Piero della Vigna
(Huillard-Bréholles, *Pierre*, p. 404).[1]

SINCE the end of January 1239 the Emperor, accompanied by the Empress, had been in Padua where he awaited the season for the resumption of the war against the Lombard League. There for a period of three months he engaged in the pastimes which he so greatly enjoyed, especially in hunting, while also seeking to pacify some of his former foes. In Padua his court life had the splendour of that of an oriental prince; he often made his appearance in the robes of royalty, while observing the court ceremonies typical of his reign. At times he appeared surrounded by the nobility and the courtiers at great feasts. In Padua he had assembled his falcons, cheetahs, and hunting-dogs, with their keepers, ready at all times for himself and his guests on their hunting expeditions.

But business was combined with pleasure throughout these months of waiting. Frederick had summoned to Padua the perennial foes, Ezzelino of Romano and Azzo the Marquis of Este, and a dubious reconciliation was temporarily effected. The two enemies, under a pretext of friendliness, employed the occasion for intrigues profitable to their own interests. In his attempt to reconcile them Frederick had brought about a marriage of Azzo's son, Reginald, with Adelheid, the daughter of Alberigo of Romano, the brother of Ezzelino. But almost immediately he had offended both parties to this agreement by sending the newly married couple into Apulia to be held as hostages.[2] This action could

---

[1] I believe that Gregory, known as the ninth,
    Was a Pope pious and virtuous,
    But, throughout the regions of the earth he created unrest
    Because he was always excessively prone to make war.

[2] *Rolandini Patavini Chronica* (Muratori, *RIS*, new edn.), viii, part 1, 314 ff.; vii, part 1, 65; F. Stieve, *Ezzelino von Romano*, 43 f.

only be interpreted as a decision in favour of Ezzelino in opposition to both Azzo of Este and Alberigo of Romano who, unlike his brother, was friendly towards Azzo. Henceforth, Alberigo was to reveal himself as a most dangerous enemy of the Emperor. His enmity was heightened by the neglect of his daughter. At first attended by a eunuch and some servants, she was found later in such need that the Emperor himself gave orders that she was to be adequately provided for.[1]

Together with Azzo of Este, Alberigo succeeded on 4 May 1239 in driving James of Morra, the imperial *podestà*, from Treviso and in taking possession of the city.

Meanwhile, on Palm Sunday 1239, the day of the death of Hermann of Salza, who for so many years had successfully represented Frederick II in negotiations with the papacy, Gregory IX excommunicated the Emperor for the second time.[2] This action of the Pope was not unexpected. In anticipation of the papal decree, Frederick had taken advantage of a traditional gathering of the citizens of Padua on Holy Thursday (20 March), in a plain or meadow, *Pratum Valis* (Prato della Valle), outside the city, to appear before the people, apparently as a gesture of goodwill. Here he was joined by the eloquent Piero della Vigna, Justice of the Superior Court, and later logothete, who delivered an address calculated to promote good relationships between the citizens and their sovereign.[3] Shortly afterwards, when it became known in Padua that the Emperor had been excommunicated, he summoned the people to the palace of Padua where again he appeared before them accompanied by Piero della Vigna. On this occasion it was the mission of the learned Justice to present to the citizens a defence of the Emperor against the papal accusations. Appropriately he chose as his text two verses from the *Heroides* of Ovid (v, lines 7–8):

> One ought to bear patiently that
> which one suffers, if it is merited.
> It is the punishment that is inflicted
> upon us unjustly that brings sorrow.

The content of the address was clearly anticipated in the text. Piero told of the prejudices of the Pope and spoke of the recklessness with which a benevolent sovereign, who governed the Empire with a justice comparable to that of the Great Charles, had been unjustly attacked. If the sentence were based upon justice, said the speaker, the Emperor would not hesitate to confess his wrongdoing and to seek absolution. But if he failed to do this, no one should be surprised at his complaints

---

[1] Huillard-Bréholles, v, part ii, 891.
[2] Huillard-Bréholles, v, part i, 286 ff., *Rolandini Patavini Chronica* (Muratori, *RIS*, new edn. viii, part i), 313.

against the head of the Church. For, where no wrong has been committed it is unjust to inflict punishment.[1]

Of the sixteen complaints brought against Frederick in the articles of excommunication, eleven had to do with his alleged misdeeds committed in the Kingdom of Sicily. Here, as in the first excommunication of 1227, it is apparent that the true cause of the bitter hostility of Pope and Curia was not Frederick's alleged immorality and infidelity or other misdeeds, but their determination to prevent the union of Sicily and the Empire. The articles pertaining to Sicily have to do chiefly with Frederick's obstructing the filling of vacancies in the Sicilian bishoprics, churches, and monasteries, the imprisonment of the clergy, alleged robbery of the churches, unjust extortion of taxes from the clergy, and abuse of adherents of the papal party in the Kingdom. Frederick was charged also with interfering in the missions of papal legates; with inciting the Romans to rebellion against the Pope; with the seizure of Church lands in Northern Italy; with despoiling the Templars and Hospitallers; with hindering the recovery of the Holy Land; and with the detention of the nephew of the King of Tunis, naïvely believed by Gregory IX to be *en route* to Rome to seek baptism.[2]

Following the proclaiming of the ban, Gregory commanded the Christian princes, the prelates, and rectors of communes to give it wide publicity.[3] The Pope also found a use at this time for the brothers of the Minorite order whose activities he had zealously sponsored since his authorization as their protector by Honorius III. He now called upon many of the brothers to spread throughout Italy and Germany as propagandists, preaching against the excommunicated Emperor, seeking, in the language of one contemporary observer, to persuade the people 'that through unfaithfulness they would be faithful, obedient through disobedience'.[4]

The verbal conflict, the war of propaganda, between the two great rivals for world dominance, following the proclaiming of the ban has rarely been equalled in bitterness. The polemics exchanged between the papal and imperial chanceries are of the utmost significance because, far more than contemporary chronicles, they reveal the relentlessness, the acrimony, with which each of the antagonists contended.[5] Only a few weeks after Frederick's excommunication, on 20 April 1239, his chancery released a stinging broadside against Gregory IX. Throughout this exceptionally long polemic the colourful rhetoric of Piero della

[1] The address is reported, although not quoted, by *Rolandini Patavini Chronica* (Muratori, *RIS*, new edn. viii, part 1), 65.
[2] Huillard-Bréholles, v, part i, 287.
[3] *MGH, Epist. Pont.* i. 640–1.
[4] Matthew Paris, *Chronica majora*, iii. 621.
[5] F. Graefe, *Die Publizistik in der letzten Epoche Kaiser Friedrichs II.*, 4 ff.

Vigna is discernible. Addressed as a letter to various princes, spiritual and temporal, this remarkable composition pleaded with them 'to cast your eyes around you, hearken with your ears! Weep over the scandals of the world, the dissensions of the peoples, the deplorable extinction of justice.' And these, explained the polemic, have their origin in 'an unfaithful man in your midst, a prophet of unwholesome mind, a priest who defiles the Church, who acts unjustly in defiance of the law.' Towards the close of the letter its author turned to a subject often to be repeated by Frederick II in his correspondence with the kings of Europe. He concedes that the wickedness of a Pope such as Gregory IX is felt more keenly by the Emperor than by kings but, he adds, 'in the end our shame is shared by you also: When a fire is raging in your neighbourhood hasten with water to your own house . . . for the submission of all other kings and princes is thought to be easy if first the power of the Emperor of the Romans . . . is destroyed.' In this letter, as in his letters addressed to the cardinals just before the proclaiming of the ban, the author continues to distinguish between the individual, Gregory IX, and the College of Cardinals as a whole, saying: 'The Pope acted in opposition to the saner of his brothers, among whom only the Lombard cardinals advised our excommunication.'[1] In this letter the author also advanced the opinion that the cardinals are superior to the Pope, a concept which Frederick II, henceforth, never ceased to expound. What he and his juristically educated advisers refused to recognize was that it was in their own era, as if it were before their very eyes, that the extreme canonists succeeded in attributing jurisdiction of the Holy See in canonical legislation and in dispensative authority exclusively to the Pope.[2] Moreover, nowhere would these jurists have found a principle of canon law establishing the cardinals or 'brothers' as anything other than counsellors to be employed at the discretion of the Pope. It is a tribute to Frederick II and his legal advisers that they were several generations in advance of their era in recognizing the dangers inherent in this tradition and in making an effort to substitute in its stead the legal validity of the oligarchical concept of Church government.

On the side of the Emperor this propagandist battle reached its zenith in a letter of Piero della Vigna (*Epist.* i. 1), a masterpiece of sarcasm and ridicule, directed at the Pope and Curia:

The pharisees and prelates assembled and held council together against their Lord, the Roman Emperor. 'What shall we do', they asked, 'now that this man is so triumphant over his enemies?—If we give him a free hand he

---

[1] *MGH, Const.*, ii. 290 ff. See also W. Seegrün, 'Kirche, Papst und Kaiser nach den Anschauungen Kaiser Friedrichs II.' (*Hist. Zeitschr.*, 207, 1968), 16 ff.

[2] P. Hinschius, *System des katholischen Kirchenrechts mit besonderer Rücksicht auf Deutschland*, iii. 734 ff., and especially p. 740. See also J. B. Sägmüller, *Kirchenrecht*, i. 102 ff.

will crush the Lombards completely and, in the manner of Caesar, he will not long delay in routing us from our position, and he will destroy our species. He will entrust the vineyards of the Lord Sabaoth to other labourers and condemn and destroy us without tribunal. Therefore, let us resist from the outset lest, indeed, the tiny spark burst into an all-consuming flame and the sickness which has begun to spread penetrate to the very marrow . . . Then, disregarding the words of this prince, let us attack the enemy, they said, let neither our tongues nor our arrows lie hidden, but come forth, so that they will strike; strike so that will wound; let him be so wounded that he falls, so falls that he cannot again arise—so that he will perceive the futility of his dream.

Gregory IX recognized the threat that lay in the revolutionary thinking of his great antagonist. At any cost he must prevent its spread to other regions of the Christian world; it must be fought with every available weapon, without consideration of the ethical or the scrupulous. Frederick must be made to appear the monstrous heretic, the Antichrist, capable of every crime, and guilty of every sin. Accordingly the Pope's polemical manifesto, released only a few weeks after Frederick's appeal to the princes (21 May 1239), has few parallels in passionate propaganda in the Middle Ages. It brings into play all the emotionalism and wild fantasy of the Apocalypse.

'Out of the sea', he writes, 'comes a beast filled with words of blasphemy, which, formed with the feet of a bear, the mouth of an enraged lion and, in the rest of its body, shaped like a panther, opens its mouth in blasphemy of the Divine Name, nor does it fail to attack with similar shafts the Church and the saints who dwell in heaven.' Throughout the letter these apocalyptic attributes are made characteristics of Frederick II, who is depicted as seeking to destroy the Christian faith, as revolting against the Redeemer of the World. Thus, the Pope bids the world 'examine closely the head, the torso, and the extremities of this beast, the so-called Emperor', this 'creator of lies, oblivious of all modesty, untouched by the blush of shame . . . a wolf in sheep's clothing . . . blustering in greatness, and intoxicated with power . . . a scorpion with a sting in its tail . . . unsound of faith'. Reverting to Frederick's delayed expedition to the Holy Land in 1227 in the company of his friend the Landgrave of Thuringia, the Pope did not shrink from suggesting that the Emperor had poisoned his noble companion, adding the soft touch of the common gossip-mongers, 'so everyone says' (*sicut mundus clamat*). As the letter proceeds with mounting viciousness, the Emperor is described as 'the dragon formed to deceive us', the 'hammer of the earth . . . desiring to transform the earth into a desert', this 'robber of Church property', 'this man who takes pride in being called the forerunner of the Antichrist'. Then, digging deep into the unsavoury gossip of the time, the Pope repeated Frederick's alleged characterization of Christ as an impostor; his reported scoffing at the Virgin birth; his vicious habits of thought and lascivious ways of life. The letter closed with an exhortation to princes and prelates 'fully and faithfully to publicize the above-mentioned among the clergy and the people subject to you'.[1]

Frederick was well aware that this letter of the Pope could have a most damaging effect upon his cause. To his mind Gregory had delivered a foul blow in representing him as heretic, as blasphemer, and as moral pervert. A letter in self-defence now became a necessity.

Is it possible [he asked] that the Apostolic See believes that we deviate from the Catholic faith, since whatever it may be in our heart the true belief is firmly rooted? If, however, he charges that we—far from truth—do not cling to the true faith, so also we can say that the Pope acts contrary to the faith. For, if he were the image of him—who when cursed did not curse, and when he suffered did not threaten—he would not have hurled at us from ambush projectiles of malediction.

It is in this letter that Frederick's own interpretation of the figure of speech of the sun and moon was set forth:

At the creation of the world, that wise and ineffable wisdom, whose counsel is inscrutable, placed two great lights in the heavens, a larger and a smaller, the larger to rule the day, the lesser to rule the night. Both of these move in such manner and describe their orbits so peacefully that neither impinges upon the other but, on the contrary, the lesser constantly receives its light from the greater. Similarly, also, the same eternal provision desired that two powers govern the sphere of the earth, a sacerdotal and an imperial, one to teach the other to chastise to the end that man, who is composed of two differing elements, would be restrained by two reins.

And then, exclaimed the author of the letter: 'What an unprecedented phenomenon! The sun endeavours to obscure the moon and to deprive it of its light . . .'[2]

In another letter singularly resembling the one just cited and most certainly the work of Piero della Vigna, written on behalf of the Emperor, the attack upon the Pope is even less restrained. Gregory IX is here depicted as 'the great dragon who has led the world astray', a second Balaam, 'the Antichrist'; drawing from the Apocalypse, the author likens Gregory to 'another horse that was red: and power was given him that sat thereon to take peace from the earth'. It was in this letter that a complete defence of Frederick against the charge of heresy was made. For here, indeed, was an unrestrained profession of Christian

---

[1] *MGH, Epist. Pont.* i, no. 750, pp. 646 ff. See also H. M. Schaller, 'Die Antwort Gregors IX. auf Petrus Vinea' (*Deutsches Archiv*, xi, 1954–5), 140 ff.

[2] Winkelmann, *Acta*, i, no. 355, p. 314.

faith. To the charge that Frederick had described Moses, Christ, and Muhammad as the three 'charlatans' or 'deceivers', the author makes Frederick reply that 'no such words have ever passed our lips'. On the contrary, he continues, 'We recognize the only son of God as co-eternal and co-existent with the Father and the Holy Spirit, our Lord Jesus Christ, who was begotten from the beginning and before all time; that he was sent below for the redemption of mankind . . . was born of the venerated Virgin Mother, to suffer, to die according to the flesh . . . to rise again on the third day.' As to his honouring Muhammad by including him in the trio of charlatans, he replied: 'we believe that Muhammad disappeared into thin air, swept away by demons; his soul, however, is tormented in hell because his acts were of darkness and contrary to the laws of the All Highest.' The author acknowledged also that Frederick accepted Moses 'as the friend and confidant of God, who spoke with his Lord on Mount Sinai, to whom God appeared in a burning bush, giving to the Hebrew people their laws and afterwards with others of the Elect was called to his glory'.[1]

The Pope moved rapidly, following the excommunication, in his efforts to gain the advantage for his cause among the people and the princes of Christendom. Not only did he make the fullest possible use of the Minorite brothers as agents in the attempted destruction of his dangerous adversary, but his legates, already present or else swiftly dispatched to strategic positions throughout the West, were entrusted with the task of destroying the prestige of the Emperor. Few men were more clever than the newly chosen Lombard legate and arch-intriguer, Gregory of Montelongo, in carrying out the mission of injuring the prestige. of the Emperor. In the Romagna and Emilia the legatine activity was most effective. Bologna now displayed extraordinary zeal in preparing for an attack on the Emperor. Azzo of Este, already alienated from the Emperor since the spring of 1239 after an attempted reconciliation with Ezzelino of Romano at Padua, joined the enemy forces in June. Treviso had succumbed to the attacks of anti-imperial forces in May. Far more serious was the loss of Ravenna. Again it was the papal legate in that region, Cardinal Sinibald Fiesco of San Lorenzo in Lucinia, later to become Pope Innocent IV, who induced Ravenna to desert to the side of the Pope. Strategically, Ravenna had been of special importance to the Emperor as a connecting link by sea with the ports of the Kingdom of Sicily. For the moment Ferrara and Bertinora remained faithful, although exposed always to the intrigues of papal agents. Meanwhile, the skilful diplomacy of Gregory of Montelongo had changed the somewhat tenuous *rapprochement* between the papacy and the Lombard League into a formal alliance. Milan and Piacenza,

---

[1] Huillard-Bréholles, v, part i, 348 ff.

already allied with Genoa, now entered into an alliance in which the contracting parties agreed to conclude no peace with the Emperor save with the consent of the Pope or his successor. This treaty complemented that which in November 1238 Genoa and Venice had made with each other and which subsequently had been extended, through the efforts of the papal nuncio, Berard, to an offensive alliance with the Pope against the Emperor.[1]

While taking these energetic measures in Italy the Pope had lost no time in seeking to injure the Emperor also in other countries of the West, especially in England, Germany, and France. The King of England, although the brother-in-law of Frederick, was incapable of any positive action on one side or the other. While offering no opposition to the ban against the Emperor, he assumed a passive attitude towards each of the opposing parties. Frederick in his letter to King Henry expressed astonishment that he had permitted the excommunication to be broadcast 'in his most Christian country' (*in sua christianissima terra*) without any opposition. He reproached the King with 'disregarding the marriage agreement and the friendship entered into at the time of the marriage of Isabella, now the Empress'. He demanded, therefore, that the papal legate, then active in England, be expelled.[2] Despite the indifference of the weak King, the presence of the papal legate in England, engaged in extorting money from both temporal and ecclesiastical princes to aid in financing the war against Frederick II, did not fail to arouse opposition to Gregory IX or sympathy for the Emperor. When the letter of the Emperor defining his position became known and when the Pope's letter was widely publicized the popular reaction was favourable to Frederick. 'What is the meaning of this?' the people are said to have inquired. 'Before this time the Pope made the charge that the Emperor was more in agreement with Muhammad and the Saracen law than with Christ and the Christian law. But now in his polemical letter he accuses him of calling Muhammad as well as Jesus and Moses—horrible as it is to mention—a charlatan (*baratator*).' In contrast with this, they said, 'the Emperor speaks of God humbly and in the manner of a Catholic, save that in his last letter he disparages the person of the Pope, not the office. Nor, in so far as we are aware, does he give utterance to anything heretical or profane, neither does he send usurers and extortioners among us.'[3]

In Germany the Pope endeavoured to alienate the Emperor's subjects

---

[1] *Annales Placentini Gibellini* (*MGH, SS.* xviii), 481.

[2] Matthew Paris, *Chronica majora*, iv. 4–5.

[3] Ibid. iii. 609. While one might be tempted to regard this report as a fabrication of Matthew, it is an accurate reflection of the sentiments of many Englishmen towards the papal demands and towards the legate, Otto. See also *Annales prioratus de Dunstaplia* (*Annales Monastici*, iii), 147 ff., and *Annales monasterii de Oseneia* (ibid. iv), 84 ff.

through the activities of his legate, Albert of Beham (Bohemia), as clever and unscrupulous as his counterpart in Lombardy, Gregory of Montelongo. It has been said of him that he well understood how to turn things topsy-turvy in Germany, 'how to punish obedience and reward disobedience'.[1] Fortunately, the cause of the Emperor was still faithfully represented by Conrad of Thuringia, the recently elected successor to Hermann of Salza as Grand Master of the Teutonic Order. The Diet at Eger which the Emperor had summoned for June, following his excommunication, offered Albert of Beham what he believed an excellent opportunity for injuring the Emperor's prestige in Germany.[2] The Pope had instructed his agents in Germany, Albert of Beham and Philip of Assisi, as to their procedure: 'Because Frederick, the so-called Emperor, although repeatedly and urgently admonished to atone for his many and serious excesses, far from trying to make atonement, committed in his calloused sensibilities worse offences, we have, with the advice of our brothers, deemed it necessary to excommunicate and anathematize him and all those who have given him aid, encouragement, and counsel in these or other excesses against the Roman Church.' The Pope then ordered the dissolution of the oath of fealty to the Emperor, at the same time placing under the interdict all places, cities, castles, towns, etc., where he stayed. He instructed his legates also that all patriarchs, archbishops, and bishops in Germany were to publish this sentence to the accompaniment of the ringing of bells and under the light of candles and to punish with excommunication all persons, lay or ecclesiastic, who gave aid to the Emperor with or without weapons. He instructed the legates, moreover, that any of the archbishops or others who neglected to carry out these commands of the Pope were to be excommunicated.[3]

The efforts of Albert of Beham at Eger had met with little sympathy. The princes present at the Diet, conscious of their obligations to the Emperor, determined, instead, to seek a reconciliation between him and the Pope.[4] Despite the threat of excommunication, many bishops refused to publish the ban; one of them, the Patriarch of Aquileia, openly sided with the Emperor.[5] Many bishops who had bound themselves at Eger to seek a reconciliation between Pope and Emperor had been excommunicated by Albert of Beham with the result that there was some delay in their effort to obtain access to Pope Gregory. It was not until the spring of 1240, during April and May, that Conrad of Thuringia, the new Master of the Teutonic Order, was sent to the Pope with letters

[1] W. Schirrmacher, *Kaiser Friedrich II.*, iii. 111.
[2] For the calling of the Diet see *Annales Erphordenses* (*MGH, SS.* xvi), 33.
[3] *Albertus von Beham* (ed. C. H. Höfler), 8–9.
[4] *Annales Erphordenses*, loc. cit.
[5] Raynaldus, *Annales*, xiii. 482.

from German princes pleading for the ending of hostilities. In general, the letters were similar in content, calling attention to the spread of heresy, to the many seditions, to the petty wars, and, above all, to the wide-spread prevalence of crime. These ills, they advised, could be checked only with the restoration of peace between the Pope and the Emperor. They deplored the injurious effect of the continued conflict upon conditions in the Holy Land and the irreparable damage to the Catholic faith which arose from the continued strife.[1]

The Pope appealed to the princes of Germany to choose a new Emperor, but in this he met with no success. As some of the princes now wrote to him, 'it was not his legal right to make a substitution for the Emperor, but merely to crown such as the princes elected'. For, 'as is well known, the choice lies with them'.[2] Despite this clear enunciation by the princes of the legal procedure in the election of a German King, Gregory persisted in his arbitrary efforts to find a successor to Frederick II. First he offered the crown to Abel, the son of King Waldemar of Denmark, who refused it. It was then offered to Otto, Duke of Brunswick, who also declined, saying that he did not wish to die in the manner of his uncle the Emperor Otto.[3]

Gregory next endeavoured to transfer the imperial crown to a French prince, hoping to find in Louis IX support for his plan. To this end he sent one of the bitterest foes of Frederick II, Cardinal James of Palestrina, as papal legate to France. Gregory wrote to King Louis:

After deliberation and careful consideration with all our brothers, we have condemned and expelled the so-called Emperor Frederick from the imperial dignity and have chosen in his stead Count Robert, brother of the King of France . . . Do not hesitate, therefore, for any reason whatsoever to accept with open arms so great a gift, offered voluntarily, and to obtain which we will give support, both in effort and in abundance of money. For, as the world now knows, the multitude of crimes of the aforesaid Frederick have condemned him irreversibly.

The reply of the French King to this offer is indicative of the unfavourable reaction of a temporal sovereign to the presumptuous proceedings of the Pope. Louis IX reminded Gregory that Frederick had not been convicted nor had he confessed to alleged criminal acts. And, even if he merited to be deposed, 'he could not be deprived of his crown, save by the decision of a general council'. Thus, once more, the concept of the superiority of a general council was suggested, giving further evidence that during the first half of the thirteenth century this method of re-

---

[1] *MGH, Const.* ii, nos. 225–32, pp. 313 ff.
[2] *Annales Stadenses* (*MGH, SS.* xvi), 367.
[3] *Gesta Abbatum Horti Sanctae Mariae* (*MGH, SS.* xxiii), 595; *Chronica Albrici Trium Fontium* (*MGH, SS.* xxiii), 949.

straining the autocracy of the Pope was seriously advanced. That the reply was gratifying to the Emperor is apparent in the observation of Louis IX that Frederick is, 'to us, still innocent, and, indeed, a good neighbour; nor have we seen anything sinful in his loyalty to the Church or in his faith'. As to the offer of the crown, the King is said to have replied: 'We do not wish to place ourselves in such great jeopardy by attacking so powerful a prince . . . If the Pope should crush him either through us or through others, he would then destroy all the princes of the world . . . inasmuch as he had conquered the great Emperor Frederick.' This alleged reply, reported only by Matthew Paris, doubtless reflects more or less accurately the sentiments of King Louis IX, although its authenticity may be seriously questioned. It has all the ear-marks of a paraphrase by the chronicler of a letter addressed by Frederick II to Henry III (King of England) warning him of the dangers to all temporal sovereigns inherent in the extreme canonistic interpretation of the papal authority.[1] Whether or not the report of Louis IX's reply is verbally accurate, the refusal of the offer by the King of France is amply reported by other contemporary sources.[2]

These hostile acts of Pope Gregory were effectively countered, however, by the Emperor. Already in 1239 he had recognized the dangers from the propagandist activities of the preaching monks and Minorites. All such monks and Minorites who originated in Lombardy or in the revolting cities of the north were ordered to be driven from the Kingdom; exceptions were made only of those who were in the personal service of Cardinal Thomas of Sabina, recognized as an active promoter of peace, and of the papal notary John of Capua. Frederick now ordered rigorous punishments, including the death penalty, against people bringing papal letters into Sicily and against those who, without special permit from the Master Justiciar, visited the papal court. Persons making such visits, whether men or women, were forbidden to return to the Kingdom. Members of the clergy carrying out the papal mandate to suspend religious services were to be punished by the confiscation of their church property.[3] Angered especially by the heavy collections of money being made in England by the papal legate, Cardinal Otto of St. Nicholas, Frederick protested to King Henry III. Henry offered the excuse that he did not dare to oppose the Pope, at the same time he appeared to intimate that he might have been more sympathetic to the Emperor's protest if his sister, Isabella, had been duly crowned as Empress. On another occasion, however, in replying

---

[1] Matthew Paris, *Chronica majora*, iii. 624 ff.

[2] See, for example, *Chronica regia Coloniensis*, 273–4, and *Vie de Saint Louis par Guillaume de Nangis* (*RHGF*, xx), 330–2.

[3] Richard of San Germano, 200. See also Huillard-Bréholles, iii. 51 (incorrectly dated; for correction see BFW, *Reg.* v, Abt. i, no. 2438).

to Frederick's protests against the activities of the papal legate in England, King Henry revealed the true cause of his timidity when he wrote that 'he was constrained to obey the mandates of the Pope and the Church more than other princes of the world because, as it is obvious, he is a subject or vassal of the Pope'.[1] In his various protests to the Kings of England and of France, Frederick frequently reminded them that 'these things have no more to do with us than with other kings and princes'.[2]

Frederick's retaliatory measures against the papal acts proved useful also in providing income for the royal treasury. He did not hesitate to levy fines against the recalcitrant bishops and abbots for their refusal to permit the holding of divine services or for other acts hostile to him. When forfeiture of all property was not feasible or desirable, a third of their incomes might be confiscated or else their properties were declared vacant and the income accrued to the royal treasury during the vacancy.[3] It was inevitable that procedures such as these would be seized upon by the Pope and made to count heavily against Frederick at the time of his deposition during the Council of Lyons.

They became all the more objectionable in the eyes of the Pope when Frederick succeeded in winning to his side Elias of Cortona, Minister-General of the Franciscan Order. Brother Elias, much maligned by contemporaries and by strongly partisan historians of later centuries, had been an intimate and trusted associate of St. Francis, first in Syria and subsequently in Italy where his policies and activities, although at variance with those of St. Francis, were in part responsible for making the Franciscan Order a powerful influence throughout the Christian world.[4] Although too respectful towards the simple and pious founder of the Order openly to offend him, Elias seems from the outset to have been aware that Franciscans could not become a source of influence in the world if their regulations were such as Francis had insisted upon in the formulation of his *Rule*. It was doubtless this, as well as Elias's awareness of the cultural capabilities of the Order, that caused him to become an intimate of Frederick II and of others whose religious and political

[1] Matthew Paris, *Chronica majora*, iv. 4–5, 16–19; Huillard-Bréholles, v, part i, 464.

[2] See the elaboration of this by W. von den Steinen, *Staatsbriefe*, 45 ff. The legatine mission of Otto of St. Nicholas in England at this time has been treated in detail by H. Weber, *Über das Verhältnis Englands zu Rom während der Zeit der Legation des Kardinals Otto in den Jahren 1237–1241*.

[3] Huillard-Bréholles, v, part i, 437 ff.

[4] Concerning Elias and his activities in relation to St. Francis and the Franciscan Order and also concerning St. Francis himself, see the following: R. B. Brooke, *Early Franciscan Government*; O. Engelbert, *St. Francis of Assisi* (2nd English edn., by I. Brady and R. Brown, Chicago, 1965). Still highly useful also are the older works of Father Cuthbert, *Life of St. Francis of Assisi*, especially pp. 308 ff.; P. Sabatier, *Vie de S. François*, especially pp. 260, 271; E. Lempp, *Frère Élie de Cortona*; H. J. Rybka, *Elias von Cortona*. Pertinent also is H. Hefele, *Die Bettelorden*, especially pp. 55 ff.

ideas were in sharp contrast to the autocratic concepts of the Pope and Curia. Like Frederick II, Brother Elias enjoyed the pleasures of life, as evidenced by his luxurious 'cell' in Cortona, by his splendidly caparisoned horses, and the exotic delicacies which he habitually enjoyed at the table.[1] It was said of him that he openly charged the Church of Rome with usury, simony, and robbery, 'asserting that the Pope was wrathfully attacking the rights of the Empire, that he was covetous of money, extorting it by means of various arguments . . . that he employed fraudulently the money collected for the aid of the Holy Land'. In language reminiscent of that employed by Frederick in his letters to the cardinals and others, Elias is said to have charged Pope Gregory IX with sealing documents in his private chamber, in accordance with his own pleasure, without obtaining the approval of his brothers.[2] If Elias accepted the Franciscan doctrine of poverty, he did so much as the popes and cardinals of his era accepted the teachings of humility of Jesus and the Apostles: as essential to the masses of Christian laymen, but incompatible with the lives and duties of prelates. To him the mission of the Order was not so much to spread the doctrines of poverty, humility, and of self-abnegation, as to work for the glorification of the Christian faith through splendid monuments or through artistic representations of the ideals of the simple Christ-like founder of the Franciscan Order. In the long list of faults or defects of Elias, enumerated by his contemporary, Salimbene, none was greater than his habitual association with Frederick II, whom he served as counsellor. Indeed, when at length Elias was excommunicated by Pope Gregory IX, he continued his intimate association with the Emperor. As if holding in contempt the decrees of the Pope, he is said to have absolved those whom the Pope had excommunicated.[3]

After his retaliatory measures against the activities of the Pope, his legates, and the Minorite agents of papal propaganda, and after obtaining the support of some of the bolder spirits of the Church, Frederick continued his military efforts against the Lombard communes. He abandoned all plans for the retaking of Treviso, following the defection of Azzo of Este and Alberigo of Romano. Instead, he gave the city and its environs to the faithful Paduans, believing they would be able with but little effort to obtain possession. Meanwhile, he continued his military activities in the north, although with only minor successes, the chief of which was the capture of several castles in the vicinity of Bologna.[4] The somewhat precipitous abandonment of the attack on the March of Treviso was undoubtedly due to Frederick's desire to secure

---

[1] Salimbene, *Chronica*, 157; see also O. Engelbert, pp. 250 f.
[2] Matthew Paris, *Chronica majora*, iii. 628.   [3] *Cronica*, 160.
[4] *Annales S. Justinae Patavini* (*MGH, SS.* xix), 157.

a dependable route for the passage of troops from Sicily to the region of the Po valley. The main route, the ancient Via Aemilia, which normally would have offered easy access to the Po, was blocked by two powerful cities of the League, Bologna and Faenza. Two other routes, one along the eastern coast and through Ravenna and Ferrara, and the other to the west, traversing the coast of the Ligurian Sea and through the Cisa Pass to Parma, were far less direct. It was of the utmost importance, therefore, for Frederick to overcome the opposition of the two cities, Ravenna and Ferrara, which had recently fallen under the influence of the papal–Genoese–Venetian diplomatic triangle. Meanwhile, Ezzelino, in a successful incursion into the region of Verona, gained possession of a defile north of the city, thus making possible a connecting route between Italy and Germany.[1]

On 16 September Frederick began his operations against the city of Milan with a considerable army consisting of German, Sicilian, and Tuscan troops, including many bowmen and probably as many as 8,000 cavalrymen, while the Milanese mounted troops are said to have numbered about 5,000. Frederick's plan was not aimed primarily at storming the city, an undertaking for which he was not at that time equipped; he endeavoured rather to draw the Milanese into open battle. But, firmly entrenched as they were behind their massive walls and in the fortifications surrounding the city, they refused to engage in open battle. In their defensive measures they were greatly aided by the surrounding terrain. The streams in that area could be swiftly utilized as barriers because of the ease with which their courses could be altered.[2] After repeated attempts to draw the Milanese into the open, and recognizing the futility of an attack against the powerfully walled city, Frederick withdrew his troops on 22 October across the Ticino river, moving his army to the vicinity of Piacenza where he succeeded in taking possession of a bridge across the Po, temporarily cutting the direct route between Piacenza and Milan. In this region, however, his operations were shattered by five days of torrential rains which forced him to withdraw from the flooded area and to sacrifice many of his vehicles and much heavy equipment. The sole gains from his expedition into Lombardy were derived from the voluntary surrender of Como and Lecco.[3] After several weeks in Lodi the Emperor proceeded late in November to Cremona, thence via Parma and the Cisa Pass, near Pontremoli, he moved southwards into Tuscany. As the year 1239 was drawing to a close with the record of military failure in Lombardy, and

[1] *Rolandini Patavini Chronica* (*MGH*, *SS*. xix), 74.

[2] *Memoriae Mediolanenses* (*MGH*, *SS*. xviii), 402; Galvanus Flamma, *Chronica* (Muratori, *RIS* xi), col. 675; *Annales Placentini Gibellini* (*MGH*, *SS*. xviii), 482.

[3] *Annales Placentini Gibellini* (*MGH*, *SS*. xviii), 482; *Memoriae Mediolanenses* (*MGH*, *SS*. xviii), 402; Galvanus Flamma, *Chronica* (Muratori, *RIS* xi), col. 675.

at a time when the full wrath of the Pope had descended upon him, Frederick found a temporary respite in Pisa, where he celebrated the Christmas festivities. There, in defiance of the ban, he attended divine services, and it was said that he mounted the pulpit and preached a sermon on the subject of peace.[1]

As the Emperor looked back upon the events since his victory at Cortenuova, when his future success seemed assured by the brilliance of that victory, he must have recognized that the inexorable force of history was against him. Again and again he had been made to feel that the new era of the communes, with their wealth, their love of independence, their capacity for self-defence, boded nothing but ill for his dream of Empire. Brescia, Treviso, Bologna, Milan, and Piacenza had defied his efforts to subdue them. Indeed, there were moments in the course of his conquests in Lombardy when he could not fail to recognize that each of these communes, fortified and well armed, and, above all, with the spirit to resist, was capable of holding its own against the full power of the Empire. Certainly he must have been made aware that the immediate task before him was not so much the subjection of the hostile cities of the Lombard League as it was to check the communal movement before it swept away the cities that still remained loyal to the imperial rule.

[1] *Vita Gregorii IX* (Muratori, *RIS* iii), 586; also in *Liber Censuum*, ii. 34.

II

FREDERICK II AT THE GATES
OF ROME

De prelatorum captura papa dolebit,
Sed de iactura rerum cruciamen habebit,
Per mare, per terras papam casura docebit,
Quam formam pacis guerarum finis habebit.

Prophecy of Michael Scot (ed. O. Holder-Egger,
Neues Archiv, xxx, 1904–5), 364–5.[1]

THE events of the year 1239 convinced Frederick that a far more vigorous policy was necessary, not only in opposing the aggression of the Pope, but in preventing further defections among the loyal communes. He recognized also that the most effective measures possible must be taken to defend the Kingdom of Sicily. For some time it had been apparent that he looked more and more to the assistance of his natural son, Enzio, recently become King of Sardinia, for the carrying out of his future plans. In July 1239 Frederick had bestowed upon Enzio the title *Vicar for the Whole of Italy* and had given him almost unlimited powers. In his letter of authorization he stated as his object in making this appointment: the establishment of peace in the whole of imperial Italy. In this letter to Enzio he wrote also: 'We grant to you unlimited *imperium* and the power of the sword . . . for the detection and punishment of malefactors.' This authorization included jurisdiction in both civil and criminal justice with specific mention of questions pertaining to the alienation of ecclesiastical property, save in cases specifically reserved for the Emperor. Above all, Enzio was admonished to ensure peace and tranquillity and to see that the rights of the Crown were unimpaired.[2] This designation of Enzio was but an initial step in a vast plan for the reorganization of imperial Italy which Frederick felt necessary because of the Pope's determination to oppose him. The aim of his new policy is set forth in his reply to the Archbishop of Messina who had urged him to make peace with the Pope: 'We believe it necessary to

[1]   The Pope will sorrow over the capture of the prelates,
       Also from the course of events he will be aggrieved,
       His misfortunes by sea and by land will teach him
       The kind of peace the end of war will bring.
[2] *MGH, Const.* ii, no. 217, pp. 301–2.

adopt a different procedure from that which we have previously followed. Accordingly, renouncing the forbearance, which has availed us nothing with him, we shall now resort to force. We firmly resolve to take into our hands and reannex to the Empire the Duchy [Spoleto], the March [Ancona], and the other lands which the empire held long, and were stolen . . .'[1]

By September 1239 Enzio had already made substantial progress in regaining control over the March of Ancona in his conflict with Cardinal John Colonna, who had been sent there by Pope Gregory IX to establish the authority of the Holy See.[2] The Cardinal, whose want of military skill was so conspicuously demonstrated in 1229 in conflict with the imperial troops in Sicily and Apulia, was no match for the young and brilliant Enzio. Almost immediately upon the arrival of the imperial vicar, the cities of Jesi and Macerata, which previously had been compelled to submit to the Cardinal, opened their gates to the imperial forces. Both men and money were thus made available to Frederick for the further prosecution of the conquest.[3]

The Duchy of Spoleto was less easily conquered and, in the end, yielded more readily to bribery skilfully employed by Andrew of Cicala, an imperial captain, than to military conquest. The citizens of Rieti in particular, either through cupidity or because of preference for imperial rule, proved eager subjects for the inducements offered by the imperial captain and promised to surrender the city upon the arrival of the Emperor.[4] When, on 22 February 1240, Frederick made his appearance in the upper valley of the Tiber the resistance in much of that region collapsed. Only the cities of Perugia, Assisi, Spoleto, and Terni remained loyal to the papal party.[5] Foligno, where Frederick had spent the first years of his infancy, now gave him an enthusiastic welcome. It was at about this time also that Viterbo, long faithful to the Pope, opened its gates to the Emperor. Shortly afterwards, either through preference or through force, Civita Castellana, Corneto, Sutri, Montefiascone, and other cities of the *patrimonium* submitted.[6] The whole of the papal territory in the immediate vicinity of Rome was now in the hands of the Emperor, who stood in a threatening position just outside the city. He pictured himself about to enter the Eternal City in triumph and acclaimed by the entire Roman populace, eagerly waiting to crown his

[1] Huillard-Bréholles, v, part ii, 709.

[2] Concerning John Colonna see K. Wenck, 'Das erste Konklave der Papstgeschichte' (*QF* xviii, 1926), 118 ff., H. Zimmermann, *Die päpstliche Legation in der ersten Hälfte des XIII. Jhds.*, pp. 48 ff.; J. Maubach, *Die Kardinäle und ihre Politik*, 4 f.

[3] In late October 1239 Enzio confirmed privileges to Jesi and, in November, to Macerata. See Huillard-Bréholles, v, part i, 463 f. and 539 ff. See BFW, *Reg.* v, Abt. i, 2616, 2675, 2862, 2947, 2948.   [4] Huillard-Bréholles, v, part ii, 679.

[5] *Vita Gregorii IX* (Muratori; *RIS* iii), 586; also in *Liber Censuum*, ii. 35.

[6] Richard of San Germano, 205.

victorious eagles with laurels.[1] The Pope was thoroughly alarmed; a contemporary describes him as 'abandoning all hope for his cause', and as 'falling into the depth of despair'. Moreover, we are told also that many of the cardinals deserted him 'when they saw that he was moved more by his own passions than by the restraints of reason and discretion'.[2]

As Frederick travelled from Viterbo towards Rome, convinced that the moment was propitious for the realization of his hopes, it is understandable that he could write: 'It remains therefore, with the whole Roman people favouring us and rejoicing, as it began to do at our coming, that we should make ready to enter the city auspiciously, to revive the ancient festivals of the Empire and the triumphal laurels, befitting our victorious eagles . . .'[3] But the Roman citizens, less susceptible to the allurements of ancient Rome than the Emperor, were more readily moved to the acceptance of his plans by the power of gold.[4] It is said that as Frederick stood with his troops outside the gates of Rome, following the surrender of many of the cities of the *patrimonium*, the Romans cheered his coming, shouting: 'Veniat, veniat imperator et accipiat urbem!'[5]

Although for some time in exile because of the unfriendly attitude of the populace and the hostility of some of the noble families, especially the Frangipani, Gregory IX had returned to Rome in mid-November 1239. His position there, however, grew ever more precarious as the fickle inhabitants, now revealing unusual friendliness towards the Emperor, clamoured for Frederick's admission. There developed also within the College of Cardinals unmistakable dissatisfaction with the militant policy of Gregory IX. It was in the midst of these days of near-despair that the aged Pope, by an act of rare courage, saved the day. On 22 February he appeared unexpectedly outside his palace surrounded by archbishops, bishops, abbots, and by all ranks of the Roman clergy wearing their sacred vestments and bearing in their midst the relics of the cross and 'the heads of the apostles Peter and Paul'. Singing hymns of devotion, this brilliantly caparisoned procession moved through the jeering throng of hostile Ghibellines, on its way from the Lateran to St. Peter's, where the Pope, octogenarian that he was, boldly faced the hostile crowd and spoke with firmness and with dignity. He told of the sufferings of the Church, born of the madness of the Emperor, and, uncovering the sacred relics, he said: 'Behold, these are the relics for which your city is venerated!' Then, removing his tiara from his head, and

---

[1] Huillard-Bréholles, v, part ii, 763, 845.

[2] Matthew Paris, *Chronica majora*, iv. 16.

[3] Huillard-Bréholles, v, part ii, 763. See also K. Burdach, *Rienzo*, ii, part 1, 385f.

[4] See, for example, BFW, *Reg.* v, Abt. i, nos. 2476, 2515, 2523, 2524, 2809, etc.; Winkelmann (*FzDG* xvi, 1876), 287.

[5] *Annales Placentini Gibellini* (*MGH, SS.* xviii), 483.

placing it upon the relics, he exclaimed: 'O saintly ones! Defend Rome, since no longer will the men of Rome defend her!' Thereupon the major portion of the mob was silenced, unable to respond save by making the sign of the cross, indicating their defence of the Church.[1] This act of sheer bravado by the aged but undaunted Pope stopped the over-confident Emperor in his tracks. Frederick was forced to the conclusion that the Romans were not yet prepared to yield voluntarily to imperial authority or to abandon their loyalty of a thousand years to the See of Peter. In March 1240 Frederick withdrew from the *patrimonium* to his Kingdom. It is a striking feature of this singular episode that Frederick II had made his appeal to the citizens as patriots of the ancient pagan Empire, while the Pope, by his dramatic revealing of the relics, had recalled them to their loyalty to Christian Rome. Temporarily checked in his effort to obtain control of the Eternal City, Frederick now turned his attention to the Kingdom of Sicily and imperial Italy.

So great were the differences now separating the Pope and the Emperor that the latter abandoned the pretence of honouring the promises he had made recognizing the Kingdom of Sicily as a fief from the Pope. Accordingly, as he returned to the Kingdom in 1240, he determined to push through the far-reaching reforms which would establish the Kingdom of Sicily and imperial Italy as a unified state, firmly bound to a centralized administrative system. These reforms had been partially implemented in 1238–9 when he appointed his son Enzio as vicar for the whole of Italy and Andrew of Cicada as imperial captain for the region between the Porte Roseta and the border of the Kingdom, virtually the whole of peninsular Sicily. Meanwhile, he had placed loyal Sicilian barons as *podestàs* over the subjugated cities of Northern and Central Italy, thus binding them closely to the central administrative system, and had also named Marquis Manfred Lancia as his vicar-general in the Piedmontese province.[2] The reorganization at Foggia emphasized especially the strengthening of all available military forces and the ensuring of the maximum employment of the resources of the Kingdom. The old regency, which had been authorized at the time of Frederick's Lombard expedition and his visit to Germany, was dissolved and the administration taken over directly by the Emperor and his court of highly trained officials whose jurisdiction extended over all Sicily and imperial Italy. The *magnae curiae magister justitiarius* or Grand High Justiciar henceforth would adjudicate not only petitions within

---

[1] Ibid. See also *Vita Gregorii* (*Liber Censuum*, ii), 34 ff., and the letter of Gregory IX, Huillard-Bréholles, v, part ii, 778.

[2] For the earlier administrative changes see first Richard of San Germano for the year 1239 and then E. Jordan, *Origines*, Introduction, pp. iv f. For the further changes, made during the Diet of Foggia, see the thorough study of E. Winkelmann, 'Zur Geschichte Kaiser Friedrichs II. in den Jahren 1239–1241' (*FzDG* xii, 1872), 523 ff., especially p. 529.

the Kingdom but also within imperial Italy. The new High Court of Justice would be supreme in both Sicily and imperial Italy. A central court of reckoning or 'exchequer court' under the control of the central administrative system was established at Melfi. For the remainder of Frederick's reign there was a continuous movement, most manifest in 1244 and 1247, towards the extension and perfection of this administrative system.

In May Frederick returned to the vicinity of Capua with his newly organized and newly equipped army. From there he continued to the borders of the Tuscan patrimony with the intention of renewing the attack upon that region. Just at this time, however, the Grand Master of the Teutonic Order, Conrad of Thuringia, as emissary for the German princes, arrived in Rome with urgent plans for the peaceful settlement of the conflict between Pope and Emperor. It was the cardinals rather than the Pope who now resumed negotiations at the urgent insistence of Conrad of Thuringia.[1] Two cardinals participating in these negotiations (Reginald of Ostia and John Colonna) were known to favour a peaceful settlement. But Gregory, irritated by Frederick's moving his troops into a threatening position on the outskirts of Rome, stiffened his resistance. Interpreting Frederick's movement as a threat to continue the war, Gregory ordered the city of Velletri to furnish troops to protect the Campagna.[2] His determination to continue his resistance is emphasized in a letter written at this time in which he assured the Count of Provence that no peace negotiations with the Emperor had taken place or would take place.[3]

It was about this time that he engaged in an altercation with Cardinal John Colonna. Gregory is reported to have said to the Cardinal, who had carried on the negotiations: 'I am ashamed of having granted a truce to Frederick, the enemy of the Church . . . Go immediately to him and say that I am not disposed to honour the truce. In defiance of him, say that henceforth I shall be his enemy, as I now am and as I have been in the past.' To this, John Colonna, who had made a sincere effort to conclude an honourable peace, replied angrily: 'On no account will I assent to this dishonourable procedure, but firmly oppose it.' Gregory, irked at this disobedience, exclaimed: 'I no longer consider you as my cardinal.' Whereupon John replied: 'And I no longer honour you as Pope.'[4] But, notwithstanding the impatience of John Colonna and the obduracy of the Pope, more conciliatory cardinals continued their efforts to find an acceptable formula for peace. At their urgent insistence, Frederick promised to abstain from further devastations in the Cam-

---

[1] Huillard-Bréholles, v, part ii, 985 ff., 1038. See above, pp. 435 f.
[2] BFW, *Reg.* v, Abt. iii, no. 7300.   [3] Winkelmann, *Acta*, i, no. 664, p. 530.
[4] Matthew Paris, *Chronica majora*, iv. 59.

pagna. He seems to have been persuaded that, in return for his cessation of hostilities there, the Pope would consent to further negotiations and that he was eager for peace.[1] Frederick was either deceived in this or else—and this seems more likely—he desired to place the onus for continued hostilities on the Pope. It is apparent throughout the negotiations that it was the cardinals who kept the negotiations alive, and it was they who were in agreement that the differences could be resolved only through the calling of a General Council.[2] Here also the efforts of the peacefully inclined cardinals were doomed to failure, for it was almost immediately apparent that there could be no agreement between Emperor and Pope as to the composition of the Council. Every attempt to find a compromise on this vital issue failed and the negotiations collapsed in mid July 1240. Even while the negotiations were taking place, the Pope condemned as rebels all persons who continued loyal to the Emperor. A few weeks later, Gregory, upon his own initiative, and in accordance with his own ideas as to its constituent members, summoned a General Council to be held during the Easter festivities of 1241.[3] The insuperable difficulty was Gregory's insistence that representatives of the Lombards and other enemies of the Emperor must be included.[4] To this the Emperor was unalterably opposed. In his letters summoning the Council Gregory left no doubt as to his belief that he alone was endowed by the will of God with unlimited power in all questions pertaining to the governance of the Church—that he alone was, therefore, authorized to call a Council and to determine its composition.[5] It was obvious that a Council summoned by a hostile Pope, who thus assumed full authority to exclude from it all persons friendly to the Emperor, placed him in the secure position of serving simultaneously as plaintiff and as judge.[6] This in itself would have been sufficient to exclude all further negotiations. Although Frederick had been first to suggest the appeal to a Council, he had never accepted the expressed belief of Gregory that this was solely a papal prerogative. Moreover, Frederick complained of the Pope's arbitrary choice of a date for the meeting. He held that the decision of a Council would not be valid unless its members were chosen by both Emperor and Pope: that the Pope had evaded the actual purpose of calling it by using the vague phraseology 'to settle the

---

[1] Huillard-Bréholles, v, part ii, 1059.

[2] Matthew Paris, *Historia Anglorum* (Rolls Series), ii. 434. See also the letter of Frederick to the King of England, Huillard-Bréholles, v, part ii, 1038: 'nos universale concilium et specialiter nunciorum vestrorum presentiam petissemus.'

[3] *MGH, Epist. Pont.* i. 677–9.

[4] Huillard-Bréholles, v, part ii, 1014 f.; Matthew Paris, *Chronica majora*, iv. 65 ff.

[5] Thus in his letter he said (see *Epist. Pont.* i, no. 781): 'Eterna providentia . . . ut uni pastori potestatis plenitudinem obtinenti ceteri partem sollicitudinis assumentes tanquam membra capiti.'

[6] See especially B. Sütterlin, *Die Politik Kaiser Friedrichs II. und die römischen Kardinäle*, 35.

arduous business of the Church'. For these and for other reasons Frederick recognized that the Council as it was visualized by the Pope had as its sole aim the ruin of the Emperor and the Empire.[1] In a letter addressed to the Cardinal Bishop Reginald of Ostia, but obviously intended for all the cardinals, Frederick again expounded his ideas concerning the supremacy of the College of Cardinals.

We have such firm faith in your sense of justice and consider you and your brothers of such steadfast character that, no matter how closely you are bound to the Roman pontiff by the bonds of reverence and love . . . as the hinges of the world, and as its most inflexible pillars, you will not be easily coerced into obstructing our just cause or into impairing our rights.

And however much you may yield at first to the present turmoil, to avoid as we believe the loss resulting from a schism, we believe that you really wish to find a fundamental solution by whose power the evils which have arisen may be healed and the troubles stirred up in the world may be quietened.[2]

Although he avoided the threat of force in his letter to the cardinals Frederick's letters to the Kings of England and France leave no doubt of his intention to employ all means at his disposal, including methods of violence, to prevent the delegates summoned by Gregory from reaching Rome. To the King of England he wrote: 'We exhort your Highness, therefore, by these letters to make known our imperial proclamation to each and all of the prelates of your Kingdom that no one is to set out for this council in the expectation of obtaining safe-conduct from us.'[3] Frederick thus defied the authority of the Pope in a matter of prerogative in which tradition had long since established the jurisdiction of the Holy See. Since the eleventh century, custom had decreed that a General Council could be summoned only by the Pope.[4] Aware, as he must have been, of the general acceptance of this as a papal prerogative, Frederick could not have failed to recognize the danger to which he had exposed himself when he advocated the summoning of a Council. Pope Gregory lost little time in calling attention to this.[5] The position of the Pope was not without weakness. At the Council of Lyons, some years later, Thaddeus of Suessa, who so eloquently defended the Emperor, emphasized the fact that 'the Pope had summoned the declared enemies of the Empire, even laymen, supported by armed force'.[6]

---

[1] The chief source for Frederick's opposition to the Council is Matthew Paris, *Chronica majora*, iv. 68 ff.

[2] Huillard-Bréholles, v, part ii, 1028–9.

[3] Matthew Paris, *Chronica majora*, iv. 68.

[4] *Dictatus Papae*, par. 16: 'quod nulla synodus absque precepto eius debet generalis vocari.' See also S. Löwenfeld, 'Der Dictatus Papae Gregors VII. und eine Überarbeitung desselben im XII. Jahrhundert' (*Neues Archiv*, xvi, 1890–1), 198.

[5] *MGH, Epist. Pont.* i. 717.

[6] Matthew Paris, *Chronica majora*, iv. 438.

Meanwhile the papal legate Gregory of Montelongo was working towards the consolidation of the opposition to the Emperor. For the moment his efforts seem to have checked the petty local quarrels of the Lombard cities by inducing them to direct their combined efforts towards the destruction of the imperial authority. The most vulnerable area for the Emperor in the midsummer of 1240 was in the Romagna. Not only Ravenna, which had deserted the Emperor the previous year, but also Ferrara had been won over by the papal party more by trickery than by force or by the convictions of the citizenry. Repeatedly the octogenarian leader of the citizens, Salinguerra, had repelled the attacks of neighbouring cities and their allies, Azzo of Este and Alberigo of Romano. Even the Doge of Venice, who, angered by the failure of his lieutenants and allies, had assumed the leadership of the assault on Ferrara, met with no success. But Salinguerra had enemies within the city itself. A hostile faction, led by Hugo Ramperti, yielding to Venetian bribery, made it possible for the Doge to take possession of the city. The aged Salinguerra, although menaced by his captors, was at length taken to Venice where he was permitted to live in honour until his death in July 1244.[1]

These reverses in the Romagna had weakened Frederick's prestige in that region at the moment when he most needed the support of all loyal subjects. The deterioration of his interests caused him to direct his attention to Bologna and Ravenna. Although Bologna appears to have been the focal point of his expedition, he could not safely leave the strongly fortified Faenza in his rear. Moreover, shortly after his arrival in that area the inhabitants had expelled the Ghibelline faction from the city. Avoiding the hazards of a direct attack, Frederick placed a blockade around Faenza while he prepared winter quarters for his troops by erecting a veritable wooden city outside the walls. It was during this siege that Frederick, confronted with a shortage of money with which to pay his troops, ordered the stamping of leather coins, later to be redeemed with gold at face value from the royal treasury. It was while engaged in this leisurely siege that he corrected the translation which Master Theodore, 'Todre le philosophe', was making from an Arabic book on falconry. The siege endured for six months when starvation compelled the inhabitants to surrender on 14 April 1241. The terrified citizens, expecting the direst of punishments from the Emperor whom they had so often offended, could register only surprise when Frederick, doubtless because he wished to devote himself to more pressing matters, displayed the greatest magnanimity towards them.[2] In a letter to

[1] See especially A. Frizzi, *Memorie per la Storia di Ferrara*, iii. 130 ff. See also *Annales Placentini Gibellini* (*MGH, SS.* xviii), 483; *Memoriale Mediolanenses* (*MHG, SS.* xviii), 402.
[2] For Frederick's account of the siege see Savioli, *Annali Bolognesi*, iii, part 2, 188; Fantuzzi,

Ezzelino Frederick told of his leniency to the rebels, 'With extended arms of clemency we accept the submission of the faithful.'[1]

While still in the vicinity of Faenza, the Emperor had, in March 1241, appointed as admiral of the fleet to succeed the late Nicholas of Spinola, a Genoese seaman, Ansaldus de Mari. Under his direction the final preparations of the fleet had moved forward rapidly for the impending conflict with the combined Venetian and Genoese fleets, which were now attempting to carry out the mission of escorting the prelates from various parts of Europe to Rome. Despite warnings from the Emperor, as well as from neutral observers, the prelates, admonished and encouraged by the Pope, determined to undertake the perilous voyage. The Pope had counselled them to hold in contempt the threats of temporal authority and to obey the spiritual father.[2]

Among the warnings to the prelates appearing at this time is a singular letter, thought to be the work of an anonymous priest, evidently designed to give pause at least to the more faint-hearted of its readers. The author told of the great perils to be encountered on the land, on the sea, and from the foul and pestilential air, which the prudence of mankind was incapable of avoiding. He dwelt especially upon the hazards of the sea: the indigestible sea-bread, the turbid wine, ceaselessly agitated by the turbulent sea; the corrupt water made unfit to drink by teeming vermin. Of the city of Rome, the destination of the prelates, he wrote that its heat was unbearable, its food coarse and bad, its atmosphere heavy and filled with mosquitoes, the ground alive with scorpions, the people filthy and repulsive. He said also that the city was undermined and from its snake-filled catacombs there arose a fatal vapour.[3] But heedless of all such warnings, the prelates, escorted by the Genoese fleet, began their fateful voyage on 25 April 1241. On 3 May Admiral Ansaldus, with elements of the Sicilian and Pisan fleets, overhauled the Genoese ships between the islands of Monte Cristo and Giglio and inflicted upon them a crushing defeat which virtually annihilated them. The battle has been described as one of the great sea battles of the Middle Ages.[4] The Genoese, unaccustomed to such reversals on the sea, were stunned. A Genoese chronicler, who describes the battle in some detail, introduces his annals with the remark: 'In this same

---

Monumenti Ravennati, iii. 81–2; Annales Placentini Gibellini (MGH, SS. xviii), 484. See also R. Davidsohn, Geschichte von Florenz, ii, part i, 268–9. For the translating of the Arabic work on falconry at this time see above, p. 310, note 5.

[1] Huillard-Bréholles, v, part ii, 1113.
[2] Matthew Paris, Chronica majora, iv. 121.
[3] The letter appears in Stephani Baluzii Miscellaneorum, Lib. I, 485 ff., Huillard-Bréholles, v, part ii, 1077.
[4] W. Cohn, Die Geschichte der sizilischen Flotte, 49 ff. See also Graefe, Publizistik, 84–5, and the detailed account of R. Davidsohn, Florenz, ii, part i, 272 ff.; C. Manfroni, Storia della Marina Italiana, i. 396 ff.

year [1241] it pleased God that many misfortunes should overtake the city.'[1]

More than a hundred prelates were taken captive, including Cardinal Otto of St. Nicholas, whose 'extortions' of money in England had so offended the Emperor, and James of Palestrina, the leader of the hostile faction of cardinals. The captives were taken by the Sicilian fleet to Pisa. During the voyage of a week's duration this 'prelate swarm', as they were scornfully described by Frederick, suffered all the inconveniences, and more, that had been depicted in the priestly warning. They were exposed to the unrestricted brutal abuse of the besotted sailors, their shoes and clothing stripped from their bodies, and their most cherished personal belongings taken from them.[2] Arriving at Pisa in a deplorable condition, the cardinals were turned over to the custody of Enzio whose more hospitable treatment gave them a momentary respite.[3] What appears to have been an order from the Emperor, however, brought an end to this leniency and, regardless of the law promulgated under Pope Honorius III in November 1225 declaring such mistreatment of cardinals as *lèse-majesté*, they were again subjected to abuse:[4] they were loaded with chains and held first in the Castle of San Miniato and later in various prisons in Apulia. The full fury of imperial wrath was visited upon Cardinal James of Palestrina 'who had so often stirred hatred' against Frederick. In a letter to the King of England, Frederick said of him: 'Let this man who bears the form of a wolf in the clothing of a sheep, cease thinking that he carries God within himself, and let him understand that God is with us, seated upon his throne and dispensing justice.'[5] Sharing this punishment with James of Palestrina during the first months of their captivity was Cardinal Otto of St. Nicholas. This treatment of the captive cardinals can only be described as an example of a short-sighted policy of vengeance which, although the result of heavy provocation, left an indelible stain upon Frederick as sovereign. One of the most injurious charges against Frederick II, and one which contributed to his deposition at the Council of Lyons, was this act of sacrilege committed through the imprisonment and brutal treatment of the cardinals.[6]

Yet, momentarily, he had gained an advantage: the deposition of the Emperor, the chief object of the projected Council, had been made temporarily impossible. Frederick had obtained a respite of several

[1] *Annales Janvenses* (*Fonti*, iii), 103 ff.

[2] Huillard-Bréholles, part ii, 1120 ff., 1127; See also *Ex Annalibus Melrosensibus* (*MGH, SS.* xxvii), 440.

[3] Davidsohn, *Florenz*, ii, part i, 273–4. See also BFW, *Reg. v*, no. 3200*a* and Abt. iv, no. 13370*a*.

[4] *MGH, Epist. Pont.* i. 208.   [5] Matthew Paris, *Chronica majora*, iv. 128–9.

[6] Ibid. 448.

years in which to seek a peaceful settlement or else to achieve his aims
by the force of arms. There is evidence also that among some contemporaries the prestige of the Emperor, in contrast with that of the
Pope, whose hostile intentions had been thwarted, was actually improved. A zealous Ghibelline poet and prophet could tell of the Pope's
grief at the imprisonment of the prelates. The same poet rashly prophesied that 'the "boy of Apulia" will hold the lands in peace'.[1] Matthew
Paris in relating the capture of the prelates quotes the Sibylline prophecy,
taken from the so-called *Dicta Merlini*: 'The sea will be crimsoned with
the blood of the saints.'[2] Even among some of the clergy the victories of
Frederick at Faenza and over the Genoese in the battle at sea were
looked upon as portents that the God of the earth and the sea had
revealed himself as the ally of the Emperor.[3] The lot of the unfortunate
prelates became more unbearable as time passed. A three weeks' sea
voyage from their prison near Pisa again exposed them to every form of
discomfort and to torture. Some succumbed to the inhuman treatment,
the remainder, sick and emaciated, were imprisoned temporarily in a
castle near Naples until, at length, they were separated and sent to
various prisons in Sicily.[4] But Frederick II, oblivious alike of the praise
and the censure of his contemporaries and in the full confidence of
victory, left no doubt of his determination to wring a peaceful settlement
from the Pope, if need be, by the force of arms.[5] The belief now prevailed in Italy that the Pope would be compelled to seek for peace. The
feeling that a peaceful settlement was imminent was heightened by the
profound impression made by the reports of the Tatar invasions in
the Orient. Shortly after the fall of Faenza, Frederick, writing of the
threatening approach of the Tatars, said: 'We cannot remain silent on a
matter which concerns not merely the Roman Empire, whose responsibility it is to care for the spread of the Gospel, but it touches also all
the kingdoms of the world that practise Christian worship, and threatens
the destruction of the whole of Christendom.'[6] The imprisoned prelates,
doubtless in the conviction that continued obstinate resistance by the
Pope could redound only to the detriment of the Church, also advised
him to make peace. A letter of Gregory's consoling the cardinals reveals
an unmistakable note of discontent. Moreover, a determined peace
faction among the cardinals now made earnest efforts towards the
establishment of peace.[7]

---

[1] O. Holder-Egger, 'Italienische Prophetieen des 13. Jahrhundert' (*Neues Archiv*, xxx, 1904–5), 351–2, 364–5.

[2] Matthew Paris, *Chronica majora*, iv. 130.

[3] Huillard-Bréholles, v, part ii, 1146.   [4] Richard of San Germano, 210.

[5] Huillard-Bréholles, v, part ii, 1141 ff., 1145.

[6] Matthew Paris, *Chronica majora*, iv. 112.

[7] *MGH, Epist. Pont.* i, no. 820, p. 721. As B. Sütterlin, *Die Politik Kaiser Friedrichs*, 43, has

It was about this time also that Richard, Earl of Cornwall, the brother-in-law of the Emperor, who had recently arrived at the Sicilian court on his return from a crusade, visited Rome in the hope of bringing about a peaceful settlement of the conflict between Gregory IX and Frederick II. In Rome, however, his reception was anything but hospitable. Everywhere he was exposed to injuries and insults and found no disposition for peace on the part of the Pope and Curia. 'After seeing . . . much which justly displeased him', he returned to the Emperor.[1]

It would be difficult to imagine conditions more unfavourable to the well-being of the Church than those which existed at the moment in 1241 when Gregory IX, heedless of all warnings and advice, determined to consider no basis for peace except unconditional surrender by the Emperor. The provinces of the Church had submitted to Frederick; the city of Rome was completely dominated by the ruthless senatorial dictator, Matthew Orsini; several of the cardinals were absent from the papal court, languishing in imperial prisons, and unlikely to obtain release until the Emperor had forced the Pope to accept his terms.[2] The members of the College of Cardinals still free to act were hopelessly split into two factions: those who stood firmly with the Pope in his policy of last-ditch resistance, and those who, if not supporting Frederick, at least desired a peaceful settlement. Cardinal John Colonna's desertion of the pro-papal party had served to heighten the tension among the cardinals and among the nobility and magnates in the city of Rome. The outspoken antagonism of the noble family of Colonna, the 'most arrogant *optimates* of Rome',[3] to the family of Orsini (now headed by the dictatorial senator, Matthew) contributed to the schisms, both in the College of Cardinals and among the citizens. The fickle populace, egged on by the Orsini faction, succeeded in driving Cardinal John Colonna from Rome; he was forced to take refuge in the fortified Palestrina, located on the Colonna family estate and dominating the route between Rome and the Campagna, where he received assistance from the Emperor.[4]

John, the second cardinal of the family of Colonna, now broke completely with Gregory IX and joined the Ghibelline faction.[5] It is impossible to attribute the defection of the proud Colonna either to selfishness or to greed. In an era so characterized by trickery, selfishness, and malice he apparently acted solely in honest protest against the

pointed out, the peace efforts of the cardinals can be assumed from a passage in a letter, Huillard-Bréholles, v, part ii, 1147.

[1] Matthew Paris, *Chronica majora*, iv. 147.
[2] See the letter of Frederick to the King of Hungary in *MGH, Const.* ii, 352–3.
[3] K. Burdach, *Rienzo*, ii, part i, 123.
[4] Richard of San Germano, 210.
[5] K. Wenck, 'Das erste Konklave' (*QF* xviii, 1926), 118–36.

irrational obstinacy of Gregory IX.[1] John Colonna seems also to have reached the conclusion that the well-being of the Church, no less than the peace of Rome and, indeed, of the Western world, could be attained only by the restoration of the Empire in the pattern of Roman antiquity. Frederick II himself was as astonished as he was gratified at the Cardinal's attitude, which, in a letter to his new supporter, he attributed 'to a noble desire for noble things and the burning zeal of noble blood'. In this letter Frederick assured John Colonna 'that you are a man after our heart. We will not only honour and esteem you, but also have confidence in your counsel in great and difficult matters. That which we recognize as originating in pure motives shall not be without influence.'[2] It can only be assumed that the advice of the Cardinal which met such warm approval from the Emperor could have been nothing less than the urging of Frederick to take possession of the city of Rome. Advice such as this, coming from one who had long been recognized as the 'foremost member of the College of Cardinals', could only strengthen Frederick's conviction of the righteousness of his cause. In the face of what was a veritable military alliance between Frederick II and John Colonna in August 1241, and with troops from the Kingdom of Sicily occupying strongholds of the Cardinal at the very gates of Rome, it could have been only a matter of time before the city itself fell. It is not improbable that the Cardinal and the Emperor were together in the Colonna castle, only twelve miles from the city, when they received news of the death of Gregory IX. The aged Pope, accustomed to escape from the summer heat of Rome to the cooler mountain air of Anagni or Viterbo, found himself unable to break through the siege of the city. Some years later the propagandist, Cardinal Rainer of Viterbo, charged Frederick II with causing Gregory's death by forcing him to remain in the enervating heat of Rome.[3]

---

[1] For an interpretation of his action see especially K. Wenck, 'Das Kardinalcollegium' (*Preussische Jahrbücher*, liii, 1884), 439.

[2] Huillard-Bréholles, v, part ii, 1155 ff.

[3] F. Graefe, *Publizistik*, 109. For the close association of Frederick and the Cardinal in Aug. 1241 see K. Wenck, 'Konklave', 135–6.

III

FREDERICK II AND THE CHOICE OF A SUCCESSOR TO POPE GREGORY IX

Nullus papa potest esse Ghibellinus.
Galvanus Flamma, *Chronica* (Muratori), *RIS* xi), col. 680.[1]

As Piero della Vigna, the imperial High Court Justice, had written in July 1241, the force of arms was to determine the outcome of the conflict between Emperor and Pope. But Frederick himself had repeatedly declared that he was in conflict neither with the Church nor with Rome—his efforts had been directed solely against the obstinate and unjust Gregory IX. In a letter to Christian princes Frederick wrote: 'On the 22nd of the present month of August news arrived at our camp that the Pope had died; that he who had refused to accept peace, desiring instead universal dissension, had narrowly escaped the vengeance of Augustus through death.' While acknowledging that the deceased Pope merited only his hatred, Frederick regretted that Gregory had not lived longer in order that he might have repaired the manifest wrongs and malicious persecution incited by him. 'But', he continued, 'God, who knows the secret thoughts of the wicked, decreed otherwise. Yielding to the pleas of the whole of Christendom, he will now cause to ascend to the Apostolic Throne a man after his own heart who will correct the errors and right the wrongs of his predecessors.'[2] In the same letter Frederick also expressed his desire for a reconciliation with the Church. This he now regarded as essential because of the threat from the Tatars.

But the hope for peace was hardly to be realized merely from the passing of Frederick's old antagonist, Gregory IX. In his hatred of the latter, he seems to have failed to perceive that the controversy had advanced far beyond the personal quarrel between two men—that it was now a fight unto death between the *sacerdotium* and the *imperium*, the spiritual rule of priests and the temporal rule of monarchs. Behind the activities of Gregory IX was the powerful support of an evolving canonical interpretation of the unlimited power of the Pope which far

---

[1] No Pope can be a Ghibelline.
[2] Piero della Vigna, *Epist.* i. 11; *Albertus van Behan* (ed. Höfler), 59.

transcended the policies of an individual. Frederick must face the subtle but inexorable force of the changing concept of the role of the *sacerdotium*. The Christian world anxiously awaited the all-important decision of the Emperor: would he release the imprisoned cardinals whose presence was now generally recognized as essential to ensure the election of a new Pope?[1]

At the time of the death of Gregory IX there were only nine cardinals present at the papal court; two were held captive by the Emperor; one, John Colonna, now an imperial partisan, stood with Frederick outside the gates of Rome. In the city the ruthless Matthew Orsini ruled with the unrestrained authority of a self-chosen dictator under the pretext of defending the city against the aggression of the Emperor.[2] Determined to dictate the election of the new Pope, Matthew subjected the cardinals who were in Rome to every possible pressure. Holding them prisoner in the ancient *Septizonium*, he ordered them to be bound hand and foot and subjected them to the most brutal treatment, in order to impose his will upon them. Here in a dilapidated room of the palace they had no protection from the rain which penetrated the crumbling roof or from the excrement of the guards who, stationed in a room above them, employed the cracked ceiling as a latrine. Into this foul prison, in the course of time, came also Cardinal John Colonna, under guarantee of safe conduct from the cunning senator Matthew Orsini.[3] After protracted deliberations the cardinals found themselves at an impasse, unable to agree upon a choice.

Five of the members present were able to agree on one of their colleagues, Godfrey Castiglione of Santa Sabina, a Milanese, as the new Pope. The five thus agreeing were John Colonna, Stephen of Santa Maria in Trastevere, Giles of Torres, a Spaniard, Rainer of Viterbo, later to become the chief papal propagandist, and Robert of Somercote, an Englishman, who succumbed shortly afterwards to the intolerable filth and brutal treatment of his prison. This group, although not necessarily friendly towards Frederick, was, above all, desirous of peace. It may well be that John Colonna, now the friend of the Emperor, exerted great influence upon his colleagues, perhaps ascertaining in advance that Godfrey, although of Milanese origin, would be acceptable to the Emperor. The other three cardinals, Reginald of Ostia (later Pope Alexander IV), Sinibald Fiesco of San Lorenzo (later Pope Innocent IV), and Richard Annibaldi, dissenting, chose Romanus of Porto, already well known as an implacable enemy of the Emperor.

[1] Richard of San Germano, 211.

[2] Concerning the Orsini, including Matthew, see D. Sternfeld, *Kardinal Johann Gaëtan Orsini*, 2 ff. See also P. Brezzi, *Roma e l'impero medioevale, 774–1252*, 445 ff.

[3] K. Hampe, *Ein ungedruckter Bericht über das Konklave von 1241 im römischen Septizonium*, especially pp. 4 ff., and p. 27.

Matthew Paris relates that the Emperor opposed Romanus not only as one who had kept alive the quarrel between the Emperor and the Pope, but also as a disreputable man who was said to have debauched Blanche of Castile, the Queen of France, and to have oppressed the University of Paris. His election as Pope could have served only to perpetuate the unhappy conditions that had so long prevailed in the relations between the papacy and Empire. Because of this impasse the assembled cardinals appealed to the Emperor to release their 'brothers' on whatever terms he would agree to in order that the welfare of the Church might be served. The reply of the Emperor, thanks to the advice of Richard of Cornwall and, probably, of John Colonna, was conciliatory. He imposed the condition, however, that unless Cardinal Otto of St. Nicholas, who during his imprisonment had been reconciled with the Emperor, was elected Pope, the two cardinals were to return to their imprisonment.[1]

The two cardinals who had been chosen by rival factions voluntarily resigned during the negotiations with the Emperor. For the moment at least Frederick could be hopeful of an election favourable to his interests.[2] But, unfortunately, Matthew Orsini now intervened. He spared no effort to ensure that the Emperor could exert no influence either upon the citizens of Rome or upon the candidates. Thanks, however, to the magnanimous action of the two nominees, the cardinals had been able to agree upon a third candidate whose identity has not been established, but who apparently was not one of their own number.[3] This compromise candidate was unacceptable to Matthew Orsini, who compelled the cardinals to repudiate their choice and to choose one of their own number who could emerge from the conclave wearing the customary mitre, symbol of the Apostolic authority. He threatened, in the event of their failure to choose one of their own number, to exhume the body of the late Gregory IX and to place it in their midst in order that its putrefaction might serve as a stimulus to hasten their decision. Under these threats, the cardinals now agreed to the choice of Godfrey Castiglione, Cardinal Bishop of Santa Sabina, who had previously been supported by five of the collegians. The newly elected Pope, characterized chiefly by his dignified bearing and by his conciliatory policies, assumed the name of Celestine IV.[4] Although old and infirm, the new Pope was known to favour a peaceful policy in settling the conflict with the Emperor.

---

[1] Matthew Paris, *Chronica majora*, iv. 164 f.: 'nisi Otto in Papam eligeretur.' See also K. Hampe, *Konklave*, 12 ff. The role of Romanus (Romano, Cardinal of S. Angelo) in the affairs of the University is mentioned briefly by H. Rashdall, *Universities*, i. 335 ff.

[2] *Annales Stadenses* (*MGH, SS.* xvi), 367; Huillard-Bréholles, vi, part i, 5.

[3] K. Wenck, 'Konklave', 146 ff., offers the conjecture that this compromise choice was a Tuscan, Humbertus de Romanis, Prior of the Dominican Order. There is no corroborative evidence of this.   [4] Hampe, *Konklave*, 14 ff.

The election did not ease the tension in Rome and the senator Matthew Orsini, outraged at the defiance of the cardinals, seized and imprisoned John Colonna, despite the guarantee of safe conduct which he had given to him.[1] After the home of another cardinal was plundered, Celestine IV proclaimed the ban against the turbulent senator. Seventeen or eighteen days after his election Pope Celestine IV died.[2] Some of the cardinals now made their escape from the city, taking refuge in Anagni. Apart from the imprisoned John Colonna, only two cardinals remained in Rome, apparently Sinibald Fiesco and Richard Annibaldi.[3]

The prospects for a new election were now far from bright, with the cardinals widely scattered, and three of them imprisoned. On 18 November those remaining in Rome appealed to their colleagues in Anagni to return in order that the election might proceed. In their letter they also informed the Anagni refugees that 'the venerable brother John [Colonna]', when asked to participate in the election, stated that in his prison he was not in a position to participate, nor did he have the freedom of will or the desire to do so. Accordingly he abstained from offering any counsel.[4] The reply of the Anagni cardinals to this urgent appeal to return to Rome not only explains their unwillingness to do so, but provides a vivid account of their sufferings during the conclave in the *Septizonium*. After describing these sufferings, the sickness and death of some of their colleagues, the filth of their surroundings, they, in turn, appealed to the cardinals in Rome to meet them in a mutually convenient place in the *patrimonium* where, in safety and in freedom, they could proceed with the election in conformity with the decretal, *In Nomine Domini*, of Pope Nicholas II of the year 1059, which provided that: 'if the wickedness of depraved men shall so prevail that a pure, sincere, and free election cannot be held in the city, they shall have the right to elect the pontiff of the Apostolic See wherever they shall judge most suitable'. The Anagni group stated also in their reply that, if their colleagues in Rome insisted upon proceeding with the election despite their absence from the city of Rome, they would call for the meeting of a General Council.[5]

As the factions among the cardinals continued their exchanges of invitations and threats, the Emperor became more insistent that the

---

[1] *Annales Placentini Gibellini* (*MGH, SS.* xviii), 485; Matthew Paris, *Chronica majora*, iv. 168.

[2] Nicholas of Carbio, *Vita Innocentii IV* (*Archiv. Soc. Rom.* xxi, 1898), 79. For the excommunication of the senator see K. Hampe, *Konklave*, p. 16 and note 39: 'propter hanc causam et alias excommunicationis vinculo innodati'.

[3] *Annales Placentini Gibellini* (*MGH, SS.* xviii), 485: 'Omnes cardinales preter duos de urbe Rome fugierunt . . .'; Matthew Paris, *Chronica majora*, iv. 194: 'sex vel septem cardinales Romae remanserunt.' See, however, the remarks of K. Hampe, *Konklave*, 18–19.

[4] Hampe, *Konklave*, 26–7.

[5] Hampe, *Konklave*, 31. For the decretal of Pope Nicholas see *MGH, Const.* i, no. 382, p. 540.

dissensions should end and a new Pope be elected. It was in conformity with this desire that he had Cardinals Otto of St. Nicholas and James of Palestrina transferred to Capua, apparently in anticipation of their ultimate release, in order that they might participate in the election 'in a secure and convenient place'.[1] Other sources also exerted pressure upon the cardinals. A letter, probably originating in the French court, appealed to the cardinals to proceed to a new election 'as the hinges of the world and the supporters of the faith'. This letter, certainly from an independent source, places the blame for the continued vacancy of the Holy See equally upon the Romans, the cardinals, and the Emperor.

The protracted vacancy in the papal office inevitably gave rise to some doubt as to the authority of the College of Cardinals to act upon official business as head of the Church. This question became all the more important because of the absence of several of the members. In a letter addressed to the Abbot of Wardon the cardinals themselves left no doubt that, in their opinion, the power resided in the College in the event of a vacancy. Such was the growing pressure upon them that the cardinals felt the necessity for positive action. From France came the warning that, if the College persisted in its negligence, the French themselves would provide a sovereign pontiff whom they would be sworn to obey, justifying their action through the ancient privilege granted to St. Denis by St. Clement, who released the apostleship to the Western world.[2]

The imprisonment and harsh treatment of Cardinal James of Palestrina remained always a serious hindrance to a reconciliation of Frederick and the cardinals. Several times they had appealed through Piero della Vigna for the 'restoration of the son to his mother', or else for a more humane treatment of the imprisoned Cardinal. But despite such appeals, the treatment of the Cardinal of Palestrina became more rigorous in retaliation for his unyielding defiance of the Emperor. In contrast, Otto of St. Nicholas, formerly regarded by Frederick as among his greatest enemies, had now become a friend and staunch ally of the Emperor. He was not only given his freedom but was also showered with gifts and with the imperial blessing. The explanation of this extraordinary reconciliation is no doubt to be found in the suggestion that 'Frederick, with the subtle skill inherent in his personality, knew how to inspire the conviction that the Empire and papacy could best carry on if they made peace and proceeded hand in hand'.[3] Otto, who only a few months before had invited the hatred of the Emperor as the papal legate extort-

---

[1] *MGH, Const.* ii, nos. 236 and 238, pp. 326, 327.
[2] Matthew Paris, *Chronica majora*, iv. 249–50; Huillard-Bréholles, vi, part i, 68 ff.
[3] C. Rodenberg, 'Die Friedensverhandlungen zwischen Friedrich II. und Innocenz IV. 1243–1244', *Festgabe für Gerold Meyer von Knonau*, 167.

ing funds from the reluctant clergy and nobles of England, now won his praise as 'our foremost friend among all the cardinals of the Church of Rome'.[1]

With the coming of the spring of 1243 Frederick pushed his campaign more persistently against the city of Rome. His military superiority, the poverty of the Curia,[2] the tyranny of the autocratic senator, Matthew Orsini, the chaotic conditions in Rome, and, most of all, the recent death of Cardinal Romanus of Porto, the spearhead of the anti-imperial faction—all these contributed to the growing demand for conciliation. Although Frederick's ambassadors succeeded several times in reaching the cardinals in Anagni and in Rome, the negotiations continued well into the summer of 1243. Again the cardinals in Anagni pleaded with their colleagues in Rome to join them so that the election might proceed without molestation. But the cardinals in Rome offered the excuse that they could not leave the city as long as the Emperor with an army stood at the gates. Thereupon the Anagni group sent an embassy to Frederick requesting his withdrawal, 'so that the filling of the vacancy might not be hindered or delayed'. They assured him also that immediately after the freeing of Cardinal James of Palestrina the election would take place. It is to be assumed that the cardinals in Rome had made this an indispensable condition for the acceptance of the Anagni invitation. It is probable that there had also been an agreement between the Emperor and the Anagni embassy as to the prelate to be chosen, or, at least, the assurance that the individual chosen would not be hostile to him and to the Empire.[3] Without such assurance it is most unlikely that Frederick would have agreed to release the imprisoned prelates, including the obdurate Cardinal James of Palestrina, whom he sent to join his colleagues now assembled in Anagni.[4]

In exchange for the release of the Cardinal, Frederick had demanded the recall of Gregory of Montelongo, the agent of the Curia active in fomenting opposition to Frederick in the Romagna and elsewhere in Northern Italy. But the cardinals gave only a vague assurance that they would comply with this demand, saying that, with God's help, they would do so as soon as possible—a promise which, after his election, the new Pope refused to honour.[5] In return it was proposed that Frederick make restitution to the Church for everything for which he had been

[1] Huillard-Bréholles, vi, part i, 143.

[2] Ibid. 87 f., 95 f. For the poverty of the Curia and the deplorable conditions in Rome see Nicholas of Carbio, *Vita*, pp. 81–3.

[3] Huillard-Bréholles, vi, part i, 90–4, 96–7. See also Winkelmann, *Acta*, i, no. 374, p. 331: 'ut mundo pacificum, nobis et nostro imperio non infestum sedes Petri reciperet successorem.'

[4] Richard of San Germano, 216; *Annales Placentini Gibellini* (*MGH, SS.* xviii), 486.

[5] See the letter of Innocent IV to the Archbishop of Rouen of Aug. 1243, *MGH, Epist. Pont.* ii. 9; *MGH, Const.* ii, no. 241, p. 330.

excommunicated—obviously the seizure of the *patrimonium*. Meanwhile, he withdrew his troops from the vicinity of Rome, with the exception of a small guard detachment.[1] For Frederick II the release of the Cardinal of Palestrina had been a most difficult decision. As if to satisfy his own conscience because of this act of weakness in releasing an objectionable antagonist, he asserted that his magnanimity resulted from his having in mind the well-being of the whole of Christendom, rather than his personal interests. In a letter to the Emperor of Constantinople he claimed that no such 'God-inspired clemency' could be found in the annals of the Caesars.[2]

On 25 June 1243 Sinibald Fiesco, Cardinal Priest of the Church of San Laurentius in Lucina, was unanimously chosen as Pope and three days later was consecrated under the somewhat prophetic name of Innocent IV.[3] The choice of Sinibald Fiesco was the signal for widespread rejoicing in the world of Christendom. The Emperor himself ordered services of thanksgiving throughout the Kingdom of Sicily. He hastened to congratulate the newly elected Pope, saying of him that from an old friend he had now become a father.[4] He notified Innocent IV that he was sending an embassy which he had authorized to negotiate a peace settlement. The chief members of the embassy were Gerard of Malperg, Master of the Teutonic Order in Jerusalem, Ansaldus de Mari, admiral of the Sicilian fleet, the two Justices of the High Court, Pierro della Vigna and Thaddeus of Suessa, and other important personages from the Kingdom of Sicily.[5] In letters to the kings and princes of Europe the Emperor expressed his satisfaction over the election.[6] He had some reason to believe that the new Pope, coming from the distinguished family of Hugh, Count of Lavagna, who had received his title from the Emperor and was regarded as a nobleman of the Empire, would follow a conciliatory policy.[7]

The sequel to the election, however, gives little reason to assume that Pope Innocent IV was disposed to make concessions to the Emperor. On the contrary, his complete devotion to legal studies, especially to canon law, made of him one of the foremost defenders of the unrestricted power of the Pope. Frederick must have anticipated the difficulties that lay before him; the remark allegedly made by him, whether authentic or not, may well express his misgivings: 'I fear I have lost a friend among the cardinals and will find once more a hostile Pope! No Pope can be

---

[1] Huillard-Bréholles, vi, part i, 97.
[2] Ibid. 91.
[3] Nicholas of Carbio, *Vita*, 79–80.
[4] *MGH, Const.* ii, no. 239, pp. 328–9: 'Vetus amicus, novum creatus in patrem.'
[5] Nicholas of Carbio, *Vita*, 82.
[6] *MGH, Const.* ii, no. 253, p. 353: 'gavisi fuimus gaudio magno.'
[7] Nicholas of Carbio, *Vita*, 80.

a Ghibelline!' Temporarily, the new Pope may have been disposed to accept a conciliatory settlement because of serious financial difficulties of the Church resulting from the long conflict with the Emperor. Early in his pontificate he complained in a letter to the clergy in the East of 'the great and serious need' of the Church.[1] If in the early days of his pontificate necessity impelled him towards conciliation, this was but momentary and was speedily abandoned as he began more fully to grasp the latent power, indeed, the obligation, inherent in the office of the Holy See.

It is difficult at times in recording the policies of Innocent IV in his long conflict with Frederick II to see him as other than an ambitious Pope, sacrificing everything in life or in his office except that which exalted him as ruler of the world. But such a characterization would be superficial. It is important to see Innocent IV against his background, his canonistic education, his ecclesiastical environment. Unlike his predecessors, his hierocratic thinking originated much more in the classical concept of a *Respublica*, a living organism in the Plutarchian sense, animated by the soul. His conduct of the papal office never ceases to appear as an attempt to apply practically the theme so logically set forth by John of Salisbury: Just as the human body is guided and directed by the soul, so the *Respublica* is oriented by the spirit. No less pertinent in explaining the conduct of Innocent IV is his literal application of the dictum of John of Salisbury that the basic feature of this corporate body is unity and the unitary principle is represented by the Pope, who alone is placed by God over nations and kingdoms.[2] Innocent IV, like his contemporary canonists, accepted the hierocratic system as sacred. As Pope his obligation to safeguard this system was even greater. To him, there was, fundamentally, but one body of laws, the laws of Christian society. So also there was but one fountain-head of all law and of all justice, the Pope who, in the language of St. Bernard of Clairvaux, had no equal. 'All drink from the public fountain, the Pope's breast.'[3]

Innocent IV's conception of his obligation, his sacred duty, in serving the interests of the Church outweighed all scrupulous restraints or what are in the temporal world described as ethical considerations. His duty was to him crystal clear. Obstacles to the fulfilment of that duty, whatever their nature, must be beaten down or ignored. He was of that group

---

[1] E. Berger, *Les Registres d'Innocent IV*, i, no. 22. See also H. Weber, *Der Kampf zwischen Innocenz IV. und Kaiser Friedrich II.*, 13–14.

[2] *Policraticus* (ed. Webb, Oxford, 1909), Lib. III, cap. 1, 171: 'Sic et Deus animam perfecte viventem totam occupat, totam possidet, regnat et viget in tota.' See also John of Salisbury, *Epist.* ccxviii (Migne, *PL* 199), col. 242; and the excellent analysis of John of Salisbury in W. Ullmann, *Growth of Papal Government*, 420 ff.

[3] *De consideratione* (Migne, *PL* 182), I, 5, col. 735 and II, ii, 4, col. 744: 'parem super terram non habes.' See also E. Kantorowicz, 'Deus per naturam, deus per gratiam, A Note on Mediaeval Political Theory' (*Harvard Theological Review*, xlv, 1952), 253 ff.

of extreme canonists who were convinced that the annihilation of the Staufen foe was essential to the preservation of the papal authority, indeed, of the *societas fidelium* itself. If at times he appeared conciliatory in his early years as Pope, it was but a manifestation of the dexterity with which he could shift his methods to the necessity of the moment. Relying upon his fullness of power, he did not hesitate to support his agents in the violation of justice and freedom, provided their actions were useful to the Church. For, in the final analysis, only the Pope could determine and decree what was just. Although adept at pursuing a coldly calculated policy, Innocent IV was capable of an opportunistic approach when confronted by sudden changes of conditions. Even in his nepotism, so patently characteristic of his rule, his favours were based upon the usefulness of the recipient in furthering the interests of the Church. Innocent acted throughout his pontificate solely upon his own counsel, yielding to no threat, to no fear, and to no sentiment. He was not unlike his great antagonist Frederick II in his obedience to a single ideal. Just as Frederick could justify the most tyrannical of his acts as essential to the restoration of a divinely ordained temporal sovereignty, so Innocent IV was driven always by his conviction of the sacredness of his cause. He saw the Staufen concept of universal empire as wholly inimical to the Vicariate, and to the hierarchical authority of the Holy See. Innocent IV was, in truth, a foremost architect in the planning of an arrogant and coercive Christian concept, destined in time to destroy itself by the extravagance of its pretensions, by the abuse of the power of the keys, and by its incapacity to adapt itself to the enlightenment of a more rationalistic era.

If Frederick had seen, or affected to see, in the election of Cardinal Sinibald Fiesco the prospect of a peaceful settlement he was soon to be disillusioned when Innocent's encyclical of 2 July 1243 revealed his true policy.[1] In this masterpiece of evasion Innocent carefully avoided references to the specific problems associated with a peaceful settlement, devoting his remarks rather to broad generalizations and spiritual platitudes, or else to an appeal for resistance to the Tatar invasions. Even more ominous for the future relations with the Emperor was Innocent's appeal to the allies of the papacy to continue their loyalty, while giving assurance of his own loyalty to former adherents of Gregory IX.[2] He had lost no time after his consecration in beginning discussions with his colleagues of the problems of peace and the choice of ambassadors to negotiate with the Emperor, designating for this mission Archbishop Peter of Rouen, William, sometime Bishop of Modena and now papal penitentiary, and the Abbot of St. Facundi, who was subsequently

[1] *MGH, Epist. Pont.* ii, no. 1, p. 1.
[2] See also H. Weber, *Der Kampf*, 9; and B. Sütterlin, *Die Politik*, 67–8.

made Cardinal. The ambassadors made their appearance at the imperial court in early August 1243.[1] They had been instructed to assure the Emperor of the desire of the Pope and Cardinals to live in peace with the whole world and, especially, with the Emperor. They were to remind him of his earlier promises to free all prisoners and appeal to him to reveal in what manner he proposed to make reparation to the Church. They were to assure him that in any way that the Church had wronged him, 'which is inconceivable', it was prepared to make compensation. If the Emperor denied his guilt then the Pope would assemble all princes and prelates in a secure place and leave to their judgement the reparation to be made by each side. Thus far the proposals of the embassy could well have afforded the basis of a lasting peace, but the Pope laid special stress upon including all 'friends of the Church' as participants in the peace settlement. It is obvious, of course, that these 'friends' included the cities of the Lombard League.

There can be no doubt that the Pope had found among his 'brothers' at this initial conference serious conflicts of opinion, the continuation of the factional differences which had characterized the College in the time of Gregory IX. It was probably the preliminary discussions within the College that determined the Pope's policy of maintaining a firm personal hold upon the negotiations.[2] This intention is apparent in his determination to include the Lombard communes as contracting parties in the peace negotiations. The Pope's attitude towards the Lombard question was further emphasized when Frederick, through the papal embassy, informed Innocent IV that Gregory of Montelongo, the legate in Lombardy, was undermining the imperial authority in that region. Frederick therefore demanded Gregory's recall. In a letter of 26 August to his ambassadors the Pope refused this demand, saying that the Roman Church was free and could send legates wherever it chose. He asserted also that he could not recall his legate without tainting himself with treason towards the Lombards, unless first the Emperor made peace with them. In the same letter he ordered his ambassadors to return to the papal court if they found the 'prince' unwilling to accept this admonition. Meanwhile, the tension between Pope and Emperor had been heightened when the embassy of Frederick II was refused audience with the Pope until first they had been absolved from the ban, inasmuch as 'the Roman pontiff has never knowingly admitted the excommunicated to an audience'.[3] After a second imperial embassy had been rebuffed by the Pope it was augmented by the addition of the Archbishop of Palermo, and Frederick again made it clear that he was willing to

---

[1] *Encyclical of Frederick* (*MGH, Const.* ii), no. 252, p. 342; Nicholas of Carbio, *Vita*, 81.

[2] See especially C. Rodenberg, 'Friedensverhandlungen', 169 ff.

[3] Berger, *Registres*, i, no. 72. *MGH, Const.* ii, no. 241, p. 330.

give satisfaction to the Church through honouring his spiritual obligations. Since the excommunication of the Emperor had not been pronounced because of the Lombard question, Innocent IV felt compelled
to yield. He notified his embassy that he would receive the agents of 'the
prince' after absolution and accordingly stated, 'we authorize you, *viva
voce*, to extend the benefits of absolution'.[1] Although yielding in a matter
which appertained to the spiritual well-being of the Emperor, the Pope
made no concession where the interests of the Lombards were concerned. Moreover, any concessions to the Lombards by himself would
have been considered by Frederick a disparagement of the Emperor and
of the honour of the Empire. The two issues which, henceforth, as before,
were to make conciliation impossible were the refusal of Frederick to
include the Lombards in the peace negotiations and his unyielding
attitude towards the Pope's demand for the restoration of the lands of
the Church.

The Pope's reply to Frederick's demand for the recall of Gregory of
Montelongo served to arouse still further the antagonism of the Emperor
when Innocent suggested that he would ascertain whether or not the
Lombards would agree. It was clear to Frederick that further negotiations about the political issues were futile—that the Pope would accept
nothing short of the unrestricted restoration of the *patrimonium*. The
Lombard question could be disposed of only if both sides submitted
their differences to the Pope as arbiter.[2]

In the midst of these unpromising negotiations hopes for conciliation
were shattered by the activities of Cardinal Rainer of Viterbo, the
obstinate and unscrupulous foe of the Emperor, and the propagandist
agent of the papacy.[3] Cardinal Rainer was a unique figure among the
cardinals of the thirteenth century. He combined the attributes of a
soldier with the base instincts of an intriguing and scheming politician.
Throughout the pontificate of Gregory IX he had kept alive among his
colleagues all the hatred and uncompromising sentiment towards the
policies of Frederick II, indeed, towards the family of Hohenstaufen,
that had characterized the papal court during the era of Henry VI and
Philip of Swabia. His life was one of ceaseless effort on behalf of the
omnipotence of the Holy See. Toward the realization of this he gave
himself unsparingly, whether as military leader, as legate, as intriguer,
or as propagandist. Fanatic that he was, he was above self-seeking,
becoming rather the dynamic instrument of the Church which he
thought of, not so much as a spiritual institution, but as a hierocratic

---

[1] *MGH, Const.* ii, no. 241, p. 332.
[2] Ibid. 341–2, 346.
[3] See E. von Westenholz, *Kardinal Rainer von Viterbo*; also the observations by F. Baethgen
(*MIöG* xxxvii, 1916), 506 ff.

state charged with the supervision of the thoughts and activities of mankind. For thirty years he served this dubious ideal valiantly and without reservations, whether physical, intellectual, or moral. He hesitated not at all in the employment of chicanery, faithlessness, vilification, and deceit. He belonged to the school of politically minded prelates, predominant throughout the thirteenth century, which subjected all ethical conduct and all precepts of morality to the material and political interests of the hierocratic state. His hatred of Frederick II knew no bounds and, not infrequently, drove him to attacks upon the Emperor of such violence and of such viciousness as to suggest an unbalanced mind.

Since February 1240, when Viterbo had voluntarily submitted to the Emperor, its citizens had remained his loyal supporters. Frederick visited the city frequently, building a palace there and, from time to time, bestowing important privileges upon the citizens. Within the city there existed the usual Ghibelline and Guelf factions characteristic of most Italian cities of the thirteenth century.[1] These partisan conflicts within the city had subsided temporarily under the conciliatory policy of Count Simon of Teate, the imperial *podestà*. Meanwhile, however, Cardinal Rainer, a native of Viterbo, who had from the outset opposed all peaceful negotiations, now found an opportunity not only to sabotage the negotiations between Pope and Emperor but also to make future conciliation impossible. He became the instigator of a conspiracy in Viterbo which seems to have been known to and tacitly approved by Innocent IV. Despite the latter's denial, there is implicating evidence that in 1243 the Pope expressed his willingness to pay some 2,500 ounces of gold to mercenaries to be employed in an attack upon the imperial garrison of Viterbo, although he is said to have warned the over-zealous Cardinal that 'we do not wish to be put to any expense in this affair'.[2] Relying upon the latent discontent within the Guelf faction in Viterbo which had recently been heightened by unpopular acts of the imperial officials in the city, Rainer secretly persuaded them to make peace with their former enemies, the Romans. With the aid of the latter, who are said to have joined the citizens of Viterbo in great numbers, they seized the imperial guards and took them as captives to Rome, substituting Roman and Viterbese in the fortified places within the city.[3] Although Rainer endeavoured to shield the Pope and Curia as parties to the conspiracy, Frederick was convinced of the guilt of Innocent IV, saying of him that 'he who we hoped would be a father . . . concealed his bow

[1] The following account is based chiefly upon the *Cronache di Viterbo* (Böhmer, *Fontes*, iv), 709 ff., and Nicholas of Carbio, *Vita*, 83–4.   [2] *MGH, Epist. Pont.* ii, no. 30, p. 24.
[3] In addition to the *Cronache di Viterbo* (Böhmer, *Fontes*, iv), 709 ff., see also Matthew Paris, *Chronica majora*, iv. 266–7. For Rainer's effort to shield the Pope see Winkelmann, *Acta*, i, no. 693, p. 547: 'supresso ecclesie nomine propter metum.'

under words of peace and prepared it for wounding us'.[1] Indeed, it is apparent that the initial opposition of the Pope to Rainer's conspiracy was not due to moral or ethical considerations but to the fact that it was likely to be expensive. The duplicity here revealed set a pattern which the Pope and his legate were to follow henceforth in their efforts to destroy the Emperor. If in the end Innocent IV yielded to Rainer's appeal for financial aid, it was because he recognized that a defeat of Viterbo by the forces of the Emperor could only be interpreted as a vindication of the latter's cause and as a serious set-back to the designs of the Holy See. Although the Pope actually provided financial assistance well in excess of what had been requested, Rainer, swept on by his fanatical hatred of the Emperor, mortgaged his own property in order to obtain necessary funds to carry on the conquest.[2]

To Frederick II also the attack on Viterbo proved an expensive enterprise, necessitating the borrowing of considerable sums from Pisan merchants, for a period of two years.[3] Additional reinforcements of the conspirators, made possible by the Pope's financial aid, enabled them to besiege the imperial castle so insistently that the *podestà*, Simon of Teate, was compelled to send an urgent appeal to Frederick for reinforcements. In September Frederick hastened in person to the relief of the garrison. His following, however, was obviously small, probably the remnant of an army which he had dismissed at the beginning of negotiations with the Pope, or else hastily assembled by his son-in-law, the Count of Caserta. Frederick's attempt to relieve the garrison resulted in an overwhelming defeat, which forced him to suspend the siege after two months.[4] Taking advantage of this turn of events, the Pope sent Cardinal Otto of St. Nicholas, who during his captivity by the Emperor had become 'the upright and true friend' of the latter, to reopen negotiations. Innocent IV had astutely chosen the one member of the College of Cardinals who was on such terms with the Emperor as to give reasonable assurance of fruitful negotiations. Thanks to the Emperor's confidence in the rectitude of Cardinal Otto, an agreement was quickly reached. The Emperor promised to withdraw his garrison, while Otto gave his sworn assurance on behalf of the Pope that the imperial partisans would be permitted to leave the city unmolested in person and in property.[5]

[1] Winkelmann, *Acta*, i, no. 374, pp. 330–1: 'sub verbo pacis arcum suum tetendit et paravit illum ad lesionem nostram.'

[2] Ibid. i, no. 693, p. 549; Huillard-Bréholles, vi, part i, 143. See also E. Westenholz, *Rainer*, pp. 90–1.

[3] H. Weber, *Der Kampf zwischen Papst Innocenz IV. und Kaiser Friedrich II.*, 42; and Huillard-Bréholles, vi, part 1, 138–9.

[4] *Cronache di Viterbo* (Böhmer, *Fontes*, iv), 709; Piero della Vigna, *Epist.* i, Lib. II, nos. 53–6, pp. 352–60. See also Richard of San Germano, 217, and E. von Westenholz, *Rainer*, 88.

[5] *MGH, Const.* ii, no. 252, p. 342.

Humiliating as was the defeat to the Emperor, he apparently had not consented to these terms without some concessions on the part of the Curia. It has been conjectured that he probably received some recognition of his territorial claims in the *patrimonium*. Unfortunately, the only clue that we have to these concessions is the somewhat indefinite remark of the Emperor in which he intimated that he was assured that the withdrawal of his garrison would redound greatly to his advantage in future negotiations.[1] The actual withdrawal of the imperial troops, however, served only to demonstrate the perfidy of Cardinal Rainer and to heighten Frederick's distrust of the integrity of the Pope himself. For the adherents of Cardinal Rainer broke their pledge: falling upon the retreating troops and other supporters of the Emperor, they killed and wounded many and robbed them of their personal property. Cardinal Otto of St. Nicholas, true to his oath, sought valiantly, even at the risk of his life, to restrain the mob. It is said that he emerged from the fray bespattered with the blood of those whom he sought to protect. As the Pope's agent and as the author of the terms of peace which the Emperor had agreed to because of his confidence in him as a friend, Cardinal Otto was shamed by this betrayal in which he, like the Emperor, must have recognized the hand of his crafty colleague, Rainer of Viterbo. The Emperor needed no reassurance from Otto, but immediately cleared him of all blame.[2]

The reaction of Innocent IV to the report of this deed of violence by his partisans in Viterbo appeared for the moment to absolve him also of any taint of guilt. He threatened both the *podestà* and the populace with heavy punishment if they failed to release the injured captives and to restore the pillaged property.[3] The Pope's action becomes somewhat suspect, however, in that he associated Cardinal Rainer with Otto of St. Nicholas in the execution of the papal order.[4] This suspicion is strengthened by the continued imprisonment of the Ghibelline citizens, many of whom were still held two years later, while others remained in exile. The distrust of the motives and of the sincerity of the Pope was still further heightened when, after repeated efforts to spur Innocent to compel the freeing of the imprisoned citizens, Frederick was put off with the excuse that the Pope would freely do everything possible to make amends were it not for his fear of losing the city.[5] This attitude of the Pope, no less than his obvious connivance at the conspiratorial undertakings of Cardinal Rainer, shattered the faith of the Emperor in the

---

[1] *MGH, Const.* ii, loc. cit.; C. Rodenberg, 'Friedensverhandlungen', 181. I find no adequate support of this conjecture.

[2] Huillard-Bréholles, vi, part i, 144.

[3] Winkelmann, *Acta*, i, no. 693.

[4] C. Pinzi, *Storia della città di Viterbo*, i. 445 f.

[5] *MGH, Const.* ii, no. 252, p. 342.

honesty of his papal antagonists. The affair of Viterbo was to burn deep into his heart and to stir him to one of his most extravagant statements that 'if one foot stood in paradise he would withdraw it if in so doing he could revenge himself on the Viterbians'.[1]

[1] Winkelmann, *Acta*, i, no. 720, p. 567.

PART X

THE CLOSING YEARS
DEATH OF THE EMPEROR

I

POPE INNOCENT IV FLEES
TO LYONS

Fugit impius, nemine persequente.
Flores Historiarum (attributed to Matthew of West
minster; Rolls Series), ii. 277; Proverbs 28 : 1.[1]

So great was the resentment of Frederick II at the loss of Viterbo
that it was most unlikely that further negotiations with the Pope
would have been undertaken upon his initiative. The reopening of
negotiations seems to have come about at the instance of King Louis IX
of France, who had taken the cross in 1244. The loss of Jerusalem to
the Khorezmians on 23 August 1244, followed in less than two months
by the crushing defeat of the combined Christian and Muslim forces
near Gorza, must have driven the pious Louis IX to his decision. The
losses of the Christians, largely French, were variously estimated by
contemporary chroniclers as between 5,000 and 16,000 men.[2] The
Christians of Syria had now sacrificed the gains made by the diplomacy
of Frederick II in 1229, the crusade of Theobald of Novare in 1239–40,
and by the efforts of Richard of Cornwall in 1240–1. In the West the conflict between Frederick II and the Pope made it virtually impossible for
either the Germans or the Italians to undertake an expedition to relieve
their fellow Christians in the Orient. France alone was in a position to
undertake such an expedition.[3]

It was fortunate for both the King of France and Frederick II that
Raymond of Toulouse had been with the Emperor since September
1242 and that he was active, with the support of Louis IX, on behalf of
a peaceful settlement between the Pope and Frederick II. On 2 December
1243 the Pope had authorized the Archbishop of Bari, a faithful supporter of Frederick II, to release Raymond from the ban. He was thus
in a position to accompany Frederick's emissaries, Piero della Vigna and

---

[1] The wicked fleeth, none pursuing.
[2] Matthew Paris, *Chronica majora*, iv. 307–11; Joinville, *Histoire de Saint Louis* (ed. M.
Natalis Wailly), 61 f.
[3] See especially J. R. Strayer, 'The Crusade of Louis IX' (*The Crusades*, ii: *The Later
Crusades*, ed. R. L. Wolff), ii. 489 ff.

Thaddeus of Suessa, with plenipotential authority, to negotiate with the Pope.[1]

On Maundy Thursday (31 March 1244), in a public ceremony in which the imperial ambassadors, representatives of the Lombard cities, the cardinals, the Emperor of Constantinople, and the senate and citizens of Rome participated, a provisional peace was agreed to. Somewhat prematurely, Frederick hastened to inform his son Conrad of the anticipated peace, expressing his satisfaction that the Pope, in a sermon before thousands of people, had alluded to the Emperor as the 'devoted son of the Church and Catholic prince'. In the same letter Frederick ordered his son to give wide publicity to the good news in the whole of Germany.[2] A glance at the chief articles of the proposed agreement, however, affords little reason to believe that they could have become the basis for a lasting peace.[3]

With regard to territory, an agreement was suggested which was satisfactory to both parties (*qui placet utrique parti*) ensuring the restoration to the Church and to adherents of the papal party of all lands which they possessed at the time of the excommunication of the Emperor. As to his alleged 'contempt for the keys' (*contemptu clavium*), the Emperor was to proclaim throughout the whole earth that he did not treat with contempt the sentence pronounced by Gregory IX; that his resistance had arisen only because the action of the Pope was not in the requisite form and because obedience was not obligatory until this action was duly made known to him. Frederick is said to have admitted that he had conducted himself badly with respect to the sentence. He acknowledged the full power of the Pope in spiritual matters over him, as over all other Christians of whatsoever degree. In atonement for his misconduct he agreed to provide such military and financial assistance to any prince of Christendom as the Pope might deem fitting; to give alms, and to keep fasts as the Pope might decree; and humbly and devotedly to accept the sentence of excommunication pending his absolution. The Emperor was to restore all property that could still be found which had fallen into his hands at the time of the capture of the prelates on their way to the Council. Furthermore, he agreed to compensate those who had suffered as a result of this offence and to atone for his wrongdoing by the building and endowing of hospitals and churches in accordance with the wishes of the Pope. As to all other damages suffered by the churches and by the clergy since the excommunication was pronounced, the Emperor agreed to abide by the judgement of the Pope, in so far as

[1] Letter of Frederick II in Matthew Paris, *Chronica majora*, iv. 331 ff.; C. Rodenberg, 'Friedensverhandlungen', pp. 184–5; *MGH, Epist. Pont.* ii 31.

[2] Huillard-Bréholles, vi, part i, 176–7; Savioli, *Storia di Bologna*, iii, part ii, no. 632.

[3] *MGH*, Const. ii. 334–7; Matthew Paris, *Chronica majora*, iv. 332 ff.

such judgement did not impinge upon his honour or in any way diminish his realms. Those who had adhered to the papal party after the commencement of the quarrel were to be forgiven all injury inflicted by them, both before and after the quarrel (*offensa tam ante quam post*). Their possessions, rights, and honours were to be restored, even though these had been granted to others (*etsi aliis sint concessa*). Frederick agreed also to revoke all bans and all sentences pronounced against them, while releasing them from obligations for all gifts, contracts, or bonds which they had made to him since the promulgation of the sentence of excommunication, or after their adherence to the Church party. This general amnesty was to apply equally to those who were in rebellion before the dispute arose. Noblemen, who, during the recent wars, were partisans of the Holy See (among them the Marquis of Montferrat), were not to be required to fulfil the feudal obligations to the Emperor in person, but by proxy. Nicholas of Carbio, the papal chaplain, is responsible for the statement that Frederick II proposed a marriage alliance between his son Conrad and a niece of Pope Innocent IV in return for lands of the Church which he had appropriated during the conflict.[1]

Hazardous as were these terms as the basis of an enduring peace, they were destined to be nullified by the obstinate resistance of the Lombards, who continued to demand that their conflict with the Emperor must be terminated solely by the Pope. Now, as before, Innocent IV yielded to their demand and agreed that the negotiations would be reopened only on that condition. Innocent himself could not have failed to recognize that in accepting the demands of his allies he was closing the door upon reconciliation with the Emperor. The Pope further jeopardized the negotiations by his premature publication of the tentative agreement in which he did not scruple to make changes both in substance and in form. Like his predecessor, Innocent IV had obviously decided that the conflict with the Staufen was one of survival. There appears to have been in his mind neither hope nor desire for a peaceful coexistence—only the triumph, absolute and undisputed, of the *sacerdotium* over the *imperium*. But in implementing this all-or-nothing policy the Pope must still reckon upon the opposition of the cardinals who deplored his submission to the Lombard demands as well as his premature publication of the tentative agreement.[2] These dissenting cardinals were now Frederick's only hope for separating the question of his absolution from the purely political issue of the conflict with the Lombards. But Innocent IV had no intention of delegating to the cardinals decisions as to policy. They might serve as the agents through whom the negotiations were to be carried on, but ultimate decisions were to be his alone.

[1] *Vita*, 85.
[2] *MGH, Const.* ii, no. 252, pp. 345, 347, 350.

Upon the return of Piero della Vigna and his fellow High Court Justice, Thaddeus of Suessa, to the papal court shortly after Easter 1244, Innocent suddenly demanded, in addition to the inclusion of the Lombards in a peace settlement, the restoration of the lands of the Church as a surety for the Emperor's absolution.[1] The restoration of these lands before first obtaining absolution for his spiritual offences would have left the Emperor in a position of helplessness, while giving Innocent IV every possible advantage. As long as Frederick retained control of the *patrimonium* he could feel hopeful that the Pope would want to continue the negotiations. Accordingly, he requested Innocent, as pastor, to give him absolution in return for his submission to the purely spiritual demands, while leaving negotiations with regard to the *patrimonium* for future settlement. Innocent affected to see in this request only evidences of evasion and even of perjury. The astute High Court Justices, however, supported by the Emperor of Constantinople, who had for some time been actively pressing for peace, and by some of the cardinals, now suggested that a cardinal be delegated to absolve the Emperor.[2] Faced with this opposition, the Pope moved to strengthen his position by creating twelve new cardinals who would be sympathetic to his policies. A contemporary chronicler says that Innocent made this decision because he had so few colleagues who were sympathetic to his designs.[3] Only one of the new cardinals, Peter of Albano, was disposed towards a peaceful settlement. Innocent could now be reasonably sure that in the future he would find a sympathetic and subservient support from a majority of the cardinals.

The attitude that the Pope affected towards Frederick's perjuring himself by refusing to surrender the *patrimonium* before receiving absolution, placed the latter in a most difficult, if not impossible, position. He could see no means of escaping the impasse save through a personal meeting with the Pope. In order to achieve this, he offered the immediate restoration of a part of the lands of the Church, provided the Pope would come into the Campagna for a conference. After some hesitation and further negotiations Innocent agreed to accept the invitation but expressed a preference for Narni as the meeting-place.[4] Apparently in the conviction that some trickery was involved in the Emperor's proposal, Innocent suddenly changed his plans, or else carried out a long-contemplated decision to take flight from Italy and find a safe refuge beyond the Alps. He proceeded not to Narni but to

---

[1] Nicholas of Carbio, *Vita*, 85: 'Postmodum vero ut terras Ecclesie restitueret, quas occupare presumserat.' See also *MGH, Const.* ii. 345.

[2] Nicholas of Carbio, *Vita*, 85; *MGH. Const.* ii. 345.

[3] Matthew Paris, *Chronica majora*, iv. 354; Nicholas of Carbio, *Vita*, p. 85: 'duodecim cardinalium'. See also J. Maubach, *Die Kardinäle und ihre Politik*, ch. iii, pp. 13 ff.

[4] *MGH, Const.* ii, no. 252, pp. 347, 351.

Civita Castellani. His conduct after reaching Civita Castellana suggests well-planned preparations for a projected flight. Meanwhile, Cardinal Otto of Porto, ignorant of the Pope's intentions to take flight, continued on his mission to Narni. Frederick received confirmation from Otto of what he must have already perceived was the Pope's attitude: 'that if no remedy could be found for the hidden sickness, that is to say the Lombard business, then peace could not possibly proceed.'[1] It was soon obvious that the purpose of the Pope's apparently conciliatory attitude was to conceal his preparations for his flight from Italy.

The motives behind Innocent's flight are not far to seek. Recollection of the serious threat to Rome and to the Pope resulting from the presence of an imperial army outside the city gates during the last days of Gregory IX was still vividly before him. What now if, under similar conditions, the forces of Frederick should enter Rome, virtually holding the Lateran in a state of siege? Even if the Pope, accompanied by the cardinals, were to leave the city, where in Italy could they find a secure refuge? Once outside Italy, would it not be possible, particularly in France, the traditional protector of menaced popes, to obtain the necessary assistance to oppose the forces of the Emperor? Upon receiving the Pope's request to enter France, King Louis IX, after consulting with the magnates, denied it, partly because of the traditional friendship with the Hohenstaufen but also because of the dangers inherent in having 'two great luminaries in his country'.[2] Meanwhile, the Pope, disguised as a soldier and accompanied by his nephew James and William Fiesco and a few loyal followers, fled secretly during the night to Sutri, leaving behind all the other cardinals. Proceeding then to Civitavecchia, he boarded the flagship of the Genoese galleys, which had awaited his arrival, and set sail for the friendly city of Genoa,[3] arriving there on 7 July.

On the following day he was received in the city with honour and rejoicing. Here also he was reunited with four or five of the cardinals; others had gone, on orders from the Pope, by the land route to Susa (Segusio) to await Innocent's arrival in Lyons. Four others remained in Italy as representatives of the Pope in the affairs of the Church.[4]

It is doubtful whether the Pope was able to participate in the gay festivities held in honour of his arrival in Genoa. His chaplain, Nicholas

---

[1] Ibid. 347. See also C. Rodenberg, 'Friedenverhandlungen', 198 f.

[2] Matthew of Westminster, *Flores Historiarum* (Rolls Series), ii. 283: 'Nec permitterent duo magna luminaria in suo climate apparere.'

[3] For the details of the flight see especially the account of Nicholas of Carbio, *Vita*, 86–9; and the *Annales Janvenses (Fonti*, iii), 153. See also *Flores Historiarum*, ii. 276; *MGH*, *Const*. ii. 351.

[4] *Annales Janvenses*, iii. 154. See also Nicholas of Carbio, *Vita*, 88 f. The *Annales Janvenses* mentions four cardinals, while Nicholas of Carbio names five. For the movements of Cardinal Otto of Porto and other cardinals see Matthew Paris, *Chronica majora*, iv. 393.

of Carbio, who accompanied him, relates that the voyage had scarcely begun when severe storms arose, compelling the ships to seek refuge at Porto Veneri where they waited for three days for the fury of the storm to abate before proceeding to Genoa. Innocent was so seriously stricken with fever and dysentery that he was forced to spend three months recuperating in the monastery of St. Andrew outside the city of Genoa. It was only towards the end of the year, in early December, that he finally reached Lyons.[1] In Italy the Pope had made arrangements for handling the affairs of the Church; he left Cardinal Rainer of the Church of Santa Maria in Cosmedin as papal representative in the *patrimonium*, Spoleto, Ancona, and Tuscany; Reginald, Cardinal Bishop of Ostia, with no specific assignment; Richard of St. Angelo as Count of the Campagna; and Stephen of Santa Maria Trastevere as representative in Rome.[2]

The flight of the Pope could be made invaluable in the propagandist battle which the Curia was to wage so successfully against the Emperor. Frederick could now be represented as the irresponsible perjurer, the ruthless and brutal despot aiming at nothing short of annihilation of the See of Peter. Innocent could and did affect terror—the helpless head of the Church fleeing before the imperial assassins.[3]

On the feast of St. John the Evangelist (27 December), in a sermon following Mass, the Pope announced a 'General Council' for 24 June 1245, to be held in Lyons. In this sermon the Emperor was invited to attend the Council, but Frederick's invitation was verbal—not a formal summons.[4] While thus excluding the Emperor from the list of formally invited participants, the Pope sent numerous letters to prelates and kings throughout Christendom. In these letters he described the turbulent conditions threatening the Church and endangering the Christian religion, saying that he was calling a Council to the end that peace might be restored. He mentioned also the sad plight of the Holy Land, of the Greek Empire, and the devastation wrought by the Tatar invasion. Finally he indicated that the business pending between the Church and the 'princeps' was to be considered. Innocent IV habitually abstained henceforth from designating Frederick as Emperor, employing instead the title 'princeps'.[5]

There can be little doubt that Frederick had been greatly disconcerted by the flight of the Pope. Far from desiring to injure him, as Nicholas of Carbio intimates,[6] Frederick was in need of a peaceful settlement with

---

[1] Nicholas of Carbio, *Vita*, 88, 90; *Chronica regia Coloniensis*, 286.
[2] *MGH, Epist. Pont.* ii, no. 89.
[3] U. Tammen, *Kaiser Friedrich II. und Papst Innocenz IV. in den Jahren 1243–1245*, 37–8.
[4] *Vita*, 93. See also the encyclical of Innocent IV, Huillard-Bréholles, vi, part i, 248.
[5] For the form of the invitation see *MGH, Epist. Pont.* ii, no. 78, pp. 56–7; A. Folz, *Kaiser Friedrich II. und Papst Innocenz IV.*, 9 ff.   [6] *Vita*, 86.

the Pope and also of a sympathetic understanding of the conflict by the world of Christendom. The rumour, current at the time of Innocent's flight from Italy, that three hundred knights were on the way to arrest him may therefore be dismissed as insidious propaganda.[1] In a letter to the King of France in 1247 Frederick indignantly refused the charge that he sought to injure the Pope: 'For who, in his right mind, would believe that we would wish to put to death one whose murder would bring to ourselves and our posterity perpetual strife?'[2] How greatly Frederick was in need of a *rapprochement* with the Pope is apparent in his letter to Cardinals Otto of Porto and Peter of Albano shortly after Innocent's flight: 'We, because of the reverence which we have for the Mother Church, still hope for peace and for absolution.' To this end he appealed to the friendly cardinals to continue to seek an agreement, although cautioning them against any concession which would injure the dignity of the Empire or do injustice to the imperial majesty. As a gesture of goodwill he offered the cardinals and prelates still remaining in Italy, and other members of the clergy, safe conduct to Genoa.[3]

Thus the year 1244 ended with the conflict between Pope and Emperor no less threatening to the peace of Europe than it had been during the last year of Gregory IX. From the Orient also came repeated reports of the advance of the Tatars. The arrival of the Patriarch, Albert of Antioch, at the court of Frederick in the autumn of 1244 served to emphasize the growing danger in the East. Frederick, making use of the Patriarch as his emissary, redoubled his efforts to obtain a peaceful settlement with the Church. In an encyclical letter to all princes of Christendom he called upon them to aid him in his efforts, and with the support of his 'special friend and faithful adherent', the Patriarch, he approached the Pope with a new plan for peace. Frederick had again expressed his desire to fulfil the peace terms which he had agreed to on Maundy Thursday of the previous year and suggested additional concessions, provided that the Pope would act in conformity with the wishes of some of his colleagues.[4] He suggested also that a representative of the Pope, preferably a cardinal, be sent to him to negotiate.

The peace proposals submitted by the Patriarch and subsequently amended by the Grand Master of the Teutonic Order, as representative of the German princes, were so far-reaching as to evoke a feeling of incredulity. They were tantamount to an unqualified capitulation on the part of the Emperor. His action can be explained only as originating in a desperate need for peace. He was conscious at this time, as on several

[1] Matthew Paris, *Chronica majora*, iv. 354.
[2] Huillard-Bréholles, vi, part i, 516.
[3] *MGH, Const.* ii, no. 254, pp. 353–4; *Breve chronicon de rebus Siculis*, 907.
[4] *MGH, Epist. Pont.* ii, no. 110, p. 78. See also Matthew Paris, *Chronica majora*, iv. 332 ff.

occasions afterwards, that his continued resistance to the Holy See might well endanger the succession of his son. It was doubtless this haunting desire to ensure the succession of his son and the continuation of the Hohenstaufen line of emperors that led him in 1246 to offer to depart for the Holy Land, never to return, promising that he would reside there for the remainder of his life fighting for Christ, provided his son should be elevated to the imperial dignity in his stead.[1] Nothing so well illustrates how fully the temporal ambitions of the Curia transcended its spiritual obligations as the Pope's reply to this offer of an abject surrender. He demanded that all Frederick's proposals be carried out in advance of his absolution. In short, the Pope now responded as he had a year before when he had required that Frederick first make amends for the misdeeds for which he had been banned, including the surrender of the *patrimonium* and the freeing of all captive adherents of the papal party. Moreover, he demanded that the release of the prisoners and the restoration of the lands of the Church must be made in accordance with an adjudication by a Council.[2] The negotiations had been further influenced by the appearance before the Curia of Henry of Hohenlohe, Master of the Teutonic Order, with what appear to have been additional concessions providing for the guarantees by the princes of Germany which the Pope had demanded. Unfortunately, there exists no positive source revealing the exact nature of these concessions, although they were probably the same as the six proposals mentioned later in a propagandist letter of Cardinal Rainer of Viterbo.[3]

In return for the lifting of the ban Frederick would agree to give up his Empire and his imperial dignity and would immediately fall under the ban if again he opposed the Church, blasphemed the sacrament, or failed to fulfil what he had promised. He is said to have agreed also to the surrender of the lands of the Church, the release of all prisoners, and full compensation for all damages. Finally, he is said to have promised to undertake a crusade to the Holy Land, pledging himself to remain there for three years, unless permitted by the Pope to return. Kings and princes (obviously the Kings of England and France and the princes of Germany) were to give security for his pledge. So all-inclusive were these alleged concessions that the suspicion arises that they were made for their propagandist value and in the conviction that the Pope, now against any peaceful settlement, would not accept them—that Innocent intended to accept nothing save the complete annihilation of the temporal Empire. That Frederick's abject surrender was offered solely for

---

[1] Matthew Paris, *Chronica majora*, iv. 523: 'Ita scilicet ut, filio suo loco ipsius in imperiali dignitate substituto . . .'

[2] *MGH, Epist. Pont.*, no. 110, p. 79.

[3] Winkelmann, *Acta*, ii, no. 1037, i, p. 716. These terms were probably similar also to those later mentioned by Thaddeus of Suessa at the Council of Lyons. See below, p. 485.

propagandist purposes is further borne out by his devastation in the *patrimonium* at the very moment when the Grand Master of the Teutonic Order was presenting his far-reaching proposals to the Curia. Whatever its object may have been, this ill-timed military action in the vicinity of Viterbo offered the hostile faction an excellent opportunity to vilify the Emperor.[1] Cardinal Rainer of Viterbo eagerly seized this opportunity to accomplish what he had long sought, the complete discrediting of Frederick II in the eyes of his colleagues. He attacked the Emperor in a pamphlet with a viciousness unparalleled in the history of propaganda. This first of a series of inspired attacks appeared in the spring and summer of 1245 and was cleverly aimed at forestalling the projected marriage of the Emperor and Gertrude, the niece of Duke Frederick II of Austria. In March 1245 a marriage agreement between Gertrude and the Emperor had been concluded in Vienna through the mediation of Berthold, Patriarch of Aquileia; in this agreement, in return for the hand of Gertrude, the Emperor promised to elevate Austria to the status of a kingdom.[2] But while these negotiations were in progress the insidious attack upon the Emperor appeared, depicting him as a veritable Bluebeard holding his three former wives in close imprisonment and ultimately poisoning them. The author proceeded to predict a similar fate for the fourth wife, clearly a reference to his affianced Gertrude of Austria.[3] It can hardly be doubted that the sudden refusal of Gertrude to accept the marriage was the result of Frederick's excommunication and, as Karl Hampe has remarked, 'our pamphlet itself is a link in the chain of this influence'.[4] The author also made the most of the unhappy relationship between Frederick II and his son Henry (VII) whose imprisonment and ultimate suicide were presented as evidence of the Emperor's unnatural cruelty. In this and in other pamphlets obviously emanating from the same source, the actual causes of the conflict between the Emperor and the Pope, such as the Lombard question, were virtually ignored. Instead, these defamatory screeds were directed against the person of the Emperor: his 'ingratitude', his 'bloodthirsty tyranny', his 'blasphemy', his 'heresy'.[5]

The object of these pamphlets seems to have been to influence members of the College of Cardinals who were disposed to be conciliatory towards the Emperor and, at the same time, to besmirch his reputation in the eyes of Christendom. The most defamatory of these

---

[1] Winkelmann, *Acta*, i, no. 718, p. 565; and K. Hampe, 'Über die Flugschriften zum Lyoner Konzil von 1245' (*Hist. Vierteljahrschr.* xi, 1908), 308 and note 1.

[2] Huillard-Bréholles, vi, part i, 274; BFW, *Reg.* v, Abt. i, no. 3478. See also nos. 3478b and 3475.

[3] *Albertus von Beham* (ed. Höfler), 73–9; K. Hampe, 'Flugschriften', 311–12. See also Graefe, *Publizistik*, 115 ff.

[4] 'Flugschriften', 312.   [5] Graefe, *Publizistik*, 112–15.

tracts was sent, with an accompanying letter, to Emperor Baldwin of
Constantinople and to the Patriarch of Antioch some time between 12
and 15 June 1245.[1] The letter opened with a description of the sufferings
of the *patrimonium* and of the city of Rome where 'the ruler had delivered
the sons of the Church to the ungodly'. The author then directed his
attack against the cardinals who had befriended the Emperor: these
'leaders of the bride' who 'tread their feet upon the honour and the
freedom of the Church, giving heed to the voice of Herod [Frederick II]
rather than to Jesus Christ'.

The letter was but the preliminary effort of the fanatical author.
Apparently accompanying it was an extraordinary pamphlet, a lengthy
screed, singularly wrought from Apocalyptic quotations and from the
extravagant phraseology of a mind unbalanced by hatred. The pamphlet
opens with references to Isaiah 3:10–11 and 28:17: 'Judgement also
will I lay to the line, and righteousness to the plummet: and the hail
shall sweep away the refuge of lies, and the water shall overflow the
hiding place.' After sermonizing upon the punishment and misdeeds of
the wicked the author proceeded to a devastating attack upon 'the
prince of tyranny' (Frederick II), 'the destroyer of the doctrine of the
Church', 'the denier of the faith', 'the master of cruelty', 'the corrupter
of the world', 'the disturber and the hammer of the whole earth'. He
compared Frederick with a serpent venting its poison here and there.
He then gave wide publicity to the falsehood that Frederick had
threatened Pope Gregory IX and the cardinals with murder if they excommunicated him. He told how Frederick had persistently defied the
ban, denying the prerogative of the heirs of St. Peter to bind and loose.
He declared that Frederick had called himself the 'Vicar of the All
Highest', claiming the right to dethrone popes, and to force prelates and
bishops to bow before his will 'as if he were seated like a God in the
temple of the Lord'. He compared Frederick to the fourth beast in the
Book of Daniel (7:19), 'whose teeth were of iron and his nails of brass;
which devoured, broke in pieces, and stamped the residue with his feet'.
The author dwelt at length upon Frederick's capture of the prelates
en route to the Council, his brutal abuse of them; how Frederick now
sought to dethrone the Pope and to force the Apostolic See to subject
itself to him. And, since he, like the beast in Daniel, has a 'horn of power
and a mouth speaking great things, he thought that he could change
laws and alter the course of events'. Then, obviously referring to
Frederick's alleged ridicule of some of the rites of the Catholic Church,
he accused him of seeking to restore the heresy of the Sadducees: that
there is no resurrection; that there are neither angels nor spirits.[2]

---

[1] Winkelmann, *Acta*, i, no. 723, pp. 568 ff. See also Graefe, *Publizistik*, 119 ff.

It would be erroneous to attach too great importance to the effect of the propagandist pamphlet of Rainer in the ending of negotiations between Pope and Emperor. Long before, Innocent IV had obviously determined the course that he was to pursue. His aim had long been precisely what was actually accomplished after the death of Frederick II: the destruction of the Hohenstaufen and the subjugation of the Empire to papal dominance. The significance of this pamphlet, and of others from the unscrupulous pen of Rainer of Viterbo, lay in the paralysing effect it had upon the friends of the Emperor in the College of Cardinals, its temporary strengthening of the hand of the Pope in what he had already determined to accomplish. Its greatest significance lay in the fact that it sketched a picture of Frederick which for centuries was to serve as a distorting mirror. Only in the nineteenth century was the picture rectified so that the distortion which fanaticism and insane hatred had wrought could be eradicated and the just image restored. In no age in history has propaganda been more insidious or more effective in beclouding the true course of a great controversy. Coming as it did on the eve of the opening of the Council of Lyons, it served to render impossible a calm and deliberate consideration of the questions at issue.

THE COUNCIL OF LYONS
DEPOSITION OF FREDERICK II

. . . flectere si nequeo superos, Acheronta movebo.

Aeneid, VII. 310–12.[1]

AFTER a preliminary meeting on 26 June in the refectory of the monks of St. Just, the Council was formally opened two days later in the cathedral of St. John.[2] The number of prelates in attendance was small, perhaps 145 or 150 at most. Those who had come from Germany departed early. None came from war-ravaged Hungary and but few from Sicily, chiefly the special representatives of the Emperor. In addition to the prelates there were present the Patriarchs of Constantinople and Antioch, the Patriarch of Aquileia and Venice, the Emperor of Constantinople, the Count of Toulouse, various proxies of the King of England, and representatives of the abbeys and cathedral chapters. Although summoned as a 'General Council', the absence of numerous prelates and others who were eligible to attend reduced its constituent membership to representatives primarily from Spain, France, and England. There were few in attendance who could be regarded as supporters of the Emperor's cause. From the outset it was apparent that the Council would act in obedience to the desires of the Pope and Curia.

In the midst of the gathering Innocent IV was seated upon an elevated throne, flanked on his right by the Emperor of Constantinople and on his left by lesser temporal princes, secretaries, and notaries. In the nave of the cathedral were the cardinals, occupying elevated seats, and, below them, the archbishops, bishops, abbots, representatives of the

---

[1] If Heaven I cannot bend, then Hell I will arouse.

[2] The chief sources for the Council of Lyons are: Matthew Paris, *Chronica majora* (Rolls Series), iv. 410–15, 419, 420, 430–79; *Brevis nota eorum quae in primo concilio Lugdunensi generali gesta sunt* (*MGH, Const.* ii), 513–16. Supplementary to the above also is *Documents illustrative of English History in the Thirteenth and Fourteenth Centuries, selected from the Records of the Department of the Queen's Remembrancer of the Exchequer* (ed. Sir Henry Cole), 351. See also C. J. Hefele, *Histoire des conciles* (Nouv. traduction française, Paris, 1907), v, part 2, 1633 ff.; Karajan, 'Zur Geschichte des Concils von Lyon 1245' (*Denkschriften der Kaiserlichen Akademie der Wissenschaften*, ii, 1851), 67–118; and A. Folz, *Kaiser Friedrich II. und Papst Innocenz IV.*, 40–54. For a critical survey of the sources see W. E. Lunt, 'The Sources of the First Council of Lyons, 1245' (*EHR*, xxxiii, 1918), 72 ff.

cathedral chapters, and the proxies of numerous kings and princes. In front of these and nearest to the Pope were the patriarchs. After the Pope had opened the session with the *Veni creator spiritus*, he preached his famous sermon on his 'five sorrows', taking as his text, Lamentations 2:12: 'Behold, and see if there be any sorrow like unto my sorrow.' Of all these 'sorrows' it was the last, the persecutions by the Emperor, Frederick II, that claimed his special attention. He spoke of the many complaints against the Emperor: his heresy, cruelty, sacrilege; his friendliness to the Saracens, his lusts with Saracen women; his violations of his sacred oaths. As so often in the past, the Pope showed special concern for the Emperor's misdeeds in the Kingdom of Sicily and Apulia, described by him as properties of the Holy See, held by Frederick II merely as vassal.

Representing the Emperor was the Justice of the Sicilian Supreme Court, Thaddeus of Suessa, described by a contemporary as 'a man of unusual wisdom and eloquence, a knight, and doctor of law'. Thaddeus set forth the concessions which the Emperor was prepared to make to the Pope in the interest of peace. As if in response to the pleas of the Patriarch of Antioch, he stated that Frederick would restore the whole of Greece to the unity of the Roman Church, pledging himself personally to oppose the Tatars, the Saracens, and other enemies of the Church, and to undertake at his own expense an expedition to the Holy Land. Moreover, Thaddeus announced the willingness of the Emperor to restore the possessions of the Church which he had taken from it, giving full satisfaction for the alleged wrongs which he had inflicted upon it. Then, 'valiantly and unperturbed', Thaddeus continued his brilliant defence. Despite the initial damage wrought by the unscrupulous attacks of Cardinal Rainer, the able defence won many, temporarily, to the support of Frederick II. But the unyielding attitude of Innocent IV was soon to destroy the hopes of those who saw in these generous offers the prospect of a peaceful settlement. Innocent dismissed these offers as merely delaying tactics. He demanded to be informed who would stand security for Frederick to compel him to fulfil these promises. To Thaddeus' reply that they would be secured by the Kings of England and France, Innocent refused to accept them. He did so, as he is reported to have said, because of his conviction that in the future the Emperor would either repudiate or modify his pledge 'as he had frequently done', and the Pope would be compelled to censure the royal guarantors, thus making three enemies where there had been but one.[1]

As to other charges which the Pope had presented to the Council, Thaddeus refuted them with a reasonableness which could only have impressed his auditors favourably. The charge of heresy, which he described as 'a most serious one', he opposed by saying, 'No one can be

[1] Matthew Paris, *Chronica majora*, iv. 432.

fully convinced of this unless the Emperor himself be present', for that which was locked in the bosom of the Emperor could be ascertained only from his own confession. Thaddeus then spoke of Frederick's alleged familiarity with the Sultan and with the Saracens whom he permitted to dwell within his Kingdom, describing it as a deliberate policy of prudence. Moreover, his employment of Saracen troops on his various expeditions was justifiable in that in making use of them he was preventing the unnecessary effusion of Christian blood. The alleged lusts with Saracen women, he refuted, first by asking, 'who can prove it?' and then by admitting that the presence of such women at the court was for the purpose of entertaining the Emperor and his associates. This argument of Thaddeus was all the more convincing since it was well known that Frederick, in seeking entertainment for his court, employed Saracen dancers, acrobats, jugglers, and musicians. This had previously been noted by the Earl of Cornwall during his visit to the Kingdom of Sicily in 1241.[1]

Thaddeus' claim that Frederick must be present to defend himself against the charge of heresy apparently took the Pope unawares, leaving him no recourse but to consent to a delay of the proceedings pending the personal appearance of the Emperor or his plenipotentiary.[2] But upon further reflection, or else upon contrary advice from the Curia, the Pope repudiated his agreement to await the Emperor's arrival. During the sitting of the Council on 17 July 1245, without awaiting the arrival of the Emperor or his representatives, Innocent pronounced the sentence of deposition, declaring Frederick deprived of all his honours and of his imperial office. At the same time the Pope freed all subjects of the Kingdom and Empire of their oaths of allegiance.[3] He accompanied this action by a lengthy review of the peace negotiations, including a re-statement of all Frederick's past misdeeds, real or alleged. Here again he omitted the actual cause of the conflict, the Lombard question. He preferred, instead, to present charges against the Emperor's character which, as the propagandist pamphlets of Cardinal Rainer had revealed, could make more plausible the damnation and deposition. Deceived by the Pope's repudiation of his promise to delay the proceedings, Thaddeus declared the action null and void and appealed for the intervention of a future Pope and General Council to rectify the injustice of Innocent IV. To Thaddeus this session of the Council was 'a day of anger, of misfortune, of calamity'.[4] The Pope himself was obviously not without some misgivings as to the correctness of his procedure. Shortly

[1] See above, p. 336.
[2] *Brevis nota* (*MGH, Const.* ii), 515. Matthew Paris, *Chronica majora*, iv. 436.
[3] See the *Bulla Depositionis* (*MGH, Const.* ii), no. 400, pp. 508–12; *MGH, Epist. Pont.* ii. 88 ff.
[4] *Brevis nota*, 516; Matthew Paris, *Chronica majora*, iv. 456, 473.

afterwards he found it expedient to reassure the Cistercian abbots, who were meeting in a general session, as to the justice of his action. He appealed to them not to permit the criticisms of 'ignorant and truthless men' to induce them to believe that the sentence against the Emperor had been pronounced 'hastily and without a deliberate and thorough consultation with our "brothers" and many other prudent men'. He continued, 'Therefore we are prepared to stand firm, even unto death, in behalf of this cause . . . and for it, both we as well as our brothers are prepared to die unyieldingly, for God and for his Church.'[1]

The news of his deposition reached Frederick at Turin. Matthew Paris reports that, 'hearing of these proceedings, the Emperor Frederick, scarcely able to restrain himself, burst into a violent rage'. According to the chronicler he ordered his portable treasure chests brought before him and, selecting one of his crowns, he placed it upon his own head, 'and when he was thus crowned he arose, and with threatening eyes and awful voice filled with emotion, he exclaimed: "I have not yet lost my crown, nor will I be deprived of it by any action of the Pope or synod without a bloody conflict." ' Frederick himself was not unaware that the most crucial moment of his struggle with the Pope had arrived, that he was now freed from all bonds of affection and veneration and from the obligation of seeking a reconciliation. At this moment his profound conviction of his own God-ordained superiority reasserted itself. He saw himself as the temporal prince of transcendent greatness, 'without an equal'.[2]

But Frederick was aware also that he now stood alone in his great conflict. No longer could he hope for the open support of the few cardinals who in the past had befriended him. They were now intimidated by the harsh accusations of Cardinal Rainer of Viterbo or by the unreasoning hatred of the Pope. Frederick had long hoped that his concept of oligarchical rule by the cardinals, as opposed to the autocratic rule of the Pope, would prevail and that, through the voice of reason of the 'brothers', peace would at last be restored. The action of the Council of Lyons shattered this hope. Despite his isolation, however, Frederick was fully informed, clandestinely, by his adherents in the College of Cardinals, about the papal policies.[3]

Frederick II alone among the princes of Europe during the first half of the thirteenth century recognized what the action of the Council of Lyons portended for the temporal sovereignty. He perceived clearly at that time a tendency which, in modern times, Otto Gierke has so pertinently described:

[that] always more plainly the Principle of Unity begins to appear as the

---

[1] Matthew Paris, *Chronica majora*, iv. 480. [2] Ibid. 474.
[3] Huillard-Bréholles, vi, part i, 392.

philosophical groundwork of that theory which, from the days of Gregory VII onwards, was demanding—now with more and now with less rigour—that all political arrangements should be regarded as part and parcel of the ecclesiastical organization. The 'argumentum unitatis' becomes the key-stone of all those arguments, biblical, historical, legal, which support the papal power over temporal affairs . . . The Pope is the wielder of what is in principle an Empire (*principatus*) over the Community of Mortals. He is their Priest and their King; their spiritual and temporal Monarch; their Law-giver and Judge in all causes supreme.

It was precisely in support of this concept that Innocent IV had written: 'We rule upon the earth with *plenitudo potestatis* of the King of Kings, which was bestowed upon the Apostles and upon us without limitation, and with absolute authority to bind and loose, and thereby nothing is excluded.'[1] On more than one occasion Frederick had sounded a warning concerning this encroachment by the papal hierarchy upon the temporal authority. Thus he wrote to his brother-in-law, the King of England: 'Faced by such a sacerdotal prince, what will then remain in your kingdoms for each of you not to fear if he endeavours to depose us who have been chosen through solemn election by the princes and with the approval of the entire Church, and, as it were from heaven, to wear the imperial crown?' And then, with a sharp note of warning, he continued: 'But we are not the first, nor yet the last (*nec primi sumus nec ultimi*), indeed, whom this sacerdotal abuse of power threatens and seeks to cast down from the summit.'[2]

In the same letter Frederick returned also to a favourite theme: his desire to induce the clergy, especially those of highest rank, to lead an apostolic life, 'imitating our Lord's humility' (*humilitatem dominicam imitantes*). For, he continued, 'these men, devoted to worldly things and intoxicated by its pleasures, put God aside and, because of the abundance of their wealth, religion is suffocated'. But in his criticisms of the papal aspirations to temporal authority Frederick was in open revolt against the predominant concept of the papal office. In the prevailing view of the mid-thirteenth-century canonists, Frederick was in revolt against the will of God. As Innocent IV wrote in reply to Frederick's complaints: 'Christ founded not merely a sacerdotal but a monarchical sovereignty and committed to St. Peter and his successors both the temporal and the spiritual realms.'[3]

---

[1] *Political Theories of the Middle Ages* (tr. F. W. Maitland, Cambridge, 1900), 11–12. See also the letter of Innocent IV to Frederick II (Winkelmann, *Acta*, ii. 1035); also W. Ullmann, *Medieval Papalism*, especially pp. 116–20.

[2] Matthew Paris, *Chronica majora*, iv. 475 ff.

[3] Winkelmann, *Acta*, ii, no. 1035, p. 698; *Albertus von Beham* (ed. Höfler), 86–92, see especially p. 88. See also Ullman, *Medieval Papalism*, 185 ff.

Although Louis IX of France failed at this time to grasp the full significance of Frederick's warning, the restoration of peace was of the utmost importance to him in furthering his crusading plans. Aware of the Emperor's willingness to submit to the spiritual demands of the Pope and of his promise to go on a crusade after the restoration of peaceful relations and, above all, desirous of Frederick's assistance in the supplying of troops, ships, and provisions, Louis endeavoured to persuade the Pope to lift the ban. In a secret conference at Cluny on 30 November 1245, which is said to have continued for seven days, King Louis IX and Blanche the Queen Mother tried vainly to convince the Pope of the sincerity of Frederick's proposals and of the necessity for a peaceful settlement in consideration of the crusade. But on this occasion, as in future conferences with the King of France, Innocent IV obstinately refused to yield.[1] Louis IX must have recognized after this first meeting with the Pope that henceforth the advances of papal authority were to be made within the framework of the most extreme canonical concept which would brook no resistance from subordinate temporal kings. The bestowal of the red hat upon the cardinals during the Pope's residence in Lyons was in itself an announcement to the world of Christendom that the College, no less than the Pope, was pledged to fight even unto death for the aims of the papacy.[2] Early in this year 1246 Frederick submitted to examination by a group of prelates and abbots designed to test his constancy in the Christian faith. Satisfied with the results of their examination, these prelates appeared before the Curia bearing a letter and prepared to report favourably on their findings. Lest the Pope refuse to receive them, they gave assurances to the Curia that they came, not as agents of the Emperor, an excommunicate, but as simple Christians. When, after much delay, the examiners were admitted to the presence of the Pope, he declined to accept the proof of orthodoxy, saying that it was not valid because it had not been established in the right place or with reference to the right questions.[3] He then asserted that if Frederick would clear himself of the charge of heresy in the presence of the Pope and at a convenient place he would hear him, provided he came at a specified time, unarmed, and with but a small retinue. The Pope promised also to give safe conduct to him and his followers. It is doubtful, however, that Frederick, under any conditions prescribed by the Pope, would have accepted terms which, at best, would have led only to another Canossa. It is equally doubtful that Innocent believed for a moment that Frederick would accept them. They serve rather to

[1] Matthew Paris, *Chronica majora*, iv. 484. As to Innocent's obduracy in future conferences see Nicholas of Carbio, *Vita*, 99. For a detailed treatment of the relation between Louis IX and the Pope from 1244 see Meyer, *Ludwig IX. von Frankreich und Innocenz IV.*

[2] Ehrhard, *Das Mittelalter und seine kirchliche Entwicklung*, 121.

[3] *MGH, Epist. Pont.* ii, no. 187, pp. 141–2.

emphasize the determination of the Pope to put an end to attempts at negotiation.

But in the midst of these futile efforts to negotiate, a conspiracy against the life of Frederick was detected which, in its far-flung ramifications, strongly suggests that the Pope himself was implicated.[1] The conspiracy was directed by a group of the highest prelates of the Church and by their henchmen. Through their machinations, faithful servants of the Emperor, many of whom had long been his most reliable supporters, were induced to participate in the conspiracy. At first glance it is somewhat baffling to find an explanation for the defection of these men who were so deeply indebted to the Emperor. Undoubtedly the incessant wars of the past several years, with the accompanying heavy taxes and other obligations imposed upon the nobility, had led to a general deterioration of morale. Also, since Frederick's second excommunication in 1239, the constant tendency towards centralization of authority and the growth of a bureaucratic system had deprived the nobility of many of their traditional privileges. The active agents of the conspiracy were chiefly men from the Capitanata, holders of extensive properties there, and deeply indebted to Frederick for numerous past favours and for many evidences of confidence in their loyalty. Conspicuous among them were Pandulf of Fasanella, for several years the imperial vicar of Tuscany; James of Morra, vicar of the March of Ancona and son of Henry of Morra, the late Justiciar; and Tibaldi Franciscus, imperial *podestà* of Parma. The vitalizing force behind the conspiracy was Bernardo Orlando Rossi, brother-in-law of Pope Innocent IV, and formerly an intimate of Frederick II, of whom Salimbene said: 'He was the greatest friend of the Emperor and esteemed by him.'[2]

Early in the year 1246, while the Emperor was in Grosetto, two of the arch-conspirators were present at his court, charged by their co-conspirators with directing the actual plans for the murder. Other members of the conspiracy, notably Tibaldi Franciscus, Pandulf of Fasanella, and William of San Severino, remained in the Kingdom prepared to assume direction of affairs there as soon as they were informed that the murder had been accomplished. But, meanwhile, the conspiracy was detected, and Frederick learned of it from the Count of Caserta or else from the latter's wife, Violante, a natural daughter of the Emperor. Secretly informed that their intentions had been discovered, Pandulf of Fasanella and James of Morra fled to the protection

---

[1] The most enlightening treatment of this conspiracy and the most plausible evidence of Innocent's knowledge of and sympathy with it are to be found in K. Hampe, *Papst Innozenz IV. und die sizilische Verschwörung von 1246* (*Sb. H. Ak.*, viii *Abhandlung*, 1923).

[2] *MGH, SS.* xxxii, 201. For the chief conspirators and their activities see *Annales Placentini Gibellini* (*MGH, SS.* xviii), 492. See also Huillard-Bréholles, vi, part i, 408 ff.

of the cardinals who were in Rome. They failed, however, to inform their co-conspirators of the discovery. In a letter to the King of England Frederick II, in relating the incidents of the conspiracy, described Pandulf and James as its leaders and told of their sudden flight from the court. When they heard of the failure of the murder plot Tibaldi Franciscus, William of San Severino, and others in the Kingdom, unable to escape to Rome or elsewhere, took possession of two imperial castles, Capaccio and Sala, under pretext of being faithful servants of the Emperor. Prompt action by Frederick forced the surrender of Sala within a few days, while the conspirators in Capaccio succeeded in holding out for some time. Most of the prisoners were summarily blinded, mutilated, or consigned to the flames. Some, after mutilation, were exposed in different parts of the Kingdom as examples of the fate of the treasonable. In his letter to the King of England Frederick attributed the defection of his faithful adherents to 'extravagant promises made by our well-known enemy (*per publicum adversarium nostrum*) . . . The name and office of which adversary we would prefer to pass over in silence, if the gossip of the street did not reveal it and if the evidence of what has been done did not accuse him.' In the same letter Frederick also revealed that the Minorite brothers who had accompanied some of the conspirators, and who had preached a crusade against the Emperor, were responsible for the defection of his erstwhile faithful officials. It was these Minorites, so it was said, who assured the conspirators that they had been authorized by the Pope to oppose Frederick. Some of the interrogated captives openly declared that they had acted on behalf of the Holy Roman Church, their mother, thus insinuating 'that the Supreme Pontiff was the instigator of the aforesaid attempt upon our life'. The statement of the Emperor could be attributed merely to suspicion on the part of one who felt himself to be greatly wronged by the Pope, were it not for other evidence which appears seriously to implicate the Pope. The Bishop of Bamberg, returning to Germany after a visit to the papal court, is said to have predicted the impending disgraceful death of the Emperor at the hands of his *familiares* and servants.[1]

More convincing evidence of the Pope's knowledge of the conspiracy comes from his own correspondence with the cardinals who remained in Rome or elsewhere in Italy (Reginald of Ostia, Stephen of Santa Maria Trastevere, and Richard of St. Angelo); in this he urged them to continue their support and protection of the conspirators who had fled to Rome 'in the praiseworthy manner in which you have previously done'.[2] The active role of the Pope in furthering the conspiracy, if not

---

[1] Matthew Paris, *Chronica majora*, iv. 573: 'predicavit, quod nos infra breve tempus per familiares et domesticos nostros occidi morte turpissima debeamus.'

[2] *MGH, Epist. Pont.* ii, no. 164, p. 124.

the murder itself, is supported by a somewhat cryptic letter written by Cardinal Richard of St. Angelo in which, after a bitter attack upon the Emperor, he made reference to a letter of Innocent IV which gave instructions as to the procedure to be followed in freeing the unfortunate in the Kingdom and concerning the projected invasion of the Romans there. In his letter Cardinal Richard assured the Pope that he would devote himself to these things to the best of his ability and in accordance with the Pope's wishes and instructions. There can be little doubt that the 'unfortunates from the Kingdom' who were to be liberated were the conspirators who had failed to escape, or that the Roman troops destined for the invasion of the Kingdom were to assist in the revolt against the Emperor. It is apparent also from the letter of Cardinal Richard that he and his 'brothers' in Rome were fully aware of and active participants in the plans of the Romans and that it was one of their functions to keep Innocent informed on that phase of the conspiracy. At the conclusion of the letter the Cardinal expressed the belief that the 'Cardinals S. and R.' (certainly Stephen and Rainer) will report [to the Pope] in their letters what appears to be the status of the negotiations with the Romans and 'the amount of the loan'. Here again the somewhat vague and conspiratorial nature of the closing sentence of the letter suggests that whatever business was afoot had to do with the invasion of the Romans in the Kingdom. This extraordinary letter, which refers to the recipient in such terms as *reverentissime domine, beatissime pater,* could have been intended for none other than the Pope; it thus involves him beyond reasonable doubt as an accessary to the conspiracy, if not to the actual murder plot.[1]

Whether or not the Pope was privy to the murder plan or merely to the instigation of the conspiracy (that is, to the revolt in the Kingdom) can perhaps never be established definitively. The circumstantial evidence appears strongly to implicate him in both; all the more so because among the agents fomenting the conspiracy were not only the cardinals in Rome but also the kinsmen of Innocent IV. The close liaison between the Pope and the cardinals in Rome was further emphasized in the Pope's reply to one of the letters from his cardinal agents there, when he wrote: 'In accordance with your laudable advice we will, after consulting with our "brothers", take care etc., etc.' Finally, it would be quite impossible to clear the Pope of guilt or to deny his complicity in the conspiracy when, in a letter to the two arch-conspirators, Pandulf of Fasanella and James of Morra, after their escape to Rome, he extended

---

[1] K. Hampe, *Verschwörung*, 5–6 ff. It is especially noteworthy that this letter, discovered by K. Hampe (see his *Verschwörung*, 1), and his penetrating analysis serve to shatter the previously widely accepted opinion of C. Rodenberg, *Innozenz IV. und das Königreich Sicilien,* 43: '... deswegen kann die Verschwörung weder von ihm angezettelt sein noch mit seinen übrigen Plänen in Verbindung gestanden haben.'

his congratulations 'that you escaped from the hands of Pharaoh and betook your persons safely to the bosom of the Apostolic See'. Greatly pleased with the activities of his agents in Rome, 'men endowed both with wisdom and conspicuous for various virtues', the Pope was soon to reward them by appointment as legates in the Tuscan *patrimonium*, the Duchy of Spoleto, and in the whole Kingdom.[1]

As Innocent IV now rallied all his forces to strike a devastating blow against the Emperor he concerned himself no less with Germany than with the imperial possessions in Italy. The efforts of Albert of Beham (Bohemia), the papal legate, following Frederick's excommunication in 1239, to arouse opposition in Germany had proved futile. The great majority of temporal and ecclesiastical princes had remained faithful to the Emperor.[2] Albert had achieved some small measure of success in 1242 when he won the support of three archbishops in the valley of the Rhine who, in the future, were to constitute the core of the anti-Staufen party in Germany.[3]

It was only after the elevation of Innocent IV to the pontificate that conditions in Germany changed; he called into play every resource of the Church, spiritual and material, to undermine the prestige, to destroy the authority of the Emperor, and to foster disloyalty among the German people. Once more, as in the days of Innocent III, the protests of the German princes were scornfully swept aside when the Pope sent a special legation to Germany, abundantly supplied with gold, to carry on a devastating propagandist drive against Frederick II. The German clergy were enlisted in a campaign of defamation and of opposition to the imperial authority. Twice each month the bishops were to assemble the faithful in a specified place and there preach a crusade against the 'erstwhile Emperor', his son Conrad, and all their adherents. Both Franciscan and Dominican friars were effectively employed as propagandist agents of the papal party, as disseminators of hate and defamation against the Emperor.[4] To counteract this concerted effort by a vast hierarchical organization the Emperor was at a disadvantage. For the moment he was powerless to meet the subversive attacks of an ostensibly spiritual institution transformed into a political machine determined to destroy the temporal Empire.

Innocent IV well understood the importance of Germany in any successful military enterprise of Frederick II. For the first time in the

---

[1] *MGH, Epist. Pont.* ii, nos. 168–73, pp. 126–30.

[2] For the activities of Albert of Beham, Archdeacon of Passau, as legate in Germany, the chief source is *Albertus von Beham* (ed. Höfler), 55 ff. See also M. Stimming, 'Kaiser Friedrich II. und der Abfall der deutschen Fürsten' (*Hist. Zeitschr.*, 120, 1919), 210 ff.

[3] For the progress of the anti-Staufen movement in Germany see M. Stimming, op. cit. 231 ff.; and K. Hampe, *Kaisergeschichte*, 311 ff.

[4] *Cronica S. Petri Erfordensis Moderna* (*MGH, SS.* xxx, part 1), 395.

long conflict between the Emperor and the Pope, Innocent IV now
achieved, temporarily, what was tantamount to a separation of Kingdom and Empire. In the final phase of his struggle for survival Frederick
was limited, in large measure, to Italy. The Pope devoted himself unsparingly to the attainment of this end.[1] Oblivious of all scrupulous
considerations, ever willing to resort to bribery or to the perversion of
the power of dispensation, extravagant in the promise of benefices, often
in excess of the capabilities of the Holy See, Innocent succeeded in gaining the support of the German clergy. By means of threats, interdictions,
suspensions of the right of free elections by the cathedral chapters 'the
backbone of the German Church was completely broken'.[2] Through
the subornation of the German clergy, the Rhenish archbishops, as
agents of the Pope, and the papal legate Philip of Ferarra succeeded in
obtaining the election of the feeble and subservient Henry Raspe as
rival king in Germany. The Pope was lavish in his expenditures of the
treasure of the Holy See in bringing about the election. Innocent's
chaplain and biographer, Nicholas of Carbio, relates that 15,000 silver
marks were said to have been sent to the rival king, Henry Raspe. Other
contemporaries mention varying sums, all indicative, however, of lavish
expenditures.[3]

Through papal bribery, and the treason of some of the Swabian
counts normally faithful to the Hohenstaufen, Henry Raspe succeeded
in obtaining a victory in an encounter with the forces of King Conrad in
the vicinity of Frankfurt on 5 August 1246.[4] Few of the temporal princes
participated in the battle, assuming what appears to have been an
attitude of studied neutrality. It was doubtless this apathy on their part
that led Frederick to seek the support of the Duke of Austria, taking up
once more the plans for a marriage alliance with the Duke's niece. As
has been mentioned above, this plan was shattered as a result of the
deposition and excommunication of Frederick at the Council of Lyons.

---

[1] M. Stimming, 'Abfall', 236–8.

[2] K. Hampe, *Kaisergeschichte*, 312; A. Hauck, *Kirchengeschichte Deutschlands*, iv (Leipzig,
1903), 831 ff. (3rd and 4th edns., Leipzig, 1913), 866. See also P. Aldinger, *Die Neubesetzung
der deutschen Bistümer unter Papst Innocenz IV.* For the loss of freedom of election by the cathedral
chapters see especially A. Diegel, *Der päpstliche Einfluss auf die Bischofswahlen in Deutschland
während des 13. Jahrhunderts.* Pertinent also are the remarks of F. Graefe, *Publizistik*, 236.

[3] *Vita*, 97; Matthew Paris, *Chronica majora*, iv. 544–5:' Promisit igitur eidem pecuniare et
militare subsidium copiosum.' *Cronica S. Petri Erfordensis moderna*, 396: 'XXV milia [marcarum]
argenti'. Concerning the election of Henry Raspe see *Chronica regia Coloniensis*, 289; and R.
Malsch, *Heinrich Raspe, Landgraf von Thüringen und deutscher König*; K. Weller, 'König Konrad
IV. und die Schwaben' (*Württemberg. Vierteljahrshefte*, vi, 1897), 113–27. For a detailed
account of Philip Fontana's activities in Germany see O. W. Canz, *Philip Fontana im Dienste
der Kurie unter Päpsten Gregor IX. und Innocenz IV.* (Leipzig, 1910), 8–34.

[4] For a detailed account see G. Egelhaaf, 'Die Schlacht bei Frankfurt am 5. August 1246'
(*Württembergische Vierteljahrshefte*, Neue Folge, xxxi, 1925), 45–53. See also K. Weller ibid.
vi. 113 ff.

Moreover, it was made objectionable, if not impossible, by the calumnious pamphlet of Cardinal Rainer of Viterbo.[1] Despite the shattering of the marriage plans, the death of Duke Frederick of Austria without direct heir in 1246 opened the way for the Emperor's seizure of the Duchy as an imperial fief. He immediately strengthened this hold by assigning to it a captain-general or vicar as governor. With the acquisition of Austria Frederick's hold upon southern Germany was once more secure, save in the territories held by a few disgruntled Swabian barons who had been induced to support the Landgrave of Thuringia as the papally approved king. How little the Swabians generally sympathized with the desertion of the treasonable barons was, in some measure, revealed by a violent though futile demonstration against the Pope, the prelates, the secular clergy, and especially against the Minorities, whom they regarded as the chief agents of the Pope's nefarious plans. It was perhaps inevitable that this Swabian heresy, like other heretical movements appearing in many parts of Europe at this time, denied the right of the Pope to forbid divine services and declared heretical those clergymen who obeyed the papal interdict. They condemned the Franciscans, the Dominicans, and Cistercians as false teachers, insisting that indulgences could come only from God, not from the Pope, because of his perverted life. While not necessarily inspired by the conflict between the Pope and Emperor, these heretics, nevertheless, identified themselves with it, calling for prayers 'on behalf of the Lord Emperor and his son Conrad, who are upright and just'. They preached also that the Pope, because he did not live an apostolic life, was incapable of binding and loosing.[2] Limited as it was, this heretical movement in Swabia was significant as a sporadic manifestation of the religious unrest and the active sympathy for the Hohenstaufen cause in Germany.

The sudden death of Henry Raspe in 1247 brought to an end the nominal rule of this feeble hireling of the Pope, whose lands now returned to the sphere of influence of the Hohenstaufen. The right of inheritance to this region now fell to the son of Margrave Henry of Meissen, Albert, who was affianced to the Emperor's daughter Margarete.[3] Six months were to pass before the ecclesiastical princes of the Rhine valley succeeded in electing young William of Holland as king. Although distinguished by courage and by a chivalrous bearing, William, like his weak predecessor, was recognized only for what he was,

---

[1] See above, pp. 481 f.; and K. Hampe, 'Flugschriften zum Lyoner Konzil von 1245' (*Hist. Vierteljahrschr.* xi, 1908), especially pp. 311 ff.; and G. Juritsch, *Geschichte der Babenberger und ihrer Länder*, especially p. 644.

[2] This movement is described in considerable detail by *Annales Stadenses* (*MGH, SS.* xvi), 371.

[3] K. Hampe, *Kaisergeschichte*, 314 and note 2.

a puppet-king of the Pope.[1] Each of these ghost-kings fell short of the expectations of the Pope and the spiritual princes who had induced them to accept the ill-starred role. As long as Frederick II lived the Curia failed, notwithstanding its strenuous efforts, to overthrow the Staufen authority in Germany.[2]

The effort of the papal party to separate Germany from imperial control was, at most, of secondary importance in the world-shaking conflict between the *imperium* and the *sacerdotium*. Only in Italy could the outcome of the rivalry be decided. There, amidst the perennially fighting Guelfs and Ghibellines, where violent emotions not infrequently exploded into scurrilous charges and counter-charges, into murderous attempts and gruesome acts of vengeance, the papal agents found little resistance in stirring revolts among the people. It is difficult to measure, yet impossible to ignore, the far-reaching effects of the papal machinations of this era upon the future of the Christian faith in Italy or, indeed, in the whole of the Western world. But it is not difficult to perceive how the policies of Innocent IV, the intrigues of his cardinal legates, and, above all, the perversive activities of the Minorites influenced in Italy the rebirth of a pagan spirit. Just as in England and Germany the seeds of the Reformation were widely scattered and deeply rooted by the abuses of the legatine agents of the Roman Church during the thirteenth century, so in Italy, never wholly deprived of its urbanity, these same abuses called into being a pagan outlook reminiscent of ancient Rome. During the last years of Frederick II, between his deposition and his death, there was never a moment when he was not conscious of the threat of revolt, of sabotage, of conspiracy, or of threats of murder to himself. It could not have improved the moral atmosphere of Italy and Sicily during these years that the source of much of this pollution was to be found in the cardinal legates or in other papal agents, widely scattered and ceaselessly active as defamers and saboteurs. It could not have been surprising when, in such surroundings, Frederick exclaimed: 'I have been the anvil long enough . . . henceforth, I shall be the hammer.'[3] Frederick had witnessed too long the abuse of the apostolic power: the extravagant and sometimes trivial proclamations of the bans of excommunication and interdict. On more than one occasion he had heard malediction proclaimed against himself. It is unthinkable that he could have regarded it any longer as other than a vindictive weapon wielded irresponsibly and in the spirit of hatred. If the world of Christendom still continued to think of this much-abused weapon as ordained of God, even when wielded by an ambitious Pope clad in the

---

[1] See O. Hintze, *Das Königtum Wilhelms von Holland*; also J. Kempf, *Geschichte d. Deutsch. Reich.*, 40–90: 'Die Gegenkönige Konrad und Wilhelm'.

[2] K. Hampe, *Kaisergeschichte*, 314–15.   [3] Huillard-Bréholles, vi, part ii, 710.

dissembling vestments of a spiritual pastor, and if, in obedience to this belief, it joined in branding Frederick II as the Antichrist, what recourse was left him save the wielding of shattering blows as the 'hammer of the earth'—the crushing of 'all rebels between the anvil and the hammer'?[1]

It is not surprising that Frederick II treated with contempt the sentences of excommunication and deposition pronounced by Gregory IX and Innocent IV, supported, as they were, in their temporal ambitions by arch-intriguers such as Rainer of Viterbo, Gregory of Montelongo, James of Palestrina, and Albert of Beham. The power of binding and loosing had been too often employed for selfish and political ends, as an instrument of papal advantage, to be longer accepted, when so used, as a divinely ordained power. Henceforth Frederick must fight his way through barriers erected by these men. Each year, therefore, following his deposition, the conflict between Pope and Emperor continued increasingly as one based upon distrust and hatred. Long before the Council of Lyons the Pope's hatred, and that of some of the cardinals, for Frederick, or, indeed, for any concept of temporal Empire, had been unrestrained. Hate begets hate, and so it was with Frederick II, and with Innocent IV. Frederick was now determined to wield the sword of vengeance in the spirit which had once led him to say of the citizens of disloyal Viterbo, 'The hate that now consumes us will be satisfied only with their complete annihilation.'[1]

[1] BFW, *Reg.* v, Abt. i, no. 3470.

III

FREDERICK'S FINAL EFFORT AGAINST
THE LOMBARDS
HIS DEFEAT AT PARMA

Ab hoste Victoria dicta et constructa,
per Dei victoriam funditus destructa,
docet, ut sit anima quelibet instructa,
quod nulla resistere potest Deo lucta.

Carmina Triumphalia de Victoria Urbe Eversa, ii
(*MGH, SS.* xviii), 794.[1]

IT was in this atmosphere of reciprocal hatred that Frederick II now launched a new policy which evoked from hostile critics his condemnation as 'scourge of the world'. His unrestrained vengeance made him, no less than the Pope, responsible for the evils which were long to plague Italy and Germany. Like Innocent IV, Frederick contributed to the growing cynicism, the deep-seated hatred which possessed the warring factions in Italian cities, to the suspicion and distrust of men and motives which now plagued both Italy and Germany and, indeed, the whole of Christendom.[2] But Frederick was not alone in the role of 'scourge of the world'. Associated with him was his son-in-law, Ezzelino of Romano, destined to leave his stamp deeply impressed upon Italy, a forerunner and prototype of a host of despots of the era of the Italian Renaissance.[3]

This intractable man, so intimately associated with Frederick during the last decade of the latter's life, was born in Treviso in 1194, actually a descendant of a distinguished German line. Energetic, bold, cruel, self-confident, and inordinately proud, he surpassed, if possible, the Emperor himself in his lust for power, involving him in almost ceaseless

---

[1]
     Victoria, named and built by the enemy,
     Completely destroyed by the victory of God,
     Teaches, as let the mind of anyone comprehend,
     That no struggle can withstand God.

[2] See especially the numerous complaints from both England and France against the Pope, the higher clergy, and the Minorites, in Matthew Paris, *Chronica majora* (Rolls Series), iv. 557 ff.

[3] For a study of the career and personality of Ezzelino see *Studi Ezzelianiani* (Rome, 1963). The individual contributions are cited under the names of their respective authors. See also F. Stieve, *Ezzelino*.

conflicts with numerous rivals in various Lombard communes. His extravagant cruelties, his mastery of the most exquisite forms of torture, his capacity for duplicity and greed, his monstrous ways of life, especially during his later years, inevitably gave rise to legends which have served through the centuries to make his name synonymous with tyranny. His own cruelties, no less than his intimacy with Frederick II, made his name anathema to the clergy. It is upon their pens, particularly that of an annalist of the monastery of St. Justina in Padua, that we are compelled to rely for a contemporary account of his life.[1]

If we accepted at face value this exaggerated picture we could only describe Ezzelino as a monster, a man 'hostile to the human race', finding his chief diversion in the mutilation of men, women, and children, for the sheer joy of the pastime. We are told of his especial penchant for castrations, for inflicting suffering upon noble matrons and young girls, many of whom perished in his foul prisons, victims of horrible diseases. Contemporaries wrote of the screams of the tortured rending the air around his castles by day and by night. Well-to-do merchants, wise judges, venerable prelates, distinguished clergymen, comely youths, delicate maidens, were said to have been tortured or destroyed by him so that their properties might be appropriated or disposed of in a manner useful to Ezzelino's own ends. For, says the chronicler of St. Justina, 'his thoughts were constantly occupied with the destruction of mankind, and each day he deliberated how he could annihilate his victims'. It may not be overlooked, however, that Ezzelino, like Frederick II, was a special target for the papal propagandists. His cruelty was unquestionable, but even the smallest of his misdeeds led to exaggeration. The worst of these were often committed in retaliation for the intolerable machinations of the papal legates. Ezzelino must be judged as the 'authentic child of his era', activated, as were the popes and cardinals, by codes of conduct which were but little influenced by standards of morals and ethics approved by civilized men of the present day. The role in which he cast himself was that of successful tyrant. If acts of cruelty could contribute to the perfection of that role he hesitated not at all to employ them. It has perhaps been justly said of him that he was one 'who had within himself the elements of a great ruler, and only through an unhappy working together of his intractable nature and the savage era in which he lived did he become the scourge of God of his century'.[2] But, unfortunately, the Ezzelino of history and of fiction will doubtless always be influenced by the picture drawn of him by the

---

[1] *MGH, SS.* xix, especially p. 162. F. Stieve, 'Der Charakter des Ezzelino von Romano in Anekdote und Dichtung' (*Hist. Vierteljahrschr.* xiii, 1910), 171 ff.

[2] A. Bassermann, *Dantes Spuren in Italien*, 392. See also Raumer, *Geschichte der Hohenstaufen*, iii. 341 ff., iv. 252.

clergy of his era whose hopes and ambitions were thwarted by his ruthless opposition. It is this characterization that Dante perpetuated when, in his description of the first round of the seventh circle of Hell, he wrote:

> We moved onwards with our trusty guide,
> along the border of the purple
> boiling, wherein the boiled were making
> loud shrieks.
> I saw people down in it even to the
> eyebrows; and the great Centaur said: 'These
> are tyrants, who took to blood and plunder.
> Here they lament their merciless offences;
> here is Alexander; the fierce Dionysius, who
> made Sicily have years of woe;
> and that brow which has hair so
> black is Azzolino . . .'[1]

Another of the *aides* of Frederick II who, like his sovereign and Ezzelino of Romano, deserved to be called the 'scourge of Italy' was the Marquis Hubert Pallavicini, vicar-general of Lombardy.[2] His family was among the oldest and most prominent of Italy; 'neither fable nor legend was necessary to contribute to its fame in the early centuries.' While sharing Ezzelino's contempt for both Pope and cardinals, and equally indifferent to the Christian religion, Pallavicini impressed his contemporaries especially by his unusual physical appearance. Deprived of one eye, which, according to legend, had been plucked out by a cock while he was still an infant,[3] Pallavicini was also remarkable for his abundance of blackest hair. Of medium height, he is said to have possessed extraordinary physical strength. His relentless fight against the temporal ambitions of the papacy continued long after the death of Frederick II when, in the manner of Ezzelino, he succeeded in extending his authority over several regions of Italy; at times he dominated not only Cremona, but also Piacenza, Pavia, Vercelli, Milan, Alessandria, Crema, and Tortona.[4] With the military assistance of Ezzelino, Enzio, and Hubert Pallavicini, Frederick made substantial gains in retaliation for the conspiracy against his life, greatly strengthening his position in some regions. The conspiracy had offered an opportunity and provided an excuse for the tightening of the royal administrative and judicial systems throughout Italy.

---

[1] *Inferno*, Canto XII, lines 109–10: 'E quella fronte c' ha'l pel cosi nero è Azzolino.'

[2] See Z. Schiffer, *Markgraf Hubert Pallavicini. Ein Signore Oberitaliens im 13. Jahrhundert*, 9 ff., 20 ff.; Muratori, *Delle antichità estensi ed italiane*, i. 260.

[3] Salimbene, *Cronica (MGH, SS.* xxxii), 344.

[4] K. Hampe, *Geschichte Konradins von Hohenstaufen*, 85–91. See also Z. Schiffer, op. cit. 44 ff.

Meanwhile, Innocent IV, probably misled by the optimistic reports of his cardinal representatives in Rome, became over-confident of his ability to regain possession not only of the *patrimonium*, which Frederick's representatives had occupied, but of Sicily as well. In April 1246 Innocent's recently appointed cardinal legates, Stephen of Santa Maria Trastevere and Rainer of Santa Maria in Cosmedin, had begun their activities in the March of Ancona and the Duchy of Spoleto. Where the Kingdom of Sicily was concerned, he limited their authority, reserving for himself the granting of temporalities, villages, cities, booty, lands, church properties, as well as all spiritualities such as prebends, ecclesiastical benefices, and the filling of all church vacancies.[1] In his efforts to conquer the Duchy of Spoleto, undertaken at the instance of the traitor, James of Morra, Rainer had been disastrously defeated by the imperial vicar-general, Marinus of Eboli.[2] Many of the Cardinal's troops were killed or taken captive and imprisoned in Apulia. In the months following the shattering of the conspiracy Frederick's son Enzio and the Margrave Lancia returned to Parma and there inflicted heavy punishment upon those who had participated in the conspiracy. The fortified towers occupied by Guelfs were destroyed and many knights, followers of the Pope's brother-in-law, Bernard Orlando Rossi, were taken as hostages to Cremona and Reggio. Others succeeded in escaping to Piacenza and Milan where they were soon in alliance with the papal legate, Gregory of Montelongo, and were later successfully employed by him in an attack on the city of Parma.[3]

By the close of the year 1246 the papal interests in Italy had been seriously threatened. In contrast, the prospects of the Emperor were greatly improved. Frederick had personally crushed the rebellion in Sicily, and by midsummer 1246 he could inform Ezzelino that the Saracens in Sicily, who had taken advantage of the unrest during the conspiracy to revolt, had been compelled to submit. In November he re-established a Grand Master Justiciar in the Kingdom of Sicily, an office which had remained vacant since 1242. In consequence of this change, the office of Captain-General of Sicily, formerly held by Andrew of Cicala, one of the conspirators of 1246, was abolished. Before the end of the year Frederick felt free to devote his attention once more to the rebels of Italy.[4] In the second week of February 1247 he set out from the Kingdom of Sicily via the Duchy of Spoleto, where he seems to have held court at Terni before proceeding northward. It was probably there

[1] *MGH, Epist. Pont.* ii, no. 171, pp. 129 ff. See also Rodenberg, *Innozenz IV.*, 45 f.

[2] Huillard-Bréholles, vi, part i, 406. See also ibid. 517; and Matthew Paris, *Chronica majora*, iv. 574.

[3] *Chronicon Parmense* (Muratori, *RIS*, new series ix, part 9), 13; *Annales Placentini Gibellini* (*MGH, SS.* xviii), 493; *Annales Janvenses* (*Fonti*), iii. 171.

[4] Huillard-Bréholles, vi, part i, 471–92.

that he conferred upon his young son Henry, the nephew of Henry III of England, the title of King, and also provided a group of counsellors as governors of Sicily during his own absence.[1] Aware of the importance of the Emperor's successes in Spoleto and in the north, Innocent IV, in a letter of October 1246, ordered Cardinal Stephen, one of his legates in Italy, to preach a crusade against the Emperor in Rome, the Campagna, and in the Maritima.[2] But even as this crusade was being preached against Frederick and his associates, King Louis IX of France continued his efforts to find a basis for a peaceful settlement of the papal—imperial conflict. A letter of Frederick II to Louis IX written towards the close of the year 1246 thanked the French King for his efforts in behalf of peace, giving assurance of his willingness to submit to the Pope in all spiritual things.[3]

In the spring of 1247 King Louis IX suggested to the Emperor that he name an embassy, provided with plenipotential authority to conclude peace. Frederick had answered that he would comply with the French King's suggestions immediately were it not that he wished first to hasten to Germany where on the feast of St. John (24 June) he would confer with the German princes. Thereafter, in accordance with the advice of the princes, he would send the plenipotentiaries.[4] There appears also to have been at this time a revival of an active conciliatory movement among some of the cardinals and other members of the clergy. It was in the knowledge of this movement that Frederick wrote to the King of England in March 1247 that he had delayed the baptism of his son because his friends in the Curia had so advised him, to the end that, after the restoration of peace, the Pope himself might baptize the young King.[5] This optimism of the friendly cardinals could only have originated in wishful thinking, for, only a short time before Frederick's letter to the English King, the Pope had written to the Bishop of Strassburg that he would not make peace with Frederick as long as he remained Emperor or King.[6]

The Pope could not have been unaware, even before the end of year 1246, of Frederick's intention to lead an expedition to Lombardy to compel the hostile communes to submit, and thence into Germany to restore the imperial authority. In a letter to the King of England, Master Walter Ocra, a notary and chaplain of the Emperor, reported that Frederick had sworn he would proceed to Germany about Easter-

---

[1] See first BFW, *Reg.* v, Abt. i, no. 3609a, and then Huillard-Bréholles, vi, part i, 502 f., Matthew Paris, *Chronica majora*, iv. 613. See also the letter of young Henry to his uncle, Henry III (Huillard-Bréholles, vi, part i, 504).

[2] *MGH, Epist. Pont.* ii. 184f.

[3] Huillard-Bréholles, vi, part i, 472–3.

[4] Ibid. 514 ff.

[5] Ibid. 503.

[6] *MGH, Epist. Pont.* ii, no. 277, p. 208.

time (1247) with a large body of troops.[1] While in Cremona, where he had summoned a diet, he altered his plans, probably on receipt of news of the death of Henry Raspe. He now planned to go first to Lyons in order to meet the Pope personally; afterwards, he would continue leisurely into Germany. This change of plans may have resulted in part from Frederick's knowledge of the activities of the King of France and some French bishops who were ardently desirous of a personal meeting between the Emperor and the Pope.[2] But, obviously, Frederick had no intention of appearing before the Pope unarmed and with but a small following, as Innocent had earlier required. Supported as he was by both the King of France and the Emperor of Constantinople, Frederick would have had a decided advantage in negotiating in person. Innocent's position was made all the more difficult by a peace proposal which, if we may accept a questionable contemporary report, Frederick was prepared to offer. It was said that he was now willing to depart for the Holy Land and that he would there pass the remainder of his life 'fighting for Christ and would make every effort to restore the entire Kingdom to the Christian faith'. In return for this he required that his son Conrad be confirmed in the imperial office in his stead. Absolution, with full pardon, must be granted the Emperor for all his alleged transgressions and his good name must be restored. The refusal of the Pope to entertain this or any other formula for a peace settlement is said to have angered Louis IX, who had found so little humility in the servant of the servants of God.[3]

Recognizing the awkwardness of his position in the face of a proposal which could not fail to improve Frederick's position in the eyes of the Christian world, Innocent now affected to fear that the approach of Frederick with a large army, albeit the obvious destination of the army was Germany, would not be without danger to himself. This anxiety of the Pope was made known to Louis IX by the legates Cardinals Otto of Tusculum and Peter Albano. Probably as a gesture of reassurance, and in order to remove the Pope's objection, Louis IX, although disposed to maintain a neutral position, pledged his protection, volunteering to lead the forces of opposition personally if Frederick molested the Pope and Curia in Lyons. There can be little doubt that the promise made by Louis IX was nothing more than an assurance of protection of the Pope in the event of an actual invasion of Lyons. The exuberant expression of gratitude, however, with which the Pope received the assurance of aid suggests that he found it expedient to construe the reply

[1] Matthew Paris, *Chronica majora*, iv. 576. See also Huillard-Bréholles, vi, part i, 457, and *Bartholomaei Scribae Annales* (*MGH, SS.* xviii), 221.

[2] Matthew Paris, *Chronica majora*, vi. 131. See also Huillard-Bréholles, vi, part i, 528–9, part ii, 556.

[3] Matthew Paris, *Chronica majora*, iv. 523 f.

as an indication that the King of France was prepared to support the papal interests against the encroachments of Frederick II in both Italy and Germany.[1] It is to be assumed, however, from some of the restrictions imposed upon Louis IX (especially the stipulation that he was to advance into Italy only with the consent of the Pope) that the Pope's enthusiastic letters were intended to deter the Emperor from any hostile action that would endanger the papal interests.[2]

The Pope now displayed a new energy in his efforts to crush the Hohenstaufen authority in Germany. Already in mid March 1247 he had sent Cardinal Peter Capoccio as an 'angel of peace' to Germany to bring about the election of an acceptable rival king in place of the deceased Henry Raspe. Authorized to 'tear down and to destroy, to build and to establish', it was soon apparent that his chief mission was to prepare the way for the preaching of a crusade against Frederick II, his son Conrad, and all their adherents.[3] About the same time Innocent took other steps to prevent Frederick's visit to Lyons and Germany. To this end he sent Cardinal Ottaviano Ubaldini to Italy, accompanied by an armed following of some 1,500 men, to support the legate, Gregory of Montelongo, in his fight for the papal interests in Lombardy and the Romagna.[4] Even as the troops of Ottaviano were being assembled in Burgundy during May, Innocent reiterated what previously he had written to the Bishop of Strassburg, but this time he included the Emperor's son Conrad: that he would not make peace with the one-time Emperor as long as he and his son continued as Emperor and King.[5]

In Italy Innocent made full use of his relatives in preparing his offensive measures. Once more Bernard Orlando Rossi, the brother-in-law of Innocent IV, prepared the way for a revolt against the Emperor, this time in Parma. There also a nephew of the Pope, Albert San Vitale, Bishop of Parma, was granted authority to occupy all Church property in the city and diocese as long as the threat from the Emperor existed.[6] A contemporary chronicler states that Innocent had encouraged the Parmesans to revolt, promising them a large sum of money and effective aid. As a consequence of the 'wise management of the Pope', the whole of the province of Parma, formerly faithful to Frederick, now suddenly entered into an alliance with the Milanese who opposed the Emperor.[7] Cardinal Ottaviano, who had been chosen by Innocent IV to lead the

---

[1] *MGH, Epist. Pont.* ii, nos. 394–6, pp. 288 ff.

[2] *MGH, Epist. Pont.* ii. 288. See also W. Kienast, *Die deutschen Fürsten im Dienste der West-mächte*, ii. 115 f.

[3] *MGH, Epist. Pont.* ii, no. 304, pp. 231, 235.   [4] Ibid. 238.

[5] Ibid. ii. 251 (4 May). See a similar letter of 12 May, ibid. 359, 266.

[6] For the Pope's nepotism, especially as illustrated in Parma, see *Annales Placentini Gibellini* (*MGH, SS.* xviii), 493; Matthew Paris, *Chronica majora*, iv. 598; and Salimbene, *Cronica*, 61; and ibid. 199, 362.

[7] Matthew Paris, *Chronica majora*, iv. 637.

expedition in support of Gregory of Montelongo, was another striking example of the worldly cardinals so frequently employed as agents of the Popes of the thirteenth century.[1] Ottaviano came from the noble family of Ubaldini whose lands included the strategically important pass between Tuscany and the Romagna. The chronicler Salimbene, whose love for scandal may well have misled him, states that 'it was said that he [Ottaviano] was the son of the Lord Pope Gregory IX'.[2] Although later associated with the Ghibellines, the Ubaldini were adherents of the Pope, and at the same time, foes of long standing of the neighbouring city of Florence. As a youth Ottaviano had been made subdeacon by Pope Gregory IX. Dante, who placed him in Hell along with Frederick II, mentions him merely as 'the Cardinal': 'Here is the second Frederick, and here the Cardinal; concerning the others I am silent.'[3] The unfavourable opinion of Ottaviano expressed by some of his contemporaries probably resulted from the premature choice of him by Pope Gregory IX as Bishop of Bologna at the age of twenty-two, some four years before he attained the age of eligibility. Innocent IV elevated him to the dignity of Cardinal of Santa Maria in Via Lata. By virtue of an exceptionally long tenure as cardinal he exercised a far-reaching influence upon the Church. Politically, his career was one of vacillation between Ghibellines and Guelfs; he shifted his party allegiance for reasons of expediency. He is said to have remarked: 'If there is a soul I have lost mine through the Ghibellines.'[4] His political affiliations, like his personal friendships, originated not in his convictions or in his affections, but rather in opportunist considerations. He lived for and by political intrigue and was but little troubled if his methods were unscrupulous. He was both egoist and hedonist, glorying in his purple raiment. The pleasures of life enticed him inordinately and he denied himself nothing either in the delicacies of his table or in the allurements of love. He was notorious for his want of orthodox religious convictions, choosing his associates from among the leading heretics of his day. His legatine assignments offered him an endless opportunity for the amassing of the wealth so essential to his luxurious habits of life. His palace, Montaccianico, in Mugello was one of the most splendid, affording him a congenial environment in which to satisfy his aesthetic tastes and to indulge his baser instincts. He was an ardent connoisseur of artistic treasures, especially of exotic utensils and ornaments of silver and gold,

[1] See A. Hauss, *Kardinal Oktavian Ubaldini*; R. Davidsohn, *Florenz*, ii, part 1, 327; G. Levi, 'Cardinal Ottaviano degli Ubaldini' (*Archivio Soc. Rom.*, xiv, 1891), 231 ff.

[2] *MGH, SS.* xxxii. 385. See also G. Levi, 'Cardinal Ottaviano', 232.

[3] *Inferno*, Canto X, lines 119–20: 'qua entro è lo secondo Federico, e il Cardinale, e degli altri mi taccio.'

[4] Boccaccio, *Commento alla Divina Commedia*, iii. 65: 'Se anima è, perduta l'ho per li ghibellini.'

collected widely from Greece, Africa, Spain, and elsewhere. His silver table service was made to his order in Paris and was especially notable for a chalice of rare beauty and exquisite workmanship. Among his treasures was a crown intricately designed and adorned with rubies and sapphires. His wash-basin was said to have been studded with pearls and precious stones.[1]

On 18 May 1247 Cardinal Ottaviano left the papal court in Lyons with his following of 1,500 men on his way to cross the Alps by the St. Bernard Pass.[2] But Frederick was not unprepared for this move by the Pope and his cardinal legate. Long conscious of his need for the control of the Alpine passes, he had regained the stronghold of Rivoli and, through the marriage of his natural son Manfred, with Beatrice, the daughter of Amadeus of Savoy, in early May 1247, he won the Savoyards to his side.[3] Frederick's position in this region was further strengthened when he regained the dubious support of the unreliable Marquis of Montferrat, who had broken his faith with the Emperor in 1242, restoring to him all his fiefs and privileges. In early February 1247, at the instance of, and under the guarantee of Count Amadeus of Savoy and Enzio, King of Sardinia and imperial Vicar for Italy, the Marquis of Montferrat agreed not only to submit to the Emperor but also to aid him as long as the war with the Lombard rebels continued.[4] It was of this unreliable marquis that the troubadour, Lanfranc Cigala, warned Frederick when he wrote:

> If I were his lord he could not swear
>   allegiance to me in the customary way.
> For I know he would not remain true to me;
> Nor could he ever again kiss me on the
>   cheek with his mouth,
> For once he kissed me with it in Pavia,
> Then, in the same manner he kissed the Pope.
> But since he betrays his every loyalty
>   with lies
> I would not believe him if he made either
>   a promise or covenant,
> So he could kiss me only on the behind.[5]

---

[1] As source for the above account see Matthew Paris, *Chronica majora*, v. 723; Boccaccio, *Commento*, ii. 242; G. Levi, *Archiv. Soc. Rom.*, xiv, 1891, 231, 297–303, containing an inventory of the precious articles of Ottaviano, made in 1262. See also R. Davidsohn, *Florenz*, ii, part 1, pp. 327–9, and especially note 1, p. 329.

[2] *MGH, Epist. Pont.* ii, no. 334, p. 251. Nicholas of Carbio, *Vita*, 98.

[3] BFW, *Reg. v*, Abt. i, nos. 3626, 3748a. See also *Annales Janvenses (Fonti)*, iii. 172; S. Hellmann, *Die Grafen von Savoyen und das Reich bis zum Ende der staufischen Periode* (Innsbruck, 1908), pp. 169 ff.; and F. Hayward, *Histoire de la Maison de Savoie (1000–1553)* (Paris, 1941), 67.   [4] Huillard-Bréholles, vi, part ii, 673, 916.

[5] As O. Schultz-Gora, 'Die Lebensverhältnisse der ital. Trobadors' (*Zeitschr. f. roman.*

Frederick's diplomacy in Savoy, as in the March of Montferrat, had opened to him the routes across the Alps while endangering the lines of communication between the Pope and Curia, now in Lyons, and their representatives in Italy. Papal messengers were captured and robbed, and Cardinal Ottaviano found his route to Lombardy blocked by the Savoyards.[1] Ottaviano, a pretentious but incompetent soldier, was unwilling to risk the hazards of battle. He remained idle in the foot-hills of the Alps until his troops, wearied by idleness and discontented with the withholding of their pay, returned to their homes. With the utmost difficulty, and only through stealth, did Ottaviano secretly—defenceless and but little in the manner of a commander—make his way into Lombardy.[2] His failure to bring with him the expected reinforcements occasioned great disappointment. Yet, despite this failure, he was far from powerless. He had been given extraordinary authority by the Pope, strikingly similar to that given by Innocent IV to Cardinal Peter Capoccio in Germany.[3]

The defection of the Savoyard region to the side of the Emperor and the failure of Ottaviano's mission had presented the Pope with a most unpromising outlook. Meanwhile, Frederick, believing the whole of Central Italy to be safely in his hands, again announced his intention of going first to Lyons and then into Germany.[4] He stood poised in the foot-hills of the Alps ready to set out on his long-planned expedition. But his plans were rudely shattered when intelligence reached him that the city of Parma had been captured by enemy forces under the leadership of the Pope's brother-in-law, Bernard Orlando Rossi, and the archintriguer Gregory of Montelongo.[5] Stunned and angered, Frederick was compelled to abandon his projected expedition and hasten to the aid of his son Enzio before the walls of Parma. He had expected the recapture of the city to be quickly accomplished and that, after an annoying but

---

Philol. vii, 1883), 217 f., has pointed out, the probable date of the poem is 1245. The text of the poem is from F. Wittenberg, *Die Hohenstaufen im Munde der Troubadours*, 109:

> S'eu fos seingner, ja no'm feir' homenatge
> adrechamen, car sai que'l no'm tenria,
> ni'm baisera mais de boch' el visatge,
> car autra vetz la'm baiset a Pavia,
> pois en baiset lo papa eissamen;
> donc pois aisi tota sa fe desmen,
> s'ab me ja mai fezes plai ni coven,
> si no'm baises en cul, ren no'l creiria.

[1] Huillard-Bréholles, vi, part ii, 555 f.
[2] Ibid. 570 (Frederick's letter to the captains of Sicily).
[3] *MGH, Epist. Pont.* ii, nos. 292–6, 313, 315, 317–19, 323, 325, 336, 341.
[4] Huillard-Bréholles, vi, part i, 526 ff.
[5] Nicholas of Carbio, *Vita*, chs. 25–8; O. Holder-Egger (*Neues Archiv*, xxxvii, 1912), 189 f.; and *Chronicon Parmense* (Muratori, *RIS*, new edn., ix, part 9), 13.

necessary delay, he could proceed as planned across the Alps.[1] But he had counted too much upon what he believed to be a weak and poorly armed garrison and had underestimated the cunning of Gregory of Montelongo. Unlike most of the cardinals designated for military missions, who revealed at best but little military skill, Gregory of Montelongo was well trained in the art of war (*doctus ad bellum*). He was equally skilled in the art of dissimulation.[2] By intrigue he had brought about the defection of Parma and through his military prowess he was now to defy successfully all attempts of the Emperor to regain the city.

The loss of Parma, however, was not the result merely of Gregory's skill, but equally of the carelessness of Enzio, who had been charged with guarding the city. In a decision revealing poor judgement and little knowledge of his opponent, Enzio had undertaken an expedition against the Brescian castle of Quinzono, leaving Parma inadequately guarded. At this time also wedding festivities were in progress in the city of Parma, absorbing the attention of many of the most prominent citizens and thus affording the crafty legate an excellent opportunity for carrying out his long-prepared plans. A considerable body of Parmesan exiles, previously driven from the city by the imperial sympathizers, and now led by the Pope's brother-in-law Bernard Orlando Rossi, marched upon Parma and seized and occupied its towers. Henry Testa of Arezzo, the imperial *podestà*, hastily gathered a small following from the imperial garrison but was powerless to expel the invaders. He himself fell in a battle which took place on 16 June. Enzio, when told of the invasion, instead of hastening back to Parma which, if we can accept the observation of Salimbene, he could have retaken easily by an immediate attack,[3] went to Cremona to gather reinforcements from that city and from Pavia and Bergano. The interval thus provided afforded an opportunity to the rebels to reinforce the city strongholds through extensive construction of trenches and palisades.[4] Powerless to retake the city, Enzio awaited the arrival of the Emperor, while making preparations for a large-scale siege. Meanwhile, Gregory of Montelongo, recognizing that a long siege was in prospect, appealed once more to Ottaviano, as papal emissary, for substantial reinforcements. Ottaviano obviously wanted to make amends for his original failure, and being well supplied with

---

[1] Huillard-Bréholles, vi, part ii, 554, 557, 558, 564.

[2] See especially G. Marchetti-Longhi, 'La Legazione de Gregorio da Monte Longo' (*Archivio Soc. Rom.* xxxvii, 1914), xi, 'Ribellione di Parma all'Impero', 225–66; H. Frankfurth, *Gregorius de Montelongo*. See also the penetrating description of Gregory in Salimbene, *Cronica*, 387 ff., and *Chronicon Parmense* (Muratori, *RIS*, new edn. ix, part 9), 13.

[3] *Cronica*, 193.

[4] *Chronicon Parmense* (Muratori, *RIS*, new edn. ix, part 9), 16–17; *Annales Placentini Gibellini* (*MGH, SS.* xviii), *Annales Janvenses* (*Fonti*), iii. 171 f. See also G. Marchetti-Longhi, 'Legazione' 225–49 for a full account.

money, assembled a new mercenary army comparable to that which he had abandoned at the foot of the Alps.[1]

As Ottaviano set out from Mantua, where he had assembled his mercenaries, accompanied by a flotilla on the river Po, the hopes of the besieged Parmesans were buoyed up by the anticipation of imminent aid. But shortly before, Enzio and Ezzelino had captured Brescello on the Po, north of Parma, and had blocked the transport of provisions by throwing a barrier across the river. Deprived of provisions from the outside, the Parmesans found themselves in a desperate condition. Repeatedly Gregory of Montelongo appealed to Cardinal Ottaviano to hasten his relief of the city as the inhabitants were rapidly becoming demoralized.[2] But Ottaviano, never skilled in the manœuvring of troops, after crossing the Po, found himself in a cul-de-sac between the Po and the Tagliata canal which connected Guastalla, on the south bank of the Po, with Reggio. There he was held immobile for two months by the forces of Enzio and Ezzelino who dominated the routes to Parma.[3]

With the continued delay of Ottaviano conditions in Parma became increasingly serious. The chronicler Salimbene relates that Gregory of Montelongo found difficulty in maintaining discipline within the threatened city and in bolstering the morale of the starving citizens. On one occasion he is said to have arranged a banquet to which he invited the chief knights and other prominent personages. While the guests were at table a messenger arrived loudly clamouring for admission and displaying every indication of a long and hasty journey. After receiving the message from the 'weary' messenger, Gregory sent him away for refreshments and rest. He then opened the message and, with simulated delight, read to the assembled guests what he himself had penned, announcing that help was on the way. The guests, upon their departure, spread the news throughout the city. Salimbene says, with obvious amusement, that the letter had been prepared secretly in Gregory's chamber the previous evening, adding that when this story was worn out the astute legate invented another.[4]

Fortunately for Gregory of Montelongo and his supporters, the Mantuans and Ferrarese succeeded on All Saints' Day in piercing the blockade and in delivering supplies to the city. But Cardinal Ottaviano, unable or unwilling to advance, released his army and returned to Mantua. This second failure inevitably gave rise to serious charges, even

---

[1] *Annales Janvenses (Fonti)*, iii. 172. *Annales Placentini Gibellini (MGH, SS.* xviii), 495: 'cardinalis congregatis 1000 militibus . . .'

[2] Huillard-Bréholles, vi, part ii, 570. See also G. Marchetti-Longhi, 'Legazione', 242.

[3] *Chronicon Parmense* (Muratori, *RIS*, new edn. ix, part 9,), 17. For Ottaviano's ineptitude as a soldier see A. Hauss, *Oktavian*, 16. For the activities of Ezzelino and Enzio see also F. Stieve, *Ezzelino*, 56.

[4] *Cronica*, 389–90.

the implication of treason, for, as rumour had it, Ottaviano's inactivity was said to be the result of a secret agreement with the Emperor. Salimbene, who rarely overlooked any morsel of scandalous gossip, tells of a conversation he had with Cardinal Deacon William Fiesco who, he says, 'asked me what the Parmesans were saying about Ottaviano. I answered him and said: "The Parmesans say that he was a traitor to Parma as he was to Faenza." "Ah, by God! that is not to be believed," replied William.—I answered him and said: "Whether or not it is to be believed, I do not know, but the Parmesans say so."'[1] The defensive measures of Gregory of Montelongo proved formidable; month after month the siege continued and, despite the want of provisions, the garrison obstinately resisted. It is apparent throughout the operation that Frederick II was largely dependent upon mercenary troops,[2] while Gregory of Montelongo had at his command citizen-soldiers deeply concerned for the safety of their city and for their own freedom.

With the approach of autumn Frederick began the erection of a siege-city outside the walls of Parma to which he gave the name, somewhat over-optimistically, of Victoria.[3] It is apparent, however, that he intended Victoria to be something more than a temporary city—probably a permanent memorial to what he confidently anticipated would be a decisive victory. Like the cities of antiquity, Victoria was laid out ceremoniously under the auspices of the court astrologers. It was to be a city large and populous, 800 rods in length, slightly less in breadth.[4] Within its walls Frederick planned the erection of a splendid cathedral in honour of St. Victor. Here also he established his chancery, his courts of law, and other agencies of the royal court. It was said that he had brought there his menagerie, including elephants, dromedaries, panthers, lions, cheetahs, lynxes, and white bears, also his hunting dogs, birds of various kinds, including goshawks, gyrfalcons, and owls. Here also was his harem, women of great beauty, held captive in pleasure gardens under the surveillance of eunuchs. On the outskirts of the city were villas, vineyards, and orchards.[5]

But with all these preparations so confidently undertaken, Frederick, like his son Enzio, greatly underestimated his opponent Gregory of Montelongo who soon found an opportunity to strike the Emperor a

---

[1] *Cronica*, 384; A. Hauss, *Oktavian*, 17. See also J. Maubach, *Die Kardinäle und ihre Politik*, 34–5.

[2] J. Mikulla, *Der Söldner*, 47–8, 66–7.

[3] *Annales Placentini Gibellini* (*MGH, SS*. xviii), 495. See also G. Marchetti-Longhi, 'Legazione', 247 ff.

[4] Matthew Paris, *Chronica majora*, iv. 637 f.: 'civitatem grandem et populosam'. P. Collenuccio, *Historia Neapolitana*, 97. See also for Collenuccio's probable source P. Scheffer-Boichorst, *Zur Geschichte*, 283; *Rolandini Patavini Chronica* (*MGH, SS*. xix), 495.

[5] F. Biondo, *Historiarum ab inclinatiōe romano imperio decades III*, 294; *Carmina triumphalia de Victoria Urbe Eversa*, ii (*MGH, SS*. xviii), 795.

shattering blow. Gregory must clearly have been well informed about the activities within the city of Victoria and of the movements of Frederick, whose absence on a hunting expedition gave the Parmesans the chance for a successful assault.[1] The garrison of Parma, emerging from the city and making a sortie in the direction of the Apennines, succeeded in enticing the Margrave Lancia, the only military commander left in Victoria, to pursue them. At the same time other Parmesan troops, together with a motley throng of citizens with their wives and children, suddenly attacked the siege-city, killing or else putting to ignominious flight the defending forces. They razed and burned the city of Victoria, capturing Thaddeus of Suessa, the learned Justice. With him they also captured an inestimable treasure. The chronicler of Parma asserts that before his imprisonment and death Thaddeus' hands had been amputated and that he was led away half alive (*semivivus*).[2] The Cremonese were also routed and their *carroccio* captured. In addition, the victorious Parmesans carried away many prisoners as well as nearly 15,000 head of cattle, numerous saddle-horses, pack-horses, mules, and oxen, 'so that, beyond all expectations, their city abounded in wealth of every kind.'[3] In his account Salimbene says that the booty taken by the Parmesans included 'large quantities of gold, silver, and precious stones, vases, and vestments; they took also all of the jewellery and household furnishings and the imperial crown of great weight and value, constructed entirely of gold embroidered with precious stones and ornamented with engraved figures and embossed designs.' In circumference it was said to be as large 'as a cooking-pot, for it was more of a display and museum piece than an ornament for the head'. Of this crown Salimbene, who once held it in his hands when it was deposited in the sacristy of the Cathedral of the Holy Virgin in Parma, says that it was of such great size that 'it would have covered entirely the face and head, save for the support of a cross-piece which would hold it securely above the head'.[4] Lost also was the royal seal; it was either carried away by the victors or else, as Frederick stated in a letter to the officials in Palermo, 'the seal of the Kingdom and the stamp of the golden bull . . . were destroyed in the burning of the camp'.[5]

Serious as were these losses, no less disturbing to Frederick was the loss of an exquisitely decorated manuscript of his book on falconry, which was subsequently described in a letter of Guilielmus Bottatus of Milan to Charles of Anjou as skilfully decorated with gold and silver

[1] *Chronica regia Coloniensis*, 295.
[2] *Chronicon Parmense* (Muratori, *RIS.*, new edn. ix, part. 9), 18; Matthew Paris, *Chronica majora*, v. 13–15, vi. 147; *Bartholomei scribae Annales*, 224–5.
[3] *Annales Placentini Gibellini* (*MGH, SS.* xviii), 496; and *Chronica regia Coloniensis*, 295.
[4] *Cronica*, 203.
[5] Winkelmann, *Acta*, i, no. 397, p. 345; and no. 398, p. 346.

designs and with a likeness of his imperial majesty.[1] Salimbene says of Frederick's reactions to these losses that he 'raged as a she-bear robbed of her cubs in the forest';[2] while Matthew Paris says, 'he groaned openly and inwardly with repeated sighs as though deeply wounded; for the death of Thaddeus and the insult of the Pope wounded the heart of Frederick even to bitterness, more than all other losses'.[3] Returning hastily from his hunting expedition upon receiving news of the catastrophe, Frederick saw that further efforts to save Victoria would be futile, what with the raging fire in the city and his surviving forces in flight. He and his retinue, leaving the blazing city behind them, moved first to Borgo San Donnino and then, on the same day, to Cremona.[4]

[1] The text of this letter is given by C. H. Haskins, *Med. Science*, 308–9: 'auri enim et argenti decore artificiose politus et imperatorie maiestatis effigie decoratus.'

[2] *Cronica*, 211.

[3] Matthew Paris, *Chronica majora*, v. 15.

[4] *Cronica regia Coloniensis*, 295; *Thomae Tusci Gesta* (*MGH, SS*. xxii), 514–15; Collenuccio, *Historia Neapolitana*, 99.

IV

FROM ADVERSITY TO THE THRESHOLD
OF VICTORY
DEATH OF THE EMPEROR

Si Probitas, Sensus, Virtutum Gratia, Census,
  Nobilitas Orti Possent Resistere Morti,
Non Foret Extinctus Fredericus, Qui Jacet Intus.
  Early inscription on sepulchre of Frederick II.[1] *Riccobaldi Ferra-*
  riensis Chronicon Romanorum Imperatorum (Muratori, *RIS.* ix. 249)

CRUSHING as was the defeat at Parma, the Emperor lost little
time in sorrowing over the disaster. He rapidly reassembled his
scattered army and, on 22 February, three days after the destruction of Victoria, he crossed the Po apparently with the intention of
resuming the siege of Parma. His immediate return, and the attack
by his son Enzio on the ships laden with provisions for the starving
Parmesans, so terrified the enemy troops that they took flight, leaving
behind much booty and some 300 prisoners. It is said that the unfortunate captives were summarily hanged along the banks of the Po.[2]
Frederick at first seriously considered renewing the siege at once, re-
establishing the old camp at Victoria and devastating the region in
the vicinity of Parma. On the site of the ruined siege-city of Victoria he
'held a great council', and afterwards departed, thus leaving the Parmesans in fear that it was his intention to rebuild the siege-city. Apparently as a result of this council of war, the project of an immediate
resumption of the siege was abandoned.[3] Frederick now turned his
attention to securing the Cisa Pass near Pontremoli, essential to keeping open his lines of communication between the Kingdom of Sicily
and Northern Italy.[4] It was while he was still lingering in this region
that forces sent to harass his withdrawal were attacked and defeated
by Margrave Lancia with a group of Parmesan knights, refugees from

[1]   If probity, reason, abundance of virtue, wealth,
          Nobility of birth, could forfend death,
          Frederick, who is here entombed, would not be dead.
  [2] Huillard-Bréholles, vi, part i, 594; Winkelmann, *Acta*, i. 345 ff.
  [3] *Chronicon Parmense* (Muratori, *RIS*, new edn.) ix, pt. 9, 19: 'reversus fuit in loco civitatis
Victorie, et ibi fecit magnum consilium et postea recessit.'
  [4] *Annales Placentini Gibellini*, 498.

the city, who were loyal to the Emperor. Among the captured was
Bernard Orlando Rossi, brother-in-law of the Pope, 'the head and tail
of the whole opposition' (*totius partis adverse caput et cauda*), who was
brutally cut to pieces by his captors.[1]

But the capture and execution of a treasonable enemy was poor
compensation for the shattering blow dealt the Emperor by the capture
and burning of Victoria. So serious was this defeat that it was long
treated by historians, certainly erroneously, as a turning-point in the
life of Frederick II, leaving him a defeated and broken man. On the
contrary, one is astonished rather by the speed with which he rearmed
and by the successes won thereafter, if not by himself, by his lieutenants.
True, the immediate results of his spectacular defeat appear to have
opened the way for a far-reaching victory of the papal party and, for the
moment, regions such as Romagna, the March of Ancona, and some
cities of Spoleto, were freed from imperial control. Where previously
Cardinal Rainer had achieved but little success, he now renewed his
activity, temporarily regaining several cities for the Pope.[2] It was not
broken spirit, however, but scarcity of money that had given pause to
the Emperor. Accordingly, in June 1248 he wrote to his faithful subjects that only the want of money prevented his achieving a complete
victory.[3] It was this want of funds that necessitated the levying of an unusually heavy *collecta*, not only upon his lay subjects but also upon all
churches and monasteries, 'not in his own interests, but for the good
of the people and for crushing the rebellion'.[4]

There is evidence also that to meet this need some citizens of the
Kingdom made voluntary offerings. In a letter to the inhabitants of one
city which had proffered financial aid, Frederick, while thanking them
for their generosity, replied that in consideration of the heavy financial
burdens already imposed, he felt constrained to decline their offer.[5]
Once more the silver mine of Montieri, as during the siege of Viterbo
in 1243, served as security for an important financial arrangement, not
as on the previous occasion, with Florentine merchants, but with the
Sienese, in which the produce of the mine was mortgaged to the bankers
of that city pending the repayment of a loan.[6] Through the minting
of new coins in Brindisi, and their exchange, considerable sums were
brought into the royal treasury.[7] There is probable evidence also that

---

[1] Huillard-Bréholles, vi, part ii, 609.

[2] E. Westenholz, *Kardinal Rainer von Viterbo*, see especially pp. 143 ff.

[3] Huillard-Bréholles, vi, part ii, 634 f.

[4] Ibid. vi, part i, 361. For the date see BFW, *Reg.* v, Abt. i, no. 3681.

[5] Huillard-Bréholles, vi, part ii, 633. See also BFW, *Reg.* v, Abt. i, no. 3692, for the date of
this letter.

[6] Huillard-Bréholles, vi, part ii, 936. For the earlier arrangement with the Florentines see
ibid., part i, 138.

[7] Winkelmann, *Acta*, i, no. 930, p. 707.

Frederick was aided during this period of extreme financial stringency by his son-in-law, John Vatatzes, the Greek Emperor.[1]

As Frederick marked time while replenishing his treasury, the Pope, believing his enemy no longer capable of serious resistance, grew over-confident of ultimate victory. The legates Gregory of Montelongo, Ottaviano Ubaldini, and Rainer of Viterbo renewed their propagandist attacks, not only through the preaching of a crusade against the Emperor, but also by proclaiming the ban once more against his kinsmen and allies, emphasizing especially the misdeeds of Ezzelino of Romano.[2] Cardinal Rainer, moved by Frederick's execution of the treasonable Bishop Marcellina of Arezzo, who, although a vassal of the Emperor, was active as a legate of the Pope, issued another of his vitriolic attacks on Frederick, 'the vicar of Satan, the forerunner of the Antichrist'. This pamphlet, surpassing Rainer's earlier efforts in defamation, depicted Frederick as the 'inventor and perpetrator of all cruelties', 'the defiler and assailant of the anointed of the Lord'.[3] That this attack injured the cause of Frederick is suggested in the remark of Matthew Paris that 'it wounded the hearts of many'; but he hastens to add that it would have caused them to oppose Frederick, had it not been that his papal enemies were sullied by greed, simony, usury, and other vices.[4]

Superficially, Frederick's fortunes appeared to be at their lowest at midsummer 1248. He personally took little action in pushing the re-conquest of his lost territories. Central Italy seemed destined to fall into the hands of the papal representatives. Frederick's activities in Northern Italy during the summer caused much speculation as to his motives. Salimbene, ever ready to seize upon any suggestion of the sensational, reports the Guelf-inspired rumour that Frederick was *en route* to Lyons with the object of taking captive the Pope and Cardinals.[5] It is much more probable that, in response to the efforts of Louis IX, who at that time was again with the Pope, Frederick anticipated the reopening of negotiations with Innocent IV. King Louis, eager for a peaceful settlement before his departure for the Holy Land, had again urged the Emperor to send ambassadors, accredited with full authority, with peace proposals.[6] But the recent reversals of the Emperor offered no suitable background for further negotiations. Innocent IV obviously felt he could turn a deaf ear to all proposals of peace short of unconditional surrender by the Emperor. In his response to the French King

---

[1] Collenuccio, *Compendio* p. 99; idem, ed. A. Saviotti, p. 141.
[2] *MGH, Epist. pont.* ii, no. 545, p. 348; ibid. 413.
[3] Matthew Paris, *Chronica majora*, v. 61 ff.   [4] Ibid. 67.
[5] *Cronica*, 53.
[6] *Annales Janvenses* (Fonti), iii. 182. See also BFW, *Reg.* Abt. i, no. 3716a and Abt. iii, no. 8030.

he reiterated that he would never conclude peace with Frederick or his offspring. Unpromising also for a future peace was the Pope's statement that peace without the inclusion of the Lombards was impossible.[1]

With dogged determination to resist all pleas for a peaceful settlement, Innocent IV now turned to the conquest of the Kingdom of Sicily, not only with the intention of reasserting the control of the papacy there, but also with the object of distracting Frederick from his expedition against Lyons. Again he ordered Stephen, his vicar in Rome, to initiate the preaching of a crusade against Frederick, in Rome, in the Campagna and the Maritima, and to excommunicate clerics in the Kingdom who were adherents of Frederick, depriving them of all their benefices. In addition, all cities that persisted in adhering to Frederick after the arrival of the papal army were to be denied their freedom; all temporal magnates loyal to the Emperor were to forfeit their rights and their property without hope of restitution through the grace of the Apostolic See.[2] Not content with a crusade against Frederick and his immediate adherents, the Pope charged his vicar also to proclaim the interdict over the entire Kingdom of Sicily as long as it adhered to the Emperor.

It has been observed that the Pope's proclaiming the interdict over the entire Kingdom of Sicily, an extraordinary step in singular contrast to its employment in other regions of Italy and Germany, is attributable to Innocent's recognition that the Church had nothing to lose there— that there was in Sicily no province in which inhabitants sympathetic to the papal cause so predominated as to require special consideration. Already the Sicilians had long shown their loyalty to the excommunicated Emperor and his adherents, just as the clergy had continued, despite the papal ban, to conduct divine services. The Pope's object appears to have been primarily to emphasize before the world of Christendom that he had been driven to extreme measures by the obstinate resistance of the King and his subjects. The rigorous measures to which he resorted are especially apparent in his pronouncement that belated repentance on the part of those who had once submitted to Frederick or to his sons was to be ignored.[3]

Unfortunately, we have little information as to what actually took place in the papal party during the months following this order of the Pope. It is to be presumed that Cardinal Stephen and his associates, authorized to represent the Pope in Italy, were occupied with assembling the crusading army and with other preparations for the projected crusade against the Kingdom. Now, as before, however, it was apparent that Innocent had no intention of granting the legates full authority

---

[1] Huillard-Bréholles, vi, part ii, 644, 645.
[2] *MGH, Epist. Pont.* no. 585, pp. 413 ff. (30 Aug. 1248).
[3] Huillard-Bréholles, vi, part ii, 616; C. Rodenberg, *Innozenz IV.*, pp. 60-2.

within the Kingdom of Sicily. This was to remain the special province of the Pope, as was clearly indicated by an incident which took place in Jesi, the birthplace of Frederick II. Early in the year 1248 this city had submitted to Cardinal Rainer in exchange for promises of liberal privileges.[1] Subsequently, however, the Pope refused to confirm these privileges, explaining that his remoteness from that region made it impossible for him to act until the re-establishment of peace when, as lord, he could give due consideration to it.[2] It may be concluded that, in the opinion of Innocent IV, there was no justification for the granting of privileges to a city merely for fulfilling its obligations to the Pope as its rightful lord. It is probable also that this rebuke to Rainer for his presumption in granting these privileges—an action exceeding his authority—contributed to his loss of favour at the papal court. Although subsequently entrusted with minor missions in Central Italy, and retaining the title of legate, Rainer was obviously no longer charged with tasks comparable to that which he had undertaken in Jesi. Already he was growing old; he had been named as Cardinal by Innocent III in 1216 while Abbot of the Monastery of Trois-fontaines.[3] Shortly after the suspension of his activities in Central Italy he was recalled to Rome where he died towards the end of the year 1250. Matthew Paris says of him: 'Rainer of Viterbo, a Cardinal and Chamberlain of the Pope, went the way of all flesh—a man of great wealth and noble blood who had been the persistent persecutor and defamer of Frederick.'[4]

Innocent did not immediately announce the appointment of a successor as legate in the Kingdom of Sicily. As if in anticipation of future successes there, he issued in early December 1248, 'after careful deliberation with the cardinals', an edict (or, more accurately, a programme) for future arrangements in Sicily.[5] In substance the proposed statutes directed:

1. All laws, ordinances, and all arrangements of Frederick II with regard to ecclesiastical matters, which were disadvantageous to the Church, were to be declared null and void, and all property and all privileges taken from the Church by Frederick were to be restored.

2. Elections to vacated churches were to be free and canonical; neither before nor after the election should the concurrence of the king be solicited.

[1] Rodenberg, *Innozenz IV.*, p. 63.

[2] C. Ciavarini, *Collezione di documenti storici antichi . . . delle città e terre Marchigiane, etc.*, v. 101, no. 92; and 117, no. 107: 'Donec nos Dominus cum pace'.

[3] Berger, *Registres*, nos. 4247–53; 4271–4; 4408. For his earlier activities and his ascent to the cardinalate see J. Maubach, *Die Kardinäle und ihre Politik*, 5 f.

[4] *Chronica majora*, v. 146.

[5] *MGH, Epist. Pont.* ii, no. 613, pp. 434 ff.: 'Statuta edita per dominum Innocentium papam quartum pro ecclesiastica libertate in regno Sicilie.'

3. Neither the King nor other temporal lords were to exact oaths of fealty from prelates who did not hold regalia from them.

4. No person of the estate of the clergy could henceforth be haled before a temporal court in criminal or civil complaints—even if the case had to do with high treason.

5. No clergyman or layman under the ban of excommunication was to be admitted before a spiritual or temporal tribunal prior to his absolution.

6. Bishops and other prelates were to have the right in places included within their spiritual jurisdiction to judge and to punish, in accordance with canon law, in cases of adultery and other violations by clergymen and laymen, unobstructed by the jurisdiction of temporal lords; and the right to pronounce judgement over marital and all other causes belonging to the ecclesiastical court.

It is apparent that these pre-arrangements set forth by Pope and Curia ignored completely the customary law of Sicily which was based upon the old Norman code, save where the Norman procedure coincided with the proposed statutes of Innocent IV. The form in which these proposed regulations appeared suggests that they were to serve as the basis for future agreements under which the Kingdom of Sicily would be granted to a foreign prince.[1] The chief immediate value of the proposed regulations lay in their appeal to the Sicilian clergy who could anticipate, through their implementation, virtually complete freedom from temporal interference.

To initiate his far-reaching new policies in the Sicilian Kingdom Innocent at last chose, in April 1249, Cardinal Deacon Peter Capoccio of San Giorgio in Velabro to replace Cardinal Rainer. Member of a prominent Roman family, long distinguished for its faithful service to the papacy, Peter Capoccio recommended himself particularly by virtue of his recent legatine mission to Germany where he was instrumental in bringing about the election of William of Holland as King. Innocent IV saw in him a man possessed of skill and integrity, prudent in council —a man proven in many and difficult missions.[2] Chosen as cardinal by Innocent IV, perhaps for his military prowess rather than for his spiritual qualities, he was made Cardinal Deacon of St. George ad velum aureum. Already, in the time of Pope Gregory IX, he had distinguished himself while suppressing a rebellion in Rome. Under Pope Innocent IV, to whom he was closely bound by ties of friendship,

---

[1] Rodenberg, op. cit. 67.

[2] *MGH, Epist. Pont.* ii, 681, pp. 487 ff. See also Matthew Paris, *Chronica majora*, v. 79. For the service of Peter's family, especially his father, see Gregorovius, *Rom.* iv. 595, note 1; and the English edn. (London, 1896), iv, part ii, 634. For a more detailed study of Cardinal Peter see F. Reh, *Kardinal Peter Capocci*, 92 ff.

he was destined to exercise great influence upon the affairs of the Church.[1]

In a series of letters from the papal chancery Peter was authorized 'to pull down, to destroy, to overthrow, to ruin, to build, and to transplant' in the Kingdom of Sicily, not only in spiritual but in temporal matters as well. He was given plenary authority in Sicily, in imperial Tuscany, the Duchy of Spoleto, the *patrimonium*, the Sabina, the Campagna, the Maritima, and in various individual provinces within the Papal State, excluding only the city of Rome.[2] Peter's authorization was unique in its comprehensiveness, having no precedent in previous documents. His over-all task was to free Sicily from imperial control, and no significant limitations were placed upon his procedure. He was authorized to raise money, to levy troops in the Papal State, to tax exiled Sicilians and all bishops and other clergymen. He was to assure all within his jurisdiction that the Church would never make peace with Frederick of such a nature as to permit either him or his sons to remain as King or Emperor.

In contemplating these extraordinary powers, singularly in contrast with his own limited authority, Cardinal Reginald of Ostia, legate at large in Italy since the flight of Innocent IV, must have felt the sting of the Pope's implied want of confidence. This sensitiveness was increased when the Pope excused his action by suggesting to the Cardinal that, because of his age, the legatine burdens were too arduous for him.[3] It would have been something of a shock to Innocent IV if he could have foreseen that four years later Reginald of Ostia would be chosen as Pope Alexander IV. Richard Annibaldi, Cardinal Deacon of St. Angelus who, after the flight of Innocent IV to Lyons, served as the papal representative in the Campagna and the Maritima, and Stephen, papal legate in Rome, were also relieved of their legatine functions and called to the papal court. The letter of recall was couched in such language, however, as to leave in the minds of those faithful servants the conviction of the Pope's capacity for ingratitude. For the only explanation offered to Cardinal Richard Annibaldi was the alleged rumour that the Cardinal had expressed his desire to serve at the papal court.[4]

While the Pope was thus making preparations for the conquest of the much-coveted Kingdom of Sicily and was seeking to open all avenues of assistance to his newly appointed legate, Frederick II, who since midsummer 1248 had been in Piedmont, returned early in 1249 to

---

[1] See especially J. Maubach, *Die Kardinäle*, 22, and D. Waley, *The Papal State*, 147 f.

[2] *MGH, Epist. Pont.* ii, no. 681, pp. 486 ff.; nos. XII, XIII, XVII, XIX, XXIX. See also C. Rodenberg, *Innozenz*, 69 ff.; and J. Maubach, *Die Kardinäle*, 36 f.

[3] *MGH, Epist. Pont.* ii, no. 681, viii, p. 491: 'Quod grave tibi nimis tanti onus negotii extitisset.' See also J. Maubach, op. cit. 36 and (for his original assignment in Italy) p. 26.

[4] *MGH, Epist. Pont.* ii, no. 681, xviii, p. 492.

Cremona. Serious as had been his defeat at Victoria and the loss of his faithful Lord Chief Justice, Thaddeus of Suessa, he was now to suffer an even greater blow in that he was finally persuaded of the treasonable conduct of his protonotary and logothete who had been intimately bound to him by ties of friendship and congeniality. Rarely have the lives of two men been more closely and intricately interwoven than those of Frederick II and Piero della Vigna.[1] Educated in the ornate style of rhetoric and oratory fashionable in his era, as well as in both Roman and canon law, Piero della Vigna rose rapidly in the esteem of Frederick II from the moment of his entrance into the service of the Sicilian court in 1221. Long a High Court Justice, an office which he shared with Thaddeus of Suessa, and often entrusted with the most delicate diplomatic missions, Piero was finally elevated in 1247 to the joint offices of protonotary and logothete of Sicily. In these offices he was, in fact, head of the chancery, adviser and trusted agent to the Emperor in matters diplomatic, fiscal, and political, as well as judicial. Next to Frederick himself, Piero was the most powerful official of the Sicilian court. As such he was exposed to every temptation of a man known to be privy to the conscience of the King—often permitted by his sovereign to act arbitrarily and upon his own intiative. How far would a man in such a position be influenced by tempting gifts or by extravagant bribes? Even though impervious to such temptations, how could he avoid the suspicion of envious nobles who saw in him a parvenu, usurping their traditional privileges as counsellors of the King?

The bond between these two remarkable men was much more than that of sovereign and faithful servant. Their abilities, their tastes, their outlook upon life, their concepts of empire, their cultural attributes as a whole, coincided so completely as to make them inseparable in the cultural, intellectual, and political history of thirteenth-century Sicily. At every step in the constitutional development of the Kingdom, Piero della Vigna was at the side of his sovereign. In the intimate scholarly, literary, and artistic life of the Sicilian court he was the congenial associate of his royal master, whether in the cultivation of the art of poetry, the pursuit of Arab-Greek philosophy, or in shaping the policies to be pursued in relations with the papacy. Thaddeus of Suessa and Piero della Vigna shared with Frederick II the dream of empire which was the activating force behind all his achievements. The passing of these two men, each under tragic circumstances, and within a few months of each other, was, in some measure, prophetic of the shattering of the imperial dream soon after the death of Frederick II.

---

[1] The alleged treason, the imprisonment and death of Piero della Vigna, are dealt with in detail by Huillard-Bréholles, *Pierre de la Vigne*, especially pp. 55–90.

The alleged treason of Piero della Vigna is shrouded in mystery and may well have resulted solely from Frederick's growing distrust of all men, which had been intensified by the conspiracy of 1246. Suspicion feeds upon suspicion, and so it appears to have been with Frederick II. Unquestionably also this suspicion was constantly fed by the malicious gossip of the court nobility. As Piero's influence over the Emperor increased, contemporaries professed to see in him the *deus ex machina* guiding the actions of his sovereign. To his friends he was 'a second Joseph' to whom, as the faithful interpreter of his will, this great Emperor 'whose power is admired by sun and moon' entrusted the reins of the terrestrial globe as governor. To his enemies he was 'a second Ahithophel', whose counsels, to the detriment of the princes, guided his imperial majesty and governed the state.[1]

His foes overlooked no opportunity to cast suspicion upon his official conduct. He became all the more vulnerable to the shafts of his enemies when, in the most critical period of Frederick's reign, he was given the extraordinary powers inherent in the joint offices of protonotary and logothete. His 'treasonable acts' consisted in cupidity—the avarice of a man already abundantly wealthy for greater wealth and for greater power, to be obtained from selling justice for his own profit. It was this that Frederick alluded to in a letter to his son-in-law the Count of Caserta when he admonished him to take care that his accounts were accurate and in conformity with the facts, reminding the Count of the fate of Piero, 'a second Simon, who, to the end that he might possess and fill his own coffers, had transformed the staff of justice into a serpent who, by habitual falsifications, pushed the empire towards an abyss in which we might have been engulfed at the bottom of the sea with the army of Pharoah and the chariots of Egypt'.[2] Rightly or wrongly, Frederick was convinced of the guilt of his most trusted friend and official. But there remains always the possibility that at a moment when he was most sensitive to his own financial difficulties, Frederick lent his ear too readily to calumniators who affected to see in Piero della Vigna the fortunate embezzler that they themselves might have been. That he was guilty of peculation there can be no reasonable doubt; his trial and the sentence imposed appear to have confirmed his guilt. Peculation, however, was a crime not uncommon among the much-tempted officials of Frederick's court. The question remains, did not Frederick, influenced by envious foes of his protonotary, exaggerate the magnitude of Piero's guilt when he alleged that it threatened the

[1] Huillard-Bréholles, *Pierre*, 'Pièces justificatives', 289–94; *Vita Greg. IX* (Muratori, *RIS* iii), col. 581; or in *Liber Censuum*, ii. 28.

[2] Huillard-Bréholles, vi, part ii, 700. For a carefully considered analysis of the alleged malfeasance of Piero della Vigna see F. Baethgen, 'Dante and Petrus de Vinea' (*Sb. Bayer. Ak.*, 1955, Heft iii).

solvency of the Empire? Salimbene, notorious as the purveyor of scandalous gossip, and master of harmful innuendo, inspired by rumours of Piero's fabulous riches, intimates that Frederick sought his faithful official's ruin in order to confiscate his wealth. It was Salimbene who attributed to Frederick the sordid dictum: 'Never have I fed a hog from which I could not extract the lard.'[1]

It was perhaps inevitable that contemporaries, including the generally well-informed Matthew Paris, should associate this accusation of Piero della Vigna with the nearly contemporary effort to poison the Emperor, and to represent this as an additional cause of Piero's disgrace.[2] In the formal sentencing of him, however, no mention was made of his implication in the attempted murder. Indeed, one is constrained to accept the conclusion that the association of Piero with the poison plot was merely an effort on the part of hostile contemporaries to deepen 'the ditch into which he was to fall from favour'.[3] Undoubtedly the attempted poisoning did take place, and much in the manner described by Matthew Paris, save that there is no reliable evidence that either Pope Innocent IV or Piero della Vigna was an accomplice. Certainly so heinous a crime would not have passed unnoticed in the sentence condemning Piero to death. Matthew relates that the Emperor, having become ill, was advised to take a specially prepared physic and to follow it with a medicated bath. It was said that Piero della Vigna, yielding to bribes by the Pope, induced the attending physician to mix a strong and deadly poison in both the physic and the bath. Just before the administration of the dose Frederick was warned of the intended crime. Turning to Piero and the physician, as if in a jocular mood, he entreated them 'not to give me, who confide in you, poison instead of medicine'. He then bade the physician 'drink half of the potion with me'. Astonished and terrified, the physician affected to stumble, spilling the greater part of the poisoned drink. Frederick ordered the remnant to be given to some condemned criminals who are said to have died instantly.

In an era fraught with suspicion, born of the long conflict between Pope and Emperor, in which Piero della Vigna was so deeply involved, it is not surprising that hostile contemporary gossip associated both him and Innocent IV with the murder plot. It is apparent, however, that more judicious contemporary opinion was not so ready to accept either the alleged treasonable conduct of Piero or the allegation of murder. This opinion is reflected in a passage of the *Inferno* (Canto XIII) in which Dante, in depicting this tragic downfall of Frederick's long-

---

[1] *Cronica*, 439: 'Nunquam nutrivi porcum, de quo axungiam non habuerim.'
[2] Huillard-Bréholles, *Pierre*, 77 ff.
[3] Matthew Paris, *Chronica Majora*, v. 68.

faithful servant and his suffering among the suicides in Hell, has Piero relate the cause of his self-inflicted death:

> . . . so great fidelity I have to the glorious office, that I lost thereby both sleep and life.
> The harlot, that never from Caesar's dwelling turned her adulterous eyes, common bane, and vice of courts,
> inflamed all minds against me; and these [being inflamed,] so inflamed Augustus, that my joyous honours were changed to dismal sorrows.
> My soul, in its disdainful mood, thinking to escape disdain by death, made me, *though* just, unjust against myself.[1]

As late as January 1249 Piero della Vigna continued to carry on his duties at the court and was with Frederick in Cremona when he was suddenly seized and imprisoned.[2] So great was the hatred of the Cremonese towards the unfortunate protonotary that he was transferred during the night, under guard and in chains, first to Borgo San Donnino and, subsequently to San Miniato, where, already blinded, he crushed his skull by hurling himself headlong against a stone column to which he was chained.[3]

Slightly more than a month after Piero's suicide Frederick suffered the greatest of sorrows when, during a battle at Fossalta between Modena and Bologna, his son Enzio, his steed shot from under him, was taken prisoner, together with many of his followers and those of his allies from Cremona and Modena. The brave and talented young King, among the most trusted of Frederick's lieutenants, and a favourite son, was destined to remain a prisoner for the rest of his life.[4] The Emperor entered at once into negotiations for the release of his son, and these negotiations were still being actively pressed at the moment of Frederick's death in the following year.[5] Like the defeats of Frederick at Brescia and Parma, the capture of Enzio had far-reaching repercussions, seriously affecting his prestige. Defection after defection now took place among the once-faithful cities. The strategically important Cisa Pass near Pontremoli, connecting Lombardy and Tuscany, was lost. On 19 July 1249 Como, as the result of an agreement with Milan, deserted.[6] In mid December Modena also, after enduring a long siege by Bologna, abandoned the cause of the Emperor.[7] The one fortunate

---

[1] *Inferno*, Canto XIII, lines 61–72 (from the Temple Classics edn.).

[2] *Annales Placentini Gibellini* (*MGH, SS.* xviii), 498: 'Imperator . . . equitavit Cremonam, ubi capi fecit Petrum de Vinea eius proditorem.'

[3] Matthew Paris, *Chronica majora*, v. 69.

[4] *Chronicon Parmense* (Muratori, *RIS*, new edn. ix, part 9), 19. For detailed accounts of his imprisonment see L. Frati, *La prigionia de re Enzio* (*Bibl. Stor. Bologna*, vi, 1902), 88 ff.; and H. Blasius, *König Enzio*, especially pp. 127 ff.

[5] Matthew Paris, *Chronica majora*, v. 200; Huillard-Bréholles, vi, part ii, 737 ff.

[6] *Annales Placentini Gibellini* (*MGH, SS.* xviii), 498; BFW, *Reg.* v, Abt. i, no. 3785.

[7] Ibid., no. 3793a.

incident in the affairs of the Emperor in this fateful year of 1249 occurred in the autumn, when the Counts of Bagnacavallo regained the strategically important city of Ravenna.[1]

It is not surprising that Innocent IV, in contemplating the various reverses of the Emperor during these months, should have considered the time propitious for the launching of a campaign against the Kingdom of Sicily. Peter Capoccio, who had been long delayed in Lyons, found no difficulty in entering the March of Ancona to begin his hostile operations. In September 1249 he was encamped with his troops on the river Aso some three miles from the border of the Kingdom of Sicily (*in castris supra Asum*).[2] However, in a border encounter with imperial troops he was defeated with heavy losses, and about 4 October he had apparently withdrawn to the northernmost region of the March. He had met unexpected resistance as he was making preparations for an expedition into the Kingdom. Matthew Paris, writing of the activities of Peter Capoccio during the winter months of 1249–50, says that numerous troops which he had acquired through bribery, and through the granting of plenary indulgences for sins, did serious injury to Frederick and seduced many nobles from allegiance to him.[3]

It was during these winter months, also, when Peter was marking time in the March of Ancona, apparently because of the inability of the Pope to supply him with sufficient funds, that Innocent, in a desperate effort to obtain financial assistance, summoned Richard of Cornwall to Lyons. The extraordinary reception given to the Earl and the numerous honours showered upon him indicate the importance that the Pope attached to this visit. Matthew Paris, who reports this in detail, relates that after breakfasting together the two men engaged in many 'secret and lengthy conferences' and that 'all who witnessed the proceedings marvelled at them'.[4] Circumstantial evidence suggests that the Pope at this time may have offered Richard the Sicilian crown. This appears all the more probable because in a later report (in 1252) Matthew, recalling Richard's previous meeting with the Pope at Lyons, conjectured that 'the Pope, aware that Earl Richard . . . was far wealthier than other noblemen of the West', sought to have him chosen as sovereign over Apulia, Sicily, and Calabria.[5] It is most unlikely, however, that Earl Richard, the brother-in-law of Frederick II, would have permitted himself to become party to a scheme which

---

[1] *Annales Placentini Gibellini* (*MGH, SS.* xviii), 499; *Annales Caesenates* (Muratori, *RIS* xiv), col. 1101; and Savioli, *Annali Bolognesi*, iii. 263.

[2] G. Colucci, *Della Antichità Picene*, xviii, App. 24, n. 13. See also C. Rodenberg, *Innozenz IV.*, 81 ff., and M. Natalucci, *Ancona traverso i Secoli*, i. 341 f., and Hagemann, 'Jesi im Zeitalter Friedrichs II.' (*QF* xxxvi, 1956), 185 ff.

[3] *Chronica majora*, v. 79.

[4] Ibid. v. 111.   [5] Ibid. v. 346–7.

would have been dishonourable in that it would have deprived his nephew Henry of his birthright.[1]

After the capture of Enzio, Frederick had withdrawn into Sicily where he lingered until early in 1250 because of ill health. In various letters of this time he mentioned casually that he was recovering his strength.[2] The mere suggestion of illness was sufficient to cause his enemies once more, as during his crusade in 1228–9, to spread rumours that he was dead.[3] But, if he was ill during these months, he was not wholly inactive. For, with the resources of Sicily at his command, he prepared for renewed expeditions against the various hostile and defecting regions of Italy.[4] He was especially sensitive to the successes of Peter Capoccio who, despite his initial failure to cross the border into the Kingdom, had persuaded a number of the cities of Ancona to desert the Emperor. In one of his letters to his son-in-law Vatatzes, Frederick complained bitterly of these priests 'who grasp the spear instead of the crozier . . . one calls himself duke, another margrave, and still another calls himself count. One of them organizes phalanxes, another sets up cohorts, still another incites men to war . . . Such today are the pastors in Israel: not priests of the Church of Christ, but rapacious wolves, wild beasts, who devour the Christian folk.'[5]

Despite these successes of the papal legate in parts of the March of Ancona, a sudden upsurge in the affairs of the Emperor occurred in the spring of 1250, both in Italy and in Germany. Frederick did not re-enter the field personally. In the March of Ancona his capable lieutenant Walter of Manupello began operations against Peter Capoccio. In June he had taken possession of S. Elpidio in the vicinity of Fermo, and in August he successfully attacked the papal armoury at Cingoli, where Peter Capoccio, in command there, narrowly escaped capture through precipitous flight, 'in the disguise of a beggar'. Before the end of the summer the castles of Fermo, Macerata, and Osimo were compelled to surrender to the imperial forces.[6] By early autumn

---

[1] Matthew Paris was well aware of this when he wrote: 'quid inhonestum videretur nepotem suum Henricum supplantare . . .', ibid. 347.

[2] Huillard-Bréholles, v, part ii, 992; and vi, part i, 505. See also G. Verci, *Storia degli Ecceleni*, iii. 304.

[3] In a letter to his son-in-law Vatatzes, Emperor of Nicaea (Huillard-Bréholles, vi, part ii, 790), Frederick wrote: 'illi qui Ecclesiae praesidere dicuntur, contra nos machinantur et mendacia quae cotidie de certitudine mortis nostrae divulgabant.' See also G. Wolff, *Vier griech. Briefe*, 54; Festa, 'Le Lettre Grechi di Federigo II' (*Archivio stor. Ital.*, 5th ser., xiii), 29.

[4] Winkelmann, *Acta*, i, no. 427.

[5] Huillard-Bréholles, vi, part ii, 773 f. See also G. Wolff, *Vier griech. Briefe*, 45; Festa, op. cit. 24 f.

[6] Winkelmann, *Acta*, i, no. 425, p. 364; no. 430, pp. 367–8; Huillard-Bréholles, vi, part ii, 791 ff.; see also G. Wolff, *Vier griech. Briefe*, pp. 55 ff.; and F. Reh, *Kardinal Peter Capocci*, 102 ff.

1250 the March of Ancona, the Duchy of Spoleto, and the Romagna were for the most part securely in the hands of the imperial forces.

During the summer also Hubert Pallavicini, operating in Lombardy, delivered a crushing defeat to his Parmesan adversaries on what was long remembered by the inhabitants of that city as the 'evil Thursday' ('la malzobia'), 18 August 1250. Few successes of this year gave greater satisfaction to the Emperor than this; for the humiliation of the Parmesans took place on the very site of the ill-fated siege-city of Victoria. It is said that 3,000 of the Parmesan troops were slain or captured, and their *carroccio* (*Biancarda*), was taken. Pallavicini, long notorious for his inhuman cruelties, now gave full play to his love of torture, inflicting upon his captives various newly invented punishments calculated to prolong their sufferings before finally succumbing.[1]

At about the same time also Conrad led an expedition in Germany down the valley of the Rhine against the adherents of the 'Pope-King', William of Holland, and the hostile bishops of the lower Rhine, forcing the latter to agree to an armistice.[2] Wherever the imperial forces operated they now achieved significant military gains. If the previous year had brought reversals and great sorrow to Frederick II, the year 1250 saw almost continuous victories. For a few brief months it appeared that the clouds had lifted over the whole of Italy and that peace under imperial sovereignty would at last be realized. Peter Capoccio, despite a few initial gains, had failed in his mission. In October 1250 he was recalled as legate.[3] Once more Innocent turned to Cardinal Ottaviano whose previous performances in the attempted relief of Parma had so strikingly revealed his incompetence as a military leader. It is perhaps a sign of the Pope's desperate situation that he now turned to this man. Certainly it could have been only with most serious misgivings that he wrote to the citizens of S. Ginesio that he had chosen to protect them and other faithful followers in Ancona a reliable person, who would be sent to them by Cardinal Deacon Ottaviano of Santa Maria in Via Lata.[4]

By the late autumn of 1250 the affairs of the papacy were most unpromising. Defeat had followed defeat, and, in a vain effort to check the imperial advances, the treasury of the Pope was emptied. Moreover, each year the resistance of the clergy throughout the West to the end-

---

[1] For the details of this victory see *Annales Placentini Gibellini* (*MGH, SS.* xviii), 502; *Chronicon Parmense* (Muratori, *RIS* ix, part 9, new edn.), 19; *MGH, SS.* xviii, 675 f.; Salimbene, *Cronica*, 335: 'Et inventores novorum tormentorum tunc temporis extiterunt.' See also Z. Schiffer, *Markgraf Hubert Pallavicini*, 46 ff.

[2] Huillard-Bréholles, vi, part ii, 794; G. Wolff, *Vier griech. Briefe*, 57 ff. See also *Annal. Wormat.* (*MGH, SS.* xvii), 52.

[3] C. Rodenberg, *Innozenz IV.*, 87; J. Maubach, *Die Kardinäle*, 37.

[4] Colucci, *Antichità Picene*, xix, 33, no. 24; see also C. Rodenberg, op. cit. 87.

less demands for money had grown more obstinate. The position of the Pope became all the more difficult when reports arrived of the disastrous defeat and capture of King Louis IX at Mansura on 6 April 1250. Innocent IV could not fail to recall that his own obstinacy in refusing to make peace with the Emperor prior to the departure of Louis for the Holy Land was probably the decisive factor in the ill-fated crusade. Propagandistically, the defeat of Louis IX was of the greatest advantage to the Emperor. The Pope was widely blamed for the disastrous failure. His contribution to the defeat became all the more apparent in that he, the heir to the Prince of the Apostles, instead of devoting his efforts to a crusade against the infidel by supporting the reconquest of the Holy Land, had preached a crusade against the Emperor of the Holy Roman Empire. The embarrassment of the Pope was further heightened when Louis IX, obtaining his release from captivity by the payment of a huge ransom, sent his brothers Charles of Anjou and Alfonso of Poitou, together with Duke Henry IV of Burgundy, to the papal court to insist upon a peaceful settlement with the Emperor. Now threatened by Frederick II, by the rising pressure of public opinion, and by 'the most Christian King of France', but determined to hold his defiant position, Innocent IV appealed to the King of England for domicile in Bordeaux.[1]

Never since his deposition had the outlook of Frederick II appeared more favourable for the winning of universal support among the princes of the West. Indeed, never had his prospects for victory in the conflict with the Pope appeared brighter. It is almost incredible that the Pope continued to cling to the position that no peaceful settlement was possible which did not include the Lombards.[2] Some six days after Innocent IV had repeated this assurance to several Tuscan nobles, and at a moment when Frederick stood near to the realization of his dream of empire, he died suddenly of a persistent attack of dysentery at the Castel Fiorentino in the Capitanata some fifteen miles from his residential palace at Foggia, on 13 December 1250. Matthew Paris, in relating the events of that day, wrote: 'Then, about this same time, Frederick, the greatest of the princes on the earth . . . died in Apulia, absolved of the sentence passed upon him . . . clothed as a Cistercian.'[3] His absolution, however, was pronounced not by the Pope but by Archbishop Berard of Palermo who, since Frederick's hazardous journey in 1212 to receive the crown, had been one of his most intimate associates and counsellors.

---

[1] Matthew Paris, *Chronica majora*, v. 188.

[2] *MGH, Epist. Pont.* iii, no. 25, p. 19; Berger, *Les Registres*, no. 4948.

[3] Matthew Paris, *Chronica majora*, v. 190; *Necrologia Panormitana* (*FzDG* xviii, 1878), 474. See also the parallel accounts of Collenuccio and Calco as set forth in F. Güterbock, 'Eine Biographie Friedrichs II.' (*Neues Archiv*, xxx, 1904–5), 78–83. For the cause of Frederick's

If, as Matthew Paris relates, Frederick was clad in the garments of a Cistercian at the time of his absolution, he was much more luxuriously attired at the time of his burial. When, in 1782, his sepulchre was opened, his body was found to be wrapped in rich Arabic fabrics of red silk embroidered with cryptic arabesque designs. On his left shoulder he wore a cross in token of his crusade of 1228–9.[1]

The passing of a dominant and colourful figure such as Frederick II inevitably gave rise to a multitude of legends, associated both with the day of his death and with the fifty-six years of his life. It was said that years before he had been warned in a prophecy that he would die *sub flore* and that, consequently, he had shunned the city of Florence (Florentia) only to find too late that not Firenze (Florentia = Florence), but Firenzuola (Fiorentino) was destined to be the place of his death. An often repeated legend, derived from the *Sibylla-Erythraea*, was that of Frederick's immortality; the unwillingness to accept the report that he, the Antichrist, was dead. For the Erythraean prophecy had said (perhaps meaning only that he survived in his son, in the sense that 'the King never dies'): 'He lives' and 'he does not live'.[2] The belief that Frederick was the Antichrist, so often proclaimed, even by the popes during his lifetime, was widely publicized by the pseudo-Joachimite writings. Only reluctantly did the disciples of Joachim of Floris accept the proof of Frederick's death. Some of them, including Salimbene, who had believed firmly that Frederick was the Antichrist, were disillusioned with regard to all prophesying, while others were convinced that the veritable Antichrist was Alfonso X of Castile.[3]

Legend also associated Frederick's place of retreat with Mount Etna, believed to be the seat of Satan's empire. A Minorite brother, while at

---

death see Nicholas of Carbio, *Vita*, c. xxix, p. 102: 'laborans gravibus dissenteriis'. For the day of Frederick's death see the critical statement of BFW, *Reg.*, v, Abt. i, no. 3835a.

[1] See F. Daniele, *I regali sepolcri del Duomo di Palermo*, 99.

[2] For the Fiorentino legend see R. Malespini (Muratori, *RIS* viii), col. 788; and G. Villani, *Cronica*, vol. ii, ch. xli); also *Anonymi Vaticani Historia Sicula* (Muratori, *RIS* viii), col. 780, and *Franciscus Pipinus, Chron.* (Muratori, *RIS* ix), col. 660. Pertinent also are the extracts from Collenuccio and Calco in F. Güterbock, 'Eine Biographie Friedrichs II.' (*Neues Archiv*, xxx, 1904–5), 79 ff. For Frederick's association with the Antichrist see Salimbene, *Cronica*, pp. 174, 243, and especially 347: 'Hinc fuit, quod multi crediderunt eum non esse mortuum, cum vere mortuus esset; et ex hoc impletum fuit Sibille vaticinium, que dicit: Sonabit et in populis: "Vivit" et "non vivit" et premittit, quod mors eius esset abscondita.'

See also O. Holder-Egger, 'Italienische Prophetieen des 13. Jahrhundert' (*Neues Archiv*, xv, 1889–90), 168: 'Oculos eius morte claudet abscondita supervivetque, sonabit et in populis: "Vivit, non vivit", uno ex pullis pullisque pullorum superstite. Hinc galli cantus usque Trinacrim audietur.' See also idem, *Neues Archiv*, xxx, 1904–5, 334, and xxxiii, 1907–8, 138. Most enlightening on this whole subject is E. Kantorowicz, 'Zu den Rechtsgrundlagen der Kaisersage' (*Deutsches Archiv*, xiii, 1957), 127 ff.

[3] See the remarkable conversation between Salimbene and Brother Ghiradinus de Buego Sancti Donnani in the chronicle of the former (*MGH, SS.* xxxii), 455 ff., and O. Holder-Egger, loc. cit.

prayer in Sicily, reported that he had seen an army of 5,000 horsemen ride into the sea, whereupon, as if these troops were clothed in red-hot armour, a hissing sound arose from the water. One of these horsemen, the leader, was identified in the hallucination of this visionary friar as none other than Frederick II, 'For it was at this moment that Frederick died.'[1]

To Innocent IV the death of his unconquerable foe was a profound relief. 'Let heaven exult and the earth rejoice', he wrote to the prelates, barons, and citizens of Sicily. The papal legate, Peter Capoccio, who had failed in his mission in the Sicilian Kingdom, wrote to the commune of Bologna of the death of the 'prince of darkness'. But it was the papal chaplain, Nicholas of Carbio, who most accurately expressed the satisfaction of the papal party when he wrote:

At length God, from his sacred throne on high, seeing the bark of Peter floundering in the waves and being dashed to pieces by various oppressions and misfortunes, snatched away, in the midst of life, the tyrant and son of Satan, Frederick ... who ... died horribly, deposed and excommunicated, suffering excruciatingly from dysentery, gnashing his teeth, frothing at the mouth, and screaming, at the castle Fiorentino in Apulia, in the year of Our Lord 1250.[2]

Present at the bedside of the dying Emperor were many of his court officials, who apparently had been hastily summoned to Castel Fiorentino. In addition to Archbishop Berard, who had absolved him, there were present also Frederick's son-in-law, Count Richard of Caserta, and his young son Manfred, who wrote to his half-brother, Conrad: 'The sun of the world which illuminated mankind has set—the sun of justice has gone down; the author of peace has passed away.'[3] Present also was the court physician, John of Procida, one of the signatories of Frederick's testament, later to be associated, albeit in a half-legendary role, with the Sicilian Vespers, allegedly as organizer of the Aragonese agents who led the rebellion.[4]

A day or two prior to his death Frederick dictated his will to his notary, Nicholas of Brindisi. Conrad, the eldest surviving son, was to inherit the Empire and the Kingdom, to be succeeded by Henry, the son of Isabella; Manfred was to succeed in the case of the death of both Conrad and Henry. In the event that Conrad remained in Germany

---

[1] *Ex Thomae de Eccleston Libro de Adventu Minorum in Angliam* (*MGH, SS.* xxviii), 568. See also F. Schneider, 'Kaiser Friedrich II. und seine Bedeutung für das Elsass' (*Elsass.-Lothr. Jahrb.* ix, 1930), 149ff.

[2] Nicholas of Carbio, *Vita*, 102. For other reactions of the enemies of Frederick at the report of his death see *MGH, Epist. Pont.* iii. 24, and BFW, *Reg.* v, Abt. iv, no. 13796.

[3] Huillard-Bréholles, vi, part ii, 811.

[4] For a recent treatment of the conflicting opinions concerning John of Procida see S. Runciman, *The Sicilian Vespers* (Cambridge, 1958), 288 ff.

or was otherwise absent from the Kingdom of Sicily, Manfred was
to serve as governor there. Also, Manfred was to receive the principality of Tarento, several counties and other property as fiefs from
Conrad, together with a sum of 10,000 ounces of gold for expenses. A
grandson of the Emperor, Frederick, son of the late Henry (VII), was
to become Duke of Austria and the March of Styria, and Henry, the
son of Isabella of England, was to have either the Kingdom of Arles
or the Kingdom of Jerusalem, the choice to be left to Conrad. In addition, Henry was to receive 100,000 ounces of gold for the reconquest of
the Kingdom of Jerusalem. After making various bequests, restitutions
of property, abatements of taxes, and release of prisoners (excepting
traitors), the Emperor devised that the property of the Church was to
be restored, save that which would impinge upon the rights or compromise the honour of the Empire.[1] He stipulated also that, if the
present illness should prove fatal, his body was to be entombed in the
Cathedral of Palermo beside his parents, the Emperor Henry VI
and the Empress Constance. There he reposes in a red porphyry
sarcophagus, originally intended for King Roger II. The sarcophagus
is mounted upon four cryptically carved lions, 'closely related to Oriental
prototypes', and reflecting antique, Byzantine, and Islamic influences.
The supporting lions, although originally symbolizing the victories of
Roger II, are, like the lions surmounting the columns of the portals of
the Castel del Monte, appropriate emblems of Frederick II.[2]

[1] *MGH, Const.* ii, no. 274, pp. 382–9.
[2] For an excellent study of this and other tombs see J. Deér, 'The Dynastic Porphyry
Tombs of the Norman Period in Sicily' (*Dumbarton Oaks Studies*, v, 1959).

EPILOGUE

FREDERICK II has been subjected to the most varied and conflicting judgements by his contemporaries and by historians of succeeding generations. In his own time he was depicted as both paragon and monster: 'the wonder of the world' and 'the bloodthirsty tyrant', 'the author of peace' and 'the scourge and hammer of the earth', 'the sun of the world illuminating mankind' and the 'Antichrist'. And yet the bitterest of his contemporary foes recognized in him supreme courage, exceptional learning, unparalleled capacity for 'apprehension through his potential intellect'. By some of his more intimate associates, aware of his true virtues, he was praised for his 'noble heart'. Simple and pious men saw in him a unique figure, destined to bring about justice upon earth. They believed implicitly that after death he would return to restore and purify the corrupt and decaying Church, to punish the wicked clergy, to redistribute wealth, to bestow upon widows and orphans the comforts of which they had been deprived.

To the learned men of succeeding generations he appeared, in the words of Boccaccio, as 'Marviglioso Uomo' and 'Gran Letterato'. Benvenuto of Imola said of him, 'no emperor since Charles the Great was more brilliant or more powerful, even though he was more concerned with terrestrial than with celestial things'. But it is a tragedy of history, indeed of life itself, that the evil of which men are accused inevitably survives and flourishes in the minds of succeeding generations more readily than their virtuous and noble deeds. It is doubtless the recognition of this that has caused more recent historians, at times, to exaggerate the virtues and to minimize the evil deeds of Frederick II. With Burckhardt they are wont to see in him 'the first modern man on the throne', or else to accept the observation of E. A. Freeman that 'it is probable there never lived a human being with greater natural gifts, or whose natural gifts were, according to the means afforded him by the age, more sedulously cultivated'. It is but natural when confronted by the presence of Frederick II in the thirteenth century that one is constrained, by the very singularity of his attributes, to associate him with the Renaissance rather than with the Middle Ages. But it is misleading to insist unduly upon the presence of Renaissance attributes in isolated individuals. The term is properly applied to or descriptive of a movement, not sporadic but continuous. But Frederick was not part of a continuous movement. Like Dante, St. Thomas

Aquinas, and Roger Bacon, he belongs to no movement and to no era. He was neither Medieval nor Renaissance—nor was he Modern. He revealed attributes of all these eras, but he belonged to none. More recent historians, aware of the dangers of associating him too narrowly with any era, have satisfied themselves with the less definite characterization, 'stupor mundi Fredericus', or with such descriptive phrases as 'the amazing Frederick', or 'transformer of the world'. It is unnecessary to conceal the vices or the evil deeds of Frederick II in order to appraise his virtues. A great danger is that he will be judged in conformity with moral and ethical standards approved by our own era. A still greater danger is that, out of respect for a religious ideal, the biographer may be unwilling to recognize in the popes and cardinals of the thirteenth century the very same vices that he discovers so abundantly in Frederick II. The conflict of papacy and Empire waged, on the one hand, by such Popes as Innocent III, Gregory IX, and Innocent IV and, on the other, by Frederick II, his sons, and his adherents, affords little opportunity for favourable moral judgements on either party to the conflict. Greed, ambition, faithlessness, unscrupulousness, ruthlessness are attributes displayed by papal and imperial parties alike. It was the advantage of the Pope that, as the Vicar of Christ, his actions, however evil or ambitious in appearance, could be legitimately weighed only on his own scales of justice. The problem of judging Frederick's conduct accurately is complicated by the difficulty of finding in his ecclesiastical antagonists the preoccupation with spiritual interests which is to be expected in those who presume to be the representatives of Christ and the successors of the First of the Apostles.

It is no disparagement of the qualities of greatness of Frederick II to suggest that there was in his conduct a median between the extremes of virtue and wickedness, of superiority and depravity. The qualities of greatness in biographies are measured generally in terms of achievements in statesmanship, in military prowess, in scientific accomplishments, in conspicuous attainments in the realms of the arts and letters, or in other outstanding services to mankind. Few men achieve greatness in all or even in several of these realms of action. It is a distinguishing attribute of Frederick II that he achieved greatness in most of them and that, in a sense, he identified himself with all of them. Among the most admirable of his accomplishments was his statesmanship: superior wisdom in directing public affairs, together with exceptional aptitude in associating himself with men highly skilled in the art of government. An eternal monument to each of these is his *Liber Augustalis* or *Constitutiones*, embodying the loftiest concepts of government and exemplifying the noblest principles of law. Here are brought together in discriminating manner the best of Anglo-Norman, Byzantine, Arabic, and ancient Roman law. But most of all, the *Liber Augustalis* embodies a wealth of human experience and the mature wisdom of judiciously trained men—principles of legislation which, in defiance of misguided tradition, embodied new concepts capable of furthering the achievements of mankind. It is a tribute to Frederick that many of the most worthy principles and administrative procedures of his *Constitutiones* have survived in the governmental systems of the modern world.

No less permanent were Frederick's achievements as scholar and as patron of scholars. Supreme among his scholarly attributes was his intellectual integrity, his willingness to break through the most cherished traditions, to question the established concepts of faith, if these were obviously obstacles to truth. A single sentence of his *De Arte Venandi cum Avibus* serves to establish his position among the scholars of the ages: 'Our work is to represent things that are as they are.' No less significant is another of his utterances, so defiant of the intellectual standards of his age: 'One should accept as truth only that which is proved by nature and by the force of reason.' Indeed, a remark of his which signals a turning-point from Western man's subserviency to tradition and his approach to the methods of modern science appears in the Preface of his book on falconry: 'We discovered by hard-won experience that the deductions of Aristotle, which we followed when they appealed to our reason, were not entirely to be relied upon.' With this remark Frederick stood, intellectually, in opposition to his age, invited the condemnation of the tradition-minded theocracy of the thirteenth century, made himself liable to the relentless hostile propaganda of the Roman Church. While not alone in his century in the search for truth, Frederick was conspicuous in that he alone among the sovereigns of the era dared to support these concepts against the obstinate resistance of the prevailing dogmatism. It is only regrettable that he, in his enlightened search for truth, in his exaltation of the intellectual potentialities of mankind, did not, in the manner of St. Thomas Aquinas, recognize that there may be realms of impenetrable mystery which the mind of man is incapable of exploring.

But far more important than his own ventures into the realms of science and learning was Frederick's incomparable service as patron of scholars: philosophers, mathematicians, natural scientists, and of poets. He alone among the sovereigns of his era seems to have recognized that scientific discoveries may briefly flourish and as quickly perish, if left in isolation, the singular achievements of obscure individuals. It was one of his supreme services and one of his greatest attributes as sovereign, that he sought out the true scholars of his age, regardless of place of residence, of race, or religion, or condition of life, and brought them together at his court or, if unable to bring them there in person, invited their scholarly contributions through continuous correspondence. For the first time in Western Europe in the Middle Ages Jews, Muslims, and Christians were encouraged by sovereign authority, and by an emperor who was himself a scholar, to explore jointly the fields of learning. Even more than in Spain, the language barrier was swept away at the Sicilian court and, what is far more important, the obstacles of racial and religious prejudices were reduced to a minimum. The search for truth was temporarily unimpeded by the seemingly impenetrable wall of tradition.

As in scientific scholarship, so also in belles-lettres the influence of Frederick II was great as it was permanent. Deeply sensitive to literary style himself, whether in poetry or in prose, and versatile in his use of languages—Latin and Greek, French and German, Arabic and Italian —he made his court a veritable magnet for the literati of all lands. Under his patronage there flourished schools of Latin poetry, or Latin prose style, and, even more significant, a new school of the vernacular, the cradle of the Italian language and literature.

If, indeed, one is tempted to see in Frederick II a man of the Renaissance, this is most vividly suggested by his artistic interests, especially in architecture and in sculpture. Like his Renaissance successors, he found his criterion of artistic taste in the models preserved from antiquity. It is impossible to contemplate the mutilated remnants of his magnificent bridge-tower at Capua without recognizing the extraordinary impact of antiquity upon his artistic tastes. In the splendid sculptural works, the ruins of the statue of Frederick himself, the busts probably erroneously believed to be representations of his high court justices, Piero della Vigna and Thaddeus of Suessa, in the colossal feminine bust, plausibly conjectured as symbolizing the *Justitia Caesaris*, there is apparent indisputable evidence of antique inspiration. And yet there are present also certain traditional motifs of the Middle Ages, clear evidence of the duality of Frederick's tastes. He, like Dante, although finding in antiquity more perfect models, was not oblivious of the enduring artistry of the Middle Ages.

There is an unfortunate tendency in biography, as in history, to attribute to men of conspicuous achievement in some field or fields of endeavour the quality of greatness in all things. Thus Frederick II has often been adjudged a great soldier. And yet one searches in vain through the records of his well-nigh continuous warfare for most of the attributes essential to a great soldier. In his early years of conflict with his imperial rival Otto IV he won not a single victory on the field of battle. His conquest of northern Germany in 1213, undertaken with a force of some 60,000 men, far superior in numbers to the forces of

Otto, ended in humiliating failure. He had neglected the first requirement of a successful expeditionary force: continuous access to necessary provisions and supplies. During more than six years of unremitting war with Otto such success as Frederick achieved came not as a result of superior military prowess, but solely through fortuitous circumstances. Only the death of Otto IV from natural causes, but while securely entrenched behind the walls of his city of Brunswick, freed Frederick from the Welf threat. In Italy his wars with the cities of the Lombard League ended, with but few exceptions, in disastrous failures. His one conspicuous success, his victory at Cortenuova, was actually a minor triumph the significance of which Frederick and his partisans exaggerated out of all proportions. In contrast with this, his operations against Brescia and Parma, characterized by carelessness and ineptitude, were shocking failures. As Emperor of the Holy Roman Empire, possessing superior resources, he was powerless to subdue permanently the least formidable of the cities of the Lombard League. Successful as was his expedition to the Holy Land when measured by its accomplishment of the desired end, this was achieved, not through military skill, but through diplomacy and, one might add, as a result of serious disunity among the Arabs. His successful reconquest of the Kingdom of Sicily after his return from the crusade was not marked by spectacular military success. Much more, it was the result of the loyalty of the citizens themselves and of the feeble effort of the papal armies when informed of Frederick's return. The mere knowledge of his presence among them was a far more decisive factor than his military operations. In short, any analysis of Frederick as a military leader could result only in an unfavourable judgement. The only excuse and the only extenuating circumstances which might be advanced as the causes of his want of greatness in military achievement are that neither the science of logistics nor the effectiveness of siege-weapons had developed sufficiently to make possible either a large-scale military expedition or a successful siege-operation against a well-fortified city.

In a man of transcendent superiority, however, in so many realms of action, such as Frederick II was, the want of military greatness, at best of transient significance, is of relatively minor importance. Far more important as a contribution to cultural progress were Frederick's efforts to define and to separate the legitimate spheres of action of the *sacerdotium* and the *imperium*. He alone among the sovereigns of the first half of the thirteenth century perceived the danger inherent in the temporal ambitions of the papacy. He saw this not merely as an encroachment on the prerogatives of the temporal princes, but as a destructive force to the spiritual office itself. Like Joachim of Floris and St. Francis of Assisi, Frederick was deeply aware of this weakness and sought vigorously to check it. In this effort, however, he was far in advance of his age. Clearly and forcefully as he depicted this growing danger to his contemporaries among the princes, he was powerless, against the weight of tradition, to make his warning heard.

While it is difficult to determine accurately the religious beliefs of Frederick II, it is always apparent that he was not antagonistic to the Christian religion. Actually he saw in Christianity something far more spiritual than it had become in the interpretation of contemporary theologians, canonists, and popes. The irrational conduct of Pope Gregory IX with regard to Frederick's crusading efforts of the years 1227–9; the obvious unfairness of Pope Innocent IV in choosing the constituent members of the so-called General Council, summoned with the predetermined intention of condemning and deposing the Emperor; the complicity of Innocent IV in the conspiracy and, probably, in the murder plot against Frederick; and, finally, the Pope's open defiance of all constitutional procedure in setting up Henry Raspe and, after his death, William of Holland, as German Kings—all of these could serve only to subject the Holy See to the gravest suspicions as to its motives and methods. At no point in the conflict is it possible to find in Frederick's utterances evidence of opposition to the papal office. Always he studiously avoided attacks on the office, but levelled them at what he believed to be the misguided efforts of individual popes to usurp the temporal authority of the Emperor. Perhaps as early as his first excommunication in 1227, and the continued persecution by the Pope after he had obtained possession of the Holy City, Frederick recognized that the sacred office of the papacy could, at times, fall into the hands of the most worldly and ambitious of men. Whatever else Frederick's attitude may have been towards Gregory IX and Innocent IV, he could not, as a rational human being, continue to regard them with reverence or look upon them as worthy vicars of God. While providing an explanation of his hostility toward his papal antagonists, the procedures of Gregory IX and Innocent IV do not render less reprehensible Frederick's own acts of retaliation. His treatment of the captive prelates, seized when *en route* to a General Council, his encroachments upon the rights and privileges of the clergy which he had repeatedly sworn to protect—these and innumerable misdeeds committed in the name of vengeance leave no room for favourable moral or ethical judgements of his relations with his antagonists. On the other hand, there could never be an objective or unbiased judgement of the guilt or innocence of the opposing parties if the popes and their adherents were permitted, because of their sacerdotal association, to claim immunity to the moral and ethical codes to which Frederick II and his partisans are habitually subjected.

The hostile attitude of Frederick towards individuals who had been elevated to the papal office, together with the tolerant spirit displayed by him toward non-Christian peoples, has at times given rise to the charge that he was more favourably disposed towards the Muslim faith than towards Christianity. This charge has no foundation in fact. There can be no question that he saw much in the Islamic faith to admire, or, more accurately, he saw much to admire in the intellectual and moral outlook of many votaries of Islam. He admired especially the unequivocal acceptance by his Muslim associates of the methods of the natural sciences and their intelligent appreciation of the scholarly and scientific achievements of Greek antiquity. To a mind such as that of Frederick II the timid and fearful utilization of antique science and learning by medieval Christianity could only have given rise to the conviction that, intellectually, his fellow Christians were in a far more primitive stage of development than were their Muslim contemporaries. To a man of the unfettered faculties of Frederick II, of his cosmopolitan outlook, of his instinctive tolerance of the ideas of non-Christian peoples, even though contrary to the accepted doctrines of Christendom, the flourishing scientific learning of Islamic lands could have evoked only sentiments of sympathy and approval.

To our era there is nothing either shocking or incomprehensible in the religious views of Frederick II. To him religion could be only spiritual. Any venture of its leaders into the realm of the temporal inevitably invited corruption and decay. There could be no place in Western society for an organized religion the leader of which contemplated both temporal and spiritual supremacy. In this regard Frederick's attitude was merely prophetic of future generations. He could comprehend only a religion wholly spiritual in outlook, but recognizing in the temporal head of the state its divinely ordained protector. The unmistakable clue to his concept of the relationship of the temporal and spiritual authorities, of the *imperium* and the *ecclesia*, is to be found in his *Liber Augustalis*. There it is always apparent that the association of these two institutions is comparable to that of body and soul. The body complements the soul even as the soul gives spiritual motivation to the body. Frederick never ceased to recognize that the light of the sun to which he, like his papal antagonists, compared the spiritual authority, was greater than the reflected light of the moon, which was the light of the Emperor. At the same time he insisted that each of these, in accordance with the will of their Creator, was designed to move independently within its own orbit, never impinging upon the sphere of the other. The superiority of the Pope lay solely in the greater intensity of his spiritual enlightenment, not in his temporal power.

The unrestrained bitterness of Frederick toward the popes who opposed him, often expressing itself in violent hatred and in ruthless acts of vengeance, originated solely in his belief that the Pope, in the guise of God's Vicar on earth, and oblivious of his spiritual obligations towards mankind, was determined to appropriate to himself the God-ordained functions of the Emperor. His concept of the essential equality in the sight of God of the *imperium* and the *ecclesia* explains also Frederick's attitude towards heresy. Whosoever opposed the order ordained of God upon earth was guilty of heresy. But the Emperor and the Empire, no less than the Pope and the Church, were a part of the Divine Order. The Emperor, as the guardian of the Church and as the arbiter of justice upon earth, was obligated to punish those who presumed to oppose what God had ordained. Opposition to, or the rejection of, either the spiritual authority of the Church or the temporal authority of the Empire was heretical. It was the function of the Pope to decree the punishment to be imposed upon those who defied the spiritual order, just as it was a function of the Emperor to decree the penalty to be imposed upon those who defied the temporal authority. But in each case it was the function of the Emperor to inflict the punishment. Here is to be found the explanation of Frederick's willingness, although seemingly contrary to his intelligence and to his instinctive tolerance, to consign to the flames those unfortunate individuals who, scornful of all earthly authority, professed obedience to God alone. At no time did Frederick question the Pope's spiritual jurisdiction over him or over other princes of Christendom. What he did question and what he opposed with all the resources at his command was the Pope's employment of spiritual punishment as a means of compelling the surrender of temporal prerogatives which Frederick regarded as the sacred responsibility of kings and emperors. Even his unrestrained ruthlessness towards the Lombard cities and his brutal treatment of prisoners taken in the Lombard wars and in other conflicts in Italy often originated in his conviction that their resistance was inspired by the machinations of the Pope or his legatine agents. There were few characteristics of Frederick II that the Pope resented more than the extreme dignity that he as Emperor imparted to the sovereign authority of a temporal prince. By Frederick's insistence that he as Emperor was arbiter of justice upon earth, he defied the long-cherished concept of the canonists that justice is that which the Pope decrees.

Certainly it was Frederick's desire to employ his rare gifts peacefully, and to do so with the aid of the Church. He believed that the Empire must rest upon a foundation sustained by the joint efforts of Pope and Emperor, of *ecclesia* and *imperium*. His desire to reform the outward structure of the Church has led to the popular misconception that he had Caesaro-papal ambitions, that he sought to grasp in his own hands the spiritual as well as the temporal government of the earth. Far from this, there is abundant evidence in his writings: in his *Liber Augustalis*, in his letters, and his laws, that his concept of World Empire contemplated a dual administration of Pope and Emperor, which he believed to be inherent in the teachings of Gelasius in the fifth century of the Christian era. Thus Frederick saw the Church, not as a universal state, or as a state within a state, but as the spiritual agency responsible for the ultimate salvation of the Christians within a temporal state in which the Emperor was the divinely ordained head, but subject, spiritually, to the guidance of the Pope. As opposed to this, Innocent III and his successors in the thirteenth century visualized an all-powerful 'State of the Church', thus making impossible the co-operation of temporal and spiritual authorities. As Emperor, Frederick was forced to strengthen the bonds of temporal union of Germany, Italy, and Sicily. It has often been observed that the summoning of Frederick II from Sicily by the Pope to become King of the Romans and Emperor made inevitable the territorial conflict which followed. Save through a firm union of Germany, Italy, and Sicily, a temporal Empire would have been impossible. Their union in the hands of the Pope, or their temporal as well as spiritual dominance by the Pope, could have resulted only in the elimination of the Emperor as an obstacle to the papal ambitions. Yet in reviewing this tedious history of territorial conflict, it is apparent that neither Pope nor Emperor could have emerged as permanent victor. The insuperable difficulties of uniting Sicily and Germany, or Italy and Germany—of welding together German principalities and Italian communes, Sicilian traditional absolutism and German regional particularism, made impossible any successful effort towards unification. The time had long since passed when it would have been possible—if indeed it ever was possible—to check either the growing independence of the German principalities or of the Italian communes. If at times each of these appeared to be subservient to the will of the Pope, this was because, for the moment, the support of the papacy was useful in checking the more immediate threat of imperial dominance. The historical sequel was soon to give proof that a permanent alliance with Rome was irksome to principalities and communes alike. Independence, unhampered and complete, was the goal of each.

Frederick II has no counterpart or near counterpart in history. He was a man of pronounced individuality in an age that insisted upon conformity. It was his unwillingness to accept this, his insistent opposition to it, that made possible his astonishing achievements. Only his imperial goal was beyond his reach—beyond the reach of any man. The task that lay before him from the moment of his summons from Sicily to Germany was an impossible one. It was not within the power of a single individual, nor was it possible in the limited span of a human life, to accomplish what Frederick had emphasized in the preamble of his *Liber Augustalis* as within the power of the Emperor: to change the condition of his age. He might make new laws, or even point the way to a change and an improvement in mankind's habits of life and thought, but time alone could bring to fruition his ambitious plans, no matter how clearly, when seen in retrospect, they reflect his superior wisdom.

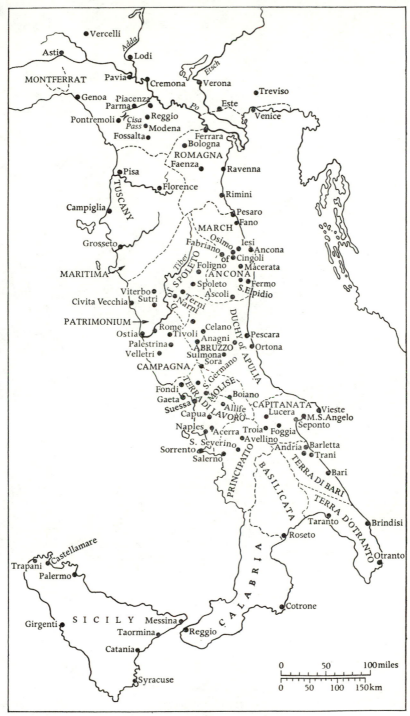

MAP 5. Italy in the era of the Hohenstaufen

SOURCES AND BIBLIOGRAPHY

COMMENTARY ON THE PRIMARY SOURCES

I. THE GERMAN SOURCES

Chronicles and Related Sources

Virtually all German chronicles or annals of the thirteenth century are of some use in relation to the Frederician era. The following list includes only the most useful ones.

Basic to any study of the German sources for the Hohenstaufen era are the two works of Otto of Freising: his *Chronica* or *Historia de Duabus Civitatibus* (ed. A. Hofmeister in *SRG in usum scholarum*) and *Gesta Friderici Imperatoris* (ed. G. Waitz, ibid.). In these two works we have not only the high point in the development of historiography of the twelfth century, but an account of the life and achievements of Frederick Barbarossa that is an essential introduction to the policies of the Hohenstaufen era as a whole.

By virtue of Otto's exceptional education (chiefly in Paris), his tenure as Abbot of the Cistercian monastery of Morimond in Burgundy, his advantageous position as Bishop of Freising, but, most of all, his kinship and intimate association with both the Margrave of Austria and the Swabian Hohenstaufen, his record of the events of Barbarossa's reign, to the year 1157, is of the greatest possible value.

Otto's philosophy of history, which reflects the views of Augustine and Orosius, is discernible not only in the policies and concepts of Barbarossa, but to some degree projects itself also into those of Frederick II. Though Otto's philosophy in his *Chronica* is deeply pessimistic, other-worldly to a degree, and anticipating the imminent end of the world, the advent of Frederick I opened a new and optimistic outlook. Moreover, the influence of Otto is strikingly apparent in the work of succeeding German chroniclers, a salutary influence upon the historiography of the thirteenth century.

Few chroniclers of the Middle Ages were as fortunate in their continuators as was Otto of Freising. In Rahewin, or Ragewin, he had a faithful protégé who, in the *Gesta*, maintained the quality of the content and of the literary structure of his own work throughout the years 1157–60. It is difficult to trace the transition from master to disciple: the distinguishing characteristic is to be found merely in Rahewin's strict attention to historical narrative and in the complete absence of the philosophizing which was the hallmark of his master. As contemporary biography the work of each is unequalled in the Middle Ages.

Another Otto, he of St. Blaise, proved a worthy continuator of the *Chronica* in annalistic form to 1209: *Ottonis de Sancto Blasio Chronica* (ed. A. Hofmeister in *SRG in usum scholarum*). His method regularly reflects that of his predecessor and master. Like Otto of Freising, Otto of St. Blaise also was influenced by the historians of Roman antiquity, thus fostering the concept that the sovereignty of Germany was a continuation of that of the Caesars—a concept that was to permeate the German chroniclers of the thirteenth century and to appear consistently in the policies of both Henry VI and Frederick II.

To an astonishing extent, Otto of St. Blaise managed to appear to maintain a nonpartisan view, although he was unmistakably in fact a strong Staufen partisan. His capacity for objectivity is apparent throughout his *Chronica*, notably when he is writing about Otto of Brunswick; when the tide turned in favour of Philip of Swabia he continued his narrative with equal objectivity. It is regrettable, therefore, that his *Chronica* ends with Otto of Brunswick's succession in 1209, although he continued as Abbot of St. Blaise until his death in 1223.

No less important for the same years, and for the succeeding years to 1249, is the *Chronica regia Coloniensis* (ed. G. Waitz in *SRG in usum scholarum*). Although conceived by its original unknown author as a record of world events from the era of Adam and Eve, it became, after 1144, in the hands of a variety of Colognese authors, an intimate record of the activities of the Hohenstaufen kings and emperors, reflecting not only the importance of Cologne as the foremost German city culturally and economically but also, and more importantly, providing an intimate record of Frederick Barbarossa, Reginald of Dassel, Henry VI, Philip of Swabia, Otto of Brunswick, Henry (VII), and Frederick II to 1249.

Its several authors were, without exception, intimately associated with the royal court. Edited variously as *Annales maximi Colonienses* (*MGH, SS.* xvii) and as *Chronica regia Coloniensis*, as noted above, it is the most important of all the German chronicles of the Hohenstaufen era.

A source of importance for the thirteenth century, and a valuable supplement to the *Chronica regia Coloniensis*, is the *Vita sancti Engelberti Archiepiscopi Coloniensis*, historically the most important work of Caesar of Heisterbach (ed. J. F. Böhmer in *Fontes*, ii). Its author, a monk in the monastery of Heisterbach in the Siebengebirge or Seven Hills, not far from Bonn, was a man of superior education, refinement, and charm. He was at times closely associated with Archbishop Engelbert and was much at home in the city of Cologne. A penetrating observer, he described Engelbert's virtues and foibles entertainingly and not without a sense of humour. For the years of the minority of Henry (VII) and for the events in Germany during the regency, his *Vita* is indispensable.

A second work of Caesar of Heisterbach, his *Dialogus Miraculorum* (ed. J. Strange) is of lesser importance historically, but is not without value as a preserver of the legendary and the miraculous—a monkish interpreter of the events of the era, evangelistic, visionary, mythological, as well as fabulous. It is a Cistercian outlook on the world. Historically, the work is useful for the 'Hungerjahre' of the late twelfth century in Germany, for its portraits of Bernhard of Saxony and Berthold as possible Kings of the Romans following the death of Henry VI.

Of comparable importance to the *Chronica regia Coloniensis*, although obviously biased in favour of the Hohenstaufen, is *Burchardi Praepositi Urspergensis Chronicon* (ed. O. Holder-Egger and B. von Simson in *SRG in usum scholarum*). It is of special value as a source from 1152 to 1228, although often a bitter critic of papal policies. It is of great usefulness for the conflict of Philip of Swabia and Otto of Brunswick, for the election of Frederick II by the German princes, and for his coronation as Emperor in 1220. It continues to be useful for the excommunication of Frederick in 1227 and for the beginning of the crusade in 1228. Its author, an abbot of Ursperg, was a native of Biberach in Württemberg, south of the city of Ulm, and was an eyewitness to various events in the time of Innocent III.

The *Annales Marbacenses* (ed. H. Bloch in *SRG in usum scholarum*), the Alsatian *Annales* of the Hohenstaufen era, is a strongly partisan work, favouring the Hohenstaufen. Notwithstanding its bias, it is of the greatest value, notably for Henry VI's conquest of Sicily, the Sicilian conspiracy of 1197, the conflict of Philip of Swabia and Otto of Brunswick. The author was an unknown monk of the Monastery of Neuburg near Hagenau. He is thought to have been present at Strassburg in 1186 when a crusade was preached in the presence of Barbarossa and to have witnessed the departure of Henry VI for the conquest of Sicily in 1194. He reveals a special admiration for Philip of Swabia, probably because of the latter's intended ecclesiastical career. The *Annales* continues to 1238 and is especially valuable for its eyewitness accounts.

Closely associated with Frederick Barbarossa as imperial notary and, to a lesser degree, with Henry VI, was Godfrey of Viterbo (1120–96), born in Germany, although sometimes described as a native of Viterbo. He was unquestionably educated in Bamberg. A prolific writer, Godfrey's one work of historical importance is his *Gesta Friderici I* (ed. G. Waitz, together with Godfrey's *Pantheon* and a *Gesta Heinrici VI* attributed to Godfrey, and other works, in *MGH, SS.* xxii). His poetical *Vita* describes the deeds of Barbarossa between 1155 and 1180, many of which Godfrey witnessed, either in the company of the Emperor or as ambassador in the service of the latter in Sicily, Provence, Spain, France, and elsewhere. His *Pantheon* is of lesser value historically, but influential in the perpetuation of legendary material. Both these works are chiefly important in the present study of Frederick II for background material.

Another poetical work, useful in much the same way as that of Godfrey of Viterbo, is the *Ligurinus*, a heroic poem describing in great detail the events of the life of Frederick Barbarossa up to 1160 (ed. C. C. Bümge, Heidelberg, 1812; see also Migne, *PL* 212, for *Ligurium, sive de Rebus Gestis Impr. Caesaris Friderici Aug.*). Attributed, but doubtfully, to Gunther of Paris, and obviously written in an effort to win the favour of Barbarossa and his sons, it is chiefly valuable for its enlightening remarks about the education of the latter.

For northern Germany, Saxony, and Thuringia there are several sources of value both monastic and municipal. Chief among them is *Arnoldi Abbatis Lubecensis Chronicon* (ed. I. M. Lappenberg in *MGH, SS.* xxi). It is a continuation of *Helmoldi Presbyteri Bozoviensis Cronica Slavorum* from 1209. Apart from its special significance for Henry the Lion, it assumes a place of first importance, as a source after the submission of Henry, for the crusade and death of Frederick Barbarossa, the succession of Henry VI and his conquest of Sicily, the conspiracy of 1197 against Henry VI, and his death. A strong feature of the *Chronicon* is its account of the conflict of Philip of Swabia and Otto of Brunswick, the murder of Philip, the Diet of Frankfurt of 1208, and the consecration of Otto as Emperor. Though loosely organized, it is a well-informed and highly useful chronicle.

Among the sources for northern Germany is the *Chronica Reinhardsbrunnensis* (originally ed. Wegele, ed. O. Holder-Egger, in *MGH, SS.* xxx). Although essentially a compilatory chronicle, it is outstanding for its wealth of material. Like most medieval chronicles of northern Germany, it is characterized by a certain provincialism, leading to very full accounts of regional events and to a tendency to abbreviate external events, save when Otto of Brunswick, Hermann and Louis of Thuringia, and other personages of Saxony and Thuringia are involved. Accordingly, it is a source of importance for the double election and the ensuing conflict of Otto of Brunswick and Philip of Swabia. Other events treated reliably and in adequate detail are the election, deposition, and concluding years of Otto of Brunswick, the arrival of Frederick II in Rome in 1212, his policy of generosity upon entering Germany, and his relations with the King of France. It is also an extremely useful source for the abortive crusade of 1227 and the death of Louis of Thuringia in Otranto and, consequently, a prime source for Elizabeth of Thuringia and for the activities of Conrad of Marburg.

Similarly provincial is the *Cronica S. Petri Erfordensis Moderna* (ed. O. Holder-Egger in *MGH, SS.* xxx). In large part a compilatory and excerptive chronicle, it is a source of importance for northern Germany. Brief in its treatment of the crusade and death of Frederick Barbarossa and such external events as Henry VI's expeditions to Sicily in 1191 and 1194, it is quite full when dealing with ecclesiastical affairs in the Landgravate of Thuringia. It is a good source for the conflict of Otto of Brunswick and

Philip of Swabia, for the murder of Philip, and for the brief succession and early deposition of Otto of Brunswick. Characteristically, however, when personages of Saxony and Thuringia are not involved, it is inadequate in recording such events as Frederick II's crusade in 1227–8. It is an essential source for the heresies in Germany from 1232, for the activities of Conrad of Marburg, and for the translation of the body of Elizabeth of Thuringia. With similar provincialism, it is useful on the election of Henry Raspe of Thuringia as a papal selection to succeed the deposed Emperor, Frederick II.

The *Annales Stadenses* (ed. I. M. Lappenberg in *MGH, SS*. xvi) extends, as the author says, 'abcondito orbe usque ad annum Jesu Christi 1256'. Its author, born during the mid twelfth century and originally a monk in Rosenfeld, became in 1240 abbot of the Benedictine monastery at Stade. It was apparently about this time that he began his chronicle, which continues to 1256; it was later extended to 1264. Like most annals of that era, the earlier part of the work is based upon such works as Bede's *Historia Ecclesiastica*, the Chronicle of Ekkehard, the *Sächsische Weltchronik*, and others. Many entries in the chronicle are merely brief notices which leave much to be desired in the way of detail. Moreover, these annalistic notices often prove unreliable when checked against other sources, all the more so because of the author's inclusion of the fabulous and the miraculous. Despite these defects, however, the work is useful for the era of Frederick II, at least for the years 1240–50.

The *Sächsische Weltchronik* (ed. L. Weiland *MGH, Deutsch. Chron.* ii) is the oldest prose account of world history in the German language. Like most of the so-called World Chronicles of the Middle Ages, the early part relies heavily upon the Chronicle of Ekkehard and similar works. From approximately 1237 much of the useful material is the author's own and reflects his own observations and, obviously, his authentic knowledge of the included material. It is unfortunate that the observed events are often treated scantily as if the author was fearful of prevaricating or misinforming. This results also in his giving the impression of knowing much more than he reveals.

He is likely to be uncritical of his early sources, incorporating them in his own work as though there could be no question of their authenticity. With equal assurance he includes the fabulous and the miraculous which he finds in these earlier sources. On the other hand, he seems always to shun the fabulous and the miraculous in writing of contemporary events. He is shrewd in his judgements of the conflict between the popes and the emperors and succeeds, for the most part, in maintaining his objectivity. There are times when this attempt to avoid partisanship results in a paucity of detail; it leaves much to be desired in his account of such events as the excommunication and deposition of Frederick II. Perhaps because of his access to more complete information, his account of the capture of King Waldemar of Denmark and the ensuing negotiation is surprisingly detailed.

Among the German municipal chronicles in the German language the *Magdeburger Schöppenchronik* (ed. K. Janicke) is useful for supplementary and corroborative purposes. Written much later than the events which it describes, the chronicle is largely dependent upon earlier sources, in particular Eike von Repgow in the *Sächsische Weltchronik* for materials relating to the Hohenstaufen era. It is useful for the years 1212 to 1218 as a supplementary source for the events in northern Germany, especially Otto of Brunswick's attacks on the Archbishop of Magdeburg and for Frederick II's expedition to aid the Archbishop, his ally.

Although not a chronicle, the *Conceptbuch und Regesten Papst Innocenz IV.* of Alberius Archdeacon of Passau (ed. C. Höfler) is an essential source for papal relations with Germany in the years following the second excommunication of Frederick II in 1239. The Archbishop, better known as Albert von Beham (Bohemia), was in fact of Bavarian origin and assumed, or was given, the appellation 'Beham' because of his occasional residences in Bohemia. He served as papal and curial counsellor or *advocatus* under Popes Innocent III and Honorius III and in 1239–40 he was sent by Pope Gregory IX as legate to Germany, charged with destroying the prestige of Frederick II there. He was especially active in that capacity during the Diet of Eger following the excommunication and is, therefore, a first-rate source for the papal policies of that era and for the reaction of the German clergy and people. He was again active at the papal court under Innocent IV during the Council of Lyons. His intimate knowledge of the relations of Frederick II with four popes during the thirteenth century, as well as his knowledge of conditions in Germany, makes him, although highly partisan as a papal favourite, an invaluable source for the conflict between Pope and Emperor.

For Lorraine, the *Reineri Annales* (ed. Pertz, *MGH, SS*. xvi) is a source of great value for a limited period. Beginning with the year 1194, it is a continuation of the *Annales Lamberti Parvi*, also edited by Pertz in the same volume. It is primarily useful for the years preceding 1220; thereafter it is of questionable reliability. While of some use for the period of Otto of Brunswick and Philip of Swabia, it is of exceptional value for the years 1212 to 1215, for the battle of Bouvines, for the coronation of Frederick II in Aachen, for his tribute to Charles the Great, and for the peaceful submission of Cologne. It is probable that Reiner witnessed some of these events. Of equal importance is his report on the Diet of Frankfurt and the election of Henry (VII) as King of the Romans. Reiner was a penetrating and much-travelled observer and a faithful reporter.

The *Annales Wormatienses* (assembled by Böhmer, *MGH, SS*. xvii) was written by various municipal officials and is, in large measure, an authorized or official record of the city of Worms, but, incidentally, of considerablei mportance for Germany as a whole. In its present form the work is a mosaic of fragments of varying condition. Nevertheless it is an important and usable source for the Empire as well as for Germany and the city during the eras of Philip of Swabia, Frederick II, and Henry (VII). It is most useful for the years of conflict between Frederick II and his recalcitrant son Henry (VII), for the inquisitorial persecutions, and for the murder of Conrad of Marburg, for Frederick's visit to Germany in 1235, and for the punishment of Henry (VII) during the Diet of Worms.

The poetry of Walther von der Vogelweide and the troubadours is also a useful source for various episodes in the life of Frederick II. The closeness of Walther to the court circles from the time of Frederick Barbarossa to Frederick II enabled him to depict in his *Sprüche* the conflicts of Welfs and Hohenstaufen, the papal–imperial conflict, and various episodes of the crusades.

So too the troubadours, especially Aimeric de Peguilhan, and Guillem de Figueira, create in their poetry something of the friendly atmosphere in Germany into which the 'boy of Apulia' was welcomed. Several troubadours—Huon de Saint-Quentin, Guillaume le Clerc de Normandie, Peirol—together with the German minnesinger, Freidank, are useful sources for the crusades.

II. THE ITALIAN SOURCES

Chronicles and Related Sources

As a result of their growing self-consciousness and their aspirations for independence, there is a wealth of source material in the chronicles of the Italian communes, especially those of Lombardy, in the Hohenstaufen era. The chief stimuli for such chronicles and annals in the late twelfth century were the expeditions of Frederick Barbarossa into Italy and his efforts to regain the regalian rights which had been lost by default to the communes. After about 1160 these municipal chronicles become a major source and they continue to grow in importance thereafter. There were but few communes that did not produce one or more such chronicles or annals, and each of them, as will be observed in the citations, has something, even though of no great importance, to contribute to the Hohenstaufen era. Only the more important ones, or those that deal most fully with the era of Frederick II, are included in this commentary.

In contrast to their German counterparts, most of these Italian communal sources are the works of lay authors, often notaries, town clerks, or other municipal officials, while the German authors, with but few exceptions, are monks or other members of the clergy.

Outstanding among the Italian communal chronicles and annals are the *Annales Placentini Guelfi* (1012–1235) and *Annales Placentini Gibellini* (1154–1284), the latter, the more important, obviously written by a citizen (probably an official of the commune) who was exceptionally well informed. Both are edited by P. Jaffé, in *MGH, SS.* xviii. The former has been revised and corrected by O. Holder-Egger as *Johannis Codagnelli Annales Placentini* in *SRG in usum scholarum*.

The *Annales Guelfi* is strongly biased, bitterly hostile to Frederick II and sympathetic towards Milan. Its most objective treatment is its report of Frederick's visit to Rome on his way to Germany in 1212. Its bias becomes apparent after 1220, notably, for example, 'When the Pope drew forth his spiritual sword "contra perfidiam ac nequitiam imperatoris"'. While a highly useful source for Piacenza and for the relations of that city with other cities of Lombardy, it must be employed with the utmost caution because of a clear tendency to falsify events in such manner as to injure Frederick II.

The *Annales Placentini Gibellini*, while favouring the Ghibelline faction and the interests of Frederick II, is more objective, and is less restricted to the affairs of Piacenza, embracing the whole of Lombardy and extending to parts of Southern Italy. For the Staufen period, both in its Lombard and papal relations, it is an indispensable source. It is at its best in its treatment of the events of 1235–7, in Verona, Vicenza, Cortenuova, and the description of the *Triumphus* in Cremona. It is useful and generally reliable in its report of Frederick's Lombard expedition in 1226, the conspiracy of 1246, the siege of Parma, and the events in Lombardy thereafter.

Comparable to the Piacenza *Annales* in its usefulness is *Rolandi Patavini Chronica* (ed. P. Jaffé in *MGH, SS.* xix). Its author, a native of Padua, was educated in the schools of Bologna and was a student of Buoncompagno, whose rhetorical flourishes occasionally reappear in the writing of Roland. As a schoolmaster, and as a notary in Padua, he sometimes permitted his rhetoric to obscure his factual accounts; but his *Chronica* is superior in its literary style, in its richness of content, and in its colourful presentation. It is of greatest usefulness for Frederick's sojourn in Padua in 1239, for his second excommunication and, thereafter, for the activities of Ezzelino, Frederick's captain and vicar. It continues as a prime source for the siege of Parma, for the Council of Lyons, and for the last years of Frederick II. Roland was an eyewitness of Ezzelino's entrance into Padua. Although a Guelf and, nominally, an adherent of Azzo of Este, Roland at times revealed a certain admiration for Frederick II.

Another work emanating from Padua, but written by a monk of the monastery of S. Justina, is *Annales S. Justinae Patavini* (1207–70) (ed. P. Jaffé in *MGH, SS.* xix). Apart from its invaluable treatment of Ezzelino, who, at times, is harshly judged by the author, the work is generally characterized by extraordinary frankness and reflects the spirit of freedom and independence characteristic of the Lombard communes of the thirteenth century.

Basic for the history of Ezzelino of Romano in his relations with Frederick II is *Gerardi Maurisii Vicinteni Historia de Rebus Eccelini da Romano* (1183–1237) (in Muratori *RIS.* viii. 1 ff.). Written by a member of a distinguished Ghibelline family of Vicenza, which was known for its hostility to the popes and the family of Este, Maurisius' *Cronica* presents the lives of Ezzelino and other Romanos in the most favourable light prior to 1237. Maurisius's account, although biased, is useful for the events surrounding Ezzelino's activities in Verona, Treviso, and Padua. He was fortunate in writing of Ezzelino's career prior to the years of cruelty and tyranny which characterized the latter part of his life.

Serving in some measure as a counterweight to Maurisius' *Cronica* is the *Cronica di Antoni Godi* (Muratori, *RIS*, new ed., viii, part 2). Also of a noble family of Vicenza, Antonio Godi was bitterly hostile to Frederick II and to Ezzelino. It is rather extraordinary, therefore, that his *Cronica*, prior to 1237, is based almost exclusively upon that of Maurisius. His entries after 1237 are relatively unimportant, other than as a record of Ezzelino's cruelties and, finally, of Ezzelino's capture in 1259.

In many respects the most informative, and certainly the most comprehensive, of the Italian communal chronicles and annals is the *Annales Janvenses (Fonti)*. Save for the earlier years (1099–1163), when it was begun by Cafaro, it is the work of various authors commissioned by the city of Genoa. In this manner, it was extended to 1293. The parts of the *Annales* most relevant to the era of Frederick II are those written by Ottobonus, Marchisius, and Bartholomäus, all citizens of importance and officials of the city. While concentrating heavily on internal affairs of Genoa, the work is of first importance for all events and situations involving the cities with the Empire. It is replete with material relevant to Frederick's visit to Genoa while *en route* to Germany in 1212. It is especially well informed for the years 1215 ff., and it provides one of the fullest accounts of Frederick's return to Italy in 1220 for his imperial coronation and, thereafter, for his policies as King of Sicily, particularly his economic policies affecting the northern communes. It is a first-rate source also for many events affecting Italy as a whole and for many of the activities of Frederick II as Emperor, including the siege and capture of Faenza, the naval battle resulting in the capture of the prelates *en route* to the General Council, the flight of the Pope to Genoa, and the Council of Lyons. Because of its official character as a communal history, it is in many ways the most satisfactory of the Italian chronicles originating in the municipalities.

A chronicle of limited usefulness is the *Chronicon Parmense* (Muratori, *RIS*, new edn., ix; edited, also as *Annales Parmenses Maiores* by P. Jaffé in *MGH*, *SS.* xviii). It is sometimes attributed to John Oddi, a canon of Parma Cathedral, although the actual authorship is doubtful. In general, the work is narrowly restricted to the commune of Parma, its *podestàs*, its military leaders, its conflicts with other cities. It is, however, a prime source for the siege of Parma in 1248 by Frederick II and Enzio and includes a detailed description of the siege-city of Victoria, its construction and its spectacular fall before the assault of the irate citizens and soldiers of Parma.

Of unusual interest among thirteenth-century chronicles of Italy is the *Chronica Fratris Salimbene de Adamo* (ed. O. Holder-Egger in *MGH*, *SS.* xxxii). Although born in Padua in 1221, Salimbene was a much-travelled Minorite, appearing from time to time in many cities—Cremona, Siena, Pisa, Lyons, Paris. Apparently he began the writing of his *Cronica* in Ferrara in 1250. Much of it is important for France as well as for Italy. His accounts are lively, observant, shrewd in character analysis, often gossipy and, at times, scandalous. He had unusual opportunities to witness the events he describes, and, generally, he is impartial in his accounts, except where his hostility towards Frederick II warped his judgement, or where his suspicions of Cardinal Ottaviano and others led him to spread damaging gossip. His chronicle is always colourful and his knowledge of important personages, both ecclesiastical and lay, is astonishing.

A source somewhat similar to Salimbene's chronicle is *Thomae Tusci Gesta Imperatorum et Pontificum* (ed. E. Ehrenfeuchter, *MGH*, *SS.* xxii), or, as edited by Böhmer (in *Fontes*, iv), *Chronicon Pontificum et Imperatorum*. It was probably written or assembled by its author *c.* 1300 and spans the years from the beginning of the Christian era to 1278. Its author was a much-travelled Florentine monk who obviously had a wide acquaintance among persons in positions that enabled them to give him trustworthy accounts. While he often gives the impression of reporting as an eyewitness, it seems more likely that he was using reasonably authentic accounts that he had been given by others. He is especially useful for the events following Cortenuova, including the negotiations with Milan. His account, when checked by other contemporary sources, is generally accurate. He employs a topical organization, dealing respectively with Frederick I, Otto IV, Frederick II, Henry VII, etc., which, at times, is confusing and repetitious.

The *Chronica* of Riccardus Sangermanensis, covering the years 1189–1243, has been edited several times, in part or as a whole. It was first completely edited by A. Gaudenzi (Naples, 1888), including the *Chronica Priora*. It has appeared, although without the prior chronicle, as *Ryccardi de S. Germano Annales* (ed. Pertz in *MGH, SS.* xix), and, as Richard of San Germano's *Chronica*, in Muratori, *RIS* vii, part 2, in its complete form. The latter edition is usually cited in this book. The author was a notary, and probably a municipal clerk for San Germano in the Campagna. He expressed a desire to preserve accurately for posterity what he had seen and heard, and throughout his chronicle one is impressed by the sincerity of his effort. He has organized his entries by the year and by the respective months of each year. Even so, he is at times confused as to the year, although his simple, straightforward accounts leave little reason to doubt their authenticity as to substance. He says of the scope of his *Chronica* that it extends from the death of William II to the era of Frederick II, and that it is intended to include all the events of the Kingdom of Sicily, 'vel ubique per orbem'. It is the most valuable single source for Sicily, including the eras of Tancred of Lecce, Henry VI and Constance, and Frederick II to 1243.

The *Breve Chronicon de Rebus Siculis* (Huillard-Bréholles, i, part ii, *Additamenta*) was written after the death (probably *c.* 1272) of Frederick II by an anonymous author. It is obvious, however, that the author had been a close associate of Frederick II and had accompanied him on the crusade in 1228: he left a detailed diary or log of the expedition from Brindisi and Otranto to Cyprus. Of all the chronicles or annals of the era, his is the least partisan. With but few exceptions, he confines himself strictly to a factual account. Unfortunately, he is sometimes misleading as to chronology, which is all the more surprising, since he is meticulous in recording the events themselves, briefly, concisely, accurately.

The *Annales Ceccanenses* (ed. Pertz, *MGH, SS.* xix), also described as *Chronicon Fossae Novae*, is the work of John of Ceccano towards the end of the twelfth century and the beginning of the thirteenth. It was evidently written in the monastery of Fossa Nova in the Campagna, near Ferentino, the locale of many of the conflicts for the control of Sicily and Apulia after the death of Henry VI. The early part is briefly annalistic and compilatory, with very short entries from the time of Caesar Augustus. It continues, however, with increasing usefulness to 1217. It is especially valuable for the conquest of Sicily by Henry VI in 1194, and his coronation in Palermo; it includes a lengthy poetical chronicle describing the events of the conquest in minute detail. The last years of the *Annales*, from the succession of Otto of Brunswick in 1209, his progress through Italy and early deposition, and the succeeding events to 1217, are the most useful.

The *Annales Casinenses* (ed. Pertz, in *MGH, SS.* xix) begins with the usual brief annalistic entries from the year 1000, the work of Albericus of Monte Cassino, to 1153. Thereafter it is written by continuators to 1212. The last of these continuators was responsible for the events of the years 1183 to 1212, the years for which it becomes relevant to the Hohenstaufen. It takes note of the peace between William II and

Frederick Barbarossa in 1185. From then until 1212 it is a source of first-rate importance for Henry VI, Constance of Sicily, and for Frederick II to the year of his election as King of the Romans. It is a prime source for the details of Henry VI's conquest of Sicily, his coronation, the conspiracy of 1197, and for the conflicts for the control of Sicily after the death of Henry VI, as well as for Frederick II's succession as King of Sicily and his marriage to Constance of Aragon.

For the first half of the pontificate of Pope Innocent III the *Gesta Innocentii III* (Migne, *PL.* 214) is an essential source. The author, a clergyman and, probably, a relative of the Pope, wrote what frequently appears to be a panegyric. It is apparent throughout the *Gesta* that the author was closely associated with Innocent III and that he had access to the papal letters. At times his entries are taken from them verbatim. Inevitably a biography made in this manner is strongly biased in favour of the Pope, and as a source it must therefore be employed with the utmost caution. The author assumes from the outset that one of the chief tasks of the Pope was the recovery of the *Patrimonium Petri* which 'Henricus . . . imperator occupaverat usque ad portas urbis'. The author is much concerned also with the 'perfidissimus Marcualdus', who never ceases to be the *bête noire* of the Pope. On the other hand, Walter of Brienne, who is fully treated in the *Gesta*, is always the 'vir utique fortis, nobilis, strenuus, magnanimus'. Important also is the *Gesta*'s treatment of the papal relations with Germany, primarily with Philip of Swabia and with Chancellor Conrad of Hildesheim. Apart from the bias and the plethora of derogatory adjectives applied to the enemies of the Pope, the essential facts are clearly set forth, making of the *Gesta* a useful and an essential source.

For an intimate and detailed account of the pontificate of Gregory IX the *Vita Gregorii IX Papae* (Muratori, *RIS* iii), also in P. Fabre *et al.* (edd.), *Le Liber Censuum de l'Église Romaine*, ii. 18–36, is indispensable, despite its strong bias in favour of the Pope and, at times, an uncompromising hostility to Frederick II. It was written by someone who was in almost daily association with the Pope and an eyewitness to many of the events recounted. The work is written in the style characteristic of the papal chancery of the thirteenth century. It focuses attention upon the alleged hypocrisy and cunning of Frederick II. Its most useful feature is the accurate reflection of the prevailing sentiment in the papal Curia and the conditions in the Papal State. Despite its obvious prejudicial treatment, it is of the utmost usefulness for the election of Gregory IX as Pope, the failure of Frederick II's crusade in 1227 and the resultant excommunication, and for Frederick at the gates of Rome on the eve of Gregory's death.

Comparable in its value as a source for papal history of the thirteenth century is the 'Vita Innocentii IV' (ed. F. Pagnotti, in *Archivio della R. Società Romana di Storia Patria*, xxi, Rome, 1898). Written by Gregory's chaplain and confessor, Nicholas of Carbio, who was intimately associated with the Pope during his most trying days, the work is a source of the greatest possible usefulness from the convocation of a Great Council by Gregory IX and the resultant captivity of the Prelates, to the 'most terrible death of Frederick' (*De morte pessima Frederici*).

It is one of the most dependable sources for the death of Gregory IX and for the vacancy of the See of Rome, the details of the election of Innocent IV, the ensuing negotiations between Pope and Emperor, and the flight of Innocent to Genoa and Lyons. Thereafter, it becomes a prime source for the Council of Lyons and the deposition of Frederick II. It is, of course, at all times, strongly biased in favour of the papacy and consistently hostile to Frederick II, but nevertheless it is an indispensable source for the relations of Innocent IV and Frederick II.

For Norman Sicily and its institutions influencing the court of Frederick II, two sources are of primary importance: *Romualdi Salernitani Chronicon* (Muratori, *RIS* vii), or, as edited by Arndt, *Romoaldi Annales* (*MGH, SS.* xix); and Hugo Falcandus, *La Historia o Liber de Regno Sicilie e la Epistola ad Petrum Panormitane Ecclesie Thesaurium* (ed. G. B. Siragusa, in *Fonti*).

Romuald, Archbishop of Salerno (1153–81), was a chronicler of first-rate importance. He was a member of a Lombard family long distinguished in the affairs of Southern Italy. Author of many books, mostly of a religious nature, his chief historical work is his *Chronicon sive Annales*, which extends from the creation of the world to 1178. Up to the tenth century it is based largely upon earlier chronicles, including Bede, Isidore of Seville, Paul the Deacon, and others. The important part is the contemporary history of which Romuald was an actual observer and participant. As Archbishop of Salerno and a frequent participant in the events which he describes, he was exceptionally well situated and admirably qualified to write the history of the Norman monarchy and to portray the important personages with whom he was intimately associated. He is especially valuable as a source because of his objectivity, even when writing of events and of persons to whom he was unsympathetic or opposed. He has been justly criticized, however, for ignoring in his *Chronicon* events which displeased him. Unlike Falcandus, he concerned himself but little with court intrigues. He possessed a clear instinct for that which was of permanent historical significance, and of such events his accounts are accurate and dependable.

Hugo Falcandus (obviously a pseudonym) in his *Liber de Regno Sicilie* is concerned with events in Sicily or, more accurately, with affairs of the Sicilian court, between the years 1154 and 1169. Like his name, the events of his life are shrouded in mystery. Miss Evelyn Jamison, in her excellent work on Admiral Eugene of Palermo, has most plausibly dispelled the mystery and credited the learned Admiral with both the *Liber de Regno* and the *Epistola*. But whether or not the mystery is permanently dispelled, the two works are useful sources: the *Epistola ad Petrum* as a reflection of hostile Sicilian reaction to the marriage of Constance, heiress to the Sicilian crown, to Henry of Swabia and the anticipated extension of Hohenstaufen dominance over the Kingdom; and the *Liber de Regno* as a record of the ceaseless court intrigues in which Falcandus took an active part. This interest in court intrigues deprives the work of much of its value as a comprehensive history of Sicily, while, at the same time, it enhances its value as a record of the historically less important partisan conflicts within the court circles. Falcandus' method of approach to the history of the era leads, inevitably, to the discussion of personalities and to characterizations of leading court personages. Examples are his accounts of the roles of Admiral Maio and the leading conspirators with whom he had to contend. For the most part, Falcandus was a partisan historian. Used by itself, therefore, the *Liber de Regno Sicilie* can be most misleading, but when employed with the *Chronicon* of Romuald, it often proves of exceptional supplementary value, perhaps by supplying some unsavoury details which the more scrupulous Romuald ignored. What Romuald concealed, Falcandus revealed.

III. OTHER SOURCES

A. *English and French Chronicles and Annals*

Most of the chronicles and annals of thirteenth-century England and France contain some material pertinent to the era of Frederick II of Hohenstaufen. A few of them provide much that is essential to the study of the policies of Frederick II as Emperor in his relations with the world outside Germany and Italy, especially his relations with England and France. Four of these must be considered essential sources, namely: *Matthaei Parisiensis, Monachi Sancti Albani Chronica Majora* (7 vols., ed. H. R. Luard, Rolls Series); *Rogeri de Wendover Chronica sive Flores Historiarum* (5 vols., ed. H. O. Coxe);

Guillaume de Nangis, *Vie de Saint Louis* (*RHGF* xx); Guillelmus Armoricus, *De Gestis Philippi Augusti* (*RHGF* xvii).

The *Chronica majora* of Matthew Paris, one of the least dispensable and yet one of the most adversely criticized of sources, is the work of an English monk from the Benedictine monastery of St. Albans, well known as a centre for historical writing through the work of Roger of Wendover, a superior chronicler, noted for his simplicity, directness, and dependability. Matthew's *Chronica majora* is, in fact, an elaboration and a continuation of the chronicle of Roger, from which it derives some of its best features. By incorporating the work of Roger into his own, Matthew makes his chronicle extend from the year *one* to 1273. It is most unfortunate that he adorned and elaborated the entries of his predecessor, often disadvantageously. The reader is frequently confronted with the task of separating the authentic from the distorted. Moreover, there is always in Matthew's work a deep-seated and uncompromising hostility towards the popes and the papal Curia which is likely to distort his accounts of papal–imperial relations. On the other hand, his *Chronica* is replete with essential documents and letters, to which he had access through his intimacy with the King (Henry III) and the King's brother, Earl Richard of Cornwall. One is never quite sure, however, to what extent Matthew may have tampered with the documents. But it is generally true that he rarely tampered with authentic official letters. He did not hesitate, however, to interpolate letters into his chronicle if they served to illustrate or strengthen his point of view. In his favour it can be said that, as a rule, the information which he obtained from the Earl of Cornwall about Frederick II and the Pope, both of whom the Earl visited in 1241, appears to be reliable. There can be but little doubt also as to the accuracy of his account, and of that of Roger of Wendover, of the marriage of Isabella, the sister of King Henry and Earl Richard.

After 1235, when the chronicle of Roger ends, it becomes increasingly necessary to check Matthew's accounts against other contemporary sources. In some instances, notably the capture of the prelates *en route* to the General Council in 1241, and the proceedings of the Council of Lyons in 1245, the essential facts, as stated by Matthew, are found to be accurate. On the other hand, his accounts of the siege of Brescia and the expedition against Milan in the following year are faulty, especially as to chronology. These are typical examples of the frequent weaknesses of his *Chronica*.

Further evidence of his unreliability is his practice of fabricating conversations purporting to reflect the reactions of the English people to papal injustices and extortions, and his interpolating letters attributed to the King of France, ostensibly reported verbatim, and intended to interpret the policy of the King concerning the alleged offer of the imperial crown to his brother, Count Robert. Nevertheless, while recognizing these and others as fabrications, one is disposed to tolerate them much in the spirit of the remark of a well-known classicist about the speeches that Thucydides introduced into his History: 'He was merely making thought and motive vivid in a way natural to simple ages.' Despite all his shortcomings, Matthew was deeply conscious of his obligation to inform posterity accurately about what he had seen and heard. There is, indeed, a calculated risk in employing Matthew Paris as a source; but many of the events and episodes in the relations of Popes and Emperors would be drab without the adornments and without the vivid portrayals of this penetrating observer and his shrewd interpretations of motives.

Of the French sources the *De Gestis Philippi Augusti* of Guillelmus Armoricus is of first importance for the early years of Frederick II in Germany. The author was born in Brittany about 1165. Quite early he became a chaplain of Philip Augustus with whom he lived in intimate association and for whom he was, at times, a trusted ambassador to Rome and elsewhere. He was exceptionally well placed and intellectually qualified to report accurately and fully the activities of his sovereign, whom he accompanied even on military expeditions. He was an eyewitness of the battle of Bouvines, and, in so far as it is possible for a single observer, a clergyman at that, to comprehend all that takes place on a battlefield, his detailed account is useful. The most useful part of his chronicle, however, for Frederick II is his account of the events in Germany between 1212 and 1215, including the part played by Philip Augustus in the deposition of Otto, the choice of Frederick II as King of the Romans, and the events in Aachen and Cologne during and after the coronation.

Less useful, because of its brevity, is most of the *Vie de Saint Louis* of Guillaume de Nangis. The author, a monk of Saint Denis, archivist and librarian, was also well placed for the pursuit of his career as historian. His brief accounts are chiefly useful for corroborative purposes. He mentions, for example, such incidents as the meeting of Frederick II and Count Robert, the brother of Louis IX, at Vaucouleurs, the contention between Frederick II and the Pope in 1239, the mission of Cardinal James of Palestrina to France to give emphasis to the excommunication of Frederick. His best entry has to do with some aspects of the Council of Lyons, including a most detailed listing of the articles of deposition, and, after the Council ended, he takes note of the visit of Louis IX and the Queen Mother, Blanche, to the Pope at Cluny.

Two other sources, both continuations of William of Tyre, the *Chronique d'Ernoul et de Bernard le Trésorier* (ed. M. L. de Mas-Latrie, Paris, 1871) and *L'Estoire de Eracles Empereur et la Conquest de la Terre d'Outremer* (*RHC: Hist. occ.*, ii) are useful for various episodes in the life of Frederick II, but are of primary value where the crusades are concerned. The identity of the authors has long been a subject of controversy, and it can only be said with assurance that they were among several chroniclers who undertook the continuation of the chronicle of William of Tyre, which ended in 1184, some of them evidently with the French crusaders in Syria, others in France or in Italy. While each of the two chronicles touches briefly upon most of the important events of Western Europe, often much better covered in other sources, they occupy a unique position as chroniclers of the Fifth Crusade and the Crusade of Frederick II, including such events as Frederick's marriage to Isabella of Brienne, his quarrel with John of Brienne, the father of Isabella, Frederick's visit to Cyprus and his relations with the Ibelins and other Franco-Syrian families, and the capture and subsequent loss of Damietta. Both chroniclers are exceptionally well informed with respect to Syria and Egypt during the years 1215 ff.

B. *Imperial Registers, Letters, Documents, etc.*

Of first importance among the imperial registers is the *Regesta Imperii*, vol. v: *Die Regesten des Kaiserreichs unter Philipp, Otto IV., Friedrich II., Heinrich (VII.), Conrad IV., Heinrich Raspe, Wilhelm und Richard, 1198–1272* (ed. Böhmer, Ficker, Winkelmann). Both charters and letters are to be found in J. L. Huillard-Bréholles, *Historia Diplomatica Friderici Secundi* (6 vols.). Constitutional documents, mandates, edicts, etc., are in *Monumenta Germaniae Historica: Constitutiones et acta publica imperatorum et regum*, vol. ii, 1198–1272 (ed. L. Weiland). Additional documents and some letters are in J. F. Böhmer, *Acta Imperii Selecta* and in E. Winkelmann, *Acta Imperii Inedita Saeculi XIII*. There are several important documents, as well as letters, in various German and Italian periodicals, especially *Quellen und Forschungen aus italienischen Archiven und Bibliotheken*. For the letters of Piero della Vigna (Petrus de Vineis) the available edition is that of J. R. Iselius. For an interesting and often unique series of letters see K. Hampe's collection, chiefly in *Mitteilungen aus der Capuaner Briefsammlung*, i–iv, and for others of the Hampe collection see the list in *QF* xx. 40.

The Sicilian laws of Frederick are to be found in C. Carcani, *Constitutiones regum regni utriusque Siciliae, mandante Friderico II Imperatore*, and in Huillard-Bréholles, iv.

Other letters are in Huillard-Bréholles's *Vie et Correspondance de Pierre de la Vigne* (Paris, 1865). Important letters of Frederick II are also to be found in various chronicles and annals, notably in Matthew Paris's *Chronica majora* (ed. Luard).

The documents of the Norman-Sicilian kings that are occasionally referred to in the footnotes of the present work are edited by K. A. Kehr, *Die Urkunden der Normannisch-Sicilischen Könige*; the documents of the German kings and emperors, predecessors of Frederick II, are listed in Stumpf.

The Greek letters of Frederick II are edited by N. Festa, 'Le Lettre Greche di Federigo II' (*Archivio storico italiano*, 5th series, xiii) and by G. Wolff, *Vier griechische Briefe Kaiser Friedrichs des Zweiten* (Berlin, 1855).

c. *Papal Registers, Letters, Documents, etc.*

The papal documents prior to 1198 are calendared in P. Jaffé (ed.), *Regesta Pontificum Romanorum* (2nd edn., S. Löwenfeld *et al.*, 2 vols., Leipzig, 1885–8), and P. F. Kehr (ed.), *Regesta Pontificum Romanorum* (7 vols., Berlin, 1906–25). For the *Registrum Domini Innocentii III super Negotio Romani Imperii* see Migne, *PL* 216. The letters of Innocent III are also to be found in Migne, *PL*, vols. 214, 215, 216, 217. The Register of Pope Honorius III is in C. A.H oroy, *Honorii III Romani Pontificis Opera Omnia* (5 vols., Paris, 1879–82); that of Gregory IX, in L. Auvray, *Les Registres de Grégoire IX* (*Bibliothèque des Écoles françaises d'Athènes et de Rome*, Paris, 1896 ff.); those of Innocent IV have been edited by E. Berger, *Les Registres d'Innocent IV* (4 vols., Paris, 1884–1921). For a summary of the papal registers see A. Potthast, *Regesta Pontificum Romanorum A.D. 1198–1304* (2 vols., Berlin, 1874–5), and for a brief outline of the register of Honorius III see P. Pressutti, *Regesta Honorii Papae III* (2 vols., Rome, 1888–95).

The most important letters of the Popes are in *Monumenta Germaniae Historica: Epistolae Saeculi XIII e Regestis Pontificum Romanorum Selectae* (3 vols., ed. C. Rodenberg, Berlin, 1883–7).

d. *The Arabic Sources*

The Arabic sources have been edited and translated into Italian by M. Amari, *Bibliotheca Arabo-Sicula* (Turin and Rome, 1880–9), and into French in *Recueil des Historiens des Croisades: Historiens orientaux* (12 vols., Paris, 1893–1911).

BIBLIOGRAPHY—PART I

PRIMARY SOURCES

Abd-oul-Ḥaqq ibn Sabīn, *Correspondance philosophique avec l'empereur Frédéric II de Hohenstaufen* (ed. S. Yaltkaya, Paris, 1941). Sometimes cited also Abd-al-Ḥaġġ: or as Ibn Sabin Abd-oul-Ḥaqq, and Abd al Ḥakk.

Abū'l-Fidā', *Kitāb al-mukhtasar fī akhbār al-bashar* (extracts tr. in *RHC: Hist. or.* i). See also Amari, 'Extratti del Tarih Mansuri' (*Archivio*, ix).

Abū-Shāmah, *Kitāb ar-rauḍatain* (Cairo, 1870–1; extracts tr. in *RHC: Hist. or.* iv–v).

Acta Pacis ad S. Germanum (ed. K. Hampe: *MGH Epistolae Selectae*, iv, Berlin, 1926).

Acta sanctorum (new ed., vols. i ff., Paris, 1863 ff.).

Affò, I., *Storia della città di Parma* (4 vols., Parma, 1792–5).

Albertano of Brescia, *Liber Consolationis et Consilii* (ed. T. Sundby under the auspices of the Chaucer Society, 1873).

Albertus von Beham und die Regesten Papst Innocenz IV. (hrsg. von C. Höfler, *Bibliothek des literarischen Vereins in Stuttgart*, 16/2, 1847).

Albertini Milioli Notarii Regini Liber de Temporibus (*MGH, SS.* xxxi).

Albrici monachi Trium Fontium Chronica (*MGH, SS.* xxiii).

Alexander Telesinus, *De rebus gestis Rogerii Siciliae regis libri IV* (ed. G. Del Re, *Cronistie scrittori*, i, Naples, 1845). Also in Muratori, *RIS* v.

Al-Makín, G., *Historia Saracenica* (ed. and tr. T. Erpinus, Leiden, 1625).

Al-Maqrīzī, *Akhbar Misr* (tr. E. Blochet as *Histoire d'Égypte*, *ROL* vi, viii–xi, 1898, 1901–8).

Amari, M. (ed.), *Bibliotheca Arabo-Sicula, versione italiana* (2 vols., Turin and Rome 1880–9).

—— 'Extratti del Tarih Mansuri' (*Archivio Storico Siciliano*, new series—Anno IX, 1884).

—— and Schiaparelli, C. (trs.), *L'Italia descritta nel Libro del Re Ruggero* (Rome, 1883).

Andreae Danduli Chronicon (Muratori, *RIS*, new ed., xii, part i).

Andreae Ungari Descriptio Victoriae a Karolo comite Provinciae reportatae a. 1245–1266 (*MGH, SS.* xxvi).

Annales Admuntenses, Continuatio Garstensis (*MGH, SS.* ix).

Annales Altahenses (*MGH, SS.* xx).

Annales Aquenses (*MGH, SS.* xxiv).

Annales Argentinenses (*MGH, SS.* xvii).

Annales Bergomates (*MGH, SS.* xviii).

Annales Bremenses (*MGH, SS.* xvii).

Annales Brixienses (*MGH, SS.* xviii).

Annales Caesenates (Muratori, *RIS* xiv).

Annales Casinenses (*MGH, SS* xix).

Annales Cavenses (*MGH, SS* iii).

Annales Ceccanenses (*MGH, SS* xix).

Annales Cisterciensium. See Manrique, A.

Annales Colmarienses minores (*MGH, SS.* xvii).

Annales Cremonenses (*MGH, SS.* xviii).

Annales Erphordenses (*MGH, SS.* xvi).

Annales Januenses (*Fonti*, 11–14, 14 *bis*, 1890–1926).

Annales Magdeburgenses (*MGH, SS.* xvi).

Annales Mantuani (*MGH, SS.* xix).

Annales Marbacenses (*SRG in usum scholarum*, revised by H. Bloch, Hanover and Leipzig, 1907); ibid. (*MGH, SS.* xvii).

Annales Mediolanenses breves (*MGH, SS.* xviii).

Annales Mediolanenses minores (*MGH, SS.* xviii).

Annales Mellicenses (*MGH, SS.* ix).

Annales Melrosenses or *Chronicon Mailrosensis Monasterii: Ex Annalibus Melrosensibus* (*MGH, SS.* xxvii).

Annales Monasterii de Oseneia (*Annales Monastici*, iv, ed. H. R. Luard, Rolls Series, 1965, reprinted).

Annales Monasterii de Waverleia (*Annales Monastici*, ii, ed. H. R. Luard, Rolls Series, 1865).

Annales Parmenses maiores (*MGH, SS.* xviii). See also *Chronicon Parmense.*

Annales Pegavienses (*MGH, SS.* xvi).

Annales Pisani. See *Bernardi Maragonis.*

Annales Placentini Gibellini (*MGH, SS.* xviii).

Annales Placentini Guelfi (*MGH, SS.* xviii). See Codagnellus, John.

Annales Pragenses (*MGH, SS.* iii).

Annales Prioratus de Dunstaplia (*Annales Monastici*, iii, ed. H. R. Luard, Rolls Series, 1866).

Annales Prioratus de Wigornia (*Annales Monastici*, iv, ed. H. R. Luard, Rolls Series, 1866).

Annales Reineri (*MGH, SS.* xvi).

Annals Ryenses (*MGH, SS.* xvi).

Annales Sancti Georgii in Nigra Silva (*MGH, SS.* xvii).

Annales Sancti Gereonis Coloniensis (*MGH, SS.* xvi).

Annales S. Justinae Patavini (*MGH, SS.* xix).

Annales Sancti Rudberti Salisburgenses (*MGH, SS.* ix).

Annales Scheftlarienses maiores (*MGH, SS.* xvii).

Annales Scheftlarienses minores (*MGH, SS.* xvii).

Annales Siculi (*MGH, SS.* xix).

Annales Stadenses auctore Alberto abbate (*MGH, SS.* xvi).

Annales S. Trudperti (*MGH, SS.* xvii).

Annales Veronenses (*MGH, SS.* xix); also as Parisius de Cereta, *Chronicon Veronense* (Muratori, *RIS* viii).

Annales veteres Mutinensium (Muratori, *RIS* xi).

Annales Wormatienses (*MGH, SS.* xvii).

Annales Wormatienses breves (*MGH, SS.* xvii).

Annales Zwifaltenses (*MGH, SS.* x).

Anonymi Vaticani Historia Sicula ab ingressu Normannorum in Apuliam usque ad a. 1282 (Muratori, *RIS* viii).

Antonelli, G. (ed.), *Statuti di Spoleto del 1296* (*Studi dell'Accademia Spoletina*, Florence, 1962).

Antoninus archiepiscopus Florentinus, _Chronicon sive opus historiarum sive summa historialis ab O.C.–1547_ (3 vols., Lyons, 1586).

Archives de l'Orient latin (2 vols., Paris, 1881–4).

Arnoldi abbatis Lubecensis Chronica Slavorum (_MGH, SS._ xxi); also (_SRG in usum scholarum_).

Assises de Jérusalem, 2 vols., ed. Count Beugnot, Paris, 1841–3 (_RHC_, Lois).

Auvray, L., _Les Registres de Grégoire IX: Bibliothèque des écoles françaises d'Athènes et de Rome_ (4 vols., Paris, 1890–1955).

Bacon, Roger, _Compendium studii philosophiae_ (ed. J. S. Brewer, Rolls Series, 1859).

—— _Opus Majus_ (2 vols., ed. J. H. Bridges, Oxford, 1897).

Badr-ad-Dīn al-'Ainī, '_Iqd al-jamān_ (extracts tr. in _RHC: Hist. or._ ii).

Baronius, C., _Annales Ecclesiastici_ (contin. by O. Raynaldus 1198–1565, 34 vols., ed. J. D. Mansi, Lucca, 1734–46). See also the new edition (Bar-le-Duc, 1864–83).

Bartholomai scribae Annales Januenses (_MGH, SS._ xviii). See _Annales Januenses_.

Battaglia, G., _I diplomi inediti relativi all'ordinamento della proprietà fondiaria in Sicilia_ (_Documenti per servire alla storia di Sicilia_, Diplomatica, xvi, 1895–6).

Benvenuti Imolensis Commentaria in Dantis Comoediam (Muratori, _Antiq._ i).

Benzonis Episcopi Albensis ad Henricum IV imperatorem libri VII (_MGH, SS._ xi).

Berger, É., _Les Registres d'Innocent IV_ (1243–54) (4 vols., Paris, 1884–1921).

Bernard of Clairvaux, _De Consideratione libri quinque ad Eugenium Tertium_ (Migne, _PL_ 182).

Bernardi Maragonis Annales Pisani (_MGH, SS._ xix).

Blancard, L., _Documents inédits sur le commerce de Marseille au moyen-âge_ (2 vols., Marseilles, 1884, 1885).

Boccaccio, Giovanni, _Comento alle 'Divina Commedia'_ (ed. D. Guerri, 3 vols., Bari, 1918).

Böhmer, J. Fr., _Acta imperii selecta_ (Innsbruck, 1870).

—— _Fontes rerum Germanicarum_ (4 vols., Stuttgart, 1843–68).

—— _Regesten zur Geschichte der Mainzer Erzbischöfe_ (2 vols., Innsbruck, 1877–86).

—— Ficker, J., and Winkelmann, E., _Regesta Imperii V. Die Regesten des Kaiserreichs unter Philipp, Otto IV., Friedrich II., Heinrich (VII.), Conrad IV., Heinrich Raspe, Wilhelm und Richard_ (Innsbruck, 1881 ff.).

Boncompagni, B. (ed.), _Scritti di Leonardo Pisano_ (2 vols., Rome, 1857–62).

Braunschweigische Reimchronik (_MGH, Deutsch. Chron._ ii).

Breve chronicon de rebus Siculis (Huillard-Bréholles, i, part ii).

Brevis nota eorum quae in primo concilio Lugdunensi generali gesta sunt (_MGH, Const._ ii).

Brunetti Latini, _Li Livres dou Tresor_ (ed. P. Chabaille, Paris, 1863). See also the critical edition by F. J. Carmody (University of California Press, 1948).

Bulla Depositionis (_MGH, Const._ ii).

Burchardi et Cuonradi Urspergensium Chronicon (_MGH, SS._ xxiii); also as _Burchardi prepositi Urspergensis Chronicon_ (_SRG in usum scholarum_, hrsg. von O. Holder-Egger und B. Simson, Hanover and Leipzig, 1916).

Caesar of Heisterbach, _Dialogus miraculorum_ (2 vols., ed. J. Strange, Cologne, Bonn, and Brussels, 1851).

—— _Vita S. Engelberti archiepiscopi Coloniensis_ (Böhmer, _Fontes_, ii).

Campano, Giovanni Antonio, _Opera_ (Leipzig, 1734): _De rebus gestis Andreae Brachi Perusini, Lib. IV_; idem (Muratori, _RIS_, new edn., xix, part 4).

Canonicorum Pragensium Continuationes Cosmae Chronicon Boemorum (_MGH, SS._ ix).

Carmen Placentini (*MGH, SS.* xviii).

Carmina triumphalia tria de Victoria urbe eversa, ii (*MGH, SS.* xviii).

Catalogi archiepiscoporum Coloniensium (*MGH, SS.* xxiv).

Chartularium Universitatis Parisiensis (4 vols., ed. H. Denifle and E. Chatelain, Paris, 1889–97).

Chronica Albrici Monachi Trium Fontium (*MGH, SS.* xxiii).

Chronica ignoti monachi Cisterciensis S. Mariae de Ferraria, ed. Gaudenzi, Società Napoletana di storia patria (*Monumenti storici,* Series I, *Cronache,* Naples, 1888).

Chronica monasterii Casinensis (*MGH, SS.* vii). See also Migne, *PL* 173.

Chronica regia Coloniensis (*SRG in usum scholarum,* revised by G. Waitz, Hanover, 1880); idem (*MGH, SS.* xvii, xxii, xxiv).

Chronica universalis Mettensis (*MGH, SS.* xxiv).

Chronica varia Pisana (Muratori, *RIS* vi).

Ex Chronico Turonensi (*RHGF* xviii).

Chronicon Ebersheimense (*MGH, SS.* xxiii).

Chronicon Estense (Muratori, *RIS,* new edn., xv, part 3).

Chronicon Hildesheimense (*MGH, SS.* vii).

Chronicon Leodiensi (*RHGF* xviii).

Chronicon Magni presbiteri Reichersbergensis (*MGH, SS.* xvii).

Chronicon Montis Sereni (*MGH, SS.* xxiii).

Chronicon Parmense (Muratori, *RIS,* new edn., ix, part 9).

Chronicon Tolosani canonici Faventi (*Documenti di storia italiana: cronache dei secoli XIII e XIV,* vol. i); idem (Muratori, *RIS,* new edn., xxviii, part 1).

Chronicon Universale Anonymi Laudunensis, 1154–1219 (hrsg. von A. Cartellieri, Paris, 1909).

Chronik des Stiftes S. Simon und Judas in Goslar (*MGH, Deutsch. Chron.* ii).

Chronique d'Ernoul et de Bernard le Trésorier (ed. M. L. de Mas-Latrie, Paris, 1871).

Chuonradi Schirensis Annales (*MGH, SS.* xvii).

Ciavarini, C., *Collezione di documenti storici antichi, inediti ed editi rari, delle città e terre marchigiane* (5 vols., Ancona, 1870–84).

Codagnellus, John, *Annales Placentini* (*SRG in usum scholarum,* revised by O. Holder-Egger, Hanover and Leipzig, 1901).

Compendio dell'istoria del regno di Napoli di Pandolfo Collenuccio . . . di Mambrino Roseo . . . et di Tommaso Costo (3 vols., Naples, 1771). See also later edition . . . a cura di A. Saviotti (Bari, 1929).

Confoederatio cum principibus ecclesiasticis, 1220 (*MGH, Const.* ii). Or *Privilegium in Favorem Principum Ecclesiasticorum* (*MGH, Const.* ii).

Conrad of Fabaria, *Casus de S. Galli* (*MGH, SS,* ii).

Constitutio pacis or *Mainzer Landfriede, 1235* (*MGH, Const.* ii).

Constitutiones Regni Siciliae (Huillard-Bréholles, iv, part i).

Constitutiones regum regni utriusque Siciliae mandante Friderico II. Imperatore per Petrum de Vinea concinnatae (ed. C. Carcani, Naples, 1786).

Continuatio Admuntensis (*MGH, SS.* ix).

Continuatio Chronico ex Pantheo excerpti (*MGH, SS.* xxii).

Continuatio Claustroneoburgensis (*MGH, SS.* ix).

Continuatio Cremifanensis (*MGH, SS.* ix).

Continuatio Eberbacensis (MGH, SS. xxii).

Continuatio Funiacensis et Eberbacensis (MGH, SS. xxii).

Continuatio Garstensis (MGH, SS. ix).

Continuatio Guilelmi Tyrensis (RHC: Hist. occ. ii, Paris, 1859).

Continuatio Lambacensis (MGH, SS. ix).

Continuatio Sancrucensis secunda, i and ii *(MGH, SS.* ix).

Continuatio Weingartensis. See *Hugonis Chronici.*

Continuatio Zwetlensis, iii *(MGH, SS.* ix).

Coquelines, C., *Bullarum, privilegiorum ac diplomatum romanorum pontificum amplissima collectio* (14 vols., Rome, 1736–64).

Coronatio Aquisgranensis: Ordo Coronationis (MGH, Legum, ii).

Cronaca Altinate (Muratori, *RIS* vii); also *Chronicon Venetum quod vulgo dicitur Altinate (MGH, SS.* xiv).

Cronaca di Antonio Godi (Muratori, *RIS,* new edn., viii, part 2).

Cronache e statuti della città di Viterbo (ed. I. Ciampi: *Documenti di storia italiana,* v, Florence, 1872).

Cronica Dominorum Ecelini et Alberici fratrum de Romano Gerardi Maurisii (Muratori, *RIS,* new edn., viii, part 4).

Cronica Fratris Salimbene (MGH, SS. xxxii).

Cronica Pontificum et Imperatorum S. Bartholomaei in Insula Romani (MGH, SS. xxxi).

Cronica Reinhardsbrunnensis (MGH, SS. xxx, part 1).

Cronica S. Petri Erfordensis Moderna (MGH, SS. xxx, part 1); idem (in Monumenta Erphesfurtensia saec. XII, XIII, XIV *(SRG in usum scholarum,* ed. O. Holder-Egger, Hanover and Leipzig, 1899).

Croniche di Viterbo (Böhmer, *Fontes,* iv).

Cusa, S., *I diplomi greci et arabi di Sicilia pubblicati nel testo originale* (Documenti degli Archivi Siciliani, Palermo, 1868 ff.).

Dante Alighieri, *De Monarchia* (ed. G. B. Giuliani, *Le opere latine di Dante Alighieri,* vol. i, Florence, 1871).

—— *De Vulgari Eloquentia* (ed. G. B. Giuliani, *Le opere latine di Dante Alighieri,* vol. i, Florence, 1871).

—— *La Divina Commedia* (3 vols., ed. G. A. Scartazzini, Leipzig, 1874–82).

De Advocatis Altahensibus (MGH, SS. xvii).

Decretales Gregorii Noni Pontificis, cum epitomis, divisionibus, et glossis ordinariis (Lyons, 1558).

De la Porte du Theil, M., 'Notice des differens articles qui sont contenus dans le manuscrit de la bibliothèque du Roi, No. 5696', Art. IX (*Notices et Extraits des Manuscrits de la Bibliothèque du Roi,* vol. ii, Paris, 1789).

Delaville le Roulx, J., *Cartulaire général de l'ordre des Hospitaliers de S. Jean de Jérusalem,* i, ii (Paris, 1894, 1897).

Delectus ex Epistolarum Honorii III Papae (RHGF xix).

Delectus Epistolarum Innocentii III Papae (RHGF xix).

Delehaye, H., 'Catalogus codicum hagiographicorum graecorum monasterii S. Salvatoris nunc Bibliothecae Universitatis Messanensis' (*Analecta bollandiana,* xxiii, 1904).

Deliberatio domini papae Innocentii super facto imperii de tribus electis, videlicet Friderico puero, Philippo et Otto (Huillard-Bréholles, i, part ii); ibid. (Migne, *PL* 216).

Delisle, L., *Catalogue des actes de Philippe-Auguste avec une introduction sur les sources, les caractères et l'importance historique de ces documents* (Paris, 1856).

—— *Inventaire des manuscrits de la Bibliothèque Nationale: Fonds de Cluni* (Paris, 1884).

Del Re, G., *Cronisti e scrittori sincroni della dominazione normanna del regno di Puglia e Sicilia* (Naples, 1845–65).

Denifle, H., and Chatelain, E., *Chartularium Universitatis Parisiensis* (4 vols., Paris, 1889–97).

De rebus Alsaticis ineuntis saeculi XIII (MGH, SS. xvii).

Descriptio Alsatie (MGH, SS. xvii).

Dictatus Papae (ed. M. Doeberl) (*Monumenta Germaniae Selecta*, vol. iii, Munich, 1889).

Die Chroniken der niedersächsischen Städte: Magdeburg, i (ed. K. Janicke, *Die Chroniken der deutschen Städte*, 14 vols., Leipzig, 1862 ff., vii).

Disputatio Carmine Conscripta inter Romam et Papem de Ottonis IV. Destitutione (G. W. Leibniz, *Scriptores rerum Brunsvicensium*, 3 vols., Hanover, 1707–11, ii).

Documenti per servire alla storia di Sicilia (pubblicati a cura della Società Siciliana per la Storia Patria, Palermo, 1876 ff.).

Eckhart, J. G. von, *Gesta Friderici II. ejusque filiorum* (*Corpus historicum Medii Aevi*, i, Leipzig, 1723).

Egidi, P., *Codice diplomatico dei Saraceni di Lucera (1285–1343)* (Naples, 1917).

Epistolae Innocentii III. Papae (Migne, *PL* 214–16).

Epistolario di Coluccio Salutati, ii, iii (*Fonti*, 15, 18, 1887).

L'Estoire de Eracles empereur et la conquète de la terre d'outremer, c'est la translation de l'estoire de Guillaume arcevesque de Sur (*RHC: Hist. occ.* ii).

Excerpta ex necrologio Hildesheimensis ecclesiae veteri (Leibniz, *SS. Bruns.* ii).

'Extraits de l'histoire des patriarches d'Alexandrie relatifs au siège de Damiette' (tr. E. Blochet in *ROL* xi, 1908).

Extraits des Chroniques de S. Denis (RHGF xvii).

Fabre, P., and Duchesne, L., *Le Liber Censuum de l'église romaine* (2 vols., Paris, 1889–1910).

Facius, B., *De Rebus gestis ab Alphonso primo Neapolitanorum Rege* (Naples, 1769).

Falcandus, Hugo, *La Historia o Liber de Regno Sicilie e la Epistola ad Petrum Panormitane Ecclesie Thesaurarium* (ed. G. B. Siragusa: *Fonti*, 22, 1897).

Falco, B. de, *Chronicon* (ed. G. Del Re, *Cronista e scrittori sincroni napoletani* . . ., i, 1845).

Fantuzzi, M., *Monumenti Ravennati de' secoli di mezzo, per la maggior parte inediti* (6 vols., Venice, 1801–4).

Fazzello, T., *De rebus Siculis decades duae* (3 vols., ed. V. W. Amico and Stotella, Catania, 1749–53).

Fedele, P., *Fonti per la storia di Arnaldo da Brescia* (Rome, 1938).

Foerster, R., *Scriptores Physiognomonici Graeci et Latini* (Leipzig, 1893).

Fragment de la Chronique Rimé de Philippe Mousket (*RHGF* xxii).

Franciscus Pippini Chronicon (Muratori, *RIS* ix).

Freidank, *Bescheidenheit* (ed. L. Sandvoss, Berlin, 1877).

Friderici Romanorum Imperatoris secundi: De arte venandi cum avibus (ed. and tr. C. A. Wood, and F. M. Fyfe, Boston and London, 1955).

Friedrich II., *De arte venandi cum avibus* (ed. L. Schneider, Leipzig, 1788). See also the more recent edition (ed. C. A. Willemsen, Leipzig, 1942).

Galvaneus Flamma, *Manipulus Florum sive Historia Mediolanensis Chronica* (Muratori, *RIS* xi).

Garufi, C. A., 'Documenti dell'epoca sveva' (*QF* vii, 1905).

—— *I documenti inediti dell'epoca normanna in Sicilia* (*Documenti per servire alla storia di Sicilia*, First Series, xviii).

Gaudenzi, A. (ed.), *Bibliotheca iuridica medii aevi: Scripta anecdota glossatorum* (3 vols., Bologna, 1888–1901).

Gaufredus Malaterra, *Historia Sicula* (Muratori, *RIS* v).

Gelasius, *Epistolae et decreta* (Migne, *PL* 59).

Genealogiae ducum Brabantiae (*MGH, SS.* xxv).

Genuardi, L., 'Documenti inediti di Federico II' (*QF* xii, 1909).

Gerardo, Pietro, *Vita e Gesti di Ezzelino terzo da Romano* (ed. A. Bonardi, Venice, 1894).

Gesta abbatum Horti Santae Mariae (*MGH, SS.* xxiii).

Gesta episcoporum Halberstadensium (*MGH, SS.* xxiii).

Gesta episcoporum Leodiensium abbreviata (*MGH, SS.* xxv).

Gesta Innocentii III (Migne, *PL* 214).

Gesta Romanorum (ed. H. Oesterley, Berlin, 1872).

Gesta Treverorum continuatio quarta (*MGH, SS.* xxiv).

Giraldus Cambrensis, *Opera*, vol. viii (ed. G. F. Warner, Rolls Series, 1891).

Gisleberti Chronicon Hanoniense (ed. W. Arndt, *SRG in usum scholarum*, Hanover, 1869); idem (*MGH, SS.* xxi).

Godfrey of Viterbo, *Gesta Friderici I imperatoris metrice* (*MGH, SS.* xxii).

—— (attrib.) *Gesta Heinrici VI* (*MGH, SS.* xxii).

—— *Pantheon* (*MGH, SS.* xxii).

Guillelmus Armoricus, *De Gestis Philippi Augusti* (*RHGF* xvii).

—— *Philippidos* (*RHGF* xvii).

Guillermi Apuliensis, *Gesta Roberti Wiscardi* (*MGH, SS.* ix). See also Mathieu, M.

Gunther of Paris (attrib.), *Ligurinus sive de Rebus Gestis Imp. Caesaris Friderici I* (Migne, *PL* 212).

Güterbock, F., 'Die Urkunden des Corio' (*Neues Archiv*, xxiii, 1897–8).

Hampe, K., *Ein ungedruckter Bericht über das Konklave von 1241 im römischen Septizonium* (*Sb. H. Ak.*, Jahrgang, 1 Abhandlung, 1913).

Hermann Altahensis, *Annales* (*MGH, SS.* xvii).

Holsteinische Reimchronik (*MGH, Deutsch. Chron.* ii).

Hoogweg, H. (ed.), *Die Schriften des Kölner Domscholasticus, späteren Bischofs von Paderborn und Kardinal-Bischofs von Sabina, Oliverus* (*Bibliothek des literarischen Vereins in Stuttgart*, ccii, Tübingen, 1894).

Horoy, C. A. (ed.), *Honorii III Romani Pontificis Opera Omnia quae extant* (5 vols., Paris, 1879–82).

Hostiensis, *Summa aurea super titulis Decretalium* (Lyons, 1588; Cologne, 1612).

Hugonis Chronici Continuatio Weingartensis (*MGH, SS.* xxi).

Huillard-Bréholles, J. L., *Historia diplomatica Friderici II* (6 vols. in 12, Paris, 1852–61).

—— *Rouleaux de Cluny* (*Notices et extraits de la bibliothèque impér.* xxi, 1865).

Ibn-al-Athīr, *Al-kamil fī-t-ta' rīkh* (extracts tr. in *RHC: Hist. or.* ii, part 1).

Innocenti III epistolae (Migne, *PL* 214–16).

Innocenti III registrum super negotio Romani imperii (Migne, *PL* 216).

Innocent III, *Sermo III: In consecratione Pontificis maximi* (Migne, *PL* 217).

Innocent IV, *Commentaria in V libros Decretalium* (Venice, 1578).

Inveges, D. Agostino, *Annali . . . di Palermo* (3 vols., Palermo, 1649–51).

Isidori Hispalensis Episcopi Etymologiarum sive Originum Libri XX (2 vols., ed. W. M. Lindsay, Oxford, 1911).

Italia Pontificia. See Kehr, P. F., *Regesta Pontificum Romanorum*.

Jacobi Malvecii Chronicon Brixianum (Muratori, *RIS* xiv).

Jaffé, P., *Regesta Pontificum Romanorum* (2 vols., 2nd edn., curaverunt S. Löwenfeld, F. Kaltenbrunner, P. Ewald, Leipzig, 1885–8).

James of Viterbo, *De Regimine Christiano* (ed. H. Arquillière, Paris, 1926).

Jansen Enikels Weltchronik (*MGH, Deutsch. Chron.* iii).

Jean d'Ibelin, 'Documents relatifs à la successibilité au trône et à la régence' (*Assises de Jérusalem*, ii, Paris, 1843).

Johannes Saresberiensis, *Opera Omnia* (6 vols., ed. J. A. Giles, Oxford, 1848; reprinted in Migne, *PL* 199).

——*Policraticus* (2 vols., ed. C. I. Webb, Oxford, 1909).

Johannis Vitordurani Chronica (ed. F. Baethgen, *MGH, SRG, nova series, III*, Berlin, 1924).

John of Paris, *De potestate regia et papali* (ed. J. Leclercq, in *Jean de Paris et l'ecclésiologie du XIIIe siècle*, Paris, 1942).

John of Viterbo, 'De Regimine Civitatum' (ed. G. Salvemini, *Bibliotheca Juridica Medii Aevi*, iii, 1901).

Joinville, *Histoire de Saint Louis* (ed. N. Wailly, Paris, 1874).

Jordanus de Jano, *Chronica sive memorabilia* (*Collection d'études et de documents*, vi, 1908). See also *Archivum Historicum Franciscanum*, iii.

Die Kaiserchronik eines Regensburger Geistlichen mit Fortsetzungen (*MGH, Deutsch. Chron.* i).

Kalbfuss, H., 'Urkunden und Regesten zur Reichsgeschichte Oberitaliens' (*QF* xv, 1913; xvi, 1914).

Kehr, K. A., *Die Urkunden der Normannisch-Sicilischen Könige* (Innsbruck, 1902).

Kehr, P., 'Das Briefbuch des Thomas von Gaeta Justitiars Friedrich II.' (*QF* viii, 1905).

Kehr, P. F., *et al.*, *Regesta Pontificum Romanorum* (9 vols., Berlin, 1906 ff.; vols. vi and vii in two parts).

Lachmann, K., and Kraus, C. von, *Gedichte Walthers von der Vogelweide* (10th edn., Berlin and Leipzig, 1936).

Lacomblet, T. J., *Urkundenbuch für die Geschichte des Niederrheins* (4 vols., Düsseldorf, 1840–58).

Leclercq, J., *Jean de Paris et l'ecclésiologie du XIIIe siècle* (Paris, 1942).

Lejeune, A., *L'Optique de Claude Ptolémée dans la version latine d'après l'arabe de l'émir Eugène de Sicile* (Louvain, 1956).

Leopoldinum (*Urkundenbuch zur Geschichte der Babenberger in Österreich*, ii, vorbereitet von Oskar Frh. von Mitis, bearbeitet von H. Fichtenau und E. Zöllner, Vienna, 1955).

Levi, G., *Registri dei cardinali Ugolino d'Ostia e Ottaviano degli Ubaldini* (*Fonti*, 8, 1890).

Liber censuum de l'église Romaine (2 vols., ed. P. Fabre and L. Duchesne, Paris, 1899, 1910).

Liber Pontificalis (2 vols., ed. L. Duchesne, Paris, 1886, 1892).

Ljubić, S., *et al.* (eds.), *Monumenta spectantia historiam Slavorum meridionalium* (Agram, 1868 ff.).

Lodi, Defendente, *Discorsi historici in materie diverse appartenenti alla città di Lodi* (Lodi, 1629).

Lucas de Penna, *Commentaria in tres posteriores Libros Codicis Justiniana* (Lyons, 1528).

Mabillon, J., *Acta sanctorum ordinis S. Benedicti* (9 vols., Paris, 1668–1702).

Magdeburger Schöppenchronik (ed. K. Janicke, *Die Chroniken der deutschen Städte*, vii).

Mahn, C. A. F., *Gedichte der Troubadours, in provenzalischer Sprache* (4 vols., Berlin, 1856–73).

Malaspina, Saba, *Historia de rebus Frederici Imperatoris* (*Bibliotheca historica regni Siciliae*, 2 vols., Panormi, 1723, ii); idem (Muratori, *RIS* vii).

Malaterra, Gaufred, *Historia Sicula* (Muratori, *RIS* v); idem (*RHGF* ii).

Malespina, Ricardano, *Historia Florentina* (Muratori, *RIS* viii).

Manrique, A., *Cisterciensium annales* (4 vols., Lyons, 1642 ff.).

Mansi, J. D., *Sanctorum conciliorum nova et amplissima collectio* (53 vols., Paris, Leipzig, Arnheim, 1901–27; reprinted, 1960–2).

Marafioti, G., *Chroniche et antichità di Calabria* (Padua, 1601).

Marsilius de Padua, *Defensor Pacis* (ed. C. W. Previté-Orton, Cambridge, 1928).

Martin-Dairvault, H. (ed.), *Le Livre du Roi Dancus: Texte français inédit du XIIIᵉ siècle suivi d'un traité de fauconnerie également inédit d'après Albert le Grand avec une notice et des notes* (Paris, 1883).

Martino da Canale, *La Chronique des Veniciens* (ed. A. Zon, *Arch. stor. ital.*, series I, vol. viii, 1845).

Mathieu, M. (ed. and tr.), *Guillaume de Pouille: La Geste de Robert Guiscard* (Istituto Siciliano de Studi Bizantini e Neoellenici, Testi IV, Palermo, 1961).

Matthew of Westminster (reputed author), *Flores Historiarum* (3 vols., ed. H. R. Luard, Rolls Series, 1890).

Mecklenburgisches Urkundenbuch (24 vols., Schwerin, 1863 ff.).

Memoriae Mediolanenses (*MGH, SS.* xviii).

Memoriale potestatum Regiensium gestorumque iis temporibus a 1154–1290 auctoreanon ymo Regiensi (Muratori, *RIS* viii).

Michaud, J. M., *Bibliothèque des Croisades* (2nd edn., 4 vols., Paris, 1829–30).

Mongitore, A. *Bullae, privilegia et instrumenta panormitanae ecclesiae* (Palermo, 1734).

Monumenta Boica (ed. Academia Scientiarum Maximilianea Monachi; 1763 ff.).

Monumenta Germaniae Historica. Constitutiones et acta publica imperatorum et regum (Hanover, 1893 ff.).

Monumenta Germaniae Historica. Deutsche Chroniken (6 vols., 1887–1909).

Monumenta Germaniae Historica. Epistolae saeculi XIII e regestis pontificum Romanorum selectae (3 vols., Berlin, 1883–7).

Monumenta Germaniae Historica. Legum (Hanover, 1875–89; vols. i–iv; reprinted in Leipzig, 1925).

Monumenta Germaniae Historica. Scriptores (Hanover, 1826 ff.).

Monumenta Germaniae Historica. Scriptores rerum Germanicarum in usum scholarum ex monumentis Germaniae historicis separatim editi (Hanover, 1839 ff.).

Monumenta Raitenhaselacensia (*Monumenta Boica*, iii).

Moscato, G. B., *Cronaca dei Musulmani in Calabria* (San Lucido, 1902).

Moses Ben Maimon (Maimonides), *Dalât al-Hairin: le guide des égarés* (ed. S. Munk, Arabic and French, 3 vols., Paris, 1856–66).

Muratori, L. A., *Antiquitates Italicae medii aevi* (6 vols., Milan, 1738–42; new edn., Milan, 1905 ff.).

—— *Delle antichità estensi ed italiane* (2 vols., Modena, 1717–40).

—— *Rerum Italicarum Scriptores* (24 vols., Milan, 1723–51; new edn. by G. Carducco and V. Fiorini, Città di Castello, 1900 ff.).

Necrologia Panormitana (*FzDG* xviii, 1878).

Nemesi episcopi premnon physicon . . . a N. Alfano archiepiscopo Salerni in Lat. transl. (ed. C. Burkard, Leipzig, 1917).

Nicholas of Jamsilla, *Historia de rebus gestis Friderici II imp.* (Muratori, *RIS* viii).

Nicholas Smeregus, *Annales civitatis Vincentiae* (Muratori, *RIS*, new edn., ix, part 5).

Nicolaus de Carbio, 'Vita Innocentii IV' (ed. J. Pagnotti, *Archivio della R. Società Romana di Storia Patria*, xxi, 1898).

Niese, Hans, 'Normannische und staufische Urkunden aus Apulien. I' (*QF* ix, 1906).

Niketas Choniates, *Byzantina Historia* (ed. J. Bekker, *Corpus scriptorum historiae Byzantinae*, Bonn, 1835).

Notae Eberbacenses (*MGH, SS.* xvii).

Notae Sancti Emmerammi (*MGH, SS.* xvii).

Notae Sancti Georgii Mediolanensis (*MGH, SS.* xviii).

Notices et Extraits des MSS., de la Bibliothèque du Roi (later *Impériale, Nationale*) *et autres bibliothèques* (Paris, 1787 ff.).

Novae Constitutiones regni Sicilie (Huillard-Bréholles, iv, part i).

Origines Guelficae. See Scheidius.

'Ortneit und Wolfdietrich nach der Wiener Piaristenhandschrift' (hrsg. von Dr. Justus Lunzer Edlen von Landhausen: *Bibliothek des Literarischen Vereins in Stuttgart*, vol. ccxxxix, Tübingen, 1906).

Otto Bishop of Freising, *Chronica sive Historia Duabus Civitatibus* (*SRG in usum scholarum*, revised by A. Hofmeister, Hanover and Leipzig, 1912).

Otto Bishop of Freising and Rahewin, *Gesta Friderici I Imperatoris* (*MGH, SS.* xx); idem (*SRG in usum scholarum*, 3rd edn., ed. G. Waitz, curavit B. Simson, Hanover and Leipzig, 1912).

Otto of St. Blaise, *Chronica* (*MGH, SS.* xx); idem (*SRG in usum scholarum*, ed. A. Hofmeister, Hanover and Leipzig, 1912).

Ozanam, A. F., *Documents inédits pour servir à l'histoire de l'Italie depuis le VIIIe siècle jusqu'au XIIIe siècle* (Paris, 1850).

Paris, Matthew, *Chronica majora* (7 vols., ed. H. R. Luard, Rolls Series, 1872–83).

—— *Historia minor* (3 vols., ed. F. Madden, Rolls Series).

Peter the Deacon, *Chronica monasterii Casinensis* (*MGH, SS.* vii). Also in Migne, *PL* 173.

—— *De viris illustribus Casinensis coenobii* (Migne, *PL* 173).

Philippe de Novare, *Mémoires* (ed. C. Kohler, Paris, 1913).

Piero della Vigna (Petrus de Vineis), *Epistolarum libri VI* (2 vols., ed. J. R. Iselius, Basel, 1740).

Pietro de Eboli, *Liber ad honorem Augusti* (ed. G. B. Siragusa, *Fonti*, 39, 1900).

Pinzi, C., *Storia della città de Viterbo, illustrata con note e nuovi documenti in gran parte inediti* (4 vols., Rome, 1897–1913).

Pipinus, Franciscus, *Chronica* (Muratori, *RIS* ix).

Pirri, Rocco, *Chronologia Regum Siciliae* (Palermo, 1643).

—— *Sicilia Sacra* (3rd edn., by A. Mongitore, 2 vols., Palermo, 1733).

Potthast, A., *Regesta pontificum Romanorum* (2 vols., Berlin, 1874–5).

Pressutti, P., *Regesta Honorii Papae III* (2 vols., Rome, 1888–95).

Ptolemaeus Lucensis, *Annales* (Muratori, *RIS* xi). See also *Die Annalen des Tholmeus von Lucca* (*SRG, nova series,* viii, Hanover and Leipzig, 1930); and in *Cronache dei sec. XIII e XIV,* Florence, 1876.

Radulphus de Coggeshall, *Chronicon Anglicanum* (ed. J. Stevenson, Rolls Series, 1875)·

Radulphus Diceto, *Ymagines Historiarum* (2 vols., ed. W. Stubbs, Rolls Series, 1876).

Raynaldi continuatio Annalium Caesaris Baronii ab anno 1198 usque ad annum 1534 (Cologne, 1694 ff.).

Raynaud, G. (ed.), *Les Gestes des Chiprois. Recueil de chroniques françaises écrites en Orient aux 13ᵉ et 14ᵉ siècles* (Geneva, 1887).

Regesten der Bischöfe von Strassburg (hrsg. von A. Hessel und M. Krebs, vol. i, 2, ii).

Registrum Domini Innocentii III super Negotio Romani Imperii (Migne, *PL* 216).

Relation française du mariage de Frédéric II avec Isabelle de Brienne et ses démêlés avec le Roi Jean (Huillard-Bréholles, ii, part ii).

Riccardi comitis Sancti Bonifacii Vita (Muratori, *RIS* viii).

Richard of San Germano, *Chronica* (Muratori, *RIS,* new edn., vii, part 2); idem (*MGH, SS.* xix).

Richeri Gesta Senoniensis ecclesiae (*MGH, SS.* xxv).

Ricobaldi Ferrariensis Chronicon Romanorum Imperatorum (Muratori, *RIS* ix).

Rieder, K., 'Das sizilianische Format und Ämterbuch des Bartholomäus von Capua' (*Rom. Quartalschrift,* xx, 1906).

Ries, R., 'Regesten der Kaiserin Konstanze' (*QF* xviii, 1926).

Roberti Autissidorensis Chronicon Continuationes (*MGH, SS.* xxvi).

Rockinger, L. von, *Briefsteller und Formelbücher des XI. bis XIV. Jahrhunderts* (*Quellen und Erörterungen zur bayerischen und deutschen Geschichte,* ix, 1863–4 (2 vols.); reprinted 1961).

Roger of Hoveden, *Chronica* (4 vols., ed. W. Stubbs, Rolls Series, 1871).

Roger of Wendover, *Chronica, sive Flores historiarum* (4 vols., ed. H. O. Coxe, English Historical Society, London, 1831–44).

Rolandino of Padua, *Chronica* (*MGH, SS.* xix). Also in Muratori, *RIS,* new edn., viii, part 1.

Romualdi Salernitani Chronicon (Muratori, *RIS,* new edn., vii, part 1); *Romoaldi Annales* (*MGH, SS.* xix).

Rotuli litterarum clausarum in Turri Londoniensi asservati (ed. T. D. Hardy, vol. i, 1204–24, London, 1833).

Rotulus misae 1212–1213 (in *Documents illustrative of English History in the Thirteenth and Fourteenth Centuries,* ed. H. Cole, London, 1844).

Rouleaux de Cluny. See Huillard-Bréholles.

Rymer, T., and Sanderson, R., *Foedera, conventiones, litterae et cuiuscunque generis acta publica inter reges Angliae et alios quosvis imperatores, reges, pontifices, principes, vel communitates* (4 vols. in 7, edd. A. Clarke, F. Holbrooke, *et al.,* London, 1816–69).

Sächsische Weltchronik (*MGH, Deutsch. Chron.* ii).

St. Thomas Aquinas (probable author of Book I and three chs. of Book II), *De Regimine Principum* (*Opuscula Selecta,* vol. iii, Paris, 1881).

Salimbene, *Cronica* (*MGH, SS.* xxxii).

Savioli, L., *Annali Bolognesi* (3 vols., Bassano, 1784–95).

Schäfer, D. (ed.), *Württembergische Geschichtsquellen im Auftrage der Württembergischen Kommission für Landesgeschichte* (Stuttgart, 1894 ff.).

Schaller, H. M., 'Die Antwort Gregors IX. auf Petrus de Vineas I, 1: "Collegerunt pontifices" ' (*Deutsches Archiv*, xi, 1954–5).

—— 'Unbekannte Briefe Kaiser Friedrichs II. aus Vat. lat. 14204' (*Deutsches Archiv*, xix, 1963).

Scheidius, C. L., *et al.*, *Origines Guelficae* (5 vols., Hanover, 1750–8). Cited as *Origines Guelficae*.

Schott (Schottus), A., *et al.* (eds.), *Hispaniae illustratae, seu rerum urbiumque Hispaniae, Lusitaniae, Aethiopiae et Indiae scriptores varii* (4 vols., Frankfurt, 1603–8, folio).

Sententia contra Communiones (*MGH, Const.* ii).

Series instrumentorum super renovatione Societatis Lombardiae (Huillard-Bréholles, ii, part ii).

Sicardi Episcopi Cremonensis Cronica (*MGH, SS.* xxxi).

Sifridi Presbyteri de Balnhusin Historia universalis et Compendium historiarum (*MGH, SS.* xxv).

Sigeberti Gemblacensis Chronica, continuatio Aquicinctina (*MGH, SS.* vi).

Spicilegium Ravennatis historiae (Muratori, *RIS* i, part ii).

Stephanii Baluzii Miscellaneorum (7 vols., Paris, 1678–1715).

Stumpf-Brentano, K. F., *Die Reichskanzler vornehmlich des X., XI. und XII. Jahrhunderts* (vol. iii, *Acta imperii adhuc inedita*, Innsbruck, 1881).

Suger, *Vie de Louis VI le Gros* (ed. and tr. H. Waquet, Paris, 1929).

Tafel, G., and Thomas, G., *Urkunden zur älteren Handels und Staatsgeschichte der Republik Venedig* (*Fontes rerum Austriacarum*, 12–14, Vienna, 1856–7).

Tallone, A., 'Regesto dei Marchesi d. Saluzzo, 1091–1340' (*Bibl. della Soc. stor. Subalpine*, xvi, 1906).

'Tareh Mansuri' (*Arch. stor. sic.* ix, 1884). See Amari, M.

Telesinus, Alexander. See Alexander Telesinus.

Theiner, A. (ed.), *Codex diplomaticus dominii temporalis S. Sedis* (3 vols., Rome, 1861–2).

—— *Commentatio de Romanorum Pontificum Epistolarum Decretalium antiquis collectionibus et de Gregorii IX P. M. Decretalium codice* (Leipzig, 1829).

Thesaurus anecdotorum novissimus (6 vols., ed. B. Pez, Augusta Vindelicorum, 1721–9).

Ex Thomae de Eccleston Libro de adventu fratrum Minorum (*MGH, SS.* xxviii).

Thomae Tusci Gesta Imperatorum et Pontificum (*MGH, SS.* xxii).

Tilander, G. (ed.), *Dancus Rex, Guillelmus Falconarius, Gerardus Falconarius: Les plus anciens traités de fauconnerie de l'Occident publiés d'après tous les manuscrits connus* (Lund, 1963).

Translatio S. Julianae (Mabillon, *Acta Sanctorum*, 16 February).

Ughelli, F., *Italia sacra* (2nd edn., by G. Coletti, 9 vols., Venice, 1717–22).

Urkundenbuch zur Geschichte der Babenberger in Österreich, ii (vorbereitet von Oskar Frh. von Mitis, bearbeitet von H. Fichtenau und E. Zöllner, Vienna, 1955).

Vie de Saint Louis par Guillaume de Nangis (*RHGF* xx).

Villani, G., *Cronica* (ed. G. Dragomanni, vol. i, Milan, 1848). Also *La Cronaca di Giovanni Villani* (*Illustri storici italiani dal secolo XIII al XIV*, Venice, 1833).

Ville-Hardouin, Geoffroi de, *Conquête de Constantinople* (ed. N. de Wailly, Paris, 1862); idem (*RHGF* xviii).

Vita Gregorii IX (Muratori, *RIS*, iii); idem in *Liber Censuum*, vol. ii.

Vita Ricciardi comitis S. Bonifacii res inter ipsum et Eccelinos gestas complectens (authorship doubtful, 1184–1253) (Muratori, *RIS* viii).

Walter of Coventry, *Memoriale* (ed. W. Stubbs, Rolls Series, 1873).

Walther von der Vogelweide (10th edn., edd. Lachmann and Kraus, Leipzig, 1936).

Watterich, J. M. (ed.), *Pontificum Romanorum qui fuerunt inde ab exeunte saeculo IX usque ad finem saeculi XIII vitae ab aequalibus conscriptae* (2 vols., Leipzig, 1862).

Winkelmann, E., *Acta imperii inedita* (2 vols., Innsbruck, 1880–5).

Zeumer, K., *Quellensammlung zur Geschichte der deutschen Reichsverfassung im Mittelalter und Neuzeit* (Leipzig, 1904). See also the newer edition, 1913.

BIBLIOGRAPHY—PART II

A CLASSIFIED LIST OF
SECONDARY WORKS

LISTED UNDER THE FOLLOWING HEADINGS:

1. Art and Architecture in Southern Italy	*pages* 569–70
2. Biographical Works	570–5
3. Byzantine Influence in Southern Italy	575–6
4. Cities and Communes	576–8
5. Crusades	578–9
6. Cultural Developments (General Aspects)	579
7. German Cities and Principalities	579–82
8. German Vernacular Literature	582
9. Germany and Austria (General History)	582–3
10. International and Interregional Legatine and Ambassadorial Missions	583–4
11. Italy, Sicily, and Sardinia	584–5
12. Jews (Cultural Influence)	585
13. Latin Literature and Literary Style	585–6
14. Medicine, Medical History, and the School of Salerno	586
15. Mendicant Orders, Heresy, and the Inquisition	586–7
16. Military Concerns and Battles	587
17. Monte Cassino in the Norman Era	587
18. Normans in Sicily	587–8
19. Papal–Imperial Relations	588–93
20. Prophets, Prophesying, and Mysticism	593
21. Royal and Imperial Coronations and Imperial Emblems	593
22. Saracens in Sicily	594
23. Sicilian Government and Administration	594–5
24. Trade and Commerce (Routes of Trade Mountain and Passes).	596
25. Translations: Greek, Arabic, Hebraic	596
26. Troubadours and Lyric Poets in Southern Italy	597–8
27. Universities	598

1. *Art and Architecture in Southern Italy*

Agnello, G., 'L'architectura militare, civile e religiosa nell'età sveva' (*Arch. stor. pugliesa*, xiii, 1960); Avena, A., *Monumenti dell'Italia meridionale* (Rome, 1902); Bertaux, É., *L'Art dans l'Italie méridionale*, vol. i (Paris, 1904); Bottari, S., *Monumenti svevi di Sicilia* (Palermo, 1950); Carotti, G., *A History of Art: Italian Art in the Middle Ages* (London, 1933); Chierici, G., *La Porta di Capua* (in *Miscellanea di storia dell'arte in onore di I. B. Supino*, Florence, 1933); Crowe, J. A., and Cavalcaselle, C. B., *A New History of Painting in Italy* (new edn. by Murray, 6 vols., London, 1903 ff.); Daniele, F., *I regali sepolcri del Duomo di Palermo riconosciuti e illustrati* (Naples, 1784); Deér, J., 'Adler aus der Zeit Friedrichs II.: *victrix aquila*' (P. Schramm, *Kaiser Friedrich II. Herrschaftszeichen*, Göttingen Abh., 3rd series, 1955); Deér, J., 'The Dynastic Porphyry Tombs of the Norman Period in Sicily' (*Dumbarton Oaks Studies*, v, Cambridge, Mass., 1959); Dehio, G., 'Die Kunst Unteritaliens aus der Zeit Kaiser Friedrichs II.' (*Hist. Zeitschr.* 95, 1905); Diehl, C., *L'Art byzantin dans l'Italie méridionale* (Paris, 1894); Enlart, C., *Origines françaises de l'architecture gothique en Italie* (Paris, 1894); Fabriczy, C. von, 'Zur Kunstgeschichte der Hohenstaufenzeit' (*Zeitschrift für bildende Kunst*, xiv, 1879); Frey, K., 'Ursprung und Entwicklung staufischer Kunst in Süditalien' (*Deutsche Rundschau*, lxviii, 1891); Gaudenzi, A., 'Il Templo della Giustizia a Ravenna e a Bologna' (*Mélanges Fitting*, Montpellier, 1908, vol. ii); Geymüller, Baron Heinrich von, *Friedrich II. von Hohenstaufen und die Anfänge der Architektur der Renaissance in Italien* (Munich, 1908); Giacomo de Nicola, 'Un disegno della Porta di Capua di Federico II' (*L'Arte*, xi, 1908); Gravina, D. B., *Il duomo di Monreale* (Palermo, 1859–67); Haseloff, A., *Die Bauten der Hohenstaufen in Unteritalien*, vol. i (Berlin, 1920); Haseloff, A., *Die Kaiserinnengräber in Andria* (Rome, 1905); Hettner, H., 'Streitfrage über Nicola Pisano' (in *Italienische Studien*, Brunswick, 1879); Huillard-Bréholles, J. L., *Recherches sur les monuments des Normands et de la maison de Souabe dans l'Italie méridionale* (Paris, 1844); Kaufmann, K. M., *The Baths of Pozzuoli: A Study of Medieval Illuminations of Peter of Eboli's Poem* (London, 1959); Koehler, W., 'Byzantine Art in the West' (*Dumbarton Oaks Papers*, 1, 1940); Luynes, Duc de, *Monuments et Histoire des Normands et de la maison de Souabe* (Paris, 1844); Nietzsche, F., 'Götzen-Dämmerung oder wie man mit dem Hammer philosophiert' (*Gesammelte Werke*, xvii, Munich, 1926); Paeseler, W., and Holtzmann, W., 'Fabio Vecchioni und seine Beschreibung des Triumphtors in Capua' (*QF* xxxvi, 1956); Salazaro, D., *L'arco di trionfo con le torri di Federico II a Capua* (Caserta, 1877); Salazaro, D., *Notizie storiche sul Palazzo di Federico II a Castel del Monte* (Naples, 1870); Salazaro, D., *Studi sui monumenti de la Italia meridionale dal IVᵉ al XIIIᵉ secolo*, Part I (Naples, 1874); Schubring, P., 'Schloss- und Burgbauten der Hohenstaufen in Sizilien' (*Die Baukunst*, II. Serie, Heft V, Stuttgart and Berlin); Schulz, H. W., *Denkmäler der Kunst des Mittelalters in Unteritalien* (2 vols., 2nd Atlas, Dresden, 1860); Shearer, C., *The Renaissance of Architecture in Southern Italy* (Cambridge, 1935); Sola, J. N., 'De Codice Laurentiano X plutei V' (*Byzant. Zeitschr.* xx, 1911); Thomasso de Masi, *Memorie degli Auranci* (Naples, 1761); Thümmler, H., 'Die Baukunst des 11. Jahrhunderts in Italien' (*Römisches Jahrbuch für Kunstgeschichte*, iii, 1939); Valentiner, W. R., *The Bamberg Rider: Studies in Mediaeval German Sculpture* (Los Angeles, 1956); Vasari, G., *Vite dei più eccellenti pittori, scultori e architettori* (new edn. by K. Frey, vol. i, Munich, 1911; also trans. J. Foster, *Lives of seventy of the most eminent painters, sculptors, and architects*, 5 vols., London, 1850–64); Venturi, A., *Storia dell'arte italiana*, vol. iii (Milan, 1904); Vitzthum, G., Graf, *Malerei und Plastik des Mittelalters in Italien* (*Handbuch der Kunstwissenschaft*, Potsdam, 1914–24); Willemsen, C. A., *Castel del Monte* (Insel-Verlag, 1955); Willemsen, C. A., *Kaiser Friedrichs II. Triumphtor zu Capua* (Wiesbaden, 1953); Willemsen, C. A., and Odenthal, D., *Apulia: Imperial Splendor in Southern Italy* (trans. D. Woodward, New York, 1959).

2. *Biographical Works*

Abel, H. F. O., *König Philipp der Hohenstaufe* (Berlin, 1852); Allshorn, L., *Stupor Mundi. The Life and Time of Frederick II* (London, 1912); Amari, M., 'Sulla data degli sponsali di Arrigo VI con la Constanza erede del trono di Sicilia e sui divani dell'azienda normanna in Palermo' (*Atti della R. Acad. dei Lincei*, 3rd Series, ii, 1877); Ancelet-Hustache, J., *Sainte Élisabeth de Hongrie* (Paris, 1946); Antichkof, E. V., *Joachim de Flore et les milieux courtois* (Rome, 1931); d'Arbois de Jubainville, 'Catalogue d'actes des comtes de Brienne' (*Bibl. de l'École de chartes*, xxxiii, 1871); *Atti del Convegno Internazionale di Studi Federiciani* (Palermo, 1952); *Atti del Convegno Internazionale di Studi Ruggeriani* (2 vols., Palermo, 1955); Baethgen, F., 'Dante und Petrus de Vinea' (*Sb. Bayer. Ak.*, Heft 3, 1955); Baethgen, F., 'Zu Mainardino von Imola' (*Neues Archiv*, xxxviii, 1913); Baeumker, C., *Petrus de Hibernia* (*Sb. M. Ak. Philosoph.-Philolog.-Hist.-Klasse*, Munich, 1920); Balan, P., *Storia di Gregorio IX* (3 vols., Modena, 1872); Beck, J., *Konrad von Marburg* (Diss., Breslau, 1871); Berger, E., *Saint Louis et Innocent IV* (Paris, 1893); Bergmann, A., *König Manfred von Sizilien. Seine Geschichte vom Tode Urbans IV. bis zur Schlacht bei Benevent, 1264–6* (*Abhandlungen zur mittleren und neueren Geschichte*, 23, Heidelberg, 1909); Bett, H., *Joachim of Flora* (London, 1931); Biehringer, F. J., *Kaiser Friedrich II.* (Eberings Historische Studien, 102, Berlin, 1912); Bienemann, F., *Conrad von Scharfenberg, Bischof von Speier und Metz und kaiserlicher Hofkanzler, 1200–1224* (Diss., Strassburg, 1886); *Biographisches Lexikon der hervorragenden Ärzte aller Zeiten und Völker*, unter Mitwirkung zahlreicher Fachgelehrter herausgegeben von A. Hirsch *et al.* (2nd edn., by W. Haberling *et al.*, 6 vols., Berlin, 1929–35); Blasius, H., *König Enzio. Ein Beitrag zur Geschichte Kaiser Friedrichs II.* (Breslau, 1884); Boehm, L., *Johann von Brienne, König von Jerusalem und Kaiser von Konstantinopel* (Diss., Heidelberg, 1938); Bonnard, A., *Saint François d'Assisi* (Paris, 1929); Brackmann, A., 'Kaiser Friedrich II.' (*Gestalter Deutscher Vergangenheit*, hrsg. von P. R. Rohden, Berlin, undated); Brackmann, A., 'Kaiser Friedrich II. in "mythischer Schau"' (*Hist. Zeitschr.* 140, 1929); Braun, P., *Beichtvater d. Heiligen Elisabeth und deutscher Inquisitor Konrad von Marburg, † 1233* (*Beiträge zur Hessischen Kirchengeschichte*, iv, 1909/11, and Diss., Jena, 1909); Brem, E., *Papst Gregor IX. bis zum Beginn seines Pontifikats* (Heidelberg, 1911); Brion, M., *Frédéric II de Hohenstaufen* (Paris, 1948); Brischar, J. N., *Papst Innozenz III. und seine Zeit* (Freiburg i/B., 1883); Brown J. W., *An Enquiry into the Life and Legend of Michael Scot* (Edinburgh, 1897); Buonaiuti, E., *Gioacchino da Fiore, i tempi, la vita, il messaggio* (Rome, 1931); Busse-Wilson, E., *Das Leben der heilige Elisabeth von Thüringen: das Abbild einer mittelalterlichen Seele* (Munich, 1931); Caemmerer, E., 'Zur Charakteristik Heinrich Raspe, Landgrafen von Thüringen und Deutschen Königs' (*Bulletin f. dt. Landgeschichte*, 89, 1952); Cantù, C., *Ezelino da Romano* (new edn., Milan, 1901); Canz, O., *Philipp Fontana, Erzbischof von Ravenna (1240–70)* (Leipzig, 1910); Carra de Vaux, Baron A., *Avicenne* (Paris, 1900); Cartellieri, A., *Philipp II. August, König von Frankreich* (4 vols., Leipzig, 1899–1922); Cipolla, Carlo, 'Ricerche su Eugenio l'Emiro' (*Arch. stor. sic.*, Series 3, i, 1946); Clausen, J., *Papst Honorius III., 1216–1225* (Bonn, 1895); Cohn, W., 'Die Gestalt des Stauferkaisers Friedrich II. im Lichte der gegenwärtigen Geschichtsauffassung' (*N. Jahrbücher für Wissenschaft und Jugendbildung*, vi, 1940); Cohn, W., 'Heinrich von Malta' (*Hist. Vierteljahrschr.* xviii, 1917–18); Cohn, W., *Hermann von Salza* (Abhandlungen der Schleswiger Gesellschaft für vaterländische Kultur, iv, 1930); *Convegno Internazionale di Studi Federiciani* (10–18 decembre, 1950); Creuz, R., 'Der Arzt Constantinus Africanus von Montekassino. Sein Leben, sein Werk und seine Bedeutung für die mittelalterliche Medizin' (*Studien und Mitteilungen zur Geschichte des Benediktinerordens und seiner Zweige*, xlvii, 1949); Curtis, E., *Roger of Sicily and the Normans in Lower Italy 1016–1154* (New York, 1912); Father Cuthbert, *Life of St. Francis of Assisi* (London and New York, 1912); Davidsohn, R., *Philipp II. August von Frankreich und Ingeborg* (Stuttgart, 1888); Delbrück, R., 'Ein Porträt Friedrichs II. von Hohenstaufen' (*Zeitschrift für bildende Kunst*, Neue Folge, xiv, 1902–4); Del Giudice, G., *Riccardo Filangieri sotto il regno di Federico II di Corrado e di Manfredi* (Naples, 1893); Della Valle, P., *Lettere Sanesi* (Venice, 1782);

Duff, A. B., 'Frédéric II de Hohenstaufen' (A. B. Duff and F. Galy, *Hommes d'état*, ii, Paris and Bruges, 1936); Elkan, H., *Die Gesta Innocentii III. im Verhältnis zu den Regesten desselben Papstes* (Diss., Heidelberg, 1876); Engelbert, O., *Saint Francis of Assisi* (2nd English ed. revised and augmented by O. F. M. Brady and R. Brown, Chicago, 1965); Falco, G., 'Un vescovo poete del sec. XI: Alfano di Salerno' (*Archivio della R. Società Romana*, 35, 1912); Fedele, P., 'Un diplomatico dei tempi di Federico II, Tommaso da Gaeta' (*Arch. stor. per le provincie napoletane*, xxxi, 1906); Felten, J., *Papst Gregor IX.* (Freiburg i/B., 1886); Ferretti, G., 'Roffredo Epifanio da Benevento' (*Studi medievali*, iii, 1909); Festa, N., 'Le lettre greche di Federigo II' (*Arch. stor. ital.*, Series V, xiii, 1894); Ficker, A., *Herzog Friedrich II. der letzte Babenberger* (Innsbruck, 1884); Ficker, J., *Engelbert der Heilige, Erzbischof von Köln und Reichsverweser* (Cologne, 1853); Ficker, J., *Reinald von Dassel, Erzbischof von Köln* (Cologne, 1850); Fink, E., *Siegfried III. von Eppenstein, Erzbischof von Mainz, 1230–49* (Diss., Rostock, 1892); Fischer, H., *Der heilige Franziskus von Assisi während der Jahre 1219–1221* (Freiburg, 1907); Foerster, H., *Engelbert von Berg, der Heilige* (Elberfeld, 1925); Fournier, P., *Études sur Joachim de Flore et ses doctrines* (Paris, 1909); Francke, H., *Arnold von Brescia und seine Zeit* (Zürich, 1825); Francona, R., *Il Cancelliere Matteo d'Ajello* (Palermo, 1920); Frankfurth, H., *Gregorius de Montelongo* (Marburg, 1898); Frati, L., *La prigionia de re Enzo* (*Bibl. stor. Bolognese*, vi, 1902); Funck, C. W. F., *Geschichte Kaiser Friedrichs des Zweiten* (Zullichau und Freystadt, 1792); Garufi, C. A., 'Ruggiero II' (*Arch. stor. sic.*, new series, lii, 1931); Geiger, A., *Moses ben Maimon* (Breslau, 1850); Geroges, É., *Jean de Brienne, empereur de Constantinople et roi de Jérusalem* (Troyes, 1858); Giesebrecht, Wilhelm von, *Geschichte der deutschen Kaiserzeit*, v–vi: *Die Zeit Kaiser Friedrichs des Rothbarts* (edn., Leipzig, 1895); Gillis, F. M., 'Mathilda, Countess of Tuscany' (*The Catholic Historical Review*, iv, 1918); Gittermann, J. M., *Ezzelin von Romano*, vol. i: *Die Gründung d. Signorie (1194–1244)* (Stuttgart, 1890); Grabmann, H., 'Thomas von Aquino und Petrus von Hibernia' (*Philos. Jahrbuch*, 43, 1920); Grundmann, H., *Kaiser Friedrich II.* (in *Die Grossen Deutschen*, i, 1935); Güterbock, F. 'Eine zeitgenössiche Biographie Friedrichs II.: Das verlorene Geschichtswerk Mainardinos' (*Neues Archiv*, xxx, 1905); Haller, J., 'Kaiser Heinrich VI.' (*Hist. Zeitschr.* 113, 1914); Hampe, K., 'Aus der Kindheit Kaiser Friedrichs II.' (*MIöG* xxii, 1901); Hampe, K., *Beiträge zur Geschichte der letzten Staufer. Ungedruckte Briefe aus der Sammlung des Magisters Heinrich von Isernia* (Leipzig, 1910); Hampe, K., 'Beiträge zur Geschichte Kaiser Friedrichs II.' (*Hist. Vierteljahrschr.* iv, 1901); Hampe, K., 'Das neueste Lebensbild Kaiser Friedrichs II.' (*Hist. Zeitschr.* 146, 1932); Hampe, K., *Geschichte Konradins von Hohenstaufen* (Innsbruck, 1894); Hampe, K., 'Kaiser Friedrich II.' (*Hist. Zeitschr.* 146, 1932); Hampe, K., *Kaiser Friedrich II. in der Auffassung der Nachwelt* (Rektorsrede zur Jahresfeier der Universität Heidelberg, Nov. 1924; also published as separate pamphlet, Berlin and Leipzig, 1925); Hartwig, O., 'Über den Todestag und das Testament Friedrichs II.' (*FzDG*, xii, 1872); Haskins, C. H., 'Magister Gaulterius Esculanus' (*Mélanges Ferdinand Lot*, Paris, 1925); Haskins, C. H., 'Michael Scot and Frederick II' (*Ibis*, iv); Haskins, C. H., 'The "de arte venandi cum avibus" of the Emperor Frederick II' (*EHR* xxxvi, 1921); Hauss, A., *Kardinal Oktavian Ubaldini, ein Staatsmann des 13. Jahrhunderts* (Heidelberg, 1913); Hayward, F., *Histoire de la Maison de Savoie (1000–1553)* (Paris, 1941); Heinemann, L. von, *Heinrich von Braunschweig, Pfalzgraf bei Rhein* (Gotha, 1882); Henke, E. L. T., *Konrad von Marburg, Beichtvater der heiligen Elisabeth und Inquisitor* (Marburg, 1861); Hirsch, F., 'Desiderius von Montecassino als Papst Viktor III.' (*FzDG* vii, 1867); Höfler, C., *Kaiser Friedrich II.* (Munich, 1844); Höhler, M., *Kaiser Friedrich II. Eine Lebens- und Characterskizze* (Frankfurt, 1880); Holtzmann, W., 'Berard Erzbischof von Messina' (*QF* xxxix, 1959); Holtzmann, W., 'Zum Itinerar Heinrichs VI.' (*Deutsches Archiv*, xiv, 1958); Huddy, M. E., *Matilda, Countess of Tuscany* (London 1905); Huillard-Bréholles, J. L., *Vie et correspondance de Pierre de la Vigne* (Paris, 1865)

Hurter, F., *Geschichte Papst Innozenz III. und seiner Zeitgenossen* (4 vols., Hamburg, 1834–42; vol. i in 3rd edn., 1841; ii–iv in 2nd edn., 1842–4; also trans. A. de Saint-Chéron and J. B. Heiber, *Histoire du Pape Innocent III*, 3 vols., Paris, 1838; 2nd edn., 1855); Ipser, K., *Kaiser Friedrich der Zweite, Leben und Werk in Italien* (Leipzig, 1942); Jacobs, W., *Patriarch Gerold von Jerusalem* (Aachen, 1905); Jamison, E., *Admiral Eugenius of Sicily* (London, 1957); Janelli, G., *Pietro della Vigna di Capua* (Caserta, 1886); Kaltner, B., *Konrad von Marburg und die Inquisition in Deutschland* (Prague, 1882); Kantorowicz, E., *Kaiser Friedrich der Zweite* (dritte unveränderte Auflage, 2 vols., Berlin, 1931); Kaufmann, A., *Cäsarius von Heisterbach* (2nd edn., Cologne, 1862); Kingston, T. L., *History of Frederick II, Emperor of the Romans* (2 vols., London, 1862); Kleist, W., *Der Tod des Erzbischofs Engelbert von Köln, eine kritische Studie* (Diss., Berlin, 1914); Kloos, R. M., 'Ein Brief des Petrus de Prece zum Tode Friedrichs II.' (*Deutsches Archiv*, xiii, 1957); Koch, A., *Hermann von Salza, Meister des Deutschen Ordens* (Leipzig, 1885); Lafitau, P. J. F., *Histoire de Jean de Brienne* (Paris, 1727); Langerfeld, G., *Kaiser Otto IV. der Welfe* (Hanover, 1872); Langosch, K., *Caesarius von Heisterbach, Leben, Leiden und Wunder des heiligen Erzbischofs Engelbert von Köln* (Weimar, 1955); La Piana, G., 'Joachim of Flora: A Critical Survey' (*Speculum*, vii, 1932); Lejeune, P., *Walther von Palearia, Kanzler des normannisch-staufischen Reiches* (Diss., Bonn, 1906); Lempp, E., *Frère Élie de Cortone: Étude biographique* (Paris, 1901); Le Nain de Tillemont, L. S., *Vie de Saint Louis, Roi de France* (6 vols., Paris, 1847–57); Levi, G., 'Cardinal Ottaviano degli Ubaldini' (*Arch. Soc. Rom.* xiv, 1891); Levy, E., *Guilhem Figueira, ein provenzalischer Troubadour* (Diss., Berlin, 1880); Loparco, L., *Federico II. di Svevi e la sua corte* (Florence, 1871); Lorck, A., *Hermann von Salza. Sein Itinerar* (Diss., Kiel, 1880); Lorenz, O., 'Kaiser Friedrich II.' (*Hist. Zeitschr.* 11, 1851); Löwe, H., *Richard von San Germano und die ältere Redaktion seiner Chronik* (Halle, 1894); Luchaire, A., *Innocent III* (6 vols,. Paris, 1905–8); Malsch, R., *Heinrich Raspe, Landgraf von Thüringen und deutscher König* (†*1247*) (Halle, 1911); Mandalari, M. T., 'Enrico Aristippo, Arcidiacono di Catania nella vita culturale e politica del sec. XII' (*Bolletino storico catanese*, 1923–4 I–II, 1936/XIV, 1937/XV, 1938/XVI); Manongiu, E., 'Note federiciane' (*Studi medievali*, new series, 18, 1952); Manselli, R., 'Ezzelino da Romano nella politica italiana del sec. XIII' (*Studi ezzeliniani*, 1963); Marx, J., *Die Vita Gregorii IX.* (Berlin, 1889); Maschke, E., *Das Geschlecht der Staufer* (Munich, 1889); Masson, G., *Frederick II of Hohenstaufen. A Life* (London, 1957); Mattei-Cerasoli, L., 'I genitori di Piero della Vigna' (*Arch. stor. napoletane*, new series, x, 1924); Mauerer, W., 'Zum Verständnis der heiligen Elisabeth von Thüringen' (*Zeitschrift für Kirchengeschichte*, 65, 1934–5); Mayr, J., *Markward von Anweiler, Reichstruchsess und kaiserlicher Lehensherr in Italien* (Innsbruck, 1876); Meyer, W., *Ludwig IX. von Frankreich und Innocenz IV., 1244–1247* (Diss., Marburg, 1915); Mielke, H., *Die heilige Elisabeth* (*Sammlung gemeinständlicher Vorträge* hrsg. von R. Virchow und W. Wattenbach, Neue Folge, Serie VI, Heft 125, 1891); Mitis, G., *Storia d'Ezzelino IV. da Romano* (Maddaloni, 1896); Mitrović, B., *Federico II. considerato como principe protettore* (Trieste, 1879); Momigliano, E., *Federico II. di Svevia* (Milan, 1948); Montalambert, C. R. F., *Histoire de Sainte Élisabeth de Hongrie, Duchesse de Thuringe* (*1207–31*) (3rd edn., Paris, 1841, also in Eng. as *The Life of Saint Elizabeth of Hungary*, trans. F. D. Hoyt, New York, 1904); Montcarmet, E. de, *Jean de Brienne, Roi de Jérusalem et Empereur de Constantinople* (Limoges, 1856); Morghen, R., 'Il cardinale Matteo Rosso Orsini' (*Arch. Soc. Rom.* xlvi, 1923); Münster, Th., *Konrad von Querfurt, kaiserlicher Hofkanzler, Bischof von Hildesheim und Würzburg* (Diss., Leipzig, 1890); Neumann, R., *Die Colonna und ihre Politik 1288–1328* (Langensalza, 1914); Niese, H., 'Materialien zur Geschichte Kaiser Friedrichs II.' (*Nachrichten von der königlichen Gesellschaft der Wissenschaften zu Göttingen: Phil.-Hist.-Klasse*, 1912); Nitschke, A., 'Friedrich II. Ein Ritter des hohen Mittelalters' (*Hist. Zeitschr.* 194, 1957); Oke, R., *The Boy from Apulia* (London, 1936); Overmann, A., *Gräfin Mathilde von Tuscien. Ihre Besitzungen. Geschichte ihres Gutes von 1115–1230 und ihre Regesten* (Innsbruck, 1895); Paolucci, G., 'La giovinezza de Federico II di Svevia' (*Atti della R. Accademia di Palermo*, 3rd series, vi, 1900 ff.); Pappadopoulos, J. B., *Théodore II Lascaris, empereur de Nicée* (Paris, 1908); Pfister, K., *Kaiser Friedrich II.* (Munich, 1942); Pieri, P., *Federico II de Svevia* (Turin, 1962); Powell, J. M., 'Frederick II's Knowledge of Greek' (*Speculum*, xxxviii, 1963); Powicke, F. M., *King Henry III and the Lord Edward* (2 vols., Oxford, 1947); Prinz, P., *Markward von Anweiler* (Emden, 1875); Prutz, H., *Heinrich der Löwe, Herzog von Bayern und Sachsen* (Leipzig, 1865); Puttkamer, G., *Papst Innocenz IV. Versuch einer Gesamtcharakteristik aus seiner Wirkung* (Münster, 1930); Querfeld, A. H., *Michael Scot und seine Schrift de Secretis Naturae* (Diss., Leipzig, 1919); Ratzinger, G., 'Albert Böheim' (in the author's *Forschungen zur bayrischen Geschichte*, Kempten, 1898); Reh, F., *Kardinal Peter Capocci, ein Staatsmann und Feldherr des XIII. Jahrhunderts* (Berlin, 1933); Reinhold, P., *Die Empörung König Heinrichs (VII.) gegen seinen Vater* (Leipzig, 1911); Renan, E., *Averroës et l'Averroisme* (3rd edn., Paris, 1866; 4th edn., 1882); Reuter, H., *Geschichte Alexanders des Dritten und der Kirche seiner Zeit* (2nd edn., 3 vols., Leipzig, 1860–4); Ridola, D., 'Federico d'Antiochia e i suoi discendenti' (*Arch. stor. napoletane*, xi, 1886); Russell, J. C., 'Master Henry of Avranches as an international Poet' (*Speculum*, iii, 1928); Rybka, H. H. J., *Elias von Cortona der Zweite General der Franziskaner* (Diss., Leipzig, 1874); Sabatier, P., *Vie de S. François d'Assise* (4th edn., Paris, 1894; trans. L. S. Houghton, *Life of St. Francis of Assisi*, London, 1894); Salvatorelli, L., *The Life of Saint Francis of Assisi* (trans. from the Italian by E. Sutton, New York and London, 1928); Schaller, H. M., *Kaiser Friedrich II. Verwandler der Welt* (Göttingen, 1964); Scheffer-Boichorst, P., 'Über Testamente Friedrichs II.' (*Zur Geschichte des XII. und XIII. Jahrhunderts*, Berlin, 1897); Schiffer, Z., *Markgraf Hubert Pallavicini. Ein Signore Oberitaliens im 13. Jahrhundert* (Leipzig, 1910); Schirmer, F., *Beiträge zur Geschichte Kaiser Friedrichs II.* (Diss., Friedland, 1904); Schirrmacher, F. W., *Albert von Possemünster, genannt d. Böhme* (Weimar, 1871); Schirrmacher, F. W., 'Beiträge zur Geschichte Kaiser Friedrichs II.' (*FzDG* xi, 1871); Schirrmacher, F. W., *Die letzten Hohenstaufen* (Göttingen, 1871); Schirrmacher, F. W., *Kaiser Friedrich der Zweite* (4 vols., Göttingen, 1859–65); Schmidt, H., *Erzbischof Albrecht II. von Magdeburg* (Diss., Halle, 1880); Schneider, F., *Beiträge zur Geschichte Kaiser Friedrichs II. und Manfreds* (*QF* xv, 1912); Schneider, F., 'Kaiser Friedrich II. und seine Bedeutung für das Elsass' (*Elsass-Lothringisches Jahrbuch*, ix, 1930); Schott, E., 'Joachim, der Abt von Floris' (*Zeitschrift für Kirchengesch.* xxii, 1901); Schrötter, F., *Über die Heimat des Hugo Falcandus* (Eisleben, 1880); Scipa, M., 'Alfano I, Arcivescovo di Salerno' (*Salerno*, 1880); Slaughter, G., *The Amazing Frederick* (New York, 1937); Steinen, W. von den, *Das Kaisertum Friedrichs des Zweiten nach den Anschauungen seiner Staatsbriefe* (Berlin and Leipzig, 1922); Sternbach, L., 'Eugenio von Palermo' (*Byzantinische Zeitschrift*, xii, 1903); Sternfeld, R., *Kardinal Johann Gaëtan Orsini (Papst Nicolaus III), 1244–1277* (Berlin, 1905); Stieve, F., 'Der Charakter des Ezzelino von Romano in Anekdote und Dichtung' (*Hist. Vierteljahrschr.* xiii, 1910); Stieve, F., *Ezzelino von Romano* (Leipzig, 1909); Stradowitz, S. K. von (see 'Die Abstammung der Kaiserin Konstanz, der Gemahlin Kaiser Heinrich VI. etc.' in *Familiengeschichte Blätter*, xxii, 1924); Sutter, C., *Aus Leben und Schriften des Magisters Buoncompagno* (Freiburg and Leipzig, 1893); Testa, F., *De Vita et Rebus Gestis Frederici II Siciliae regis* (Palermo, 1775); Tillmann, H., *Papst Innocenz III.* (Bonn, 1954); Toeche, Th., *Kaiser Heinrich VI.* (*Jahrbücher der deutschen Geschichte*, Leipzig, 1867); Tosti, L., *La Contessa Matilde e i Romani Pontifici* (Florence, 1859); Van Cleve, T. C., *Markward of Anweiler and the Sicilian Regency* (Princeton, 1937); Verci, G., *Storia degli Ecelini* (3 vols., Bassano, 1779); Walz, A., *Saint Thomas D'Aquin* (Louvain, 1962); Wegele, F. X., 'Die heilige Elisabeth von Thüringen' (*Hist. Zeitschr.* 5, 1845); Weller, K., 'König Konrad IV. und die Schwaben' (*Württembergische Vierteljahreshefte für Landesgeschichte*, Neue Folge, vi, 1897); Wenck, K.,

'Die Heilige Elisabeth' (*Hist. Zeitschr.* 69, 1892); Wenck, K., 'Die heilige Elisabeth' (Tübingen, 1908); Wenck, K., *Franz von Assisi* (Leipzig, 1908); Westenholz, Elisabeth von, *Kardinal Rainer von Viterbo* (*Abhandlungen zur mittleren und neueren Geschichte*, 34, Heidelberg, 1912); White, L. T., Jr., 'For the biography of William of Blois' (*EHR* l, 1935); Winkelmann, E., 'Bischof Harduin von Cefalù' (*MIöG*, Ergänzungsband I, 1885); Winkelmann, E., *Kaiser Friedrich II.* (2 vols., Leipzig, 1889–97); Winkelmann, E., *Philipp von Schwaben und Otto IV. von Braunschweig* (*Jahrbücher der deutschen Geschichte*, 2 vols., Leipzig, 1873–8), cited as *P. von S.*, and *O. von B.*; Winkelmann, E., 'Über die Herkunft Dipolds des Grafen von Acerra und Herzog von Spoleto' (*FzDG* xvi, 1876); Winkelmann, E., 'Zum Leben König Enzios' (*FzDG* xxvi, 1886); Winkelmann, E., 'Zur Geschichte Kaiser Friedrichs II. in den Jahren 1239 bis 1241' (*FzDG* xii, 1872); Wolff, G. (ed.), *Stupor Mundi. Zur Geschichte Kaiser Friedrichs II. von Hohenstaufen* (Darmstadt, 1966); Wolff, G., *Vier griechische Briefe Kaiser Friedrichs des Zweiten* (Berlin, 1855); Wolfschläger, C., *Erzbischof Adolf von Köln als Fürst und Politiker (1193–1205)* (Diss., Münster, 1905); Zeitlin, S., *Maimonides: a biography* (New York, 1935); Zeller, J. S., *L'Empereur Frédéric II et la chute de l'empire germanique au moyen âge* (*Histoire de l'Allemagne*, v, Paris, 1885); Ziegler, H. de, *Vie de l'empereur Frédéric II de Hohenstaufen* (Paris, 1935); Zingarelli, N., *La vita, i tempi e le opere di Dante* (4th edn., 2 vols., Milan, 1944).

3. *Byzantine Influence in Southern Italy*

Aar, E., *Gli studi storici in Terra d'Otranto* (Florence, 1888); Aliquo, L., *et al.*, *Gli scrittori calabresi dizionario bio-bibliografico* (2nd edn., 4 vols., Reggio di Calabria, 1955 ff.); Amato, G. M., *De principe templo Panormitano libri XIII* (Palermo, 1728), folio; D'Avino, V., *Cenni storici sulle chiese del regno delle Due Sicilie* (Naples, 1848); Batiffol, P., *L'Abbaye de Rossano* (Paris, 1891); Bonsari, S., 'Federico II e l'Oriente bizantino' (*Riv. stor. ital.* 63, 1951); Bonsari, S., *Il monachismo bizantino nella Sicilia e nell'Italia meridionale prenormanne* (Naples, 1963); Lancia di Brolo, D. G., *Storia della Chiesa in Sicilia nei dieci primi secoli del cristianesimo* (2 vols., Palermo, 1880–4); Crusius, M., *Turco-Graeciae libri octo* (Basel, 1584); Diehl, C., *Le Monastère de Saint Nicolas de Casole* (Rome, 1886); Diehl, C., *Palermo et Syracuse* (Paris, 1907); Fabricius, J. A., *Bibliotheca Graeca* (4th edn., 12 vols. Hamburg, 1790–1809); Fiore, G., *Della Calabria illustrata* (Naples, 1734); Gabrieli, F., 'Greeks and Arabs in the Central Mediterranean Area' (*Dumbarton Oaks Papers*, 18, 1964); Gay, J., 'Jusqu'où s'étend, à l'époque normande, la zone hellénisée de l'Italie méridionale?' (*Mélanges Bertaux*, Paris, 1924); Gay, J., *L'Italie méridionale et l'empire byzantin depuis l'avènement de Basile I jusqu'à la prise de Bari par les Normands* (Paris, 1904); Gay, J., 'Notes sur la conservation du rite grec dans la Calabre et la terre d'Otranto au XIVe siècle' (*Byzant. Zeitschr.* iv, 1895); Gay, J., 'Notes sur l'hellénisme sicilien de l'occupation arabe à la conquête normande' (*Byzantion*, i, 1924); Geanakoplos, D. J., *Greek Scholars in Venice: Studies in the Dissemination of Greek Learning from Byzantium to Western Europe* (Cambridge, Mass., 1926); Gigante, M. (ed.), *Poeti italobizantini del secolo XIII* (*collana di studi greci diretta da Vittorio de Falco*, xxii, Naples, 1953); Giunta, F., *Bizantini e bizantinismo nella Sicilia normanna* (Palermo, 1950); Guillou, A., 'Inchiesta sulla popolazione greca della Sicilia e della Calabria nel Medioevo' (*Riv. stor. ital.* 75, 1963); Guillou, A., *Les Actes grecs de S. Maria di Messina: Enquête sur les populations grecques d'Italie du sud et de Sicile (XIe–XIVe siècles)* (Istituto Siciliano di Studi Bizantini e Neoellenici, Testi 8, Palermo, 1963); Guldencrone, Baroness D. de, *L'Italie byzantine. Étude sur le haut moyen âge, 400–1050* (Paris, 1914); Hartmann, L. M., *Untersuchungen zur Geschichte der byzantinischen Verwaltung in Italien (540–750)* (Leipzig, 1889); Hartwig, O., *Aus Sicilien, Cultur- und Geschichtsbilder* (2 vols. in one, Cassel and Göttingen, 1867); Heiberg, J. L., review of F. Loparco, 'Scolario-Saba bibliofilo italiota' (*Byzant. Zeitschr.* xxii, 1913); Heisenberg, A., *Aus der Geschichte und Literatur der Palaiologenzeit*

(*Sb. München Akad.* 9, 1900, and ibid. 10, 1920); Horna, K., 'Metrische und text-kritische Bemerkungen zu den Gedichten des Eugenios von Palermo' (*Byzant. Zeitschr.* xiv, 1905); Jordan, E., *Monuments byzantins de Calabre* (Rome, 1889); Krumbacher, K., *Geschichte der byzantinischen Literatur von Justinian bis zum Ende des oströmischen Reiches, 527–1453* (2nd edn., Munich, 1897); Ladomersky, N., 'The Influence of Basilian Greek Monasticism on the Cultural Life of Southern Italy' (*Unitas*, Oct. 1951); Lake, K., 'The Greek Monasteries in Southern Italy' (*Journal of Theological Studies*, iv, 1903); Lenormant, F., *A travers l'Apulie et la Lucanie* (2 vols., Paris, 1883); Lenormant, F., *La Grande Grèce* (3 vols., Paris, 1881–4); Loparco, F., 'Scolario-Saba bibliofilo italiota, vissuto tra l'XI e il XII secolo e la biblioteca del monastero basiliano del SS. Salvatore di Bordonaro pressa Messina' (*Atti della R. Accademia di Archeologia, Lettere e Belle Arti*, Società Reale di Napoli, N.S. i, 1910); Ménager, L.-R., 'La "byzantinisation" religieuse de l'Italie méridionale (IXᵉ–XIIᵉ siècles) et la politique monastique des Normands d'Italie' (*Revue d'histoire ecclésiastique*, 59, 1958–9); Mercati, S. G., 'Sul testo dei tetrastici di Nattario di Casole in Lode dei suoi predecessori nella direzione del monastero' (*Studi bizantini e neoellenici*, iii, 1931); Michel, A., *Die Kaisermacht in der Ostkirche (843–1204)* (Darmstadt, 1959); Orsi, P., 'Byzantina Siciliae' (*Byzant. Zeitschr.* xix, 1910); Orsi, P., *Le chiese basiliane della Calabria* (with historical appendix by A. Caffi, Florence, 1929); Pardi, G., 'La popolazione della Sicilia attraverso i secoli: periodo normanno, 1066–1198' (*Arch. stor. sic.* xlix, 1928); Parthey, G. von, *Hierocles Synecdemus et notitiae Graecae episcopatuum. Accedunt Nili Doxapatrii notitia patriarchatuum* (Berlin, 1866); Pratesi, A., *Carte latine di abbazie calabresi proveniente dall'Archivio Aldobrandini* (*Studi e testi*, 197, Vatican City, 1958); Renucci, P., *L'Aventure de l'humanisme européen au moyen âge (IVᵉ–XIVᵉ siècles)* (Paris, 1953); Rodotà, P. P., *Dell'origine, progresso, e stato presente del rito greco in Italia* (3 vols., Rome, 1758–63); Rohlfs, G., *Das Fortleben des antiken Griechentums in Unteritalien* (Cologne, 1933); Rohlfs, G., *Griechen und Romanen in Unteritalien* (Geneva, 1924); Rühl, F., 'Bemerkungen über einige Bibliotheken von Sicilien' (*Philologus*, xlvii, 1889); Scaduto, M., S.J., *Il monachismo basiliano nella Sicilia medievale. Rinascita e decadenza, secoli XI–XIV* (Rome, 1947); Schlumberger, G., *L'Épopée byzantine à la fin du dixième siècle* (3 vols., Paris, 1890–1905); White, L. T., Jr., 'The Byzantinization of Sicily' (*EHR* xlii, 1936); Zuretti, C. O., 'Contrasto fra Taranto e Otranto' (*Centenario della nascita di Michele Amari*, Palermo, 1910).

4. Cities and Communes

Abegg, E., *Die Politik Mailands in den ersten Jahrzehnten des 13. Jahrhunderts* (*Beiträge zur Kulturgeschichte des Mittelalters und der Renaissance*, ed. W. Goetz, vol. 24, Leipzig, 1918); Angelis, C. N. de, *Le origini del comune meridionale* (Naples, 1940); Appelt, H., 'Friedrich Barbarossa und die italienischen Kommunen (*MIöG* lxxii, 1964); Baer, A., *Die Beziehungen Venedigs zum Kaiserreiche in der staufischen Zeit* (Innsbruck, 1888); Bernini, F., *I comuni italiani e Federico II di Svevia* (Turin, 1950 ff.); Brezzi, P., 'I comuni cittadini italiani e l'impero medioevale' (*Nuove Questioni di storia medioevale*, Milan, 1964); Brezzi, P., *I comuni medioevali nella storia d'Italia* (Turin, 1965); Butler, W. F., *The Lombard Communes* (New York, 1906); Calco, T. (Tristani Calchi), *Mediolanensis Hist. patriae* (Milan, 1627); Campi, P. M., *Dell'historia ecclesiastica di Piacenza* (Piacenza, 1651); Campo, A., *Cremona fedelissima* (new edn., Milan, 1645); Canale, M. G., *Nuova istoria della repubblica di Genova, del suo commercio e della sua letteratura* (4 vols., Florence, 1858–64); Colucci, G., *Delle antichità picene* (31 vols., Fermo, 1786–94); Corio, B., *Historia di Milano* (riveduta e annotata, 3 vols., Milan, 1855–7); Dahm, G., *Untersuchungen zur Verfassungs- und Strafrechtsgeschichte der italienischen Stadt im Mittelalter* (Hamburg, 1941); Davidsohn, R., *Forschungen zur Geschichte von Florenz* (4 vols., Berlin,

1896–1908); Davidsohn, R., *Geschichte von Florenz* (4 vols., Berlin, 1896–7); Davis, J. C., *The Decline of the Venetian Nobility as a Ruling Class* (*Johns Hopkins University Studies in Historical and Political Science*, lxxx, 2, Baltimore, 1962); Dupré Theseider, E., *L'idea imperiale di Roma nella tradizione del Medio Evo* (Milan, 1942); Ficker, J., *Zur Geschichte des Lombardenbundes* (*Sb. Wien*, 60, 1868); Franchini, U., *Saggio di ricerche sull'istituto del podestà nei comuni medioevali* (Bologna, 1912); Frizzi, A., *Memorie per la storia di Ferrara* (2nd edn., 5 vols., Ferrara, 1847–50); Gianani, F., *I comuni* (1000–1300) (Milan, 1900); Giannone, P., *Istoria civile del regno di Napoli* (4 vols., Naples, 1723); Giovanni, V. di, *La topografia antica di Palermo dal secolo 10 al 15* (2 vols., Palermo, 1889–90); Gräf, F., *Die Gründung Alessandrias* (Diss., Berlin, 1887); Güterbock, F., *Der Friede von Montebello und die Weiterentwicklung des Lombardenbundes* (Diss., Berlin, 1895); Hagemann, W., 'Jesi im Zeitalter Friedrichs II.' (*QF* xxxvi, 1956); Halphen, L., *Études sur l'administration de Rome au moyen âge, 751–1282* (Paris, 1907); Hegel, C. von, *Geschichte der Städteverfassung von Italien seit der Zeit der römischen Herrschaft bis zum Ausgang des zwölften Jahrhunderts* (2 vols., Leipzig, 1847), vol. ii; Hessel, A., *Geschichte der Stadt Bologna von 1116 bis 1280* (*Hist. Studien*, Heft lxxvi, Berlin, 1910); Hutton, E., *The Cities of Lombardy* (New York and London, 1912); Jiriček, C., *Die Bedeutung von Regusa in der Handelsgeschichte des Mittelalters* (Vienna, 1899); Kretschmayr, H., *Geschichte von Venedig* (3 vols., Gotha, 1920–34); La Mantia, G., *Sugli studi di topografia palermitana del Medio Evo* (Palermo, 1919); Langer, O., *Politische Geschichte Genuas und Pisas im 12. Jahrhundert* (Leipzig, 1882); Lanzani, F., *Storia dei comuni italiani dalle origini al 1313* (Milan, 1882); Lenel, W., *Studien zur Geschichte Paduas und Veronas im 13. Jahrhundert* (Strassburg, 1893); Lizier, A., *Note intorno alla storia del comune di Treviso* (Modena, 1901); Manaresi, C., *Gli atti del comune di Milano fino all'anno MCCXVI* (Milan, 1919); Masi, T. de, *Memorie istoriche degli Aurunci antichissimi popoli d'Italia, e delle loro principali città Aurunca e Sessa* (Naples, 1761); Monti, S., *Il Comune di Como nel Medio Evo* (Como, 1905); Natalucca, M., *Ancona traverso i secoli* (Città di Castello, 1960); Noyes, E., *The Story of Ferrara* (London, 1904); Noyes, E., *The Story of Milan* (London, 1908); Perifano, C., *Cenni storici su la origine della città di Foggia, con la narrativa della portentosa invenzione, ed apparizione di Maria Santissima della Icona-Vetere* (Foggia, 1831); Picone, G., *Memorie storiche agrigentine* (6 vols., Agrigento, 1866 ff.); Pinzi, C., *Storia della città di Viterbo illustrata con note e nuovi documenti in gran parte inediti* (4 vols., Rome, 1887–1913); Pirenne, H., *Medieval Cities* (trans. from the French by F. D. Halsey, Princeton, 1939); Poggiali, C., *Memorie storiche della città di Piacenza* (12 vols., Piacenza, 1757–66); Poupardin, R., *Étude sur les institutions politiques et administratives des principautés lombardes de l'Italie méridionale* (*IX – XIe siècles*) (Paris, 1907); Ranghiaschi, L., *Bibliografia storica della città e leoghi dello stato pontifico* (2 vols. in one, Rome 1792–3); Rialdo, C., *Memorie istoriche della città di Capua* (2 vols., Naples, 1753–5); Roncioni, R., 'Delle istorie Pisane' (*Arch. stor. ital.* vi, 1848); Salzer, E., *Über die Anfänge der Signorie in Oberitalien* (*Hist. Studien*, Heft 14, Berlin, 1900); Schipa, M., *Sicilia e Italia sotto Federico II* (Naples, 1929); Seeger, H., *Die Reorganisation des Kirchenstaates unter Innocenz III.* (Kiel, 1937); Sudhoff, K., 'Salerno, eine mittelalterliche Heil- und Lehrstätte' (*Sudhoffs Archiv für Gesch. d. Medizin*, xxxi, 1929); Tenckhoff, F., *Der Kampf der Hohenstaufen um die Mark Ancona und das Herzogtum Spoleto von der zweiten Exkommunikation Friedrichs II. bis zum Tode Konradins* (Paderborn, 1893); Tronci, P., *Memorie istoriche della città di Pisa* (Leghorn, 1682); D'Urso, R., *Storia della città di Andria* (Naples, 1842); Valsecchi, F., *Comune e corporazione nel Medio Evo italiano* (Milan, 1948); Vergottini, G. de, *Il 'popole' nella costituzione del comune di Modena sino alla metà del secolo XIII* (Sienna, 1931); Vicini, E. P., *I podestà di Modena 1156–1796* (Rome, 1913); Vignati, C., *Storia diplomatica della Lega Lombarda* (Milan, 1866); Villani, G., *Foggia al tempo degli Hohenstaufen e degli Angioina* (Trani, 1894); Volpe, G., *Questioni fondamentali sull'origine e solgimento dei comuni italiani sec. 10–14* (Pisa, 1905); Waley, D., *The Papal State in the Thirteenth Century* (London,

1961); Zdekaufr, L., 'Il parlemento cittadino nei comuni delle Marche' (*Atti e Memorie Deputazione storia patria per le Marche*, x).

5. Crusades

Bertaux, É., 'Les Français d'outremer en Apulie et en Épire au temps des Hohenstaufen d'Italie' (*Revue historique*, 85, 1904); Bréhier, L., *L'Église et l'Orient: les croisades* (5th edn., Paris, 1928); Cahen, C., *La Syrie du nord à l'époque des croisades et la principauté franque d'Antioche* (Paris, 1940); Delaville le Roulx, J., *Les Hospitaliers en Terre Sainte et à Chypre 1100–1310* (Paris, 1904); Dodu, G., *Histoire des institutions monarchiques dans le royaume latin de Jérusalem, 1099–1291* (Paris, 1894); Ducange, C. D., *Les Familles d'Outremer* (ed. E. G. Rey, Paris, 1869); Flugi van Aspermont, C. H. C., *De Johanniter-Orde in het Heilige Land (1100–1292)* (Assen, 1957); Gottschalk, H. L., *Al-Malik al-Kāmil von Ägypten und seine Zeit* (Wiesbaden, 1958); Grousset, R., *Histoire des croisades et du royaume franc de Jérusalem* (3 vols., Paris, 1934–6), vol. iii; Hertzberg, G. F., *Geschichte der Byzantiner und des osmanischen Reiches bis gegen Ende des sechszehnten Jahrhunderts* (Berlin, 1883 ff.); Hill, G. F., *A History of Cyprus* (4 vols., Cambridge, 1940–52); Hoogeweg, H., 'Die Kreuzpredigt des Jahres 1224 in Deutschland mit besonderer Rücksicht auf die Erzdiöcese Köln' (*Dt. Z f. Gwiss.* iv, 1890); Howorth, H. H., *History of the Mongols* (5 vols., London, 1876–1927); Kestner, E., *Der Kreuzzug Friedrichs II.* (Diss., Göttingen, 1873); King, E. J., *The Knights Hospitallers in the Holy Land* (London, 1931); Lamma, P., *Comneni e Staufer* (2 vols., Rome, 1955–7); Lamonte, J. L., *Feudal Monarchy in the Latin Kingdom of Jerusalem, 1100–1291* (Cambridge, Mass., 1932); Lamonte, J. L., *The Wars of Frederick II against the Ibelins in Syria and Cyprus*, with verse translation by M. J. Hubert (New York, 1936); Löher, F. von, *Kaiser Friedrichs II. Kampf um Cypern* (*Abh. München*, 1879); Longnon, J., *Les Français d'outremer au moyen âge* (Paris, 1929); Mas-Latrie, J. M. J. L. de, *Histoire de l'Île de Chypre sous le règne des Princes de la maison de Lusignan* (3 vols., Paris, 1856–61); Reinhard, J. P., *Vollständige Geschichte des Königreichs Cypern* (2 vols., Erlangen and Leipzig, 1766–8); Rey, E. G., *Essai sur la domination Française en Syrie durant le moyen âge* (Paris, 1886); Rey, E. G., *Les Colonies franques de Syrie aux XIIᵉ et XIIIᵉ siècles* (Paris, 1883); Rey, E. G., *Recherches géographiques et historiques sur la domination des Latins en Orient* (Paris, 1877); Richter, P., 'Beiträge zur Historiographie in den Kreuzfahrerstaaten, vornehmlich für die Geschichte Kaiser Friedrichs II.' (*MIöG* xiii, 1892; xv, 1894); Röhricht, R., *Beiträge zur Geschichte der Kreuzzüge* (2 vols. in one, Berlin, 1874–8); Röhricht, R., *Die Deutschen im heiligen Lande* (Innsbruck, 1894); Röhricht, R., *Die Kreuzfahrt Kaiser Friedrichs des Zweiten* (Berlin, 1872; reprinted with corrections and revisions in R.'s *Beiträge zur Geschichte der Kreuzzüge*, i, Berlin, 1874); Röhricht, R., *Geschichte des Königreichs Jerusalem, 1100–1291* (Innsbruck, 1898); Röhricht, R., *Regesta Regni Hierosolymitani, 1097–1291* (2 vols., Innsbruck, 1893–1904); Runciman, S., *A History of the Crusades* (3 vols., Cambridge, 1951–4); Schindler, H., *Die Kreuzzüge in der Altprovenzalischen und mittelhochdeutschen Lyrik* (Dresden and Neustadt, 1889); Setton, K. M. (ed.-in-chief), *A History of the Crusades*, vol. i: *The First Hundred Years* (ed. M. W. Baldwin and H. W. Hazard, Philadelphia, 1955), vol. ii: *The Later Crusades, 1189–1311* (ed. R. L. Wolff and H. W. Hazard, Philadelphia, 1962); Strayer, J. R., 'The Political Crusades of the Thirteenth Century' (*A History of the Crusades*, vol. ii, ed. R. L. Wolff et al.); Stubbs, W., *The Medieval Kingdoms of Cyprus and Armenia* (Oxford, 1878); Throop, P. A., 'Criticism of Papal Crusade Policy in Old French and Provençal' (*Speculum*, xiii, 1938); Throop, P. A., *Criticism of the Crusade. A Study of Public Opinion and Crusade Propaganda* (Amsterdam, 1940); Traub, E., *Der Kreuzzugsplan Kaiser Heinrichs VI. im Zusammenhang mit der Politik der Jahre 1195–1197* (Diss., Jena, 1910); Van Cleve, T. C., 'The Crusade of Frederick II' (*A History of the Crusades*, vol. ii: *The Later Crusades*, ed.

R. L. Wolff *et al.*); Van Cleve, T. C., 'The Fifth Crusade' (*A History of the Crusades*, vol. ii: *The Later Crusades*, ed. R. L. Wolff *et al.*); Wentzlaff-Eggebert, F. W., *Kreuzzugsdichtung des Mittelalters: Studien zu ihrer geschichtlichen und dichterischen Wirklichkeit* (Berlin, 1960).

6. Cultural Developments (General Aspects)

Baeumker, C., *Der Platonismus im Mittelalter* (Munich, 1916); Bernheim, E., *Mittelalterliche Zeitanschauungen in ihrem Einfluss auf Politik und Geschichtsschreibung*, vol. i (Tübingen, 1918); Burckhardt, J., *Die Kultur der Renaissance in Italien* (15th edn., Leipzig, 1926; a reprinting of the original edition); Burdach, K., *Rienzo und die geistliche Wandlung seiner Zeit* (*Vom Mittelalter zur Reformation*) (*Forschungen zur Geschichte der Deutschen Bildung*, ii, part 1, Berlin, 1913 ff.); Clerval, A., *Les Écoles de Chartres au moyen âge du Ve au XVIe siècle* (Chartres, 1895); Comparetti, D., *Vergil in the Middle Ages* (trans. E. F. M. Beneck, London, 1895); Gilbert, A. H., 'Notes on the Influence of the *secretum secretorum*' (*Speculum*, iii, 1928); Grabmann, M., *Der lateinische Averroismus des 13. Jahrhunderts und seine Stellung zur christlichen Weltanschauung* (*Sb. Bayer. Ak.* Jahrgang 1931, Heft iii); Grabmann, M., *Mittelalterliches Geistesleben: Abhandlungen zur Geschichte der Scholastik und Mystik* (Munich, 1926); Haskins, C. H., *The Renaissance of the Twelfth Century* (Cambridge, Mass., 1927); Haskins, C. H., *Studies in Medieval Culture* (Oxford, 1929); Haskins, C. H., *Studies in the History of Medieval Science* (Cambridge, Mass., 1937); Hauber, A., 'Kaiser Friedrich der Staufer und der langlebige Fisch' (*Archiv für Geschichte der Naturwissenschaften*, iii, 1911); Hauréau, B., *Histoire de la philosophie scolastique* (2nd edn., 3 vols., Paris, 1872–80); Kampers, F., *Kaiser Friedrich II. Der Wegbereiter der Renaissance* (Bielefeld and Leipzig, 1929); Karl, L., 'Recherches sur quelques ouvrages scientifiques du moyen âge' (*Revue des bibliothèques*, xxxviii, 1928); Lagarde, G. de, *La Naissance de l'esprit laïque au déclin du moyen âge* (6 vols., Paris, 1934–46); Langlois, Ch. V., *La Connaissance de la nature et du monde* (Paris, 1927); Niese, H., 'Zur Geschichte des geistigen Lebens am Hofe Kaiser Friedrichs II.' (*Hist. Zeitsch.* 108, 1912); Renan, E., and Paris, G., 'La Fontaine de Toutes Sciences: Du Philosophe Sidrach' (*Histoire Littéraire de la France*, vol. xxxi, Paris, 1893); Sarton, G., *Introduction to the History of Science* (5 vols., Washington, 1931–52); Schmutzerus, J. G., *De Friderici secundi I.R.C.A. in rem litterariam meritis dissertatio* (Leipzig, 1740); Stefano, A. de, *Federico II e le correnti spirituali del suo tempo* (Rome, 1922); Stefano, A. de, *La Cultura alla corte di Federico II. imperatore* (new edn., Bologna, 1950); Strunz, F., *Geschichte der Naturwissenschaften im Mittelalter* (Stuttgart, 1910); Thorndike, L., *History of Magic and Experimental Science* (8 vols., New York, 1923–58); Vossler, K., *Mediaeval Culture: an introduction to Dante and his times* (2 vols., New York, 1929); Werth, H., 'Altfranzösische Jagdlehrbücher nebst Handschriften-Bibliographie der abendländischen Jagdliteratur überhaupt' (*Zeitschr. für Romanische Philologie*, xii, 1859); Wiedemann, E., 'Fragen aus dem Gebiet der Naturwissenschaften, gestellt von Friedrich II.' (*Archiv für Kulturgeschichte*, xi, 1914).

7. German Cities and Principalities

Aldinger, P., *Die Neubesetzung der deutschen Bistümer unter Papst Innozenz IV., 1243–1254* (Leipzig, 1900); Barthold, F. W., *Geschichte der deutschen Städte und des deutschen Bürgerthums* (2 vols., Leipzig, 1850–3); Below, G. von, *Der deutsche Staat des Mittelalters* (2nd edn., Leipzig, 1925); Below, G. von, *Territorium und Stadt* (2nd edn., Berlin, 1923); Berchtold, J., *Die Entwicklung der Landeshoheit in Deutschland in der Periode von Friedrich II. bis zum Tode Rudolfs von Habsburg* (Munich, 1863); Blondel, G., *Études sur la politique de l'empereur Frédéric II en Allemagne et sur les transformations de la constitution allemande dans la première moitié du 13e siècle* (Paris, 1892); Börger, R., *Die Belehnungen der deutschen geistlichen Fürsten* (Diss., Leipzig, 1900); Bosl, K., *Die Reichsministerialität der Salier und Staufer: ein Beitrag zur Geschichte des hochmittelalterlichen deutschen Volkes, Staates und Reiches* (2 vols., *MGH, Schriften*, x, Stuttgart, 1950–1); Brackmann, A., *Der mittelalterliche Ursprung des Nationalstaaten* (*Sb. Ber. Ak.*, no. xiii, 1936); Brackmann, A., 'Die Wandlung der Staatsanschauungen im Zeitalter Kaiser Friedrichs I.' (*Hist. Zeitschr.* 145, 1931); Brackmann, A., 'The National State' (ed. and trans. G. Barraclough, *Medieval Germany*, ii); Brunner, H., *Deutsche Rechtsgeschichte* (2 vols., Leipzig, 1887; 2nd edn., 1906); Brunner, O., *Land und Herrschaft* (3rd edn., Brünn, 1943); Conrad, H., *Deutsche Rechtsgeschichte*, vol. i: *Frühzeit und Mittelalter* (Karlsruhe, 1954); Diegel, A., *Der päpstliche Einfluss auf die Bischofswahlen in Deutschland während des 13. Jahrhunderts* (Diss., Berlin, 1932); Dungern, O. Frhr. von, 'Constitutional Reorganization and Reform under the Hohenstaufen' (ed. and trans. G. Barraclough, *Medieval Germany*, ii); Dürre, H., *Geschichte der Stadt Braunschweig im Mittelalter* (Wolfenbüttel, 1875); Ebengreuth, A. Luschin von, 'Der deutsche Text des Mainzer Landfriedens und das österreichische Landesrecht' (*Neues Archiv*, xxv, 1900); Eggert, U., *Studien zur Geschichte der Landfrieden* (Diss., Göttingen, 1875); Eichmann, E., *Acht und Bann im Reichsrecht des Mittelalters* (Paderborn, 1909); Eichhorn, K. F., *Deutsche Staats- und Rechtsgeschichte* (4th edn., 4 vols., Göttingen, 1834–6); Ennen, L., *Geschichte der Stadt Köln* (5 vols., Cologne, 1863–80); Ernst, V., 'Die Entstehung der Württembergischen Städte' (*Württemberg. Studien, Festschrift zum 70. Geburtstag von Prof. E. Nägele*, 1926); Fein, H., 'Die staufischen Städtegründungen im Elsass' (*Schriften des Wissenschaft. Inst. der Elsass-Lothringer im Reich an der Universität*, Frankfurt, Neue Folge, xxiii, 1939); Ficker, J., *Vom Reichsfürstenstande* (2nd edn., Innsbruck 1911; orig. edn., Innsbruck, 1861); Franzel, E., *König Heinrich (VII.), Studien zur Geschichte des 'Staates' in Deutschland* (Prague, 1929); Frey, C., *Schicksale des königlichen Gutes in Deutschland unter den letzten Staufern seit König Philipp* (Berlin, 1881); Geffcken, H., *Die Krone und das niedere deutsche Kirchengut unter Kaiser Friedrich II. 1210–1250* (Diss., Jena, 1890); Hartung, J., 'Die Territorialpolitik der Magdeburger Erzbischöfe Wichmann, Ludolf und Albrecht 1152–1232' (*Geschichtsblätter für Stadt und Land*, xxi, Magdeburg, 1886); Hauck, A., *Kirchengeschichte Deutschlands* (5 vols. in 6, Leipzig, 1887–1920; vols. i–iv in 3rd and 4th edns.); Hegel, K., *Die Entstehung des deutschen Städtewesens* (Leipzig, 1898); Hegel, K., *Städte und Gilden der germanischen Völker im Mittelalter* (2 vols., Leipzig, 1891); Heil, B., *Die deutschen Städte und Bürger im Mittelalter* (Leipzig, 1903; no. 43 of *Aus Natur und Geistewelt*); Heimpel, H., 'Reich und Staat im deutschen Mittelalter' (*Arch. d. öffentl. Rechts*, Neue Folge, xvii, 1936); Heusler, A., *Deutsche Verfassungsgeschichte* (Leipzig, 1905); Heusler, A., *Institutionen des deutschen Privatrechts* (2 vols., Leipzig, 1885–6); Heyck, E., *Geschichte der Herzoge von Zähringen* (Freiburg i/B., 1891); His, R., *Das Strafrecht des deutschen Mittelalters*, i–ii (Leipzig, 1920–5); Hotz, W., 'Die staufischen Reichsburgen' (*Deutsches Volkstum*, 1937); Kalisch, H. K., *Über das Verhältnis des Geleitregals zum Zollregal* (Diss., Berlin, 1901); Kallen, G., 'Friedrich Barbarossas Verfassungsreform und das Landrecht des Sachsenspiegels' (*ZfRG, Abteil.* lviii, 1938); Keutgen, F., *Beiträge zur deutschen Territorial- und Stadtgeschichte* (3 vols., Kassel, 1896–7); Keutgen, F., *Der deutsche Staat des Mittelalters* (Jena, 1918); Keutgen, F., *Untersuchungen über den Ursprung der deutschen Stadtverfassung* (Leipzig, 1895); Kienast, W., 'Lehnrecht und Staatsgewalt im Mittelalter, Studien zu dem Mitteis'schen Werk' (*Hist. Zeitschr.* 158, 1938); Kirmse, J., 'Die Reichspolitik Hermanns I., Landgrafen von Thüringen und Pfalzgrafen von Sachsen, 1190–1217' (*Zeitschrift für Thüringische Geschichte*, 27, 28 (Neue Folge 19, 20), 1909/11); Kirn, P., 'Der mittelalterliche Staat und das geistliche Gericht' (*ZfRG* xlvi, 1926); Kirn, P., 'Die Verdienste der staufischen Kaiser um das Deutsche Reich' (*Hist. Zeitschr.* 164, 1941); Kist, J., *Fürst- und Erzbistum Bamberg: Leitfaden durch ihre Geschichte von 1007 bis 1960* (*Historischer Verein Bamberg*, 3rd edn., Bamberg, 1962); Klingelhöfer, E., *Die Reichs-*

gesetze von 1220, 1231–32 und 1235, ihr Werden und ihre Wirkung im deutschen Staat Friedrichs II. (Weimar, 1955); Knöpp, F., *Die Stellung Friedrichs II. und seiner beiden Söhne zu den deutschen Städten* (*Hist. Studien*, 181, Berlin, 1928); Koehne, C., *Der Ursprung der Stadtverfassung in Worms, Speier und Mainz* (Breslau, 1890); Koller, H., 'Zur Diskussion über die Reichsgesetze Friedrichs II.' (*MIöG* lxvi, 1958); Krabbo, H., *Die Besetzung der deutschen Bistümer unter der Regierung K. Friedrichs II.* Teil i (*Eberings Historische Studien*, 25, Berlin, 1901); Krammer, M., 'Das Kurfürstenkolleg von seinen Anfängen bis zum Zusammenschluss im Renser Kurverein des Jahres 1338' (*Quellen und Studien z. Verfassungsgeschichte d. deutschen Reiches*, v, 1, 1913); Kurth, G., *La Cité de Liège au moyen âge* (3 vols., Brussels, 1910); Löher, F. von, *Fürsten und Städte zur Zeit der Hohenstaufen, dargestellt in den Reichsgesetzen Friedrichs II.* (Halle, 1846); Maurer, G. L. von, *Geschichte der Städteverfassung in Deutschland* (4 vols., Erlangen, 1869–71); Meister, A., *Deutsche Verfassungsgeschichte von den Anfängen bis ins 15. Jahrhundert* (3rd edn., Leipzig, 1922); Meister, A., *Die Hohenstaufen im Elsass* (Diss., Strassburg, 1890); Metz, W., *Staufische Güterverzeichnisse* (Berlin, 1964); Mitteis, H., *Der Staat des hohen Mittelalters* (4th edn., Weimar, 1953); Mitteis, H., *Deutsche Rechtsgeschichte* (5th edn., Munich and Berlin, 1958); Mitteis, H., *Lehrecht und Staatsgewalt* (Weimar, 1933); Mitteis, H., 'Zum Mainzer Reichslandfrieden von 1235' (*ZfRG*, German. Abt. lxii, 1942); Molitor, E., 'Zur Entwicklung der Munt' (*ZfRG*, German. Abt. lxiv, 1944); Niese, Hans, *Die Verwaltung des Reichsgutes im 13. Jahrhundert. Ein Beitrag zur deutschen Verfassungsgeschichte* (Innsbruck, 1905); Niese, H., *Prokurationen und Landvogteien. Ein Beitrag zur Geschichte der Reichsgüterverwaltung im 13. Jahrhundert* (Diss., Strassburg, 1904); Nitzsch, K. W., *Ministerialität und Bürgerthum im 11. und 12. Jahrhundert* (*Vorbereitung zur Geschichte der staufischen Periode*, vol. i, Leipzig, 1859); Planitz, H., 'Forschungen zur Stadtverfassungsgeschichte', 1–3 (*ZfRG*, German. Abt. lx, 1940; lxiii, 1943; lxiv, 1944); Preuss, H., *Die Entwicklung des deutschen Städtewesens* i (Leipzig, 1906); Prochnow, F., *Das Spolienrecht und die Testierfähigkeit der Geistlichen im Abendlande bis zum 13. Jahrhundert* (*Eberings Historische Studien*, 136, Berlin, 1919); Rietschel, S., *Markt und Stadt im rechtlichen Verhältnis* (Leipzig, 1897); Rütimeyer, E., *Stadtherr und Stadtbürgerschaft in den rheinischen Bischofsstädten* (Stuttgart, 1928); Schaab, K. A., *Geschichte der Stadt Mainz* (4 vols., Mainz, 1841–51); Scheffer-Boichorst, P., *Das Gesetz Kaiser Friedrichs II. Das Gesetz Kaiser Friedrichs II. De resignandis privilegiis* (*Sb. Ber. Ak.* 1900); Schmeidler, B., 'Die Stellung Frankens im Gefüge des alten deutschen Reiches bis ins 13. Jahrhundert' (trans. G. Barraclough, *Medieval Germany*, ii); Schneider, F., 'Bistum und Geldwirtschaft' (*QF* ix, 1906); Scholz, R., *Beiträge zur Geschichte der Hoheitsrechte der deutschen Könige zur Zeit der ersten Staufer 1138–1197* (*Leipziger Studien aus dem Gebiete der Geschichte*, vols. 2, 4, edd. E. Brandenburg, G. Seelinger, and U. Wilcken, 1896); Schrader, E., *Das Befestigungsrecht in Deutschland von den Anfängen bis zum Beginn des 14. Jahrhunderts* (Göttingen, 1909); Schrader, E., *Ursprünge und Wirkungen der Reichsgesetze Friedrichs II. von 1220, 1231/32* (*ZfRG*, German. Abt. lxviii, 1951); Schröder, R., ed. and continued Eberhard Frhr. von Kunssberg, *Lehrbuch der deutschen Rechtsgeschichte* (7th edn., Leipzig, 1932); Schwineköper, B., 'Die Provienienz der goldenen Bulle Kaiser Friedrichs II. ⟨Statutum in favorem principum⟩ im Stadtarchiv Halle a.d. Saale' (*Archivalische Zeitschrift*, 49, 1953); Sohm, R., *Die Entstehung des deutschen Städtewesens* (Leipzig, 1890); Spangenberg, H., *Vom Lehnstaat zum Ständestaat* (Munich, 1912); Stabbe, O., *Geschichte der deutschen Rechtsquellen* (Leipzig, 1860); Steinacker, H., 'Der lateinische Entwurf zum Mainzer Landfrieden König Heinrichs (VII.) von 1234' (*MIöG* xlvi, 1932); Voltelini, H. von, 'Die deutsche Fassung des Mainzer Landfriedens' (*Zeitschr. des Hist. Vereins für Steiermark*, xxvi, 1931: *Festschrift für Luschin von Ebengreuth*); Waitz, G., *Deutsche Verfassungsgeschichte* (2nd edn., 8 vols., Berlin, 1880–96); Weiland, L., 'Friedrichs II. Privileg für die geistlichen Fürsten' (*Hist. Aufsätze zum Andenken an G. Waitz*, Hanover, 1886); Weller, K., 'Die staufische Städtegründung in Schwaben' (*Württembergische Vierteljahreshefte für Landes-*

geschichte, Neue Folge, xxxvi, 1930); Weller, K., 'Zur Organisation des Reichsgutes in der späteren Stauferzeit' (*Festschrift für D. Schäfer*, Jena, 1915); Winkelmann, E., 'Ungedruckte Urkunden und Briefe zur Reichsgeschichte des 13. Jahrhunderts' (*MIöG* xiv, 1893); Zeumer, K., 'Der deutsche Urtext des Landfriedens von 1235' (*Neues Archiv*, xxviii, 1903).

8. German Vernacular Literature

Bezzenberger, H. E. (ed.), *Fridankes Bescheidenheit* (Halle, 1872); Fischer, R., *Das Vernhältnis Walthers von der Vogelweide zu Friedrich II.* (Progr. Hamm, 1893); Henrici, E. (ed.), *Das deutsche Heldenbuch* (Berlin and Stuttgart, 1887); Koberstein, C. A., *Grundriss zur Geschichte der deutschen Nationalliteratur* (6th edn., revised by K. Bartsch, Leipzig, 1884); Koch, F., *Geschichte deutscher Dichtung* (5th edn., Hamburg, 1942); Kraus, C. von, *Die Gedichte Walthers von der Vogelweide* (zehnte Auflage mit Bezeichnung der Abweichungen von Lachmann und mit seinen Anmerkungen neu herausgegeben, Leipzig, 1936); Kuhn, H., *Minnesangs Wende* (*Hermae: Germanistische Forschungen*, Neue Folge, i, Tübingen, 1952); Meyer, E. H., 'Quellenstudien zur Mittelhochdeutschen Spielmannsdichtung' (*Zeitschrift für deutsches Altertum und deutsche Literatur*, hrsg. von E. Schröder und Gustav Roethe, Neue Folge, 38, 1894); Müllenhoff, K., 'Das Alter des Ortnit' (*Zeitschrift fur deutsches Altertum und deutsche Literatur*, i, 1867); Nellmann, E., *Die Reichsidee in deutschen Dichtungen der Salier- und früher Staufenzeit* (Berlin, 1963); Scherer, W., *Geschichte der deutschen Literatur* (11th edn., Berlin, 1910); Scherer, W., *Geistliche Poeten der deutschen Kaiserzeit* (2 vols., Strassburg, 1874 ff.); Schneider, H., *Heldendichtung, Geistlichendichtung, Ritterdichtung* (Heidelberg, 1925; enlarged edn., 1943); Wechssler, E., *Das Kulturproblem des Minnesangs* (2 vols., Halle, 1909 ff.).

9. Germany and Austria (General History)

Barraclough, G., *Medieval Germany* (2 vols., Oxford, 1938); Below, G. von, *Deutsche Reichspolitik einst und jetzt* (Tübingen, 1922); Below, G. von, *Die italienische Kaiserpolitik des deutschen Mittelalters mit besonderer Hinblick auf die Politik Friedrich Barbarossas* (Munich and Berlin, 1927); Bosl, K., *Zur Geschichte der Bayern* (Darmstadt, 1965); Bühler, J., *Die Hohenstaufen. Nach zeitgenössischen Quellen* (Leipzig, 1925); Cloüet, Abbé L., *Histoire de Verdun depuis l'origine de cette ville jusqu'en 1830*, i (Verdun, 1838); see also idem, *Histoire de Verdun et du pays verdunois* (3 vols., Verdun, 1867–70); Dehio, G., *Geschichte der deutschen Kunst* (6 vols., Berlin and Leipzig, 1919–26); Dehio, G., *L'Influence de l'art rançais sur l'art allemand au XIIIe siècle* (Ann. Int. Hist. Congrs., Paris, 1900, sec. 7); Ebengreuth, A. Luschin von, *Grundriss der österreichischen Reichsgeschichte* (Bamberg, 1899); Ebengreuth, A. Luschin von, *Österreichische Reichsgeschichte des Mittelalters* (2 vols., Bamberg, 1895–6); Gerbert, M., *Historiae nigrae silvae* (3 vols., S. Blaise, 1783–8); Grauert, H., *Die Kaisergräber im Dome zu Speier* (Sb. d. Bayer. Ak. 1900); Hantsch, H., *Geschichte Österreichs* (Graz and Vienna, 1951); Heinemann, L. von, *Die Welfischen Territorien seit dem Sturze Heinrichs des Löwen bis zur Gründung des Herzogthums Braunschweig-Lüneburg* (Diss., Leipzig, 1882); Hotz, W., *König und Verschwörer, Männer und Mächte um Heinrich (VII.) von Hohenstaufen* (*Deutsches Volkstum*, i, 1940); Hugelmann, K. G., *Die Wahl Konrads IV. zu Wien im Jahre 1237* (Weimar, 1914); Jastrow, J., and Winter, G., *Deutsche Geschichte im Zeitalter der Hohenstaufen, 1125–1273* (2 vols., Berlin, 1893–1901); Juritsch, G., *Geschichte der Babenberger und ihrer Länder, 976–1246* (Innsbruck, 1894); Källström, O., 'Das Reliquiar in Stockholm mit den von Friedrich gestifteten Kronen und seinem "Becher" ' (P. Schramm, *Kaiser Friedrichs II. Herrschaftszeichen*); Ketrzynski, W. von, *Die deutschen Orden und Konrad von Masovien, 1225–1235* (Lemberg, 1904); Kienast, W., *Die deutschen Fürsten im Dienst der Westmächte* (2 vols., Utrecht, Leipzig, and Munich, 1924–31); Kozak, C., *Über den Streit des österreichischen Herzogs Friedrich II. von Babenberg* *mit Kaiser Friedrich II.* (Czernowitz, 1896); Lavisse, E., *De Hermanno Salzensi Ordinis Teutonici Magistro* (Paris, 1875); Lhotsky, A., *Quellenkunde zur mittelalterlichen Geschichte Österreichs* (Vienna, 1963); Lindemann, H., *Die Ermordung des Herzogs Ludwig von Bayern und die päpstliche Agitation in Deutschland* (Diss., Rostock, 1892); Lindner, Th., 'Über die Entstehung des Kurfürstentums' (*MIöG* xvii, 1896); Lintzel, M., 'Die "Entstehung des Kurfürstenkollegs" ' (*Sb. Leipzig, Phil.-Hist.-Klasse*, 99, Heft 2, 1952); Meyer, Hans, *Die Militärpolitik Friedrich Barbarossas in Zusammenhang mit seiner Italienpolitik* (*Eberings Historische Studien*, 200, Berlin, 1930); Michael, E., *Geschichte des deutschen Volkes seit dem 13. Jahrhundert bis zum Ausgang des Mittelalters* (6 vols., Freiburg i/B., 1852–1917): *Politische Geschichte*, vol. vi; Nitzsch, K. W., *Deutsche Studien. Gesammelte Aufsätze und Vorträge zur deutschen Geschichte* (Berlin, 1879); Nitzsch, K. W., 'Staufische Studien' (*Hist. Zeitschr.* 3, 1843); Öhler, M., *Geschichte des deutschen Ritterordens*, vol. i (Elbing, 1908); Patze, H., 'Zur Chemnitzer Fälschung auf Friedrich II. zu 1226, April 30, Parma' (*Forschungen aus mitteldeutschen Archiven. Zum 60. Geburtstag von Hellmut Kretzschmar*, Berlin, 1953); Prutz, H., *Die geistlichen Ritterorden* (Berlin, 1907); Quidde, L., *Die Entstehung des Kurfürstencollegiums* (Frankfurt a/M., 1884); Raumer, F. von, *Geschichte der Hohenstaufen und ihrer Zeit* (3rd edn., 6 vols., Leipzig, 1857–8; reprinted, Berlin, 1943); Reuss, R., *De Scriptoribus Rerum Alsaticarum Historicis* (Strassburg, 1898); Rodenberg, C., 'Kaiser Friedrich II. und die deutsche Kirche' (*Historische Aufsätze, dem Andenken an Georg Waitz gewidmet*, Hanover, 1886); Rohden, J., 'Der Sturz Heinrichs (VII.)' (*FzDG* xxii, 1882); Rosbach, O., *Die Reichspolitik der trierischen Erzbischöfe vom Ausgange der Regierung Friedrichs I. bis zum Ende des Interregnums* (Trier, 1883–91); Rössler, H., *et al.*, *Biographisches Wörterbuch zur deutschen Geschichte* (Munich, 1952); Schäfer, D., *Deutsche Geschichte* (2 vols., 8th edn., Jena, 1921); Schmidt, M. G., 'Die Pfalbürger' (*Zeitschrift für Kulturgeschichte*, ix, 1902); Schwemer, R., *Innocenz III. und die deutsche Kirche während des Thronstreites von 1198 bis 1208* (Strassburg, 1882); Stälin, C. F., *Wirtembergische Geschichte* (4 vols., Stuttgart and Tübingen, 1841–73); Stimming, M., 'Kaiser Friedrich II. und der Abfall der deutschen Fürsten' (*Hist. Zeitschr.* 120, 1919); Thiel, F., *Kritische Untersuchungen über die im Manifest Kaiser Friedrichs II. vom Jahre 1236 gegen Friedrich II. von Österreich vorgebrachten Anklagens* (*Prager Studien aus dem Gebiete der Geschichtswissenschaft*, xi, 1905); Trautmann, C., *Heinrich VI. und der Lütticher Bischofsmord* (Cottbus, 1912); Uhlirz, K., *Handbuch der Geschichte Österreich-Ungarns bis 1526* (2nd edn., Leipzig, 1964); Ussermann, A., *Episcopatus Wirceburgensis* (S. Blaise, 1774); Voigt, J., *Geschichte des deutschen Ritterordens* (2 vols., Berlin, 1857–9); Wackernagel, R., *Geschichte des Elsass* (Freiburg i/B., 1940); Waldburg-Wolfegg, Hubert Graf von, *Vom Nordreich der Hohenstaufen* (Munich, 1961); Waldburg-Wolfegg, Hubert Graf von, *Vom Südreich der Hohenstaufen* (Munich, 1955); Winkelmann, E., 'Die Wahl König Heinrichs (VII.), seine Regierungsweise und sein Sturz' (*FzDG* i, 1860); Zallinger, O. von, *Ministeriales und Milites. Untersuchungen über die ritterlichen Unfreien zunächst in bayerischen Rechtsquellen des XII. und XIII. Jahrhunderts* (Innsbruck, 1878); Zeller, J. S., *Histoire d'Allemagne* (7 vols., Paris, 1872–92).

10. International and Interregional Legatine and Ambassadorial Missions

Cartellieri, A., 'Das deutsch-französische Bündnis von 1187 und seine Wandlungen' (*Hist. Vierteljahrschr.* xxvii, 1932); Clerc, E., *Essai sur l'histoire de la Franche-Comté* (2 vols., Besançon, 1840–6; 2nd edn., Besançon, 1870); Febvre, L., *Histoire de Franche-Comté* (Paris, 1912); Francesco, U. A. de, *Enrico III d'Inghilterra, Bonifacio di Savoia e la loro politica verso Federico II di Svevia* (Naples, 1939); Friedländer, I., *Die päpstlichen Legaten in Deutschland und Italien am Ende des XII. Jahrhunderts, 1181–1198* (*Eberings Historische Studien*, 177, Berlin, 1928); Ganshof, F. L., *Le Moyen Âge* (*Histoire des relations internationales*, i, Paris, 1958); Hampe, K., *Das Hochmittelalter, Geschichte des*

Abendlandes von 900–1250, mit einem Nachwort von Gerd Tellenbach (4th edn., Cologne, 1953); Hofmeister, A., *Deutschland und Burgund im früheren Mittelalter* (Leipzig, 1914); Jamison, E., 'Alliance of England and Sicily in the Second Half of the Twelfth Century' (*Journal of the Warburg and Courtauld Institutes,* vi, 1943); Jordan, E., *L'Allemagne et l'Italie aux XIIe et XIIIe siècles (Histoire du Moyen Âge IV,* i, ed. G. Glotz, Paris, 1939); Kantorowicz, E., 'Petrus de Vinea in England' (*MIöG* li, 1937); Kienast, W., *Deutschland und Frankreich in der Kaiserzeit, 900–1270* (Leipzig, 1943); Kienast, W., *Die deutschen Fürsten im Dienst der Westmächte bis zum Tode Philipps des Schönen von Frankreich* (2 vols., Utrecht, Leipzig, and Munich, 1924–31); Marchetti-Longhi, G., 'La legazione in Lombardia di Gregorio da Montelongo negli anni 1238–51' (*Arch. Soc. Rom.* 36–8, 1913–15); Mariotte, J.-Y., *Le Comté de Bourgogne sous les Hohenstaufen, 1156–1208* (Paris, 1963); Menzel, V., *Deutsches Gesandtschaftswesen im Mittelalter* (Hanover, 1892); Pirenne, H., *Histoire de l'Europe* (Paris, 1936); Queller, D. E., 'Thirteenth-Century Diplomatic Envoys: *Nuncii* and *Procuratores*' (*Speculum,* xxxv, 1960); Ruess, K., *Die rechtliche Stellung der päpstlichen Legaten bis Bonifaz VIII.* (Paderborn, 1912); Schwann, M., 'Ludwig der Heilige von Frankreich und seine Beziehungen zu Kaiser und Papst' (*Zeitschrift für allgemeine Geschichte,* iv, 1887); Sybel, H. von, 'Deutschland und Dänemark im dreizehnten Jahrhundert' (*Hist. Zeitschr.* 12, 1852); Tanner, T., *Bibliotheca Britannico-Hibernica* (London, 1748); Usinger, R., *Deutsch-dänische Geschichte, 1189–1227* (Berlin, 1863); Zimmermann, H., *Die päpstliche Legation in der ersten Hälfte des XIII. Jahrhunderts, 1198–1241* (Paderborn, 1913).

11. *Italy, Sicily, and Sardinia*

Besta, E., *La Sardegna medioevale* (2 vols., Palermo, 1908–9); Bocca, F., *Biblioteca storica italiana* (Turin, 1881); Camera, M., *Annali delle Due Sicilie* (2 vols., Naples, 1841–60); Capasso, B., *Le fonti della storia delle provincie napoletane dal 568 al 1500* (*Arch. stor. napoletana,* 1876–1877–1880; see also later edn. with notes by E. Mastrojanni, Naples, 1902); Caruso, A., 'Indagini sulla legislazione di Federico di svevi per il Regno di Sicilia — le leggi pubblicate a Foggia nell'aprile 1240' (*Arch. stor. pugliese,* iv, 1951); Caruso, G. B., *Bibliotheca historica regni Siciliae* (2 vols., Palermo, 1719–23); Cipolla, C., *Per la storia d'Italia e de' suoi conquistatori nel Medio Evo più antico* (Bologna, 1895); Cotterill, H. B., *Medieval Italy during a Thousand Years (305–1313)* (London, 1915); Fasoli, G., *Aspetti della politica italiana di Federico II* (Bologna, 1964); Gonzenbach, L., *Sizilianische Märchen* (Leipzig, 1870); Gregorio, R., *Considerazioni sopra la storia di Sicilia* (2nd edn., 4 vols., Palermo, 1831–9; also a 3rd edn., 1845); Hahn, H., *et al., Hohenstaufenburgen in Süditalien* (Ingelheim, 1961); Hartmann, L. M., *Geschichte Italiens im Mittelalter* (6 vols., Leipzig, 1897 ff.; vol. iii appeared in 1911); Haskins, C. H., 'England and Sicily in the Twelfth Century' (*EHR* xxvi, 1911); Hayward, F., *Histoire de la Maison de Savoie, 1000–1553* (Paris, 1941); Hellmann, S., *Die Grafen von Savoyen und das Reich bis zum Ende der staufischen Periode* (Innsbruck, 1900); Heskel, A., *Die Historia Sicula des Anonymus Vaticanus und des Gaufredus Malaterra* (Kiel, 1891); Hochholzer, H., 'Sizilien als Beispiel der mittelmeerischen Kulturschichtung' (*Hist. Zeitschr.* 155, 1936–7); Jordan, É., *Les Origines de la domination angevine en Italie* (Paris, 1909); Klewitz, H. W., 'Studien über die Wiederherstellung der römischen Kirche in Süditalien durch das Reformpapsttum' (*QF* xxv, 1933–4); Manno, G., *Storia di Sardegna* (3rd edn., 2 vols., Milan, 1835); Niese, H., 'Das Bistum Catania' (*Gött. Nachrichten,* 1913); Piazza, F., *Le colonie e i dialetti lombardo-siculi* (Catania, 1921); Previté-Orton, C., *The Early History of the House of Savoy, 1000–1233* (Cambridge, 1912); Ruhrmohr, C. F. von, *Italienische Forschungen* (Berlin, 1827–31); Runciman, S., *The Sicilian Vespers* (Cambridge, 1958); Schmeidler, B., 'Der sogenannte Cusentinus bei Tolomeus von Lucca' (*Neues Archiv,* xxxii, 1906–7), used in connection with Romuald's

Annales; Tomassetti, G., *La Campagna Romana antica, medioevale e moderna* (4 vols., Rome, 1910–26); Volpe, G., *Il Medioevo italiano* (2nd edn., Florence, 1928); Waern, C., *Mediaeval Sicily* (New York, 1911); Zeller, J. S., *Histoire de l'Italie depuis l'invasion des Barbares jusqu'à nos jours* (Paris, 1853; 2nd edn., 1865).

12. *Jews (Cultural Influence)*

Beugnot, A., *Les Juifs d'Occident* (Paris, 1824); Caro, G., *Sozial- und Wirtschaftsgeschichte der Juden im Mittelalter und der Neuzeit* (2 vols., Leipzig, 1908); Fernández, A. A., *Literatura Rabinica Española del siglo XIII* (Barcelona, 1898); Graetz, H., *Geschichte der Juden* (4th edition, 13 vols., Leipzig, 1897–1911; Eng. trans., 6 vols., Philadelphia, 1891–8); Güdemann, M., *Geschichte des Erziehungswesens und der Cultur der abendländischen Juden in Italien* (Vienna, 1884); *Jewish Encyclopaedia* (12 vols., New York, 1901–6); Renan, E., 'Les Rabbins français' (*Hist. littéraire de la France*, xxvi, Paris, 1873); Robert, U., *Les Signes d'Infamie au Moyen Âge* (Paris, 1889); Straus, R., *Die Juden im Königreich Sizilien unter Normannen und Staufern* (Heidelberg, 1910).

13. *Latin Literature and Literary Style*

Clötta, W., *Komödie und Tragödie im Mittelalter: Beiträge zur Literaturgeschichte des Mittelalters und der Renaissance* (2 vols., Halle, 1890–2); Cohn, E. S., 'The Manuscript Evidence for the Letters of Peter of Blois' (*EHR* xli, 1926); De Ghellinck, J., *L'Essor de la littérature latine au XIIe siècle* (2 vols., Brussels and Paris, 1946); Du Méril, É., *Poésies inédites du moyen âge* (Paris, 1854); Gröber, G., 'Lateinische Literatur' (*Grundriss der Romanischen Philologie*, Strassburg, 1886–1901), ii, part i; Hampe, K., *Mitteilungen aus der Capuaner Briefsammlung* (*Sb. Heidelberger Ak.* 1910–12, no. 13 (i–ii) and 14 (iii–iv)); Hampe, K., and Hennesthal, R., 'Die Reimser Briefsammlung in cod. 1275 der Reimser Stadtbibliothek' (*Neues Archiv*, xlvii, 1928); Hanauer, G., 'Material zur Beurteilung der Petrus de Vinea-Briefe' (*MIöG* xxi, 1900); Hartmann, F., *Die Literatur von Früh- und Hochsalerno* (Diss., Leipzig, 1919); Haskins, C. H., 'Latin Literature under Frederick II' (*Speculum*, iii, 1928); Heckel, R. von, *Das päpstliche und sicilische Registerwesen* (*Archiv für Urkundenforschung*, i, 1908); Heilin, M., *A History of Medieval Latin Literature* (trans. J. C. Snow from *Littérature d'Occident: Histoire des lettres du moyen âge*, Brussels, 1943); Heller, E., 'Die *ars dictandi* des Thomas von Capua' (*Sb. Heidelberger Ak.* 1928–9); Heller, E., 'Zur Frage des kurialen Stileinflusses in der sizilischen Kanzlei Friedrichs II.' (*Deutsches Archiv*, xix, 1963); Herter, F., *Die Podestaliteratur Italiens im 12. und 13. Jahrhundert* (*Beiträge zur Kulturgeschichte des Mittelalters und der Renaissance*, ed. W. Goetz, vii, Leipzig and Berlin, 1910); Huillard-Bréholles, J. L., 'Notice sur le véritable auteur du poème "De balneis Puteolanis" ' (*Mémoires de la Société des antiquaires de France*, i, 1807); Kantorowicz, E., 'The Prologue to *Fleta* and the School of Petrus de Vinea' (*Speculum*, xxxii, 1957); Ladner, G., 'Formularbeihelfe in der Kanzlei Kaiser Friedrichs II. und die "Briefe des Petrus de Vinea" ' (*MIöG, Ergänzungsband* xii, 1933); Lehmann, P., *Pseudo-antike Literatur des Mittelalters* (Leipzig, 1927); Levi, E., 'L'ultimo re de Giullari' (*Studi medievali*, new series, i, 1928); Maccarrone, N., *La vita del latino in Sicilia fino all'età normanna* (Florence, 1915); Manitius, M., *Geschichte der lateinischen Literatur des Mittelalters*, iii (Munich, 1931); Mercati, S. G., 'Deux poésies dialogiques sur les fables d'Héro et Léandre et d'Apollon et Daphné' (*Byzantinoslavica*, ix, 1937); Norden, E., *Die antike Kunstprosa vom 6. Jahrhundert v. Chr. bis in die Zeit der Renaissance* (2 vols., new edn., Leipzig, 1909); Pagano, A., *Studi di letteratura latina medievale* (Nicotera, 1931); Panneborg, A., 'Über der Ligurinus' (*FzDG* xi, 1871); Procopo, E., 'I bagni di Pozzuoli' (*Arch. stor. napoletane*, xi, 1886); Raby, F. J. E., *A History of Secular Latin Poetry in the Middle Ages* (2nd edn., 2 vols., Oxford, 1934); Rand, E. K., 'The Classics in the

Thirteenth Century' (*Speculum*, iv, 1929); Rockinger, L. von, *Briefsteller und Formelbücher des XI. bis XIV. Jahrhunderts* (*Quellen und Erörterungen zur bayerischen und deutschen Geschichte*, ix, 1863–4 (2 vols.); reprinted 1961); Rockinger, L. von, 'Über *ars dictandi* und die *summae dictaminis* in Italien' (*Sb. Bayer. Ak.* i, 1861); Rockinger, L. von, *Über Formelbücher vom dreizehnten bis zum sechzehnten Jahrhundert als Rechtsgeschichte* (Munich, 1855); Santifaller, L., *Beiträge zur Geschichte der Beschreibstoffe im Mittelalter mit besonderer Berücksichtigung der päpstlichen Kanzlei* (*MIöG, Ergänzungsband* xvi/i, 1953); Schaller, H. M., 'Zur Entstehung der sogenannten Briefsammlung des Petrus de Vinea' (*Deutsches Archiv*, xii, 1956); Schillmann, F., *Die Formularsammlung des Marinus von Eboli*. 1. *Entstehung und Inhalt* (Rome, 1929); Schmale, F.-J., 'Die Bologneser Schule der *Ars dictandi*' (*Deutsches Archiv*, xiii, 1957); Schmeidler, B., *Italienische Geschichtsschreiber des XII. und XIII. Jahrhunderts* (Leipzig, 1880; 2nd edn., 1900); Ullmann, B. L., *The Humanism of Coluccio Salutati* (*Medioevo e Umanesimo*, 4, 1963); Voigt, G., *Die Wiederbelebung des classischen Alterthums* (2 vols., 3rd edn., ed. M. Lehnerdt, Berlin, 1893), vol. ii; Wattenbach, W. (ed.), *Universis animalibus eadem lege viventibus fere bestie de regno Apulie gressus elegere tuciores* (*Sb. Ber. Ak.* 1892); Wieruszowski, H., 'A Twelfth-Century "Ars dictaminis" in the Barberini Collection of the Vatican Library' (*Traditio*, xviii, 1962); Winkelmann, E., 'Drei Gedichte Heinrichs von Avranches an Kaiser Friedrich II.' (*FzDG* xviii, 1878); Young, K., *The Drama of the Medieval Church* (Oxford, 1933); Zezschwitz, G. von, *Das mittelalterliche Drama vom Ende des römischen Kaisertums und von der Erscheinung des Antichrists* (Leipzig, 1877).

14. *Medicine, Medical History, and the School of Salerno*

Archiv für Geschichte der Medizin (later *Sudhoff's Archiv* ...) (hrsg. von der Puschmann-Stiftung, red. von K. Sudhoff, 4, Leipzig, 1908 ff.); Capparoni, P., *Il 'De quattuor humoribus corporis humani' di Alfano I, archievescovo di Salerno* (Rome, 1928); Gould, G. M., and Pyle, W. L., *Anomalies and Curiosities of Medicine* (Philadelphia, 1897); Holmes, U. T., and Weedon, F., 'Peter of Blois as Physician' (*Speculum*, xxxvi, 1962); Hönger, F., *Ärztliche Verhaltungsmassregeln auf dem Heerzug ins Heilige Land für Kaiser Friedrich II. geschrieben von Adam von Cremona* (Diss., Leipzig, 1913); Moulé, L. *Histoire de la médecine vétérinaire*: 2nd part, *au moyen âge* (Paris, 1898); Puschmann, T., *et al.*, *Handbuch der Geschichte der Medizin*, mit einem Vorwort von G. Rath (Jena, 1902–5); Renzi, S. de, *Collectio salernitana* (5 vols., Naples, 1852–9); Renzi, S. de, *Storia documentata della Scuola Medica di Salerno* (Naples, 1857); Sudhoff, K., 'Ein diätetischer Brief an Kaiser Friedrich II. von seinem Hofphilosophen Magister Theodor' (*Archiv für Geschichte der Medizin*, x, 1916); Thorndike, L., *Notes on Medical Texts in Manuscripts at London and Oxford* (offprint from *Janus*, xlviii, no. 3, Leiden, 1959).

15. *Mendicant Orders, Heresy, and the Inquisition*

Brooke, R. B., *Early Franciscan Government: Elias to Bonaventura* (Cambridge, 1959); Ehrhard, A., *Das Mittelalter und seine kirchliche Entwicklung* (Mainz and Munich, 1908); Förg, L., *Die Ketzerverfolgung in Deutschland unter Gregor IX.* (*Hist. Studien*, 218, Berlin, 1932); Gratien, B., *Histoire de la fondation et de l'évolution de l'ordre des Frères mineurs au XIIIe siècle* (Paris, 1928); Grundmann, H., *Religiöse Bewegungen im Mittelalter* (Berlin, 1935); Hansen, J., *Zauberwahn, Inquisition und Hexenprozess im Mittelalter* (Munich, 1900); Hefele, H., *Die Bettelorden und das religiöse Volksleben Ober- und Mittelitaliens im 13. Jahrhundert* (*Beiträge zur Kulturgeschichte der Renaissance*, hrsg. von W. Goetz, Heft ix, Leipzig and Berlin, 1910); Lea, H. C., *A History of the Inquisition in the Middle Ages* (3 vols., New York, 1888); Monticelli, G., *Vita religiosa italiana nel secolo XIII* (Turin, 1932); Müller, K., *Die Anfänge des Minoritenordens und der Bussbruderschaften*

(Freiburg i/B., 1885); Sutter, C., *Johann von Vicenza und die italienische Friedensbewegung im Jahre 1233* (Freiburg i/B., 1891); Volpe, G., *Movimenti religiosi e sette ereticali nella società medioevale italiana secoli xi–xiv* (Florence, 1922).

16. *Military Concerns and Battles*

Baltzer, M., *Zur Geschichte des deutschen Kriegswesens von den letzten Karolingern bis auf Kaiser Friedrich II.* (Leipzig, 1877); Delbrück, H., *Geschichte der Kriegskunst im Rahmen der politischen Geschichte* (6 vols., Berlin, 1920–9); Egelhaaf, E., 'Die Schlacht bei Frankfurt am 5. August 1246' (*Württembergische Vierteljahrshefte*, Neue Folge, xxxi, 1925); Erben, W., *Kriegsgeschichte des Mittelalters* (*Hist. Zeitschr.*, Beiheft 16, 1929); Hadank, K., *Die Schlacht bei Cortenuovo* (Berlin, 1905); Köhler, G., *Die Entwicklung des Kriegswesens und der Kriegsführung in der Ritterzeit von der Mitte des 11. Jahrhunderts bis zu den Hussitenkriegen* (3 vols., Breslau, 1886–90); Mikulla, J., *Der Söldner in den Heeren Kaiser Friedrichs II.* (Diss., Breslau, 1885); Niese, H., 'Zur Geschichte des deutschen Soldrittertums in Italien' (*QF* viii, 1905); Schmitthenner, P., *Das freie Söldnertum im abendländischen Imperium des Mittelalters* (Munich, 1934).

17. *Monte Cassino in the Norman Era*

Bloch, H., *Monte Cassino, Byzantium and the West in the Earlier Middle Ages* (*Dumbarton Oaks Papers*, 3, 1946); Caspar, E., *Petrus Diaconus und die Monte Cassineser Fälschungen* (Berlin, 1909); Caspar, E., 'Zur ältesten Geschichte von Monte Cassino' (*Neues Archiv*, xxxiv, 1909); Dantier, A., *Les Monastères bénédictins d'Italie* (2 vols., Paris, 1866); Garufi, C. A., 'Le Benedettine in Sicilia da San Gregorio al tempo svevo' (*Bollettino dell'Istituto Storico Italiano*, xlvii, 1932); Gattola, E., *Historia Abbatiae Casinensis* (2 vols., Venice, 1733), and *Ad historiam Abbatiae Casinensis accessiones* (2 vols., Venice, 1734); Inguanez, Dom M., 'Montecassino e l'Oriente nel Medioevo' (*Atti del IV Congresso Nazionale di Studi Romani*, i, Rome, 1938); Klewitz, H. W., 'Petrus Diaconus und die Montecassinenser Klosterchronik des Leo von Ostia' (*Archiv für Urkundenforschungen*, xiv, 1936); Palmarocchi, R., *L'abbazia di Montecassino et la conquista normanna* (Rome, 1913); Smidt, W., 'Guido von Monte Cassino und die "Fortetzung" der Chronik Leos durch Petrus Diaconus' (*Festschrift für A. Brackmann*, Weimar, 1931); Smidt, W., 'Über den Verfasser der drei letzten Redaktionen der Chronik Leos von Monte Cassino' (*Papsttum und Kaisertum: Festschrift für Paul Kehr*, Munich, 1926); Tosti, L., *Storia della badia di Monte Cassino* (3 vols., Naples, 1842–3).

18. *Normans in Sicily*

Behring, W., 'Sicilianische Studien: I, Die Anfänge des Königreiches; II, Regesten des normannischen Königshauses (1130–1197)' (*Progr. des kgl. Gymnasiums zu Elbing*, 1882, 1887); Caspar, E., *Die Gründungsurkunden der sicilischen Bistümer und die Kirchenpolitik Graf Rogers I., 1082–1098* (Innsbruck, 1902); Caspar, E., *Roger II. und die Gründung der normannisch-sicilianischen Monarchie* (Innsbruck, 1904); Cerone, F., *L'Opera politica e militare di Ruggiero II in Africa ed in Oriente* (Catania, 1913); Chalandon, F., *Histoire de la domination normande en Italie et en Sicile* (2 vols., Paris, 1907); Clementi, D. R., 'Some Unnoticed Aspects of the Emperor Henry VI's Conquest of the Norman Kingdom of Sicily' (*Bull. of the John Rylands Library*, xxxvi, 1953–4, 328–59); Cohn, W., *Das Zeitalter der Normannen in Sizilien* (Bonn and Leipzig, 1920); Delarc, O., *Les Normands en Italie, depuis les premières invasions jusqu'à l'avènement de S. Grégoire VII (859–862, 1016–1073)* (Paris, 1883); Dodati, L., *Delle monete che si nominano nelle constituzioni delle Due Sicilie* (Naples, 1788); Dondorff, H., *Die Normannen und ihre Bedeutung für das europäische Culturleben im Mittelalter* (Berlin, 1875); Engel, A., *Recherches sur la numismatique et la sigillographie des Normands de Sicile et d'Italie* (Paris, 1882); Freeman, E. A., 'The Normans at Palermo' (*Historical Essays*, 3rd series, London, 1871–92); Fréville, R. de, 'Étude sur l'organisation judiciaire en Normandie aux XIIᵉ et XIIIᵉ siècles' (*Nouvelle Revue historique de droit*, 1912); Garufi, C. A., 'Sull'ordinamento amministrativo normanno in Sicilia: exhiquier o diwan?' (*Arch. stor. ital.*, 5th series, xxxvii, 1901); Hartwig, O., 'Re Guiglielmo e il suo grande ammiraglio Majone di Bari' (*Arch. stor. per le provincie napoletane*, viii, 1883); Haskins, C. H., *The Normans in European History* (Boston and New York, 1915); Heinemann, L. von, *Geschichte der Normannen in Unteritalien und Sicilien bis zum Aussterben des normannischen Königshauses* (vol. i, Leipzig, 1894); Holach, F., *Die auswärtige Politik des Königreichs Sizilien vom Tode Rogers II. bis zum Frieden von Venedig* (Basel, 1892); *Il regno normanno. Conferenze tenute in Palermo per l'VIII centenario dell'incoronazione di Ruggero a re di Sicilia* (Messina, 1932); Jamison, E., 'The Norman Administration of Apulia and Capua more especially under Roger I and William I, 1127–1166' (Papers of the British School at Rome, vi, no. 6, 1913); Kehr, P., *Die Belehnungen der süditalienischen Normannenfürsten durch die Päpste (1059–1192)* (*Abh. der Preuss. Akad. Phil.-Hist.-Klasse*, 1934, no. 1); La Lumia, I., *Storia della Sicilia sotto Guglielmo il Buono* (Florence, 1867); La Mantia, G., 'La Sicilia ed il suo dominio nell'Africa settentrionale' (*Arch. stor. sic.* xliv, 1922); La Mantia, G., 'Sull' uso della registrazione della cancelleria del Regno di Sicilia dei normanni a Federico III d'Aragona, 1130–1377' (*Arch. stor. sic.* xxxi, 1906); Leicht, P. S., 'Lo stato normanno' (*Il Regno normanno*, 1932); Lopez, R. S., 'The Norman Conquest of Sicily' (*A History of the Crusades*, vol. i, eds. M. W. Baldwin and H. W. Hazard); Monti, G. M., *Lo stato normanno svevo. Lineamenti e ricerche* (Trani, 1934; also a new edition, 1945); Marongiu, A., 'L'héritage normand de l'état de Frédéric II de Souabe' (*Studi medioevali in onore di Antonio de Stefano*, Palermo, 1956); Niese, H., *Die Gesetzgebung der normannischen Dynastie in Regnum Siciliae* (Halle, 1910); Ottendorf, H., *Die Regierung der beiden letzten Normannenkönige, Tankreds und Wilhelms III. von Sizilien, und ihre Kämpfe gegen Kaiser Heinrich VI.* (Diss., Bonn, 1899); Palomes, A., *La storia di li Nurmanni 'n Sicilia* (4 vols., Palermo, 1883–7); Panzer, F., 'Die italienischen Normannen in der deutschen Heldensage' (*Deutsche Forschungen*, Heft i, Frankfurt, 1925); Pontieri, E., 'I Normanni dell'Italia meridionale e la Prima Crociata' (*Arch. stor. ital.* cxiv, 1956); Pontieri, E., 'I Normanni e la fondazione del Regno di Sicilia' (*Il Regno normanno*, 1932); Schack, A. F. von, *Geschichte der Normannen in Sicilien* (2 vols., Stuttgart, 1889); Schipa, M., 'Storia del principato longobardo di Salerno' (*Arch. stor. per le provincie napoletane*, xii, 1887); Siragusa, G. B., *Il Regno di Guglielmo I in Sicilia* (2 vols., Palermo, 1885–6; 2nd edn., 1929); Stefano, A. de, *La cultura in Sicilia nel periodo normanno* (new edn., Bologna, 1954); Théophane de Taormine, *Homiliae in Evangelia dominicalia et festa totius anni* (ed. P. Francesco Scorso, Lutetiae Parisiorum, 1644); Villars, J. B., *Les Normands en Méditerranée* (Paris, 1951); White, L. T., Jr., *Latin Monasticism in Norman Sicily* (Cambridge, Mass., 1938); Wieruszowski, H., 'Roger II of Sicily, *Rex-Tyrannus*, in Twelfth Century Political Thought' (*Speculum*, xxxviii, 1963); Willemsen, C. A., *Apulien, Land der Normannen, Land der Staufer* (Leipzig, 1944); Winckler, A., 'Gregor VII. und die Normannen' (*Sammlung gemeinverständlicher wissenschaftlicher Vorträge*, vol. x, Heft 234, 1875).

19. *Papal–Imperial Relations*

Acquacotte, C., *Memorie de Matelicz* (Ancona, 1838); Audisio, G., *Sistema politico e religioso di Federico II e di Pier della Vigna* (Diss., Rome, 1866); van den Baar, P. A., *Die kirchliche Lehre de Translatio Imperii Romani bis zur Mitte des 13. Jahrhunderts* (*Analecta Gregoriana*, lxxviii, Rome, 1956); Baethgen, F., 'Der Anspruch des Papsttums auf das Reichsvikariat' (*ZfRG*, Kan. Abt. xli, 1920); Baethgen, F., *Die Regentschaft Papst*

Innocenz III. im Königreich Sizilien (Heidelberg, 1914); Balan, P., *La prima lotta di Gregorio IX con Federigo II* (Modena, 1871); Baldwin, J. W., 'The Intellectual Preparation for the Canon of 1215 Against Ordeals' (*Speculum*, xxxvi, 1961); Barry, W., *The Papal Monarchy from St. Gregory the Great to Boniface XIII (595–1303)* (London, 1922); Baumann, J. J., *Die Staatslehre des heiligen Thomas von Aquino* (2 vols., Leipzig, 1873 and 1909); Bernheim, E., 'Politische Begriffe des Mittelalters im Lichte der Anschauungen Augustins' (*DZfG*, Neue Folge, i, 1896–7); Bernini, F., 'Come si preparò la rovina di Federico II (Parma. la lega medio-pedana e Innocenzo IV dal 1238 al 1247)' (*Riv. stor. ital.* lx, 1948); Biondo, Flavio, *Historiarum ab inclinato Romano imperio decades III* (2 vols., Basel, 1531); Bloch, H., review of M. Krammer, *Der Reichsgedanke des staufischen Kaiserhauses* (*GGA*, 1909); Block, F., *Reichsidee und Nationalstaaten* (Munich, 1943); Böhmer, H., *Kaiser Friedrich II. im Kampf um das Reich* (Diss., Cologne, 1937); Bretholz, B., 'Ein päpstliches Schreiben gegen Kaiser Otto IV. von 1210, Oktober 30, Lateran' (*Neues Archiv*, xxii, 1897); Brezzi, P., *Aspetti della storia dei movimenti religiosi in Italia* (Turin, 1956); Brezzi, P., *Il Papato* (Rome, 1951; 2nd edn., 1967); Brezzi, P., *Roma e l'Impero medioevale 774–1252* (*Storia di Roma*, 10, Bologna, 1947); Brolo, L. de, 'Sopra Teofano Cerameo ricerche e schiarimenti' (*Arch. stor. sic.* ii, 1877); Carlyle, R. W. and A. J., *A History of Mediaeval Political Theory in the West* (5 vols., Edinburgh and London, 1903–28); Caro, J., *Die Beziehungen Heinrichs VI. zur römischen Kurie während der Jahre 1190–7* (Diss., Rostock, 1902); Catalano, G., 'Imperio, regni, e sacerdozio nel pensiero di Uguccio da Pisa' (*Riv. di storia del diritto italiano*, 32, 1957); Cherrier, C. de, *Histoire de la lutte des papes et des empereurs de la maison souabe* (2nd edn., 3 vols., Paris, 1858–9); Cohn, W., 'Die Hohenstaufen im Urteil Dantes und der neueren Geschichtsforschung' (*Deutsches Dante-Jahrbuch*, xv, Neue Folge, vi, 1930); Dehio, L., *Innocenz IV. und England. Ein Beitrag zur Kirchengeschichte des 13. Jahrhunderts* (Berlin and Leipzig, 1914); Delisle, L., 'Mémoire sur les actes d'Innocent III' (*Bibl. de l'École des Chartes*, 4e série, 1858); Domeier, V., *Die Päpste als Richter über die deutschen Könige von der Mitte des 11. bis zum Ausgang des 13. Jahrhunderts* (*Untersuchungen zur deutschen Staats- und Rechtsgeschichte*, hrsg. von O. Gierke, 53, Breslau, 1897); Eicken, H. von, *Geschichte und System der mittelalterlichen Weltanschauung* (Stuttgart, 1887); Engelmann, E., *Der Anspruch der Päpste auf Konfirmation und Approbation bei den deutschen Königswahlen (1077–1379)* (Breslau, 1886); Engelmann, E., *Philipp von Schwaben und Papst Innocenz III. während des deutschen Thronstreites, 1198–1208* (Berlin, 1896); Erler, A., 'Die Ronkalischen Gesetze des Jahres 1158' (*ZfRG*, German Abt. lxi, 1941); Eubel, E., *Hierarchia catholica medii aevi* (3 vols., Münster, 1898–1910; vol. i, 2nd edn., Münster, 1913); Falco, G., 'I preliminari della pace d. S. Germano, Novembre 1229–Juglio 1230' (*Arch. soc. rom.* xxxiii, 1910); Fehling, F., *Kaiser Friedrich II. und die römischen Kardinäle in den Jahren 1227–1239* (*Eberings Historische Studien* 21, Berlin, 1901); Felz, A., *Untersuchungen zur Geschichte der ersten Konzils von Lyon* (Diss., Strassburg, 1905); Ficker, J. F., 'Der Einfalls Reinalds von Spoleto in den Kirchenstaat' (*MIöG* iv, 1883); Ficker, J., *Über das Testament Kaiser Heinrichs VI.* (Vienna, 1871); Fiebach, J., *Die augustinischen Anschauungen Papst Innocenz III. als Grundlage für die Beurteilung seiner Stellung zum deutschen Thronstreit, 1198–1208* (Diss., Greifswald, 1914); Folz, A., *Kaiser Friedrich II. und Papst Innocenz IV. Ihr Kampf in den Jahren 1244 und 1245* (Strassburg, 1905); Folz, A., *Untersuchungen zur Geschichte des Ersten Konzils von Lyons* (Diss., Strassburg, 1905); Folz, R., *L'Idée d'Empire en occident du Ve au XIVe siècle* (Paris, 1953); Frantz, T., *Der grosse Kampf zwischen Kaisertum und Papsttum zur Zeit des Hohenstaufen Friedrich II.* (Berlin, 1903); Gennrich, P., *Die Staats- und Kirchenlehre Johannes von Salisbury* (Gotha, 1894); Gierke, O., *Das deutsche Genossenschaftsrecht* (4 vols., Berlin, 1868–1913; part of vol. iii trans. F. W. Maitland, *Political Theories of the Middle Ages*, Cambridge, 1900); Gierke, O., 'Die Theokratische Idee des Mittelalters' (in *Johannes Althusius und die Entwicklung der naturrechtlichen Staatstheorien*, 2nd edn., Breslau,

1902); Graefe, F., *Die Publizistik in der letzten Epoche Kaiser Friedrichs II. Ein Beitrag zur Geschichte der Jahren 1239–50* (Heidelberg, 1909); Graf, A., *Roma nella memoria e nelle imaginazioni del Medio Evo* (2 vols., 1882–3; revised edn., 1915); Gregorovius, F., *Geschichte der Stadt Rom im Mittelalter* (8 vols., 5th edn., Stuttgart, Berlin, 1903–22); Greinacher, A., *Die Anschauungen des Papstes Nikolaus I. über das Verhältnis von Staat und Kirche* (Diss., Freiburg, 1909); Hahn, L., *Das Kaisertum* (Leipzig, 1913); Halbe, M., *Friedrich II. und der päpstliche Stuhl bis zur Kaiserkrönung (Nov. 1220)* (Berlin, 1888); Haller, J., *Das Papsttum* (3 vols., Stuttgart, 1934 ff.); Haller, J., *Die Epochen der deutschen Geschichte* (Stuttgart, 1939); Haller, J., 'Heinrich VI. und die römische Kirche' (*MIöG* xxxv, 1914); Haller, J., 'Innozenz III. und Otto IV.' (in A. Brackmann (ed.), *Papsttum und Kaisertum*, Munich, 1926); Haller, J., *Papsttum und Kirchenreform: Vier Kapitel zur Geschichte des ausgehenden Mittelalters* (Berlin, 1903); Hampe, K., 'Deutsche Angriffe auf das Königreich Sicilien im Anfang des 13. Jahrhunderts' (*Hist. Vierteljahrschr.* vii, 1904); Hampe, K., *Deutsche Kaisergeschichte in der Zeit der Salier und Staufer* (10th edn., hrsg. von Friedrich Baethgen, Heidelberg, 1949); Hampe, K., 'Eine Schilderung des Sommeraufenthalts der römischen Kurie unter Innocenz III. in Subiaco 1202' (*Hist. Vierteljahrschr.* viii, 1905); Hampe, K., 'Kritische Bemerkungen zur Kirchenpolitik der Staufernzeit' (*Hist. Zeitschr.* 93, 1904); Hampe, K., 'Papst Innozenz IV und die sizilische Verschwörung von 1246' (*Sb. d. H. Akad.: Phil.-Hist.- Klasse*, VIII. Abhandlung, Heidelberg, 1923); Hampe, K., 'Über die Flugschriften zum Lyoner Konzil von 1245' (*Hist. Vierteljahrschr.* xi, 1908); Hauck, A., *Der Gedanke der päpstlichen Weltherrschaft bis auf Bonifaz VIII.* (Leipzig, 1904); Hauck, A., *Kirchengeschichte Deutschlands* (5 vols. in 6, Leipzig, 1887–1920; vols. i–iv in 3rd and 4th edns.); Hefele, C. J., *Histoire des conciles* (Nouvelle traduction française faite sur la 2e éd. allemande, corrigée et augmentée avec notes critiques et bibliographiques, par un religieux Bénédictin de l'abbaye Saint-Michel de Fransborough, 10 vols., Paris, 1907 ff.); Hinschius, P., *Das Kirchenrecht der Katholiken und Protestanten in Deutschland*: part i, *Das katholische Kirchenrecht* (6 vols. in 7, Berlin, 1869–97); Hintze, O., *Das Königtum Wilhelms von Holland* (Leipzig, 1885); Hof, A., ' "Plenitudo potestatis" und "Imitatio imperii" zur Zeit Innozenz' (*ZfKG*, 66, 1954–5); Hofmeister, A., *Die nationale Bedeutung der mittelalterlichen Kaiserpolitik* (Greifswald, 1923); Holtzmann, R., 'Dominium mundi und imperium merum. Ein Beitrag zur Geschichte des staufischen Reichsgedanken' (*ZfKG*, 61, 1942); Holtzmann, R., *Die Weltherrschaftsgedanke des mittelalterlichen Kaisertums und die Souveränität der europäischen Staaten* (Munich, 1938); Holtzmann, W., *Beiträge zur Reichs- und Papstgeschichte des hohen Mittelalters* (*Bonner Historische Forschungen*, ed. M. Braubach, vol. viii, Bonn, 1957); Honig, R., *Rapporti tra Federico II e Gregorio IX rispetto alla spedizione in Palestina* (Bologna, 1896); Jacqueline, B., 'Bernard et l'expression "plenitudo potestatis" ' (*Bernard de Clairvaux*, Paris, 1952); Jordan, K., *Der Reichsgedanke der deutschen Kaiserzeit* (*Kiel Blätter*, 1942); Kampers, F., *Dantes Kaisertraum* (Breslau, 1908); Kampers, F., 'Die Fortuna Caesarea Kaiser Friedrichs II.' (*Historisches Jahrbuch*, xlviii, 1928); Kantorowicz, E., 'Deus per naturam, deus per gratiam, a note on Mediaeval Political Theory' (*The Harvard Theological Review*, xlv, 1952); Kap-Herr, H. von, 'Die unio regni ad imperium' (*DZfG*, i, 1889); Karajan, Th. G. von, 'Zur Geschichte des Concils von Lyon 1245' (*Denkschriften der Kaiserlichen Akademie der Wissenschaften: Phil.-Hist.-Klasse*, ii, Vienna, 1851); Kehl, P., *Die Steuer in der Lehre der Theologen des Mittelalters* (Berlin, 1927); Kempf, F., *Papsttum und Kaisertum bei Innocenz III.: die geistigen und rechtlichen Grundlagen seiner Thronstreitpolitik* (Rome, 1954); Kempf, J., *Geschichte des deutschen Reiches während des grossen Interregnums, 1245–1273* (Würzburg, 1893); Keutner, A., *Papsttum und Krieg unter dem Pontifikat des Papstes Honorius III. 1216–1227* (*Münsterische Beiträge zur Geschichtsforschung*, dritte Folge, Heft x, Münster, 1935); Kissling, W., *Das Verhältnis zwischen sacerdotium und imperium nach den Anschauungen der Päpste von Leo d. Grossen bis Gelasius I.*

(Paderborn, 1920); Kloos, R. M., 'Nikolaus von Bari, eine neue Quelle zur Entwicklung der Kaiseridee unter Friedrich II.' (*Deutsches Archiv*, xi, 1954); Knabel, W., *Kaiser Friedrich II. und Papst Honorius III. in ihren gegenseitigen Beziehungen von der Kaiserkrönung Friedrichs bis zum Tode des Papstes 1220–1227* (Münster, 1905); Koehne, C., 'Die Konstitutionen des ersten Allgemeinen Konzils von Lyon' (*Studia et Documenta Historiae et Juris*, vi, 1940); Köhler, C., *Das Verhältnis Kaiser Friedrichs II. zu den Päpsten seiner Zeit* (*Untersuchungen zur deutschen Staats- und Rechtsgeschichte*, hrsg. von O. Gierke, 24, Breslau, 1888); Koster, W., *Der Kreussblass im Kampfe der Kurie mit Friedrich II.* (Diss., Münster, 1913); Krabbo, H., 'Ottos IV. erste Versprechungen an Innocenz III.' (*Neues Archiv*, xxvii, 1901); Krammer, M., *Der Reichsgedanke des staufischen Kaiserhauses. Untersuchungen zur deutschen Staats- und Rechtsgeschichte* (Breslau, 1908); Krauth, K., 'Die Verschwörung von 1246 gegen Friedrich II.' (unpubl. Diss., Heidelberg, 1922); Kühne, A., *Das Herrscherideal des Mittelalters und Kaiser Friedrich I.* (*Leipziger Studien*, V: 1898); Ladner, G. B., 'The concepts of "ecclesia" and "christianitas" and their relation to the idea of papal "plenitudo potestatis", from Gregory VII to Boniface VIII' (*Sacerdozio e regno da Gregorio VII a Bonifacio VIII*: Misc. hist. pont. 18, 1954, 49–77); Lewis, E., *Medieval Political Ideas* (2 vols., London and New York, 1954); Löwenfeld, S., 'Der *Dictatus Papae* Gregors VII. und eine Überarbeitung desselben im XII. Jahrhundert' (*Neues Archiv*, xvi, 1891); Lunt, W. E., 'The Sources of the First Council of Lyons, 1245' (*EHR* xxxiii, 1918); Maccarrone, M., *Chiesa e Stato nella dottrina di Pape Innocenzo III* (Rome, 1940); Maccarrone, M., 'Potestas directa e potestas indiretta nel teologi del XII e XIII sieclo' (*Sacerdozio e regno da Gregorio VII a Bonifacio VIII*: Misc. hist. pont. 18, 1954); Manselli, R., *Federico II ed Alatrino, diplomatico pontificio del secolo XIII* (*Studi romani*, 6, 1958); Martini, G., 'La politica finanziaria dei papi in Francia intorno alla metà del secolo XII' (*Memorie della Accademia dei Lincei etc.*, Series 8, vol. 3, 1956); Maschke, E., *Der Kampf zwischen Kaisertum und Papsttum* (Darmstadt, 1953); Maubach, J., *Die Kardinäle und ihre Politik um die Mitte des XIII. Jahrhunderts* (Diss., Bonn, 1902); Mayer, T., 'Papsttum und Kaisertum im hohen Mittelalter' (*Hist. Zeitschr.* 187, 1959); Meyer, E. W., *Staatstheorien Papsts Innocenz III.* (*Jenaer Historische Arbeiten*, Heft ix, Bonn, 1919); Michiels, G., 'Pouvoir spirituel et pouvoir temporel' (*Bulletin de théologie ancienne et médiévale*, 8, 1958); Mitteis, H., *Die Rechtsidee in der Geschichte* (in *Gesammelte Abhandlungen und Vorträge*, Weimar, 1957); Morrall, J. B., *Political Thought in Medieval Times* (New York, 1962; originally published in England, 1958); Paolucci, G., 'Documenti inediti sulle relazione tra chiesa e stato nel tempo svevo' (*Atti Acc. Palermo*, 3rd series, iv, 1897); Pepe, G., *Lo stato ghibellino di Federico II* (2nd edn., Bari, 1951); Pfaff, V., *Kaiser Heinrichs VI. höchstes Angebot an die römische Kurie, 1196* (Heidelberg, 1927); Poole, R. L., *The Early Correspondence of John of Salisbury* (British Academy, 1924); Post, G., *Plena Potestas* (*Traditio*, i, 1943); Post, G., *Status Regis* (*Studies in Medieval and Renaissance History*, i, 1964); Post, G., *Studies in Medieval Legal Thought: Public Law and the State 1100–1322* (Princeton, 1964); Pouzet, P., 'Le Pape Innocent IV à Lyon. Le Concile de 1245' (*Revue d'histoire de l'Église de France*, 15, 1929); Rivière, J., *Le Problème de l'église et de l'état au temps de Philippe le Bel* (Paris, 1926); Rocquain, F., *La Cour de Rome et l'esprit de réforme avant Luther* (3 vols., Paris, 1893 ff.); Rocquain, F., *La Papauté au Moyen Âge* (Paris, 1881); Rocquain, F., 'Quelques mots sur les "Dictatus Papae" ' (*Bibl. de l'École des Chartes*, xxxiii, 1872); Rodenberg, C., 'Die Friedensverhandlungen zwischen Friedrich II. und Innocenz IV. 1243–1244' (*Festgabe für Gerold Meyer von Knonau*, Zürich, 1913); Rodenberg, C., *Innocenz IV. und das Königreich Sizilien 1245–1254* (Halle, 1892); Rodenberg, C., 'Die Vorverhandlungen zum Frieden von S. Germano' (*Neues Archiv*, xviii, 1896–7); Rost, K., *Die Historia pontificum Romanorum aus Zwettl* (*Greifswalder Abhandlungen zur Geschichte des Mittelalters*, 2, Greifswald, 1932); Rupp, J., *L'Idée de chrétienté dans la pensée pontificale des origines jusqu'à Innocent III* (Paris, 1929); Rüsen, W., *Der Weltherrschaftsgedanke und das deutsche Kaisertum im Mittelalter* (Diss., Halle, 1913); Sägmüller, J. B., *Die Tätigkeit und Stellung der Kardinäle bis Papst Bonifaz VIII.* (Freiburg, 1896); Sägmüller, J. B., *Lehrbuch des katholischen Kirchenrechts* (Freiburg i/B., 1914); Schelenz, E. M., *Studien zur Geschichte des Kardinalats im 13. und 14. Jahrhunderts bis zur Aufstellung der ersten Wahlkapitulation im Jahre 1352* (Diss., Marburg, 1913); Schneider, F., *Rom und Romgedanken im Mittelalter, die geistigen Grundlagen der Renaissance* (Munich, 1926); Schramm, P. E., *Kaiser, Rom und Renovatio* (2 vols., Leipzig, Berlin, 1929); Schulte, J. F. von, *Die Geschichte der Quellen und Literatur des kanonischen Rechts* (3 vols., Stuttgart, 1875–80); Schulte, J. F. von, 'Die Decretalen zwischen den Decretales Gregorii IX. und dem Liber Sextus Bonifacii VIII.' (*Sb. d. Kaiser. Akad.* iv, 1867); Schulte, J. F. von, *Lehrbuch der deutschen Reichs- und Rechtsgeschichte* (Stuttgart, 1892); Schulze, A., *Kaiserpolitik und Einheitsgedanke in den Karolingischen Nachfolgestaaten, 876–962* (Berlin, 1926); Seegrün, W., 'Kirche, Papst und Kaiser nach den Anschauungen Kaiser Friedrichs II.' (*Hist. Zeitschr.* 207, 1968); Sohm, R., *The Institutes: A Textbook of the History and System of Roman Private Law* (3rd Eng. edn., Oxford, 1907); Stefano, A. de, *Innocenzo III e la riforma religiosa agli inizi del secolo XIII* (Rome, 1917); Stefano, A. de, *L'idea imperiale de Federico II* (new edn., Bologna, 1952); Stickler, A. M., '*Imperator vicarius Papae*: die Lehren der französischen deutschen Dekretenschule des 12. und beginnenden 13. Jahrhunderts über die Beziehungen zwischen Papst und Kaiser' (*MIöG* lxii, 1954); Stickler, A. M., 'Sacerdozio e regno nelle nuovo ricerche attorno ai secoli XII e XIII nei decretisti e decretalisti' (*Misc. hist. pont.* 18, 1954); Stieglitz, I. L., *Die Staatstheorie des Marsilius von Padua* (Leipzig, 1914); *Studia Gratiana* (ed. G. Forchielli and A. M. Stickler, 1953 ff.); Sugenheim, S., *Geschichte der Entstehung und Ausbildung des Kirchenstaates* (Leipzig, 1854); Sütterlin, B., *Die Politik Kaiser Friedrichs II. und die römischen Kardinäle in den Jahren 1239 bis 1250* (Heidelberg, 1929); Tammen, U., *Kaiser Friedrich II. und Papst Innocenz IV. in den Jahren 1243–1245* (Diss., Leipzig, 1886); Tangl, G., 'Zur Entstehungsgeschichte der Deliberatio Innocenz III.' (*Archiv für Urkundenforschung*, x, 1928); Tangl, M., *D. Deliberatio Innocenz III.* (*Sb. Ber. Ak.* 1919); Tangl, M., *Die päpstlichen Kanzleiordnungen 1200–1500* (Innsbruck, 1894); Tenckhoff, F., *Der Kampf der Hohenstaufen um die Mark Ancona und das Herzogtum Spoleto von der zweiten Exkommunikation Friedrichs II. bis zum Tode Konradins* (Paderborn, 1893); Tierney, B., *Foundations of the Conciliar Theory: The Contribution of the Medieval Canonists from Gratian to the Great Schism* (Cambridge, 1955); Tillmann, H., 'Das Schicksal der päpstlichen Rekuperationen nach dem Friedensabkommen zwischen Philipp von Schwaben und der römischen Kirche' (*Hist. Jahrbuch*, li, 1931); Ullmann, W., *Medieval Papalism: The Political Theories of the Medieval Canonists* (London, 1949); Ullmann, W., *Principles of Government and Politics in the Middle Ages* (New York, 1961); Vehse, O., *Die amtliche Propaganda in der Staatskunst Kaiser Friedrichs II.* (*Forschungen zur mittelalterlichen und neueren Geschichte*, I, Munich, 1929); Vergottini, G. de, *Lezioni di storia del diritto italiano. Il diritto pubblico italiano nei secoli XII–XV* (3rd edn., 2 vols., Milan, 1960); Vogt, F., *Das Kaiser- und Königsideal in der deutschen Dichtung des Mittelalters* (Marburger Akad. Reden, 19, 1908); Waley, D. P., 'Papal Armies in the Thirteenth Century' (*EHR* lxxiii, 1957); Watt, J. A., 'The Early Medieval Canonists and the Formation of Conciliar Theory' (*Irish Theological Quarterly*, xxiv, 1957); Watt, J. A., *The Theory of Papal Monarchy* (New York, 1965); Weber, H., *Der Kampf zwischen Innocenz IV. und Friedrich II. bis zur Flucht des Papstes nach Lyon* (*Eberings Historische Studien* 20, Berlin, 1900); Weber, H., *Über das Verhältnis Englands zu Rom während der Zeit der Legation des Kardinals Otto in den Jahren 1237–1241* (Berlin, 1883); Wenck, K., 'Das erste Konklave der Papstgeschichte, Rom, August bis Oktober 1241' (*QF* xviii, 1926); Wenck, K., 'Das Kardinalcollegium' (*Preussische Jahrbücher*, liii, 1884); Wenck, K., 'Die römischen Päpste zwischen Alexander III. und Innocenz III.' (*Papsttum und Kaisertum*, ed. A. Brackmann, Munich, 1926); Wesener, G., *De actionibus inter Innocentium IV. Papam, et Fridericum II. a 1243–44 et Concilio Lugdunensi*

(Diss., Bonn, 1870); Wissowa, A. F., *Die politischen Beziehungen zwischen England und Deutschland bis zum Untergange der Staufer* (Diss., Breslau, 1889); Zerbi, P., *Papato, impero e 'respublica christiana' dal 1187 al 1198* (Milan, 1955).

20. *Prophets, Prophesying, and Mysticism*

Alexandre, C., *Oracula Sibyllina* (2 vols., Paris, 1869); Bloomfield, M. W., and Reeves, M. E., 'The Penetration of Joachism into Northern Europe' (*Speculum*, xxix, 1954); Frauenholz, E. von, 'Imperator Octavianus Augustus in der Geschichte und Sage des Mittelalters' (*Historisches Jahrbuch*, xlvi, 1926); Grundmann, H., *Studien über Joachim von Floris* (*Beiträge zur Kulturgeschichte des Mittelalters*, ed. W. Goetz, Leipzig and Berlin, 1927); Hampe, K., 'Eine frühe Verknüpfung der Weissagung vom Endkaiser mit Friedrich II.' (*Sb. H. Ak.* vi, 1917); Holder-Egger, O., 'Italienische Prophetieen des 13. Jahrhunderts' (*Neues Archiv*, xv, 1889–90, xxx, 1904–5, xxxiii, 1907–8); Kampers, F., *Alexander der Grosse und die Idee des Weltimperiums in Prophetie und Sage* (Freiburg i/B., 1913); Kampers, F., 'Der Waise' (*Hist. Jahrb.* xxxix, 1918–19); Kampers, F., *Die deutsche Kaiseridee in Prophetie und Sage* (Munich, 1896: a second edn. of *Kaiserprophetieen und Kaisersagen im Mittelalter*, *Hist. Abhandlungen*, viii, Munich, 1895); Kampers, F., *Vom Werdegang der abendländischen Kaisermystik* (Leipzig and Berlin, 1924); Kantorowicz, E., 'Zu den Rechtsgrundlagen der Kaisersage' (*Deutsches Archiv*, xiii, 1957); Koch, E., *Die Sage von Kaiser Friedrich im Kyffhäuser* (Leipzig, 1886); Mercati, S. G., 'E stato trovato il testo greco della Sibilla Tiburtina' (*Mélanges Henri Grégoire I: Annuaire de l'Institut de Philologie et d'Histoire orientales slaves*, Brussels, 1949); Paton, L. A., *Les Prophecies de Merlin* (2 vols., New York, London, 1926–7); Pomtow, M., *Über den Einfluss der altrömischen Vorstellungen vom Staat auf die Politik Kaiser Friedrichs I. und die Anschauungen seiner Zeit* (Diss., Halle, 1885); Preger, W., *Geschichte der deutschen Mystik im Mittelalter* (3 vols., Leipzig, 1874–93); Preuss, H., *Die Vorstellungen vom Antichrist im späteren Mittelalter, bei Luther, und der konfessionellen Polemik* (Leipzig, 1906); Sackur, E., *Sibyllinische Texte und Forschungen* (Halle, 1898); Schultheiss, F. G., *Die deutsche Sage vom Fortleben und der Wiederkehr Kaiser Friedrichs II.* (*Hist. Stud.* xciv, Berlin, 1911); Wadstein, E., *Die eschatologische Ideentruppe Antichrist, Weltsabbat, Weltende und Weltgericht in den Hauptmomenten ihrer christlich-mittelalterlichen Gesamtentwicklung* (Leipzig, 1896); Weber, W., *Der Prophet und sein Gott. Eine Studie zur vierten Ekloge Vergils* (*Beihefte zum 'Alten Orient'*, Heft iii, Leipzig, 1925); Zarncke, F., 'Zur Sage vom Priester Johannes' (*Neues Archiv*, ii, 1877).

21. *Royal and Imperial Coronations and Imperial Emblems*

Bloch, H., *Die staufischen Kaiserwahlen und die Entstehung des Kurfürstentums* (Leipzig, 1911); Deér, J., *Der Kaiserornat Friedrichs II.* (Dissertationes Bernenses Historiam Orbis Antiqui Nascentisque Medii Aevi Elucubrantes edendas curavit A. Alföldi, Series ii, fasc. 2, Bern, 1952); Diemand, A., *Das Zeremoniell der Kaiserkrönung von Otto I. bis Friedrich II.* (*Hist. Abhandlungen aus dem Münchner Seminar*, iv, Munich, 1894); Eichmann, E., *Die Kaiserkrönung im Abendland. Ein Beitrag zur Geistesgeschichte des Mittelalters* (2 vols., Würzburg, 1942); Klewitz, H. W., *Die Festkrönung der deutschen Könige* (Weimar, 1939); Maurenbrecher, W., *Geschichte der deutschen Königswahlen vom zehnten bis zur Mitte des dreizehnten Jahrhunderts* (Leipzig, 1889); Mitteis, H., *Die deutsche Königswahl. Ihre Rechtsgrundlage bis zur Goldenen Bulle* (2nd edn., Brünn, Munich, and Vienna, 1944); Schramm, P. E., *Herrschaftszeichen und Staatssymbolik* (Stuttgart, 1954–6); Schramm, P., *Kaiser Friedrichs II. Herrschaftszeichen* (*Abt. d. Ak. d. Wiss. in Gött., Phil.-Hist.-Klasse*, dritte Folge, no. 36, Göttingen, 1955); Schulte, A., *Die Kaiser- und Königskrönungen zu Aachen* (Bonn, 1924); Schwarzer, J., 'Die Ordines der Kaiserkrönung' (*FzDG* xxii, 1882).

22. *Saracens in Sicily*

Amari, M., 'Estratti del Tarih Mansuri' (*Arch. stor. sic.*, new series, ix, 1884); Amari, M., 'Questions philosophiques adressées aux savants Musulmans par l'Empereur Frédéric II' (*Journal Asiatique ou Recueil de Mémoires d'Extraits et de Notices Relatifs à l'Histoire, à la Philosophie, aux Langues et à la Littérature des Peuples Orientaux*, 5th series, i, 1870); Amari, M., *Storia dei Musulmani di Sicilia* (3 vols., Florence, 1854–72; 2nd edn., 3 vols., 1937–9); Amari, M., *Un periodo delle istorie Siciliane del secolo XIII* (Palermo, 1842); Archibald, R. C., *Euclid's Book on Divisions of Figures, with a Restoration based on Woepeke's Text and on the Practica Geometriae of Leonardo Pisano* (Cambridge, 1915); Bennici, G., *L'Ultimo dei trovatori arabi in Sicilia* (Palermo, 1874); Broadhurst, R. J. C., *The Travels of Ibn Jubayr* (London, 1952); *Centenario della nascita di Michele Amari* (2 vols., Palermo, 1910); Duhem, Pierre, *Le Système du monde* (new printing, 4 vols., Paris, 1958; see also the old edn., 5 vols., Paris, 1913–17); Egidi, P., 'La colonia Saracena di Lucera e la sua distruzione' (*Arch. stor. per le provincie napoletane*, xxxvi, 1911); Gabrielli, F., 'Federico II e le cultura musulmana' (*Riv. stor. ital.* lxiv, 1952); Gregorio, R., *Rerum Arabicarum, quae ad historiam Siculam spectant, ampla collectio* (Palermo, 1790); Grünebaum, G. E. von, *Der Islam im Mittelalter* (Zürich, 1963); Hitti, P. K., *History of the Arabs* (2nd edn., London, 1940); La Primaudaie, F. É. de, *Les Arabes en Sicile et en Italie. Les Normands en Sicile et en Italie* (Paris, 1868); McClenon, R. B., 'Leonardo of Pisa and His *Liber Quadratorum*' (*The American Mathematical Monthly*, xxvi, 1920); Marcais, G., *Les Arabes en Berbérie du XIe au XIVe siècle* (Constantine and Paris, 1913); Miles, G. C., *Fātimid Coins* (New York, 1951); Wedel, T. O., *The Mediaeval Attitude toward Astrology* (*Yale Studies in English*, lx, New Haven, 1920); Wolf, R., *Geschichte der Astronomie* (Munich, 1877); Wolfson, H. A., 'The Twice-Revealed Averroës' (*Speculum*, xxxvi, 1961).

23. *Sicilian Government and Administration*

Baumgarten, P. M., *Aus Kanzlei und Kammer* (Freiburg, 1907); Boss, A., *Die Kirchenlehen der Staufischen Kaiser* (Diss., Munich, 1886); Brandileone, F., *Il diritto romano nelle leggi normanne e sveve del regno di Sicilia* (Turin, 1884); Bresslau, H., *Handbuch der Urkundenlehre für Deutschland und Italien* (2 vols., Leipzig, 1889); Brünneck, W. von (ed.), *Siciliens mittelalterliche Stadtrechte* (Halle, 1881); Cahen, C., *Le Régime féodal de l'Italie normande* (Paris, 1940); Capasso, B., *Historia diplomatica regni Siciliae ab 1250 ad 1266* (Naples, 1874); Capasso, B., *Sulla storia esterna constituzioni del regno di Sicilia promulgate da Federico II* (Naples, 1869); Caruso, A., 'Le Leggi di Federico II pubblicata a Barletta nel mese di ottobre del 1246' (*Studi in onore di Riccardo Filangieri*, i, Naples, 1959); Cohn, W., *Das Zeitalter der Hohenstaufen in Sizilien, ein Beitrag zur Entstehung des modernen Beamtenstaates* (Breslau, 1925); Compagnoni, P., *La Reggia Picena, ouero de' presidi della Marca. Historia universale . . . Parte prima* (Macerata, 1661); Darmstadter, P., *Das Reichsgut in der Lombardei und Piemont (568–1250)* (Strassburg, 1895); Ebhardt, B., *Die Burgen Italiens* (6 vols., Berlin, 1900–27); Fasoli, G., 'La feudalità siciliana nell'età di Federico II' (*Riv. di storia del dir. ital.* xxvi, 1951); Fasoli, G, 'Problemi di storia medievale siciliana' (*Siculorum Gymnasium*, new series, iv, 1951); Fatteschi, G. C., *Memorie istorico-diplomatiche riguardanti la serie de' duchi e la topografia de' tempi di mezzo del ducato di Spoleto* (Camerino, 1801); Ficker, J., 'Erörterungen zur Reichsgeschichte des 13. Jahrhunderts' (*MIöG* iii, 1882); Ficker, J., *Forschungen zur Reichs- und Rechtsgeschichte Italiens* (4 vols., Innsbruck, 1868–74); Ficker, J., *Reichshofbeamten der Staufischen Periode* (Vienna, 1863); Fiesel, L., 'Zum früh- und hochmittelalterlichen Geleitsrecht' (*ZfRG, German. Abt.* xli, 1920); Flach, J., *Études critiques sur l'histoire du Droit romain au Moyen Âge, avec textes inédits* (Paris, 1890); Gagner, S., *Studien zur Ideengeschichte der Gesetzgebung* (Stockholm, 1960); Garcia-Pelayo, M., *Frederico II de Suábia e o nascimento do estado moderno* (trans. A. de Castro: in *Estudos sociais e políticos*, xv); Garufi, C. A., 'Sulla curia stratigoziale di Messina nel tempo normanno-suevo' (*Arch. stor. Messinese*, v, 1904); Gaudenzi, A., 'La Constitutione di Federico II che interdice lo studio bolognese' (*Arch. stor. ital.*, 5th series, xlii, 1908); Hagemann, W., 'Studien und Dokumente zur Geschichte der Marken im Zeitalter der Staufer: II. Chiarvalle di Fiastra' (*QF* xli, 1961); Hampe, K., 'Zu der von Friedrich II. 1235 eingesetzten sizilischen Regentschaft' (*Hist. Vierteljahrschr.* xxii, 1922); Hampe, K., 'Zum Erbkaiserplan Heinrichs VI.' (*MIöG* xxvii, 1906); Heinemann, L. von, *Zur Entstehung der Stadtverfassung in Italien* (Leipzig, 1896); Hellmann, S., *Die Grafen von Savoyen und das Reich bis zum Ende der staufischen Periode* (Innsbruck, 1900); Heupel, W. E., *Der sizilische Grosshof unter Kaiser Friedrich II.* (Leipzig, 1940); Hofmann, Max, *Die Stellung des Königs von Sizilien nach den Assisen von Ariano, 1140* (Münster, 1911); Huillard-Bréholles, J. L., *Étude sur l'état politique d'Italie depuis la paix de Constance au milieu du XIVᵉ siècle, 1183–1355* (Paris, 1873); Kehr, K. A., 'Staufische Diplome im Domarchiv zu Patti' (*QF* vii, 1904); Klewitz, H. W., 'Cancellaria' (*Deutsches Archiv*, i, 1937); Mayer, E., *Italienische Verfassungsgeschichte von der Gothenzeit bis zur Zunftherrschaft* (2 vols., Leipzig, 1909); Ménager, L.-R., *Amiratus—ἀμηρᾶς, L'Émirat et les origines de l'Amirauté, XIᵉ–XIIIᵉ siècles* (Paris, 1964); Mor, C. G., 'Le "assise" ruggeriane non accolte nel "Liber Augustalis"' (*Atti del Convegno Internazionale di Studi Ruggeriani*, Palermo, 1955); Natale, F., *Avviamento allo studio del Medio Evo siciliano* (*Pubblicazioni a cura dell'Istituto di Storia Medioevale e Moderna dall'Università di Messina*, ii, Florence, 1959); Ohlig, M., *Studien zum Beamtentum Friedrichs II. in Reichsitalien von 1237–1250* (Diss., Frankfurt, 1936); Paolucci, G., 'Il parlamento di Foggia' (*Atti della R. Accademia di Palermo*, 3rd series, iv, 1897); Philippi, F., *Zur Geschichte der Reichskanzlei unter den letzten Staufern Friedrich II., Heinrich (VII.) und Konrad IV.* (Münster, 1885); Powell, J. M., 'Frederick II and the Church in the Kingdom of Sicily 1220–1240' (*Church History*, xxx, 1961); Pybus, H. J., 'Frederick II and the Sicilian Church' (*The Cambridge Historical Journal*, iii, 1929); Ruck, W., 'Die Besetzung der sizilischen Bistümer unter Kaiser Friedrich II.' (unprinted Heidelberg Diss., 1923; used here in abstract only); Samanek, V., *Kronrat und Reichsherrschaft im 13. und 14. Jahrhundert* (Berlin and Leipzig, 1910); Schaller, H. M., 'Die staufische Hofkapelle im Königreich Sizilien' (*Deutsches Archiv*, xi, 1954–5); Scheffer-Boichorst, P., 'Urkunden und Forschungen zu Regesten der staufischen Periode' (*Neues Archiv*, xxvii, 1902); Scheffer-Boichorst, P., *Zur Geschichte des 12. und 13. Jahrhunderts: diplomatische Studien* (*Eberings Historische Studien*, viii, Berlin, 1897); Schneider, F., *Toskanische Studien* (Rome, 1910; also in *QF* xi–xiii); Stengel, E. E., 'Hochmeister und Reich' (*ZfRG*, German. Abt. lviii, 1938); Sthamer, E., *Die Verwaltung der Kastelle im Königreich Sizilien unter Kaiser Friedrich II. und Karl I. von Anjou* (*Die Bauten der Hohenstaufen in Unteritalien. Ergänzungsband*, i, Leipzig, 1914); Sthamer, E., 'Eigenes Diktat des Herrschers in der sizilischen Kanzlei des 13. Jahrhunderts' (*Festschrift für A. Cartellieri*, Weimar, 1927); Thieme, H., 'Die Funktion der Regalien im Mittelalter' (*ZfRG*, German. Abt. lxii, 1942); Trifone, R., 'Il testo greco delle constituzione di Federico II' (*Arch. stor. per la Sicilia orientale*, vii, 1910); Tuček, E., *Das Testament Heinrichs VI.* (Karlsburg, 1912); Vecchio, A. del, *Intorno alle legislazione di Federico II Imperatore. Saggio* (Florence, 1872); Vecchio, A. del, *La Legislazione di Federico II Imperatore illustrata* (Turin, 1874); Vergottini, G. de, *Studi sulla legislazione imperiale di Federico II in Italia: le leggi del 1220* (Pubblicazioni straordinarie dell'Accademia delle Scienze di Bologna, sci.-mor. cl. 11, Milan 1952); Wilde, H., *Zur sicilischen Gesetzgebung, Steuer und Finanzverwaltung unter Kaiser Friedrich II. und seinen normannischen Vorfahren* (Diss., Halle, 1889); Winkelmann, E., *De regni Siculi administratione qualis fuerit regnante Friderico II* (Diss. Berlin, 1859); Winter, A., *Der Erbfolgsplan und das Testament Kaiser Heinrichs VI.* (Diss., Erlangen, 1908); Zechbauer, F., *Das mittelalterliche Strafrecht Siziliens nach Friedrichs II. Constitutiones Regni Siciliae und den sizilischen Stadtrechten* (Berlin, 1908).

24. Trade and Commerce (Routes of Trade and Mountain Passes)

Blochet, E., 'Relations diplomatiques des Hohenstaufen avec les sultans d'Égypte' (*Rev. historique*, lxxx, 1902); Brătianu, G. I., *Recherches sur le commerce génois dans la Mer Noire au XIIIᵉ siècle* (Paris, 1929); *The Cambridge Economic History of Europe from the Decline of the Roman Empire* (ed. J. H. Clapham and E. Power, Cambridge, 1941 ff.); Carabellese, F. (and A. in vol. ii), *Le relazioni commerciali fra la Puglia e la republica di Venezia dal secolo X al XV*. Ricerche e documenti (2 vols., Trani, 1897-8); Chone, H., *Die Handelsbeziehungen Kaiser Friedrichs II. zu den Seestädten Venedig, Pisa, Genua* (Berlin, 1902); Ciccaglione, F., 'La vita economica siciliana nel periodo normanno-svevo' (*Arch. stor. per la Sicilia orientale*, x, 1913); Cohn, W., *Die Geschichte der sizilischen Flotte unter der Regierung Friedrichs II., 1197-1250* (3 vols., Breslau, 1910-26); Heyd, W., *Geschichte des Levantehandels im Mittelalter* (2 vols., Stuttgart, 1879; trans. F. Raynaud, *Histoire du commerce du Levant au moyen âge*, 2 vols., Leipzig, 1885-6); Hüllmann, K. D., *Geschichte des byzantinischen Handels bis zum Ende der Kreuzzüge* (Frankfurt a. d. O., 1808); Kulischer, J., *Allgemeine Wirtschaftsgeschichte*, i: *Mittelalter* (Munich and Berlin, 1928); Lenel, W., *Die Entstehung der Vorherrschaft Venedigs in der Adria* (Strassburg, 1897); Manfroni, C., *Storia della marina italiana dalle invasioni barbariche al trattato di Ninfeo, 1261* (Leghorn, 1899); Mas-Latrie, L. de, *Traités de paix et de commerce et documents divers concernant les relations de chrétiens avec les Arabes d'Afrique septentrionale au Moyen Âge* (Paris, 1886); Minotto, A. S., *Acta et Diplomata e R. Tabulario Veneto* (4 vols., Venice, 1870-83); Mitrović, B., *Il commercio medioevale dell'Italia col Levante. Epoca delle crociate* (Trieste, 1882); Öhlmann, E., 'Die Alpenpässe im Mittelalter' (*Jahrb. für schweizerische Gesch.* iii and iv, Zürich, 1878-9); Powell, J. M., *Medieval Monarchy and Trade* (reprinted from *Studi Medievali*, 3rd series, iii, 1962); Rauers, R., *Zur Geschichte der alten Handelsstrassen in Deutschland* (Gotha, 1906); Sapori, A., *Le Marchand italien au moyen âge* (Paris, 1952); Schaube, A., *Handelsgeschichte der romanischen Völker des Mittelmeergebietes bis zum Ende der Kreuzzüge* (Munich-Berlin, 1906); Schutte, L., *Der Apenninenpass des Monte Badone und die deutschen Kaiser* (*Eberings Historische Studien*, Heft 27, Berlin, 1901); Simonsfeld, H., *Der Fondaco dei Tedeschi in Venedig und die deutsch-venetianischen Handelsbeziehungen* (2 vols., Stuttgart, 1887); Stein, W., *Handels- und Verkehrsgeschichte der deutschen Kaiserzeit* (ed. O. Held, Leipzig and Berlin, 1922); Thompson, J. W., *An Economic and Social History of the Middle Ages* (New York, 1928); Tyler, J. E., *The Alpine Passes in the Middle Ages 962-1250* (Oxford, 1930); Weber, M., *Zur Geschichte der Handelsgesellschaften im Mittelalter* (Stuttgart, 1889); Wright, J. K., *The Geographical Lore of the Time of the Crusades* (New York, 1925); Yver, G., *Le Commerce et les marchands dans l'Italie méridionale au XIIIᵉ et au XIVᵉ siècle* (Bibliothèque des Écoles Françaises d'Athènes et de Rome, fasc. 88, Paris, 1903).

25. Translations: Greek, Arabic, and Hebraic

Bagrow, L., *Die Geschichte der Kartographie* (Berlin, 1951); Brockelmann, C., *Geschichte der arabischen Literatur* (2 vols., Weimar and Berlin, 1898-1902); Cantor, M., *Vorlesungen über Geschichte der Mathematik* (3rd edn., 4 vols., Leipzig, 1899-1908); Carmody, F. J., *Arabic Astronomical and Astrological Sciences in Latin Translations. A critical bibliography* (Berkeley, Calif., 1956); Cipolla, M., 'Il contributo italiano alla rinascita della matematica nel'200' (*Circolo Matematico di Catania*, viii, 1934); Fobes, F. H., 'Medieval Versions of Aristotle's Meteorology' (*Classical Philology*, x, 1915); Gabrieli, F., 'Arabi di Sicilia e Arabi di Spagna' (*Al-Andalaus*, xv, 1950); Grabmann, M., *Forschungen über die lateinischen Aristotelesübersetzungen des XIII. Jahrhunderts* (Münster, 1916); Günther, S., *Geschichte der Mathematik* (Leipzig, 1902); Hartwig, O., 'Die Übersetzungsliteratur Unteritaliens in der normannisch-staufischen Epoche' (*Zentralblatt für Bibliothekswesen*, iii, 1866); Haskins, C. H., 'The Translations of Hugo Sanctelliensis'

(*Romanic Review*, ii); Haskins, C. H., and Lockwood, P., *The Sicilian Translators and the First Latin Version of Ptolemy's Almagest* (*Harvard University Studies in Classical Philology*, xxi, 1920); Heiberg, J. L., 'Les sciences grecques et leur transmission, II. L'œuvre de conservation et de transmission des Byzantins et des Arabes' (*Scientia*, xxxi, 1922); Heiberg, J. L., 'Noch einmal die mittelalterliche Ptolemäusübersetzung' (*Hermes*, xlvi, 1911); Jourdain, A., *Recherches critiques sur l'âge et l'origine des traductions latines d'Aristote, et sur les commentaires grecs ou arabes employés par les docteurs scolastiques* (2nd edn., Paris, 1843); Kordeuter, V., and Labowsky, C. (eds.), *Meno, Interprete Henrico Aristippo* (*Plato Latinus*, vol. i of *Corpus Platonicum Medii Aevi*, ed. R. Klibansky, London, Warburg Institute, 1940); Lagumina, B., *Catalogo delle monete arabe esistenti nella Biblioteca Comunale di Palermo* (Palermo, 1892); Minio-Paluello, L. (ed.), *Phaedo, Interprete Henrico Aristoppo* (*Plato Latinus*, vol. ii of *Corpus Platonicum Medii Aevi*, ed. R. Klibansky, London, Warburg Institute, 1950); Rose, V., 'Die Lücke in Diogenes Laërtius und der alte Übersetzer' (*Hermes*, i, 1866); Rose, V., 'Ptolemäus und die Schule von Toledo' (*Hermes*, viii, 1873); Steinschneider, M., *Die arabische Literatur der Juden* (Frankfurt, 1902); Steinschneider, M., *Die hebräischen Übersetzungen des Mittelalters und die Juden als Dolmetscher* (Berlin, 1893); Walzer, R., *Arabic Transmission of Greek Thought to Medieval Europe* (Manchester, 1945; a reprint from the *Bulletin of the John Rylands Library*); Wüstenfeld, F., *Die Geschichtsschreiber der Araber und ihre Werke* (Göttingen, 1882).

26. *Troubadours and Lyric Poets in Southern Italy*

Aston, S. C., *Peirol, Troubadour of Auvergne* (ed. and trans., Cambridge, 1953); Bartholomeis, V. de, 'Osservazioni sulle poesie Provenzali relative a Federico II' (*Memorie accad. Bologna*, First Series, xi, 1911); Bartsch, K., *Grundriss zur Geschichte der provenzalischen Literatur* (Elberfeld, 1872); Bartsch, K., and Horning, A., *La Langue et la littérature françaises* (Paris, 1887); Bassermann, A., *Dante's Spuren in Italien* (Munich and Leipzig, 1898); Battisti, C., 'La poesia aulica siciliana e la corte di Federico II' (*Arch. stor. pugliese*, xiii, 1960); Bédier, J., *Les Chansons de Croisade* (Paris, 1909); Bertoni, G., *Il Duecento* (Milan, 1910); Bertoni, G., *I trovatori d'Italia* (Modena, 1915); Bertoni, G., 'L'iniziane francese nel poeti meridianali della scuola siciliana' (*Festschrift Camille Chabineau*, Erlangen, 1907); Casini, T., *Geschichte der italienischen Literatur* (trans. from the Italian by H. Schneegans in G. Gröber, *Grundriss der romanischen Philologie*, vol. ii, part ii, Strassburg, 1914); Cesareo, G. A., *La poesia siciliana sotto gli Svevi* (Catania, 1894); Cesareo, G. A., *Le origini della poesia lirica e la poesia siciliana sotto gli Svevi* (2nd edn., Milan, 1924); Diez, F., *La Poésie des Troubadours* (Paris, 1845); Diez, F., *Leben und Werke der Troubadours* (Leipzig, 1882); Faral, E., *Les Arts poétiques du XIIe et du XIIIe siècle* (Paris, 1924); Gaspary, A., *Geschichte der italienischen Literatur* (2 vols., Strassburg, 1855–88); idem (Eng. trans. by H. Oelsner, London, 1901); Jeanroy, A., 'Les Troubadours dans les cours de l'Italie du Nord aux XIIe et XIIIe siècles' (*Revue historique*, 1930); Jeanroy, A., *Un Sirventes contre Charles d'Anjou (1268)*, 1903; Langley, E. F., 'The Early Sicilian Poets' (*Publications of the Modern Language Association of America*, xxviii (new series xxi), 1913); Langley, E. F., 'The Extant Repertory of the Sicilian Poets' (*Publications of the Modern Language Association of America*, xxviii, 1913); Longnon, J., 'Les Troubadours à la Cour de Montferrat' (*Revue de synthèse historique*, July–Dec., 1948); Meyer, W., *Gesammelte Abhandlungen zur mittellateinischen Rhythmik* (2 vols., Berlin, 1905); Monaci, E., 'Elemente francesci nella più antica lirica italiana' (in *Scritti di storia di filologia e d'arte*, Naples, 1907); Monaci, E., 'Per la storia della scuola poetica siciliana' (*Accademia dei Lincei*, Series v, 5, 1896); Napolski, M. von, *Leben und Werke des Troubadours Ponz de Capduoill* (Halle, 1879); Novati, F., *Freschi e minii del Dugento* (Milan, 1908); Novati, F., *L'influsso del pensiero latino sopra la civiltà italiana del Medio Evo* (Milan, 1897); Novati, F., 'Rapports littéraires de l'Italie et de la France' (*Académie des Inscriptions et Belles Lettres: Comptes Rendus des Séances de l'Année 1910*); Novati, F., *Storia Letteraria d'Italia: Le Origini* (Milan, 1926); Panvini, B., 'La scuola poetica siciliana' (*Archivum Romanicum*, xliii, 1963); Scandone, F., *Ricerche novissime sulla scuola poetica siciliana del sec. XIII* (Avellino, 1900); Schultz-Gora, O., *Die Briefe des Troubadors Raimbaut de Vaqueiras an Bonifaz I., Markgrafen von Montferrat* (Halle, 1893); Schultz-Gora, O., 'Die Lebensverhältnisse der italienischen Trobadors' (*Zeitschrift für Roman. Philol.* vii, 1883); Schultz-Gora, O., *Ein Sirventes von Guilhem Figueira gegen Friedrich II.* (Halle, 1902); Shepard, W. P., and Chambers, F. M., *The Poems of Aimeric de Péguilhan* (Evanston, 1950); Tallgren, O. J., 'Les poésies de Rinaldo d'Aquino' (*Mémoires de la Société néophilologique de Helsingfors*, vi, 1917); Thornton, H. H., 'The Poems Ascribed to Frederick II and "Rex Fredericus" ' (*Speculum*, i, 1926); Thornton, H. H., 'The Poems Ascribed to King Enzio' (*Speculum*, i, 1926); Tiraboschi, G., *Storia della Letteratura italiana* (16 vols., Milan, 1822–6); Torraca, F., *Studi su la lirica italiana del Duecento* (Bologna, 1902); Wilkins, E., 'The Derivation of the Canzone' (*Modern Philology*, xii, 1915); Wilkins, E., 'The Invention of the Sonnet' (*Modern Philology*, xiii, 1916); Willemsen, C. A., *Kaiser Friedrich II. und sein Dichterkreis* (Krefeld, 1947); Wittenberg, F., *Die Hohenstaufen im Munde der Troubadours* (Münster, 1908); Zingarelli, N., *Intorno a due trovatori in Italia* (Florence, 1899).

27. *Universities*

Caputo, M. C., 'Il servataggio della R. Biblioteca Universitaria di Messina' (*Zentralblatt für Bibliothekswesen*, xxvi, 1909); Denifle, H., *Die Entstehung der Universitäten bis 1400* (Berlin, 1885); Hampe, K., 'Zur Gründungsgeschichte der Universität Neapel' (*Mitteilungen aus der Capuaner Briefsammlung*, v: *Sb. d. H. Ak.: Phil.-Hist.-Klasse* x, 1923); Kaufmann, G., *Die Geschichte der deutschen Universitäten* (2 vols., Stuttgart, 1888–96); Paetow, L. J., *The Arts Course at Mediaeval Universities* (Urbana, 1910); Rashdall, H., *The Universities of Europe in the Middle Ages* (new edn. by F. M. Powicke and A. B. Emden, 3 vols., Oxford, 1936); Sorbelli, A., *Storia della Università di Bologna* (Bologna, 1940); Vergottini, G. de, 'Lo studio di Bologna, l'imperio, il papato' (*Studi e memorie per la storia dell'Università di Bologna*, new series, i, 1954); Winkelmann, E., 'Über die ersten Staatsuniversitäten' (Programm Heidelberg, 1880).

NOTE

Since this book went to press the following work has appeared and should be included in the Bibliography: Powell, J. M., *The Liber Augustalis or Constitution of Melfi Promulgated by the Emperor Frederick II for the Kingdom of Sicily in 1231* (Syracuse, N.Y., 1971).

INDEX

Aachen, 96
Abel of Denmark, 436
Abu-Zacharia, Sultan of Tunis, 271
Adam of Cremona, 317
Adelasia of Sardinia, 417, 418
Adolf of Cologne, Archbishop, 29, 30, 31, 33, 51, 74
Adolf of Holstein, 354
Advocati, 117
Aimeric de Peguilhan, 84, 88
Aimeric de Pequlhan, 327
Alaman, Count, 271
Alaman da Coasta, 135, 148
Alatrin, 114
Alberia, 42, 43
Alberigo of Romano, 398, 427, 428, 439, 449
Albert IV of Bogen, Count, 397
Albert of Antioch, 479
Albert of Beham, 311, 435, 493, 497
Albert of Brabant, 6
Albert of Catania, Master, 255
Albert of Magdeburg, Bishop, 206
Albert of Meissen, 495
Albert of Orlamunde, Count, 353
Albert Malaspina, 327
Albert San Vitale, 504
Albertano of Brescia, 320, 322
Aldobrandino of Este, 126
Alem-ed-Din-Hanefi, 306
Alexander III, Pope, 5
Alexander IV, Pope, *see* Reginald of Ostia
Alfanus of Salerno, Archbishop, 286–9, 297
Alfonso X of Castile, 528
Alfonso of Poitou, 527
Alfonso of Provence, Count, 65, 66
Al-Kamil, Sultan, 202, 203, 205, 216, 218, 219, 224, 271, 306
al-Mu'azzam, Sultan, 202, 205, 216
Amadeus of Savoy, Count, 506
Amaury of Bethsan, 227
Amaury of Jerusalem, 214
Amaury Barlais, 227
Ancona, March of, 73, 168, 170, 209, 230
Andrea Dandolo, 13
Andreas the Justiciar, 81
Andrew of Cicala, 443, 445, 501
Andrew of Hungary, 339
Angelo Frisario, 276
an-Nāṣir Dā'ūd, 205, 216
Ansaldus de Mari, 272, 450, 461

Anselm of Justingen, 75, 78–80, 158, 379, 393
Antoninus of Florence, Archbishop, 340
Apulia, 46
Aquileia, Diet of, 362
Aragon, Frederick II marriage agreement with, 57
  negotiations with, 49
Architecture, 337–41
  military, 340, 344–6
Aristippus, Henry, 295–6, 299
Arnold of Brescia, 3
Arnold of Chur, Archbishop, 83
Art and sculpture, 333–6
Ashraf, Sultan of Damascus, 305
Astrology, 307–9
Augustales of Frederick, 277
Austria, 393, 397, 400, 495
Azzo of Este, Marquis, 76, 81, 397, 400, 427–8, 433, 439, 449

Bacon, Roger, 306
Baldwin of Constantinople, Emperor, 482, 484, 503
Balian of Sidon, 163, 216, 218, 227
Bartholomeo, 283
Bartholomew of Foggia, 338
Beatrice, daughter of Philip of Swabia, 68, 69, 78
Beatrice of Rethel, 18
Beatrice of Savoy, 506
Ben-Abbed, Emir, 152
Berard of Bari, Archbishop of Messina, 36, 81, 82, 83
Berard of Palermo, Archbishop, 376, 527, 529
Bernard of Carinthia, 161
Bernard of Clairvaux, 34, 35, 201, 222, 462
Bernard Orlando Rossi, 490, 501, 504, 507–8, 514
Bernhard of Saxony, 30
Berthold, Patriarch of Aquileia, 481
Berthold of Zahringen, Duke, 25, 29–31, 111
Bertrand Thessy, 218
Bohemond of Taranto, 300
Boniface VIII, Pope, 422, 424
Bouvines, battle of, 94–5, 98
Brescia, siege of, 415–18
Brown, Thomas, 294
Buoncompagno, Master, 293
Burckhardt, 531
Burkart of Hohenfels, 327

Calabria, 48
Calamandrinus, 415
Capua, administration of justice, 142
   assizes of, 139–44, 206, 241, 257
   strengthening of royal power, 143
   surrender of castles, 140
   surrender of privileges, 139
Cardinals, capture by Frederick, 451
Castel del Monte, 344
Cathari, 191
Celestine III, Pope, 38
Celestine IV, Pope, 190, 458
Charles of Anjou, 527
Cinthius of San Lorenzo, Cardinal, 52
Collenuccio, Pandolf, 15–16
Cologne, 97
Conrad II, 1
Conrad, Burgrave of Nurnberg, 393
Conrad, son of Frederick, King of the
   Romans, 206, 261, 373, 400, 402, 414, 474,
   475, 494, 503, 564, 526, 529
Conrad of Hildensheim, Chancellor, 22, 184,
   185, 253
Conrad of Mainz, 351
Conrad of Marburg, 367, 368, 369
Conrad of Marlenheim, 54–5
Conrad of Metz and Speyer, Bishop, 68, 85,
   86, 105, 350, 351, 380
Conrad of Porto, Bishop, 161
Conrad of Regensburg, 87
Conrad of Spoleto, 25
Conrad of Strassburg, Bishop, 29, 30
Conrad of Thuringia, 435, 446
Conrad of Urach, 184
Conrad of Urslingen, 21, 22, 49, 114
Conrad of Winterstettin, 351
Constance, Empress of Henry VI, 7, 13–14,
   21, 24, 25, 28, 36, 38, 39, 132
   abrogation of Sicilian rights, 37
   birth and upbringing, 18
   capture by Sicilians, 6
   hatred of Germans, 37
   marriage to Henry VI, 5, 17
   renunciation of Frederick's imperial
      claims, 37
Constance of Aragon, 65–6, 79, 80, 107, 126
Constance, Peace of, 4, 168, 396
Constance, treaty of, 183
Constantine, Donation of, 1, 395, 417
Constantine Africanus, 288
Constitutio in Favorem Principum, 359, 363
Constitutio Pacis, 382–4
Constitutiones of Frederick, 135
Constitutiones Regni Siciliae, 143; see also
   Liber Augustalis
Constitutions of Melfi, 129
Cortenuova, battle, 405–7, 413, 415

Council of Lyons, 497
Cremona, Diet of, 129, 168, 180, 185, 188,
   241
Crusade, fifth, 97, 109, 113
   postponement by Frederick, 146
   preparations, 159, 194
Cyprus, 213

Damietta, surrender of, 158
Dante, 15, 260, 328, 330, 331, 421, 505, 522
Denmark, 352
   Frederick's treaty with, 95
Desiderius, Abbot of Monte Cassino (Victor
   III), 286, 289
Diepold of Hohenburg, 327
Diet of Ravenna, 363
Diethelm of Constance, Bishop, 31
Dietrich of Meissen, 111
Dipold of Acerra, 22, 25, 39, 44, 46, 48–50,
   53, 54, 66, 72, 76, 79, 126, 136–7
Doxapater, 290

Eberhard of Waldburg, 351
Eberhardt of Salzburg, Archbishop, 110
Eckbert of Bamberg, Bishop, 393, 402
Edrisi, 290
Egeno of Urach, 111
Egeno of Urach-Freiburg, 379
Eger, Diet at, 435
   Frederick's oath at, 90
Egypt, unrest in, 202–3
Elias of Cortona, Brother, 438, 439
Elizabeth of Thuringia, 367, 386, 387, 391
Emmerich, King of Hungary, 56, 67
Engelbert of Cologne, Archbishop, 111, 349,
   350, 354, 355, 366, 375
Enzio, King of Sardinia, 329, 417, 418, 442,
   445, 451, 506–10, 513, 523
Eudes of Montbeliard, 216, 228
Eugene of Palermo, Admiral, 253, 295, 297–9
Eugenius III, Pope, 3
Ezzelino of Romano, 394, 396–400, 415,
   427, 433, 440, 498, 499, 500, 501, 509, 515

Fakhr-ad-Din, 203, 217, 219, 225, 229, 346
Ferdinand of Flanders, Count, 93, 94
Franciscan Order, 438, 439
Franciscus Pipinus, 333
Frankfurt, Diet of, 123, 126, 365
Frederick II of Hohenstaufen, agreement
      with Lombard League, 189
   arrival in Rome, 81
   as lawgiver, 242–50
   baptism, 20
   birth, 16, 18
      stories relating to, 13–19
   character and appearance, 63–4

concept of imperial sovereignty, 100–2, 120, 125, 162–3, 180, 241
concept of universal sovereignty, 412
conciliation with Gregory IX, 230–3
conflict with Gregory, 200
conflict with Lombard League, 179–89, 391–424
coronation at Aachen, 96
coronation in Mainz, 86
coronation in Rome, 133
counter-measures against Gregory, 437
crowned King of Sicily, 36
de Arte Venandi cum Avibus, 314, 333, 346
death, 527
   legends relating to, 528
defeat at Parma, 511
departure for crusade, 207
deposition by Innocent, 486
early life, 21
education, 62–3
election of son as German king, 123
Emperor Elect of Germany, 80
end of Regency, 57
excommunication by Gregory, 196
fifth crusade, 213–28
first clash with papacy, 64–5
first years as King of Sicily, 61–71
German policy, 102, 103
imperial policy, 105
Italian expedition, 123–38
Italian policy, 129–30
journey to Germany, 81–4
judgement, 531–40
   artistic interests, 534
   by contemporaries, 531–40
   by succeeding generations, 531–40
   Christian beliefs, 536
   ecclesia, 538
   hostility to papacy, 536
   imperium, 538
   individuality, 539
   patron of scholars, 533
   scholar, 533
   statesmanship, 532
   want of military greatness, 535
King of Jerusalem, 158–75, 219
Liber Augustalis, 237–50
marriage agreement with Aragon, 57
marriage to Constance of Aragon, 66
marriage to Isabella of Brienne, 163
marriage to Isabella of England, 380
patron of science, 302–18
policy towards the cities, 104–6
principle of hereditary succession, 116
relations with papacy, 114–16, 170–5
relationship with son, 371
second excommunication of, 427–41

Sicilian economic policy, 264–80
Sicilian policy, 136–57
ward of the Pope, 37
will, 529–30
Frederick of Antioch, 329
Frederick of Austria, Duke, 392–94, 400, 401, 402, 495
Frederick of Tanne, 27
Frederick of Trent, Bishop, 126, 127
Frederick Barbarossa, 2, 16, 20, 47, 116, 275, 327, 350, 417, 418
   concept of *imperium*, 3–4
   death, 5
   Italian policies, 4
Freeman, E. A., 531
Freidank, 220
Fulda, Abbot of, 115, 327

Garnier l'Aleman, 227
Gaucelm Faidit, 327, 329, 378
Gauvain of Chinchi, 227
Gebhard of Arnstein, 394, 397, 398, 400
Gebhard of Querfurt, 91
Gelasian theory, 201, 539
Gelasius I, Pope, 34
Genoa, 81
Gentile of Palear, 41, 50
   guardian of Frederick, 46
George of Gallipoli, 301
Gerhard, Cardinal, 54
Gerhard of Bremen, Bishop, 111
Gerhard Allocingola, 50
German lyricists, 327
Germany, alliance with France, 355
   anti-Hohenstaufen factors, 29–33
   border conflicts with France, 110
   Burgundian succession, 111
   cities, 359, 364
   civil war, 32
   conflict between Otto and Frederick, 92
   constitutional revolution, 100
   ecclesiastical princes, 116, 119
   election of Otto IV, 67
   Frederick's early policy, 89–90
   growth of ethnic pride, 99
   growth of urban communities, 98
   local conflicts, 110
   Northern, submission of, 89–106
   papal interference, 208
   policy of Innocent IV, 493
   'pope kings', 495
   power of ecclesiastical princes, 100, 363
   regency of Engelbert of Cologne, 349–55
   regency of Louis of Bavaria, 356
   relations with Denmark, 352
   social and economic change, 103
   Southern, support for Frederick, 86–8

Gerold, Patriarch, 161, 162, 216–19, 222, 224, 226
Gertrude of Austria, 481
Ghibellines, 496, 505
  in Italian cities, 466
Giles of Torres, 456
Godfrey of Hohenlohe, 370
Godfrey of Vinsauf, 320
Godfrey of Viterbo, 19, 87, 324
Godfrey Castiglione of Santa Sabina, *see* Celestine IV
Golden Bull of Eger, 172
Goliards, 325
Goslar, 25
Gottfried of Neifen, 327
Grasso, Admiral, 42
Gregory VII, Pope, 34, 35, 287
Gregory IX, Pope, 96, 101, 154, 230, 260, 306, 307, 366, 368, 374, 380, 387, 391, 394, 396, 405, 422, 423, 424, 429, 434, 439, 444, 455, 497, 504, 532, 536
  alliance with Genoa and Venice, 419
  attack on Frederick, 197–9
  attempts to select new emperor, 436
  bitter conflict with Frederick, 429
  concept of papal authority, 190–3
  conciliation with Frederick, 230–3
  death of, 454
  dissolution of the oath of allegiance, 209
  doctrine of world dominance, 396
  hostility to Frederick, 193
  leader of resistance to Frederick, 417
  obstinacy of, 454
  open conflict with Frederick, 446–54
  papal armies in Sicily, 211
  popular hostility against, 204
  propagandist warfare, 429–32
  rebellion by Romans, 372
  succession, 190
Gregory of Montelongo, 416, 433, 435, 449, 460, 464, 465, 497, 501, 507, 508, 509, 510, 515
Gregory of Santa Maria in Porticu, 41
Gualo, Cardinal of St. Martins, 161
Guelfs, 466, 496, 501, 505
Guido Colona, 329
Guillaume de Figueira, 327
Gunzelin of Wolfenbüttel, 172
Guy Lenfant, 163

Hadrian IV, Pope, 65
Hartmann von der Aue, 100
Hartwich of Eichstadt, 87
Hauteville family, 289
Henry III, King of England, 223, 224, 355, 385, 434, 437, 502

Henry IV of Burgundy, Duke, 527
Henry VI, Emperor, 5, 64, 72, 79, 116, 136, 278, 304
  brothers, 25
  capture of Richard I, 6, 30
  concept of Empire, 7
  conquest of Sicily, 9
  death, 24
  principle of hereditary succession, 22–3
  relations with papacy, 23
  Sicilian policy, 6, 7–9, 22, 24
  testament, 28, 38, 45, 52
Henry VII, 182, 183, 184, 185, 186, 206, 322, 329, 354
  attitude towards heresy, 369
  death of, 379
  deposition, 378
  excommunication, 374
  independent rule of, 357
  invasion of Bavaria, 370
  marriage to Margaret of Austria, 355
  opposition to Frederick, 358, 361
  rebellion against Frederick, 372
Henry (son of Isabella), 529
Henry of Avranches, 304, 306, 384
Henry of Brabant, Duke, 51
Henry of Brunswick, 112
Henry of Hohenlohe, 480
Henry of Istria, 68
Henry of Kalden, Marshal, 23, 68
Henry of Limburg, Duke, 196, 201, 202, 214, 218
Henry of Lusignan, 213
Henry of Malta, 150, 158, 163, 206, 215, 218
Henry of Morra, 138, 168, 211, 246, 247, 361, 376, 414
Henry of Neifen, 75, 78–9, 373, 379
Henry of Sax, 83
Henry of Saxony, 31, 112, 113, 356
Henry of Sayn, Count, 368
Henry of Schwerin, Count, 352–4
Henry of Tanne, 351
Henry of Trubleville, 414
Henry Aristippus, 259–96, 299
Henry Raspe, 494–5, 503, 504
Heresy, 366, 495
Hermann of Salza, 160, 161, 162, 166, 184, 216, 219, 223, 231, 321, 353, 377, 378, 392, 394, 403, 404
Hermann of Thuringia, Landgrave, 109
Hermann of Wurzburg, Bishop, 380
Hohenstaufen Emperors, problems, 2–3
Honorius III, Pope, 109, 112, 113, 123, 128, 130, 146, 161, 167, 173, 189, 306, 307, 351, 353, 424, 429
  conflict with Frederick, 171, 173, 187

death, 190
relations with Frederick, 131–2, 161
Hospitallers, 218, 226, 231, 429
Hubert Pallavicini, Marquis, 500, 526
Hugh of Gibelet, 227
Hugh of Lavagna, 461
Hugo Falcandus, 292, 296
Hugo Ramperti, 449

Ibn Djubayr, 337
Innocent III, Pope, 6, 26, 28, 29, 33, 35, 36,
    40, 43, 61, 64, 67, 70, 72, 80, 90, 93,
    96–7, 115, 323, 424, 532
  agreement with Dipold, 53
  agreement with Philip of Swabia, 53
  alienation of Sicilians, 45
  alliance with Philip Augustus, 74
  breach with Walter of Palear, 44
  concept of papacy, 34–5
  crusade against Markward, 42
  death, 108
  defeat of German forces, 52
  extension of power, 98
  German policy, 105
  intervention in Germany, 67, 73–5
  negotiations with Philip of Swabia, 52
  opposition to Hohenstaufen, 39
  Sicily, 48, 55
  succession, 33
  theocratic imperialism, 34
Innocent IV, 34, 101, 387, 423, 424, 466,
    484, 492, 497, 515, 518, 532, 536
  campaign against Sicily, 524
  character, 463
  concept of papacy, 462, 488
  conflict with Frederick, 468, 475
  conspiracy against Frederick, 490–2
  deposition of Frederick, 486
  election, 461
  flight to Lyons, 477
  policy, 496
  policy in Germany, 493
  policy in Sicily, 516
  policy towards Frederick, 463–5
  policy towards Lombard League, 465,
    476
  reaction to death of Frederick II, 529
Inquisition in Germany, 367
Isabella of Brienne, 166, 190, 204, 206
Isabella of England, 374, 381, 530
  marriage to Frederick II, 380
Italian communes, 127–9, 148, 150, 181,
    320, 360
  dangers to Frederick, 441
  defection to Innocent, 523
Italy, hostility to Germany, 27
  threat to papal interests, 501

Jacob Anatoli, 313
Jacob de Magistro Milo, 276
Jamāl-ed-Dīn, 153, 154
James, Marshal, 42, 45
James of Aquino, 329
James of Capua, Archbishop, 376
James of Lentini, 329
James of Morra, 428, 490, 492, 501
James of Palestrina, Cardinal Bishop, 394,
    395, 403, 461
James Fiesco, 477
Jamison, Miss, 296, 298
Jerusalem, 5, 473
  events after treaty, 224–8
  Frederick's entry, 223
Jews, 144, 276, 401
  in Germany, 385–6
  in Sicily, 313
Joachim, 14, 19
Joachimites, 16, 19
Johannes Maurus, 256, 265, 266, 305
John, King of England, 69, 85, 86, 91, 94,
    95, 98, 160, 200
  subjection to Innocent, 92
John, King of Jerusalem, 14, 160, 161, 162;
    see also John of Brienne
John of Brienne, 165–7, 174, 183, 210, 211,
    212, 213, 218, 229
  Frederick's quarrel with, 166
  leader of papal armies, 204
  withdrawal from papal army, 229
John of Capua, 437
John of Casamara, Abbot, 253
John of Ibelin, 213, 214, 228
John of Otranto, 301
John of Procida, 529
John of Vicenza, 368
John of Viterbo, 243
John Colonna, Cardinal, 211, 228, 443, 446,
    454, 456–7
  capture, 458
  desertion of Gregory, 453
John Grasso, 301
John Vatatzes, 301
Jordan Ruffo, 316
Juda, ben Solomon Cohen, 309, 313, 346

Lambert Visconti, 417
Lancia, Margrave, 511, 513
Landolf of Worms, Bishop, 372, 378, 380
Lanfranc Cigala, 506
Lateran Council, Fourth, 105, 107, 110
Leo of Ostia, 286
Leo 'the Great', Pope, 34
Leonardo, the Jew, 346
Leonardo of Pisa, 310, 311
Leopold of Austria, 356, 360

Liber Augustalis or *Constitutiones of Frederick*, 242, 251, 256, 257, 263, 267, 273, 278, 383, 532, 537, 598
  concept of justice, 245
  concept of sovereignty, 258
  Frederick's theory of sovereignty, 257–9
  organization of Justiciary, 247–50
  sources, 242
Lombard communes, 168, 384, 410, 439, 464
Lombard League, 101, 128, 208, 210, 232, 241, 273, 360, 361, 373, 387, 392, 411, 416, 433, 464, 527
  alliance with Gregory, 209
  alliance with Honorius, 172
  growth of autonomy, 186
  hostility to Frederick, 182
  papal mediation, 188
  political aims, 181
  political demands, 184
  re-establishment, 170
Lombardy, 76, 360, 365
Louis IX, King, 436, 473, 477, 489, 502, 503, 515
  capture of, 527
Louis of Bavaria, Duke, 147, 357, 358, 360
  guardian of Henry VII, 355
  regency of Germany, 356
Louis of Loos, 110
Lucas of Bitonto, 322
Lucius III, Pope, 5, 20
Ludolf of Worms, 126
Lupold of Worms, Bishop, 51–3
Lyons, Council of, 154, 256, 303, 423, 438, 448, 451, 483–97
  Frederick's peace proposals, 485

Magdeburg, Archbishop, 91, 109
Mainardino of Imola, Bishop, 324
Mainz, Diet of 1184, 99
  Diet of 1235, 382, 385, 391
  Synod of, 369
Mainzer Landfriede, 120
Maio, Admiral, 252, 294, 296
Manerio of Palear, 50
Manfred, King, son and successor of Frederick, 283, 329, 339, 345, 506, 529, 530
Manfred Lancia, Marquis, 445
Mangold of Passau, 87
Manrique, Angello, 15
Maqrizi, 203, 217, 271
Marcellina of Arezzo, Bishop, 515
Margaret of Austria, 355, 360
Margarito, Admiral, 148
Maria, daughter of the Duke of Brabant, 52
Marino Filangieri, Canon, 171
Marinus of Eboli, 501

Markward of Anweiler, 22, 23, 25, 28, 37, 38, 41, 44, 46, 48, 62, 79, 136, 253
  alliance with Walter of Palear, 45
  arrival in Sicily, 42
  capture of Frederick, 47
  death, 49
  defeat at Monreale, 45
  excommunication, 40
  policy in Sicily, 40–1
  representative of Philip in Sicily, 39
  siege of Palermo, 46
Matilda, Countess, 4, 181
Matthew of Salerno, 252
Matthew d'Ajello, 16, 17, 19
Matthew Gentile, 248
Matthew Orsini, 453, 456, 460
Matthew Paris, 271, 316, 336, 411, 437, 452, 512, 515, 517, 522, 524, 527
Maxey-sur-Vaise, Treaty of, 85, 355
Mazzara, Bishop of, 57
Messina, assize of, 144–5, 241, 257
Messinese document of Frederick, 80
Michael Comnenus, 301
Michael Scott, 19, 306–10, 312, 314
  De verificatione motuum coelestium, 306
Minorite order, 388, 411, 429, 433, 437, 439, 491, 496
Monreale, battle of, 45
Monte Cassino, monastery of, 285–6
Montferrat, Marquis of, 128, 193, 228, 327, 475, 506
Moses ben Salomon of Salerno, 313

Naples, University of, 256, 323
  establishment by Frederick, 155–7
Navy, 150
  establishment, 149
Nicholas I, Pope, 34
Nicholas of Carbio, 420, 475, 478, 494, 529
Nicholas of Cicala, 335
Nicholas of Jamsilla, 299
Nicholas of Otranto, 301
Nicholas of Pisa, 338, 342
Nicholas of Rocca, 326
Nicholas Peglia of Giovinazzo, 313
Nicolas Spinola, 272
Nilus Doxapater, 292, 297
Norman-Sicilian Kingdom, 2
Northern Italy, civil conflicts, 397

Obert Fallamonaca, 305
Orsini, Matthew, 453, 456, 457, 460
Ortnit, legend of, 163
Ottaviano Ubaldini, Cardinal, 504–8, 515, 526
Otto II of Bavaria, 370, 371

Otto III, 1
  Empire of, 1
Otto IV, 67, 69, 76, 83, 92, 94, 95, 97, 109,
    111, 137, 174
  alliance with England, 69
  death, 112
  defection of followers, 84
  defiance of Innocent III, 72
  deprived of imperial throne, 98
  excommunication, 73
  failures against Frederick, 109
  Italian policy, 72
  marriage to Beatrice of Swabia, 78
  policy of retaliation, 111–12
  relations with papacy, 70–1
  repudiation by Germans, 86
  retaliations in Germany, 91
  support in Germany, 91
Otto of Bavaria, Duke, 379
Otto of Botenlauben, 327
Otto of Brunswick, 31, 53, 381, 436
  conflict with Philip of Swabia, 33
Otto of Burgundy, Count Palatine, 29–30
Otto of Freising, 87
Otto of Laviano, 44
Otto of Lüneburg, 205, 356
Otto of Meran, 110
Otto of Porto, Cardinal, 477, 479
Otto of St. Nicholas, Cardinal, 205, 356, 357,
    366, 373, 437, 451, 457, 459, 467, 468
Otto of Tusculum, Cardinal, 503
Otto of Wittelsbach, 68
Ottokar I, King of Bohemia, 360

Palmer, Richard, 294
Pandulf, papal chaplain, 211
Pandulf of Fasanella, 490, 492
Pandulf Collenuccio, 324
Papal succession, conflict of, 455–61
Parma, capture by imperial forces, 526
  siege of, 508–11
Pedro, King of Aragon, 63
Pedro II, King, 49, 53, 56
Peirol, 159
Pelagius, 158, 159, 212, 229
Peter of Albano, 476, 479, 503
Peter of Blois, 295
Peter of Celano, 50, 55
Peter of Hibernia, 156
Peter of Marseilles, Bishop, 275
Peter of Montaigu, 218
Peter of Ravella, Bishop, 376
Peter of Rouen, Archbishop, 463
Peter of Sasso, 105
Peter Capoccio, Cardinal, 504, 507, 518,
    524–5, 529
Peter the Deacon, 286

Peter Traversara of Ravenna, 81
Philip of Assisi, 435
Philip of Ferarra, 494
Philip of Novare, 227, 321
Philip of Swabia, 22, 24–8, 36, 38, 40, 41, 42,
    47, 49, 53, 92
  conflict with Otto of Brunswick, 33
  coronation at Aachen, 51
  death of, 67
  marriage to Irene, 26
Philip Augustus of France, 69, 73, 74, 75,
    85, 91, 92, 110, 189, 355
  alliance with Frederick, 86
  conflict with John, 93
  defeat of John, 94
Philip the Fair of France, 422, 424
Piero della Vigna, 244, 255, 256, 259, 262,
    308, 310, 322–4, 326, 327, 329, 334, 340,
    342, 380, 403, 404, 407, 408, 429, 455,
    459, 461, 473, 476, 520, 522
  accused of treason, 521–2
  bond with Frederick, 520
  guilty of peculation, 521
  Justice of the Superior Court, 428
  letters in defence of Frederick, 430
  offices held under Frederick, 520
  poetic style, 325
  suicide, 523
Pierre Vidal, 327
Pietro da Eboli, 17, 19, 308, 316, 325
Pietro Tiepolo, 406, 407
*Privilegium in Favorem Principum Ecclesiasti-
    corum*, 102, 116, 119, 120, 123
  articles of, 117
  constitutional significance, 116
  precedents, 118

Questions Siciliennes, 309

Rainer of Sartiano, Count, 136, 137
Rainer of Viterbo, Cardinal, 456, 465, 468,
    478, 480, 485, 486, 487, 495, 497, 501,
    514, 515, 517
  conspiracy against Frederick, 466
  death, 517
  propagandist warfare against Frederick,
    481–3, 515
Rambaut de Vaqueiras, 327
Rashdall, 155
Ravenna, diet of, 360, 361
Raymond of Toulouse, 473
Reginald of Aquino, 329
Reginald of Capua, Archbishop, 47, 323
Reginald of Dassel, 100
Reginald of Ostia (later Pope Alexander IV),
    403, 446, 448, 456, 478, 491, 519

Reginald of Spoleto, Duke, 161, 162, 187, 206, 209, 211, 215
Richard of Aquilia, 55
Richard of Caserta, Count, 529
Richard of Cornwall, Earl, 336, 407, 453, 457, 473, 486, 524
Richard of St. Angelo, Cardinal, 478, 491, 492
Richard of San Germano, 171, 269, 325, 335
Richard of Segni, Count, 140
Richard of Trajetto, 255, 256
Richard Annibaldi, Cardinal, 456, 458, 519
Richard Cœur de Lion, 30, 31
Richard Conti, 55
Richard Filangieri, 205, 213, 216
Rinaldo Conti of Anagni, Cardinal, 190
Rispampani, siege of, 376
Robert Guiscard, 289
Roffrido of Benevento, 203, 323, 325
Roffrido of Monte Cassino, Abbot, 40, 54
Roger I of Sicily, 289
Roger II of Sicily, 18, 132, 143, 239, 243, 246, 251, 277, 283, 284, 289, 290, 291, 319, 337
Roger of Amico, 329
Roger of Apulia, Duke, 5, 140
Roger of Celano, 211
Roger of Wendover, 321
Roger Camera, 266
Romanus of Porto, 456
Romuald of Salerno, 297
Ruffo, Jordan, 312

St. Francis of Assisi, 190, 192, 438
St. Nicola di Casole, monastery of, 299, 300
St. Thomas Aquinas, 258, 260
Salerno, plundered by Henry VI, 8–9
  school of, 285
Salimbene, 14, 19, 64, 316, 317, 318, 325, 412, 439, 490, 509, 522, 528
Salinguerra, 449
San Germano agreement, 56, 161, 163, 167, 170, 188, 195
Saracens in Sicily, 151–4, 276, 305, 501
Sardinia, 417
Sculpture and art, 333–6, 341–3
Selby, Robert, 294
Sibylla, 21, 43, 44, 211
Sicard of Cremona, 408
Sicilian Court, pursuit of learning, 299–319
Sicilian *curia regis*, 239, 264
Sicilian literary style, antecedents, 319–26
  Bolognese culture, 320
  Capuan school, 232
  Italian poetry, 326

Sicilian school of poetry, 326–32
  Frederick's influence, 329
  French influence, 327
  importance, 331
Sicily, 429, 445, 501
  Arabic culture, 293, 303, 305, 319
  bureaucratic system, 239
  contenders for dominance, 41
  development of Chancery, 252
  division of administration, 46
  effect of Frederick's policies, 149
  expedition by Frederick, 65
  fiscal administration, 264–7
    alien tax, 276
    banking, 278
    coinage, 277–8
    customs duties, 271–5
    merchant fleet, 276
    taxation, 269
    trade, 270
  Governing Council, 41
  Greek culture, 293, 304
  Jews in, 313
  Kingdom of, 115, 126, 132, 442, 516, 519
    as sovereign state, 155
    despotic bureaucracy, 251–63
    during Frederick's absence, 208–11
    Innocent's edict of government, 517–18
    papal interdict, 516
  lawlessness, 54–6, 79
  markets and fairs, aims, 279
  Norman cultural heritage, 283–98
  nucleus of the Empire, 238
  office of Admiral, 151
  organization of provincial government, 268
  papal legate in, 50
  papal regency, 135
  racial diversity, 283–4
  reconquest by Frederick, 228–30
  restoration of sovereign authority in, 139
  seizure by Gregory, 213
  struggle for control of, 38–57
  weakness of, 61
Siegfried of Mainz, Archbishop, 68, 74
Siegfried of Regensburg, Bishop, 362
Simon of Teate, Count, 466
Simon of Tournay, 421
Simon of Tyre, Archbishop, 163
Sinibald Fiesco of San Lorenzo, Cardinal (Innocent IV), 190, 433, 461
Spoleto, Duchy of, 73, 168, 170, 209, 230
Statutum, 120
Stephen II of Auxonne, 110
Stephen, Master, 210
Stephen of Perche, Count, 252, 292, 294
Stephen of Santa Maria in Trastevere, 456

Stephen of Santa Maria trans-Tiberim, Cardinal, 478, 491, 501, 516, 519
Swabian *ministeriales*, 78, 350, 351, 356, 357, 362, 366, 370, 372
Sylvester II, Pope, 1
Syria, 5
   Muslim conflicts, 216
   unrest in, 202–3

Tancred of Campiglia, 187
Tancred of Lecce, Count, 5, 7
Tancred of Lecce, Duke, 14
Tancred of Lecce, King of Sicily, 18, 21, 42, 253
Taranto, 14
Templars, 218, 222, 226, 227, 231, 429
Teresio of Atina, 326
Teutonic Order, 222, 226
Thaddeus of Suessa, 255, 256, 340, 342, 461, 474, 476, 485, 511, 512, 520
   Frederick's representative at Lyons, 486
Theobald of Novare, 473
Theodore, Master, 449
Theodore of Antioch, 305, 310, 312
Theophanes Cerameus, 290, 291
Thomas of Acerra, Count, 212, 213, 216, 218, 227, 228, 248, 361, 376
Thomas of Capua, Cardinal, 138, 231
Thomas of Celano, 136, 138, 211
Thomas of Sabina, Cardinal, 403, 437
Thuringia, Landgrave of, 91, 196
Tibaldi Franciscus, 62, 490, 491
Toledo group, 312

Ubald Visconti, 417
Ugolino of Ostia, Cardinal, 127, 135
Ulm, Diet of, 111, 355
Ulrich of Kyburg, 111
Ulrich of St. Gall, 83, 107, 108, 110
Universality, concept of, 1, 2
Ursu de Fusco, 276

Vatatzes, John, Greek Emperor, 515
Venice, Peace of, 4
Vicenza, capture of, 399
Violante, Countess of Caserta, 412
Viterbo, Frederick's defeat, 467

Waldburgs, 356, 357
Waldemar II, King of Denmark, 95, 109, 352, 353
Waldensians, 191
Walter of Brienne, 42, 43, 46
   death, 50
   defeat of German forces, 48
   Grand Justiciar, 48
   relation to heirs of Tancred, 43
   support for Innocent III, 44
Walter of Catrone, Count, 245
Walter of Manupello, 525
Walter of Palear, 37, 41, 44, 46, 48, 50, 54, 62, 126, 148, 158, 253, 254
   negotiations with Markward of Anweiler, 45
Walter of Rouen, Archbishop, 13, 21
Walter Ascoli, 323
Walter Gentile, 80
Walter Ocra, Master, 502
Walter Ophamil, 16, 17
Walther von der Vogelweide, 32, 77, 84, 99, 125, 327
Weiblingen, 32
Welfs, 32, 39, 103, 373
   defection of Philip of Swabia, 51
   Hohenstaufen alliance with, 69
   humiliation of, 95
   imperial candidate, 31
   opposition of, 109
   submission to Frederick II, 107–20
Wener of Boland, 350, 362
William I, 5, 14
William II, 16
William of Capparone, 49, 50, 53, 54, 62
William of Holland, 110, 495, 518
William of Modena, Bishop, 463
William of Revet, 227
William of San Severino, 490, 491
William of Tocca, 255
William of Tyre, 50, 66
William Fiesco, 477, 510
William Franciscus, 46, 62, 636
William Porcus, 148, 150
Winterstettins, 356, 357
Wolfgar of Aquilea, 78
Wolfram von Eschenbach, 100
Würzburg, Diet of, 105